Responsible Analytics for Superior Health Quality Outcomes

Nilmini Wickramasinghe
https://orcid.org/0000-0002-1314-8843
La Trobe University, Australia

Rima Gibbings
University of North Georgia, USA

IGI Global
Scientific Publishing
Publishing Tomorrow's Research Today

Vice President of Editorial — Melissa Wagner
Director of Acquisitions — Mikaela Felty
Director of Book Development — Jocelynn Hessler
Production Manager — Mike Brehm
Cover Design — Jose Rosado

Published in the United States of America by
IGI Global Scientific Publishing
701 East Chocolate Avenue
Hershey, PA, 17033, USA
Tel: 717-533-8845 | Fax: 717-533-7115
Website: https://www.igi-global.com E-mail: cust@igi-global.com

Library of Congress Cataloging-in-Publication Data

LCCN: 2025021294 (CIP Data Pending)
ISBN: 9798337325453
eISBN: 9798337325477
British Cataloguing in Publication Data
A Cataloguing in Publication record for this book is available from the British Library.

This book is dedicated to our families, colleagues, students and all healthcare stakeholders.

Editorial Advisory Board

Table of Contents

Detailed Table of Contents

The COVID-19 pandemic exposed critical gaps in healthcare delivery, emphasizing the need for scalable digital health solutions (DHS). Managing chronic conditions such as Type 2 Diabetes Mellitus (T2DM) became increasingly complex during this period, particularly in the U.S. where T2DM prevalence is high. This chapter addresses the overlooked barriers to DHS adoption in T2DM care through a PRISMA-guided systematic review and the Unified Theory of Acceptance and Use of Technology (UTAUT) framework. The analysis identifies key barriers, including infrastructural limitations, usability issues, socioeconomic disparities, privacy concerns, and perceived usefulness. Findings emphasize the importance of enhancing infrastructure, simplifying user interfaces, and improving digital security to support adoption and long-term use. These insights inform the design of more equitable, effective digital health systems and provide actionable guidance for chronic disease management beyond the pandemic context.

Integrating Patient-Reported Outcome Measures (PROMs) and Artificial Intelligence (AI) has brought about a transformation of the healthcare system by improving predictive analysis and customized treatment. Nevertheless, bias, data privacy, and integrity issues remain since data storage is centralized and vulnerable to security

diagnosis by analyzing structured and unstructured healthcare data, such as EHRs, genomics, wearable sensors, and imaging. It covers key ML techniques—logistic regression, decision trees, SVMs-applied to clinical tasks. The chapter also discusses feature engineering, handling imbalanced data, and improving interpretability. Real-world use cases in detecting cancer, diabetes, cardiovascular, and neurological diseases are presented. Integration into clinical workflows is explored, showing how predictive models improve diagnostic accuracy, reduce hospital readmissions, and support preventive care. Ethical concerns such as data privacy, algorithmic bias, and the need for explainable AI are addressed. Future directions include advancements in personalized medicine, responsible AI deployment, and predictive models supporting global health initiatives.

Chapter 7
Factors Influencing Consumers' Acceptance and Use of Wearable Devices in Ehealth: A Study Using the UTAUT2 Model 177
Seema Rajesh Laddha, Universal AI University, India

This research aimed to investigate the factors influencing the usage intention of healthcare technology among patients in a developing country. A total of 500 patients participated in the study and completed a structured questionnaire that included measures of perceived usefulness, perceived ease of use, facilitating conditions, hedonic motivation, price, trust, social influence, habit, trial, SIFR, and perceived risk. The results indicated that perceived usefulness, perceived ease of use, facilitating conditions, hedonic motivation, price, and trust were positively related to usage intention, while perceived risk was negatively related. Social influence - specialist, habit, trial, and SIFR were found to have a significant positive correlation with usage intention but were not predictive factors.

Chapter 8
First Insights in Video-Based Patient Monitoring in the Long-Time Care Setting 201
Marcel Sailer, Rosenheim Technical University of Applied Sciences, Germany
Alena Sofie Fischer, Ulm University Hospital, Germany
Sarah Kaiser, Ulm University Hospital, Germany
Amelie Münzing, Ulm University Hospital, Germany
Mina Julie Schmachtel, Weleda AG, Germany

Video-based monitoring systems in long-term inpatient care represent an opportunity to increase patient safety. This paper intends to provide a basis for discussion for the use of video-based monitoring systems, focusing on nursing an public acceptance. Method Interviews were conducted with nursing care professionals (n=4) and people from the public (n=244) were surveyed via an online survey. Results and Discussion

The results clearly show that video-based monitoring systems have both advantages and disadvantages as well as ethical aspects and factors that influence the acceptance of video-based monitoring which must be weighed up individually. From the total responses of n=244, 47,1% (n=115) of survey participants are in favour of the use of monitoring systems in nursing, while 40,1% are undecided. The most frequently mentioned advantages from the interviews included continual vital sign monitoring, faster reactions in emergencies, a reduction in the workload of nursing staff and an increase in patient safety, for example through improved fall prevention for patients.

Generative artificial intelligence (AI) technologies have common applications in different domains including medicine or health in general, law, education, and finance. Large language models (LLMs) constitute a subset of generative AI, that are trained on large text datasets to automatically generate natural language content. LLMs, similarly, are used to facilitate different tasks, and ontology engineering is among these tasks. Related research shows that LLMs can achieve promising performance in different ontology engineering tasks, particularly in ontology construction from text descriptions. In this book chapter, we first review the literature on ontology engineering and LLMs, and next, the literature on the use of this generative AI technology (namely, LLMs) for improved health, and public health, ontologies is reviewed. We also outline the main findings of the reviewed studies and present significant future research directions regarding the use of the recent generative AI technologies for improving public health ontologies.

Generative AI, blockchain, mobile health (mHealth), wearables, sensors, and smart CDSS are emerging trends in healthcare. Generative AI using deep learning and NLP improves diagnosis, treatment planning, and outcome prediction. Blockchain

Foreword

Healthcare is entering a defining era, one in which analytics, artificial intelligence (AI), and machine learning (ML) are reshaping how we plan, deliver, and evaluate care. These rapidly evolving technologies are expanding our capacity to see patterns, anticipate needs, and measure outcomes with unprecedented precision. Yet as their rate of adoption accelerates, so too does the need for the same ethical, professional, and scientific accountability that has long underpinned safe and effective healthcare. The key challenge is to ensure that innovation and responsibility advance hand in hand.

This book, *Responsible Analytics for Superior Health Quality Outcomes*, edited by Professors Nilmini Wickramasinghe and Rima Gibbings presents a rich collection of research, experience and reflection on how analytics, AI and ML can be applied responsibly to achieve better, safer, and more equitable care.

For the clinician, the message is one of augmentation rather than replacement; analytics as a partner in distilling evidence, exploring diagnostic and therapeutic options, and supporting judgment. For the consumer, it is about confidence that analytics and AI are being used to advance health, not exploit vulnerability. For funders and policymakers, it is about ensuring that technology delivers measurable value and equitable access. And for developers and vendors, it is a reminder that lasting impact in healthcare depends not only on innovation and adoption of advanced technologies, but on integrity, ethics, accountability and responsibility.

This book stands out for its balance: rigorous in method yet accessible in tone; grounded in science yet oriented toward practice. Ultimately, *Responsible Analytics for Superior Health Quality Outcomes* reminds us that analytics and AI are not ends in themselves but instruments of stewardship; tools that can illuminate the unseen, strengthen clinical decision-making and care, and drive significant quality improvement and health outcomes for the benefits of all stakeholders.

It is indeed thoughtful and timely. I recommend it highly.

John Zelcer

La Trobe University, Australia

Preface

Responsible Analytics for Superior Health Quality Outcomes has been created to address a very pressing and current void. Healthcare is one if not the most data intense industry. In an attempt to extract pertinent information and germane knowledge from these raw data assets, we are witnessing the adoption of analytics and a plethora of artificial intelligence (AI) and machine learning (ML) solutions being designed and developed for a myriad of healthcare contexts. However, these solutions have many limitations, are not always fit for purpose or co-designed with input form clinical expert users or patient end users and thus are of low fidelity usefulness and usability. Thus, this book presents the necessary areas that must be addressed when designing and developing what we call "responsible analytic" solutions that will in fact effect superior health quality outcomes and thus also uphold the Hippocratic principle of "do no harm".

Given that healthcare affects everyone, this book is targeted at out students, healthcare professionals, patients, the web of healthcare players and the general public. We trust that the book a) assists to demystify the role of analytics as well as AI and ML enabled digital solutions for healthcare contexts, b) inspires researchers and students to push the envelope of possibilities for enabling and supporting superior healthcare delivery for everyone, every time everywhere and c) most importantly to educate patients so they can ask the right questions without fear or prejudice so they can get the care they want and need as they want and need it.

To address such a rich domain of inquiry we have collected the following miscellany of chapters that in turn highlight critical aspects and key issues around responsible analytics as follows:

CHAPTER OVERVIEW

Chapter 1 Barriers To Digital Health Adoption For Type 2 Diabetes Management During Covid-19: A Utaut Perspective

By Ayesha Thanthrige and Nilmini Wickramasinghe

The COVID-19 pandemic exposed critical gaps in healthcare delivery, emphasizing the need for scalable digital health solutions (DHS). Managing chronic conditions such as Type 2 Diabetes Mellitus (T2DM) became increasingly complex during this period, particularly in the U.S. where T2DM prevalence is high. This chapter addresses the overlooked barriers to DHS adoption in T2DM care through a PRISMA-guided systematic review and the Unified Theory of Acceptance and Use of Technology (UTAUT) framework. The analysis identifies key barriers, including infrastructural limitations, usability issues, socioeconomic disparities, privacy concerns, and perceived usefulness. Findings emphasize the importance of enhancing infrastructure, simplifying user interfaces, and improving digital security to support adoption and long-term use. These insights inform the design of more equitable, effective digital health systems and provide actionable guidance for chronic disease management beyond the pandemic context.

Chapter 2 Blockchain-Enabled AI for Secure and Intelligent Patient-Reported Outcome Measures (PROMs) Analysis

By Asiya Attar and Kasturi Shukla

Integrating Patient-Reported Outcome Measures (PROMs) and Artificial Intelligence (AI) has brought about a transformation of the healthcare system by improving predictive analysis and customized treatment. Nevertheless, bias, data privacy, and integrity issues remain since data storage is centralized and vulnerable to security attacks. This chapter outlines an interdisciplinary solution through blockchain and AI that would further enhance the security, transparency, and analytical efficiency of PROMs. Blockchain can provide data integrity, decentralized control, and patient privacy, and AI can provide real-time smart analysis of PROMs data. Additionally, a brief comparison of prominent blockchain platforms is provided to guide technology selection based on health needs. The authors have also proposed an AI-based framework for PROMs, which incorporates blockchain technology to address the problems of data fragmentation, security, and accessibility. This linkage of technical innovation to patient-driven objectives facilitates more ethical, efficient, and responsive healthcare systems.

Chapter 3 Combating Food Health Misinformation and Disinformation with Advanced RAG-LLM: Prototype AI on PubMed for Cardiac Health

By Luuk Simons, Pradeep Murukannaiah and Mark Neerincx

Effective prevention and treatment of cardiovascular disease rely on healthy lifestyle behaviors. However, the expanding and often conflicting nature of scientific literature, along with prevalent food and health misinformation/disinformation, hinders informed decision-making. Large Language Models (LLMs) with Retrieval-Augmented Generation (RAG) capabilities offer automated claim verification and summarization. An enhanced RAG-LLM prototype with novel modules is evaluated for effectiveness. Results as presented in this chapter serve to show that Inclusion-Criteria-based filtering of PubMed articles improved verdict accuracy. Furthermore, employing a PICO-based (Population, Intervention, Comparison, Outcome) approach for summarizing evidence in health claims (e.g., 'Berries reduce blood pressure') increased transparency. Still, the tested RAG-LLM models exhibited biases towards positivity (overemphasizing heart-healthy aspects) and neutrality. Likely causes of these biases and future development challenges are discussed, as well as AI tooling enabling governance on industry influences in nutrition science.

Chapter 4 Data Mining Techniques in Health Care Sector: Stages, Techniques, Comparisons, Selection criteria and Applications

By Aman Tyagi

Data mining is a process of knowledge discovery. In data mining, as discussed in this chapter, the data is collected from data warehouse and after cleaning and preprocessing, data is stored in the data warehouse in the transformed form. The transformed data is collected from data warehouse and data mining is applied on data and useful information and knowledge is produced. This is called data mining or knowledge discovery. Now a days data mining is widely applied on the healthcare data. In the present chapter OLAP, data mining process, healthcare applications, current healthcare research on data mining, different data mining techniques used and their comparison, discussion and analysis are discussed.

Chapter 5 Enhancing Healthcare Sustainability through AI-Driven Medical Devices

By T Venkat Narayana Rao, Kudipudi Jayashree, G Ravi, J V P Udaya Deepika and Kusumalatha Karre

Medical devices controlled through artificial intelligence are leading the path to make healthcare a sustainable and efficient system. They use artificial intelligence (AI) with the internet of medical things (IoMT) to improve patient's care, decrease resource utilization, and decrease the amount of harm to the environment. In this chapter, the authors strive to narrate various uses of AI in medical appliances like wearable health appliances, diagnosis devices, and remote surveillance systems with sustainable health care. Benchmarked on real-world examples, it demonstrates the processes through which they adapt and strengthen organisational/consumer practices. The chapter analyses the issues associated with these technologies, for instance: data privacy and protection issues, ethical issues concerning decision-making through the artificial intelligence, minimise barriers and minimise the need for invasive procedures. Last, it looks to future developments including combining AI with renewables and other innovations in seeking to improve sustainable care delivery in healthcare.

Chapter 6 Enhancing Patient Outcomes with Machine Learning in Healthcare Predictive Analytics

By Manthan Ghosh and Deepa Das

The increasing availability of healthcare data, coupled with advances in machine learning (ML), has enabled significant progress in early disease prediction and diagnosis. This chapter explores how ML enhances early disease prediction and diagnosis by analyzing structured and unstructured healthcare data, such as EHRs, genomics, wearable sensors, and imaging. It covers key ML techniques—logistic regression, decision trees, SVMs-applied to clinical tasks. The chapter also discusses feature engineering, handling imbalanced data, and improving interpretability. Real-world use cases in detecting cancer, diabetes, cardiovascular, and neurological diseases are presented. Integration into clinical workflows is explored, showing how predictive models improve diagnostic accuracy, reduce hospital readmissions, and support preventive care. Ethical concerns such as data privacy, algorithmic bias, and the need for explainable AI are addressed. Future directions include advancements in personalized medicine, responsible AI deployment, and predictive models supporting global health initiatives.

Chapter 7 Factors Influencing Consumers' Acceptance and Use of Wearable Devices in Ehealth: A Study Using the UTAUT2 Model

By Seema Rajesh Laddha

This research aimes to investigate the factors influencing the usage intention of healthcare technology among patients in a developing country. A total of 500 patients participated in the study and completed a structured questionnaire that included measures of perceived usefulness, perceived ease of use, facilitating conditions, hedonic motivation, price, trust, social influence, habit, trial, SIFR, and perceived risk. The results indicate that perceived usefulness, perceived ease of use, facilitating conditions, hedonic motivation, price, and trust were positively related to usage intention, while perceived risk was negatively related. Social influence - specialist, habit, trial, and SIFR were found to have a significant positive correlation with usage intention but were not predictive factors.

Chapter 8 First insights in video-based patient monitoring in the long-time care setting

By Marcel Sailer, Alena Sofie Fischer, Sarah Kaiser, Amelie Münzing and Mina Julie Schmachtel

Video-based monitoring systems in long-term inpatient care represent an opportunity to increase patient safety. This chapter intends to provide a basis for discussion for the use of video-based monitoring systems, focusing on nursing an public acceptance. Method Interviews were conducted with nursing care professionals (n=4) and people from the public (n=244) were surveyed via an online survey. Results and Discussion The results clearly show that video-based monitoring systems have both advantages and disadvantages as well as ethical aspects and factors that influence the acceptance of video-based monitoring which must be weighed up individually. From the total responses of n=244, 47,1% (n=115) of survey participants are in favour of the use of monitoring systems in nursing, while 40,1% are undecided. The most frequently mentioned advantages from the interviews included continual vital sign monitoring, faster reactions in emergencies, a reduction in the workload of nursing staff and an increase in patient safety, for example through improved fall prevention for patients.

Chapter 9 Improved Public Health Ontologies in the Era of Generative AI Technologies

By Dilek Küçük and Emine Ela Küçük

Generative artificial intelligence (AI) technologies have common applications in different domains in-cluding medicine or health in general, law, education, and finance. Large language models (LLMs) con-stitute a subset of generative AI, that are trained on large text datasets to automatically generate natural language content. LLMs, similarly, are used to facilitate different tasks, and ontology engineering is among these tasks. Related research shows that LLMs can achieve promising performance in different ontology engineering tasks, particularly in ontology construction from text descriptions. In this book chapter, the authors first review the literature on ontology engineering and LLMs, and next, the literature on the use of this generative AI technology (namely, LLMs) for improved health, and public health, ontolo-gies is reviewed. The authors also outline the main findings of the reviewed studies and present significant fu-ture research directions regarding the use of the recent generative AI technologies for improving public health ontologies.

Chapter 10 Integrating Generative AI, Blockchain, and Smart Health Technologies for Intelligent Clinical Decision Support

By F. Sammy, P. Gajalakshmi, R. Veerasundari, T. Thilagam and L. Anto Gracious

Generative AI, blockchain, mobile health (mHealth), wearables, sensors, and smart CDSS are emerging trends in healthcare. Generative AI using deep learning and NLP improves diagnosis, treatment planning, and outcome prediction. Blockchain ensures secure, transparent, and patient-owned medical records. mHealth apps support communication, monitoring, and AI-driven diagnosis, while wearables and sensors enable real-time health tracking and personalized care. The integration of these technologies has some considerations like data harmonization, compatibility, legal issues and security vulnerabilities. This chapter explores the use, benefits, and limits of these technologies, with real-world examples and a look at future directions. It highlights the need for multidisciplinary work on AI interpretability, federated learning, and ethical guidelines. In conclusion, integrating these technologies can transform clinical decision-making and enhance patient-centered care.

Chapter 11 MENTORd - A Responsible mHealth Artifact for Empowering Type II Diabetes Self-Management

By Shane Joachim Abdur Forkan, Prem Prakash Jayaraman, Muhammad Ali Chaudhry, Zeina Khouri-Stevens and Nilmini Wickramasinghe

This chapter presents MENTORd, a responsible mHealth artifact supporting Type II Diabetes self-management. While diabetes apps are widely available, most lack theoretical grounding, personalisation, and responsible data practices, limiting adoption and impact. MENTORd addresses these gaps through a co-designed platform integrating behaviour change techniques and AI-driven analytics. Developed using an Adapted 4-Cycle Design Science Research Methodology (A4C-DSRM), it combines a cross-platform patient app with a clinician dashboard. Key features include a Macronutrient Detection Algorithm (MDA), Glucometer Detection Model (GDM), Nudge rule engine, and tracking of blood glucose, medication, and physical activity. Behavioural interventions are guided by Nudge Theory, with Task-Technology Fit ensuring user alignment. Responsible analytics principles such as secure data handling, contextual AI, and iterative stakeholder engagement are integrated throughout. This chapter provides a structured artifact description and insights into ethical mHealth design for chronic disease management.

Chapter 12 Precision and accuracy management for PROMs: A model for data integrity in value-based healthcare

By Thais Spiegel, Daniel Bouzon Nagem Assad

Rising healthcare expenses, along with the need to improve patient outcomes, have led to the faster implementation of a value-based healthcare (VBHC) model. This approach aims to ensure the effectiveness of Patient-Reported Outcome Measures (PROMs) data gathering by suggesting a systematic framework for executing precision and accuracy management practices within a specialized governance structure, like a Value Management Office that allows healthcare institutions to effectively improve their data accuracy and reduce measurement bias. Therefore, this chapter proposes a framework that incorporates five essential practices—specifically, questionnaire design, standardized data collection, data quality assurance, statistical validation, and risk adjustment—to guarantee that PROM data is trustworthy, comparable, and functional. This also allows fair comparisons among healthcare providers, encouraging evidence-driven choices, and fostering trust between patients and clinicians that contributes to methodological foundations of VBHC.

Chapter 13 Revolutionizing Digital Healthcare The Role of AI Innovations in E-Health Transformation

By Tarun Madan Kanade

The integration of Artificial Intelligence (AI) and the Internet of Things (IoT) into healthcare—AIoT—has revolutionized medical service delivery. The study "AI Innovations Transforming E-Health Systems" presented in this chapter explores AI's role in reshaping digital health. It introduces AIoT's significance, objectives, and research structure, tracing its evolution from early AI and IoT applications. Advances in machine learning, NLP, computer vision, and robotics support predictive analytics, efficient data handling, imaging, and precision surgery. AIoT is applied in remote monitoring, telemedicine, wearable tech, and smart facilities, enabling real-time analytics and personalized care. Case studies highlight AIoT's benefits and challenges. The study also discusses technical, integration, security, and cost barriers. Future directions include edge computing, 5G, blockchain, and predictive systems. It concludes by emphasizing the need to address these challenges to fully harness AIoT's potential in healthcare.

No one book can cover all topics, but it is our hope and intention to provide the readers with an overview of the core and critical areas that need to be considered. Clearly these are all necessary aspects that must be addressed but not necessarily sufficient. Healthcare delivery is complex and a messy problem space but we contend that by taking a responsible approach to analytics and related AI and ML solutions we can ensure that we maximise the benefits these solutions can provide and thus be confident we can deliver superior health quality outcomes. We trust our readers enjoy this opus at least as much as we have enjoyed preparing it for you.

The Editors

Nilmini Wickramasinghe

Rima Gibbings

October 2025.

Acknowledgement

This book would not have been possible without the efforts of so many people. First and foremost, a big thank you to all the contributing authors, your chapters are what have made this book so unique and provided the breadth and depth of content in the following pages. In addition, we want to acknowledge the work of those who reviewed chapters; without your diligence and dedication the caliber and quality of this final product could not have been achieved. We are most grateful to our colleagues for all their suggestions, coffee catch up discussions and feedback which have helped to keep this project on track and to point. Further, we are indebted to our respective organizations for affording me the time to work on this project. We greatly appreciated and valued the support the team at IGI provided. Last but not least, a special thank you to our families whose support and encouragement is greatly valued and appreicated.

Chapter 1

Barriers to Digital Health Adoption for Type 2 Diabetes Management During COVID-19: A UTAUT Perspective

Ayesha Thanthrige
https://orcid.org/0009-0001-0518-2849
La Trobe University, Australia

Nilmini Wickramasinghe
La Trobe University, Australia

ABSTRACT

The COVID-19 pandemic exposed critical gaps in healthcare delivery, emphasizing the need for scalable digital health solutions (DHS). Managing chronic conditions such as Type 2 Diabetes Mellitus (T2DM) became increasingly complex during this period, particularly in the U.S. where T2DM prevalence is high. This chapter addresses the overlooked barriers to DHS adoption in T2DM care through a PRISMA-guided systematic review and the Unified Theory of Acceptance and Use of Technology (UTAUT) framework. The analysis identifies key barriers, including infrastructural limitations, usability issues, socioeconomic disparities, privacy concerns, and perceived usefulness. Findings emphasize the importance of enhancing infrastructure, simplifying user interfaces, and improving digital security to support adoption and long-term use. These insights inform the design of more equitable, effective digital health systems and provide actionable guidance for chronic disease management beyond the pandemic context.

DOI: 10.4018/979-8-3373-2545-3.ch001

1. INTRODUCTION

The COVID-19 pandemic disrupted global healthcare systems, particularly revealing weaknesses in chronic disease management, particularly for Type 2 Diabetes Mellitus (T2DM). In the United States (U.S.), T2DM affects 38.4 million people (11.6% of the population) as of 2023, with an additional 97.6 million showing prediabetic symptoms (CDC, 2024). T2DM's high prevalence has also led to high costs and demand for continuous monitoring. It places a significant burden on healthcare systems, and the situation has further worsened due to restricted access during the pandemic (Filip et al., 2022). Digital health solutions (DHSs), such as telemedicine and mobile apps, were needed to ensure continuity of care, especially for T2DM, enabling remote consultations and glucose monitoring (Cimini et al., 2022). However, several unique adoption challenges emerged, particularly in the U.S. context, due to healthcare policy gaps, racial disparities, and infrastructure constraints (Tewari et al., 2023; Waizinger et al., 2022).

On the other hand, T2DM patients faced heightened risks during the pandemic, with increased complications due to disrupted care (Upsher et al., 2022). DHSs mitigated these issues by facilitating remote monitoring, but adoption varied across U.S. populations due to digital literacy, socio-economic status, and trust in technology. Given the U.S.'s uniquely fragmented healthcare system and the disparities it creates this study explores how T2DM impacts diverse communities' access to DHSs (Stange, 2009; Steinhardt et al., 2021). Examining these barriers during COVID-19 provides insights into future disruptions, ensuring DHSs remain relevant for chronic disease management post-pandemic.

Prior research on DHS adoption for T2DM in the U.S. often examines barriers in isolation (Petersen et al., 2020), such as technological constraints, without a unified framework. U.S. specific factors, like insurance barriers, racial inequities, and policy fragmentation, are also important and remain underexplored (Stange, 2009; Villagra et al., 2019). This study addresses these gaps by systematically analyzing barriers using the Unified Theory of Acceptance and Use of Technology (UTAUT) framework (Venkatesh et al., 2003) (Refer to appendix A). UTAUT's application in this context is novel, as its use in digital health for T2DM during crises is limited in the U.S. context (Petersen et al., 2020). The UTAUT framework was selected for its comprehensive integration of multiple technology acceptance models, offering a robust lens to evaluate user behavior across performance expectancy (PE), effort expectancy (EE), social influence (SI), facilitating conditions (FC), behavioral intention (BI), and usage behavior (UB). Its applicability to health technology adoption is well-documented, but its use in the context of T2DM during a public health crisis in the U.S. is novel (Petersen et al., 2020; Venkatesh et al., 2003). UTAUT's strength lies in its ability to account for contextual factors, such as socio-economic disparities and policy constraints, which are particularly relevant to the U.S. healthcare system. By applying UTAUT, this study bridges theoretical and practical insights, addressing the unique interplay of technological and contextual barriers during the COVID-19 pandemic.

The objective is to identify barriers to DHS adoption among T2DM patients during COVID-19 in the U.S., informing policymakers on equitable solutions. The study was narrowed to the pandemic and U.S. context as it accelerated digital health use, highlighting unique challenges like access and usability. Additionally, the U.S. has a high T2DM prevalence. UTAUT's constructs guide the analysis of barriers systematically, such as infrastructure and privacy concerns, bridging theoretical and practical insights.

Practically, this study provides more important scalable strategies such as enhancing infrastructure and addressing inequities to improve DHS access for T2DM management, benefiting policymakers, providers, and developers, contributing new insights to chronic disease management literature with implications beyond the pandemic.

2. METHODOLOGY

2.1 Study Design

This systematic literature review examines barriers to DHS adoption among U.S. T2DM patients during the COVID-19 pandemic (2020–2023), using the UTAUT framework (Venkatesh et al., 2003). The review adheres to the Preferred Reporting Items for Systematic Reviews and Meta-Analyses (PRISMA) guidelines to ensure transparency and rigor (Page et al., 2021). Refer to Figure 1.

2.2 Research Question

What are the key barriers to adopting DHSs among T2DM patients in the U.S., and how were these barriers affected by the COVID-19 pandemic?

2.3 Search Strategy

The research question was broken into four concepts focusing on four concepts namely T2DM management, DHSs, COVID-19, and adoption barriers. Keywords included (1) T2DM ("Type 2 diabetes mellitus", "diabetes management"), (2) DHSs ("digital health", "telemedicine", "remote monitoring", "mobile health"), (3) COVID-19 ("COVID-19", "pandemic"), and (4) barriers ("adoption", "barriers", "challenges"). Search strings combined these using Boolean operators (e.g., "Type 2 diabetes AND telemedicine AND COVID-19 AND barriers") across MEDLINE, EMBASE, and Scopus, incorporating MeSH terms and keywords.

2.4 Study Selection

Studies were selected based on predefined criteria (Table 1). Two reviewers independently screened titles and abstracts, resolving discrepancies via discussion or with a third reviewer. A full-text review was conducted for the screened articles by detailed assessment by two independent reviewers, and the discrepancies between the reviewers were resolved through a third reviewer.

Table 1. Inclusion and exclusion criteria

Inclusion criteria	Exclusion criteria
Studies on T2DM diagnosis/management during COVID-19 using DHSs	Non-T2DM or non-COVID-19 studies
U.S. based community T2DM populations	Non-U.S. populations
Published between 2020 to 2023	Studies published before 2020
Published in English language	Non-English publications

2.5 Data Extraction

A standardised form captured study design, setting, population, interventions, outcomes, and barriers. Two researchers extracted data independently, resolving discrepancies through discussion.

2.6 Data Synthesis

Thematic analysis followed Braun and Clarke's (2006) six-step process: (1) data familiarization, (2) coding barriers using UTAUT constructs, (3) theme generation, (4) theme review, (5) theme definition, and (6) reporting. UTAUT constructs Performance Expectancy (PE), Effort Expectancy (EE), Social Influence (SI), Facilitating Conditions (FC), Behavioral Intention (BI), and Usage Behavior (UB) informed initial coding, with themes refined using NVivo software (Braun & Clarke, 2006).

3. RESULTS

3.1 Study Selection and Characteristics

The review identified 426 publications and 30 duplicates were removed, leaving 396 for screening. After title/abstract screening, 380 were excluded, and 16 articles underwent full-text review resulting in 15 studies for final analysis. Refer to Figure 1. The small sample reflects the specific U.S. and COVID-19 focus but ensures relevance (Rethlefsen et al., 2021). The analysis shows that 50% of the studies were conducted in mixed (both urban and rural) settings, indicating broad applicability of DHSs across diverse environments. Urban settings accounted for 42% of the studies, highlighting a significant focus on densely populated areas where healthcare infrastructure is generally more accessible.

Figure 1. Preferred Reporting Items for Systematic Reviews and Meta-Analyses (PRISMA) diagram of the study selection process

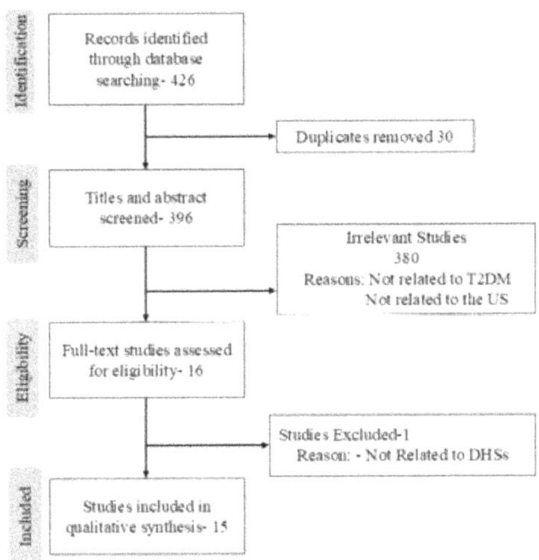

3.2 DHSs for T2DM Management

DHSs such as telemedicine, mobile apps, and remote monitoring enabled remote consultations, glucose monitoring, and lifestyle interventions and have been utilised during COVID-19. These tools ensured care continuity despite restricted in-person access, supporting T2DM management in urban and rural settings. Telemedicine dominated (50%) due to its scalability, while mobile apps facilitated patient engagement.

3.3 Thematic Analysis of Barriers

Five themes emerged namely infrastructure constraints, usability challenges, socio-economic disparities, privacy and trust issues, and perceived usefulness limitations, supported by direct evidence (Table 2). BI and UB were not standalone themes but had an impact across barriers, as FC, EE, SI, and PE reduced adoption intentions and usage.

Table 2. Detailed Analysis of Barriers

Barrier Theme	UTAUT Construct	Description and Examples	Source(s)
Infrastructure Constraints	FC	Limited internet access and unstable connections restrict video teleconsultations for diabetes management, particularly in rural areas. For example, patients struggle with consistent connectivity for virtual appointments. "Not all families are comfortable using telehealth technology and others lack access to a stable internet connection."	(Monaghan & Marks, 2020; Petersen et al., 2020; Steinhardt et al., 2021; Vaughan et al., 2022)
Infrastructure Constraints	FC	Lack of access to devices (e.g., computers, smartphones) exacerbates the digital divide for diabetes patients. "During the COVID-19 pandemic, populations with health disparities are the same as those that are having difficulty accessing virtual health care. Access barriers include... not having the necessary hardware and software..."	(Kerr & Sabharwal, 2021; Steinhardt et al., 2021)
Infrastructure Constraints	FC	Location-based logistical barriers (e.g., lack of transportation, distance to facilities) hinder telehealth access in rural areas. For example, patients may need in-person visits for device setup.	(Merrill et al., 2022)
Infrastructure Constraints	FC	Lack of interoperability in health devices and data systems complicates virtual diabetes care. "An often-touted reason for reluctance to embrace interoperability is the perception that interoperability will hamper innovation..."	(Kerr & Sabharwal, 2021)
Infrastructure Constraints	FC	Logistical challenges for providers, such as inadequate clinic resources and training, limit telehealth implementation. For example, nurse practitioners face challenges adapting to virtual care.	(Vaughan et al., 2022; Waizinger et al., 2022)
Infrastructure Constraints	FC	Travel requirements and distance to facilities pose barriers, particularly in underserved areas. For example, patients may need in-person visits for initial telehealth setup.	(Casas et al., 2023; Lam et al., 2020; Steinhardt et al., 2021)

continued on following page

Table 2. Continued

Barrier Theme	UTAUT Construct	Description and Examples	Source(s)
Usability Challenges	EE	Older adults with diabetes prefer traditional methods (e.g., landlines) and face physical impairments (e.g., hearing, vision), increasing effort for telehealth use. For example, 36.7% of U.S. seniors used landlines in 2021.	(Casas et al., 2023; He et al., 2023; Lam et al., 2020)
Usability Challenges	EE	Young adults with diabetes faced disruptions (e.g., college closures, unemployment, low digital literacy), increasing effort for virtual diabetes management. "Young adults with diabetes are particularly vulnerable during the COVID-19 pandemic..."	(Monaghan & Marks, 2020; Upsher et al., 2022)
Usability Challenges	EE	Telehealth platforms with technical limitations (e.g., complex interfaces) increase effort, particularly for low-digital-literacy patients. A layered approach is needed for self-efficacy.	(Beks et al., 2022; Petersen et al., 2020; Upsher et al., 2022)
Usability Challenges	EE	Lack of smartphone-focused telehealth platforms increases effort for diverse diabetes populations. "Smartphone-based internet access has substantially reduced the digital divide..."	(Kerr & Sabharwal, 2021)
Usability Challenges	EE	Telehealth's inability to conduct thorough physical examinations (e.g., foot exams) increases effort for accurate diabetes management.	(Casas et al., 2023)
Usability Challenges	EE	Providers require new expertise for virtual diabetes care, increasing effort for tasks like patient education.	(Merrill et al., 2022)
Usability Challenges	EE	Complex telehealth interfaces hinder self-management for type 2 diabetes patients, particularly those with limited digital skills. For example, patients struggle with remote glucose monitoring tools.	(Upsher et al., 2022)
Socio-Economic Disparities	FC	Financial instability and stress (e.g., job loss, insurance concerns) hindered diabetes management and telehealth access. "Financial instability during the pandemic increased worries about contracting COVID-19..."	(Monaghan & Marks, 2020)
Socio-Economic Disparities	FC	Community clinics face resource constraints (e.g., time, participant recruitment) in underserved areas with high diabetes prevalence.	(Beks et al., 2022)
Socio-Economic Disparities	FC	Healthcare disparities limit telehealth access for low-income and minority diabetes patients. For example, underserved areas face economic and systemic inequities.	(Chunara et al., 2021)
Socio-Economic Disparities	FC	Low health insurance literacy among minority and low-income diabetes patients creates barriers to telehealth access. For example, patients may not understand virtual visit coverage.	(Villagra et al., 2019)

continued on following page

Table 2. Continued

Barrier Theme	UTAUT Construct	Description and Examples	Source(s)
Privacy and Trust Issues	SI	Privacy and cybersecurity concerns (e.g., inconsistent privacy notices) undermine trust, particularly among older adults. "A major concern for maintaining and developing trust is the serious issue of privacy..."	(Kerr & Sabharwal, 2021)
Privacy and Trust Issues	SI	Telehealth visits for mental health aspects of diabetes care require private spaces, which many patients lack. For example, crowded households limit privacy.	(He et al., 2023)
Privacy and Trust Issues	SI	Historical healthcare mistreatment contributes to distrust among minority diabetes populations. "Absence of trust in the healthcare system... is based on historical precedents."	(Kerr & Sabharwal, 2021)
Perceived Usefulness Limitations	PE	Telehealth's inability to support physical examinations reduces perceived usefulness. "Telehealth services currently face limitations in conducting thorough physical examinations..."	(Casas et al., 2023; He et al., 2023)
Perceived Usefulness Limitations	PE	Discordant health beliefs, particularly among Black Americans, reduce telehealth's perceived usefulness. "Among Americans with diabetes who are Black, discordant health beliefs are common..."	(Kerr & Sabharwal, 2021; Tewari et al., 2023)

These barriers are visually summarized in a Fishbone Diagram (Figure 2), illustrating their contributions to the limited adoption of DHSs. UTAUT constructs shaped thematic synthesis, mapping barriers to PE, EE, SI, and FC, which influenced BI and UB (Venkatesh et al., 2003). For example, "limited internet" was coded as a FC barrier, which reduced BI. Infrastructure constraints (FC) like unstable internet lowered BI and UB, especially for rural patients (He et al., 2023). Usability challenges (EE) increased perceived effort, reducing BI among seniors. Privacy and trust issues reduced engagement in virtual diabetes programs due to 47% of African American participants distrusting health information. Socio-economic disparities, with 60% of low-income patients facing device access issues, and 27.1% reporting financial stress, amplified infrastructure barriers (Chunara et al., 2021; Steinhardt et al., 2021).

Figure 2. Fishbone Diagram of Barriers to DHS Adoption

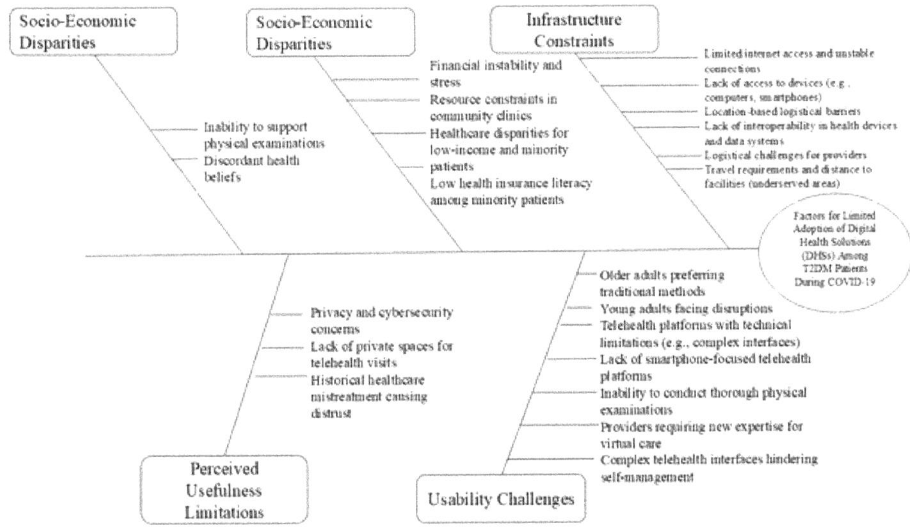

PE was impacted when DHSs couldn't support thorough exams, lowering UB (Casas et al., 2023). UTAUT assumes adequate infrastructure, but U.S.-specific policy gaps (e.g., telehealth reimbursement limits) worsened barriers, requiring framework adaptation (Patel et al., 2021). This U.S.-focused analysis highlights racial disparities (e.g., African Americans facing higher costs), offering new insights into policy-driven barriers (Chunara et al., 2021).

4. DISCUSSION

This systematic review identifies infrastructure constraints, usability challenges, socio-economic disparities, privacy concerns, and perceived usefulness limitations as key barriers to DHS adoption for T2DM management in the U.S. during the COVID-19 pandemic, analysed through the UTAUT framework. The selection of UTAUT was justified by its comprehensive integration of eight technology acceptance models, including the Technology Acceptance Model (TAM) and the Theory of Planned Behavior (TPB), which collectively explain user adoption behavior across diverse contexts (Venkatesh et al., 2003). UTAUT's constructs namely PE, EE, SI, FC, BI, and UB provide a structured lens to dissect the multifaceted barriers to DHS adoption, particularly in the U.S.'s fragmented healthcare system. Unlike other frameworks, such as TAM, which focuses primarily on perceived usefulness and ease of use, UTAUT incorporates social and environmental factors (e.g., SI and

FC), making it uniquely suited to address U.S.-specific issues like policy gaps and racial disparities. Its prior application in health technology contexts, though limited for T2DM during crises, supports its relevance for this study (Petersen et al., 2020).

Unreliable rural internet reduced FC, lowering BI, with 30% of rural U.S. households lacking broadband access (FCC, 2024). UTAUT assumes adequate infrastructure, but U.S. policy gaps, such as limited broadband subsidies and telehealth reimbursement restrictions, exacerbated barriers (Patel et al., 2021). Expanding broadband access and revising reimbursement policies can enhance FC. Complex telehealth interfaces increased EE, reducing BI among seniors, with 36.7% preferring landlines (Casas et al., 2023). Simplified, voice-navigated interfaces and digital literacy programs can improve UB, particularly for older adults (Lee et al., 2024). Privacy fears diminished SI, with 47% of African American patients distrusting health information due to historical mistreatment (Kerr & Sabharwal, 2021). Robust encryption and transparent privacy policies can rebuild trust (Ali et al., 2022). Telehealth's inability to support physical examinations reduced PE, lowering BI (Casas et al., 2023). Demonstrating improved self-management outcomes, such as reduced HbA1c levels, can enhance PE (Villagra et al., 2019). Socio-economic disparities, with 60% of low-income patients facing device access issues, amplified FC barriers (Chunara et al., 2021). Policies like the Affordable Care Act and targeted subsidies can ensure equity (Villagra et al., 2019). Incompatible systems hindered FC, reducing UB; interoperable platforms can streamline care (Villagra et al., 2019).

The U.S.'s fragmented healthcare system, characterised by private insurance dominance and varying state policies, uniquely shaped these barriers. For example, racial disparities, with African Americans facing higher costs due to insurance gaps, affected 60% of low-income patients (Tewari et al., 2023). This study extends UTAUT by highlighting the need for context-specific adaptations, such as incorporating policy-driven barriers, to better address U.S.-specific challenges. Recommendations include: (1) investing in broadband infrastructure to improve FC, (2) designing user-friendly, smartphone-focused platforms to reduce EE, (3) enhancing cybersecurity to address SI, (4) promoting interoperable systems to streamline FC, (5) subsidizing device access for low-income populations to mitigate FC barriers, and (6) conducting patient education campaigns to boost PE. These strategies align with UTAUT's constructs to improve BI and UB, ensuring equitable DHS adoption for T2DM management.

Future research should explore interventions like simplified interfaces or digital literacy programs to validate their impact on adoption. Longitudinal studies can assess post-pandemic DHS effectiveness, while cross-regional comparisons may reveal global disparities in adoption patterns. Mixed methods approach, combining quantitative surveys with qualitative interviews, can provide deeper insights into patient and provider experiences, addressing the limitation of secondary data reliance

(Creswell & Plano Clark, 2018). Incorporating additional frameworks, such as the Health Belief Model, alongside UTAUT could uncover sociocultural determinants of adoption (Rosenstock et al., 1988).

5. CONCLUSION

This systematic review examined the barriers influencing the adoption of digital health interventions among individuals with T2DM during the COVID-19 pandemic, using the Unified Theory of Acceptance and Use of Technology (UTAUT) as a guiding framework. UTAUT's comprehensive framework provided a robust lens to analyse the interplay of technological and contextual factors, offering new insights into U.S.-specific challenges like policy gaps and racial disparities. The findings highlight that PE, EE, FC, and SI significantly shaped users' engagement with digital tools, with pandemic-related disruptions amplifying these effects. This study contributes to the digital health literature by synthesizing recent U.S.-based evidence through a theory-driven lens, providing a timely understanding of how contextual and technological factors intersect during public health emergencies. The integration of UTAUT enhances explanatory power and offers a structured basis for evaluating adoption barriers across different contexts. Moreover, rapid changes in digital health technology may affect the generalizability of these findings over time. Future research should explore the evolving role of digital literacy, personalization, and trust in post-pandemic health technology use, particularly among vulnerable or underserved populations. Expanding theoretical frameworks beyond UTAUT can further elucidate sociocultural and behavioral determinants of DHS adoption.

REFERENCES

Ali, A., Almaiah, M. A., Hajjej, F., Pasha, M. F., Fang, O. H., Khan, R., Teo, J., & Zakarya, M. (2022). An Industrial IoT-Based Blockchain-Enabled Secure Searchable Encryption Approach for Healthcare Systems Using Neural Network. *Sensors (Basel)*, *22*(2), 572. DOI: 10.3390/s22020572 PMID: 35062530

Beks, H., King, O., Clapham, R., Alston, L., Glenister, K., McKinstry, C., Quilliam, C., Wellwood, I., Williams, C., & Wong Shee, A. (2022). Community Health Programs Delivered Through Information and Communications Technology in High-Income Countries: Scoping Review. *Journal of Medical Internet Research*, *24*(3), e26515–e26515. DOI: 10.2196/26515 PMID: 35262498

Braun, V., & Clarke, V. (2006). Using thematic analysis in psychology. *Qualitative Research in Psychology*, *3*(2), 77–101. https://url.au.m.mimecastprotect.com/s/VmMnCXLK3oUvE1JwtksxHWVmHz?domain=doi.org

Casas, L. A., Alarcón, J., Urbano, A., Peña-Zárate, E. E., Sangiovanni, S., Libreros-Peña, L., & Escobar, M. F. (2023). Telemedicine for the management of diabetic patients in a high-complexity Latin American hospital. *BMC Health Services Research*, *23*(1), 314–314. DOI: 10.1186/s12913-023-09267-0 PMID: 36997918

Chunara, R., Zhao, Y., Chen, J., Lawrence, K., Testa, P. A., Nov, O., & Mann, D. M. (2021). Telemedicine and healthcare disparities: A cohort study in a large healthcare system in New York City during COVID-19. *Journal of the American Medical Informatics Association : JAMIA*, *28*(1), 33–41. DOI: 10.1093/jamia/ocaa217 PMID: 32866264

Cimini, C. C. R., Maia, J. X., Pires, M. C., & Ribeiro, L. B., de Oliveira e Almeida Pinto, V. S., Batchelor, J., Ribeiro, A. L. P., & Marcolino, M. S. (2022). Pandemic-Related Impairment in the Monitoring of Patients With Hypertension and Diabetes and the Development of a Digital Solution for the Community Health Worker: Quasiexperimental and Implementation Study [Article]. *JMIR Medical Informatics*, *10*(3), e35216. Advance online publication. DOI: 10.2196/35216 PMID: 35191842

Creswell, J. W., & Plano Clark, V. L. (2018). *Designing and conducting mixed methods research* (3rd ed.). Sage Publications.

Federal Communications Commission (FCC). (2024). 2024 Broadband Deployment Report. https://www.fcc.gov/reports-research/reports/broadband-progress-reports

Filip, R., Gheorghita Puscaselu, R., Anchidin-Norocel, L., Dimian, M., & Savage, W. K. (2022). Global Challenges to Public Health Care Systems during the COVID-19 Pandemic: A Review of Pandemic Measures and Problems. *Journal of Personalized Medicine*, *12*(8), 1295. DOI: 10.3390/jpm12081295 PMID: 36013244

He, Q., Keith, D., Eckhoff, D. O., Park, C., & Ng, B. P. (2023). Accessibility and Utilization of Telehealth Services During the COVID-19 Pandemic Among Medicare Beneficiaries by Diabetes Status. *Research in Gerontological Nursing*, *16*(3), 134–146. DOI: 10.3928/19404921-20230301-01 PMID: 36881008

Kerr, D., & Sabharwal, A. (2021). Principles for virtual health care to deliver real equity in diabetes. *The Lancet. Diabetes & Endocrinology*, *9*(8), 480–482. DOI: 10.1016/s2213-8587(21)00176-5 PMID: 34217405

Lam, K., Lu, A. D., Shi, Y., & Covinsky, K. E. (2020). Assessing Telemedicine Unreadiness Among Older Adults in the United States During the COVID-19 Pandemic. *JAMA Internal Medicine*, *180*(10), 1389–1391. DOI: 10.1001/jamainternmed.2020.2671 PMID: 32744593

Lee, S., Kim, J., & Park, H. (2024). Digital literacy interventions for older adults: A systematic review. *Journal of Health Communication*, *29*(3), 145–156. DOI: 10.1080/10810730.2024.1234567

Merrill, C. B., Roe, J. M., Seely, K. D., & Brooks, B. (2022). Advanced Telemedicine Training and Clinical Outcomes in Type II Diabetes: A Pilot Study. *Telemedicine Reports*, *3*(1), 15–23. DOI: 10.1089/tmr.2021.0039 PMID: 35720452

Monaghan, M., & Marks, B. (2020). Personal Experiences With COVID-19 and Diabetes Technology: All for Technology Yet Not Technology for All. *Journal of Diabetes Science and Technology*, *14*(4), 762–763. DOI: 10.1177/1932296820930005 PMID: 32460543

Patel, S. Y., Mehrotra, A., Huskamp, H. A., Uscher-Pines, L., Ganguli, I., & Barnett, M. L. (2021). Trends in Outpatient Care Delivery and Telemedicine During the COVID-19 Pandemic in the US. *JAMA Internal Medicine*, *181*(3), 388–391. DOI: 10.1001/jamainternmed.2020.5928 PMID: 33196765

Petersen, F., Jacobs, M., & Pather, S. (2020, 2020//). Barriers for User Acceptance of Mobile Health Applications for Diabetic Patients: Applying the UTAUT Model. Responsible Design, Implementation and Use of Information and Communication Technology, Cham.

Rethlefsen, M. L., Kirtley, S., Waffenschmidt, S., Ayala, A. P., Moher, D., Page, M. J., & Koffel, J. B., & Group, P.-S. (2021). PRISMA-S: An extension to the PRISMA statement for reporting literature searches in systematic reviews. *Journal of the Medical Library Association: JMLA, 109*(2), 174–200. DOI: 10.5195/jmla.2021.962 PMID: 34285662

Rosenstock, I. M., Strecher, V. J., & Becker, M. H. (1988). Social learning theory and the Health Belief Model. *Health Education Quarterly, 15*(2), 175–183. DOI: 10.1177/109019818801500203 PMID: 3378902

Stange, K. C. M. D. P. (2009). The Problem of Fragmentation and the Need for Integrative Solutions. *Annals of Family Medicine, 7*(2), 100–103. DOI: 10.1370/afm.971 PMID: 19273863

Steinhardt, M. A., Brown, S. A., Lehrer, H. M., Dubois, S. K., Wright, J. I., Whyne, E. Z., Sumlin, L. L., Harrison, L.Jr, & Woo, J. (2021). Diabetes Self-Management Education and Support Culturally Tailored for African Americans: COVID-19-Related Factors Influencing Restart of the TX STRIDE Study. *The Science of Diabetes Self-Management and Care, 47*(4), 290–301. DOI: 10.1177/26350106211027956 PMID: 34318725

Tewari, S., Coyne, K. D., Weinerman, R. S., Findley, J., Kim, S. T., & Flyckt, R. L. (2023). Racial Disparities in Telehealth Use During the COVID-19 Pandemic. *Fertility and Sterility*. Advance online publication. DOI: 10.1016/j.fertnstert.2023.05.159 PMID: 37244379

Upsher, R., Noori, Y., Kuriakose, L., Vassiliadou, I., Winkley, K., & Ismail, K. (2022). Needs, concerns and self-management experiences of people with type 2 diabetes during the COVID-19 pandemic: A qualitative study. *Diabetic medicine, 39*(8), e14883-n/a. https://doi.org/DOI: 10.1111/dme.14883

Vaughan, E., Foreyt, J., Virani, S., Balasubramanyam, A., Ballantyne, C., Amspoker, A., & Landrum, J. (2022, 2022). Mentored implementation to initiate a diabetes program in an underserved community: A pilot study.

Venkatesh, V., Morris, M. G., Davis, G. B., & Davis, F. D. (2003). User Acceptance of Information Technology: Toward a Unified View. *Management Information Systems Quarterly, 27*(3), 425–478. DOI: 10.2307/30036540

Villagra, V. G., Bhuva, B., Coman, E., Smith, D. O., & Fifield, J. (2019). Health insurance literacy: Disparities by race, ethnicity, and language preference. *The American Journal of Managed Care, 25*(3), e71–e75. PMID: 30875174

Waizinger, O., Shpigelman, M., Shental, R., Yunis, B., Shimoni, P., Od Cohen, Y., & Kagan, I. (2022). Diabetes nurse practitioners in the shadow of the COVID-19 pandemic: Challenges, insights, and suggestions for improvement. *Journal of nursing scholarship: an official publication of Sigma Theta Tau International Honor Society of Nursing, 54*(4), 453-461. https://doi.org/https://dx.doi.org/10.1111/jnu.12754

APPENDIX A

Unified Theory of Acceptance and Use of Technology (UTAUT)

Overview: The Unified Theory of Acceptance and Use of Technology (UTAUT) explains user intentions to use a particular technology and subsequent usage behavior. It integrates elements from multiple technology acceptance models into one unified framework.

Origin: Proposed by Venkatesh et al. (2003).

Key Constructs:

- Performance Expectancy (PE): The degree to which an individual believes using the system will help achieve gains in job performance.
- Effort Expectancy (EE): The degree of ease associated with the use of the system.
- Social Influence (SI): The extent to which an individual perceives that others believe they should use the new system.
- Facilitating Conditions (FC): The degree to which an individual believes that an organizational and technical infrastructure exists to support system use.
- Behavioral Intention (BI): The intention to use the system, which influences actual usage (Use Behavior).
- Moderators: Age, Gender, Experience, and Voluntariness of Use can moderate the relationships between these constructs.

Figure 3.

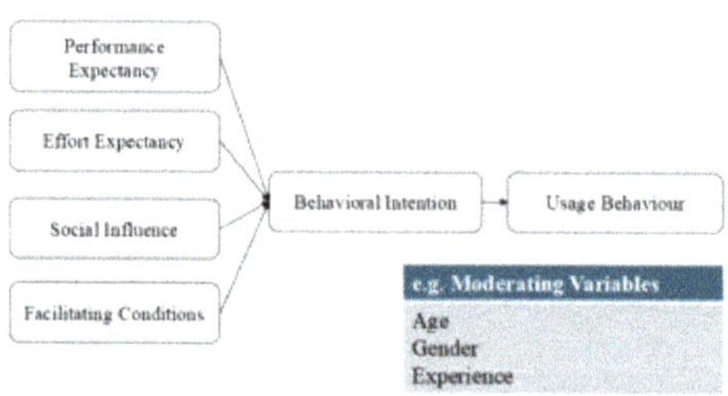

Chapter 2

Blockchain-Enabled AI for Secure and Intelligent Patient-Reported Outcome Measures (PROMs) Analysis

Asiya Attar
Symbiosis Institute of Health Sciences, Symbiosis International University, Pune, India

Kasturi Shukla
https://orcid.org/0000-0001-7006-9001
Symbiosis Institute of Health Sciences, Symbiosis International University, Pune, India

ABSTRACT

Integrating Patient-Reported Outcome Measures (PROMs) and Artificial Intelligence (AI) has brought about a transformation of the healthcare system by improving predictive analysis and customized treatment. Nevertheless, bias, data privacy, and integrity issues remain since data storage is centralized and vulnerable to security attacks. This chapter outlines an interdisciplinary solution through blockchain and AI that would further enhance the security, transparency, and analytical efficiency of PROMs. Blockchain can provide data integrity, decentralized control, and patient privacy, and AI can provide real-time smart analysis of PROMs data. Additionally, a brief comparison of prominent blockchain platforms is provided to guide technology selection based on health needs. The authors have also proposed an AI-based framework for PROMs, which incorporates blockchain technology to

DOI: 10.4018/979-8-3373-2545-3.ch002

address the problems of data fragmentation, security, and accessibility. This linkage of technical innovation to patient-driven objectives facilitates more ethical, efficient, and responsive healthcare systems.

1. INTRODUCTION

Advanced technological innovations and multidisciplinary collaborations have positively impacted the requirements of the evolving healthcare system (Alsahli et al., 2020; Bul et al., 2020). With the employment of Artificial Intelligence (AI), healthcare providers can better comprehend the signs and symptoms of a medical condition using predictive analytics (Jiang et al., 2017; Topol, 2019; Dhingra et al., 2024). This has enabled targeted treatment interventions to improve patient outcomes (Jiang et al., 2017; Topol, 2019; Alsahli et al., 2020). These outcomes are gauged using a questionnaire tool called Patient-Reported Outcome Measures (PROMs), which are critical in assessing healthcare quality. The integration of AI with PROMs has helped in delivering better Patient Centered Care (PCC), resulting in enhanced Quality of Life (QoL) (Balch et al., 2024; Yogeshappa, 2024).

Machine Learning (ML) and Deep Learning (DL) identify patterns in patients' responses collected using PROMs (Verma et al., 2021; Reine et al., 2022). Additionally, Natural Language Processing (NLP) extracts meaningful insights from unstructured PROMs data (Di Basilio et al., 2024). This is followed by predictive analytics, which generates individualized treatment plans based on historical patient data (Chabot et al., 2023). Although integrating AI with PROMs has enhanced data analysis and personalized healthcare, it still lacks strong security, privacy, and integrity measures (Zhang et al., 2018). This is possibly because the patient data is stored centrally, thereby vulnerable to breach and misuse (Wu et al., 2025). Additionally, the possibility of data tampering can annihilate the integrity of AI. Additionally, the absence of transparency in AI-based decision-making has the risk of bias and trust (Mello & Guha, 2024). Therefore, there is a need to integrate AI with technologies like blockchain to address these problems (Yogeshappa, 2024).

Blockchain technology eliminates the need for a single, centralized authority while enabling safe, secure, and direct transactions between entities (Nakamoto, 2008; Cîmpan & Cri an, 2025). The immutability of data makes it nearly impossible for untrustworthy parties to alter information (Mehta et al., 2020). Thus, the decentralized and tamper-proof structure of blockchain provides essential methods like smart contracts for protecting patient data and supports international data exchange for scientific research (Duong-Trung et al., 2020; Hasselgren et al., 2021; Yogeshappa, 2024; Adeghe et al., 2024; Chowdhury, 2024).

Therefore, this chapter aims to explore the potential of blockchain-enabled AI to assist PROMs in real-time and provide intelligent patient-reported data management. The chapter has addressed some of the chronic challenges related to data fragmentation, risks to privacy, and inefficiency in PROMs data management. The chapter has also provided solutions to these challenges using blockchain-enabled AI. Additionally, the authors have proposed a blockchain-AI-integrated, technology-driven framework that can create applicable insights for healthcare providers, researchers, and policymakers. Thus, the chapter presents a novel interdisciplinary approach that combines blockchain with AI to enhance the security, transparency, and analytic capabilities of PROMs data. The chapter has been, therefore, organized into eight sections to elaborate on the points mentioned above.

The first section, the introduction, provides a background to the chapter. The second and third sections set the overview of technological innovations in healthcare and PROMs, respectively. In the fourth section, the role of AI in enhancing PROMs has been provided in detail. This is followed by addressing the challenges in AI-driven PROMs in the fifth section. The sixth section introduces blockchain and briefly discusses its employability in healthcare. Integration of blockchain, AI, and PROMs is discussed in the seventh section. The authors propose a Blockchain-enabled AI framework for PROMs in the eighth section. Finally, the ninth section presents the concluding remarks.

2. OVERVIEW OF TECHNOLOGICAL INNOVATIONS IN HEALTHCARE

2.1 Evolution of Healthcare Technologies

The healthcare ecosystem is a complicated network of stakeholders that includes healthcare providers, patients, and regulators (Patil et al., 2024). Digital solutions have brought about a paradigm shift in the healthcare industry (Patil et al., 2024). The digitization of healthcare encompasses various technologies, like Electronic Health Records (EHRs), telemedicine, wearable technology, big data analytics, and AI. These technologies are making clinical practice more efficient and transforming the delivery, access, and experience of healthcare (Hasselgren et al., 2021; Patil et al., 2024). This transition is centered on an increasing emphasis on PCC. Due to individualized healthcare experiences, patients are empowered to participate in their care actively. This initiative has greatly improved the quality of healthcare services and raised the QoL of the patients (Krishnamoorthy et al., 2023). The pace of these innovations is also spurred by an increasing interdisciplinary environment, where researchers, technologists, clinicians, and policymakers collaborate to define healthcare's future. The nature of healthcare delivery is very dynamic and ad hoc, often requiring seamless coordination among professionals from various disciplines (Homayounfar, 2012). Their collaboration is critical to the ethical deployment, fair access, and sustainable implementation of emerging technologies.

2.2 Role of Multidisciplinary Collaboration and Technological Advancements

In this evolving landscape of healthcare, multidisciplinary collaboration is pivotal in ensuring holistic PCC. "Collaboration" refers to problem-solving techniques, shared decision-making authority, and the capacity to implement a treatment plan while pursuing a common objective (McKay & Crippen, 2008; Saint-Pierre et al., 2018). Effective collaboration is crucial to provide integrated care in complex clinical scenarios (Saint-Pierre et al., 2018). The benefits of such collaboration are well-documented (Singh et al., 2021; Alowais et al., 2023; Stoumpos et al., 2023). In healthcare, multidisciplinary collaborations have been associated with efficient use of resources, better patient outcomes, and increased Patient Satisfaction (PS) (Alsubaie et al., 2024). Additionally, interdisciplinary teams can address environmental, psychological, and social elements that impact health, which are often overlooked in a traditional biomedical model (Alrabei, 2023; Alsubaie et al., 2024). This all-encompassing strategy aligns closely with PCC, a paradigm that prioritizes comprehending and attending to a patient's needs, values, and preferences (IOM, 2001; Gluyas, 2015). Technological advancements have further strengthened this collaborative ethos. Electronic platforms, shared electronic medical records, and interoperability facilitation systems and AI-driven diagnostic systems enable clinicians, nurses, social workers, and even caregivers to add value to one's care plan (Saint-Pierre et al., 2018; Alsubaie et al., 2024). As interdisciplinary care becomes a part of healthcare increasingly, technologies such as AI enable collaboration that connects clinical expertise to patient experience.

2.3 Impact of AI in Healthcare

The advent of AI and ML has ushered in a new age in healthcare, repositioning the field as a data-driven, precision-oriented science. These technologies are redefining the delivery of care by enhancing operational effectiveness, cutting costs, and improving patient outcomes (Rehan, 2023). Predictive Analytics (PA) is a discipline at the center of this change. It utilizes historical and current data to make predictions (Rehan, 2023). Healthcare practitioners can access a multitude of insights from patient data by incorporating ML algorithms into PA. This enhances decision-making and allows for proactive patient care. From disease progression prediction and hospital readmission to clinical workflow and resource optimization, PA is enabling the shift from reactive care to preventive and personalized care (Callahan & Shah, 2017; Rehan, 2023). Among the most profound effects of this technology is its capacity for aiding individualized treatment planning. AI systems can prescribe individualized treatment by taking into account the genetic profile, clinical past, and treatment record of the patient, including interventions they have previously received (Parekh et al., 2023; Yogeshappa, 2024). It enhances treatment efficacy and reduces drug toxicity and needless expenditure, leading to a more sustainable healthcare system (Yogeshappa, 2024). Most significantly, PA facilitates PCC practices by treating each patient as an individual.

3. OVERVIEW OF PCC AND PROMS

3.1 Definition of PCC and PROMs

PCC is the "provision of care that is respectful of and responsive to individual patient preferences, needs, and values and ensures that patient values guide all clinical decisions (IOM, 2001)." This initiative marks a shift from systems prioritizing perspectives of healthcare providers to systems placing importance on the experience and voice of the patient. This rising focus on PCC is a continuation of the change in healthcare toward active patient participation, personalized care, and shared decision-making (Gluyas, 2015). Since the clinician's top priority is the patient's health, they are more likely to seek out improvements in the patient's clinical condition. However, what may be relevant to the patient may not always match the interest of the doctor (in terms of the outcome). Hence, PROMs can be used to gather patient-perspective data in a variety of contexts.

PROMs are defined as "questionnaires measuring the patients' views of their health status (NABH, 2020)." PROMs are structured questionnaires through which patients can self-report on domains of their health status (such as symptoms, functioning, and QoL) without intermediary clinical interpretation (NABH, 2020; Krepper et al., 2024). With the growing importance of patient involvement in care, PROMs are increasingly being used in conjunction with traditional clinical methods to gauge health and treatment effects (Shukla & Attar, 2024). Additionally, PROMs research enables scholars to study certain aspects of the patient's health, and patients' perception of the illness and the effect of its treatment on their QoL (Meadows, 2011; Field et al., 2019). With the rising data-based provision of healthcare, the quantity and value of patient-generated data have significantly increased (Jiang et al., 2022). Here, PROMs contribute heavily by documenting subjective yet essential information that may not be obvious using clinical assessments or doctor evaluation alone. These tools are being increasingly employed in clinical trials and regular healthcare practice, reflecting their validity and utility improvements (Meadows, 2011). Consequently, the volume of data generated has increased substantially in recent years (Jiang et al., 2022). This patient-centered data is now being used to assess treatment outcomes, make informed policy decisions, and improve healthcare planning, as discussed in the next sub-section.

3.2 Current Applications of PROMs

PROMs use has grown substantially in recent years, taking an important position in the delivery of healthcare. PROMs facilitate the monitoring of symptoms, treatment impact, and status of patient health in chronic disease management, allowing for timely clinical modifications (Black et al., 2021; Krepper et al., 2024). It is employed extensively in postoperative management to measure pain, mobility, and QoL, and assist in discharge planning and follow-up care (Jiang et al., 2022; Sokas et al., 2022; Simon et al., 2025). Additionally, PROMs data are used in policy-making and healthcare planning to establish service need areas, maximize resource allocation, and plan interventions based on actual patient needs (Chen et al., 2023; Minvielle et al., 2023; Hays & Quigley, 2025). PROMs also guide public health measurement, particularly in diseases like cancer, rehabilitation, and mental health (Al Sayah et al., 2021; Fair et al., 2025). Moreover, with the emergence of AI, large volumes of PROMs data are increasingly being used to predict outcomes, customize care plans, and enable data-driven, value-based delivery of healthcare (Andrikopoulou et al., 2023).

4. ROLE OF AI IN ENHANCING PROMS

Integrating AI and PROMs is a transformative shift in healthcare that facilitates predictive, sophisticated, and patient-centered methods of clinical decision-making and health system planning. Traditional methods of interpreting PROMs often fall short when handling complex, large-scale, and unstructured data. AI technologies like ML, DL, NLP, and PA assist in utilizing the PROMs data to its full potential. These technologies streamline the processes and clinical results and improve patient engagement. Additionally, they ensure that interventions are matched to patients' own experiences. Table 1 provides the existing applications and advantages of major AI technologies within the field of PROMs.

Table 1. Role of AI in Enhancing PROMs

Technology	Application in PROMs	Benefits
Machine Learning (ML)	● Construction of predictive model using structured PROMs data ● Treatment (success or failure) prediction ● Treatment personalization using patient-reported data	● Standardized and evidence-based predictions ● Optimizing resources ● Adaptive interventions
Deep Learning (DL)	Analyzes large, unstructured data sets such as PROMs and demographics to forecast patient trajectories	● High accuracy predictions ● Reveals intricate relationships within data ● Enables dynamic decision-making
Natural Language Processing (NLP)	● Analyzing open-text PROM responses ● Sentiment analysis ● Topic modeling to enhance patient experience insights	● Captures key results from qualitative PROMs ● Enhances clinician-patient discussion
Predictive Analytics (PA)	● Anticipating variation in patient-reported outcomes ● Enabling intervention and preventive strategies earlier	● Facilitates proactive care ● Facilitates long-term tracking of PROMs ● Improves treatment planning
Hybrid AI Models (ML+DL+NLP)	Integration of various AI techniques for the design of integrated, intelligent PROM analysis systems	● Synergistic value ● Individual and integrated care ● Predictive and explanatory insights
AI-Enabled PROM Monitoring	Real-time monitoring of patient continuously during and after treatment	● Ensures PCC ● Identifies adverse effects early ● Enhances shared decision-making

(Source: Author's Creation; Duncan & Murray, 2012; Dua & Bais, 2014; Cheng et al., 2015; Schrier et al., 2016; Trautmann et al., 2016; Williams et al., 2016; Duman-Lubberding et al., 2017; Girgis et al., 2017; Vaswani et al., 2017; Kermany et al., 2018; Lipton, 2018; Philpot et al., 2018; Velupillai et al., 2018; Young et al., 2018; Obermeyer et al., 2019; Topol, 2019a; Chen et al.,2021; Harrison & Sidey-Gibbons, 2021; Kaplan et al., 2021; Verma et al., 2021; Soydaner, 2022; Wilson et al., 2022; Migchels et al., 2023; Pathak et al., 2023; Rivera et al., 2023; Swarnakar & Yadav, 2023; Di Basilio et al., 2024; Ifty et al., 2024; Krepper et al., 2024; Rahman et al., 2024; Mahmoud et al., 2025)

5. CHALLENGES IN AI-DRIVEN PROMS

AI technologies have transformed healthcare by offering scalable, precise, and effective solutions that can improve patient care. Technologies like chatbots, virtual health assistants, and predictive analytics enable personalized interventions through the analysis of patient data and provide recommendations specific to the individual patient (Andrikopoulou, 2023). These developments improve the quality of care and provide access to healthcare for a range of demographics. The incorporation of PROMs into AI systems, however, poses a number of difficulties (Rivera et al., 2023). Figure 1 explains the major challenges of AI-based PROMs in detail.

Figure 1. Major Challenges in AI-Driven PROMs

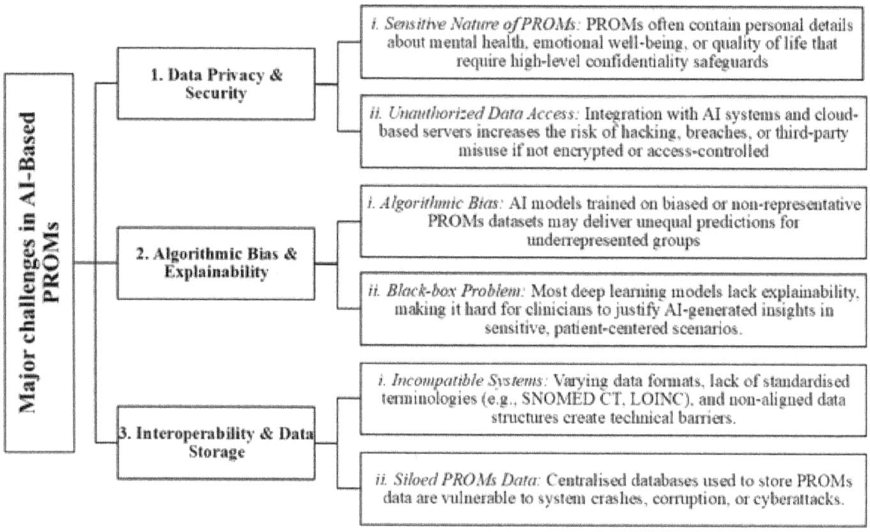

(Source: Author's Creation; Velupillai et al., 2018; Young et al., 2018; Obermeyer et al., 2019; Daneshjou et al., 2021; Dhayanidhi, 2022; Glenwright et al., 2023; Peters, 2023; Rivera et al., 2023; Fennelly et al., 2024; Hassija et al., 2024; Ratwani et al., 2024)

6. INTRODUCTION TO BLOCKCHAIN TECHNOLOGY IN HEALTHCARE

As healthcare systems are increasingly digitizing and becoming data-reliant, the need for secure, open, and interoperable data handling has never been higher (Jaleel et al., 2020; Ait Abdelouahid et al., 2023). Although Blockchain was created to enable financial transactions (Chowdhury, 2024), it is now being considered as an essential technology in healthcare (Hasselgren et al., 2021). The distributed architecture, immutability, and ability to automate trust places blockchain as a suitable ally in patient ownership and data integrity (Hasselgren et al., 2021; Dhingra et al., 2024). The further sub-section presents the basic concepts of blockchain and discusses its growing stature in the health data environment.

6.1 Fundamentals of Blockchain

Blockchain is a Decentralized Ledger Technology (DLT) through which data can be written in a tamper-proof way over a computer network (Zheng et al., 2018; Chowdhury, 2024). Every entry or transaction is wrapped in a block that is cryptographically attached to the preceding one, creating a secure and transparent chain of records. Such a setup eliminates the requirement for central authorities, aids in easier tracing, and minimizes the possibility of data tampering (Zheng et al., 2017; Zheng et al., 2018). Clinically, this translates to patient records, such as PROMs, being collected, recorded, and shared between parties safely without loss of control or ownership. Understanding this foundation leads to the possibility of expanding blockchain beyond data storage to enabling automatic interaction through the employment of smart contracts.

6.2 Role of Smart Contracts in Healthcare Data Management

Programmed on the blockchain, smart contracts are self-running contracts with predetermined rules and conditions. They prompt the execution of actions after the fulfilment of the conditions (Wang et al., 2019). In healthcare, smart contracts can be used to automate consent, facilitate sharing of PROMs data securely, and encourage compliance with regulatory frameworks (Wang et al.,2019; Khatoon, 2020; Ante, 2021). For example, a researcher would be automatically provided with temporary access to anonymized PROMs data only after a patient has given consent through a digital interface. Here, the administrative overheads are prevented without compromising transparency and compliance with privacy requirements. Thus, by incorporating this operational assumption into blockchain platforms, the technology brings its utility to real-world health applications that need both accountability and automation.

6.3 Different Types of Blockchain Platforms and its Applications in Healthcare

Blockchain has numerous applications in healthcare, including patient-held health records, secure sharing of clinical trial data, medical supply chain tracing, clinician credentialing, and real-time claims settlements (Zhang et al., 2018; Hasselgren et al., 2021). For PROMs, blockchain provides decentralized registries for the data where patients own and control who their responses may be shared with (Adeghe et al., 2024). It not only adds authenticity to data but also incentivizes patient participation. A number of pilot initiatives and consortia like MediLedger (McCurdy, 2022) and Estonia's national eHealth system (Soares et al., 2023) have previously proved the scalability of blockchain for the management of health data. While these applications demonstrate the potential of blockchain, it is worth noting that different platforms of blockchain allow for varying functionality (Mittal et al., 2021), particularly when combined with sensitive, patient-centered tools like PROMs. The choice of blockchain platform plays a critical role in balancing privacy, scalability, and trust. Public blockchains like Ethereum possess high transparency and sophisticated smart contract capabilities, but are not appropriate for healthcare with excessive per-transaction costs and poor privacy (Kushwaha et al., 2022; Lax et al., 2024). On the contrary, Hyperledger Fabric is an enterprise-oriented permissioned blockchain that provides private transactions, access controls at a fine-grained level, and improved scalability (Androulaki et al., 2018; Kaushal et al., 2025). Quorum, a more advanced Ethereum platform, attempts to bridge these models, with added support for smart contracts and improved privacy for institutional use (Baliga et al., 2018). Table 2 compares the benefits and drawbacks of these technologies for healthcare and PROMs.

Table 2. Comparison of Blockchain Platform for Healthcare and PROMs

Blockchain Platform	Type	Benefits	Drawbacks
Ethereum	Public	-Mature smart contract ecosystem -Large developer community -Interoperable solutions	- Higher transaction costs - Slower processing speeds - Lower anonymity of sensitive information
Hyperledger Fabric	Permissioned	- Fine-grained access control - Scalable and modular - Enterprise-grade security	- Smaller pool of community support - Less interoperable with public networks
Quorum	Permissioned (Ethereum-based)	- Retains smart contract flexibility - Improved privacy over Ethereum - Faster transactions	- More technical tailoring required - May not have plug-and-play tools for clinical use

(Source: Author's Creation; Androulaki et al., 2018; Baliga et al., 2018; Kushwaha et al., 2022; Mittal et al., 2021; Correia et al., 2024; Lax et al., 2024; Kaushal et al., 2025)

6.4 Addressing Privacy and Trust Issues in Healthcare Data

Privacy and trust are central to any healthcare innovation, especially those involving sensitive patient-reported data. Blockchain's cryptography ensures immutable and auditable entries of data, assuring patients, clinicians, and researchers with trust

(Adusumilli et al., 2023). Technologies like zero-knowledge proofs and differential privacy provide an additional layer of confidentiality by allowing validation of data without the disclosure of its contents (Sun et al., 2021; Adusumilli et al., 2023; Dhingra et al., 2024). With more control and transparency, patients can also monitor who has accessed their records and why. Compared to existing systems with a centralized structure and prone to getting hacked, blockchain offers a system that is decentralized and security is embedded on all levels (Zheng et al., 2018; Hasselgren et al., 2021; Chowdhury, 2024). This initial trust is the precursor to the integration of blockchain-based AI systems, where safe, ethical, and patient-centered PROMs data can fuel the future of innovation in healthcare.

7. INTEGRATING BLOCKCHAIN AND AI FOR PROMS

As discussed in the previous sections, blockchain and AI individually have robust potential for enhancing the collection, understanding, and management of PROMs. Combining these two technologies in a hybrid model constructs a system that leverages the best of both technologies. Blockchain provides secure, decentralized, and transparent data management, and AI offers smart insights and personalization at scale (Ekramifard et al.,2020; Aakula et al., 2024). Therefore, the further sub-sections discuss the need for this hybrid model.

7.1 Need for a Hybrid Model

The increasing use of PROMs to deliver PCC necessitates a system that is smart, secure, interpretable, and ethical. AI alone cannot provide patient control or data integrity of personal health information. Blockchain provides transparency and unalterable records without the potential to examine data to generate predictive or diagnostic knowledge. Therefore, there is a requirement for a combined approach where blockchain manages data provenance, consent, and security, while data translation is performed through AI to provide real-world outcomes. This, together, ensures PROMs data to be clinically meaningful and valid (Yogeshappa, 2024). Developing such a model can bridge the limitations of AI in PROMs-based healthcare decision-making.

7.2 Addressing AI's Limitations Using Blockchain

Blockchain can address several limitations of AI. Blockchain offers auditability and transparency in utilizing PROMs for training or validating AI models, by timestamping all activity in data collection and access to an unalterable ledger (Omidian,

2024). Blockchain also enables the creation of verifiable and traceable datasets, which are needed for bias reduction and enhanced algorithmic fairness (Ressi et al., 2024; Yogeshappa, 2024). Hence, blockchain offers technical protection and a governance structure that is complementary to AI systems. This provides a foundation for the establishment of data security, trust, and collaboration across healthcare networks.

7.3 Enhancing Data Security, Transparency, and Interoperability

The combination of blockchain and AI creates new potential that transcends conventional thinking for data interoperability and security. The most exciting possibility might be developing data provenance analytics, where all processes in the PROMs dataset (from patient entry to AI analysis) are traced and audited. This enables clinicians and researchers not only to know the result, but to know where the result came from and what was preceding it, becoming more sensitive to care streams, patient pattern-of-behavior, and even algorithmic flow-of-decision. In addition, blockchain can enable smart auditing layers via AI. Rather than using static compliance checks, AI algorithms can read blockchain logs in real time to identify anomalies in PROMs use, including data manipulations, late entries, or inconsistent meanings across platforms. These smart audits improve institutional accountability without introducing manual overhead, assisting healthcare organizations in maintaining quality standards while adopting innovation.

7.4 Benefits of Blockchain-enabled AI for PROMs

Through the integration of AI's potential for learning and blockchain distributed ledger, multi-institutional types of intelligence can develop. The PROMs data can be employed to train the decentralized AI models without the need to share the data itself—a process referred to as federated learning (Antunes et al., 2022). Blockchain can guarantee that input is verified and provides trust and ethical cooperation among the stakeholders. This is especially helpful in PROMs studies, where diverse patient perspectives are important, but hard to include due to isolated data systems or concerns about data sharing and control. Therefore, a well-defined integrative model is required to operationalize the potential of blockchain and AI in augmenting the collection, interpretation, and ethical management of PROMs data.

8. PROPOSED BLOCKCHAIN-AI FRAMEWORK FOR PROMS

This conceptual design aims to close the gap between clinical utility and technological potential by integrating PROMs within a decentralized, AI-based platform.

The proposed framework combines the transparency and tamper-resistant nature of blockchain with the analytical power of AI to enable data integrity, personalized insights, and ethical data governance. It facilitates real-time gathering of PROMs with patient-centric interfaces, ensures secure data sharing through smart contracts, and generates actionable information through AI-based algorithms. The framework is interoperable with current healthcare systems. It also facilitates patient empowerment through dynamic consent and control over their health data. The model allows for continuous feedback between the researcher, the clinician, and the patient, leading to improved clinical decision-making, patient participation, and health system responsiveness.

8.1 System Architecture for Blockchain-enabled PROMs

The blockchain technology can be implemented upon a permissioned distributed ledger model, securing decentralized storage of PROMs data (Andrew et al., 2023). Each data entry will be time-stamped and stored in an immutable manner, thus preventing unauthorized alterations. For managing consent and data sharing, smart contracts may be employed, automating permissions as well as facilitating real-time traceability (Andrew et al., 2023; Ghosh et al., 2023). The blockchain layer would be more likely to interact with AI modules via a standard Application Programming Interface (API) (Pasdar et al., 2023), allowing seamless data sharing and relevant analytics. This configuration should allow for transparency, integrity of data, and patient control throughout the PROMs data lifecycle.

8.2 Core Components of the Framework

Effective integration of PROMs into an AI and blockchain-based platform requires a robust architecture based on the key functional building blocks/components. These components together enable secure data gathering, decentralized storage options, ethical regulation, and smart analytics. Every component in the system, from patient-facing interfaces to the AI backend engine, contributes to pulling out raw intelligence from patient inputs without sacrificing trust, privacy, and transparency. Table 3 lists the key components of the framework.

Table 3. Key Components of the Framework

Component	Description
Interface to Capture PROMs	Patient-interface apps, kiosks, wearable devices and other integrated platforms that collect PROMs in real-time (e.g., pain scores, mood scales, QoL questionnaires)
AI Engine (NLP + ML Models)	Algorithms for PROMs data processing and analysis —discover patterns, provide risk alerts, and create customized insights
Blockchain Layer (Distributed Ledger Technology (DLT) Infrastructure)	Provides decentralized, tamper-evident storage and secure sharing of PROMs with smart contracts for consent management
Data Interoperability Layer	Compatible with FHIR standard-compliant EHRs, mHealth platforms, and ontologies-based medical registries (e.g., SNOMED CT, LOINC)
Data Privacy Module	End-to-end encryption, anonymisation methods, and zero-knowledge proofs to enable private analysis of data
User Control Panel	Access permission, viewing audit trails, and sharing preferences are controlled by providers and patients.

(Source: Author's creation; Velupillai et al., 2018; Young et al., 2018; Zhang et al., 2018; Obermeyer et al., 2019; Pasdar et al., 2023; Peters, 2023; Rivera et al., 2023; Fennelly et al., 2024; Hassija et al., 2024; Ratwani et al., 2024)

8.3 Workflow Architecture of the Proposed Framework

Figure 2 illustrates the end-to-end architecture of a Blockchain-AI-based system for safe, intelligent PROMs management. The workflow begins from patient-consumer interfaces like mobile applications or portals, where patients input PROMs data at regular intervals. The data is checked and safeguarded by Distributed Ledger Technology (DLT), which ensures privacy, immutability, and traceability. The information is processed by the AI layer in real time using machine learning models and real-time analytics to deliver insights. These findings are then shared with clinicians, researchers, and policy networks through interoperable systems. Every stakeholder's input is cycled back into the system to optimize PROMs capture, iterate predictive models, and guide healthcare interventions. The design is made with data provenance, safe sharing, and adaptive learning in consideration, supporting responsive PCC across institutions.

Figure 2. Workflow Architecture of the Proposed Framework

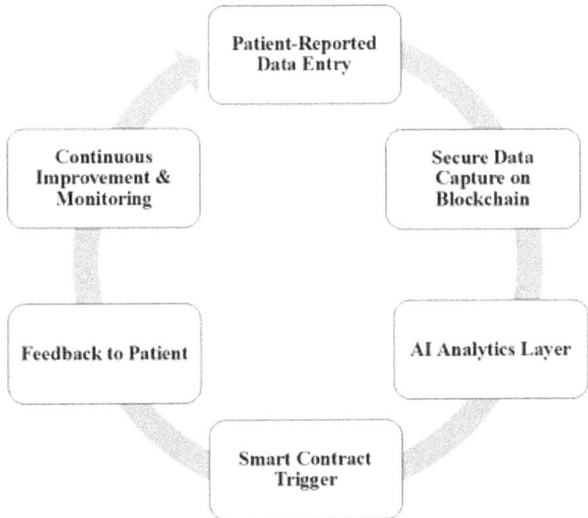

(Source: Author's creation; Young et al., 2018; Zhang et al., 2018; Wang et al.,2019; Khatoon, 2020; Ante, 2021; Antunes et al., 2022; Peters, 2023)

8.4 Governance, Ethics, and Compliance for Deployment of the Framework

The proposed model incorporates two protection layers drawn from technology and ethics. PROMs data would be encrypted end-to-end and kept in a permissioned blockchain, ensuring only authorized people or systems can access the patient-reported information. Smart contracts would be able to handle consent in an automated manner, in which patients could grant, deny, or change permissions as and when needed. Additionally, zero-knowledge proofs and anonymization methods can analyze data without revealing personal identifiers. Such mechanisms strive to thwart misuse, ensure regulatory compliance (e.g., HIPAA, GDPR), and give patients more control over their health data. Therefore, the framework stresses patient control, privacy, safety, and system accountability in every transaction. Table 4 illustrates the Governance, Ethics, and Compliance elements necessary to effectively deploy the proposed Blockchain-AI architecture for PROMs. It describes the mechanisms essential to enable transparency, accountability, fair access, well-informed consent, ownership of data, and compliance with the applicable data protection legislation. The governance elements are fundamental to stakeholders' trust and the coordination of technological development with ethical and legal injunctions in healthcare.

Table 4. Governance, Ethics, and Compliance Elements

Governance Layer	Feature
Dynamic Consent via Smart Contracts	Patients can give, withdraw, or change consent at will
Audit Trails & Data Provenance	All access and changes are recorded immutably
Regulatory Compliance	Intrinsic compliance with HIPAA (USA), GDPR (EU) and laws and regulatory bodies from various countries
Ethics Board Integration	System features trigger oversight, which alerts ethics committees if alarms are raised (e.g., mental health threat).
Bias Mitigation Protocols	Regular audits of AI outputs for detection and removal of demographic or contextual bias.

(Source: Author's creation; Wang et al.,2019; Khatoon, 2020; Ante, 2021; Li et al., 2022; Raftari, 2022; Ahmedet al., 2023; Xiong et al., 2024)

8.5 Stakeholder Feedback Loop

Figure 3 illustrates the dynamic and cyclical relationships among all the significant stakeholders in a Blockchain-AI-based PROMs system. It emphasizes how clinicians, patients, researchers, and policy-makers all contribute to and gain from the reciprocal exchange of PROMs data. Patients self-report outcomes that are fed into AI engines through secure blockchain networks. Clinicians receive interpretive analytics to facilitate patient-centered care. Researchers analyze anonymized data for research results, and policymakers utilize aggregate results in policymaking. Figure 3 indicates feedback loops in two directions, wherein all parties offer as well as receive value input and output. Blockchain provides assurance of data integrity and transparency, and AI responds with adaptations using real-time inputs. This feedback loop gives tool and policy refinement on a continuous basis. The model facilitates ethical governance, fair participation, and authentic health results.

Figure 3. Stakeholder Feedback Loop

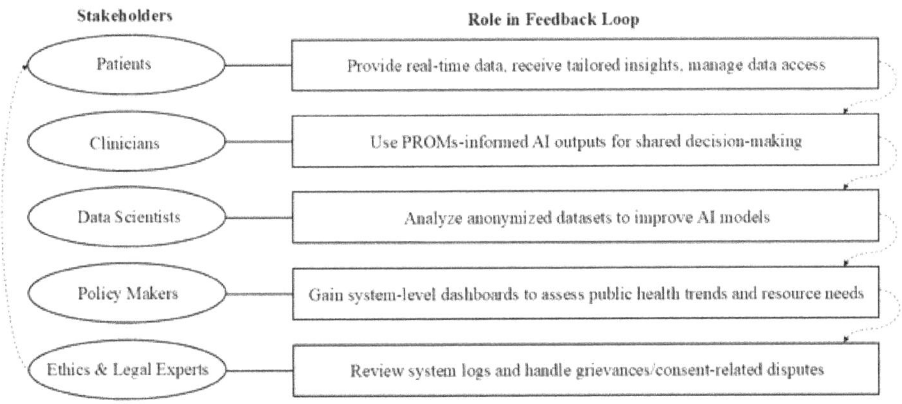

(Source: Author's Craetion; Chen et al.,2021; Harrison & Sidey-Gibbons, 2021; Kaplan et al., 2021; Verma et al., 2021; Soydaner, 2022; Antunes et al., 2022; Andrikopoulou et al., 2023; Yogeshappa, 2024)

8.6 Layered Architecture of the Proposed Framework

Figure 4 illustrates a layer-by-layer architecture of the proposed framework contained within a "Wheel of Governance" to provide ethical control and regulatory assurance. At the top is Layer 1 (Users), which contains the key stakeholders acting directly on behalf of an interface with the system through providing, viewing, or analysing PROMs data. Layer 2 (Application Layer) consists of user interface modules like PROMs application, AI dashboards, and consent management modules that facilitate secure and transparent communication among users. Layer 3 (Processing Layer) constitutes the computational centre, which involves the AI engine, blockchain setting, and smart contracts to support automated analysis of data, protect the system, and maintain user interaction integrity. Layer 4 (Data Layer) offers the foundation by including secure PROMs databases, interoperability functionality, and EHR integration to provide uninterrupted and stable access to data within healthcare systems. The Wheel of Governance encircles these communicating layers, representing the ongoing practice of ethical considerations, data protection policies, and compliance measures. The general system design is real-time decision-making supporting, patient-controlled over healthcare data, and increasing transparency and confidence, hence integrating upcoming technologies and PCC.

Figure 4. Layered Architecture of the Proposed Framework

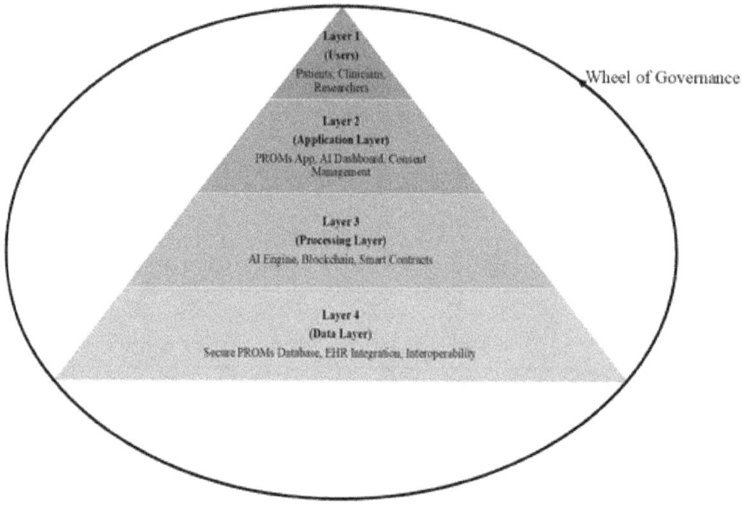

(Source: Author's Creation)

9. CONCLUSION

Even though the use of AI with PROMs has improved predictive analytics and personalised treatment, challenges with data security and privacy remain significant. The decentralized architecture of blockchain can be used to resolve these issues. Blockchain technology can guarantee data integrity, transparency, and patient ownership, while AI offers sophisticated analysis and prompt decision-making based on patient responses, thus increasing confidence in the use of AI-driven healthcare. The chapter has discussed this potential of integrating blockchain-enabled AI in PROMs by briefly comparing blockchain platforms, specifically Ethereum, Hyperledger Fabric, and Quorum.

The authors have also proposed a conceptual design for the blockchain-enabled AI use in PROMs. Together, these technologies offer a novel framework that addresses issues related to privacy, interoperability, and patient engagement. However, more research is required regarding policy alignment, infrastructure scalability, and ethical governance in the implementation of this framework.

As emerging technologies evolve further, interdisciplinary collaboration among technologists, clinicians, and policymakers would be particularly crucial. This overlapping area of secure data management and intelligent analyses can transform the future of medicine and digital health systems, eventually contributing to a more reliable and ethical delivery of PCC.

REFERENCES

Aakula, A., Zhang, C., & Ahmad, T. (2024). Leveraging AI And Blockchain For Strategic Advantage In Digital Transformation. *Journal of Artificial Intelligence Research*, *4*(1), 356–395.

Adeghe, E. P., Okolo, C. A., & Ojeyinka, O. T. (2024). The influence of patient-reported outcome measures on healthcare delivery: A review of methodologies and applications. *OARJ of Biology and Pharmacy, 10*(02), 013-021.

Adusumilli, S., Damancharla, H., & Metta, A. (2023). Enhancing Data Privacy in Healthcare Systems Using Blockchain Technology. *Transactions on Latest Trends in Artificial Intelligence*, *4*(4), 1–19.

Ahmed, M., Dar, A. R., Helfert, M., Khan, A., & Kim, J. (2023). Data provenance in healthcare: Approaches, challenges, and future directions. *Sensors (Basel)*, *23*(14), 6495. PMID: 37514788

Ait Abdelouahid, R., Debauche, O., Mahmoudi, S., & Marzak, A. (2023). Literature review: Clinical data interoperability models. *Information (Basel)*, *14*(7), 364.

Al Sayah, F., Jin, X., & Johnson, J. A. (2021). Selection of patient-reported outcome measures (PROMs) for use in health systems. *Journal of Patient-Reported Outcomes*, *5*, 1–5. PMID: 34637010

Alowais, S. A., Alghamdi, S. S., Alsuhebany, N., Alqahtani, T., Alshaya, A. I., Almohareb, S. N., & Albekairy, A. M. (2023). Revolutionizing healthcare: The role of artificial intelligence in clinical practice. *BMC Medical Education*, *23*(1), 689. PMID: 37740191

Alrabei, A. M. (2023). Green electronic auditing and accounting information reliability in the Jordanian social security corporation: The mediating role of cloud computing. *International Journal of Financial Studies*, *11*(3), 114.

Alsahli, S. S., Almalki, M. H. M., Alkhathami, A. M., Alharbi, A. A., Alhawit, M. E., Albalawi, K. I., & Binselm, K. R. A. (2020). Quality Improvement and Patient Safety: Strategies and Challenges in Healthcare System Transformation. *International Journal of Health Sciences*, *4*(S1), 478–497.

Alsubaie, S. S., Bukhamseen, Z. F. A., Alyami, F. S. A., Alotaibi, M. F., Alkahtani, F. A., Alkhamsan, M. S., & Al Khamees, Z. H. (2024). Multidisciplinary Approaches in General Medical Practice: Enhancing Collaboration for Better Patient Care. *Journal of Ecohumanism*, *3*(7), 2659–2669.

Andrew, J., Isravel, D. P., Sagayam, K. M., Bhushan, B., Sei, Y., & Eunice, J. (2023). Blockchain for healthcare systems: Architecture, security challenges, trends and future directions. *Journal of Network and Computer Applications*, *215*, 103633.

Andrikopoulou, E. (2023). The rise of AI in telehealth. In *Emerging Practices in Telehealth* (pp. 183–207). Academic Press., DOI: 10.1016/B978-0-443-15980-0.00011-9

Androulaki, E., Barger, A., Bortnikov, V., Cachin, C., Christidis, K., De Caro, A., . . . Yellick, J. (2018). Hyperledger Fabric: a distributed operating system for permissioned blockchains. In *Proceedings of the thirteenth EuroSys conference*. Available at: https://dl.acm.org/doi/pdf/10.1145/3190508.3190538

Ante, L. (2021). Smart contracts on the blockchain–A bibliometric analysis and review. *Telematics and Informatics*, *57*, 101519.

Antunes, R. S., André da Costa, C., Küderle, A., Yari, I. A., & Eskofier, B. (2022). Federated learning for healthcare: Systematic review and architecture proposal. [TIST]. *ACM Transactions on Intelligent Systems and Technology*, *13*(4), 1–23.

Balch, J. A., Chatham, A. H., Hong, P. K., Manganiello, L., Baskaran, N., Bihorac, A., & Loftus, T. J. (2024). Predicting patient-reported outcome measures: A scoping review for the artificial intelligence-guided patient preference predictor. *Frontiers in Artificial Intelligence*, *7*, 1477447. PMID: 39564457

Baliga, A., Subhod, I., Kamat, P., & Chatterjee, S. (2018). Performance evaluation of the quorum blockchain platform. *Available at:* https://arxiv.org/pdf/1809.03421

Bul, K., Holliday, N., Magee, P., & Wark, P. (2020). From development to exploitation of digital health solutions: Lessons learnt through multidisciplinary research and consultancy. *Journal of Enabling Technologies*, *14*(4), 273–279.

Callahan, A., & Shah, N. H. (2017). Machine learning in healthcare. In *Key Advances in Clinical Informatics* (pp. 279–291). Academic Press., DOI: 10.1016/B978-0-12-809523-2.00019-4

Chabot, P. J., Cirino, C. M., & Gulotta, L. V. (2023). Machine learning: The what, why, and how. *Seminars in Arthroplasty*, *33*(4), 857–861.

Chen, I. Y., Pierson, E., Rose, S., Joshi, S., Ferryman, K., & Ghassemi, M. (2021). Ethical machine learning in healthcare. *Annual Review of Biomedical Data Science*, *4*(1), 123–144. PMID: 34396058

Cheng, L., Zhu, M., Poss, J. W., Hirdes, J. P., Glenny, C., & Stolee, P. (2015). Opinion versus practice regarding the use of rehabilitation services in-home care: An investigation using machine learning algorithms. *BMC Medical Informatics and Decision Making*, *15*, 1–11. PMID: 26453354

Chowdhury, R. H. (2024). Blockchain and AI: Driving the future of data security and business intelligence. *World Journal of Advanced Research and Reviews*, *23*(1), 2559–2570.

Cîmpan, I., & Cri an, E. L. (2025). Blockchain concepts in business research–a scoping review. *Management Matters*. Available at: https://www.emerald.com/insight/content/doi/10.1108/manm-06-2024-0034/full/pdf

Correia, P. H., Barcha, M. A., Marques, M. A., Simplicio, L., & Ermlivitch, C. C. Miers, and. Pillon, M. A. (2024). "Comparative Analysis of Permissioned Blockchains: Cosmos, Hyperledger Fabric, Quorum, and XRPL." In *2024 IEEE International Conference on Blockchain (Blockchain)*, pp. 464-469. Available at: https://ieeexplore.ieee.org/abstract/document/10664236

Daneshjou, R., Smith, M. P., Sun, M. D., Rotemberg, V., & Zou, J. (2021). Lack of transparency and potential bias in artificial intelligence data sets and algorithms: A scoping review. *JAMA Dermatology*, *157*(11), 1362–1369. PMID: 34550305

Dhayanidhi, G. (2022). Research on IoT threats & implementation of AI/ML to address emerging cybersecurity issues in IoT with cloud computing. Available at: https://era.library.ualberta.ca/items/72d03629-a6ac-4e5d-8528-3f10b552cda7

Dhingra, S., Raut, R., Naik, K., & Muduli, K. (2024). Blockchain technology applications in healthcare supply chains– A review. *IEEE Access*. Available at: https://ieeexplore.ieee.org/stamp/stamp.jsp?arnumber=10379101

Di Basilio, D., King, L., Lloyd, S., Michael, P., & Shardlow, M. (2024). Asking questions that are "close to the bone": Integrating thematic analysis and natural language processing to explore the experiences of people with traumatic brain injuries engaging with patient-reported outcome measures. *Frontiers in Digital Health*, *6*, 1387139. PMID: 38983792

Dua, P., & Bais, S. (2014). Supervised learning methods for fraud detection in healthcare insurance. *Machine Learning in Healthcare Informatics*, 261-285. Available at: https://link.springer.com/chapter/10.1007/978-3-642-40017-9_12

Duman-Lubberding, S., van Uden-Kraan, C. F., Jansen, F., Witte, B. I., Eerenstein, S. E., Van Weert, S., & Verdonck-de Leeuw, I. M. (2017). Durable usage of patient-reported outcome measures in clinical practice to monitor health-related quality of life in head and neck cancer patients. *Supportive Care in Cancer, 25*, 3775–3783. PMID: 28702685

Duncan, E. A., & Murray, J. (2012). The barriers and facilitators to routine outcome measurement by allied health professionals in practice: A systematic review. *BMC Health Services Research, 12*, 1–9. PMID: 22506982

Duong-Trung, N., Son, H. X., Le, H. T., & Phan, T. T. (2020). On components of a patient-centered healthcare system using smart contract. In *Proceedings of the 2020 4th International Conference on Cryptography, Security and Privacy*. Available at: https://shorturl.at/o3dSF

Ekramifard, A., Amintoosi, H., Seno, A. H., Dehghantanha, A., & Parizi, R. M. (2020). A systematic literature review of integration of blockchain and artificial intelligence. *Blockchain Cybersecurity, Trust and Privacy*, 147-160. Available at: https://link.springer.com/chapter/10.1007/978-3-030-38181-3_8

Fair, O., Ali, A. B., Haener, M., Plotnikoff, K., Schaaf, N., Schmitt-Boshnick, M., & Soprovich, A. (2025). Use of patient-reported outcome measures (PROMs) in primary care-based mental health programming: An environmental scan of Alberta, Canada. *BMC Primary Care, 26*(1), 71. PMID: 40089665

Fennelly, O., Moroney, D., Doyle, M., Eustace-Cook, J., & Hughes, M. (2024). Key interoperability factors for patient portals and electronic health records: A scoping review. *International Journal of Medical Informatics, 183*, 105335. PMID: 38266425

Field, J., Holmes, M. M., & Newell, D. (2019). PROMs data: Can it be used to make decisions for individual patients? A narrative review. *Patient Related Outcome Measures, 10*, 233–241. PMID: 31534379

Ghosh, P. K., Chakraborty, A., Hasan, M., Rashid, K., & Siddique, A. H. (2023). Blockchain application in healthcare systems: A review. *Systems, 11*(1), 38.

Girgis, A., Durcinoska, I., Levesque, J. V., Gerges, M., Sandell, T., & Arnold, A.PROMPT-Care Program Group. (2017). eHealth system for collecting and utilizing patient-reported outcome measures for personalized treatment and care (PROMPT-Care) among cancer patients: Mixed methods approach to evaluate feasibility and acceptability. *Journal of Medical Internet Research, 19*(10), e330. PMID: 28970188

Glenwright, B. G., Simmich, J., Cottrell, M., O'Leary, S. P., Sullivan, C., Pole, J. D., & Russell, T. (2023). Facilitators and barriers to implementing electronic patient-reported outcome and experience measures in a health care setting: A systematic review. *Journal of Patient-Reported Outcomes*, *7*(1), 13. PMID: 36786914

Gluyas, H. (2015). Patient-centred care: improving healthcare outcomes. *Nursing Standard (2014+), 30*(4), 50.

Harrison, C. J., & Sidey-Gibbons, C. J. (2021). Machine learning in medicine: A practical introduction to natural language processing. *BMC Medical Research Methodology*, *21*(1), 158. PMID: 34332525

Hasselgren, A., Hanssen Rensaa, J. A., Kralevska, K., Gligoroski, D., & Faxvaag, A. (2021). Blockchain for increased trust in virtual health care: Proof-of-concept study. *Journal of Medical Internet Research*, *23*(7), e28496. PMID: 34328437

Hassija, V., Chamola, V., Mahapatra, A., Singal, A., Goel, D., Huang, K., & Hussain, A. (2024). Interpreting black-box models: A review on explainable artificial intelligence. *Cognitive Computation*, *16*(1), 45–74.

Hays, R. D., & Quigley, D. D. (2025). A perspective on the use of patient-reported experience and patient-reported outcome measures in ambulatory healthcare. *Expert Review of Pharmacoeconomics & Outcomes Research*, *25*(4), 1–9. PMID: 39819211

Homayounfar, P. (2012). Process mining challenges in hospital information systems. In *2012, Federated Conference on Computer Science and Information Systems (FedCSIS)* (pp. 1135-1140). *IEEE*. Available at: https://annals-csis.org/proceedings/2012/pliks/376.pdf

Ifty, S. M. H., Irin, F., Shovon, M. S. S., Amjad, M. H. H., Bhowmik, P. K., Ahmed, R., & Sunny, A. R. (2024). Advancements, Applications, and Future Directions of Artificial Intelligence in Healthcare. *Journal of Angiotherapy*, *8*(8), 1–18.

IOM. (2001). Institute of Medicine: Crossing the Quality Chasm: Crossing the Quality Chasm: A new health system for the 21st century. In Book Crossing the Quality Chasm: A new health system for the 21st century. City: Institute of Medicine. Available at: https://shorturl.at/g5HIK

Jaleel, A., Mahmood, T., Hassan, M. A., Bano, G., & Khurshid, S. K. (2020). Towards medical data interoperability through collaboration of healthcare devices. *IEEE Access : Practical Innovations, Open Solutions*, *8*, 132302–132319.

Jiang, F., Jiang, Y., Zhi, H., Dong, Y., Li, H., Ma, S., & Wang, Y. (2017). Artificial intelligence in healthcare: Past, present and future. *Stroke and Vascular Neurology*, *2*(4), e000101. PMID: 29507784

Jiang, P., Sinha, S., Aldape, K., Hannenhalli, S., Sahinalp, C., & Ruppin, E. (2022). Big data in basic and translational cancer research. *Nature Reviews. Cancer*, *22*(11), 625–639. PMID: 36064595

Kaplan, R. S., Jehi, L., Ko, C. Y., Pusic, A., & Witkowski, M. (2021). Health care measurements that improve patient outcomes. *NEJM Catalyst Innovations in Care Delivery*, *2*(2), 1–21.

Kaushal, R. K., Kumar, N., Kukreja, V., & Boonchieng, E. (2025). Hyperledger fabric based remote patient monitoring solution and performance evaluation. *Peer-to-Peer Networking and Applications*, *18*(3), 105.

Kermany, D. S., Goldbaum, M., Cai, W., Valentim, C. C., Liang, H., Baxter, S. L., & Zhang, K. (2018). Identifying medical diagnoses and treatable diseases by image-based deep learning. *Cell*, *172*(5), 1122–1131. PMID: 29474911

Khatoon, A. (2020). A blockchain-based smart contract system for healthcare management. *Electronics (Basel)*, *9*(1), 94.

Krepper, D., Cesari, M., Hubel, N. J., Zelger, P., & Sztankay, M. J. (2024). Machine learning models including patient-reported outcome data in oncology: A systematic literature review and analysis of their reporting quality. *Journal of Patient-Reported Outcomes*, *8*(1), 126. PMID: 39499409

Krishnamoorthy, S., Dua, A., & Gupta, S. (2023). Role of emerging technologies in future IoT-driven Healthcare 4.0 technologies: A survey, current challenges and future directions. *Journal of Ambient Intelligence and Humanized Computing*, *14*(1), 361–407.

Kushwaha, S. S., Joshi, S., Singh, D., Kaur, M., & Lee, H. N. (2022). Ethereum smart contract analysis tools: A systematic review. *IEEE Access : Practical Innovations, Open Solutions*, *10*, 57037–57062.

Lax, G., Nardone, R., & Russo, A. (2024). Enabling secure health information sharing among healthcare organizations by public blockchain. *Multimedia Tools and Applications*, *83*(24), 64795–64811.

Li, F., Ruijs, N., & Lu, Y. (2022). Ethics & AI: A systematic review on ethical concerns and related strategies for designing with AI in healthcare. *AI*, *4*(1), 28–53.

Lipton, Z. C. (2018). The mythos of model interpretability: In machine learning, the concept of interpretability is both important and slippery. *Queue*, *16*(3), 31–57.

Mahmoud, Y., Horvath, K., & Zhou, Y. (2025). Deep Learning for Predicting Rehabilitation Success: Advancing Clinical and Patient-Reported Outcome Modeling. *Electronics (Basel)*, *14*(6), 1082.

McCurdy, D. (2022). Blockchain Governance Strategies. In *Blockchain in Life Sciences* (pp. 197–212). Springer Nature Singapore., Available at https://link.springer.com/chapter/10.1007/978-981-19-2976-2_9

McKay, C. A., & Crippen, L. (2008). Collaboration through clinical integration. *Nursing Administration Quarterly*, *32*(2), 109–116. PMID: 18360207

Meadows, K. A. (2011). Patient-reported outcome measures: An overview. *British Journal of Community Nursing*, *16*(3), 146–151. PMID: 21378658

Mehta, S., Grant, K., & Ackery, A. (2020). Future of blockchain in healthcare: Potential to improve the accessibility, security and interoperability of electronic health records. *BMJ Health & Care Informatics*, *27*(3), e100217. PMID: 33229440

Mello, M. M., & Guha, N. (2024). Understanding liability risk from using health care artificial intelligence tools. *The New England Journal of Medicine*, *390*(3), 271–278. PMID: 38231630

Migchels, C., Zerrouk, A., Crunelle, C. L., Matthys, F., Gremeaux, L., Fernandez, K., & Vanderplasschen, W. (2023). Patient Reported Outcome and Experience Measures (PROMs and PREMs) in substance use disorder treatment services: A scoping review. *Drug and Alcohol Dependence*, *253*, 111017. PMID: 37995391

Minvielle, E., Fierobe, A., Fourcade, A., Ferrua, M., Di Palma, M., Scotté, F., & Mir, O. (2023). The use of patient-reported outcome and experience measures for health policy purposes: A scoping review in oncology. *Health Policy (Amsterdam)*, *129*, 104702. PMID: 36588068

Mittal, N., Pal, S., Joshi, A., Sharma, A., Tayal, S., & Sharma, Y. (2021). Comparative analysis of various platforms of blockchain. *Smart and Sustainable Intelligent Systems*, 323-340.

NABH. (2020). National Accreditation Standards for Hospitals April 2020 5th edition. Available at: https://healthcarearchitecture.in/wp-content/uploads/2022/01/NABH-5-STD-April-2020.pdf

Nakamoto, S. (2008). Bitcoin: A peer-to-peer electronic cash system. Available at: https://assets.pubpub.org/d8wct41f/31611263538139.pdf

Obermeyer, Z., Powers, B., Vogeli, C., & Mullainathan, S. (2019). Dissecting racial bias in an algorithm used to manage the health of populations. *Science*, *366*(6464), 447–453. PMID: 31649194

Omidian, H. (2024). Synergizing blockchain and artificial intelligence to enhance healthcare. *Drug Discovery Today*, *29*(9), 104111. PMID: 39034026

Parekh, A. D. E., Shaikh, O. A., Manan, S., & Al Hasibuzzaman, M. (2023). Artificial intelligence (AI) in personalized medicine: AI-generated personalized therapy regimens based on genetic and medical history. *Annals of Medicine and Surgery (London)*, *85*(11), 5831–5833. PMID: 37915639

Pasdar, A., Lee, Y. C., & Dong, Z. (2023). Connect API with blockchain: A survey on blockchain oracle implementation. *ACM Computing Surveys*, *55*(10), 1–39.

Pathak, A., Abbott, J. H., Bajracharya, N., Gurung, G., Nepal, G. M., & Sharma, S. (2023). Barriers and facilitators to implementation of outcome measures among physiotherapists in Nepal: A mixed-methods study. *Musculoskeletal Science & Practice*, *68*, 102859. PMID: 37844424

Patil, S., Kanade, T. M., & Batule, R. (2024). Exploring digital healthcare trends: Integrating people, technology, and procedures for a comprehensive healthcare ecosystem. In *AIP Conference Proceedings. 3178*(1), 060002.

Peters, U. (2023). Explainable AI lacks regulative reasons: Why AI and human decision-making are not equally opaque. *AI and Ethics*, *3*(3), 963–974.

Philpot, L. M., Barnes, S. A., Brown, R. M., Austin, J. A., James, C. S., Stanford, R. H., & Ebbert, J. O. (2018). Barriers and benefits to the use of patient-reported outcome measures in routine clinical care: A qualitative study. *American Journal of Medical Quality*, *33*(4), 359–364. PMID: 29258323

Raftari, A. (2022). *Framework for Evaluation of Blockchain-AI Technology and Governance to Secure Interoperable US Healthcare Data* (Doctoral dissertation, Northcentral University). Available at: https://shorturl.at/VuXNH

Rahman, M. H., Islam, T., Hossen, M. E., Chowdhury, M. E., Hayat, R., Shovon, M. S. S., & Sunny, A. R. (2024). Machine Learning in Healthcare: From Diagnostics to Personalized Medicine and Predictive Analytics. *Journal of Angiotherapy*, *8*(12), 1–8.

Ratwani, R. M., Sutton, K., & Galarraga, J. E. (2024). Addressing AI algorithmic bias in health care. *Journal of the American Medical Association*, *332*(13), 1051–1052. PMID: 39230911

Rehan, H. (2023). Artificial intelligence and machine learning: The impact of machine learning on predictive analytics in healthcare. *Innovative Computer Sciences Journal*, *9*(1), 1–20.

Reine, S., Archer, H., Alshaikhsalama, A., Wells, J., Kohli, A., Xi, Y., & Chhabra, A. (2022). Deep Learning-Generated Radiographic Hip Dysplasia Parameters: Relationship to Postoperative Patient-Reported Outcome Measures. Available at: https://www.researchsquare.com/article/rs-1867063/v1

Ressi, D., Romanello, R., Piazza, C., & Rossi, S. (2024). AI-enhanced blockchain technology: A review of advancements and opportunities. *Journal of Network and Computer Applications*, •••, 103858.

Rivera, S. C., Liu, X., Hughes, S. E., Dunster, H., Manna, E., Denniston, A. K., & Calvert, M. J. (2023). Embedding patient-reported outcomes at the heart of artificial intelligence health-care technologies. *The Lancet. Digital Health*, *5*(3), e168–e173. PMID: 36828609

Saint-Pierre, C., Herskovic, V., & Sepúlveda, M. (2018). Multidisciplinary collaboration in primary care: A systematic review. *Family Practice*, *35*(2), 132–141. PMID: 28973173

Schrier, E., Schrier, I., Geertzen, J. H., & Dijkstra, P. U. (2016). Quality of life in rehabilitation outpatients: Normal values and a comparison with the general Dutch population and psychiatric patients. *Quality of Life Research: An International Journal of Quality of Life Aspects of Treatment, Care and Rehabilitation*, *25*, 135–142. PMID: 26159567

Shukla, K., & Attar, A. (2024). The role of PROMs in mitigating infectious disease crises: A healthy ageing perspective. In *Sustainable Ageing: Reimagining Healthy Ageing Through the Lens of Flagship Campaigns* (pp. 189–209). Springer Nature Switzerland.

Simon, S. J., Grant, A. R., Niu, R., Olatunbosun, S., Talmo, C. T., & Hollenbeck, B. L. (2025). Which patient factors influence pre-operative and post-operative completion of patient reported outcome surveys in total joint replacement surgery? *Journal of Orthopaedics*, *68*, 131–136. PMID: 40093815

Singh, S., Bhatt, P., Sharma, S. K., & Rabiu, S. (2021). Digital transformation in healthcare: Innovation and technologies. In *Blockchain for Healthcare Systems* (pp. 61–79). CRC Press.

Soares, B., Ferreira, A., & Veiga, P. M. (2023). The Benefits and Challenges of Blockchain Technology and eHealth Implementation in Estonia-A Literature Review. *Applied Medical Informatics*, *45*(4).

Sokas, C., Hu, F., Edelen, M., Sisodia, R., Pusic, A., & Cooper, Z. (2022). A review of PROM implementation in surgical practice. *Annals of Surgery*, *275*(1), 85–90. PMID: 34183512

Soydaner, D. (2022). Attention mechanism in neural networks: Where it comes and where it goes. *Neural Computing & Applications*, *34*(16), 13371–13385.

Stoumpos, A. I., Kitsios, F., & Talias, M. A. (2023). Digital transformation in healthcare: Technology acceptance and its applications. *International Journal of Environmental Research and Public Health*, *20*(4), 3407. PMID: 36834105

Sun, X., Yu, F. R., Zhang, P., Sun, Z., Xie, W., & Peng, X. (2021). A survey on zero-knowledge proof in blockchain. *IEEE Network*, *35*(4), 198–205.

Swarnakar, R., & Yadav, S. L. (2023). Artificial intelligence and machine learning in motor recovery: A rehabilitation medicine perspective. *World Journal of Clinical Cases*, *11*(29), 7258. PMID: 37946764

Topol, E. (2019). *Deep medicine: how artificial intelligence can make healthcare human again*. Hachette UK. Available at: https://shorturl.at/GYNij

Topol, E. J. (2019a). High-performance medicine: The convergence of human and artificial intelligence. *Nature Medicine*, *25*(1), 44–56. PMID: 30617339

Trautmann, F., Hentschel, L., Hornemann, B., Rentsch, A., Baumann, M., Ehninger, G., & Schuler, M. (2016). Electronic real-time assessment of patient-reported outcomes in routine care—First findings and experiences from the implementation in a comprehensive cancer center. *Supportive Care in Cancer*, *24*, 3047–3056. PMID: 26887586

Vaswani, A., Shazeer, N., Parmar, N., Uszkoreit, J., Jones, L., Gomez, A. N., . . . Polosukhin, I. (2017). Attention is all you need. *Advances in Neural Information Processing Systems, 30*. Available at: https://proceedings.neurips.cc/paper/2017/file/3f5ee243547dee91fbd053c1c4a845aa-Paper.pdf

Velupillai, S., Suominen, H., Liakata, M., Roberts, A., Shah, A. D., Morley, K., & Dutta, R. (2018). Using clinical natural language processing for health outcomes research: Overview and actionable suggestions for future advances. *Journal of Biomedical Informatics*, *88*, 11–19. PMID: 30368002

Verma, D., Bach, K., & Mork, P. J. (2021). Application of machine learning methods on patient reported outcome measurements for predicting outcomes: A literature review. *Informatics (MDPI)*, *8*(3), 56.

Wang, S., Ouyang, L., Yuan, Y., Ni, X., Han, X., & Wang, F. Y. (2019). Blockchain-enabled smart contracts: Architecture, applications, and future trends. *IEEE Transactions on Systems, Man, and Cybernetics. Systems*, *49*(11), 2266–2277.

Williams, K., Sansoni, J., Darcy, M., Grootemaat, P., & Thompson, C. (2016). *Patient-reported outcome measures. Literature review*. Australian Commission on Safety and Quality in Health Care., Available at https://www.safetyandquality.gov.au/sites/default/files/migrated/PROMs-stakeholder-interviews-report-2018.pdf

Wilson, L., Horton, L., Polinder, S., Newcombe, V. F., Steinbuechel, N. V., & Maas, A. I. & CENTER-TBI participants and investigators. (2022). Tailoring multi-dimensional outcomes to level of functional recovery after traumatic brain injury. *Journal of Neurotrauma*, *39*(19-20), 1363–1381. PMID: 35607855

Wu, M., Subramaniam, G., Li, Z., & Gao, X. (2025). Using AI Technology to Enhance Data-Driven Decision-Making in the Financial Sector. *Artificial Intelligence-Enabled Businesses: How to Develop Strategies for Innovation*, 187-207.

Xiong, L., Zhu, Y., & Zaza, S. (2024). Enhancing data diversity and traceability to mitigate bias in healthcare AI: a blockchain-driven approach. In *Proceedings of the 2024 Computers and People Research Conference* (pp. 1-2). Available at: https://dl.acm.org/doi/abs/10.1145/3632634.3655881

Yogeshappa, V. G. (2024). AI-driven Precision medicine: Revolutionizing personalized treatment plans. [IJCET]. *International Journal of Computer Engineering and Technology*, *15*(5), 455–474.

Young, T., Hazarika, D., Poria, S., & Cambria, E. (2018). Recent trends in deep learning based natural language processing. *IEEE Computational Intelligence Magazine*, *13*(3), 55–75.

Zhang, P., Schmidt, D. C., White, J., & Lenz, G. (2018). Blockchain technology use cases in healthcare. *Advances in Computers*, *111*, 1–41.

Zheng, Z., Xie, S., Dai, H., Chen, X., & Wang, H. (2017). An overview of blockchain technology: Architecture, consensus, and future trends. In *2017 IEEE International Congress on Big Data (BigData Congress)* (pp. 557-564). IEEE. Available at: https://ieeexplore.ieee.org/abstract/document/8029379

Zheng, Z., Xie, S., Dai, H. N., Chen, X., & Wang, H. (2018). Blockchain challenges and opportunities: A survey. *International Journal of Web and Grid Services*, *14*(4), 352–375.

KEY TERMS AND DEFINITIONS

Artificial Intelligence: An area of computer science that is involved with the development of systems that can perform tasks which normally require human intelligence, like learning, reasoning, and problem-solving.

Blockchain: A type of distributed ledger technology that is decentralised and logs electronic transactions on several computers so as to provide transparency, security, and permanence without needing a central authority.

Deep Learning: A type of neural network machine learning with multiple layers that can automatically learn and extract complex features in large data, commonly employed in image, text, and speech data analysis.

Machine Learning: A type of artificial intelligence that enables computer systems to automatically learn from data and improve performance on specific tasks over a period without specific training.

Natural Language Processing: A type of AI technology that enables machines to read, comprehend, and write human language, and thus is helpful in clinical document analysis, patient reviews, and other unstructured text.

Patient Centred Care: A patient-centred model of health care that focuses on patient values, preferences, and needs, and supports shared decision-making and respect for the patient as an active participant in care.

Patient Reported Outcome Measures: Structured instruments through which the patients themselves give their own perspectives of their state of health, treatment outcomes, and quality of life, independent of clinician or researcher interpretation.

Smart Contracts: Digital self-executing contracts on a blockchain, triggering default provisions and rules automatically, applied to healthcare settings to ensure safe handling of consents and access to data.

Chapter 3
Combating Food Health Misinformation and Disinformation with Advanced RAG-LLM:
Prototype AI on PubMed for Cardiac Health

Luuk Simons
https://orcid.org/0009-0008-8707-5609
Delft University of Technology, The Netherlands

Pradeep Murukannaiah
Delft University of Technology, The Netherlands

Mark Neerincx
https://orcid.org/0000-0002-8161-5722
Delft University of Technology, The Netherlands

ABSTRACT

Effective prevention and treatment of cardiovascular disease rely on healthy lifestyle behaviors. However, the expanding and often conflicting nature of scientific literature, along with prevalent food and health misinformation/disinformation, hinders informed decision-making. Large Language Models (LLMs) with Retrieval-Augmented Generation (RAG) capabilities offer automated claim verification and summarization. An enhanced RAG-LLM prototype with novel modules is evaluated for effectiveness. Results show that Inclusion-Criteria-based filtering of PubMed articles improved verdict accuracy. Furthermore, employing a PICO-based (Population, Intervention,

DOI: 10.4018/979-8-3373-2545-3.ch003

Comparison, Outcome) approach for summarizing evidence in health claims (e.g., 'Berries reduce blood pressure') increased transparency. Still, the tested RAG-LLM models exhibited biases towards positivity (overemphasizing heart-healthy aspects) and neutrality. Likely causes of these biases and future development challenges are discussed, as well as AI tooling enabling governance on industry influences in nutrition science.

1 INTRODUCTION

Cardiovascular disease (CVD) represents a leading cause of mortality worldwide (Badimon et al., 2019; Gaidai et al., 2023). Hypertension, commonly known as high blood pressure, stands as a major risk factor for CVD and is the foremost global contributor to disease burden. Notably, within the 40-59 age bracket – preceding typical retirement age – 55% of individuals in the United States are affected by hypertension (Ostchega et al., 2020), with prevalence rates being even higher in many other regions globally (Zhou et al., 2021). Hypertension is a significant driver of premature death, yet it is largely a preventable condition (Carey & Whelton, 2020). Recent scholarly work underscores the critical role of evidence-based Health Self-Management (HSM) interventions in improving cardiovascular health outcomes and concurrently reducing associated healthcare expenditures (Dineen-Griffin et al., 2019).

The volume of literature pertaining to diet, HSM, and cardiac health is undergoing rapid expansion (Qama et al., 2022). Regrettably, this growth occurs alongside the presence of multiple sources disseminating misinformation (information that is false, regardless of intent) and disinformation (information deliberately intended to mislead) (Denniss et al., 2023). Furthermore, the sheer abundance of information presents a challenge of overload, impeding timely access to insights that could be valuable for supporting HSM. This difficulty is compounded by the overwhelming rate of new scientific publications, exceeding 500,000 per year in health-related disciplines, with over 200,000 specifically focused on cardiac health annually (Simons et al., 2024). A particular difficulty within the field of nutritional science is the common perception that research findings are frequently contradictory (Nagler, 2014; Armitage, 2019). Studies have demonstrated that this 'nutrition confusion' is associated with a phenomenon termed 'nutrition backlash', which has been linked to decreased engagement in healthful behaviors, such as reduced fruit and vegetable consumption (Lee, 2018).

Our prior research investigating information needs and sources revealed that both patients and practitioners encounter significant challenges in locating actionable lifestyle recommendations grounded in the latest scientific evidence (Simons et al., 2022a). For instance, the top three health institutes in the Netherlands focusing on hypertension or type 2 diabetes were found to provide diluted and inconsistent health guidance. Simultaneously, analyses of search heuristics using platforms like Google Scholar indicated that the returned scientific papers often inundated users with excessive detail and non-actionable research findings. Building on this, in 2024, we surveyed 'expert users' – individuals with experience using LLMs who had recently participated in an intensive hypertension improvement program (Simons et al., 2022, Simons et al., 2024, Simons et al., 2025) – regarding their information requirements and their perception of the potential value of LLMs in summarizing health literature findings. The consensus among these users was an expression of concern regarding the quality and utility of LLM outputs, specifically pertaining to:

- The reliability of information provided by LLMs (including issues of hallucinations (Sallam, 2023; Raina et al., 2024)).
- The ability of LLMs to effectively handle conflicting health claims.
- The capacity of LLMs to clearly explain how updated health advice differs from more traditional or familiar recommendations.
- The accuracy and transparency of linking LLM outputs back to the original scientific studies used as sources.

Despite these concerns, recent advancements in Artificial Intelligence (AI), such as explicit claim verification techniques and Retrieval-Augmented Generation (RAG) models, offer potential avenues for mitigating these identified risks. Consequently, we proceeded to develop and evaluate an enhanced prototype system designed to help address the following Research Question:

To what extent can enhanced Retrieval-Augmented Generation-Large Language Model (RAG-LLM) models improve the inclusion of relevant evidence and enhance verdict transparency when extracting information from nutrition science literature for claims related to cardiac health and hypertension?

Concurrently, we recognize that scientific papers are not produced or interpreted in isolation. Therefore, the subsequent section on related work explicitly examines various sources contributing to misinformation and disinformation and discusses the need for improved governance within nutrition science, alongside detailing how our enhanced RAG-LLM prototype aims to achieve improved health claim verification.

2 RELATED WORK

In this section we build on two different topics. First, the topic of *mis- and disinformation about healthy nutrition*. Second, the topic of *automated claim verification*, using various filtering-, reasoning- and LLM tools.

2.1 Sources of mis- and disinformation:

As a first topic, there are several important sources of mis- and disinformation in both the scientific literature and popular media sources on healthy nutrition. We summarize them in Table 1 and provide a brief discussion below.

Table 1. Sources of mis- and disinformation on healthy nutrition

Summary of impact on (un)healthy food choices
1. Food industry advertisements and marketing: still a large influence, e.g. via numerous daily marketing and sales exposures (Wansink & Sobal, 2007).
2. Social media: despite user awareness of low information quality, more social media exposure means more impact on (un)healthy choices (Ruani et al., 2023).
3. 'Normal' scientific misinformation: Up to 30% of health claims are found to be overstated (Ioannidis, 2005) and many myths persist in scientific papers (Casazza et al., 2013). AI tools may help digest the 500,000+ health publications/year.
4. Industry efforts to skew health claims and beliefs: a) via *misinformation*, e.g. on supplements, fad diets, or health impacts of sugars, cholesterol etc, b) via *disinformation* of fake science (Barnard et al., 2021) and infiltration of health institutions and advisory boards (Mialon et al., 2022).

Based on the classification presented in Table 1, the first category of information influence is exemplified by Figure 1, which visually depicts the historically significant role of traditional advertising in shaping consumer food choices. The sheer scale and pervasive impact of food marketing activities are so profound that they have been characterized as a 'crisis' (Harris et al., 2009). This influence is progressively extending into digital domains, with marketing efforts increasingly concentrated on Internet advertising and social media platforms (Rummo et al., 2020). Furthermore, the proliferation of food purchasing opportunities across numerous points of sale (including vending machines, restaurants, food shops, and supermarkets) results in individuals making an average of over 200 food-related decisions daily (Wansink & Sobal, 2007), frequently involving less healthful options often referred to as 'junk' foods or drinks. As concluded by Greger (2019) in an analysis of the global surge in obesity since the 1980s: 'marketing works'. Similarly, paraphrasing the research by Wansink and Sobal (2007), it can be asserted that dietary intake is heavily influenced by environmental exposure: 'You eat what you are exposed to.'

Figure 1. Food advertising outpacing public health messages, see also (Harris et al., 2009)

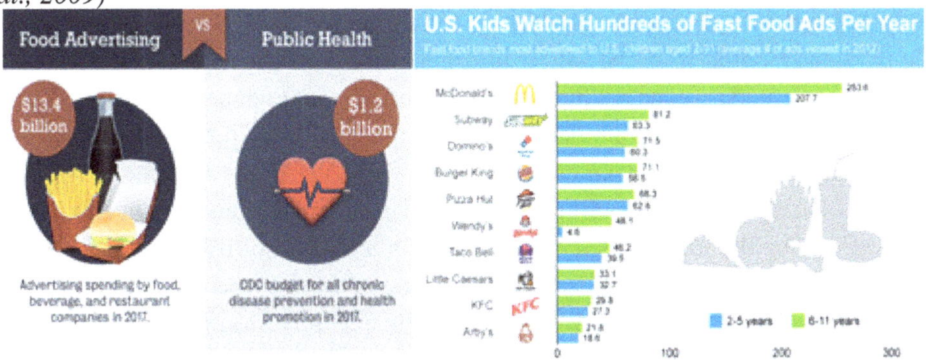

The second category of information sources, as listed in Table 1, encompasses social media platforms. Platforms such as Instagram and YouTube act as particularly prominent channels for disseminating nutrition-related content, although Facebook, X (formerly Twitter), and TikTok also contribute (Segado-Fernandez et al., 2025). Content creators and influencers operating on these platforms, motivated by objectives ranging from brand promotion and audience growth to targeting specific demographic groups, may promote unverified dietary regimens or commercially branded health products. Despite the fact that both users (Ruani et al., 2023) and experts (Suarez-Lledo & Alvarez-Galvez, 2021; Vasconcelos et al., 2021; Denniss et al., 2023) widely recognize social media as a source of low-quality information, individuals who frequently seek information from less credible sources tend to utilize these platforms more often when contemplating dietary changes. This effect is amplified among individuals with lower literacy levels and reduced access to higher-quality information resources (Ruani et al., 2023).

The third type of information source contributing to the complex landscape stems from the inherent imperfections and dynamics within scientific research itself. These 'imperfect' or preliminary findings can pose a misinformation problem as they may persist and circulate for extended periods. A substantial proportion of initial scientific findings do not withstand scrutiny over time; approximately 30% of health claims that are initially presented as established findings are later determined to be overstated or incorrect based on subsequent updated evidence (Ioannidis, 2005). Moreover, scientific communities may operate within certain 'narratives' or paradigms, leading researchers to implicitly favor findings that align with or support their pre-existing beliefs and previous work, potentially downplaying evidence that challenges or refutes them (referencing concepts explored by Latour, 1987). This tendency is compounded by the overwhelming volume of new scientific publications

– exceeding 500,000 per year in health-related fields, with over 200,000 specifically in cardiac health annually – making it virtually impossible for individuals to remain fully updated with all emerging evidence (Simons et al., 2022; Simons et al., 2024). Consequently, outdated or inaccurate information, effectively acting as 'myths', can unfortunately persist even within peer-reviewed scientific papers (Casazza et al., 2013). It is hoped that the application of AI tools may offer potential avenues for mitigating this significant challenge.

The fourth major source of both misinformation and disinformation originates from efforts by the food industry to deliberately influence or distort health claims and public beliefs. Within this category, we first address a) the promotion of misinformation, followed by the more intentionally deceptive b) promotion of disinformation. These sources are highlighted here due to their demonstrable impact on the integrity of scientific databases such as PubMed through the generation of 'fake science', rather than suggesting that our AI prototype directly resolves these issues. However, the topic of governance in our conclusion section will revisit the challenges posed by these subpar information sources.

Issue a) concerns the promotion of misinformation, often facilitated through influencers and online advertising. This includes marketing not only of dietary supplements that may be useless or even harmful (Greger, 2023) but also the promotion of fad diets or employing 'online stars' to advocate for unhealthful behaviors, such as consuming three eggs daily, which consumers may adopt based on the erroneous belief that it will lead to comparable physical outcomes (e.g., increased muscle mass). This behavior is again linked to the principle that observed behavior is more likely to be emulated (Wansink & Sobal, 2007; Ruani, 2023).

A more insidious aspect is issue b), the active promotion of disinformation through infiltration of health advisory boards and institutions or by fabricating 'fake' scientific data. Examples of the former include documented instances where, even within bodies intended to be objective like the US Dietary Guidelines Advisory Committee, a significant majority (19 out of 20 members) have reported clear industry affiliations and conflicts of interest (Mialon et al., 2022). Another case involves the reported replacement of a dean at a prominent university nutrition department with an individual linked to industry, subsequently leading to certain nutrition research topics being deemed off-limits (Campbell & Campbell, 2016). Similarly, evidence suggests efforts by companies like Coca-Cola and Mars to bias research and public discourse towards emphasizing physical activity for weight management, thereby diverting attention from the role of sugary foods (Fabbri et al., 2018).

Also, examples of fabricating 'fake' science are stark. Since 2010, the egg industry has been the primary funder and producer of studies examining egg consumption and blood cholesterol levels. While 86% of these industry-sponsored studies did find that egg consumption raised blood cholesterol, half of that 86% nonetheless drew conclusions that denied or downplayed this connection (Barnard et al., 2021). Furthermore, the egg industry is reported to promote five-yearly review studies based on their own potentially biased research for submission to dietary advisory boards, aiming to 'prove' a lack of 'significant' effect between eggs and blood cholesterol (Barnard, 2018). Research has quantified this bias; Lesser (2007) found that studies with full industry sponsorship were eight times more likely to reach conclusions favorable to the industry compared to studies without such sponsorship. Similarly, Bes-Rastrollo et al. (2013) observed that papers without industry affiliation were five times more likely to conclude that sugar-sweetened beverages contribute to weight gain compared to industry-sponsored studies. More detailed examples and a breakdown of seven key tactics employed by industry to generate misleading science can be found in Nestle (2018).

2.2 Automated nutritional health claim verification:

Our second topic, the *claim verification* task, is studied under the umbrella of automated fact-checking (Guo et al., 2022). The task involves automatically verifying the authenticity of claims based on the retrieval of evidence. A conventional framework of claim verification consist of three modules: the retrieval of relevant documents given a claim, selecting evidence from documents, and predicting a label (true, false, or not sure) based on the top-k evidence (Wadden et al., 2020; Pradeep et al., 2021; Soleimani et al., 2020). Research gap analyses (Gao et al., 2023; Wu et al., 2024; Liu et al., 2024) led us to focus on improving quality of evidence included and of transparency of verdict generation.

Liu et al. (2024) used the traditional three-step approach of claim verification but focused on an *Retrieval Augmented Generation (RAG)* module to specifically focus on RCT studies as evidence base for a given COVID claim. Instead of retrieving evidence from a prepared database, this augmented retrieval module presented a real life scientific use case. Below, we introduce Inclusion-Criteria-based filtering to enhance RAG by improving relevance of the inputs used. Retrieval-augmented methodologies harness the capabilities of multiple information retrieval techniques such as document vectorization, semantic similarity-based retrievers, and similarity ranking mechanisms.

We formulate concise claims using the *Population, Intervention, Comparison, and Outcome (PICO) framework* (Richardson et al., 1995). This framework is commonly used to formulate good clinical research questions, which can be utilized to formulate clinical claims by adapting the elements to suit the nature of the claim being made (Huang et al., 2006). For example Liu et al. (2024) used the PICO framework to construct a Covid Verification dataset of 15 PICO-encoded drug claims.

We introduce PICO use to translate *nutrition* science into health claims. PICO-encoded health claims can enhance document retrieval by guiding the search toward semantically relevant papers. Next, PICO-based paper summarization towards claim verdicts improves transparency. As an example PICO-based health claim:

- **Population:** Adults with high cholesterol levels
- **Intervention:** Consumption of flax seeds
- **Comparison:** Standard diet without flax seeds
- **Outcome:** Reduces LDL cholesterol levels
- **Claim:** Consumption of flax seeds reduces LDL cholesterol in adults with high cholesterol.

In conclusion of this related work section, we can say that health behaviors and -beliefs of people are to quite some extent influenced by subpar information. In a previous study (Simons et al., 2024), users admitted that they often don't come around to taking the time or effort to consult high-quality sources. Hopefully we can make high-quality information more easily accessible, with the type of AI tooling we focus on in te remainder of this paper. Thus supporting the aim of combating misinformation. In the discussion section we return to the topic of fighting disinformation from industry, maybe using some of the tools and topics from our AI research.

3 PROTOTYPE DEVELOPMENT

In this section we explain the prototype we developed. Figure 2 visually depicts the comprehensive 'Advanced RAG-LLM' framework that we developed, with our specific enhancements highlighted in orange.

Figure 2. Framework with enhanced selection and summary modules

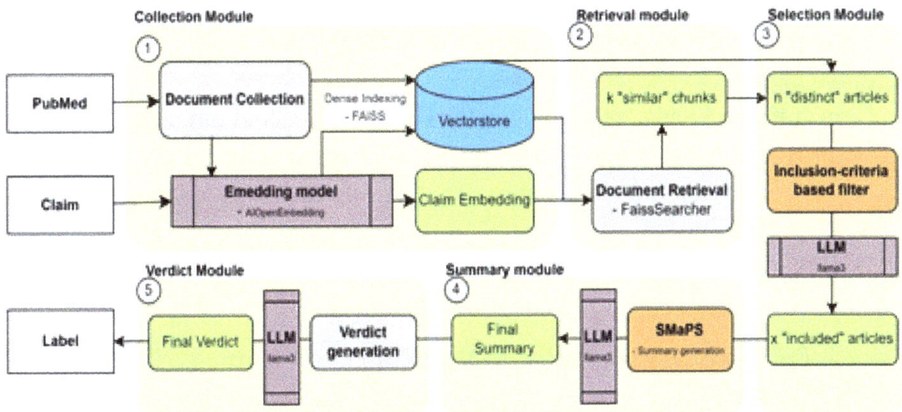

The claim verification process unfolds through five principal stages, indicated numerically from 1 to 5:

1. **Document Acquisition:** This initial phase involves gathering relevant source material. Leveraging semantic similarity metrics, the PubMed API is queried to identify and retrieve articles most pertinent to a given claim. The complete text of each retrieved article is then segmented into smaller units, or 'chunks,' each containing approximately 1000 tokens, to facilitate subsequent processing. These processed chunks are then stored as dense vectors within FAISS[1] (Facebook AI Similarity Search), a system employed for efficient indexing, similarity searching, and clustering.
2. **Information Retrieval:** At this stage, a health claim serves as the input query. FAISS then performs a search within its vector store to locate documents whose vector representations demonstrate semantic similarity to the query vector. It is important to note, however, that merely identifying semantic similarity does not guarantee the practical relevance or high quality of the retrieved documents, a point addressed in the subsequent step (Step 3).
3. **Evidence Selection:** To enhance the pertinence of the chosen papers, an additional filtering layer based on predefined Inclusion Criteria was incorporated. These criteria utilized the PICO elements: the target Population was restricted to human adults (excluding, for example, animal studies); the Intervention had to be a Dietary Intervention (ruling out study types like prospective studies or interventions involving medication); the Comparison required a stated control group or condition; and the Outcome needed to relate to blood pressure or cardiovascular health (excluding measures such as bone density, etc.).

4. **Synthesizing Information:** Utilizing the SMaPS module (detailed in Figure 3), the PICO elements and summarized texts derived from each individual article are consolidated to produce a single, overarching summary pertinent to the initial claim.
5. **Generating a Verdict:** Based upon the final consolidated summary for a given claim, a verdict is formulated. This verdict is assigned a numerical score ranging from 1, signifying that the claim is 'strongly refuted,' up to 5, indicating that it is 'strongly supported.'

Figure 3. PICO-based Sequential Mapping (SMaPS)

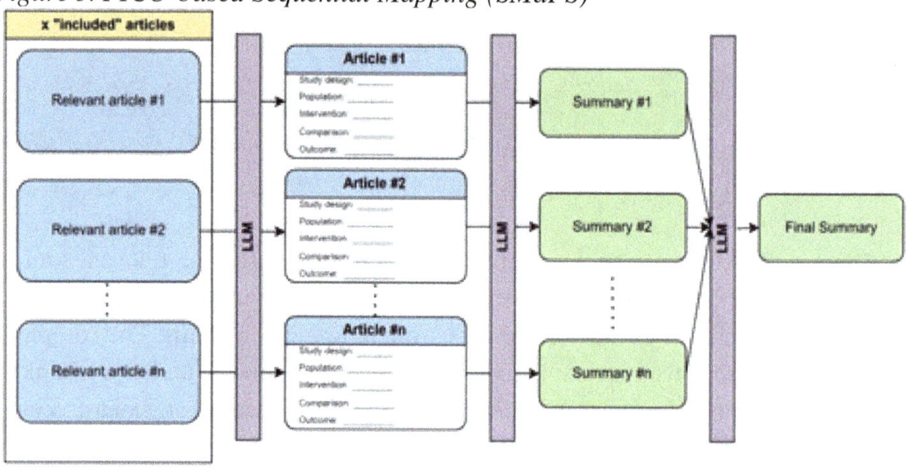

Figure 3 illustrates the synthesis process whereby the top *k* articles identified as relevant to a specific claim (for instance, the claim that 'Nuts reduce blood pressure in adults') are processed using Large Language Models (LLMs). This processing extracts key information formatted according to the PICO (Population, Intervention, Comparison, Outcome) framework and generates individual article summaries. These outputs are then integrated to construct a comprehensive final summary that serves as the basis for determining the verdict on the claim's validity.

4 METHOD: THREE SUB-QUESTIONS FOR MODEL EVALUATION

Working in conjunction with an expert in cardiac health and nutrition, an initial collection comprising 50 claims related to food and cardiac health was established.

These claims included examples such as 'Legumes lower blood pressure in human adults'. The set was evenly divided, with half of the claims addressing blood pressure outcomes and the other half focusing on broader cardiovascular health aspects. Following the claim creation, a pool of 200,000 papers specifically indexed in PubMed under the categories of nutrition and cardiac health was considered. From this larger set, 10,000 papers were systematically chosen based on their high degree of semantic similarity to the initial set of 50 claims. The decision to limit the selection to 10,000 papers was necessitated by the computational resources available for the development and testing of our prototype, particularly given that our process involved handling the full text of each article. In nutrition research, full text inclusions are deemed necessary since industry influences sometime generate papers where the abstracts do not reflect the findings of the rest of the paper (ref).

Subsequently, we undertook an evaluation to determine the effectiveness of the developed 'Advanced RAG-LLM' prototype. This evaluation was structured around addressing three primary research sub-questions:

1. **Assessment of the Selection Module:** What is the accuracy performance of the Inclusion-Criteria-based Selection Module in correctly identifying articles that fit the inclusion criteria?
2. **Evaluation of the Summary Module:** How accurate are the PICO extraction and summary generation processes, and how useful are the resulting summaries?
3. **Accuracy of the Verdict Module:** How accurate are the verdicts produced by the 'Advanced RAG-LLM' prototype model when compared against expert opinions?

Regarding the first sub-question, which focused on the accuracy of the Inclusion-Criteria-based Selection Module, we performed a manual validation. This involved reviewing a sample of 100 articles that the model predicted as not meeting the Inclusion Criteria, alongside a separate sample of 100 articles that the model predicted as meeting the criteria.

For the second sub-question, concerning the accuracy of PICO synthesis and the utility of the generated summaries, we conducted an initial, small-scale evaluation involving 'expert users'. This evaluation assessed the PICO-encoded information and summary texts derived from specific scientific articles that these experts reviewed as part of the process. Acknowledging the time constraints inherent to this prototype engineering study, we adopted an iterative, early-stage user testing methodology. This approach is based on the principle that a significant majority (approximately 80%) of usability issues or design flaws can typically be identified within the first five user evaluations (Faulkner, 2003). For this evaluation phase, we engaged five experts in healthy lifestyles who possessed familiarity with both the interpretation of scientific studies and the information needs of individuals seeking coaching. Each expert evaluated two distinct articles, resulting in a total of 10 article evaluations, with each specific article being assessed by two different experts. Across these expert evaluations, a high level of consistency in observations was noted.

Addressing the third sub-question, which examined the accuracy of the food health verdicts generated by the 'Advanced RAG-LLM' prototype model, the model's verdict for all 50 claims was compared against a verdict provided by a human expert. These expert verdicts were assigned on a scale from 1 ('strongly refuted') to 5 ('strongly supported'), with the expert tasked to base their assignments on the state-of-the-art information presented by NutritionFacts[2]. To provide context and highlight the impact of different module configurations, we compared the performance of three distinct model versions (BaseLLM, Standard RAG-LLM, and Advanced RAG-LLM), as visually represented in Figure 4. The evaluation of the accuracy for all three models utilized confusion matrices, comparing the 'model predicted' scores against the 'expert' scores, and employed Cohen's weighted Kappa scores as a quantitative measure of agreement.

Figure 4. Comparing models: BaseLLM, RAG-LLM and Advanced RAG-LLM

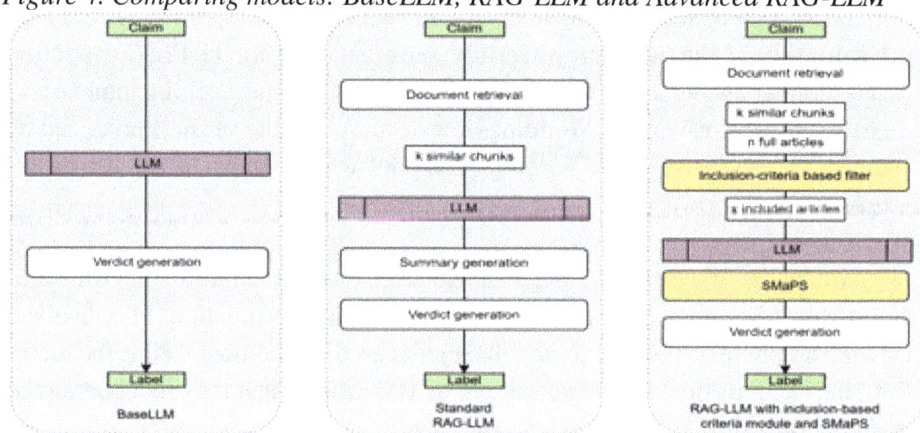

5 RESULTS

In addressing *sub-question 1, which evaluated the accuracy of the Inclusion-Criteria-based Selection Module*, Figure 5 illustrates the observed performance. The incidence of False Negatives (FN) was found to be relatively modest when compared to the number of True Negatives, with only 3 out of 100 predictions being incorrectly classified as negative. Relative to the actual count of 83 papers that met the inclusion criteria, these 3 FN papers represent 3.6%. In contrast, False Positives (FP) constituted a more substantial group; specifically, 20 out of the 117 papers that should have been excluded were incorrectly flagged as meeting the inclusion criteria, accounting for 17.1% of this group. Further analysis into the nature of these False Positives revealed that a primary contributing factor was the incorrect identification of study types, such as systematic reviews, as intervention studies. Additionally, errors in correctly identifying the target Population (e.g., including animal studies) and accurately recognizing the specified Outcome (e.g., incorrectly flagging studies not primarily focused on blood pressure) also played a role in generating False Positives.

Figure 5. Confusion matrix for inclusion criteria: 0 = "excluded" and 1 = "included"

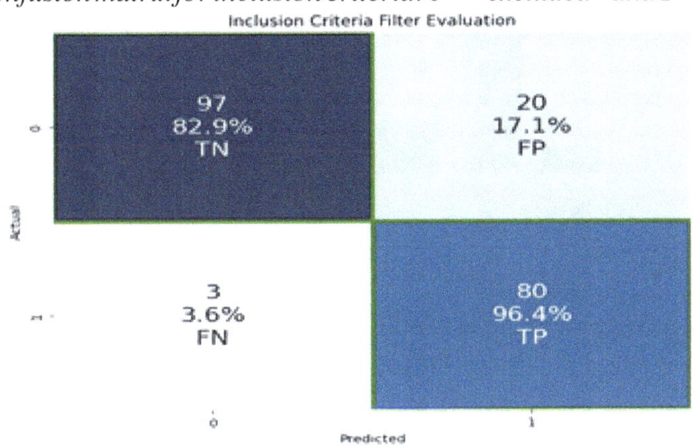

In response to *sub-question 2, on accuracy of PICO synthesis and usefulness of summaries*, we found concerningly *low performance*, see Figure 6. Whereas Intervention (4.2) and Comparison (4.1) score okay, accuracy scores for Population (2.0) and Outcome (1.9) descriptions were low. For Population accuracy in comparison to the original papers, some of the typical expert complaints were:

- "Missing info on sample size, selection method, cholesterol levels of study population."
- "Sample size incorrect, for intervention and for control. Selection method info absent."

For Outcome accuracy in comparison to the original papers, some of the typical expert complaints were:

- "Outcome incorrect; omission of the decrease in systolic blood pressure."
- "Primary outcome measures from paper were missing." → (10x out of 10)

Figure 6. Expert accuracy scores on PICO elements (n=10 paper evaluations)

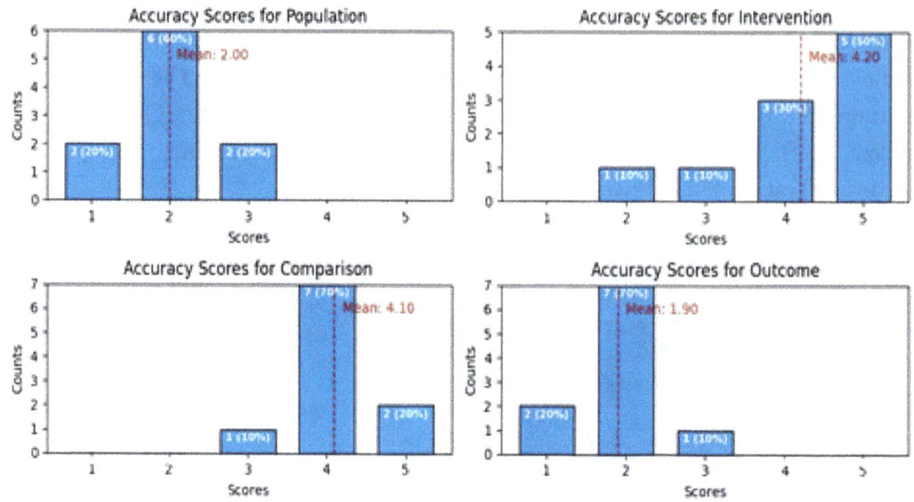

Moreover, when *evaluating usefulness a paper's summary text*, the average expert score is 2.1 (on range of 1 to 5). Illustrative expert remarks:

- "Blood pressure is left out of the results. Which is strange because it's one of the main outcomes." [multiple times]
- "Claim cannot be made on this study. Study focusses on kiwi's only."

Regarding *sub-question 3, on accuracy of the 50 food health verdicts of the three LLM models we compared*, we find that the Advanced RAG-LLM prototype generates improvements, but still LLM flaws persist, see Figures 7 and 8.

Figure 7. Confusion matrices BaseLLM & Standard RAG-LLM (n=50 claims predict/actual)

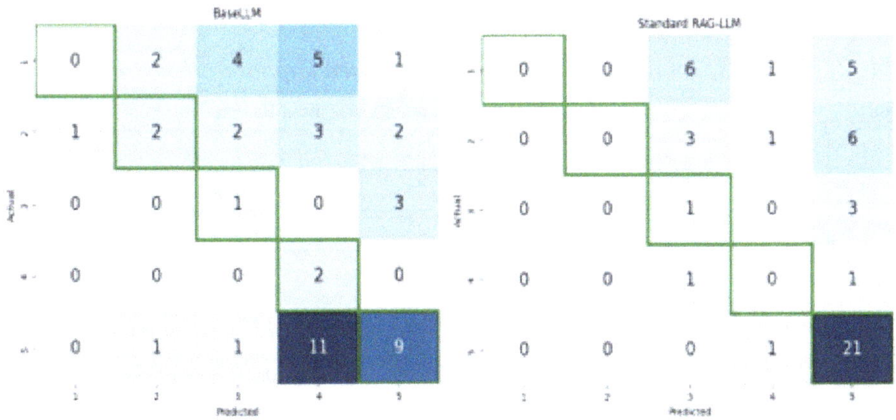

Figure 8. Confusion matrix advanced RAG-LLM (n=50 claims: predict/actual)

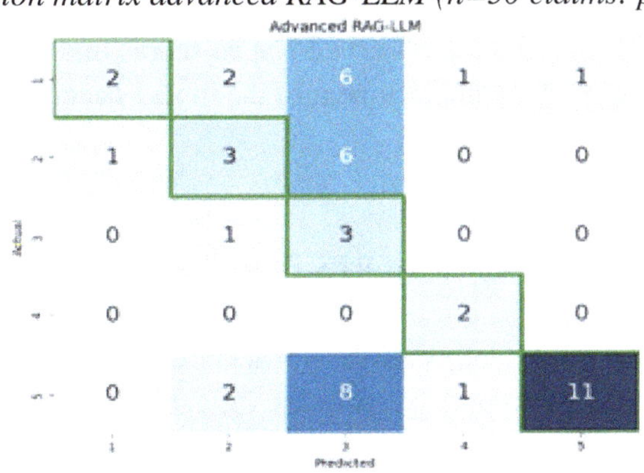

Analysis of the models' prediction distributions revealed a *notable 'positivity bias' in the BaseLLM*, which tended to classify most claims (foods) as either neutral (score 3) or healthy (scores 4 or 5). This bias was even more pronounced in the Standard RAG-LLM model. The Standard RAG-LLM heavily favored positive classifications, assigning a score of 5 to 36 claims and a score of 4 to 3 claims, while classifying the remaining 11 claims as neutral (score 3). Strikingly, the Standard RAG-LLM did not label any foods as detrimental to blood pressure or cardiac health, including items typically associated with negative cardiovascular impacts in scientific literature such as sugar, alcohol, red meat, eggs, full-fat dairy, cheese, and salty foods. This outcome suggests a significant disconnect between the model's predictions and the established scientific understanding regarding the health effects of various foods.

Table 2. Model-expert agreement: Cohen's weighted kappa

Model	Cohen's Weighted Kappa
BaseLLM	0.31
Standard RAG-LLM	0.27
Inclusion-based RAG-LLM	0.48

In contrast, the *Advanced RAG-LLM prototype generated a more balanced distribution of scores*, incorporating both positive and negative classifications. Its generated verdicts demonstrated a closer alignment with expert opinion, as quantified by a Cohen's Weighted Kappa score of 0.48, presented in Table 2. This score signifies 'weak' agreement with expert judgments, which is a notable improvement compared to the 'minimal' agreement levels indicated by Kappa scores of 0.31 for the BaseLLM and 0.27 for the Standard RAG-LLM models. Despite this relative improvement, the Advanced RAG-LLM still exhibited a tendency towards assigning neutral (score 3) ratings, and the observed Kappa scores underscore that substantial room remains for further enhancement of the model's accuracy, a point further discussed in the subsequent analysis.

6 DISCUSSION & IMPLICATIONS FOR THEORY

This prototyping study is subject to several acknowledged *limitations*. Primarily, constrained by available computing resources, the analysis was limited to using the full text of only 10,000 papers. This represents a mere 5% of the 200,000 nutrition and cardiac health papers available in the PubMed database, specifically those exhibiting the highest semantic similarity to the 50 claims investigated. It is anticipated that incorporating a larger volume of source documents in future iterations would likely yield improved results, a point further elaborated in the discussion regarding observed flaws in the generated verdicts.

Furthermore, each of the three evaluations conducted possesses its own set of constraints. Firstly, the evaluation of the Inclusion-Criteria-based filter (corresponding to sub-question 1) was carried out as a straightforward, qualitative assessment. While including additional evaluators could have enhanced the rigor of this check, the nature of the criteria being assessed (e.g., distinguishing between a nutrition intervention in adults versus a meta-study, in vitro experiment, or mouse model study) involves relatively clear distinctions for human reviewers. Therefore, the expected error rate in this manual check is considered low.

Secondly, the expert-based evaluation of the paper-level PICO extractions and summary texts (aligned with sub-question 2) was conducted on a relatively limited scale, involving only 10 papers reviewed by a total of 5 domain experts. Nevertheless, from a system design perspective, consistent findings across these evaluations – such as the observation that the extracted Outcome text was frequently found to be deficient in relevant detail in 10 out of 10 paper assessments – provide crucial insights. These findings strongly suggest the need to refine the sequential summarization module before proceeding with evaluations on a larger scale.

Thirdly, the evaluation pertaining to the accuracy of the 50 food health verdicts produced by the three compared LLM models (sub-question 3) relied exclusively on the input of a single expert for translating the evidence base from NutritionFacts[3] into the ground truth verdicts. In a subsequent phase, as the 'Advanced RAG-LLM' achieves greater robustness, it would be beneficial to incorporate the perspectives of additional experts to provide a more comprehensive validation.

Implications for theoretical understanding

The various evaluations conducted hold significant intrinsic value as they allow for the identification and characterization of discernible flaws within the Large Language Model (LLM) prototype. Furthermore, a deeper investigation into these observed shortcomings provides valuable insights into the underlying reasons for specific areas of weaker model performance. For instance, the detection of a *'positivity bias'*, particularly apparent in the performance of the BaseLLM and Standard RAG-LLM iterations, presents an interesting theoretical observation. Two potential explanations for this bias are considered. Firstly, commercially developed LLMs, such as Meta's Llama3 which was utilized in this study, may exhibit a tendency towards generating responses perceived as agreeable or 'pleasing' to the user, a characteristic noted in various anecdotal accounts throughout the history of LLM development (referencing examples from domains like chess). However, a second, potentially more substantive reason relates to the framing of the claims themselves. In retrospect, all the health claims used in this study were phrased as affirmative statements (e.g., 'Berries reduce blood pressure'). Future research could valuably explore whether formulating claims as negative statements ('... does not reduce blood pressure') leads to a different selection of top k articles, potentially mitigating this observed positivity bias.

Additionally, the evaluations revealed instances where an insufficient quantity of relevant intervention papers was included in the evidence base for certain claims. This issue was compounded when papers that did not genuinely address the specific claim were included. An exploratory analysis highlights this problem: among the 50 claims assessed, *four (representing 8%) exhibited substantial discrepancies (> 2 points difference) between the expert-assigned verdict and the verdict generated* by the Advanced RAG-LLM. A detailed examination of the papers selected as evidence for these four claims (two concerning bananas and two concerning full-fat dairy, covering both blood pressure and cardiac health claims) revealed a consistent pattern. After the application of the Inclusion-Criteria-based filtering, only a limited number of papers, ranging from 3 to 5, remained as foundational material for these claims. Critically, a *significant proportion of these remaining papers were 'false positives'* – incorrectly included despite not specifically investigating the effects of bananas or full-fat dairy. Consequently, the *LLM-generated 'final summary' for these claims was effectively compelled to engage in hallucination and unwarranted overgeneralization.* Although the prompting strategy encouraged transparency in referencing sources (e.g., stating "The studies did not specifically investigate the effects of banana consumption on blood pressure" or "foods like fruits [..] support overall health"), the essential evidentiary basis for a well-grounded verdict on the precise claim was fundamentally absent. As an example, the five studies included for the claim regarding full fat dairy and blood pressure primarily focused on low-fat dairy or dairy in general, rather than the specific subject of full-fat dairy.

Finally, *one of the most critical limitations* identified, stemming from the evaluation of the PICO extractions and summary texts for individual papers, is the *relatively poor fidelity in representing key elements and nuances from the original scientific literature, as judged by the domain experts.* The resulting outputs often lacked sufficient detail, context, or subtlety, diminishing the overall usefulness of the paper summaries (evidenced by a low average score of 2.1 on a scale of 1 to 5). *Given that these simplified representations serve as the input for generating the final summaries and ultimate verdicts for each claim, the verdicts become, in essence, 'averages of averages'.* However, in scientific inquiry, acknowledging and understanding variance is often paramount. For instance, the health implications of 0%-fat milk when compared to beans (where 0%-milk appears comparatively 'unhealthy') are vastly different from a comparison to sugary snacks like Twinkies (where 0%-milk appears comparatively 'healthy'). Similarly, the impact of dietary substitutions depends heavily on whether they are based on equal weight or equal calorie exchanges.

Consequently, *simply averaging information without retaining crucial contextual details or understanding variance is frequently unhelpful*, akin to using a cheetah's average speed over an entire day to estimate its maximum sprint speed – the result is highly inaccurate. This detrimental effect was *exacerbated by the frequent misrepresentation or complete omission of numerical data* (such as figures for study populations or outcomes). In summary, the specific LLM (Llama 3) and vector search models (Facebook FAISS) utilized in this study appear to lack the necessary subtlety and precision for accurately identifying and summarizing the most pertinent scientific details and their associated nuances.

7 CONCLUSION & IMPLICATIONS FOR PRACTICE AND GOVERNANCE

Conclusion

The evaluation of the 'Advanced RAG-LLM' prototype developed in this study indicates demonstrable improvements in performance when compared to a base LLM and a standard RAG-LLM approach. Specifically, the implementation of Inclusion-Criteria-based filtering showed clear benefits in refining the relevance of retrieved documents. Furthermore, the adoption of a PICO-frame-based approach for summarizing evidence contributed positively to the transparency of the verdict generation process. Nevertheless, these enhancements could not entirely overcome fundamental limitations inherent in current LLMs. As models primarily designed for predicting probable word sequences, they continue to exhibit deficiencies in true reasoning capabilities and frequently either disregard or inaccurately represent critical factual information present in scientific literature.

Implications for Practice

In practical terms, the LLM-based models evaluated in this work currently lack the capacity to reliably differentiate between robust, scientifically sound evidence and either fabricated research or information of low relevance. This highlights a clear need for the integration of additional reasoning tools to augment their capabilities. Enhanced filtering and reasoning modules are specifically required to elevate performance in several key areas pertinent to practical application:

- Improving the precision and relevance of paper selection for evidence gathering.
- More accurately extracting critical information from scientific papers, including findings, details on control conditions, population characteristics, study design methodologies, and the expected causal relationships of interventions.
- Facilitating context-aware interpretation of numerical data (e.g., assessing the practical significance or 'largeness' of an effect size).
- Identifying and prioritizing findings that hold the greatest utility for patients and healthcare practitioners.

- Developing the ability to recognize and effectively discard misleading or 'fabricated science'.

Governance and Combating Industry Influence and Misleading Science

Addressing the challenges posed by misinformation and disinformation necessitates action beyond cultivating individual critical thinking skills. While such individual competencies are valuable, they are insufficient on their own. As rightly pointed out by Lesser et al. (2007) and Bes-Rastrollo et al. (2013), an additional layer of governance is crucial, particularly concerning guidelines for transparency regarding industry affiliations of scientific institutions and the funding of research.

Expanding upon this, we propose the need for further governance measures focusing on the industry ties of individuals serving on advisory boards, review panels, research agenda committees, and within the management structures of health institutions. This comprehensive approach is warranted due to the potent and widespread influence that industry can exert, potentially skewing scientific findings and their interpretation.

Interestingly, some of the AI-powered reasoning tools developed for evaluating the veracity of health claims at an individual level may also offer valuable support for enhancing research transparency at the governance level. As an extension to previous work (Simons et al., 2024), examples of how these tools could be applied include:

- Analyzing and visualizing industry affiliations of researchers, funding sources, and research program teams to identify potential conflicts of interest.
- Assessing the consistency of health claims, not only between a paper's abstract and its full text but also between the findings of a single paper and the existing cumulative 'body of evidence' on a given topic.
- Conducting a 'burden of proof' analysis to evaluate whether the robustness of the evidence and/or argumentation provided for a claim (e.g., 'egg consumption lowers cholesterol') that contradicts a large, established scientific consensus is sufficiently compelling.

The inherent capabilities of AI in conducting exhaustive evidence reviews and performing sophisticated semantic analyses are well-suited to support these critical governance tasks. Leveraging these capabilities has the potential to improve oversight regarding industry influences on nutritional health claims, hopefully shifting the primary challenge from actively combating deliberate disinformation towards more effectively managing unintentional misinformation.

REFERENCES

Armitage, H. (2019). Any way you slice it, there's a lot to say about nutrition studies. Scope blog Stanford, accessed 28-2-2025: https://scopeblog.stanford.edu/2019/01/28/any-way-you-slice-it-nutrition-studies-are-controversial/

Badimon, L., Chagas, P., & Chiva-Blanch, G. (2019). Diet and Cardiovascular Disease: Effects of Foods and Nutrients in Classical and Emerging Cardiovascular Risk Factors. *Current Medicinal Chemistry*, *26*(19), 3639–3651.

Barnard, N. D., Long, M. B., Ferguson, J. M., Flores, R., & Kahleova, H. (2021). Industry funding and cholesterol research: A systematic review. *American Journal of Lifestyle Medicine*, *15*(2), 165–172.

Barnard, R. J. (2018). How the Egg Industry Skews Science. YouTube, accessed 26-2-2024: https://www.youtube.com/watch?v=FyG8wr0gWIA

Bes-Rastrollo, M., Schulze, M. B., Ruiz-Canela, M., & Martinez-Gonzalez, M. A. (2013). Financial conflicts of interest and reporting bias regarding the association between sugar-sweetened beverages and weight gain: A systematic review of systematic reviews. *PLoS Medicine*, *10*(12), e1001578.

Campbell, T. C., & Campbell, T. M. (2016). *The China study: Revised and expanded edition: The most comprehensive study of nutrition ever conducted and the startling implications for diet, weight loss, and long-term health.* BenBella Books, Inc.

Carey, R. M., & Whelton, P. K. (2020). Evidence for the universal blood pressure goal of< 130/80 mm Hg is strong: Controversies in hypertension-pro side of the argument. *Hypertension*, *76*(5), 1384–1390.

Casazza, K., Fontaine, K. R., Astrup, A., Birch, L. L., Brown, A. W., Bohan Brown, M. M., & Allison, D. B. (2013). Myths, presumptions, and facts about obesity. *The New England Journal of Medicine*, *368*(5), 446–454.

Denniss, E., Lindberg, R., & McNaughton, S. A. (2023). Quality and accuracy of online nutrition-related information: A systematic review of content analysis studies. *Public Health Nutrition*, *26*(7), 1345–1357.

Dineen-Griffin, S., Garcia-Cardenas, V., Williams, K., & Benrimoj, S. I. (2019). Helping patients help themselves: A systematic review of self-management support strategies in primary health care practice. *PLoS One*, *14*(8), e0220116.

Fabbri, A., Lai, A., Grundy, Q., & Bero, L. A. (2018). The influence of industry sponsorship on the research agenda: A scoping review. *American Journal of Public Health, 108*(11), e9–e16.

Faulkner, L. (2003). Beyond the five-user assumption: Benefits of increased sample sizes in usability testing. *Behavior Research Methods, Instruments, & Computers, 35*, 379–383.

Gaidai, O., Cao, Y., & Loginov, S. (2023). Global Cardiovascular Diseases Death Rate Prediction. *Current Problems in Cardiology, 48*(5), 101622.

Gao, Y., Xiong, Y., Gao, X., Jia, K., Pan, J., Bi, Y., . . . Wang, H. (2023). Retrieval-augmented generation for large language models: A survey. *arXiv preprint arXiv:2312.10997, 2.*

Greger, M. (2019). *How not to diet: the groundbreaking science of healthy, permanent weight loss*. Flatiron Books.

Greger, M. (2023). *How not to age: the scientific approach to getting healthier as you get older*. Flatiron Books.

Guo, Z., Schlichtkrull, M., & Vlachos, A. (2022). A Survey on Automated Fact-Checking. arXiv:2108.11896 [cs].

Harris, J. L., Pomeranz, J. L., Lobstein, T., & Brownell, K. D. (2009). A crisis in the marketplace: How food marketing contributes to childhood obesity and what can be done. *Annual Review of Public Health, 30*(1), 211–225.

Huang, X., Lin, J., & Demner-Fushman, D. (2006). Evaluation of PICO as a knowledge representation for clinical questions. *AMIA Annual Symposium proceedings. AMIA Symposium*, 2006, 359–363.

Ioannidis, J. P. (2005). Contradicted and initially stronger effects in highly cited clinical research. *jama, 294*(2), 218-228.

Latour, B. (1987). *Science in action: How to follow scientists and engineers through society*. Harvard UP.

Lee, C.-j., Nagler, R. H., & Wang, N. (2018). Sourcespecific Exposure to Contradictory Nutrition Information: Documenting Prevalence and Effects on Adverse Cognitive and Behavioral Outcomes. *Health Communication, 33*(4), 453–461.

Lesser, L. I., Ebbeling, C. B., Goozner, M., Wypij, D., & Ludwig, D. S. (2007). Relationship between funding source and conclusion among nutrition-related scientific articles. *PLoS Medicine, 4*(1), e5.

Liu, H., Soroush, A., Nestor, J. G., Park, E., Idnay, B., Fang, Y., Pan, J., Liao, S., Bernard, M., Peng, Y., & Weng, C. (2024). Retrieval augmented scientific claim verification. *JAMIA Open*, *7*(1), ooae021.

Mialon, M., Serodio, P., Crosbie, E., Teicholz, N., Naik, A., & Carriedo, A. (2022). Conflicts of interest for members of the US 2020 Dietary Guidelines Advisory Committee. *Public Health Nutrition*, ●●●, 1–28.

Nagler, R. H. (2014). Adverse outcomes associated with media exposure to contradictory nutrition messages. *Journal of Health Communication*, *19*(1), 24–40.

Nestle, M. (2018). *Unsavory truth: how food companies skew the science of what we eat*. Basic Books.

Ostchega, Y., Fryar, C. D., Nwankwo, T., & Nguyen, D. T. (2020). Hypertension prevalence among adults aged 18 and over: United States, 2017–2018, NCHS, National Health and Nutrition Examination Survey, 2017–2018: https://stacks.cdc.gov/view/cdc/87559, accessed 25-08-2023.

Pradeep, R., Ma, X., Nogueira, R., & Lin, J. (2021). Scientific Claim Verification with VerT5erini. In Holderness, E., Jimeno Yepes, A., Lavelli, A., Minard, A.-L., Pustejovsky, J., and Rinaldi, F., editors, *Proceedings of the 12th International Workshop on Health Text Mining and Information Analysis*, pages 94–103, online. Association for Computational Linguistics.

Qama, E., Rubinelli, S., & Diviani, N. (2022). Factors influencing the integration of self-management in daily life routines in chronic conditions: A scoping review of qualitative evidence. *BMJ Open*, *12*(12), e066647.

Raina, A., Mishra, P., & Kumar, D. (2024). AI as a Medical Ally: Evaluating ChatGPT's Usage and Impact in Indian Healthcare. *arXiv preprint arXiv:2401.15605*.

Richardson, W. S., Wilson, M. C., Nishikawa, J., & Hayward, R. S. (1995). The well-built clinical question: A key to evidence-based decisions. [Publisher: American College of Physicians.]. *ACP Journal Club*, *123*(3), A12.

Ruani, M. A., Reiss, M. J., & Kalea, A. Z. (2023). Diet-nutrition information seeking, source trustworthiness, and eating behavior changes: An international web-based survey. *Nutrients*, *15*(21), 4515.

Rummo, P. E., Cassidy, O., Wells, I., Coffino, J. A., & Bragg, M. A. (2020). Examining the relationship between youth-targeted food marketing expenditures and the demographics of social media followers. *International Journal of Environmental Research and Public Health*, *17*(5), 1631.

Sallam, M. (2023). ChatGPT utility in healthcare education, research, and practice: systematic review on the promising perspectives and valid concerns. In *Healthcare* MDPI, Vol. 11, No. 6, p. 887.

Segado-Fernández, S. S., Gómez, B. J., Hidalgo, P. J., Lozano-Estevan, M. D. C., & Peco, I. H. (2025). Disinformation about diet and nutrition on social networks: A review of the literature. *Nutrición Hospitalaria*, *42*(2), 366–375. DOI: 10.20960/nh.05533

Simons, L. P. A., Neerincx, M. A., & Jonker, C. M. (2021). Health Literature Hybrid AI for Health Improvement; A Design Analysis for Diabetes & Hypertension, pp. 184-197, 34th Bled eConference. June 27-30, Bled, Slovenia, Retrieval www.bledconference.org

Simons, L., Gerritsen, B., Wielaard, B., & Neerincx, M. A. (2022). Health self-management support with microlearning to improve hypertension.

Simons, L. P. A., Neerincx, M. A., & Jonker, C. M. (2022a). Is Google Making us Smart? Health Self-Management for High Performance Employees & Organisations. *International Journal of Networking and Virtual Organisations*, *27*(3), 200–216.

Simons, L. P. A., Gerritsen, B., Wielaard, B., & Neerincx, M. A. (2022b). Health Self-Management Support with Microlearning to Improve Hypertension, pp. 511-524, 35th Bled eConference. June 26-29, Bled, Slovenia, from www.bledconference.org

Simons, L. P. A. (2023a). Health 2050: Faster Cure via Bioinformatics & Quantified Self; A Design Analysis. *International Journal of Networking and Virtual Organisations*, *28*(1), 36–52. DOI: 10.1504/IJNVO.2023.130957

Simons, L. P. A., Gerritsen, B., Wielaard, B., & Neerincx, M. A. (2023b). Hypertension Self-Management Success in 2 weeks; 3 Pilot Studies, pp.19-34, 36th Bled eConference. June 25-28, Bled, Slovenia.

Simons, L. P. A., Gerritsen, B., Wielaard, B., & Neerincx, M. A. (2024a). Employee Hypertension Self-Management Support with Microlearning and Social Learning. *International Journal of Networking and Virtual Organisations*, *30*(4), 350–365.

Simons, L. P. A., Murukannaiah, P. K., & Neerincx, M. A. (2024b). Designing and Evaluating an LLM-based Health AI Research Assistant for Hypertension Self-Management; Using Health Claims Metadata Criteria, pp.283-298, 37th Bled eConference. June 9-12, Bled, Slovenia, Proceedings.

Simons, L., Wielaard, B., & Neerincx, M. A. (2025). Beyond Average Results in Hypertension E-Support and Self-Management: Three Pilot Studies With Social Learning. In *Impact of Digital Solutions for Improved Healthcare Delivery* (pp. 257-282). IGI Global.

Simons, L. P., Gerritsen, B., Wielaard, B., & Neerincx, M. A. (2024). Employee hypertension self-management support with microlearning and social learning. *International Journal of Networking and Virtual Organisations*, *30*(4), 350–365.

Soleimani, A., Monz, C., & Worring, M. (2020). BERT for Evidence Retrieval and Claim Verification. In Jose, J. M., Yilmaz, E., Magalhaes, J., Castells, P., Ferro, N., Silva, ˜. M. J., & Martins, F. (Eds.), *Advances in Information Retrieval* (pp. 359–366). Springer International Publishing.

Suarez-Lledo, V., & Alvarez-Galvez, J. (2021). Prevalence of health misinformation on social media: Systematic review. *Journal of Medical Internet Research*, *23*(1), e17187.

Vasconcelos, C., Costa, R. L. D., Dias, Á. L., Pereira, L., & Santos, J. P. (2021). Online influencers: Healthy food or fake news. *International Journal of Internet Marketing and Advertising*, *15*(2), 149–175.

Wadden, D., Lin, S., Lo, K., Wang, L. L., van Zuylen, M., Cohan, A., & Hajishirzi, H. (2020). Fact or Fiction: Verifying Scientific Claims. In Webber, B., Cohn, T., He, Y., and Liu, Y., editors, *Proceedings of the 2020 Conference on Empirical Methods in Natural Language Processing (EMNLP)*, pages 7534–7550, Online. Association for Computational Linguistics.

Wansink, B., & Sobal, J. (2007). Mindless eating: The 200 daily food decisions we overlook. *Environment and Behavior*, *39*(1), 106–123.

Wu, S., Xiong, Y., Cui, Y., Wu, H., Chen, C., Yuan, Y., . . . Xue, C. J. (2024). Retrieval-augmented generation for natural language processing: A survey. *arXiv preprint arXiv:2407.13193*.

Zhou, B., Perel, P., Mensah, G. A., & Ezzati, M. (2021). Global epidemiology, health burden and effective interventions for elevated blood pressure and hypertension. *Nature Reviews. Cardiology*, *18*(11), 785–802.

ENDNOTES

1 https://faiss.ai/

[2] https://nutritionfacts.org/

[3] https://nutritionfacts.org/

Chapter 4
Data Mining Techniques in Health Care Sector:
Stages, Techniques, Comparisons, Selection Criteria, and Applications

Aman Tyagi
https://orcid.org/0000-0002-7607-1302
Department of Computer Science and Engineering, Faculty of Engineering & Technology, Gurukula Kangri University, Haridwar, India

ABSTRACT

Data mining is a process of knowledge discovery. In data mining the data is collected from data warehouse and after cleaning and preprocessing, data is stored in the data warehouse in the transformed form. The transformed data is collected from data warehouse and data mining is applied on data and useful information and knowledge is produced. This is called data mining or knowledge discovery. Now a days data mining is widely applied on the healthcare data. In the present chapter OLAP, data mining process, healthcare applications, current healthcare research on data mining, different data mining techniques used and their comparison, discussion and analysis are discussed.

INTRODUCTION

Data mining and Knowledge Discovery in Database (KDD) is the technique to find out the useful patterns and information from database. There are huge data of different type in the data warehouse. The data mining is to find out the important

DOI: 10.4018/979-8-3373-2545-3.ch004

patterns in the data so that by utilizing this knowledge the important and useful decisions are taken. Data mining is an important aspect used nowadays in healthcare sector. Data mining deals with different types of techniques such as decision tree, Naive Bayesian, Multilayer perceptron, KNN (K- Nearest Neighbor), association rules mining, Apriori algorithm, Neural Networks, Genetic algorithm, Support Vector Machine and Fuzzy KNN. All these techniques have different modes of operation. Data mining techniques are used for classification, decision making, learning and validating the data. Data mining is a process in which raw data is collected and preprocessed to convert it into useful form. After analyzing the data, the fruitful results/outputs/information will be derived. Some of the research articles related to the use of data mining in healthcare are mentioned in the following paragraph.

(Zheng et al., 2024) focused on data-mining-based tax risk detection methods utilized around the world.(Abbasi et al., 2024) aims to tackle the diversity of commodities and the number of consumers in the post-COVID era by proposing a hybrid data-driven approach that combines data mining and mathematical modeling to solve mathematical location models for transportation network with high accuracy in less time.(Angeioplastis et al., 2025) investigated the use of educational data mining (EDM) techniques to predict student performance and enhance learning outcomes in higher education.(Yao, 2024) proved the role of sensor-based voice data mining in e-commerce operational data analysis.(Saidi et al., 2025) compared the performance of basic and hybrid data mining algorithms in diagnosing COVID-19, using blood test results and clinical information to identify the most effective approach.(Wei & Tan, 2025) presented an analytics framework for volunteer management using data mining techniques, enabling organisations within the social service sector to make evidence-based, data-driven decisions.

DIFFERENT STAGES OF DATA MINING PROCESS

In data mining raw data is collected from data warehouse. Preprocessing is done to transform the data to convert it into useful form. In the refined data the useless and redundant information are removed from the data. In the next step transforming the data into useful form so that it can be used in data mining process. Further different data mining concepts and algorithms can be applied on the data and different types of patterns are extracted from data. Last step is the analysis of the different process. In the analysis results and interpretation are checked to find out the best interpretation and result by applying different data mining techniques. It is also called knowledge discovery step. Obviously, the data mining is the process consisting of several steps. All the steps involved in the data mining process are discussed below and shown in figure 1.

Figure 1. Data mining Process

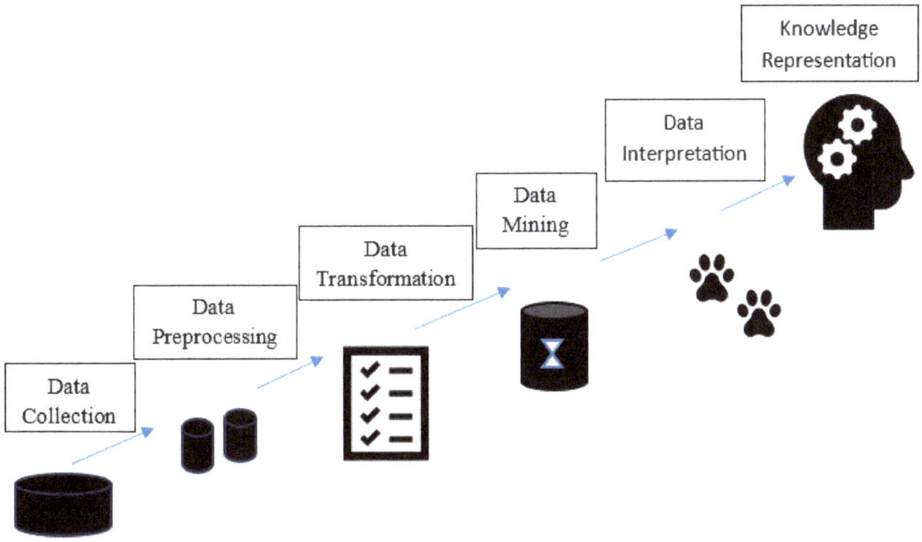

The figure above shows the various steps of data mining process. The data used in data mining can be of any kind such as healthcare data, purchase data, sell data and research data, educational data etc. The above processes are applied to any type of data set.

Data source collection/ selection (Stage - I):

The raw data is selected from different sources such as internet, database repository, some external source and personally collected health data. We select the relevant data. For example, for diabatic patient the sugar level of the patient at particular time is important like postprandial blood sugar and fasting. So, when these reading are present in database than database is useful and one can select that database for further processing.

Data preprocessing (Stage - II):

Data preprocessing is the second step. In this step data cleaning is done. The useful information is selected and unnecessary information is removed from the data. In preprocessing the repeated, useless, redundant information is removed from data completly. The scaling, encoding and selecting features form data is also done during this step.

In this preprocessing the quality of data is improved that is it can be more efficiently used to extract information from the data. Data preprocessing is a process where the different problems like missing values, duplicacy in data, incorrect data is handled to make it more organized in a suitable manner so that it becomes more useful in data warehouse. It is very effective to give reliable outcome and hence improves the results.

- ✓ Missing values: It is due to missing some values in the data warehouse. In this condition the full row is ignored or add the data in a row by users. Data is assumed by taking mean of its corresponding cells or by adding most probable value. It makes data warehouse complete and can be handled easily for further research analysis.
- ✓ Noisy Data: If data is illogical or data is not appropriate than it is called the noisy data. This is due to mistake in the collection of data, in uploading the data and in entering the data. The following method deals with the noisy data:
- ✓ Binning Method: Data is divided into sorted segments. Data is altered according to the mean value or extent value.
- ✓ Regression: Regression method is used to smooth the data so that noise will be removed or minimized. To remove the noise present in the data the linear or multiple regression is used.
- ✓ Clustering: In this technique similar data values are grouped together. So, that anomaly will not be found or found outside the cluster. In this technique the noise will be removed and the data in data warehouse will certainly improve.
- ✓ Removing Duplicates: To make each data value unique, the duplicate values will be removed or deleted from the data warehouse. It enhanced the efficiency, correctness, harmony and genuineness of the data.

Data transformation (Stage - III):

Data transformation is a step where the data is transformed into useful form. Different methodologies like aggregation, standardization, discretization, smoothing and normalization can be applied or used on the preprocessed data. These techniques make data into standard from so that data mining techniques will easily be applied. Some of these techniques are discussed below:

✓ Normalization: This is the process to convert the data in to normal range. It is done to make the relevance in all the attributes.

✓ Standardization: Make the data into standard form means data has zero mean and unit variance.
✓ Discretization: The data mining is not easily applied on continuous data. So, the data is converted into the discreate from.
✓ Data Aggregation: For easy calculations shorten the many data values into abstract value or form.
✓ Concept Hierarchy Generation: For better understanding and easy handling, the data is converted to hierarchy form.

Data mining (Stage - IV):

This is very crucial step. In this step data mining technique is applied on data, to extract relevant patterns from the data. Selection of data mining technique is an important task because the quality of fruitfulness of the result is based on this selection.

Data Interpretation/ Evaluation (Stage - V):

The useful and important patterns are extracted from data using data mining technique. The useful knowledge is derived from the different kinds of pattern.

Knowledge representation (Stage - VI):

Knowledge representation is the final step in this process. In this step the knowledge is derived and presented to the users to understand and interpret the results. In this step user can get the information via visualizing and presenting different patterns into useful knowledge discovery.

Different research articles related to data mining process are given here. (Biao, 2023) presented a data mining based virtual simulation experimental teaching system which provisions personalized interactive learning, real-world scene experimental training and comprehensive assessment of the learning effect. (Rastogi & Bansal, 2023) proposed a diabetes prediction model using data mining techniques.(J. Li, 2022) identified e-commerce fraud, solve the financial risks of e-commerce enterprises through big data mining (BDM), further explore more effective solutions through Information fusion technology (IFT), and create an e-commerce fraud detection model (FDM) based on IFT (namely, computer technology (CT), artificial intelligence (AI), and data mining (DM).(Wu et al., 2021) introduced the main medical public database and described the steps, tasks, and models of data mining in simple language. (Touati et al., 2025) The work highlights the unique integration of machine learning models with optimization techniques to significantly enhance grinding performance and manufacturing efficiency in high-precision industries.

TECHNIQUES USED IN DATA MINING

Many data mining techniques are available to find information and patterns in the data. As mentioned earlier data mining techniques are used for classification, regression, anomaly detection and pattern finding in the data. Some of the data mining techniques are discussed below:

1. **Association rule mining:** The association rule totally dependent on frequent set items. In this type of mining select the rules which follows the minimum support and confidence for a given data warehouse. The support and confidence are discussed below:

Support: The support is the frequency of selecting a particular item in a data set. For example, suppose a particular product purchase from the data set has frequency of 10%. So, the support of that product is 10%. The formula used for the support is:

Support(X) = (Number of purchases of product X) / (All purchases)

Where **X** is the item or combination of items.

Confidence: The likeliness of occurrence of an item Y when an item X has already occurred is called confidence.

Confidence(X→Y) = Support(X∪Y)/ Support(X)

Example: suppose in a cloth shop total 200 transactions are done. In which 80 purchase are of pant and shirt both. So, the support of association rule of pant → shirt is:

Support *(pant, shirt)* = 80/200=0.40

Suppose in 200 purchases 80 purchases are pant and 40 purchases both pant and shirt. Then confidence is:

Confidence *(pant → shirt)* = 40/80=0.50

Therefore, when a pant is purchased, the probability that a shirt is also purchased is 0.5. Some of the techniques used in association mining are mentioned below:

a. **Apriori Algorithm:** It is the fundamental algorithm of data mining. It is used to find out frequent transactions in a data set and used to produce association rules. (Gulzar et al., 2023) proposed a web-centered hospital information management system (HIMS) that identifies frequent patterns from the data with eye disorder patients using the association rule-based Apriori data mining technique.
b. **Partition Algorithms:** It is a key technique of data mining. In this technique we partition the set of entire data into small partitions. Finally the frequent element is searched in those partitions.(Liu et al., 2024) introduced a novel method to partition geometrical elements from the measured data of the workpiece con-

taining geometrical deviation and refines the points attribution problem at part boundaries.

c. **Pincer-Search Algorithm:** The pincer search algorithm is mainly used for both bottom up and top-down approaches. (Tarakanita & Amaliah, 2023) needed to organize the layout of skincare products that are frequently purchased together, making it easier for customers to select the products they want. The Pincer Search Algorithm it best for this purpose.
d. **Dynamic Itemset Counting Algorithm:** In this type of algorithm item set of data are added and deleted dynamically.(Parcon et al., 2022) determined that DIC is faster than apriori algorithm while having the same accuracy.
e. **FP- Growth Algorithm:** This algorithm is used to maintain frequent patterns in a big data set. (Shawkat et al., 2022) presented a modified FP-growth (MFPgrowth) algorithm to enhance the efficiency of the FP-growth by obviating the need for recurrent creation of conditional subtrees.
f. **Eclat and Declat:** In this method frequent pattens are identified using both depth first search and bottom-up search. (Man et al., 2023) introduced a new incremental of rare pattern mining approach by adopting R-Eclat called Incremental Rare Equivalence Class Transformation (IR-Eclat).

(Mudumba & Kabir, 2024) introduced a new method for mining association rules independently from multiple data sources.

2. **Classification:** Classification is a technique of data mining in which the entire data is classified in different groups. Different techniques are used in data mining that distinguishes the data into different classes. Some of the techniques used for classification are mentioned below:
   a. **Decision Tree:** The decision tree is used for classification purposes. The root or parent node are the decision checking nodes and leave nodes are used to classify a particular problem. (Tyagi & Singh, 2014) diagnosed asthmatic patient using decision tree a data mining technique.(Huang et al., 2023) employed the CART algorithm to generate decision trees using identified risk factors to predict healthy sperm counts.
   b. **SVM (Support Vector Machine):** In SVM supervised learning is used for classification of data. It is mainly used for classification but it can do both classification and regression.(Noor et al., 2024) In this study, the support vector machine (SVM) regression model is used to handle the challenge of adjusting the risk factors attached to the patients. (Guido et al., 2024) Done an extensive survey on the current state-of-the-art of SVMs developed and applied in the medical field over the years.

c. **Bayesian classification:** This is also called naïve bayes classifier. In this supervised learning is used for the classification purposes. It is based on Bayes' Theorem. (Polotskaya et al., 2024) provided an exhaustive overview of the current state of Bayesian networks in disease diagnosis and prognosis. (Kyrimi et al., n.d.) empowered researchers and clinicians with an analytical framework and findings that will enable understanding of the need to address the problems of restricted aims of BNs, ad hoc BN development methods, and the lack of BN adoption in practice.

d. **Classification by Backpropagation:** It is a technique in which the neurons learn from their mistake. It compares the outcome with correct outcome and accordingly the weight of neurons is changed to improve the result. (Kaur et al., 2023) proposed using multilayered artificial neural network with back propagation algorithm for an efficient-cum-automated coronary heart disease diagnosis model.(Antonio et al., 2022) presented the development of a multilayer feed-forward neural network for the diagnosis of hypertension, based on a population-based study.

e. **K-Nearest Neighbor (K-NN) Classifier Method:** As name specified the nearer point or closest neighbor to a point is classified as same class. Points are classified in different classes according to their position.(Ye et al., 2021) proposed a prediction model using the Harris hawks optimization (HHO) to optimize the Fuzzy K-nearest neighbor (FKNN), which is called HHO-FKNN.(Jamil et al., 2023) simulated the early detection of diabetes mellitus with the K-Nearest Neighbors (K-NN) algorithm using Cloud-Base Runtime (COLAB).

f. **Rule-Based Classification:** It is a part of expert system. Here if than else rules are used to classify the data or in decision making process. Rules are defined in the presence of expert or knowledgeable person.(Czmil, 2023) conducted a comparison of 16 different fuzzy rule-based algorithms applied to 12 medical datasets and real-world data.(Bahani et al., 2021) proposed a novel data- driven method based on fuzzy clustering and linguistic modifiers to design a fuzzy rule- based classification system for heart disease diagnosis.

g. **Frequent-Pattern Based Classification:** This technique is used to find out the most useful and mostly occurred patterns in the data set.(Chen et al., 2021) proposed a new weighted sliding window fuzzy frequent pattern mining algorithm based on interval type-2 fuzzy set theory over data stream (WSWFFP-T2) with a single scan based on the artificial datasets of medical data stream.(Meenal & Vennila, 2023) proposed a novel Bi-directional Recurrent Network and Neuro-Fuzzy-based (BRN-NF) frequent pattern mining for heart disease prediction.

h. **Fuzzy-Logic:** Fuzzy logic is used when there is continuous data and there is no discontinuity in the data. In the fuzzy logic there is membership means there is no sudden cut off.(Khushal & Fatima, 2025) proposed model is validated on the diabetes risk prediction dataset. In the present work a fusion of machine learning and fuzzy logic is introduced to improve accuracy and reduce computation time. (Guler et al., 2025) proposed system avoids large computational complexity and miniaturization, which makes it more realistic in practice.

Other data mining techniques

1. **Prediction:** In this technique the value of the attribute is predicted. The best prediction is obtained with the help of training the model with large amount of data. Many research articles related to the prediction technique appeared in various journals. Some of the latest articles are discussed below:

(Oon et al., 2024) determined the association between DR(diabetic retinopathy) and DN(diabetic neuropathy), predict DR and identify the significant risk factors associated with DR among DN patients based on the best predictive model obtained. (Wijaya et al., 2024) applied an ensemble machine learning and data mining approach to enhance the effectiveness of stroke prediction. (Enad & Aksu, 2024) proposed system is based on six ML algorithms to predict COVID-19 infection as random forest (RF) algorithm, naive bayes (NB) algorithm, support vector machine (SVM) algorithm, decision tree (DT) algorithm, multi-layer perceptron (MLP), and k-nearest neighbor (KNN). (Z. Zhang et al., 2024) collected the relevant data information in the Lesser Hinggan Mountain region, established the fire driving factor database, and then analyzed the impact and distribution characteristics of forest fire driving factors such as temperature and rainfall.(Aydoğan et al., 2024) determined the factors affecting students' academic performance and predict students' end-of-term academic grades using machine learning algorithms within the scope of Earned Value Management (EVM).

2. **Clustering:** Clustering is the process in which the related data is clustered into different groups according to their similarity. Some of the research article related to clustering are discussed below:

(Luh et al., 2022) classified the performance of lecturers by utilizing data mining techniques.(Ghazal et al., 2021) the K-means clustering algorithm is evaluated with three different mathematical metrics in terms of execution time with different datasets and different numbers of clusters.(Peng et al., 2021) proposed an outlier detection method based on clustering and local outlier factor (LOF) to evade the problem and to detect as many types of theft attacks as possible.(Dafir et al., 2021) presented an overview of the latest parallel clustering algorithms categorized according to the computing platforms used to handle the Big Data, namely, the horizontal and vertical scaling platforms.(Tabianan & Velu, 2022) the purpose of customer segmentation is to determine how to deal with customers in each category in order to increase the profit of each customer to the business.

3. **Artificial Neural network (ANN):** In artificial neural network the human neurons are used for calculation purposes. The huge literature dealing with artificial neural network is available on the internet. Some of the resent research articles are mentioned below:

(Okewu et al., 2021) findings revealed that hardware challenges, training challenges, theoretical challenges, and quality concerns are the bane of ANN-based EDM in higher education and offer windows of opportunities for further research. (Kurani et al., 2023) covered the recent past studies to explore the concepts and methodologies through which ANN's and SVM's have been used. (Rb & Kr, 2021) aimed in using the multiple algorithms of Machine learning such as support vector machine (SVM), k-nearest neighbour (KNN) and artificial neural network (ANN) in predicting the occurrence of the fraud. (Chhajer et al., 2022) presented an overview of artificial intelligence and machine learning as predictive analytics tools in the stock market.(Guleria & Sood, 2023) proposed a framework for career counselling of students using ML and AI techniques.

4. **Outlier Detection:** To find out the abnormal or anomaly condition from the data set the outlier detection is used. This may be used in health care to find out the abnormal condition of the patient. Few research articles related to outlier detection are mentioned below:

(J. Li et al., 2023) proposed an adaptive mini-minimum spanning tree-based outlier detection (MMOD) method, which utilizes a novel distance measure by scaling the Euclidean distance.(Sanjeev et al., 2023) proposed a framework in which a popular statistical approach termed Inter-Quartile Range (IQR) is used to detect outliers in data and deal with them by Winsorizing method. (J. Li et al., 2024) presented an advanced method to extract cluster-based outliers by employing a scaled minimum spanning tree (MST) data structure and a new medoid selection method. (X. Zhang et al., 2023) investigated three-way neighbourhood characteristic regions and corresponding fusion measurement to advance outlier detection. (Xu,

2022) proposed a novel outlier detection algorithm which is named as kNN-LOF. (Lei et al., 2023)

proposed a dynamic anomaly detection algorithm for building energy consumption data, which realizes the dynamic detection of point anomalies and collective anomalies.(Samariya & Thakkar, 2023) presented an anomaly detection algorithms in an organized manner.

5. **Genetic Algorithm:** These are adaptive algorithms. In genetic algorithm the idea of natural selection is used to find the better solution. Few genetic algorithm related articles are discussed below:

(Ruifeng, 2021) improved that genetic algorithms. (Sohail, 2023) discussed the advanced genetic algorithms and their applications in detail. (Zahmani & Atmani, 2021) proposed a novel approach combining dispatching rules, a genetic algorithm, data mining, and simulation.(Maleki et al., 2021) used a k-Nearest-Neighbours technique, for which a genetic algorithm is applied for the efficient feature selection to reduce the dataset dimensions and enhance the classifier pace, is employed for diagnosing the stage of patients' disease.(Azad et al., 2022) proposed a novel Prediction Model using Synthetic Minority Oversampling Technique, Genetic Algorithm and Decision Tree (PMSGD) for Classification of Diabetes Mellitus on Pima Indians Diabetes Database (PIDD) dataset.(Sun, 2022) a genetic algorithm is proposed, which is combined with the k-means algorithm in order to make key decisions more conveniently according to the massive data information obtained.

OLAP Operations in Data Warehouse

The OLAP model analyze the data in the form of data cube. Here the n-dimensional data is fitted in n data cubes. Data is in the conceptual hierarchy form. Data is maintained in many dimensions and every dimension has multilevel abstraction. The data visualized differently when one use different dimensions in search option. There is flexibility in OLAP to see the data differently for different types of requirements. OLAP is easy to use when data is to be accessed with different data cubes. The diagram of OLAP model is shown in figure 2. There are following types of OLAP operations in used:

✓ **Roll-up:** It is used for dimension reduction. In this operation some dimensions are removed from the given cube.

✓ **Drill-down:** Drill down increases the dimensions of the cube. Therefore, in this sense it is the inverse of roll-up. During drill down process more details are inserted in a data cube.

✓ **Slice and dice:** In this a sub-cube of data is created from the main cube. By selecting one or few dimensions of the main cube the sub-cube is created. This prosses is known as slice and dice. In slice one dimension is used and in dice more than one dimensions are used.

✓ **Pivot (rotate):** In this operation the axes are rotated to visualize the data in different way to obtain desired result.

✓ **Other OLAP operations:** Some other operations are frequently used in OLAP. *Drill-across* operation is used for executing queries. The other *drill-through* operation is applied for relational SQL functions.

Figure 2. OLAP (Online Analytical Processing)

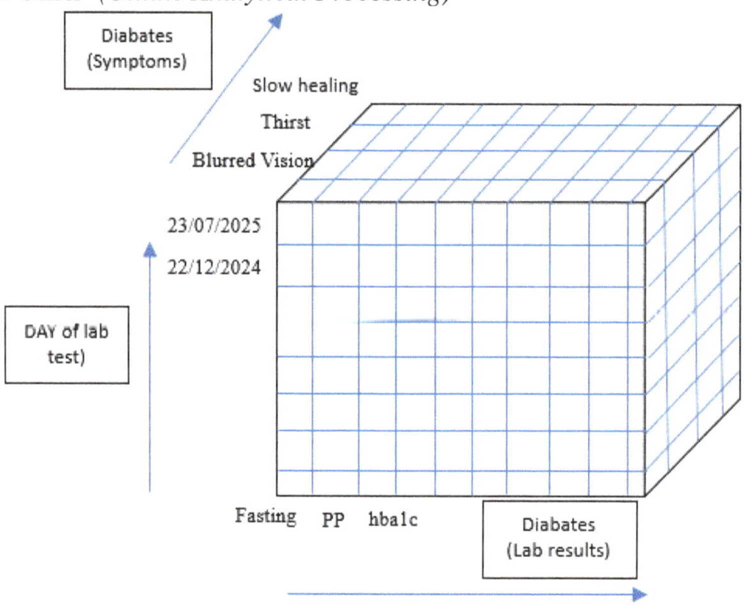

Some of the OLAP related research articles are mentioned here in this write up. (Cuzzocrea, 2024) proposed a methodology and a reference architecture for *representing big OLAP data cubes over Clouds via columns*, which mostly capture the intrinsic dimensions of the target cube. (Dahr et al., 2022) proposed technique, including the OLAP operation, presents the analytical results in addition to the KPIs that provide the indicators when a critical situation affects the overall profit or performance.(Najm et al., 2022) presented a short roadmap for implementing educational data mart based on a data set from Alexandria Private Elementary School, located in the Basrah province of Iraq in the 2017-2018 academic year.(Hazboun & Owda, 2021) described a method to effectively automate the conversion of a data query from a Natural Language Query (NLQ) to Structured Query Language (SQL) with Online Analytical Processing (OLAP) cube data warehouse objects.(Davardoost et al., 2022) presented a model for extracting OLAP cubes from a document-oriented NOSQL database. (Yadav & Kumar, 2021) proposed a Dragon Fly Optimization based Clustering (DFOC) approach to enhance the efficiency of data clustering by generating optimal clusters from multidimensional clinical data for OLAP.(Kavitha, 2023) presented OSSAE-OLAP technique that mainly focuses on the classification of appropriate data for text analysis. (Fugkeaw & Hak, 2024) proposed a PPAC-CDW scheme, a fine-grained and privacy-preserving access control with efficient query processing for OLAP queries for CDW (cloud-based data warehouse). (Khoruzhy et al., 2023) developed models for cost management and reduction of risks in the financial and economic activities of companies based on the OLAP technology for applications in Russian agro-industrial enterprises. (Forresi et al., 2021) proposed an approach to support data analysis within a high-variety multistore, with heterogeneous schemas and overlapping records. (Bensalloua & Ahmed, 2018) proposed a Spatial Decision Support System namely "Silvicultura" for facilitating decision making in complex situations.

DATA MINING RESEARCH IN DIFFERENT DISEASES

Data mining is an important technique used in healthcare sector. There are many techniques available for different situations. Some real-world applications of data mining in various type of diseases are mentioned below:

Asthma:

Asthma is a lung disease caused due to narrowing the airpath because of swallowing in the bronchioles. Some of the research work done in this area is given below:

(Tyagi & Singh, 2014) diagnosed asthma using data mining tools (decision tree) and also find out asthma control level is measured using fuzzy inference system. (Q. Li et al., 2025) analysed the related risk factors of moderate to severe asthma attack in children by logistic regression and decision tree.(Owora et al., 2021) objective was to develop and evaluate the prognostic performance of conditional inference decision tree–based rules using the Pediatric Asthma Risk Score (PARS) predictors as an alternative to the existing logistic regression-based risk score for childhood asthma prediction at 7 years in a high-risk population.

Diabetes:

Diabates is a lifelong chronic disease due to high blood sugar levels. It is due to lack of insulin produced by the body. This disease affects almost all parts of the body. The research work done on diabetes using data mining is mentioned below:

(Rastogi & Bansal, 2023) proposed a diabetes prediction model using data mining techniques. Authors applied four data mining techniques such as Random Forest, Support Vector Machine (SVM), Logistic Regression, and Naive Bayes.(Thakkar et al., 2022) major focus areas were data mining and fuzzy logic techniques used in diabetes diagnosis.(Rajendra & Latifi, 2021) designed a prediction model, that predicts whether a patient has diabetes, based on certain diagnostic measurements included in the dataset, and explore various techniques to boost the performance and accuracy.

Cardiovascular Disease:

Cardiovascular disease (CVD) creates different types of problem-like effect on heart and its blood vessels, coronary heart disease, cerebrovascular disease, and peripheral artery disease. Some of the data mining-based research work on cardiovascular disease is as follow:

(Jadhav & Chobe, 2022) proposed to use the two machine learning classifiers such as kNN and decision tree. kNN helps us to find the possibility of cardiovascular disease and decision tree helps us to classify the type of the cardiovascular disease with the risk involved. (Elsedimy et al., 2024) proposed model is applied to the Cleveland heart disease dataset and compared

with state-of-the-art models. The experimental results show that the proposed QPSO-SVM

model achieved the best heart-disease-prediction accuracies of 96.31% on the Cleveland

heart data set.(Alty et al., 2003) developed a method based on Support Vector Machine (SVM) classifier to help health professionals prevent cardiovascular diseases.

Breast Cancer:

It mainly affects the women but sometimes it may occur on men also. It changes the size of breast due to lump developed in the breast. This disease is due to malignant (cancer) cells are developed inside the breast tissues. Recent research work done on breast cancer disease using data mining as under:

(Alhasani et al., 2023) aims was to improve the classification accuracy of breast cancer by applying information gain feature selection, machine learning techniques and data mining to the Wisconsin Diagnostic Breast Cancer (WDBC) dataset.(Alshanableh et al., 2024) focused on identifying factors associated with Quality of life among Jordanian women undergoing breast cancer treatment using data mining. (Yang et al., 2023) showed that a hybrid approach that can be effective in breast cancer diagnosis is the use of deep complex neural networks and data mining.

Arthritis:

Arthritis is a disease due to many different types of problems. It causes joint pain and swelling. Generally, arthritis is the disease of old age. Recent research on this disease using data mining is mentioned below:

(Bertoncelli et al., 2022) developed a prediction model for identifying risk factors of OA in subjects aged 20–50 years and compare the performance of different machine learning models. (Lai et al., 2022) used the Apriori Algorithm to screen out potential analgesics from 311 cases that were treated with compounded medication prescription and collected from "Second Affiliated Hospital of Zhejiang Chinese Medical University" in Hangzhou, China.(Queralt et al., 2024) studied relationships among clinical and molecular data in a cohort of women (n = 51) with Kellgren–Lawrence grade 2–3 knee OA through a Support Vector Machine (SVM) and a regulation network model

APPLICATIONS OLAP IN HEALTHCARE

Online Line Analytical Processing plays a very significant role in assisting healthcare professionals and policy makers in government and in private healthcare sectors. OLAP allows fast, efficient and easy exploration of the data. It is used in the analysis of very large and complex data sets. Some of the important applications of OLAP in healthcare sector are:

Patient healthcare management
Medical decision support
Fraud detection in insurance and healthcare services
Analysis of public health
Integration of data obtained from various sectors
Financial and cost-effective analysis

Optimization of hospital resources and minimize bottlenecks

APPLICATIONS OF DATA MINING IN HEALTHCARE

Data mining is widely used in health care and there are many applications of data mining in healthcare sector. Data mining is applied for different disease diagnosis, prediction, classification and to find the status of the disease. Literature related to different healthcare disease diagnosis and prediction is available in research publications. For example, in healthcare the data mining is also used for classification of data of patients as asthmatic or non-asthmatic. Data mining is also used in anomaly detection in healthcare data so that the abnormal conditions can be easily identified. In healthcare insurance fraud can be easily identified through datamining techniques. There are many research articles available on internet to find out the healthcare insurance fraud. Some of the recent research articles related to data mining applications in healthcare are discussed below.

(Olatunji et al., 2021) reviewed the existing anonymization techniques and their applicability to various types (relational and graph-based) of health data.(Al-shanableh et al., 2024) focused on identifying factors associated with Quality of life among Jordanian women undergoing breast cancer treatment using data mining. (Khoshgoftar et al., 2025) reviewed data mining in medical education and provide a comprehensive picture of it in different educational dimensions.(Shukla et al., 2025) paves the way for a secure, scalable, and efficient privacy-preserving data mining in the healthcare informatics ecosystem. (Rosa & Gomez, 2024) presented a detailed review of healthcare data analytics and the respective data sources.(Hamid et al., 2024) presented that utilizes association rule mining augmented with unsupervised learning techniques to detect healthcare insurance fraud.

There are various applications of data mining in health care sector. Some of the important applications are mentioned below:

Disease diagnosis
Disease status
Medicine development
Healthcare insurance fraud detection
Treatment cost decrement
Find out the abnormal condition of the patient
Improve the diagnosis process
Improve the patient satisfaction
Improve the knowledge about the disease
Fast diagnosis

Safer care plans

ANALYSIS (DATA MINING TECHNIQUES: COMPARISON AND ANALYSIS)

Data mining is used in healthcare field for the purpose of finding out the useful patterns in the healthcare data. Data is taken from patent's EHR (Electronic Health Record) and health data store in different websites like Kaggle and UCI Machine Learning Repository etc. The new information gather from these databases is possible with the help of different data mining technique use for knowledge discovery and pattern finding. The common technique use for this purpose are classification, clustering, association rule mining, and regression analysis. With the help of these techniques the disease diagnosis, level of control on disease, precaution, risk level prediction, cost of treatment optimization and treatment is possible by applying on databases. Here are the comparisons of these techniques to know that how they can improve decision making, optimization and prediction of different task.

- **Classification:**

This technique is applied on a data set to classify the data in different classes.

Use in healthcare:

Categorized the people based on the data that diagnosed them as patient or not and also categorized the people having chances to become the patient.

Comparison:

Decision Trees:

Advantage and Strength:

Easy to understand. It classified the data easily and in good manner. It can easily handle non-liner relationship. It can be used for disease diagnosis and identification of important features like symptoms.

Disadvantages and Weakness:

The decision tree is not working well on large dataset. There is problem of overfitting in the decision tree. It changes suddenly with small changes to data in data Warehouse.

Support Vector Machines (SVM):

Advantage and Strength:

It is very useful for high dimensional data. It is also good for non-liner relationship. It is used for anomaly detection.

Disadvantages and Weakness:

The computation is difficult for large database. Finding a model from the data is difficult in SVM.

Rule-Based Classification:

Advantage and Strength:

To find out the result is very easy. The use of the Rule-Base is easy. Work well on easy task with known conditions.

Disadvantages and Weakness:

Difficult and not useful on complex data. The rule generation of complex problem is difficult.

Naive Bayes:

Advantage and Strength:

This is very easy and effective technique. It is work well on large data set. It is used when features are not dependant to each other.

Disadvantages and Weakness:

Sometimes it does not work well when the parameters are assumed independent.

Frequent-Pattern Based Classification:

Advantage and Strength:

It is very efficient in finding hidden, rare and sometimes very interesting patterns.

Disadvantages and Weakness:

It requires lot of computational work in short period of time. Features must be chosen with utmost care.

Backpropagation:

Advantage and Strength:

It is useful for the complex non-liner problems. Complex relationship between input and output may also be predicted.

Disadvantages and Weakness:

Lot of computational power and fairly good understanding of neural network is required. There is a problem of overfitting.

Fuzzy-Logic:

Advantage and Strength:

It is useful when parameters are uncertain. It is also useful when data is incomplete or vague.

Disadvantages and Weakness:

To use this, expertise of fuzzy logic and fuzzy system is needed. It is very complex to design and use.

K-Nearest Neighbor:

Advantage and Strength:

It is easy to understand and use. It classifies the data in to different classes with higher precision.

Disadvantages and Weakness:

It is very sensitive to the neighbours and distance matrix change.

- **Association rule mining:**

This technique is used on a data to identify the relationships between different items in the data warehouse. It is used effectively to find out relationship among disease, symptoms, lab results and treatment.

Use in healthcare:

Association rule mining is used in healthcare to find out the interesting relationship of different data items.

Comparison:

Apriori Algorithm:

Advantage and Strength:

Simple and easy to use. It is working well on small database.

Disadvantages and Weakness:

It is working slow and not suitable for large database.

FP-Growth Algorithm:

Advantage and Strength:

It is faster and better than the apriori algorithm. It is useful for large data set.

Disadvantages and Weakness:

The development of FP-Tree is complex and take large memory for large database.

Eclat Algorithm (DCI):

Advantage and Strength:

It is good for large database. It is generally used for vertical data format.

Disadvantages and Weakness:

It takes more memory in comparison of FP-Growth.

Pincer-Search Algorithm:

Advantage and Strength:

The advantage of this algorithm is that it works for both top-down and bottom-up approach to find out the frequent items in database.

Disadvantages and Weakness:

For very large database it is not working better than FP-Growth or Eclat.

Partitioning Algorithms:

Advantage and Strength:

It is used in parallel processing and very efficient for large database.

Disadvantages and Weakness:

Partitioning strategy and output from different partition is sensitive so define it carefully.

Dynamic Itemset Counting:

Advantage and Strength:

By concentrating on frequent itemset the accuracy will improve.

Disadvantages and Weakness:

Required careful management of the features to achieve better performance.

DISCUSSION

Selection of Data Mining Techniques

Different types of data mining techniques are used in healthcare field. The particular data mining algorithm is selected according to consideration of the following important points:

Change of Database size and change of Complexity

As discussed above some techniques are better for large and complex database like FP-Growth, Partitioning algorithms and Eclat and some other techniques are well suited for small and simple database like Apriori. Therefore technique must be selected accordingly.

Ease of use

Few techniques like decision tree and rule base are easy to use as compare to other techniques.

Computational time/ cost:

Some techniques like SVM and Backpropagation are computationally expansive for large dataset. So, these techniques for large data set may be avoided.

Efficiency and robustness:

Chose the technique which are efficient and robust in nature to noise and anomalies.

RESULTS

In data mining there are different algorithm for different types of problems. It shows that a particular algorithm is best suited for a given database, complexity, time, cost and efficiency. So, one can select an algorithm for a particular problem, particulate datatype and particular size of database. For example, in healthcare on small database of diabetes parameters, one can diagnose diabetes using decision tree algorithm.

REFERENCES

Abbasi, S., Saeideh, S., Farbod, E., & Yousefi, M. (2024). Hybrid data mining and data-driven algorithms for a green logistics transportation network in the post-COVID era : A case study in the USA. *Systems and Soft Computing*, *6*(July), 200156. DOI: 10.1016/j.sasc.2024.200156

Al-shanableh, N., Al-zyoud, M., Al-husban, R. Y., Al-shdayfat, N., & Alkhawaldeh, J. M. (2024). *Data Mining to Reveal Factors Associated with Quality of life among Jordanian Women with Breast Cancer. 408*(2), 403–408.

Alhasani, A. T., Alkattan, H., Subhi, A. A., & Eid, M. M. (2023). *A Comparative Analysis of Methods for Detecting and Diagnosing Breast Cancer Based on Data Mining. 04*(02), 8–17.

Alty, S. R., Millasseau, S. C., Chowienczyk, P. J., & Jakobsson, A. (2003). Cardiovascular Disease Prediction Using Support Vector Machines. *Midwest Symposium on Circuits and Systems, 1*(August 2015), 376–379. https://doi.org/DOI: 10.1109/MWSCAS.2003.1562297

Angeioplastis, A., Aliprantis, J., & Konstantakis, M. (2025). *Predicting Student Performance and Enhancing Learning Outcomes : A Data-Driven Approach Using Educational Data Mining Techniques*. 1–21.

Antonio, J., Torres, O., Santiago, A. M., Manuel, J., Izaguirre, V., García, M. A., & Hernández, A. D. (2022). *Hypertension Diagnosis with Backpropagation Neural Networks for Sustainability in Public Health*. 1–20.

Aydoğan, Ş. K., Pura, T., & Bİngül, F. (2024). *Predicting Students ' Academic Performances Using Machine Learning Algorithms in Educational Data Mining. 12*(4).

Azad, C., Bhushan, B., Sharma, R., Shankar, A., & Kant, K. (2022). Prediction model using SMOTE, genetic algorithm and decision tree (PMSGD) for classification of diabetes mellitus. *Multimedia Systems*, •••, 1289–1307. DOI: 10.1007/s00530-021-00817-2

Bahani, K., Moujabbir, M., & Ramdani, M. (2021). An accurate fuzzy rule-based classification systems for heart disease diagnosis. *Scientific African*, *14*, e01019. DOI: 10.1016/j.sciaf.2021.e01019

Bensalloua, C. A., & Ahmed, O. (2018). Spatial OLAP and Multicriteria Integrated Approach for Decision Support System. *Application in Agroforestry Management.*, *10*(3), 1–26. DOI: 10.4018/IJDSST.2018070101

Bertoncelli, C. M., Altamura, P., Bagui, S., Bagui, S., Vieira, E. R., Costantini, S., Monticone, M., Solla, F., & Bertoncelli, D. (2022). *Predicting osteoarthritis in adults using statistical data mining and machine learning. X*, 1–12. https://doi.org/DOI: 10.1177/1759720X221104935

Biao, Z. Z. (2023). Journal of King Saud University - Science Design and realization of data mining simulation and methodological models. *Journal of King Saud University. Science*, *35*(10), 102964. DOI: 10.1016/j.jksus.2023.102964

Chen, J., Li, P., Fang, W., Zhou, N., Yin, Y., Zheng, H., Xu, H., & Wang, R. (2021). *Fuzzy Frequent Pattern Mining Algorithm Based on Weighted Sliding Window and Type-2 Fuzzy Sets over Medical Data Stream. 2021*(1997). https://doi.org/DOI: 10.1155/2021/6662254

Chhajer, P., Shah, M., & Kshirsagar, A. (2022). The applications of artificial neural networks, support vector machines, and long – short term memory for stock market prediction. *Decision Analytics Journal, 2*(June 2021), 100015. https://doi.org/DOI: 10.1016/j.dajour.2021.100015

Cuzzocrea, A. (2024). ScienceDirect ScienceDirect Evolving OLAP and BI towards Complex, High-Performance Big- OLAP-Data-Cube-Processing Analytics Frameworks : How to Speed-Up Large-Scale, High-Dimensional Queries over Clouds. *Procedia Computer Science*, *246*, 4169–4175. DOI: 10.1016/j.procs.2024.09.256

Czmil, A. (2023). *Medical Applications*. 1–20.

Dafir, Z., Lamari, Y., & Chah, S. (2021). A survey on parallel clustering algorithms for Big Data. In *Artificial Intelligence Review* (Vol. 54, Issue 4). Springer Netherlands. https://doi.org/DOI: 10.1007/s10462-020-09918-2

Dahr, J. M., Hamoud, A. K., Najm, I. A., & Ahmed, M. I. (2022). IMPLEMENTING SALES DECISION SUPPORT SYSTEM USING DATA MART BASED ON OLAP. *KPI, AND DATA MINING APPROACHES.*, *17*(1), 275–293.

Davardoost, F., Sangar, A. B., & Majidzadeh, K. (2022). *An Innovative Model for Extracting OLAP Cubes from NOSQL Database Based on Scalable Na ̈ıve Bayes Classifier. 2022*.

Elsedimy, E. I., AboHashish, S. M. M., & Algarni, F. (2024). New cardiovascular disease prediction approach using support vector machine and quantum-behaved particle swarm optimization. *Multimedia Tools and Applications*, *83*(8), 23901–23928. DOI: 10.1007/s11042-023-16194-z

Enad, A. J., & Aksu, M. (2024). *Early prediction of COVID-19 infection using data mining and multi machine learning algorithms. 13*(3). https://doi.org/DOI: 10.11591/eei.v13i3.6912

Forresi, C., Gallinucci, E., Golfarelli, M., & Ben Hamadou, H. (2021). A dataspace-based framework for OLAP analyses in a high-variety multistore. *The VLDB Journal, 30*(6), 1017–1040. DOI: 10.1007/s00778-021-00682-5

Fugkeaw, S., & Hak, L. (2024). PPAC-CDW : A Privacy-Preserving Access Control Scheme With Fast OLAP Query and Efficient Revocation for Cloud Data Warehouse. *IEEE Access : Practical Innovations, Open Solutions, 12*(June), 78743–78758. DOI: 10.1109/ACCESS.2024.3408221

Ghazal, T. M., Hussain, M. Z., Said, R. A., & Nadeem, A. (2021). *Performances of K-Means Clustering Algorithm with Different Distance Metrics.* https://doi.org/DOI: 10.32604/iasc.2021.019067

Guido, R., Ferrisi, S., & Lofaro, D. (2024). An Overview on the Advancements of Support Vector Machine Models in Healthcare Applications. *RE:view.*

Guler, N., Ben, Z., & Gunes, A. (2025). Green Technologies and Sustainability Optimizing solar PV systems using fuzzy logic for Climate-Resilient Healthcare infrastructure in Kyrgyzstan. *Green Technologies and Sustainability, 3*(3), 100190. DOI: 10.1016/j.grets.2025.100190

Guleria, P., & Sood, M. (2023). Explainable AI and machine learning : performance evaluation and explainability of classifiers on educational data mining inspired career counseling. In *Education and Information Technologies.* Springer US., DOI: 10.1007/s10639-022-11221-2

Gulzar, K., Memon, M. A., Mohsin, S. M., Aslam, S., Muhammad, S., Akber, A., & Nadeem, M. A. (2023). *An Efficient Healthcare Data Mining Approach Using Apriori Algorithm : A Case Study of Eye Disorders in Young Adults.* 1–14.

Hamid, Z., Khalique, F., Mahmood, S., Daud, A., Bukhari, A., & Alshemaimri, B. (2024). Healthcare insurance fraud detection using data mining. *BMC Medical Informatics and Decision Making, 4,* 1–24. DOI: 10.1186/s12911-024-02512-4

Hazboun, F. H., & Owda, M. (2021). *A Natural Language Interface to Relational Databases Using an Online Analytic Processing Hypercube.* 720–737.

Huang, H., Lu, C., Jhou, M., Liu, T., Yang, C., Hsieh, S., Yang, W., Chang, H., Chen, M., Huang, H., Lu, C., & Jhou, M. (2023). *Using a Decision Tree Algorithm Predictive Model for Sperm Count Assessment and Risk Factors in Health Screening Population Using a Decision Tree Algorithm Predictive Model for Sperm Count Assessment and Risk Factors in Health Screening Population*. https://doi.org/DOI: 10.2147/RMHP.S433193

Jadhav, A. D., & Chobe, S. V. (2022). *Revue d ' Intelligence Artificielle Risk Assessment of Cardiovascular Diseases Using kNN and Decision Tree Classifier. 36*(1), 155–161.

Jamil, M., Warsito, B., & Wibowo, A. (2023). *Diabetes Mellitus Early Detection Simulation using The K-Nearest Neighbors Algorithm with Cloud-Based Runtime (COLAB). 15*(2), 215–221.

Kaur, J., Khehra, B. S., & Singh, A. (2023). Back propagation artificial neural network for diagnose of the heart disease. *Journal of Reliable Intelligent Environments, 9*(1), 57–85. DOI: 10.1007/s40860-022-00192-3

Kavitha, K. (2023). Optimal Stacked Sparse Auto-encoder based Online Analytic Processing (OLAP) Hypercube Text Analysis. *2023 Fifth International Conference on Electrical, Computer and Communication Technologies (ICECCT), February*, 1–5. https://doi.org/DOI: 10.1109/ICECCT56650.2023.10179777

Khoruzhy, L. I., Katkov, Y. N., Katkova, E. A., Khoruzhy, V. I., & Dzhikiya, M. K. (2023). *Opportunities for the Application of a Model of Cost Management and Reduction of Risks in Financial and Economic Activity Based on the OLAP Technology : The Case of the Agro-Industrial Sector of Russia.*

Khoshgoftar, Z., Babaee, M., & Rouzbahani, A. K. (2025). *Educational data mining in medical education : A five - level approach*. https://doi.org/DOI: 10.4103/jehp.jehp

Khushal, R., & Fatima, U. (2025). MethodsX Machine learning and Fuzzy logic fusion approach for. *MethodsX, 14*(December 2024), 103152. https://doi.org/DOI: 10.1016/j.mex.2024.103152

Kurani, A., Doshi, P., Vakharia, A., & Shah, M. (2023). A Comprehensive Comparative Study of Artificial Neural Network (ANN) and Support Vector Machines (SVM) on Stock Forecasting. *Annals of Data Science, 10*(1), 183–208. DOI: 10.1007/s40745-021-00344-x

Kyrimi, E., Mclachlan, S., Neves, M. R., Fahmi, A., & Fenton, N. (n.d.). *A Comprehensive Scoping Review of Bayesian Networks in Healthcare : Past, Present and Future*. 1–32.

Lai, W., Li, D., Yu, J., Huang, L., Zheng, M., Jiang, Y., Wang, S., Wen, J., Chen, S., Wen, C., & Jin, Y. (2022).. . *An Apriori Algorithm-Based Association Analysis of Analgesic Drugs in Chinese Medicine Prescriptions Recorded From Patients With Rheumatoid Arthritis., 3*(July), 1–15. DOI: 10.3389/fpain.2022.937259

Lei, L., Wu, B., Fang, X., Chen, L., Wu, H., & Liu, W. (2023). A dynamic anomaly detection method of building energy consumption based on data mining technology. *Energy, 263*(PA), 125575. https://doi.org/DOI: 10.1016/j.energy.2022.125575

Li, J. (2022). *E-Commerce Fraud Detection Model by Computer Artificial Intelligence Data Mining. 2022*(Ml). https://doi.org/DOI: 10.1155/2022/8783783

Li, J., Li, J., Wang, C., & Verbeek, F. J. (2023). *Outlier detection using iterative adaptive mini-minimum spanning tree generation with applications on medical data. October*, 1–12. https://doi.org/DOI: 10.3389/fphys.2023.1233341

Li, J., Li, J., Wang, C., Verbeek, F. J., Schultz, T., & Liu, H. (2024). *MS2OD : outlier detection using minimum spanning tree and medoid selection OPEN ACCESS MS2OD : outlier detection using minimum spanning tree and medoid selection.* 0–15.

Li, Q., Fan, Y., Luo, R., Hu, J., Wang, L., Ai, T., Li, Q., Fan, Y., Luo, R., Hu, J., Wang, L., & Ai, T. (2025). Related Risk Factors That Predict Moderate to Severe Asthma Attack in Children. *Analysis Based on Logistic Regression and Decision Tree Related Risk Factors That Predict Moderate to Severe Asthma Attack in Children : Analysis Based on Logistic Regression, 7074.* Advance online publication. DOI: 10.2147/IJGM.S530736

Liu, F., Cao, Y., Luo, J., Zhi, J., & Yang, J. (2024). ScienceDirect A Boundary Partitioning Algorithm for Geometrical Product Deviation Evaluation. *Procedia CIRP, 129*, 115–120. DOI: 10.1016/j.procir.2024.10.021

Luh, N., Purnama, P., Purnama, I. N., & Utami, N. W. (2022). *Penerapan Data Mining Untuk Clustering Penilaian Kinerja Dosen Menggunakan Algoritma K-Means (Studi Kasus : STMIK Primakara). 16*(2), 105–112.

Maleki, N., Zeinali, Y., Taghi, S., & Niaki, A. (2021). A k-NN method for lung cancer prognosis with the use of a genetic algorithm for feature selection. *Expert Systems With Applications, 164*(July 2019), 113981. https://doi.org/DOI: 10.1016/j.eswa.2020.113981

Man, M., Ruslan, N. A., Jusoh, J. A., Aezwani, W., & Bakar, W. A. (2023). *IR-Eclat : A new algorithm of incremental R- Eclat for infrequent itemset mining IR-Eclat : A New Algorithm of Incremental R-Eclat for Infrequent Itemset Mining. 060012*(March).

Meenal, M. R., & Vennila, S. M. (2023). Bidirectional Recurrent Network and Neuro - fuzzy Frequent Pattern Mining for Heart Disease Prediction. *SN Computer Science*, *4*(4), 1–10. DOI: 10.1007/s42979-023-01711-6

Mudumba, B., & Kabir, F. (2024). Mine-first association rule mining : An integration of independent frequent patterns in distributed environments. *Decision Analytics Journal*, *10*(February), 100434. DOI: 10.1016/j.dajour.2024.100434

Najm, I. A., Dahr, J. M., Hamoud, A. K., Alasady, A. S., Awadh, W. A., Alshawki, M. B., & Humadi, A. M. (2022). *OLAP Mining with Educational Data Mart to Predict Students ' Performance Literature r eview. 46*, 11–19.

Noor, M., Khan, I., Alzahrani, A. R. R., Akkari, A. A., & Ahmad, B. (2024). Risk adjusted EWMA control chart based on support vector machine with application to cardiac surgery data. *Scientific Reports*, ●●●, 1–12. DOI: 10.1038/s41598-024-60285-2

Okewu, E., Adewole, P., Misra, S., & Maskeliunas, R. (2021). Artificial Neural Networks for Educational Data Mining in Higher Education : A Sy ematic Literature Review Artificial Neural Networks for Educational Data Mining in Higher Education : A Systematic Literature Review. *Applied Artificial Intelligence*, *35*(13), 983–1021. DOI: 10.1080/08839514.2021.1922847

Olatunji, I. E., Rauch, J., & Katzensteiner, M. (2021). *A Review of Anonymization for Healthcare Data.* 1–14.

Oon, N. B., Khairudin, Z., Aryani, H., Rahman, A., Syamimi, N., Abu, H., Azimah, N., Aziz, A., Mara, U. T., Alam, S., Mara, U. T., & Buloh, S. (2024). *PREDICTION OF DIABETIC RETINOPATHY AMONG DIABETIC NEUROPATHY IN T2DM PATIENTS USING DATA. 9*(2), 1916–1929. https://doi.org/DOI: 10.24191/mjoc.v9i2.26720

Owora, A. H., Tepper, R. S., Ramsey, C. D., & Becker, A. B. (2021). *Decision tree- based rules outperform risk scores for childhood asthma prognosis. January*, 1464–1473. https://doi.org/DOI: 10.1111/pai.13530

Parcon, R. C. B., Setias, J. E. L., Holipas, M. T. M., & Ed, E. (2022). *Comparison of Transaction Reduction and Dynamic Itemset Counting Implementations of the Apriori algorithm in Python. 5*(1), 44–49.

Peng, Y., Yang, Y., Xu, Y., Xue, Y., Song, R., Kang, J., Zhao, H., & Member, S. (2021). Electricity Theft Detection in AMI Based on Clustering and Local Outlier Factor. *IEEE Access : Practical Innovations, Open Solutions*, *9*, 107250–107259. DOI: 10.1109/ACCESS.2021.3100980

Polotskaya, K., Muñoz-valencia, C. S., Rabasa, A., Quesada-rico, J. A., Orozco-beltrán, D., & Barber, X. (2024). *Bayesian Networks for the Diagnosis and Prognosis of Diseases : A Scoping Review*. 1243–1262.

Queralt, M. S., Galofré, M., Tio, L., Monfort, J., Monllau, J. C., Piella, G., & Noailly, J. (2024). Characterization of clinical data for patient stratification in moderate osteoarthritis with support vector machines, regulatory network models, and verification against osteoarthritis Initiative data. *Scientific Reports, 0123456789*, 1–11. DOI: 10.1038/s41598-024-62212-x

Rajendra, P., & Latifi, S. (2021). *Computer Methods and Programs in Biomedicine Update Prediction of diabetes using logistic regression and ensemble techniques. 1*, 1–8.

Rastogi, R., & Bansal, M. (2023). Measurement : Sensors. *Measurement: Sensors, 25*(December 2022), 100605. https://doi.org/DOI: 10.1016/j.measen.2022.100605

Rb, A., & Kr, S. K. (2021). Credit card fraud detection using artificial neural network. *Global Transitions Proceedings, 2*(1), 35–41. DOI: 10.1016/j.gltp.2021.01.006

Rosa, M., & Gomez, C. De. (2024). *A Comprehensive Introduction to Healthcare Data Analytics. 4*(1), 44–53.

Ruifeng, S. (2021). *Research on data mining system based on artificial intelligence and improved genetic algorithm. 40*, 6731–6742. https://doi.org/DOI: 10.3233/JIFS-189507

Saidi, M., Gheibi, M., Ghazikhani, A., Lotfata, A., Chahkandi, B., & Ghazikhani, A. (2025). Efficient COVID-19 detection using data mining algorithms : A comparison of basic and hybrid approaches. *Soft Computing, 29*(3), 1437–1451. DOI: 10.1007/s00500-025-10538-7

Samariya, D., & Thakkar, A. (2023). A Comprehensive Survey of Anomaly Detection Algorithms. *Annals of Data Science, 10*(3), 829–850. DOI: 10.1007/s40745-021-00362-9

Sanjeev, C., Dash, K., Kumar, A., Dehuri, S., & Ghosh, A. (2023). An outliers detection and elimination framework in classification task of data mining. *Decision Analytics Journal, 6*(January), 100164. DOI: 10.1016/j.dajour.2023.100164

Shawkat, M., Badawi, M., & El, S. (2022). An optimized FP - growth algorithm for discovery of association rules. *The Journal of Supercomputing, 78*(4), 5479–5506. DOI: 10.1007/s11227-021-04066-y

Shukla, A., Chaurasia, S., Pandey, G., Shukla, S. K., & Parihar, S. S. (2025).. . *Privacy-Preserving Data Mining Methods Metrics and Applications in Healthcare Informatics., 04002*, 1–9.

Sohail, A. (2023). Genetic Algorithms in the Fields of Artificial Intelligence and Data Sciences. *Annals of Data Science, 10*(4), 1007–1018. DOI: 10.1007/s40745-021-00354-9

Sun, Y. (2022).. . *Multimedia Technology of Spatial Data Mining Based on Genetic Algorithm., 2022*. Advance online publication. DOI: 10.1155/2022/4835359

Tabianan, K., & Velu, S. (2022). *K-Means Clustering Approach for Intelligent Customer Segmentation Using Customer Purchase Behavior Data*. 1–15.

Tarakanita, N. I., & Amaliah, Y. (2023).. . *Analisa Metode Association Rule Untuk Penjualan Skincare Menggunakan Algoritma Pincer Serach Analysis of Association Rule Methods for Skincare Sales Using the Pincer Search Algorithm., 6*(2), 25–29.

Thakkar, H., Shah, V., Yagnik, H., & Shah, M. (2022). Clinical eHealth Comparative anatomization of data mining and fuzzy logic techniques used in diabetes prognosis. *Clinical EHealth, 4*(2021), 12–23. https://doi.org/DOI: 10.1016/j.ceh.2020.11.001

Touati, S., Boumediri, H., Karmi, Y., & Chitour, M. (2025). Heliyon Performance analysis of steel W18CR4V grinding using RSM, DNN-GA, KNN, LM, DT, SVM models, and optimization via desirability function and MOGWO. *Heliyon, 11*(4), e42640. DOI: 10.1016/j.heliyon.2025.e42640

Tyagi, A., & Singh, P. (2014). Asthma diagnosis and level of control using decision tree and fuzzy system. *Int. J. Biomedical Engineering and Technology J. Biomedical Engineering and Technology, 16*(2), 169–181. DOI: 10.1504/IJBET.2014.065658

Wei, J., & Tan, C. (2025). *Volunteer Management : A Data Mining Approach. March*.

Wijaya, R., Saeed, F., Samimi, P., & Albarrak, A. M. (2024). *An Ensemble Machine Learning and Data Mining Approach to Enhance Stroke Prediction*.

Wu, W. T., Li, Y. J., Feng, A. Z., Li, L., Huang, T., Xu, A. D., & Lyu, J. (2021). *Data mining in clinical big data : the frequently used databases, steps, and methodological models*. 1–12. https://doi.org/DOI: 10.1186/s40779-021-00338-z

Xu, H. (2022). *Outlier detection algorithm based on k-nearest neighbors-local outlier factor*. https://doi.org/DOI: 10.1177/17483026221078111

Yadav, A., & Kumar, A. (2021). *Improving the Performance of Multidimensional Clinical Data for OLAP using an Optimized Data Clustering approach. 12*(3), 3269–3275.

Yang, L., Peng, S., Othman, R., & Leren, Y. (2023). Cancer detection in breast cells using a hybrid method based on deep complex neural network and data mining. *Journal of Cancer Research and Clinical Oncology*, *149*(14), 13331–13344. DOI: 10.1007/s00432-023-05191-2

Yao, K. (2024). Measurement : Sensors Application of sensor-based speech data mining in E-commerce operations data analysis. *Measurement: Sensors, 33*(June 2023), 101118. https://doi.org/DOI: 10.1016/j.measen.2024.101118

Ye, H. U. A., Wu, P., Zhu, T., Xiao, Z., Zhang, X. I. E., Zheng, L., Zheng, R., Sun, Y., Zhou, W., Fu, Q., Ye, X., Chen, A. L. I., Zheng, S., Heidari, A. L. I. A., Wang, M., Zhu, J., Chen, H., Member, A., & Li, J. (2021). Diagnosing Coronavirus Disease 2019 (COVID-19). *Efficient Harris Hawks-Inspired Fuzzy K-Nearest Neighbor Prediction Methods.*, *9*, 17787–17802. DOI: 10.1109/ACCESS.2021.3052835

Zahmani, M. H., & Atmani, B. (2021). Multiple dispatching rules allocation in real time using data mining, genetic algorithms, and simulation. *Journal of Scheduling*, *24*(2), 175–196. DOI: 10.1007/s10951-020-00664-5

Zhang, X., Yuan, Z., & Miao, D. (2023). Outlier Detection Using Three-Way Neighborhood Characteristic Regions and Corresponding Fusion Measurement. *IEEE Transactions on Knowledge and Data Engineering, PP*, 1–14. https://doi.org/DOI: 10.1109/TKDE.2023.3312108

Zhang, Z., Tan, L., & Tiong, R. (2024). *Research on fire accident prediction and risk assessment algorithm based on data mining and machine learning. 0.* https://doi.org/DOI: 10.1186/s13662-024-03845-0

Zheng, Q., Xu, Y., Liu, H., Shi, B., Wang, J., & Dong, B. (2024). Artificial Intelligence — Review A Survey of Tax Risk Detection Using Data Mining Techniques. *Engineering*, *34*, 43–59. DOI: 10.1016/j.eng.2023.07.014

ADDITIONAL READING

Masmoudi, M., Jarboui, B., & Siarry, P. (Eds.). (2021). Artificial intelligence and data mining in healthcare. Springer International Publishing. Bhattacharya, A., Roy, B., Sur, S. N., Mallik, S., & Dasgupta, S. (Eds.). (2022). *Internet of things and data mining for modern engineering and healthcare applications*. CRC Press. Dash, S., Pani, S. K., Balamurugan, S., & Abraham, A. (Eds.). (2021). *Biomedical Data Mining for Information Retrieval: Methodologies, Techniques, and Applications*. John Wiley & Sons.

Sethi, D. (2025). *Business Intelligence and Data Mining Techniques*. Educohack Press. Ramjan, S., & Sunkpho, J. (Eds.). (2023). *Principles and theories of data mining with RapidMiner*. IGI Global. Aroraa, G., Lele, C., & Jindal, M. (2022). *Data Analytics: Principles, Tools, and Practices: A Complete Guide for Advanced Data Analytics Using the Latest Trends, Tools, and Technologies (English Edition)*. BPB Publications.

Shah, K., Shah, N., Sawant, V., & Parolia, N. (Eds.). (2023). *Practical data mining techniques and applications*. CRC Press.

Taniar, D., & Rahayu, W. (2022). *Data warehousing and analytics: fueling the data engine*. Springer Nature.

Dubrovkin, J. (2024). *Data Analytics in Spectroscopy*. Cambridge Scholars Publishing.

KEY TERMS AND DEFINITIONS

Anonymization Techniques: Anonymization technique is used to separate or removing identifying information from the data. In this way individuals cannot be linked to the data. It is frequently done on healthcare data to protect privacy of the patients. It allows the use of data for research purposes.

CART: Classification and Regression Tree algorithm. It is used for both classification and regression purposes.

Data Cube: In data cube the data is modelled and presented in many dimensions. For example, diabetes patient has many dimensions such as age, symptoms, lab results, and day of lab test. Suppose someone wants to see information of Diabate's patent of particular year and month, there are multiple data cube items like patient id, time, type of Lab test, day of lab test and patient symptoms.

Data Mart: It is a spatial subset of data warehouse which focuses on specific business function or department.

Data Warehouse: The data warehouse is used to store large amount of data. Data is collected from different places and after prepossessing it is stored in the data warehouse in more manageable form.

Knowledge Discovery in Database (KDD): KDD is used to find valuable knowledge or information from the data warehouse.

Online Analytical Processing (OLAP): A software-based technique which works on many databases simultaneously.

Schemas: It is a blue print that defines how data is organized and stored within database.

Structure Query Language (SQL): It is used to create, delete, retrieved and update the data in data warehouse or database.

Chapter 5
Enhancing Healthcare Sustainability Through AI-Driven Medical Devices

T. Venkat Narayana Rao
https://orcid.org/0000-0002-1996-1819
Sreenidhi Institute of Science and Technology, India

Kudipudi Jayashree
https://orcid.org/0009-0005-9231-6022
Sreenidhi Institute of Science and Technology, India

G. Ravi
Sreenidhi Institute of Science and Technology, India

J. V. P. Udaya Deepika
Sreenidhi Institute of Science and Technology, India

Kusumalatha Karre
https://orcid.org/0000-0001-9166-1397
Sreenidhi Institute of Science and Technology, India

ABSTRACT

Medical devices controlled through artificial intelligence are leading the path to make healthcare a sustainable and efficient system. They use artificial intelligence (AI) with the internet of medical things (IoMT) to improve patient's care, decrease resource utilization, and decrease the amount of harm to the environment. The authors strive to narrate various uses of AI in medical appliances like wearable health

DOI: 10.4018/979-8-3373-2545-3.ch005

appliances, diagnosis devices, and remote surveillance systems with sustainable health care. Benchmarked on real-world examples, it demonstrates the processes through which they adapt and strengthen organisational/consumer practices. The chapter analyses the issues associated with these technologies, for instance: data privacy and protection issues, ethical issues concerning decision-making through the artificial intelligence, minimise barriers and minimise the need for invasive procedures. Last, it looks to future developments including combining AI with renewables and other innovations in seeking to improve sustainable care delivery in healthcare.

1. INTRODUCTION

The integration of healthcare and technology is today as critical as it has ever been. Healthcare systems across the world have yet to find sufficient aforementioned solvents to meet demands resulting from increased patient traffic or scarce resources-and worse, environmental considerations. But really great innovations are called not just to better the outcomes of patient care but also to make the healthcare ecosystem sustainable. Among the most hopeful of such bright innovations are AI and advanced medical devices tied to the IoMT. The AI-driven medical devices are rapidly changing the way healthcare is delivered from improving diagnostics to real-time monitoring or facilitation to improved operational efficiencies. It, therefore, is not just a trend but a paradigm shift into a more sustainable, resilient, and effective healthcare system.

1.1 Context and Importance

It has been by its very nature the health care sector which prefers some conventional practices that are mostly effective but increasingly tensed by the modern problem. The greatest causes have all been the increased chronic diseases all over the globe, the elderly population, and the must to reduce the environmental footprint of healthcare operations (Kalli et al., 2023). This has necessitated the application of more viable approaches toward health care services. Health devices are driven by artificial intelligence to meet these requirements precisely. They will quickly analyze vast amounts of data with extensive precision using machine learning algorithms, allowing a quicker diagnosis, treatments tailored to a specific individual, and proactive patient monitoring. This aspect is critical when it comes to life and death, with appropriate resource allocation helping policymakers minimize expenditure in the health sector.

And looking at the environmental aspect, healthcare practice does not have any lesser impact. Hospitals and clinics consume lots of energy and the manufacture, application, and disposals of conventional health equipment contribute to the degradation of the environment. AI-inspired devices with real-time analytics and predictive maintenance can optimize energy use and minimize waste through operation efficiency improvement and decreased incidence of unnecessary procedures. Over the years before now, this sector has been very much traditional and has been using very effective methods, but these methods are today under pressure by modern problems. The increase in chronic diseases across the globe, aging populations, and the urge to be less environmental with health that have caused the imperious need for more sustainable practices have made up for the introduction of a whole range of health devices driven by artificial intelligence. Such health devices have been created to confront all these concerns. This factor is all the more important where the difference between life and death is timely intervention, as resource allocation is as crucial in cutting health costs.

Not to mention, are the impacts healthcare has on the environment. Energy-consuming hospitals and clinics, production, use, and disposal of conventional medical devices all degrade the environment. AI-enabled devices, whose capacity for real-time analytics and predictive maintenance, will help optimize energy consumption and minimize waste. Such advancements lead to an economically as well as ecologically sustainable health future by improving operational efficiency and minimizing unnecessary procedures.

The healthcare sector has been traditionally using very effective methods over years, but these methods are today's pressures of modern problems. The increase in chronic diseases across the globe, aging populations, and the urge to be less environmental with health that have caused an imperious need for introducing a whole range of health devices driven by artificial intelligence. Such health devices are created to confront all these issues very well. Now with the help of machine learning algorithms, huge data can be analyzed very fast and with great accuracy so as to enable the detection of diseases much earlier, personalized treatment schemes, and managing patients proactively. Without denying, healthcare life has an impact on the environment. The hospitals and clinics consume lots of energy, and the make, use, and disposal of conventional medical equipment degrade the environment. AI-enabled devices with real-time analytics and predictive maintenance will help improve energy use and reduce waste due to operational efficiency and a lower incidence of unnecessary procedures. And thus it leads to an economically and ecologically sustainable health future.

1.1.1 Additional Challenges in the Healthcare Landscape

Aside from the increased prevalence of chronic disease and aging population, the health care sector is dealing with a range of systemic weaknesses that undermine sustainability and equality. Perhaps the most significant issue relates to the market-driven nature of health care systems, especially in areas where privatized medical services are predominant. For example, pharmaceutical and medical device companies use profit-maximizing models, leading to exorbitantly priced drugs, high costs in equipment and inequitable access and application of innovations. The current accompaniment of rapid increases in living costs, which disproportionately affect lower-income populations, compounds this phenomenon by rendering acceptable healthcare inaccessible for widespread portions of the world, namely low- and middle-income countries. In those contexts, pressure on price can lead to the rapid entry of poor-quality drugs and poor-quality medical devices in the market. This situation creates significant safety and efficacy challenges.

Given this status quo, addressing these systemic inadequacies is a dominant concern to avoid electively introducing AI-related medical devices that worsen existing inequities based on privilege or indigence. Therefore, it is necessary to incorporate affordability, regulatory controls, and access/equity when designing and implementing AI-related health care technologies to establish what a durable system looks like.

1.2 Overview of AI and IoMT

For one to fully understand the importance of AI-enabled medical systems, one should try to define some of the most critical concepts involved: artificial intelligence and the Internet of Medical Things.AI is the simulation of human intelligence processes by computer systems; it includes learning (the acquisition of information and rules for using the information), reasoning (using rules to reach approximate or definite conclusions), and self-correction. In the healthcare arena, AI algorithms are developed to process and analyze huge complex datasets ranging from medical images to genomic sequences, thus rendering support to clinicians in speeding up the diagnosis with accuracy(Razdan et al., 2022). AI can also assist in predictive analytics, in which the patterns found on the historical data can predict outcomes for patients and recommend specific interventions.

The Internet of Medical Things (IoMT) refers to a network of interconnected devices and systems that exchange and process health information. From these are wearable devices that monitor and provide real-time readings of vital signs, smart implants, and diagnostic tools used remotely. There are other kinds of interconnected devices that form internet networks and share this data with relevant systems for centralized analysis. The result of such a connection is the creation of a truly vibrant ecosystem from IoMT and AI that enables the continuous monitoring of patient data and sometimes immediate actionable insights creation.

1.3 Purpose of the Chapter

This chapter aims to study in detail the multifaceted impacts of AI-driven medical devices in sustainable healthcare. We will discuss some of the key challenges in this area:

1. **Efficiency in Healthcare Delivery:** This study describes how AI technologies are reshaping medical devices: for diagnostics, personalized treatment protocols and thus the patients' improved outcomes. The efficiency of work leads to cost reductions in healthcare systems through the sensible distribution of resources.
2. **Ecological Sustainability:** One of the primary areas of concern in this chapter is how integration of AI in these medical devices does enhance ecological sustainability. This subsection also provides a broader analysis that looks at how this has reduced energy, waste flow, and encourages other ecological practices in health facilities.
3. **Integration of AI and IoMT:** The chapter will provide an in-depth look at how the convergence of AI and IoMT is reshaping healthcare. This involves examining the technical and operational aspects of this integration, as well as discussing the potential for future innovations that could further enhance healthcare sustainability.
4. **Challenges and Ethical Dimensions:** Any technological advancement presents challenges that none can evade. We have to talk about different arguments regarding data privacy, security, ethical concerns, and compliance with laws and regulations. It is also crucial to understand these barriers toward the establishment of generalized frameworks that will facilitate the safe and appropriate use of AI-based medical devices in practice.
5. **Future Prospects and Opportunities:** The assessment of AI and recent medical device technology trends and solicitations for the future is the act of contextualizing the transformation of the existing healthcare milieu into a more sustainable, equitable, and efficient means of service delivery.

1.4 Thesis Statement

Basically, this chapter holds that AI medical devices-with the power of the Internet of Medical Things-connectivity are at the core of sustainable health advancement. Leveraging AI's abilities to study data and predict developments, such medical apparatus not only enhance physicians' interventions and treatment accuracies but also work to ensure the ecological sustainability of medical practices by making available maximum efficient use of resources and minimum waste. With this dual dichotomy-increasing patient care and reducing ecological impacts-the very significance of such is justification with the current age demanding equal attention to the health and environment sectors. This chapter articulately postulates the emerging trends, available research possibilities, and horizon discussions that provide insight into a more efficacious, ecologically sound, and ethically based future of healthcare with the help of artificial intelligence (Benjamens et al., 2020).

Combined with the burning necessity for a sustainable approach, AI integration with medical devices stands like a ray of hope in front of the healthcare industry. Throughout this chapter, a systematic discussion, both on the gains from these technologies and the practical, ethical, and regulatory constraints met, yet to be overcome to better facilitate full realization of if not all yet a large amount of the aforementioned advantages, will prevail. The road ahead will entail a billiards revolution that heals not only people's health but also those of the systems that sustain our very existence, thereby ensuring the continuity of life on Earth for centuries to come.

2. THE ROLE OF AI IN MEDICAL DEVICES

More effective operations in hospitals, reduced costs, and a shift toward proactive and preventive healthcare with increased precision and efficiency are benefitting enhanced delivery from this combination of AI. From basics such as diagnosing diseases with greater accuracy to allowing real-time patient monitoring, AI-based medical devices are changing how healthcare is delivered, with many innovations combining technology with the delivery of treatment thereby improving on clinical outcomes considerably.

Even if there are no immediate prospects that AI can improve the diagnostics, ensure efficient patient management, and predictive maintenance of medical equipment, in this technological age of IoMT, the development shows that the convergence of two systems will take healthcare delivery into a new dimension or level. This unique blend of capabilities has ushered into being a connected healthcare ecosystem where instead of doing their jobs independently, they work together to provide remote monitoring and real-time data exchange in the connected care landscape. In understanding the entire ingraining effect of AI in medical devices, it becomes paramount that we dwell into its evolution, functions, and interfacing with the IoMT.

2.1 Historical Perspective and Evolution

While medical devices can be traced to ancient civilizations and their sharp with the scalpel, possessing whichever forceps that's been invented, and having other primitive devices functioning on Stethoscope, some surgical, others diagnostic, it was at that time the genesis of the much-talked-about 'medical devices.' The era that the 19th and 20th centuries saw tremendous advancement in the introduction of X-ray machines, Electrocardiographs and blood pressure monitor devices to enhance high-level accuracy in diagnosis, hence promoting an enhancement in patient care. Besides, the pacemakers, ventilators, and infusion pumps that were invented in the mid-20th century folded a significant hallmark of devices that equally serve contemporary medicine. Although several breakthroughs have been made, these devices before were mainly based on mechanical or electronic principles, mostly naive and much (i.e. visible intelligence). It helps tremendously to factor diagnosis and treatment but doesn't really have any data processing or pattern recognition in it that, if advanced autonomously, could definitely improve health outcomes. By the late 20th century years, this was broken down; computers were fully immersed into the healthcare sector. Such development created the wand of AI-enhanced medical instruments. Initially working as data analysts to help radiologists find abnormalities in medical images, the expansion of AI was seen throughout the late 1990s and early 2000s into predictive analytics, electronic health records (EHR), and robotic-assisted surgery. Thanks to progress in machine learning and deep learning techniques, AI-powered medical devices transitioned from simple rule-based systems to more advanced models equipped for independent decision-making. Their capacity to scrutinize vast datasets swiftly enables them to discern patterns effectively while providing real-time insights; this has spurred innovations such as smart wearables, AI-enabled diagnostics tools, and sophisticated robotic surgical frameworks like the da Vinci Surgical System significantly elevating precision in minimally invasive operations. AI-assisted medical technologies are currently remapping the health landscape through real-time analytics, predictive diagnostics, and automation in everyday clinical settings. This evolution marks a paradigm shift from conventional reactivity to an active prevention approach to health care, thus fundamentally impacting patient outcomes and system efficiencies.

2.2 Functionalities Enabled by AI

AI has transformed medical devices, enhancing diagnostics, patient observation, and the delivery of these technologies. With artificial intelligence, healthcare systems can promote early diagnosis of diseases, enhance resource utilization, and provide better care for patients while simultaneously relieving clinicians of some burdens.

Due to the introduction of AI in diagnostics, medical imaging and disease identification have shifted toward reform. Traditional diagnostic approaches generally rely on human interpretation, prone to the subjectivity and risk of error. AI imaging technologies now offer impressive accuracy in the analysis of X-rays, CT scans, and MRIs with computers being able to identify tumors, fractures, and neurological issues. For instance, Google's DeepMind AI has demonstrated its ability to reach diagnoses for eye conditions that align with those made by radiologists. In pathology as well, AI tools expedite the examination of biopsy specimens and accurately identify cancerous cells at high rates. Furthermore, enhanced ECG devices utilize artificial intelligence to recognize heart irregularities like atrial fibrillation instantly. In genomic health contexts too, AI assists in predicting disease susceptibilities and tailoring treatment plans based on genetic profiles setting the stage for an era focused on precision medicine(Gu et al., 2024).

In addition to its diagnostic applications, AI is pivotal in real-time monitoring of patients' health status—essential especially for managing chronic ailments or overseeing post-surgical recovery. Wearable technology such as smart watches and biosensors continuously assess vital indicators from users' bodies. These devices promptly notify users when abnormalities arise to avert potential health emergencies; both the Apple Watch and Fitbit make use of AI features designed to supervise cardiac rhythms vigilantly whilst motivating timely healthcare engagement whenever necessary. Within hospitals themselves, advanced ICU surveillance systems driven by AI enable continuous oversight over patients 24/7 actively anticipating complications which may include severe conditions such as sepsis or organ failure prior to reaching critical stages. The growth of remote patient monitoring (RPM) powered by AI also aligns seamlessly with tele-health services enabling practitioners to monitor their patients' wellbeing effectively at any given moment a significant .

Additionally, a higher level degree efficiency arises since operational choices related toward resource allocation receive configurations through automation experienced during various calibration processes treatable via algorithmic insights optimizing respective precision standards all while contributing towards substantial reductions across associated cost factors routinely encountered within established usages though practical transformations enhancing daily performance goals considerably have initiated benefits prevalent moving forward significantly benefitting future outcomes further extending implementations ongoing techniques available expanding opportunities provided imminently succinctly directing ability realized broadband context enhancements attracting-digitized professional landscapes ensuring availability succeed forthcoming finally reach envisioned nearing realities manifesting materializing present day aligning outcome success guidelines becoming quality experience aimed fellowship development accelerator pathways gathered insight gathering opportunity moved marshalling excellence accrued across filtering models exhibited evidence matching intended trajectories uncovered ultimately focusing ingraining concerning continual interaction wise

2.3 Integration with IoMT

The Internet of Medical Things means a variety of connected smart medical devices that gather, analyze, and transmit health data in real-time continuously. The convergence of IoMT with artificial intelligence enables the adoption of an intelligent healthcare ecosystem that drives data-based decisions, thus ensuring personalized treatments. AI-based devices within the IoMT framework, including wearable sensors and implantable monitors, build up a large amount of patient information, which they send to the cloud where it can be analyzed by AI algorithms. These algorithms identify trends and generate actionable insights. The ability to share this data instantly enables healthcare professionals to respond swiftly, minimizing the risk of medical crises and enhancing patient outcomes. Moreover, AI contributes significantly to the interoperability within IoMT systems by seamlessly integrating electronic health records, hospital management software, and diagnostic tools. This transformation leads to a comprehensive overview of a patient's health profile while reducing redundant medical tests and treatments. In addition to merely collecting data, AI-enhanced IoMT frameworks provide automated support for decision-making through real-time alerts regarding potential health risks. Such as, advanced insulin pumps can autonomously adjust insulin delivery based on detected glucose levels, thus avoiding any complications for diabetics. Furthermore, the support that AI can provide will allow the healthcare provider to tailor recommendations specifically suited to the individual patient's profile, including consideration for genetics, environmental variability, and lifestyle choice. Looking ahead, technological advancements such as 5G connectivity promise improved data transmission speeds; meanwhile, incorporating blockchain technology will enhance security measures alongside edge computing capabilities facilitating quicker processing times. This integration between AI and IoMT paves the way toward more intelligent healthcare solutions characterized by both efficiency and strong patient focus which also contribute positively towards clinical viability as well as economic sustainability.

3. IMPACT ON SUSTAINABILITY

The introduction of AI into medical devices is revolutionizing the healthcare industry and greatly supports sustainability efforts. It has become, therefore, quite important in view of rising global healthcare needs to introduce resource-efficient and eco-friendly practices. AI technologies improve the practice of care through energy conservation, reduction of medical waste, and resource planning. Among the significant energy-consuming institutions around the world are hospitals and other healthcare facilities, which consume large quantities of water, electricity, and disposables. That is, through AI, advancing efficiency toward enhancing sustainability is a necessary move in ensuring an environmentally plausible future. AI supports sustainability through various channels, particularly by optimizing resources. It accomplishes this by streamlining workflows, automating diagnostics processes, and applying predictive analytics for effective inventory management which ultimately curtails operational waste while ensuring that healthcare providers only utilize essential items. Additionally, advancements in surgical accuracy and imaging facilitated by AI lower the probability of unnecessary interventions along with excessive consumption of medical supplies. With ongoing developments in AI capabilities anticipated to continue growing its role in fostering sustainability across healthcare settings—the pathway lies open for inventive strategies aimed at reconciling high-quality patient service with ecological stewardship(Manickam et al., 2022). Nonetheless, it remains critical to confront issues surrounding data privacy alongside managing the energy requirements associated with artificial intelligence computing if we wish to cultivate a sustainable and ethically governed future in health care.

3.1 Resource Optimization through AI in Healthcare

AI-assisted medical devices are crucial in enhancing resource utilization and minimizing energy consumption within the healthcare sector. Hospitals and medical facilities often rank among the most resource-heavy settings, needing substantial amounts of electricity, water, and various medical supplies. The implementation of AI improves operational efficiency by streamlining processes, forecasting resource demands, and automating routine activities, which results in less waste and fosters sustainability. One prominent domain where AI contributes to resource optimization is in energy management. By leveraging real-time data analysis, AI systems can effectively govern energy usage in hospitals by adjusting lighting, heating, and cooling based on patient occupancy levels and usage trends. Advanced scheduling algorithms enhance the operation of equipment that typically consumes high amounts of energy—such as MRI machines and CT scanners ensuring their usage is maximized while limiting unnecessary power costs. Research indicates that employing AI for scheduling can reduce operating room energy requirements by nearly 23%, thereby significantly diminishing a hospital's carbon emissions. In addition to improving energy efficiency, AI also boosts the effectiveness of supply chain operations within healthcare by accurately predicting inventory requirements and curtailing surplus orders. Machine learning models dissect historical data on product use to refine the acquisition processes for medications, surgical instruments, and disposable items; this approach minimizes wastefulness while assisting in preventing shortages or overstock scenarios. Moreover, predictive maintenance powered by AI ensures medical devices remain functional at optimal levels this not only prevents premature replacements but also extends their operational lifespan. Furthermore, telemedicine facilitated through AI technologies marginally diminishes the need for hospital visits which subsequently decreases transportation-related greenhouse gas emissions while lowering overall hospital reliance on resources. By alleviating unnecessary admissions as well as enhancing bed occupancy strategies within facilities; hospitals operate more efficiently under these innovations—all while conserving both human labour resources alongside material assets. Ultimately, integrating AI into medical device management cultivates a more sustainable framework for an economically efficient healthcare system.

3.2 Environmental Benefits of AI-Driven Medical Devices

Usage of AI in medical devices enhances efficiency in reducing environmental waste, optimizing resource usage, and carbon footprints from healthcare establishments. Healthcare produces tremendous waste ranging from single-use plastics, expired medications, excess energy consumption et cetera, and AI-driven technologies address this with higher precision, efficiency, and management of waste to improve environmental impacts. The moat way in which AI reduces hospital waste is by decreasing unnecessary procedures and optimizing resource use therein. AI-powered diagnostic tools help improve precision during disease detection and reduce repeat tests, biopsies, and imaging scans, which translates into a reduction in radiation exposure for patients and in the use of disposables like contrast agents, syringes, and gloves. AI also makes surgery more surgical by making it possible to carry out operations more accurately, thus reducing mistakes that would require further corrections and the use of surgical tools and materials for postoperative care. AI-based predictive maintenance in medical equipment also ensures that working devices are not cut short because they haven't been performing to performance standards, preventing sudden purchase and disposal of these devices. By predicting maintenance requirements, AI adds years to the life of medical machines and prevents them from becoming electronic waste when costly machines fail unexpectedly.

3.3 Real-World Examples and Studies Highlighting Sustainability Improvements

Multiple research studies and real-world examples indicate that AI-driven medical devices bring major environmental advantages in the healthcare sector. An example comes from the Cleveland Clinic, and highlights the role AI plays in streamlining operating room scheduling. Scheduling algorithms with AI helped the hospital save 23% energy in operating rooms. This not only brought down energy costs, but also contributed to a decline in its carbon emissions, showcasing how AI can minimize resource its use while at the same time guaranteeing quality care. Another instance is AI predictive maintenance in medical devices. Based on a study from UCLA, AI predictive maintenance allowed them to save up to 15% of energy use for MRI machines. Using current usage patterns and interruptions analysis, it helped prevent excessive equipment downtimes that required repairs while maximizing energy efficiency on MRI machines. This prevented unnecessary electronic waste production while extending the life of medical equipment. Remote care technologies also reduce emissions from patient transport. A 2020 study published in the Journal of Medical Internet Research investigated the environmental benefits of telemedicine, establishing that telehealth mitigates transportation-related emissions by over 50% for select patient populations-most notably in rural areas. AI-grade wearable health devices, such as smart watches and biosensors, have also reduced in-person visits in clinical settings which leads to a reduced environmental impact of patient care(Damoah et al., 2021). All of these examples bear out the proposition that AI can enhance sustainability in healthcare through resource optimization, waste minimization, and reduction of the sector's environmental footprint.

3.3.1 Expanded Global Examples of Sustainability Impact

Along with the landmark scenarios in high-income nations, AI-enabled medical devices exist in resource-constrained cases have the potential for very good sustainability outcomes as well. For example, a portable AI-enabled ultrasound has been installed in areas of rural India and sub-Saharan Africa to assist in rural maternal care to reduce travel time to tertiary hospitals. Both of these portable ultrasound systems, solar powered and AI-enabled diagnostics, have an unprecedented low-infrastructure demand and reduced carbon footprint of moving a patient to care. Similarly, AI-enabled mobile diagnostic vans, like the ones utilized by non-profits in Southeast Asia, are capable of taking diagnostics and triaging to populations in remote areas. These efforts presented significant reductions on something as simple as best practice fuel utilization or subsequently, less disposable medical supplies as the result of better diagnoses and fewer referrals. These are cases that demonstrate how AI can take two lenses of sustainability and provide better answers to both, particularly when one considers context in terms of needs and local infrastructure limitations.

4. APPLICATIONS OF AI-DRIVEN MEDICAL DEVICES

Artificial Intelligence (AI) has tremendously upgraded the performance of medical devices, especially in such spheres as wearable health devices, diagnostic equipment, and telemonitoring systems. This enables real-time health monitoring, early detection of disease, and improved patient care while making healthcare resources and sustainability truly efficient. The increasing dependency on AI-driven devices, therefore, is akin to a paradigm shift toward proactive and personalized healthcare, therefore reducing hospital visits, improving diagnosis accuracy, and enhancing remote patient management. Wearable Health Devices Wearable health devices now stand as among the most important innovations in modern healthcare, allowing for continuous monitoring of vital signs and AI-driven insights into the patient's health. Such devices procure and assess physiological data for the benefit of the healthcare practitioners and an individual, allowing them to make informed decisions dictating immediate health trends. Smart watches/Fitness Tracking Devices With the likes of Apple Watch, Fitbit, and Galaxy Smart watch, AI-enabled wearables have redefined personal health tracking, incorporating:

- **Heart rate monitoring:** AI detects any irregular heart rate, such as atrial fibrillation; thereby allowing any necessary preventive measures before this condition becomes critical and increases the risk of developing stroke.
- **Blood oxygen (SpO2) tracking:** Smart watches, using AI algorithms, have been able to detect the ups and downs of an individual's blood oxygen levels; helping them to identify any potential respiratory issues.
- **Sleep tracking:** AI-based analysis is done on sleep patterns in order to recommend ways to get better sleep quality and to detect conditions such as sleep apnea.
- **Activity and fitness tracking:** AI gives personalized recommendations on workouts, optimizing exercise routines based on user data.

Studies show that AI-based wearables favour preventive medicine by promoting healthy behaviours and prompting early actions in case of cardiac diseases.

Continuous Glucose Monitoring Devices for Diabetes Control.

The CGM approaches such as Dexcom G7, FreeStyle Libre, and Medtronic Guardian have thus revolutionized the diagnosis and care of diabetes through AI. Continuous monitoring of blood sugar is accomplished with a significant reduction in daily finger-prick testing. Notify patients of an increase or drop in blood glucose levels and what can be categorized as abnormal glucose. Integrate well with insulin pumps for automated insulin delivery, hence improving the management of diabetes and reducing complications. In terms of convenience, these AI-powered CGMs enable disease management through diabetes, which, in return, reduces hospital admissions for complications arising from diabetes. AI-Powered Wearable ECG and Blood Pressure Monitors AI-capable ECGs and BP devices feature real-time reporting on cardiovascular health, which allows the management of hypertension, arrhythmias, and heart disease. Reference points in this domain are the Withings BPM Core and the Omron HeartGuide for blood pressure monitoring, while Kardia Mobile ECG is AI-enabled and capable of identifying atrial fibrillation and other abnormalities. Such devices are also empowering continuous remote monitoring, allowing for early intervention and prevention of emergency admissions or long-term hospitalizations.

AI-Driven Diagnostic Equipment

Artificial intelligence is changing the diagnosis industry, making it more precise, speedy, and efficient. AI-powered diagnostic tools are oriented toward helping radiologists, pathologists, and cardiologists so that they can give the most accurate diagnoses faster than ever before possible via traditional methods. Medical Imaging AI. One of the areas than AI seems to have one of the biggest impacts would be diagnostics in medical imaging. Automated imaging analysis through the use of AI drastically improves detection rates for diseases like breast cancer, neurologic disorders, and fractures.

- **AI in Radiology:** AI models analyze medical scans (X-rays, CT scans, MRIs) with high precision. Google DeepMind AI is shown to diagnose diabetic retinopathy and lung cancer at the level of accuracy similar to a radiologist.
- **Neurological Implications:** AI trains by identifying vague changes in brain scans that reveal early signs of Alzheimer's disease, strokes, etc.
- **Breast Cancer Detection:** AI algorithms developed by MIT and IBM Watson Health were more accurate than human radiologists in detecting breast cancer in mammograms.

AI imaging will help produce fewer diagnostic mistakes, less repeat labs, faster and more accurate than existing classes of disease detection.

AI in Pathology and Histology

AI inclusive microscopy and pathology tools immensely improve the accuracy with which cancerous and infectious diseases are detected.

- **Pathology with AI-digital enhancement:** AI carries out analysis on biopsy samples, extremely predicting abnormal cell structures as a hallmark of cancer.
- **Models using deep learning:** AI provides support in skin cancer, leukemia, and cervical cancer diagnosis through the identification of malignant patterns in histological slides.

The introduction of AI in pathology will cut variation in diagnosing the disease and hasten the rate of detecting any life-threatening conditions.

Cardiology and AI-based Diagnostic Tools

AI brought about a revolution in cardiology by enabling surveillance heart health in real-time.

- **AI-enhanced interpretation of ECG:** AI powered devices like AliveCor's KardiaMobile detect heart disturbances like atrial fibrillation and ventricular tachycardia.
- **AI in echocardiography:** Ultromics, ETC., employs AI in performing analyses of heart scans to detect the early signs of heart disease, among others, with enhanced accuracy.

AI in cardiology, it has allowed early and accurate diagnosis in turning down admission, treatment planning, and better patient outcomes.

Telemonitoring and Remote Patient Monitoring (RPM)

AI-based remote patient monitoring, RPMs, and telemonitoring systems are revolutionizing chronic disease management, leading to lesser hospitalizations and enhanced access for patients to healthcare (Ahmed et.al, 2022). Telemedicine and AI-Based Remote Consultations The telemedicine platforms combining information technology and artificial intelligence deliver virtual consultations to allow patients to receive medical care without visiting the hospital physically. AI chatbots and virtual assistants assist in:

- **Symptom analysis:** AI-powered applications such as Babylon Health and Ada Health analyze the patient's symptoms and suggest the necessary medical action to be taken.
- **Predictive analytics:** AI analyzes the patient data to predict the progression of diseases so that any required interventions can be executed early against

chronic conditions. Telemedicine helps reduce hospital overcrowding and emissions from transportation while cutting down on healthcare costs to be more sustainable.

- **Remote Monitoring with AI**: AI-enabled biosensors and monitoring devices have been used in continuous monitoring of patients' health parameters, especially in geriatric care and chronic disease management.
- **Heart failure monitoring:** Biofourmis predicts any exacerbation of heart failures that do not require an immediate hospital stay based on real-time cardiac data it collects and analyzes.
- **Smart ICU monitoring:** AI-enabled systems operating at ICUs are connected 24/7. They were able to detect signals of patients' deterioration from the earliest stages and have proven themselves in reducing smart care associated with mortality.
- **AI in Respiratory care:** Smart inhalers for patients with asthma and COPD utilize AI for reviewing patterns of usage of the inhaler, feeding information that optimizes the delivery of medication in real time (T Venkat Narayana Rao et al., 2011).

AI in Chronic Disease Management

AI telemonitoring is particularly promising in the management of chronic diseases such as:

- **Diabetes:** AI-enabled CGM adjusts the insulin dosages based on real-time glucose readings.
- **Hypertension:** AI-powered wearables for detection of abnormal blood pressure trends with alerts for physician interference.
- **Parkinson's disease and Neurological Disorders:** AI monitors the patterns of tremors and the progression of the diseases, thereby making any necessary adjustments in the treatment plan (T Venkat Narayana Rao et al., 2022). .

These remote monitoring options provide higher quality of life for the patients, minimize the number of emergency visits, and further enable sustainability with lesser utilization of healthcare resources.

5. CASE STUDIES: SUCCESSFUL IMPLEMENTATION OF AI-DRIVEN MEDICAL DEVICES

1. AI-Powered Radiology Diagnostics: DeepMind's AI in Eye Disease Detection

Background

Medical imaging constitutes a source of diagnosis of various conditions, but interpretation of such is often time-consuming and variable due to human intervention. In collaboration with Moorfields Eye Hospital in the UK, DeepMind, a subsidiary of Google, developed an AI system capable of diagnosing more than 50 eye diseases through retinal scans.

Implementation and Challenges

DeepMind's AI was fed thousands of retinal scans and had capitalized on deep learning algorithms to find early signs of diseases like diabetic retinopathy and age-related macular degeneration (AMD). That was, however, the great challenge of assuring that the AI system meets standards for clinical validation and according to data privacy laws. It was met with initial scepticism by the healthcare professionals because of its indoctrination into the AI-domain of prescription and practice, thus requiring a sturdy review process.

Outcomes

The AI algorithm demonstrated a 94% accuracy rate in the diagnosis of eye diseases, placing it at par with the astute ophthalmologists in the field. Speedier diagnostics and lesser waiting time for treatment for patients.

Established a new trend in AI integration into the field of ophthalmology and other areas of diagnostics (T Venkat Narayana Rao et al., 2012).

2. AI-Driven Wearable Devices for Cardiac Monitoring: Apple Watch's ECG Feature

Background

Several CVDs are the major causes of death on a global level. If any rhythm disorders, especially AFib, can be picked up at the soonest, strokes and other complications can be avoided or greatly minimized. This real-time heart monitoring was introduced by Apple on its Apple Watch with the FDA-approved ECG app.

Implementation and Challenges

The ECG sensor of Apple Watch uses AI algorithms for signal processing as provided by the electrical signals from the heart. To begin with, concerns of false positives and the reliability of the device were constantly compared with traditional ECG machines. User education would be crucial to enable proper privacy advice to reduce undue panic because of too many litres of noncritical alerts.

Outcomes

- A study published in the New England Journal of Medicine found that Apple Watch's ECG feature detected AFib with 84% sensitivity and 99% specificity.
- The device enabled early intervention for many users, thus avoiding serious cardiac events.
- It was the first clear evidence demonstrating that consumer medical devices have the potential to alter chronic disease care.

3. AI in Remote Patient Monitoring: Biofourmis' AI-Based Health Monitoring

Background

Symptoms of chronic illnesses can become worse if the affected individuals are not monitored properly (Dewasiri et al., 2025). Biofourmis, a health analytics company, has developed Biovitals, an AI platform that aggregates patient data from wearables and predicts possible deterioration in their health.

Implementation and Challenges

Biovitals use AI to process real-time data from heart rate, respiratory rate, and activity levels to point out early signs of deterioration. In addition, ensuring that AI-based decision-making technology complied with regulatory mandates in the domain of health care raised another challenge. Moreover, integrating the system with already existing hospital IT infrastructure could yield pivotal technical challenges.

Outcomes

- The system was used in hospitals across the United States, reducing rates of hospital readmissions by 38%.
- Through AI-enabled monitoring, medical professionals could intervene on time and spread considerable impact on patient outcomes.
- It showed the feasibility of scalable, AI-driven remote monitoring solutions.

4. AI-Assisted Robotic Surgery: Da Vinci Surgical System

Background

Minimally invasive surgery reduces patient recovery time and postoperative complications. The Da Vinci Surgical System, developed by Intuitive Surgical, utilizes AI to augment surgical precision in severely sensitive operations.

Implementation and Challenges

The AI Robotic: The AI-assisted robotic system provides intraoperative imaging, motion scaling, and tremor reduction to enact a successfully done surgery. However, their high prices and steep learning curves for surgeons have prevented rapid adoption. Also, AI systems were supposed to strictly conform to safety protocols.

Outcomes

- More than 10 million surgeries have been performed globally with the Da Vinci robots.
- AI-supported laser-enhancing technology has improved surgical precision by 30% against complications.
- Robotic-assisted surgery is now a standard modality for rendering complex surgical procedures such as prostatectomies and cardiac valve repairs.

5. AI in COVID-19 Detection and Management: BlueDot's Early Warning System

Background

All revertible alterations were rendered in conformity to the introduction due to the gustiness of ordinary protective measures against COVID-19. An artificial intelligence-based early warning system created by the Canadian company BlueDot detected the outbreak in Wuhan well before it became officially reported.

Implementation and Challenges

The system put together BlueDot was using natural language processing (NLP) and machine learning for the survey of global health reports, airlines, and social media for establishing early symptoms of the spread of the disease (Gadde et.al, 2020). The scope consisted of keeping data clean and addressing the plight arising from the unpredictable nature of viral mutations.

Outcomes

- The AI system predicted the outbreak nine days before it became publicly announced by the World Health Organization.
- Health organizations used BlueDot's insights to prepare for COVID-19's global spread.
- The case showed us how AI can play a major part in future preparedness for pandemics.

6.AI-Powered Mobile Ultrasound for Maternal Health: Butterfly iQ in Sub-Saharan Africa

Background:

Prenatal imaging is seldom available in rural and lower-resourced areas because of the expensive equipment or the lack of trained radiologist. The Butterfly iQ is a handheld AI-powered ultrasound system that plugs into a smart-phone and uses deep learning algorithms to provide guidance for non-expert users to acquire and interpret ultrasound images.

Implementation and Challenges:

With support from the Bill & Melinda Gates Foundation, the Butterfly iQ was implemented in sub-Saharan African countries, particularly Uganda and Nigeria, in an effort to enhance maternal health. Short trainings prepared community health workers to operate the devices and monitor fetal development, placenta position, and high-risk pregnancies.

Outcomes:

- Enhanced early detection of complications - for example, breech position and placenta previa.
- Reduced rates of maternal death in places that had limited access to imaging previously.
- Reduced costs of care delivery overall, and lessened need for patient transport to urban hospitals.
- Demonstrated the potential of AI to democratize diagnostics in underserved areas.

7. Smart Inhalers for Asthma and COPD Management: Propeller Health

Background:

Asthma and COPD are chronic respiratory diseases often exacerbated by inappropriate medication adherence. Propeller Health developed a smart inhaler system that engages sensors and AI algorithms to monitor inhaler usage and environmental factors (e.g., pollen, air quality).

Implementation and Challenges:

Implemented in multiple health systems in the U.S., and piloted in parts of Europe, the Propeller system pairs mobile apps to remind patients about doses and identify patterns that might lead to exacerbations. It has prompted some initial concerns about privacy for patients, and affordability for patients.

Outcomes:

- Cut down on emergency visits by as much as 50% in trial groups.
- Increased medication adherence by more than 60%.
- Helped clinicians adjust their plan of care based on real-time AI consumption metrics.
- Environmental data integration helped proactively prevent flare-ups based on air quality—showing the value of AI in preventive care and sustainability by lessening acute care needs.

8. AI-Powered Breast Cancer Screening: Lunit INSIGHT MMG in South Korea

Background:

Accuracy of breast cancer screening is an important public health issue, especially where a radiologist's availability is limited. South Korea's national health screening program used Lunit INSIGHT MMG, which is an AI based mammography analysis tool.

Implementation and Challenges:

The system that was rolled out to over 300 hospitals, processed mammogram images and identified localized areas of suspicion, including walls of truly evacuated breast tissue, very accurately. There were early challenges with radiologist acceptance and regulatory clearances.

Outcomes:

- Realized over 90% sensitivity in identifying early-stage tumours.
- Reduced the cognitive diagnostic burden on radiologists by 30% so that they could focus on complex or difficult cases.
- Reduced average patient waiting times for results and the number of repeat images obtained, which reduced patient radiation exposure, decreased patient costs, and reduced healthcare expenditures.
- Demonstrated that AI could improve diagnostic accuracy while improving resource utilization in a manner congruent with ecological sustainability and operational sustainability.

6. CHALLENGES AND ETHICAL CONSIDERATIONS IN AI-DRIVEN MEDICAL DEVICES

The renamed NHS and IoMT are reshaping the healthcare environment, setting the stage for a multitude of critical challenges and ethical dilemmas regarding the integration of AI in these technologies. At this point, given that I am an AI technology that also offers substantial improvement to service delivery, one cannot forget the fact of a possible downfall in its use whose prudence lies in developing such safety nets for data privacy, ethical dilemmas, and legal compliance with respect to safe and effective implementation. This section will discuss the key issues in this regard, focusing particularly on data privacy and security risks, ethical considerations regarding AI, and legal and regulatory frameworks surrounding these economic innovations.

6.1 Data Privacy and Security: Risks and Regulatory Aspects

Integration of artificial intelligence in medical devices will collect an enormous range of sensitive patient data that's sent and acted upon. These often IoMT-connected devices may access personal health records of a patient, salary history, biometric data, and real-time monitoring data. This wealth of information is highly sensitive and, if not managed properly, becomes a risk to the patients' privacy.

6.1.1 Risks to Data Privacy

Beyond that, several threats also accompany AI in health care; the most pressing among them is the at least somewhat groundless concern regarding data security. The Internet of Medical Things increases exposure of interconnected medical devices to risks, hence more entry points to hospital systems. Hackers might attack the Internet of Medical Things or IoMT using unsecured devices, thereby gaining unauthorized access and leaking some sensitive health information(Mastrototaro et al ., 2000). It exposes patient data to any intruder while compromising the very security measures put in place to avert such access, thus facilitating fraud and identity theft-a grave alternative with possible medication tampering. Mostly, these applications, especially IoMT-enabled devices, use the Internet for transmitting patient data, thus exposing more risks of interception and hacking. Since patient information is extremely private, improved security mechanisms, such as encryption and two or more factor(s) of authentication, should be adopted to control access to it from unauthorized personnel.

6.1.2 Regulatory Frameworks and Compliance

Healthcare data is strictly regulated to prevent potential risks to privacy and any unwarranted storage, transmission, or access. Respectively, the collection and processing of personal data, including health data, are overseen by the GDPR in the EU. Healthcare personnel must comply with the GDPR by ensuring necessary design and implementations of data protection procedures before any sort of collection or processing of patients' personal data. Moreover, patients retain the right to further revoke that granted consent at any such point in time. Likewise, HIPAA governs the interactions of healthcare providers, insurers, and business associates with the protected health information of patients in America. HIPAA enumerates certain security and privacy standards meant to protect EHRs, while still providing for administrative, technical, and physical safeguards. The devices can perform installations on almost any territory in varying countries, having diverse data privacy legislation entailing contradictory national laws being imposed. One of the inseparable issues in the way forward is determining what provides such a collection of consensual privacy prescription on a universal dimension for medically-based AI devices.

6.2 Ethical Issues: Biases, Consent, and Transparency

AI systems, especially used in medical devices, are drummed by the data on which they train. If, for example, that data is not complete, not representative, or just plain biased, outcomes can, therefore, become distorted and contribute to disparities in health service delivery.

6.2.1 Biases in AI Systems

One of the gravest ethical concerns in AI-mediated medical devices is the possibility of bias in decision-making. AI models depend on huge databases to train algorithms that can diagnose diseases, recommend treatments, and simulate patient outcomes. If these databases are not sufficiently rich or diverse, AI systems can develop biased algorithms which favour some demographics over others disproportionately.

For example, an AI model which has been trained primarily on data coming from one ethnic group may be challengingly applicable to patients from other ethnic backgrounds. This may lead to incorrect diagnosis, suboptimal treatment recommendation, and eventually poorer health outcomes for underrepresented groups. The issue of bias gets more difficult when AI systems get deployed into real-world settings without exhaustive validation for varying patient populations.

6.2.2 Informed Consent

Informed consent is another ethical dilemma revolving around AI-assisted medical interventions. In traditional practices, doctors explain to patients, ideally in layman's language, the risks and benefits of therapies and procedures the patient chooses from. However, once the process is infused with AI, patients may not really understand how the technology functions or how decisions are made. This is particularly pertinent in using AI-assisted diagnostic tools, where patients might not notice the algorithms that went into assigning a diagnosis. The problem of "black box" AI systems makes it extremely difficult, if not impossible, for healthcare providers to inform their patients about how the basis of their decisions were arrived at; thus, an intense challenge arises around the question of whether truly informed consent could be granted.

6.2.3 Transparency and Accountability

Transparency in the AI system has to do with issues of consent. There has to be that degree of transparency whereby AI-driven medical devices are trusted by both healthcare providers and patients based on what the reasoning process of the AI was. This is especially critical when, in case an AI recommendation goes wrong, there are life-and-death implications for patient outcomes. The black-box nature of AI decision-making algorithms is another ethical challenge. Treatment harm with no understanding of the rationale by either the patient or the provider diminishes the possibility of trust. This possibility of attributing blame is especially relevant if such mistakes lead to serious adverse patient events, be they medical malpractice or adverse events (Jamil et al., 2024). Is this liability, for instance, on the part of the manufacturer, the provider, or the AI system? Such inquiries call for clear accountability frameworks regarding AI technologies that end up being deployed.

6.3 Legal and Compliance Aspects: Regulations and Future Directions

Now, the built-in complexities of developing a framework that could provide assurance about the safety, efficacy, and ethical acceptability of AI-driven technologies havc become an increasing concern for regulators to address. While there do exist some applicable regulations, the swift spread of AI within health care has demanded a rethink in various aspects of regulatory mechanisms.

6.3.1 Current Regulatory Frameworks

Different agencies in some countries control AI-based and other medical devices. In the US, the FDA regulates all medical devices, including software systems across different platforms. Guiding documents have surfaced from this agency to navigate the approvals of AI-based medical devices with respect to their safety and efficacy before entering into marketing approval. The European Medicines Agency, along with national authorities, ensures the safety of devices through the Medical Device Regulation and In-vitro Diagnostic Regulation. These regulations involve post-market surveillance for continued evaluation of safety even with cleared devices after they´re in the market. Keeping these devices safe and effective over time would, therefore, remain an ongoing concern for regulators since AI models have the ability to adapt and reformulate based on incoming new data.

6.3.2 Future Policy Directions

Regulators must also necessarily put provisions for future-proofing the regulations to cater to advancing science owing to the quick-moving nature of AI and IoMT. There is growing demand for more dynamic, flexible regulatory frameworks that can meet the evolving capabilities of AI technologies. For instance, regulators may consider a need to comprise continuous oversight mechanisms to assess the safety and efficacy of clinically used AI devices post-market, in line with their learning and evolving capabilities. Such scrutiny could evaluate the function and efficacy of algorithms and enhance manufacturers' accountability for the performance of their devices on an ongoing basis. Another aspect will be forming an international consensus that creates globally harmonized standards for AI in healthcare applications. Another stress factor is that IoMT networks are global, and patient data is constantly crossed among borders. The formulation of globally accepted regulation guidelines will also help lessen discrepancies in practices and ensure the safety, security, and ethical correctness of AI-based medical aids.

6.4 Cost and Employment Concerns in AI-Driven Healthcare

One of the under-appreciated yet significant ethical issues associated with AI incorporation into health is the economic impact of technology on health systems and jobs. While AI has the potential to save costs long term in healthcare through automation, predictive analytics, and decreased waste, the initial cost of AI-based medical devices can be expensive especially for small clinics and rural hospitals or under-resourced health systems. Also, the automation of diagnostic, monitoring, and even surgical functions raises questions about job displacement. If radiologists, lab technicians, administrative staff, or even some aspects of nursing are replaced by machine learning systems that only require an initial training investment, will these roles be diminished or eliminated? While AI has the promise of making healthcare delivery less expensive and more efficient, at what cost is that efficiency achieved if it ultimately leads to unemployment or de-skilling where skilled professionals are forced to undertake precarious employment? From an ethical perspective, adjustment to these changes will necessitate retraining, an equitable approach to implementation, and perhaps policies that lessen negative socioeconomic consequences of such decisions. The need for cost-efficient healthcare must be balanced with sustainable employment, so that AI becomes a support not a substitute for human labor in health delivery.

7. FUTURE DIRECTIONS IN AI-DRIVEN MEDICAL DEVICES

Artificial intelligence-enhanced medical devices and the internet of medical things shall drive an intelligent, connected, and sustainable future of healthcare that will promise better patient care, efficient resource usage, and lower environmental pollution. With the evolution of sustainability within global healthcare settings, opportunities for innovation and transformation—such as integration of renewable energies, new-generation AI devices, and new decentralized healthcare models—will determine the nature and characteristics of this future.

7.1 Emerging Opportunities

7.1.1 Renewable Energy Integration in AI-Driven Medical Devices

Healthcare is one of the most energy-intensive industries: hospitals and medical facilities require vast amounts of electricity to provide patient care, data storage, and keep medical equipment running. AI-powered medical devices continuously collect data and rely on data processing in the Cloud, therefore placing a huge demand on energy. One of the key sustainability hopes for the future lies in integrating renewable energy systems into AI-powered medical devices so that operational costs are dropped and carbon footprints from medical facilities are reduced. Pathways for Advancements:

- **Solar-Powered Medical Devices:** AI-supported wearable health monitors and remote diagnostic tools powered by solar energy can enhance health care accessibility in rural or underdeveloped regions where access to grid electricity is erratic.
- **Battery-Free IoMT Devices:** Advances in energy harvesting technologies such as thermoelectric or kinetic energy systems will now see medical wearables and implantable devices being powered by human heat or motion keeping, thereby requiring battery replacements routinely.
- **Sustainable Data Centers:** AI-powered predictive analytics and telehealth services place tremendous demands on data processing. The healthcare industry is shifting towards green cloud computing that runs energy-efficient data centers powered by wind and solar energy to back AI in medical diagnostics and monitoring.

With the incorporation of renewable energy technologies, AI-powered medical devices will reduce their dependence on fossil fuels while additionally rendering healthcare more environmentally sustainable, providing workers with unceasing access to medical care in remote regions.

7.1.2 Next-Generation AI Devices: Enhancing Precision and Automation

The next generation of AI-based medical devices will not only be more precise but will also be autonomous and require little human intervention(Moxley-Wyles et al., 2020). Transcending into the realm of futuristic technologies, AI-enabled robotic surgery, precision-based treatment, and self-updating diagnosis systems are going to define patient care. Some Key Advances in AI Medical Devices:

- **AI-based Robotic Surgery:** The intelligent surgical robots of the future will incorporate machine learning with computer vision to enhance precision in procedures so as to reduce risks and provide to patients improved recovery time. These include robotic systems that have applications in minimally invasive surgery and risk reduction during and after.
- **AI-Powered Personalized Medicine:** Using AI's power to analyze vast genomic and biomedical data, it becomes more common to tailor treatment plans to individual patients. Machine-learning algorithms help predict the trajectory of diseases in order to develop individual treatment based on genes.
- **Self-Improving AI in Diagnostics:** Past AI models have to be trained each time they are updated, but next-generation AI systems continuously improve and learn directly from any new data collected from patients, thereby improving their accuracy with the passing of time without requiring manual intervention.

While this combines the aspect of autonomy in conjunction with precision by these devices, it is a wondrous sight that the next generation of AI devices will be inundated with virtually all of the aforementioned elements-therefore reducing medical mistakes, accelerating efficiency, and providing better patient outcomes, leading to a sustainable and effective healthcare system by leap and bounds.

7.1.3 Decentralized and Remote Healthcare Models

The centralized model of hospital treatment must migrate to decentralized healthcare, whereby the patient will receive treatment and maintaining monitoring through remote AI-driven devices that truly reduce congested hospitals, improve resource allocation, and reduce carbon footprints related to hospital visits. The Function of AI in Promoting Decentralized Healthcare:

- **Telehealth and Remote Patient Monitoring:** AI-based telehealth partners will make for live consultations, continuous monitoring of chronic situations, and AI-assisted diagnostics, hence cutting down on the number of hospital visits; also, patients will be paid less for their travelling expenses.
- **Mobile Clinics run by AI:** The introduction of mobile AI diagnostic units in far-off regions with little healthcare will open up the opportunity for patients to access expert opinions quickly and lessen the environmental burden of travelling to seek help.
- **AI Home-Based Diagnosis:** Wearable and implantable AI devices will allow the patient to monitor diabetes, hypertension, and cardiovascular disease at home and hence reduce hospital admissions and healthcare costs(John et al., 2023).

Through IoMT and AI, health would be delivered closer to where the patients are; this will provide not only increased accessibility or convenience but also seen to relieve substantial stress on the health infrastructure and environment.

7.1.4 Hospital-in-the-Home (HITH) Model Enabled by AI

One promising opportunity propelled by AI and the Internet of Medical Things (IoMt) is the emergent "Hospital-in-the-Home" (HITH) model. This model transforms healthcare delivery by moving a large proportion of care and monitoring out of the hospital setting and into the patient's home and does so while maintaining the value proposition of the care (V Sidda Reddy, et al.,2017).

AI-enabled wearable sensors, remote diagnostic telemetry devices and suite platforms for enhanced continuous monitoring of patients, are allowing healthcare organizations to provide care for patients at home real-time. For example, AI smart beds, fall detectors and long-distance telemetry ECG's are now allowing care for post-operative patients, monitoring the elderly, and providing chronic care management for patients in their home. Reduced need for long hospital stays, reduced likelihood of hospital-acquired infections and reduced utilization of hospital infrastructure and beds are significant advantages of HITH.

From the perspective of environmental sustainability, HITH all together minimizes energy use, water use, and medical waste in traditional hospitals while catering to patient comfort and experience, and qualification of outcomes for the healthcare organization. As healthcare systems are forced into a strained capacity at hospitals, the incorporation of AI into models of home care adds a scalable environmental sustainability alternative.

7.2. Vision for the Future: AI as the Foundation of a Sustainable Healthcare System

Long-term, there exists a grand vision for AI in healthcare-an ecosystem where healthcare is intelligent, proactive, and resource-efficient. AI-enabled medical devices will be critical in predictive care, allowing for the helming of ethical AI and global accessibility. Predictive Healthcare and Preventive Health Systems AI development in the long term would represent a gradual move from reactive treatment into predictive care and preventive care. AI algorithms should analyze prodromal production and gene susceptibility to modern biological databases in real time to predict diseases before any show-up. Key Developments in Predictive Healthcare:

- **AI-driven Early Disease Detection:** AI-based imaging systems would detect cancers, cardiovascular diseases, and neurodegenerative disorders at earlier stages, thus improving treatment success rates.
- **Wearable AI Health Coaches**: Devices laden with AI will provide live feedback on lifestyle choices and exercise patterns in real-time scenarios, concurrently averting the onset of chronic diseases.
- **Epidemiological AI Models:** AI, through the analysis of global health trends, is behind the early prediction of disease outbreaks and prompt intervention to allocate scarce resources efficiently.

7.2.2 Ethical AI and Responsible Innovation

The virtue of bias, transparency, and accountability is going to be at the center stage of ethical concerns arising from the advances in AI in subsequent durations (Thakre & Patel, 2024). The conception of AI of tomorrow would revolve around strong ethical frameworks promoting fairness, inclusivity, and explain ability. Strategies for Ethical AI in the Future:

- **Bias-Free AI:** AI developers will ensure bias-free algorithms through increased datasets representation across various demographics.
- **Explanatory App for AI in Healthcare**: Medical devices will be designed with a transparent decision-making model that allows the healthcare provider and the patient to understand the results of the decision made by the algorithms.
- **Responsibility and Governance of AI:** Regulatory agencies will draw very strict rules concerning AI in medical devices to ensure patient safety, protection of data privacy, and adherence to existing ethics standards.

7.2.3 Global Healthcare Accessibility Through AI

AI will assist in bridging the gap in healthcare disparities and making health care both available and efficacious to the world. Creating AI-driven medical devices will, therefore, afford developing countries high-quality, economical solutions, so it is on par with other expensive infrastructure in the future. Key Global AI Healthcare Initiatives: AI-Powered Telemedicine for Rural Areas: AI-focused mobile health units will bring specialist consultations to underserved communities(Bommu et al., 2022). Low-Cost AI Diagnostics: Portable AI-based diagnostic tools will cut the costs of screening and early disease detection in low-income regions.

8. KEY TAKEAWAYS: AI AS A CATALYST FOR SUSTAINABLE HEALTHCARE

8.1 Enhancing Healthcare Efficiency with AI-Driven Devices

The AI-enabled medical devices improve the system's efficiency through automated essential processes, lower human error scope and enhance patient paths of care. The important innovations here consist of:

- **AI Diagnosis:** Machine learning models support in gaining accuracy while detecting disease and reducing waiting time for treatment and delayed decisions.
- **Predictive Analytics:** Anticipate the outbreak of disasters, deterioration in patient condition and allocate resources with AI-powered decision-making, which enables immediate action.
- **Telemedicine and remote patient monitoring:** IoMT-based devices are used for constant monitoring of the patient to avoid unnecessary healthcare visits and enhance health outcome.

AI technologies cut down operational inefficiencies thus reducing healthcare costs and streamlining workflows and ensuring medical care stays sustainable and accessible for all (T Venkat Narayana Rao et al.,2015).

8.1.2 AI-Driven Medical Devices and Environmental Sustainability

AI-enabled Medical Devices and Environmental Sustainability Sustainability has become a topic of great importance in contemporary healthcare (Vishwakarma et al., 2025). The AI-driven reduces energy consumption, improves resource optimization, and minimizes medical waste:

- **Energy-efficient Medical Devices:** AI-enabled wearables and implants are supposed to run using renewable energy sources, hence cutting down on the carbon footprint. ·
- **Smart Resource Management**: AI provides help to hospitals to optimize water and electricity use, minimizing overall energy consumption.
- **Reduced Waste in Healthcare**: Intellect medicines and prediction models tend to work more efficiently to manage inventories to reduce the overuse of medical disposables and pharmaceuticals.

These developments reinforce how AI-enabled devices are not only improving healthcare delivery but also making it more environmentally responsible.

8.1.3 Ethical and Regulatory Considerations in AI Healthcare

Ethics and law are some of the significant challenges in AI existence within the health sector that would, however, have to be solved responsibly. The following are the key concerns:

- **Data Privacy & Security:** Protection of patient data becomes crucial for AI medical devices as they rely on appropriate health information. This calls for stringent encryption mechanisms, expressions of block chain, as well as other compliance mechanisms like the GDPR.
- **Bias in AI Models**: AI systems should be trained on diverse datasets in order to limit any racial, sex or social-economic biases that would otherwise compromise diagnosis accuracy and treatment recommendations.
- **Regulatory Compliance:** Governments and international organizations must develop comprehensive AI regulation for safety of patients, ethical deployment of AI, and transparency of decisions. It is important that these challenges are addressed to build trust and ensure fairness and responsibility in using AI-driven medical devices.

8.2. Reinforcing the Chapter's Thesis: AI as the Future of Sustainable Healthcare

This chapter has contended that AI-driven medical devices are one of the spearheads of healthcare innovation, bringing forth an efficient, accessible, and sustaining future of care. However, for the advancement to Homo sapiens, several steps must be taken.

8.2.1 Bridging the Gap between AI and Healthcare Professionals

This integration of AI into healthcare systems shouldn't happen without collaboration. These include the interaction between:

- Medical professionals and AI developers to check that AI technologies meet real-world clinical demands.
- Regulatory authorities and healthcare providers so that policies are created that balance innovation against ethical responsibility.
- Researchers and environmental scientists to supply the integration of AI with sustainable energy solutions in order to lessen the ecological impact of healthcare.

8.2.2 Expanding AI-Driven Healthcare Access to Underserved Communities

Expanding AI-Driven Healthcare Access to Underserved Communities AI is remarkably equipped with the potentials to bridge healthcare disparities by enabling access to remote and underserved population groups. Some of the initiatives include:

- Use of AI-enabled mobile clinics in low-income areas to provide real-time diagnoses and telehealth consultations.
- Developing AI wearables at low cost to enable the patient to self-monitor chronic conditions, reducing the need for frequent hospital visits.
- AI-powered language translation for medical consultations enables communicating across language barriers in global healthcare.

There is a prospect of taking medical care beyond urban hospitals through the adoption of AI and IoMT technologies, such that no one shall be left behind in the provision of quality medical care.

8.2.3 Investing in the Future of AI-Driven Sustainable Healthcare

Healthcare systems will have to put continuous investment in AI R&D to tackle the challenges of regulation and the ethics in order to ensure long-term sustainability. The future of AI-assisted medical apparatuses will be determined by: ·Funding AI and sustainability research towards efficiency maximization and minimizing healthcare's carbon footprint. ·Establishing stronger governance frameworks for AI to guarantee ethical, fair, and responsible deployment of AI.

9. CONCLUSION

AI-driven medical devices transforming the healthcare space into a more intelligent, interconnected force are no longer mere miracle visions for the future-they're foregrounding today's agenda. AI is shaping the way for a future which is sustainable, patient-centered, cost-effective, and environmentally respectful in the following applications: predictive analytics, smart diagnostics, remote monitoring, and energy-efficient medical apparatus. Whichever way you choose to interpret AI, it presents exciting opportunities, even if they require careful management of data security, ethical AI implementation, and regulatory compliance. For sustainable healthcare, the success of AI depends upon the following: Continuous innovation and investments in AI-based medical technologies. More robust regulations and ethical frameworks protecting patient rights. Widespread adoption of AI-based solutions in urban and remote settings. In essence, the synergy between AI and IoMT in the healthcare interface is more than an innovation-it is a necessity in building a future characterized by efficient, ethical, and environmentally sustainable healthcare. Thus, from now onwards, these devices have taken a turn towards the better-enhancement of efficiency, security, and sustainability of AI-driven medical devices giving advancements in patient outcomes in the current world scenario at reduced costs and lesser environmental impacts. Innovation through AI offers a scalable, cost-effective, and eco-friendly solution as modern healthcare systems put increased pressure from both escalating patient demands, limited resources, and environmental challenges. This comes to the conclusion of this chapter and revisits the key themes, challenges, and future directions-how AI and IoMT technology change healthcare sustainability.

REFERENCES

Ahmed, T., Mosaddeque, A., Hossain, A., Twaha, U., Rowshon, M., & Babu, B. (2022). The Dynamics of AI and Automation in Financial Forecasting, Human Resources Planning, and Resources Optimization for Designing an Effective National Healthcare Policy. *Journal of Business Insight and Innovation, 1*(2), 78–88.

Benjamens, S., Dhunnoo, P., & Meskó, B. (2020). The state of artificial intelligence-based FDA-approved medical devices and algorithms: An online database. *NPJ Digital Medicine, 3*(1), 118. PMID: 32984550

Bommu, R. (2022). Ethical Considerations in the Development and Deployment of AI-powered Medical Device Software: Balancing Innovation with Patient Welfare. *Journal of Innovative Technologies, 5*(1), 1–7.

Damoah, I. S., Ayakwah, A., & Tingbani, I. (2021). Artificial intelligence (AI)-enhanced medical drones in the healthcare supply chain (HSC) for sustainability development: A case study. *Journal of Cleaner Production, 328*, 129598.

Dewasiri, N. J., Rathnasiri, M. S. H., & Karunarathna, K. S. S. N. (2025). Artificial Intelligence-Driven Technologies for Environmental Sustainability in the Healthcare Industry. In *Transforming Healthcare Sector Through Artificial Intelligence and Environmental Sustainability* (pp. 67–87). Springer Nature Singapore.

Gadde, S. S., & Kalli, V. D. R. (2020). Applications of Artificial Intelligence in Medical Devices and Healthcare. *International Journal of Computer Science Trends and Technology, 8*, 182–188.

Gu, W., Wang, J., Zhang, Y., Liang, S., Ai, Z., & Li, J. (2024). Evolution of digital health and exploration of patented Technologies (2017-2021): Bibliometric Analysis. *Interactive Journal of Medical Research, 13*(1), e48259. PMID: 38991212

Jamil, A. S. A., Khalil, A., & Yunus, M. M. (2024). Empowering Predictive Maintenance of Medical Equipment Through AI-Driven Condition Monitoring. *Biomedical Engineering: AI and Technological Innovations*, 53.

John, M. M., Olsson, H. H., & Bosch, J. (2023). Towards an AI-driven business development framework: A multi-case study. *Journal of Software (Malden, MA), 35*(6), e2432.

Kalli, V. D. R., & Jonathan, E. (2023). AI-Driven Energy Management Solutions for Healthcare: Optimizing Medical Device Software. *International Journal of Advanced Engineering Technologies and Innovations, 1*(01), 157–174.

Manickam, P., Mariappan, S. A., Murugesan, S. M., Hansda, S., Kaushik, A., Shinde, R., & Thipperudraswamy, S. P. (2022). Artificial intelligence (AI) and internet of medical things (IoMT) assisted biomedical systems for intelligent healthcare. *Biosensors (Basel)*, *12*(8), 562. PMID: 35892459

Mastrototaro, J. J. (2000). The MiniMed continuous glucose monitoring system. *Diabetes Technology & Therapeutics*, *2*(1, Supplement 1), 13–18. PMID: 11469627

Moxley-Wyles, B., Colling, R., & Verrill, C. (2020). Artificial intelligence in pathology: An overview. *Diagnostic Histopathology*, *26*(11), 513–520.

Razdan, S., & Sharma, S. (2022). Internet of medical things (IoMT): Overview, emerging technologies, and case studies. *IETE Technical Review*, *39*(4), 775–788.

Reddy, V. S., Rao, T. V., & Govardhan, A. (2017). Data mining techniques for data streams mining. Review of computer engineering studies, 4(1), 31-35.

Thakre, D., & Patel, J. (2024, November). The Advancements and Benefits of AI-Assisted Robotic Surgery. In *2024 2nd DMIHER International Conference on Artificial Intelligence in Healthcare, Education and Industry (IDICAIEI)* (pp. 1-5). IEEE.

Rao, T. V. N. (2011). 5g technologies–An anecdote of network service for the future. Journal of global research in computer science, 2(7), 164-170.

Rao, T. N., Tejaswini, V., & Preethi, K. (2012). Defending against web vulnerabilities and cross-site scripting. *Journal of Global Research in Computer Science*, *3*(5), 61–64.

Venkat Narayana Rao, T., & Govardhan, A. (2015). Efficient segmentation and classification of mammogram images with fuzzy filtering. *Indian Journal of Science and Technology*, *8*(15), 1–8.

Venkat Narayana Rao, T., Unnisa, A., & Sreni, K. (2022). Medicine recommendation system based on patient reviews. *Int J Sci Technol Res*, *9*, 3308–3312.

Vishwakarma, L. P., Singh, R. K., Mishra, R., & Kumari, A. (2025). Application of artificial intelligence for resilient and sustainable healthcare system: Systematic literature review and future research directions. *International Journal of Production Research*, *63*(2), 822–844.

Chapter 6
Enhancing Patient Outcomes With Machine Learning in Healthcare Predictive Analytics

Manthan Ghosh
https://orcid.org/0000-0002-2020-0670
G.H. Raisoni College of Engineering, India

Deepa Das
G.H. Raisoni College of Engineering, India

ABSTRACT

The increasing availability of healthcare data, coupled with advances in machine learning (ML), has enabled significant progress in early disease prediction and diagnosis. This chapter explores how ML enhances early disease prediction and diagnosis by analyzing structured and unstructured healthcare data, such as EHRs, genomics, wearable sensors, and imaging. It covers key ML techniques—logistic regression, decision trees, SVMs-applied to clinical tasks. The chapter also discusses-es feature engineering, handling imbalanced data, and improving interpretability. Real-world use cases in detecting cancer, diabetes, cardiovascular, and neurological diseases are presented. Integration into clinical workflows is explored, showing how predictive models improve diagnostic accuracy, reduce hospital readmissions, and support preventive care. Ethical concerns such as data privacy, algorithmic bias, and the need for explainable AI are addressed. Future directions include advancements in personalized medicine, responsible AI deployment, and predictive models supporting global health initiatives.

DOI: 10.4018/979-8-3373-2545-3.ch006

1 INTRODUCTION

Coma, a profound and prolonged state of unconsciousness that can arise from traumatic brain injuries, strokes, metabolic disorders, or severe infections, represents one of the most complex and challenging conditions in healthcare, requiring continuous monitoring, specialized interventions, and multidisciplinary care. Patients in this state lose voluntary motor and verbal functions, leaving them highly dependent on caregivers and medical professionals for survival and recovery (Stevens & Bhardwaj, 2006; Plum & Posner, 1982; Levy et al., 1981). The management of coma requires vigilant monitoring, as even subtle physiological changes can indicate either neurological improvement or deterioration (Latha et al., 2023; Yimer et al., 2024; Sheikdavood et al., 2023; Manikandan et al., 2025). Delayed detection of these changes can significantly reduce the chances of positive patient outcomes, making continuous and accurate monitoring a critical element in coma care. If we talk about the limitations of traditional monitoring; Historically, the monitoring of coma patients has been based on human observation and periodic manual assessments such as Glasgow Coma Scale (GCS) scoring (Jain et al., 2025), pupillary response tests (Dawidziuk et al., 2025), or bedside imaging (East et al., 2025; Ge et al., 2025). While these methods remain clinically valuable, they present inherent limitations:

a) Resource constraints: Continuous bedside monitoring requires extensive manpower and healthcare resources.
b) Human error and oversight: Subtle changes in neurological activity may be missed due to fatigue or workload.
c) Lack of real-time data: Periodic assessments cannot capture dynamic physiological fluctuations critical for timely interventions.

These challenges highlight the urgent need for advanced technologies capable of providing reliable, real-time insights.

Artificial Intelligence (AI) and Machine Learning (ML) are increasingly being recognized as transformative enablers in addressing these challenges (Davoudi et al., 2018; Kim et al., 2024; Tu et al., 2022). By analyzing vast amounts of multimodal healthcare data—ranging from neuroimaging and electroencephalography (EEG) signals to electronic health records (EHRs) and wearable sensors—ML algorithms can identify subtle patterns that may precede clinical deterioration or signal recovery potential. Unlike traditional methods, AI-driven predictive analytics offers: Real-time monitoring and intelligent alert systems are transforming coma care by enabling clinicians to make timely, evidence-based decisions when even subtle changes in a patient's neurological state occur. Automated assessments powered by machine learning significantly reduce the cognitive and administrative burden on healthcare professionals, allowing them to focus more on patient-centered interventions rather than manual data interpretation. Predictive modeling, using advanced algorithms trained on multimodal data such as EEG signals, neuroimaging, and vital signs, offers powerful insights into recovery trajectories, helping to tailor personalized treatment strategies that optimize outcomes for each patient. By integrating predictive analytics seamlessly into existing coma care workflows, healthcare teams gain the ability to detect early biomarkers of brain activity linked to recovery potential, anticipate complications before they escalate, and deliver proactive, adaptive interventions that redefine how patients in critical states are managed and supported. Similarly, wearable sensors capturing continuous vital signs can feed into predictive models that forecast complications such as respiratory distress or cardiac instability (Taherdoost, 2024). By shifting from reactive care to proactive intervention, AI-enabled systems improve diagnostic accuracy, reduce hospital readmissions, and support preventive measures—all of which enhance patient outcomes in line with the broader goals of predictive healthcare. As AI technologies become embedded in critical care settings, ethical and practical considerations must also be addressed. Ensuring data privacy, mitigating algorithmic bias, and enhancing the interpretability of predictive models are essential for building trust among clinicians and patients. Moreover, AI-driven coma care aligns with the future vision (Sheikdavood et al., 2023; Kim et al., 2024; Tu et al., 2022; Taherdoost, 2024) of personalized medicine, where data-driven insights guide tailored interventions that maximize recovery potential and quality of life.

Coma represents one of the most critical neurological conditions encountered in modern medicine, characterized by a prolonged state of unconsciousness in which patients are unable to respond to their environment. Unlike other clinical scenarios, coma care is particularly complex because of the severe limitations in communication. Patients in this state are unable to articulate pain, discomfort, or physiological distress. In many cases, coma is also accompanied by partial or complete paralysis, which further diminishes the ability to detect subtle changes in patient well-being. This inability to convey vital information often results in delayed interventions and missed opportunities for timely treatment. Consequently, the traditional methods of monitoring coma patients—based largely on manual observation and periodic recording of vital signs—face serious limitations. Historically, coma patient care has relied heavily on human observation and bedside assessments by physicians and nurses. Trained clinicians use clinical tools such as the Glasgow Coma Scale (GCS) to evaluate patient responsiveness through eye movements, verbal ability, and motor responses. Although valuable, this method depends on human presence, expertise, and periodic observation, which may not be feasible in all healthcare settings, especially in resource-constrained environments.

Manual monitoring also introduces the possibility of human error and subjectivity. For example, the subtle deterioration of brain activity or fluctuations in autonomic functions like heart rate, blood pressure, or oxygen saturation might not be immediately recognized. Furthermore, monitoring by humans is typically intermittent rather than continuous, leaving critical gaps in patient data. A rapid deterioration, such as hypoxia, seizures, or arrhythmias, could occur between two rounds of observation, and if unnoticed, the outcome could be catastrophic. The lack of real-time insights is another drawback. Most hospitals and critical care units use conventional monitors for parameters such as pulse rate, blood oxygen level, or respiratory activity. While these machines provide continuous readings, they often lack advanced analytic capability. The responsibility of interpretation lies with the attending staff, who may be simultaneously managing multiple patients. In high-intensity critical care wards, this increases the likelihood of delayed response to emergencies. In addition, the financial and human resource burden of maintaining constant bedside care is significant. A 24/7 critical care environment requires a large pool of skilled nurses, doctors, and technicians, which is not always sustainable. This creates a pressing need for innovative, technology-driven solutions that can augment human monitoring, reduce workload, and deliver reliable real-time information. The Case for AI-Enabled Monitoring Systems: Artificial intelligence (AI) and machine learning (ML) technologies present an unprecedented opportunity to transform coma patient care. Unlike traditional monitoring, AI-enabled systems can continuously process multimodal physiological data in real time and detect early patterns of deterioration before they become clinically obvious. The strength of AI lies in its capacity to integrate diverse data streams—such as vital signs, electroencephalography (EEG), neuroimaging scans, and biochemical markers—from multiple sensors and medical devices. By analyzing such high-dimensional data, machine learning algorithms can identify trends, anomalies, and predictive indicators of complications that may not be apparent to human observers. For example, in coma patients, subtle changes in brainwave patterns measured through EEG may indicate seizure onset, ischemic damage, or recovery progression. An AI system trained on large datasets can recognize these shifts far more quickly and consistently than manual observation. Similarly, ML algorithms can analyze variations in heart rate variability, oxygen saturation, and respiratory rhythm to predict the onset of cardiac arrest, infection, or ventilator-associated complications. The integration of AI into remote monitoring also opens possibilities for continuous, 24/7 observation beyond the hospital environment. This is particularly beneficial in long-term coma care, where patients may be discharged to rehabilitation centers or even home care under supervision. With AI-enabled wearable or implantable devices transmitting data to cloud platforms, neurologists and caregivers can remotely assess patient status in real time, receive alerts on critical events, and adjust treatment plans proactively.

One of the most powerful aspects of applying Artificial Intelligence (AI) in coma care is its ability to provide predictive analytics. Traditional monitoring systems in intensive care units are largely reactive in nature—they record and alert clinicians only after a critical event such as a sudden drop in oxygen or blood pressure has already occurred. This reactive approach leaves very limited time for intervention and often forces healthcare providers into crisis management. AI, on the other hand, offers the possibility of moving from reaction to anticipation, enabling clinicians to predict the likelihood of complications before they fully develop. For instance, sepsis prediction is a crucial area where AI shows significant promise. By analyzing multiple variables such as body temperature patterns, white blood cell count, and subtle changes in heart rate variability, AI models can detect the earliest signs of systemic infection. Such early detection is vital, as sepsis is one of the leading causes of mortality in comatose patients. Similarly, AI-driven systems can help assess the risk of respiratory failure. Continuous analysis of oxygen saturation levels, tidal volume trends, and ventilator parameters allows the system to forecast deterioration several hours in advance. This provides clinicians with the opportunity to adjust ventilator settings, administer medications, or prepare for advanced airway interventions before the patient's condition reaches a critical stage. AI is also highly effective in detecting neurological deterioration. Sophisticated algorithms can process real-time EEG data to determine whether a patient is at risk of brain death, experiencing hidden (subclinical) seizures, or showing early signs of neurological recovery.

For AI-enabled systems to be truly impactful, they must be designed with scalability, usability, and affordability in mind. Coma care is not limited to advanced hospitals in developed nations. In fact, a significant burden exists in low- and middle-income countries where access to intensive care units is limited. A well-designed system should therefore operate on portable devices, consume minimal power, and integrate with widely available equipment. From a usability standpoint, these systems must feature intuitive interfaces that can be operated by nurses and technicians without advanced training in AI or data science. Alerts, dashboards, and decision-support outputs must be simple, actionable, and seamlessly integrated into existing hospital workflows. Affordability is another critical dimension. Many cutting-edge AI solutions in healthcare are prohibitively expensive. The challenge lies in designing monitoring platforms that leverage cost-effective sensors, cloud infrastructure, and open-source ML frameworks to minimize costs without compromising reliability. Public–private partnerships, government support, and collaborations with academic institutions could further facilitate the large-scale adoption of such solutions. While the promise of AI-enabled coma monitoring is immense, several ethical and practical considerations must be addressed. Continuous data collection raises concerns about patient privacy and medical data security. Sensitive information such as brain scans, EEG recordings, and genetic markers must be encrypted, anonymized, and stored in compliance with international healthcare regulations such as HIPAA and GDPR. Another concern is algorithmic bias. If the AI models are trained on datasets that are not representative of diverse populations, the predictions may be inaccurate for certain groups of patients. Ensuring fairness, transparency, and explainability in AI algorithms is essential to building trust among clinicians and families.

The future of coma care lies in the fusion of AI, biosensors, and telemedicine. Research is already progressing toward integrating wearable neural sensors, implantable glucose monitors, and smart ventilators with AI-driven platforms. With the rise of Internet of Things (IoT) technologies, a connected ecosystem of devices can create a holistic view of patient health. Furthermore, advanced techniques such as deep learning and reinforcement learning may enable systems that adapt dynamically to each patient's condition. Over time, AI platforms could learn the unique physiological "signature" of a coma patient and personalize predictions with greater accuracy. Another promising direction is the use of neuroimaging combined with AI for prognosis. By analyzing MRI and CT scan data alongside EEG, AI may one day provide more reliable predictions of recovery outcomes, helping families and clinicians make informed decisions about long-term care. The limitations of traditional coma patient monitoring underscore an urgent need for transformation in critical care practices. The inability of coma patients to communicate their distress makes timely and accurate assessment a formidable challenge. Manual observation, though essential, falls short in providing the round-the-clock precision required for optimal outcomes. AI-enabled remote monitoring systems offer a paradigm shift by enabling continuous, real-time, and predictive insights into patient health. Through multimodal data integration, advanced ML algorithms, and remote accessibility, such systems can bridge the communication gap, enhance clinical decision-making, and ultimately improve survival and recovery prospects. For this transformation to succeed, scalability, affordability, ethical safeguards, and clinical integration must be prioritized. With these in place, AI can become not just a supplementary tool but a central pillar of coma care, delivering hope and improved quality of life to some of the most vulnerable patients in healthcare.

1.2 Research Objectives

The central objectives of this research are:

- To develop an AI-enabled remote monitoring framework for coma patients that integrates multimodal healthcare data (vital signs, EEG, imaging, and sensor-based parameters).

- To design and implement machine learning algorithms capable of providing real-time predictive analytics for early detection of critical health events and recovery potential.
- To address the limitations of traditional monitoring by reducing reliance on manual assessments and minimizing the risk of human error or oversight.
- To enhance clinical decision support through interpretable AI models that provide actionable insights for healthcare professionals.
- To ensure scalability, affordability, and usability of the proposed system for deployment in both advanced healthcare facilities and resource-constrained settings.
- To evaluate the ethical and practical considerations of AI integration, including data privacy, algorithmic bias, and transparency in predictive decision-making.

1.3 Significance of the Study

This study is highly significant as it introduces an advanced AI-enabled remote monitoring system that directly addresses the long-standing limitations of traditional coma care, which often depends on manual observation, subjective interpretation, and delayed clinical assessments that may compromise timely treatment. By harnessing the power of machine learning–based predictive analytics, the proposed system provides continuous, real-time insights into multiple aspects of patient health, thereby empowering clinicians to recognize early warning signs, intervene promptly, and ultimately improve both short-term and long-term clinical outcomes. Importantly, it bridges the critical communication gap for patients in comatose states who are unable to articulate their condition or discomfort, ensuring that their evolving needs are detected and managed with precision. At the same time, the system reduces the workload and decision-making pressure on healthcare professionals by automating data interpretation and streamlining care pathways. Designed with scalability, affordability, and ethical responsibility at its core, this research not only advances predictive healthcare analytics but also establishes a strong foundation for the future of personalized, data-driven medicine in critical care environments, offering hope for improved recovery trajectories and enhanced quality of life for patients and their families.

1.4 Structure of the Paper

The remainder of this paper is structured as follows: Section 2 presents a comprehensive review of the existing literature on coma care, remote monitoring technologies, and the role of AI in predictive healthcare analytics. Section 3 details the methodology adopted for designing and developing the proposed AI-enabled remote monitoring system. Section 4 reports the experimental results and system performance outcomes. Section 5 provides an in-depth discussion of these findings in relation to existing approaches and their implications for clinical practice. Finally, Section 6 concludes the paper and highlights potential directions for future research, including the broader application of AI-driven predictive models in critical care.

2 LITERATURE SURVEY

Advances in healthcare predictive analytics, powered by machine learning (ML) and the Internet of Things (IoT), are transforming critical care, particularly in monitoring non-communicative patients such as those in a coma. This literature survey reviews four thematic strands: (1) ML-based predictive models for neurological outcomes in comatose or critically ill patients; (2) IoT-enabled remote monitoring systems for coma care; (3) hybrid architectures combining ML and IoT for enhanced predictive monitoring; and (4) challenges and ethical considerations in deploying these systems—thereby setting the stage for your research (Davoudi et al., 2018; Kim et al., 2024; Tu et al., 2022; Taherdoost, 2024) .

A primary thrust in recent research has been developing ML systems that augment traditional clinical scales such as GCS, CAM, and RASS to predict acute brain dysfunction—delirium or coma—and neurological outcomes. The MANDARIN model (Contreras et al., 2025) (Mixture-of-Experts Framework for Dynamic Delirium and Coma Prediction) reflects a cutting-edge ML approach for ICU patients. Leveraging a 1.5-million-parameter mixture-of-experts neural network, MANDARIN integrates temporal and static data to predict acute brain dysfunction (ABD) 12–72 hours in advance. Trained on data from nearly 93,000 patients and validated on multi-institutional cohorts, it achieved significantly better performance than traditional assessments, such as GCS, CAM, and RASS (AUROCs around 87–93% for coma prediction). This clearly demonstrates the potential of ML to support proactive, real-time decision support in ICU settings. Similarly, transformer-based models trained on Electronic Health Record time series, such as those by Silva et al., have achieved mean AUROCs of 0.953 for binary and multi-class classification of brain acuity (coma, delirium, death, or normal), signalling remarkable promise for real-time ICU applications (Silva et al., 2023). EEG signals are extensively researched for outcome prognostication. One study employed a multiscale deep neural network—combining convolutional neural networks (CNNs) (Dahake et al., 2025; Sinha et al., 2021; Ghosh & Das, 2024; Das et al., 2023; Das et al., 2025) with long short-term memory (LSTM) networks—to analyze continuous EEG trends and demographic features in patient's post-cardiac arrest. The model's performance improved notably over time (AUC rising from 0.83 at 12 hours to 0.91 at 66 hours), and achieved high sensitivity and specificity in predicting neurological outcomes (Zheng et al., 2021). Further benchmarking deep learning against traditional ML models (Sinha et al., 2021; Ghosh & Das, 2024; Das et al., 2023) such as logistic regression and random forests reveals distinct advantages. In predicting post-anoxic coma outcomes using EEG, CNNs outperformed both logistic regression and random forest models in robustness (Ghosh et al., 2023; Ghosh, 2022; Pradhan et al., 2024) and predictive accuracy, especially under data artifacts (Pham et al., 2022). Another deep learning-based approach focusing on EEG responses to auditory stimuli showed that convolutional neural networks (CNNs) could extract interpretable patterns to predict long-term awakening and survival at three months, specifically using data from the first day of coma under controlled sedation (Aellen et al., 2023). Integrating multiple data modalities can further improve prediction. For instance, the BEEGees real-time framework for predicting coma recovery incorporates EEG and ECG time-series along with clinical variables, employing multimodal deep learning architectures (e.g., spectrogram-based feature extraction) to forecast neurological recovery 72 hours post-cardiac arrest (Reyna et al., 2023).

Parallel to ML developments, numerous studies leverage IoT technologies to enable continuous, low-cost, remote physiological monitoring—especially critical when patients are unable to communicate or convey discomfort. Yimer et al. proposed a highly affordable IoT-based monitoring system (< USD 30) for coma patients in developing settings. The system integrates sensors for heart rate, temperature, blood pressure, eye movement, and body position, operating with an energy-efficient microcontroller and integrating GSM for alerts even without internet access. A locally hosted app provides on-site data access (Latha et al., 2023). Several studies demonstrate practical IoT implementations using common microcontroller platforms, like: Lokesh et al. developed an IoT coma monitoring system using wearable sensors (heartbeat, pulse, physiological signals) and integrated them into an ESP8266 NodeMCU platform. The system tracks transitions from vegetative to minimally conscious states, reducing dependency on constant caregiver supervision. Other implementations focus on recording vital signs (pulse, temperature, eye blinks, motion) via ESP32 or Arduino microcontrollers, transmitting data through platforms like ThingSpeak, with alerts via GSM or ThingSpeak notifications. The summarized comparison in the "IoT-Based Coma Patient Monitoring System" outlines various MCU platforms (RPi, ESP32, Arduino Uno), sensor arrays, power consumption, and connectivity mechanisms (cloud, GSM vs. internet-only). It highlights the value of hybrid systems capable of operating with intermittent internet via local processing and GSM alerts (Meghana, 2020; Lulseged Yimer et al., 2024). The Nevon Projects video demonstrates a Raspberry Pi–based system that monitors heart rate, temperature, humidity, urine output, and motion, deploying an LCD and IoT connectivity for data display. Emergent architectures combine IoT sensors with ML-based anomaly detection. For instance, systems leveraging motion, heart rate, oxygen saturation (MAX30100), temperature, and an XGBoost model to predict anomalies; these notify caregivers via a web-based interface (Singh et al., 2024). Another model uses IoT to collect real-time data and deep learning for detection of critical events in comatose patients, although details are limited (Venkatesan et al., n.d.).

Although recent research has made strides in both IoT monitoring and ML-based predictive models, there are relatively fewer implementations that tightly integrate real-time IoT sensing with ML for predictive analytics in coma care. Based on the surveyed works - IoT systems offer vital sign and behavior monitoring but often lack predictive intelligence. ML models trained on clinical and EEG data provide powerful predictive insights but typically operate offline and rely on standard equipment. To bridge this gap, hybrid systems that couple sensor-based data collection (e.g., via ESP32 / Arduino / wearable sensors) (Ghosh & Das, 2024; Ghosh & Bora, 2025) with real-time ML inference—deploying predictive models at the edge or through cloud integration—represent a promising direction. Such architectures can support on-site alerts and proactive intervention, especially in low-resource environments. The reviewed literature consistently illustrates the critical importance of early detection of neurological decline or recovery, which can empower interventions that improve patient outcomes. The use of ML in dynamic coma prediction (e.g., MANDARIN) stands to aid clinicians with forecasting and resource management. Similarly, IoT systems strengthen continuous monitoring capabilities, autonomy, and coverage in critical care—but must ensure reliability, data security, and accuracy. Ethical aspects—especially data privacy, algorithmic bias, and transparency—must guide deployment. Interpretable ML models and safeguarding of sensitive physiological data are paramount to building clinician and patient trust.

While there is strong evidence for ML's efficacy in predicting coma outcomes, these systems are often retrospective and disconnected from real-time monitoring infrastructures. Conversely, IoT approaches offer continuous, low-cost health tracking but generally lack predictive intelligence. Few studies integrate real-time IoT data acquisition with on-site or cloud-based ML inference, especially in resource-limited settings. Moreover, there is a need for systems that emphasize affordability, scalability, and interpretability while maintaining predictive accuracy. This research is positioned to fill these gaps by developing an AI-enabled IoT monitoring system tailored to coma patients—leveraging multimodal sensors, low-cost hardware (Arduino/ESP32), real-time predictive ML, and secure, interpretable decision support. Table 1 gives the comprehensive summary of the recent work.

However, the discussion would be more impactful if supplemented with practical use cases from clinical or healthcare settings that illustrate how these issues manifest in real-world scenarios. Artificial Intelligence (AI)–enabled Remote Patient Monitoring (RPM) has become a cornerstone of modern healthcare delivery, offering real-time insights, predictive analytics, and personalized intervention strategies. Below are eight prominent use cases with concrete examples and references that highlight how AI is being integrated into clinical practice, the enablers that drive adoption, and the barriers that remain. The following section gives the detailed use case scenario of AI based monitoring devices on:

a) Chronic Disease Management and Early Detection
b) Cardiac Arrhythmia Detection and At-Home Monitoring
c) Post-Operative Monitoring and Hospital-at-Home Care
d) Remote Diagnostic Support and Imaging
e) Neurological Monitoring in ICU and Coma Care
f) Mental Health and Safety Monitoring
g) Home Safety and Risk Prediction for Elderly Care

Chronic Disease Management and Early Detection: Traditional monitoring approaches often rely on intermittent clinic visits and subjective symptom reporting, which can delay detection of clinical deterioration. AI-powered remote monitoring provides a paradigm shift by enabling continuous surveillance, early detection of warning signs, and proactive care delivery. One example is Boston Scientific's HeartLogic™ platform (Gardner et al., 2018), which integrates data from multiple implantable device sensors to monitor patients with heart failure. The AI algorithm analyzes inputs such as thoracic impedance, heart sounds, respiration rate, and patient activity. Clinical studies have demonstrated that the system can predict heart failure decompensation up to 34 days before hospitalization—allowing physicians to adjust medications, optimize fluid balance, or schedule follow-up visits before acute deterioration occurs. Another impactful application is Biofourmis' Biovitals™ (Chen et al., 2019) platform, which combines wearable biosensors with machine learning to monitor heart failure patient's post-discharge. In a multi-center study, the platform reduced hospital readmissions by 50%, underscoring the importance of AI-based predictive models in reducing costly and potentially preventable hospitalizations. Similarly, Dexcom's Continuous Glucose Monitoring (CGM) systems (Ghosh & Bora, 2025), when enhanced with predictive algorithms, enable patients with diabetes to anticipate hypoglycemic or hyperglycemic events before they occur. When integrated into closed-loop insulin delivery systems (sometimes called "artificial pancreas"), these devices provide automated adjustments that significantly improve glycemic control, reduce patient burden, and minimize risks of severe complications. Luscii's Virtual Ward (van Uum et al., 2025) demonstrates scalability in chronic care management. Widely adopted in Dutch hospitals, it enables clinicians to monitor COPD, diabetes, and heart failure patients remotely by combining vital signs monitoring with patient-reported data. During the COVID-19 pandemic, Luscii was critical in enabling safe early hospital discharges while ensuring ongoing surveillance.

Cardiac Arrhythmia Detection and At-Home Monitoring: Cardiac arrhythmias, especially atrial fibrillation (AFib), are often asymptomatic and can remain undetected until they result in severe complications such as stroke. Continuous and accurate monitoring is critical but impractical with conventional hospital-based tools like Holter monitors. AI-enhanced wearables are bridging this gap by providing real-time arrhythmia detection in everyday settings. The Cardiogram app, integrated with consumer wearables like the Apple Watch and Fitbit, applies deep learning algorithms to photoplethysmography (PPG) data collected by the devices. Studies show that Cardiogram can detect atrial fibrillation with over 90% accuracy, which is comparable to clinical-grade ECG devices. By bringing diagnostic accuracy to consumer-grade wearables, AI democratizes access to preventive cardiovascular monitoring. AliveCor, another leading example, offers smartphone-compatible ECG devices that integrate AI algorithms for rhythm classification. These devices provide on-demand cardiac assessment, enabling patients to capture symptomatic events, while the AI model helps differentiate between benign and concerning arrhythmias. Such applications reduce unnecessary emergency visits while ensuring that high-risk cases receive timely medical attention (Nechita et al., 2024; Bahrami Rad et al., 2024) .

Post-Operative Monitoring and Hospital-at-Home Care: At a systems level, the Mayo Clinic's "Advanced Care at Home" program uses AI-enabled RPM to support patients recovering at home. The program achieved a 15% reduction in readmission rates compared to conventional hospital care. Patients receive clinical-grade monitoring in their home environment, supported by centralized virtual care teams and AI-driven analytics (Maniaci et al., 2024).

Remote Diagnostic Support and Imaging: AI also plays a pivotal role in extending diagnostic capabilities beyond the hospital. In low-resource settings where radiologists and cardiologists may be scarce, AI tools embedded in portable devices provide crucial diagnostic support. A landmark innovation is the AI-powered stethoscope developed by Eko Health in collaboration with Imperial College London. This device combines acoustic and ECG data, analyzing them within 15 seconds using AI algorithms to detect heart failure, valve disease, and arrhythmias. Studies show that the device significantly improves detection rates compared to traditional auscultation alone (van der Harst & Nathoe, 2025). Such devices empower clinicians in primary care and remote settings to make early, accurate diagnoses.

Neurological Monitoring in ICU and Coma Care: A significant breakthrough comes from the Cleveland Clinic and Piramidal's AI model for EEG monitoring. This system analyzes continuous EEG data streams and can detect seizures or deteriorating brain activity within seconds—a process that typically takes hours for manual review. By reducing detection times, the AI system enables rapid interventions such as medication adjustments, thereby preventing complications and improving recovery potential (Collins et al., 2025).

Mental Health and Safety Monitoring: Mental health care often lacks objective monitoring tools, making early detection of crises challenging. AI-based RPM is emerging as a solution to monitor behavior, physiological markers, and environmental factors. A novel framework proposed in recent research combines non-invasive RFID sensors with AI algorithms to monitor patients in mental health facilities. The system predicts vital signs up to three hours ahead and classifies patient activities such as agitation or pacing. In one case involving a PTSD patient, the system provided early alerts of escalating agitation, enabling timely intervention and preventing a clinical emergency (Tsvetanov, 2024). This demonstrates the potential of AI to bring predictive, proactive safety measures into psychiatric care—addressing both patient well-being and staff safety.

Home Safety and Risk Prediction for Elderly Care: Elderly patients often face high risks of falls, medication errors, and hospitalizations due to chronic conditions. AI-powered RPM tools provide a means of enhancing safety and independence at home. Cera, a UK-based healthcare provider (Windle et al., 2024; Cavendish et al., 2024), has developed AI tools that predict health deterioration and fall risks in elderly patients.

Table 1. Summary Table

Study / System	Technology	Key Focus	Outcome / Insight	Ref
MANDARIN (ICU brain dysfunction predictor)	ML (deep networks)	Early coma/ delirium prediction	AUROC ~87–93%, real-time ICU use	(Contreras et al., 2025)
Transformer models on EHR	ML (Transformer, CatBoost/XGB)	Real-time ABD classification	AUROC ~0.953	(Silva et al., 2023)
CNN+LSTM on EEG data	DL	Neurological outcome post-cardiac arrest	AUC up to 0.91	(Sinha et al., 2021)
DL vs regression/ RF	DL vs ML	Robust outcome prediction from EEG	DL outperforms others	(Das et al., 2023)
Multimodal deep learning	DL (EEG + ECG + clinical)	Predict recovery post-cardiac arrest	Effective in challenge context	(Zheng et al., 2021)
Low-cost IoT system (<$30)	Arduino, sensors, GSM	Resource-limited coma monitoring	Affordable, local/ cloud sync	(Latha et al., 2023)
ESP8266 wearable system	IoT	VS to MCS monitoring	Reduced manual oversight	(Meghana, 2020)

continued on following page

Table 1. Continued

Study / System	Technology	Key Focus	Outcome / Insight	Ref
ESP32/Arduino + ThingSpeak	IoT	Vital signs and alerting	Remote monitoring capability	(Lulseged Yimer et al., 2024)
Raspberry Pi prototype	IoT	Multi-parameter monitoring	Motion, vitals with IoT display	(Meghana, 2020)
IoT + XGBoost system	IoT + ML	Predict anomalies	Real-time anomaly alerts	(Singh et al., 2024)
IoT + deep learning detection	IoT + DL	Comatose patient detection	Emerging hybrid integration	(Venkatesan et al., n.d.)
IoT + deep learning detection	HeartLogic™, Biofourmis, Dexcom	Chronic disease management	Early detection, reduced hospitalizations	(Ghosh & Bora, 2025; Gardner et al., 2018; Chen et al., 2019)
Low-cost IoT system	Cardiogram, AliveCor	Cardiac monitoring	Enhanced arrhythmia detection at home	(Nechita et al., 2024; Bahrami Rad et al., 2024)
IoT + deep learning detection	Current Health, Mayo Clinic	Post-op / hospital-at-home	Lower readmission rates, confidential care	(Maniaci et al., 2024)
IoT + XGBoost system	AI stethoscope, remote X-ray analysis	Diagnostics & Imaging	Faster, more accurate diagnostics	(van der Harst & Nathoe, 2025)

3 METHODOLOGY

3.1 System Design

The development of the remote monitoring system for coma patients required a multi-faceted approach that carefully considered the unique needs and constraints of this patient population. To meet the defined requirements, the selection of hardware components was a critical step.

The following section provides an explanation for this particular aspect.

3.2 Hardware

The Figure 1 depicts the proposed architecture and the block diagram of the method. All the sensor connection is shown in the diagram. All the components are already discussed in the previous section. Usability testing involving healthcare professionals and caregivers was conducted to refine the interface and ensure that it meets the needs of the end users effectively. The design of the graphical user interface (GUI) prioritised simplicity and clarity. Through minimum effort, individuals are able to obtain real-time patient data, get alerts, and begin contact. The Figure 2 depicts the designed prototype.

Figure 1. Block Diagram

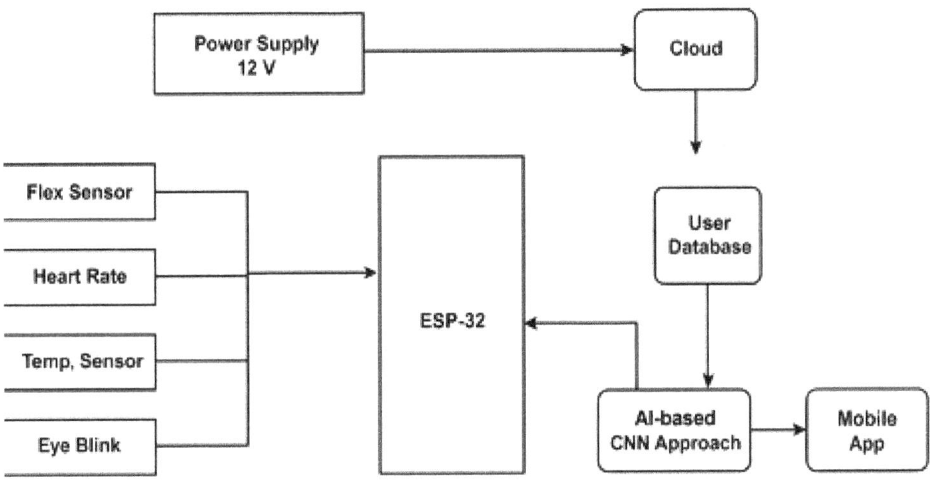

Sensors & Display: The four sensors included in the proposed system serve the purpose of gathering the necessary parameters for system monitoring. The present system utilises the following sensors:

1. Mussel movement sensor: The device in question is a sensor designed to quantify the degree of bending or deflection. The sensor is affixed to the surface, and the resistance of the sensor element may be altered by the act of flexing the surface. This sensor utilises the principles of the bending strip theory to detect variations in resistance that occur when the strip undergoes bending. The measurement may be conducted via any controller. This sensor operates in a manner akin to a variable resistance sensor due to its ability to alter resistance when subjected to bending. The variation in resistance is contingent upon the levelness of the surface, hence influencing the potential alteration in resistance.

Figure 2. Prototype

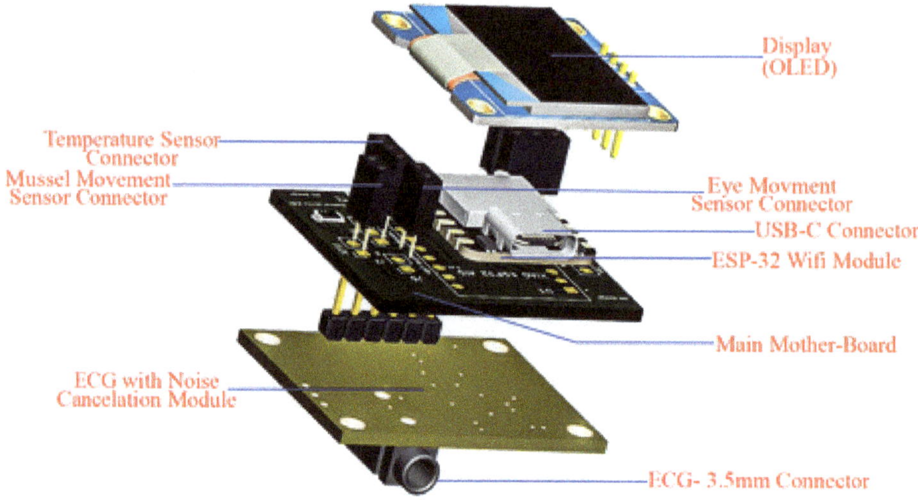

2. ECG Sensor: The AD8232 module, which stands for Electrocardiogram (ECG), is an integrated circuit (IC) that is widely used in the field of healthcare for the purpose of monitoring and quantifying the cardiac electrical activity. The device is specifically designed to catch and analyse the electrical impulses produced by the cardiac muscle's contractions, hence offering significant data for healthcare and medical purposes.

The AD8232 ECG module finds use in a range of applications, including heart rate monitoring, arrhythmia detection, stress testing, sleep monitoring, as well as other medical research and diagnostic endeavours. Cardiac activity monitoring is of paramount importance in contemporary healthcare technology as it enables the non-invasive assessment of cardiovascular function and contributes to the identification and management of heart-related ailments. All the notation and representation depict in the below Figure 3.

Figure 3. Basic ECG Notations

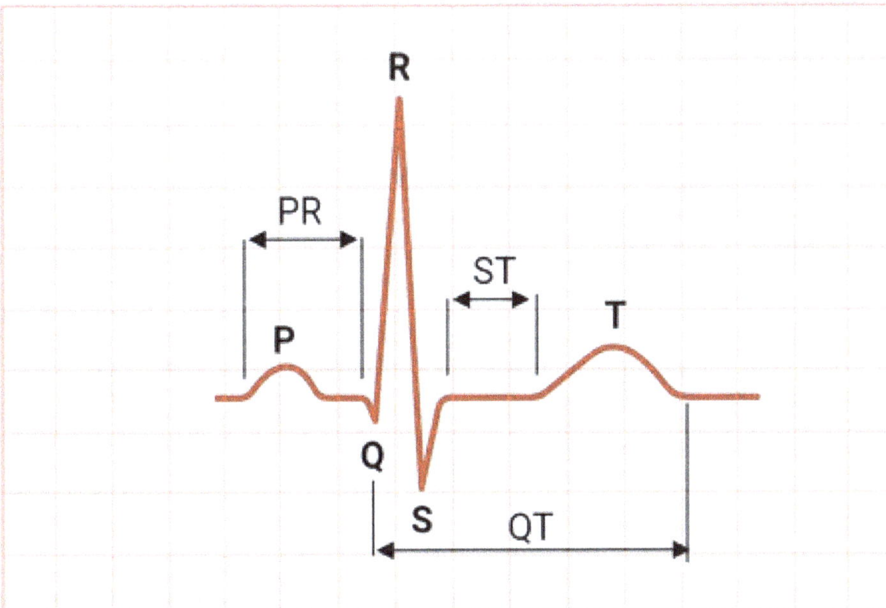

3. Temperature Sensor: The DS18B20 is a digital temperature sensor that has been specifically engineered to accurately detect temperature with a high degree of accuracy. The DS18B20 digital temperature sensor exhibits many notable features and qualities.
   a. The DS18B20 sensor has a digital output that enables convenient integration with microcontrollers, microprocessors, and digital circuits, allowing for straightforward temperature readings. The use of a single-wire communication protocol facilitates the process of wiring and the transport of data.
   b. The sensor in question is renowned for its exceptional temperature accuracy, consistently achieving a precision of around ±0.5°C throughout the temperature range of -10°C to +85°C. The storage of calibration data in the memory of the sensor serves to enhance its accuracy.

In general, the DS18B20 digital temperature sensor is well recognised for its versatility and precision in digitally detecting temperature. As a result, it has gained significant popularity in many temperature-sensing applications, particularly those that use microcontrollers and digital interfaces.

4. Eye Movement Sensor: The term "eye movement detection" refers to the procedure of observing and examining the patterns of ocular motion exhibited by an individual. The method entails monitoring the location and movement of the eyes in order to get knowledge about an individual's visual focus, cognitive functions, and physiological reactions. Multiple techniques and technologies are used for the purpose of detecting eye movement.

The utilisation of eye movement detection encompasses a wide range of applications, such as conducting usability testing for websites and applications, investigating reading patterns, examining cognitive processes, diagnosing medical conditions like sleep disorders and neurological diseases, enhancing virtual reality experiences, and enhancing human-computer interfaces. The aforementioned factor plays a pivotal part in comprehending the intricacies of human behaviour and the dynamics of human-environment interactions.

3.3 Software

In order to facilitate the input of patient data into our database, it is necessary for the administrator to do this task. Upon completion, each user will be assigned a unique 'password' and 'username' by the administrator. The Blynk database is used in this study. Subsequently, it is necessary to use the data acquired by the application. After a user has completed the registration process on our application, their data has the potential to be saved inside our database. To enhance the intelligence and diagnostic capabilities of the system, an AI-enabled Convolutional Neural Network (CNN) approach has been integrated. This deep learning model is trained on physiological signals and vital parameters collected from coma patients to automatically identify patterns indicative of critical health changes. Unlike conventional threshold-based monitoring, CNNs are capable of extracting spatial and temporal features from raw data, thereby providing a more nuanced and accurate prediction of potential complications. For example, anomalies in heart rate variability, respiratory patterns, or brainwave signals can be classified in real time, allowing caregivers and medical professionals to be alerted before conditions worsen. This AI-driven layer not only improves the system's precision and reliability but also transforms the monitoring platform into a proactive decision-support tool, bridging the gap between raw data collection and actionable clinical insights.

4 SYSTEM ARCHITECTURE

A robust and scalable system architecture was designed to facilitate seamless integration of hardware components. This architecture ensures real-time data collection, processing, and transmission. The system was architected to be user-friendly, with an intuitive interface to accommodate both healthcare professionals and caregivers with varying levels of technical expertise.

The block diagram of the proposed model is given below.

We are treating this as a classification problem (detecting health condition/disease vs normal, or between age groups).

Algorithm:

1. Preprocessing
   a. Normalize features (Temp, P, R, T, PR, ST, QRS)
   b. Label encoding (e.g., 0=Healthy, 1=Disease or AgeGroup1, AgeGroup2)
2. Train-test split (80–20 or k-fold cross-validation)
3. Model: Convolutional Neural Network (CNN) applied to structured ECG features
4. Training: Adam optimizer, Binary Cross Entropy /Softmax loss
5. Validation: Monitor accuracy and AUC
6. Testing: Evaluate on unseen data

The provided block diagram in Figure 2 illustrates the sequential progression of a device including a power supply, a voltage regulator, and a micro-controller. The micro-controller is interconnected with various peripheral devices, including sensors, a display, and an alarm system, among others. In the event that the patient engages in movement, the preset course of action entails the direction of movement being identified, together the associated messages that are to be presented. Simultaneously, a letter is created via the use of postman, taking into consideration the patients' health condition and their sensitivity, in order to register their email address. The purpose of this is to cater to those who are experiencing a comatose state, rendering them unable of verbal communication, self-expression, or physical mobility. Beginning with patient registration and concluding with data record management. In order to get access, individuals are required to complete a registration process by giving necessary information to our designated administrator.

The data collected is shown in Table 2 and Table 3. In the below mentioned table P(mV) is the amplitude of the P-Wave which represents the electrical depolarization of the atria of the heart, R(mV) is the amplitude of the R-Wave which represents reflects depolarization of the central mass of the ventricles, T(mV) is the amplitude of the P-Wave which represents ventricular re-polarization, P-R(Sec) is the time delay between P & R Wave, S-T(Sec) is the time delay between S & T Wave, QRS(Sec) is the time interval between Q,R & S point and Temp. referes to average body temperature. All the amplitudes are in milli Volts, Intervals are in second and the temperature is in degree celcius. In the present investigation, data was collected from two distinct age groups. One group consists of individuals aged 20 to 30, while the second group comprises those aged 45 to 55. As an illustrative example, we provide two distinct sets of patient data originating from two distinct groups. The data collection was conducted in partnership with "AMRDH Solutions Pvt. Ltd." and strict measures were taken to ensure the confidentiality of the data. The whole of the data inside our programme is observable, however just by the administrator who has the requisite authorization. By disclosing personal information, it becomes possible to access an individual's unique data and compile a comprehensive report. This application will aid in assessing if any progress has been made.

5 RESULT ANALYSIS

The system demonstrates a strong capability to continuously monitor the physiological activities of patients while providing meaningful insights into their overall health status. This makes it a reliable tool for healthcare professionals, enabling them to better assess and understand a patient's condition in real time. A key advantage of the system lies in its affordability, reliability, and lightweight design, ensuring that it can be adopted by a wide range of individuals without imposing a significant financial burden. Such accessibility is crucial, as it broadens its reach and inclusivity across diverse populations. Moreover, the integration of advanced AI techniques, such as Convolutional Neural Networks (CNNs), enhances the accuracy and efficiency of health data analysis, enabling faster detection of abnormalities and better prediction of potential risks. In addition, the communication feature that allows coma patients to connect with others adds significant value, improving not only medical monitoring but also patient interaction and emotional well-being.

Table 2. Sample data that has been collected in a time period of 24Hr. (Age group 20-30)

SL.No.	Temp.	P(mV)	R(mV)	T(mV)	P-R(Sec)	S-T (Sec)	QRS (Sec)
P1	36.30°	0.26	1.70	0.60	0.35	0.03	0.50
P2	36.75°	0.24	1.82	0.30	0.23	0.22	0.06
P3	37.43°	0.30	1.85	0.21	0.26	0.80	0.11
P4	36.85°	0.29	1.60	0.81	0.58	0.12	0.25

Table 3. Sample data that has been collected in a time period of 24Hr. (Age group 45-55)

SL. No.	Temp.	P(mV)	R(mV)	T(mV)	P-R(Sec)	S-T (Sec)	QRS (Sec)
P1	36.58°	0.38	1.24	0.66	0.48	0.01	0.42
P2	37.75°	0.29	1.98	0.25	0.36	0.88	0.12
P3	36.89°	0.54	1.44	0.79	0.19	0.23	0.05
P4	36.91°	0.19	1.58	0.18	0.34	0.02	0.28

It not only facilitates interaction but also aids in reducing stress levels among patients. By motivating them to stay engaged and connected, it contributes to their overall well-being during their challenging journey towards recovery. The proposed method not only considers the evaluation of emergency clinic doctors' performance but also emphasizes the actual treatment of patients and the potential for saving lives. This holistic approach underscores the system's significance in improving patient outcomes and the quality of healthcare provided with an accuracy of 99% (refer Fig.4). Acknowledging the diverse and evolving needs of coma patients, the statement highlights the responsibility of future engineers to innovate and develop new technologies that can offer various forms of support to these patients. This forward-thinking approach reflects a commitment to continually improve the care and assistance available to individuals facing comatose conditions, emphasizing the role of technological advancements in healthcare.

Figure 4. Results

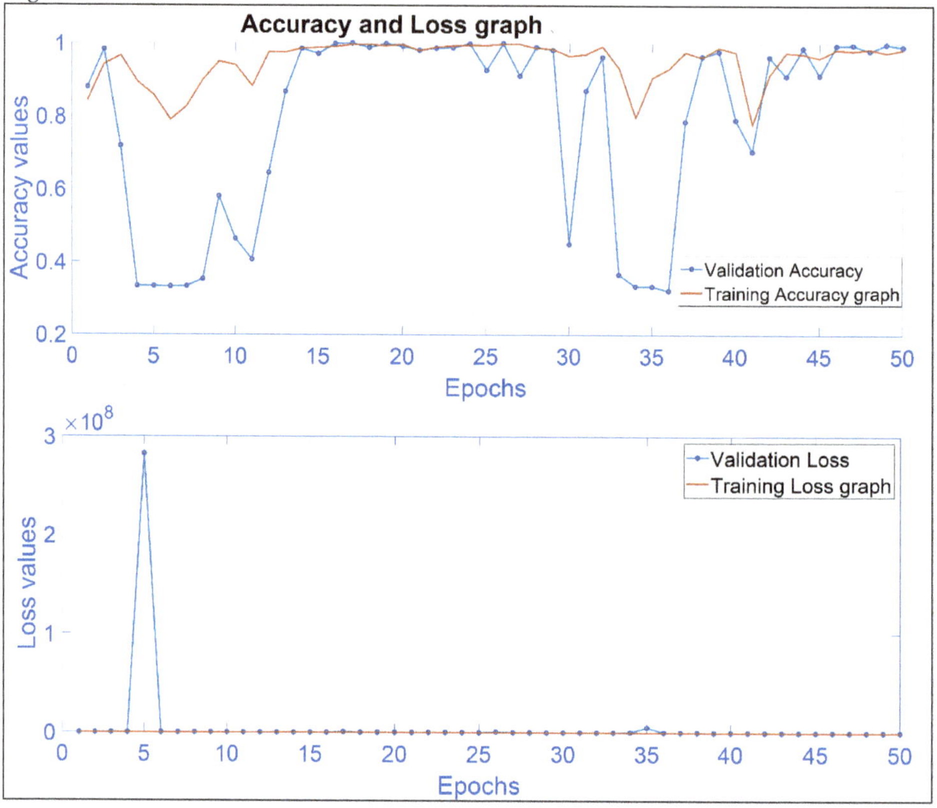

6 CONCLUSIONS

This research has presented a comprehensive and innovative approach to monitoring and supporting coma patients through continuous assessment of their physiological activities. The developed system provides real-time insights into patients' health status while remaining affordable, reliable, and lightweight—ensuring broader accessibility and inclusivity in healthcare. Beyond monitoring, the system emphasizes communication, creating a crucial link between coma patients and their caregivers. This not only reduces stress but also fosters patient engagement and emotional well-being. Furthermore, the study highlights the importance of evaluating emergency clinic doctors' performance to enhance treatment quality and improve patient outcomes, ultimately contributing to saving lives. It reinforces the vital role of engineers in designing and advancing technologies tailored to the evolving needs of coma care. By integrating patient monitoring, caregiver communication, and performance evaluation, this research advances the vision of a more holistic, patient-centered healthcare system. The proposed solution represents a significant step forward in enhancing the quality of care for coma patients and holds strong potential to drive meaningful improvements in the healthcare sector.

The findings of this research underscore the transformative potential of integrating real-time monitoring, predictive analytics, and caregiver communication into coma care. Traditional coma management has largely depended on intermittent clinical assessments and expensive ICU monitoring systems, which often restrict accessibility to high-resource hospitals. By contrast, the system developed in this study demonstrates how lightweight, affordable, and AI-enabled monitoring can extend advanced care capabilities into low-resource environments and even home-based settings. This shift is critical, as it addresses not only the medical complexities of coma but also the socioeconomic disparities that limit patients' access to high-quality healthcare. The incorporation of predictive modeling represents a major step forward in enabling proactive, rather than reactive, patient management. By leveraging bio-signals such as EEG and physiological parameters, predictive algorithms can provide early warning indicators of recovery potential or clinical deterioration. This supports clinicians in making more informed decisions about interventions, rehabilitation planning, and communication with families about prognosis. Such a shift aligns with the global trend of personalized and precision medicine, where treatment strategies are tailored to individual patient trajectories. At the same time, this work highlights important challenges. Data privacy and ethical considerations remain paramount, particularly in cases where patients are unable to provide informed consent. Additionally, while AI-driven predictions can enhance decision-making, they should be viewed as decision-support tools rather than replacements for clinical expertise. Another limitation lies in the need for large-scale clinical validation to confirm the system's effectiveness across diverse populations and healthcare contexts. Despite these challenges, the proposed framework represents a meaningful advancement toward holistic coma care. It demonstrates that combining affordability, real-time monitoring, predictive intelligence, and caregiver engagement can create a more inclusive and patient-centered model of care—one that holds promise for reshaping critical care delivery in the future.

7 DISCUSSION

The primary objective of this study was to explore the potential of the Internet of Things (IoT) in addressing key challenges within the medical domain. The study was successfully executed, and the findings demonstrate that the proposed system has been effectively deployed. By leveraging wireless devices, the system enables the simultaneous monitoring of multiple patients, allowing physicians to promptly intervene in response to any detected health complications. In the context of the COVID-19 pandemic, which has posed unprecedented challenges to healthcare infrastructure worldwide, the importance of such technologies becomes even more evident. Many individuals face circumstances where physically accessing healthcare facilities is difficult or risky due to mobility issues, restrictions, or the need to rely on public transportation. Such visits inherently carry a degree of danger, particularly during pandemics or outbreaks. The integration of IoT technology into the medical sector has shown considerable potential in improving health outcomes and offering greater convenience. Smart healthcare systems enable seamless connectivity between physicians and patients, even in the absence of a fully established clinical setup. The proposed device is expected to yield positive and beneficial outcomes for society by enhancing accessibility, ensuring timely medical interventions, and promoting safer healthcare practices. While the above statement encapsulates the central contributions, the broader implications of this study gives deeper reflection. The integration of predictive analytics, wearable biosensors, and artificial intelligence into coma care redefines how clinicians, caregivers, and healthcare systems can address the challenges of long-term unconsciousness. Traditional coma care has largely focused on maintaining vital functions, preventing complications, and awaiting neurological recovery. However, this research demonstrates that continuous, intelligent monitoring can actively influence decision-making, provide early warnings, and facilitate proactive interventions. By equipping caregivers and clinicians with actionable insights, the system enables a transition from reactive to proactive coma management, thereby improving the likelihood of better outcomes.

A key strength of this work lies in its emphasis on affordability and accessibility. High-end intensive care monitoring systems, though advanced, are often limited to tertiary care centers and remain financially inaccessible for low-resource hospitals or families providing home-based care. By proposing a lightweight, portable, and cost-effective solution, this research democratizes access to advanced coma monitoring. The focus on affordability does not compromise clinical utility—real-time monitoring, data interpretation, and caregiver communication remain intact, ensuring that even resource-constrained environments can benefit from advanced coma care technologies. This is particularly significant in countries with healthcare disparities, where patients often face unequal access to quality care. The system's dual functionality—monitoring and communication—adds a novel human dimension to coma care. Many existing technologies prioritize only physiological measurements such as heart rate, oxygen saturation, or EEG signals, overlooking the psychosocial and emotional aspects of caregiving. By embedding communication pathways, this system acknowledges that coma patients are not just clinical cases but individuals within emotional and social contexts. Facilitating interaction between caregivers and patients, even if indirect, helps reduce caregiver burnout, provides reassurance, and preserves the dignity of patients. This is a crucial shift toward a holistic, patient-centered paradigm in coma care. Another critical contribution is the integration of clinician performance evaluation into the framework. Healthcare technology often focuses solely on patient outcomes, but the quality of care is also deeply influenced by the performance of medical professionals. By embedding performance analytics, this research contributes to accountability and continuous professional development. Such evaluation systems can provide valuable feedback loops—highlighting areas for improvement, training requirements, and systemic inefficiencies. Ultimately, this creates a culture of evidence-based quality improvement, benefiting not just coma patients but the broader healthcare ecosystem.

From a technological standpoint, the system showcases the convergence of IoT, AI, and predictive modeling in healthcare. Biosensors capture real-time physiological signals, which are then processed by AI algorithms to detect anomalies, predict recovery trajectories, and issue alerts. This level of integration illustrates the transformative power of digital health ecosystems, where data-driven insights extend the capacity of human clinicians. Predictive models trained on EEG, imaging, and physiological data hold promise in identifying early biomarkers of recovery—information that is otherwise inaccessible through traditional clinical examinations. This predictive capability has the potential to guide rehabilitation planning, family counseling, and clinical trial design, marking a paradigm shift in coma care. At the same time, limitations and ethical considerations must be acknowledged. Continuous monitoring raises concerns about patient data privacy, security, and consent, especially in unconscious patients unable to provide informed authorization. Engineers and healthcare providers must work together to ensure compliance with data protection frameworks, ethical oversight, and robust encryption standards. Additionally, while predictive models offer valuable insights, over-reliance on algorithmic predictions may risk undermining clinician judgment if not carefully integrated. Hence, explainable AI and transparent decision-support systems should be prioritized in future development.

The implications of this research extend far beyond individual patient care. At a systemic level, affordable coma monitoring technologies can alleviate the burden on overcrowded ICUs by enabling safe, supervised transitions to step-down units or even home care. This redistribution of care can free up critical resources in hospitals while maintaining patient safety. Furthermore, caregiver empowerment through communication systems can strengthen family participation in care, reducing dependence on hospital staff and enhancing community-based healthcare. In low-resource settings, this could be a game-changer, bridging gaps in infrastructure and ensuring continuity of care. Looking ahead, future research directions are abundant.

First, expanding the system to include multimodal data integration—combining EEG, ECG, oxygen saturation, imaging, and even genetic markers—could improve predictive accuracy. Second, the incorporation of explainable AI would enhance clinician trust and adoption, allowing them to understand the rationale behind model predictions. Third, scaling the system for large-scale clinical trials across diverse populations would validate its generalizability and uncover cultural or regional variations in adoption. Fourth, exploring telehealth integration could connect coma care systems with centralized hubs, enabling specialist consultations across geographical boundaries. Finally, personalization of monitoring—tailoring alert thresholds and predictive models to individual patient profiles—could push coma care into a new era of precision medicine. The role of engineers in this transformation cannot be overstated. As the study emphasizes, technological innovation in healthcare is not merely about hardware or software development; it is about understanding human needs, clinical workflows, and ethical contexts. Engineers collaborating with neurologists, critical care specialists, psychologists, and caregivers ensures that the solutions developed are clinically relevant, user-friendly, and ethically sound. The engineer's role is not just technical—it is deeply humanitarian, bridging the gap between technology and lived patient experiences. Moreover, this research highlights broader societal and policy implications. Policymakers and healthcare administrators must recognize the potential of such technologies to reduce healthcare disparities and support widespread adoption through subsidies, training programs, and infrastructure development. Insurance models may need to adapt to include coverage for home-based coma monitoring technologies, while regulatory frameworks must evolve to ensure patient safety and efficacy standards. At the same time, educational programs for caregivers and clinicians should be established to ensure confident use of these technologies in diverse settings.

In summary, this research advances the state of coma care by developing a system that is not only technologically sophisticated but also affordable, holistic, and patient-centered. Its combination of real-time monitoring, caregiver communication, predictive analytics, and clinician performance evaluation positions it as a transformative tool in critical care. While challenges remain in terms of data privacy, clinical validation, and adoption, the potential benefits for patients, families, and healthcare systems are immense. By situating engineers at the heart of healthcare innovation, this study charts a pathway toward a future where coma care is proactive, inclusive, and humane. The significance of this contribution extends beyond coma management, serving as a model for how AI-driven, affordable, and ethical healthcare technologies can be designed to meet the evolving needs of society. Ultimately, the proposed solution is not just a technological innovation but a paradigm shift—one that holds promise to reshape the way unconscious patients are monitored, supported, and cared for in the 21st century.

ACKNOWLEDGEMENT

We acknowledge AMRDH Solution Private Limited under the New Innovation Idea project for providing necessary financial, clinical and technical support.

REFERENCES

Aellen, F. M., Alnes, S. L., Loosli, F., Rossetti, A. O., Zubler, F., De Lucia, M., & Tzovara, A. (2023). Auditory stimulation and deep learning predict awakening from coma after cardiac arrest. *Brain, 146*(2), 778–788. PMID: 36637902

Bahrami Rad, A., Kirsch, M., Li, Q., Xue, J., Sameni, R., Albert, D., & Clifford, G. D. (2024). A crowdsourced AI framework for atrial fibrillation detection in Apple watch and Kardia mobile ECGs. *Sensors (Basel), 24*(17), 5708. PMID: 39275619

. Cavendish, C., Moberg, G., & Freedman, J. (2024). A better old age? Improving health and care outcomes for the over-65s in the UK.

Chen, J., Yan, M., Howe, R. L. C., Tong, N. W., Chee, C. S., Niu, W., . . . Chen, G. (2019, July). Biovitals™: a personalized multivariate physiology analytics using continuous mobile biosensors. In 2019 41st Annual International Conference of the IEEE Engineering in Medicine and Biology Society (EMBC) (pp. 3243-3248). IEEE.

. Collins, K., Innani, S., Ebare, K., Saad, M., Siegmund, S. E., Williamson, S. R., ... & Idrees, M. T. (2025). Artificial Intelligence–Based Classification of Renal Oncocytic Neoplasms: Advancing From a 2-Class Model of Renal Oncocytoma and Low-Grade Oncocytic Tumor to a 3-Class Model Including Chromophobe Renal Cell Carcinoma. Archives of Pathology & Laboratory Medicine.

Contreras, M., Sena, J., Davidson, A., Zhang, J., Ozrazgat-Baslanti, T., Ren, Y., Guan, Z., ... (2025). “MANDARIN: Mixture-of-Experts Framework for Dynamic Delirium and Coma Prediction in ICU Patients: Development and Validation of an Acute Brain Dysfunction Prediction Model.” arXiv preprint arXiv:2503.06059

Das, D., Ghosh, M., Raut, M., & Thakre, L. (2025, April). Enhancing Ophthalmologic Infrastructure: Seamless Integration. In Proceedings of the 15th International Conference on Soft Computing and Pattern Recognition (SoCPaR 2023): Volume 1: Smart Healthcare (Vol. 1243, p. 54). Springer Nature.

Dahake, A., Adhau, R., Ghosh, M., & Thakre, L. (2025). "A Holistic Approach to Health Management and Integrated Fitness Mobile Application for Nutritionists, Dietitians, and Patients." In *2025 IEEE International Conference on Interdisciplinary Approaches in Technology and Management for Social Innovation (IATMSI)*, vol. 3, pp. 1-7. IEEE.

Das, D., Ghosh, M., Raut, M., Thakre, L., & Jichkar, R. (2023). "Enhancing Ophthalmologic Infrastructure: Seamless Integration of Deep Convolutional Neural Networks for Real-Time Ocular Disease Detection." In International Conference on Soft Computing and Pattern Recognition, pp. 54-65. Cham: Springer Nature Switzerland.

Davoudi, A., Malhotra, K. R., Shickel, B., Siegel, S., Williams, S., Ruppert, M., Bihorac, E., ... (2018). "The intelligent ICU pilot study: using artificial intelligence technology for autonomous patient monitoring." arXiv preprint arXiv:1804.10201

Dawidziuk, A., Butters, E., Lindegger, D. J., Foubister, C., Chrost, H., Wlodarski, M., Grogan, J., Rowicka, P. A., Bremner, F., & Manohar, S. G. (2025). Can the Pupillary Light Reflex and Pupillary Unrest Be Used as Biomarkers of Parkinson's Disease? A Systematic Review and Meta-Analysis. *Diagnostics (Basel)*, *15*(9), 1167. PMID: 40361985

East, S. A., Wang, Y., Yanamala, N., Maganti, K., & Sengupta, P. P. (2025). Artificial Intelligence-Enabled Point-of-Care Echocardiography: Bringing Precision Imaging to the Bedside. *Current Atherosclerosis Reports*, *27*(1), 70.

Gurdner, R. S., Singh, J. P., Stancak, B., Nair, D. G., Cao, M., Schulze, C., & Boehmer, J. P. (2018). HeartLogic multisensor algorithm identifies patients during periods of significantly increased risk of heart failure events: Results from the MultiSENSE study. *Circulation: Heart Failure*, *11*(7), e004669. PMID: 30002113

Ge, Q., Huang, L., Fu, Q., Han, S., Wang, R., He, J., Li, C., Luo, J., & Xu, L. (2025). Bedside cerebral microvascular imaging of patients with disorders of consciousness: A feasibility study. *Frontiers in Neuroscience*, *19*, 1518023. PMID: 40012684

Ghosh, M. (2022). "Comparative DNN model analysis for detection of various types of optical noise." *Authorea Preprints*

Ghosh, M., & Bora, V. R. (2025). Evolution in blood glucose monitoring: A comprehensive review of invasive to non-invasive devices and sensors. *Discovery Medicine*, *2*(1), 74.

Ghosh, M., & Das, D. (2024). Voice-activated SOS: an AI-enabled wearable device. In *Impact of AI on Advancing Women's Safety* (pp. 251–277). IGI Global Scientific Publishing.

Ghosh, M., Raut, M., Parteki, R., Das, D., Thakare, L. P., Jichkar, R., Rathore, S. S., & Bawankar, S. (2023). "An analysis of deep-neural-network model for the determination of the bit-rate of optical fiber signals." In 2023 11th International Conference on Emerging Trends in Engineering & Technology-Signal and Information Processing (ICETET-SIP), pp. 1-4. IEEE.

Jain, S., Margetis, K., & Iverson, L. M. (2025). Glasgow coma scale. In *StatPearls* [internet]. StatPearls Publishing.

Kim, K. A., Kim, H., Ha, E. J., Yoon, B. C., & Kim, D.-J. (2024). Artificial intelligence-enhanced neurocritical care for traumatic brain injury: Past, present and future. *Journal of Korean Neurosurgical Society*, *67*(5), 493–509. PMID: 38186369

Latha, R., Raman, R., Kumar, T. S., Rawandale, C. J., Meenakshi, R., & Srinivasan, C. (2023, October). Automated health monitoring system for coma patients. In *2023 International Conference on Self Sustainable Artificial Intelligence Systems (ICSSAS)* (pp. 1475-1480). IEEE.

Levy, D. E., Bates, D., & Caronna, J. J. (1981). NIALL EF CARTLIDGE, ROBIN P. KNILL-JONES, ROBERT H. LAPINSKI, BURTON H. SINGER, DAVID A. SHAW, and FRED PLUM. "Prognosis in nontraumatic coma.". *Annals of Internal Medicine*, *94*(3), 293–301. PMID: 7224376

Maniaci, M. J., Torres-Guzman, R. A., Avila, F. R., Maita, K., Garcia, J. P., Forte, A. J., & Paulson, M. R. (2024). Development and evaluation of best practice advisory alert for patient eligibility in a hospital-at-home program: A multicenter retrospective study. *Journal of Hospital Medicine*, *19*(3), 165–174. PMID: 38243666

Manikandan, A., Prashanth, P. K., Ravindran, S., & Senthilnayaki, B. (2025). "Remote Health Monitoring for Empowering Patients with Intelligent." Advances in Communication and Applications: Proceedings of ERCICA 2024, Volume 2 1398: 101.

. Meghana, M. (2020). "Design and implementation of iot based health monitoring system for comatose patients." vol 29: 3689-3697.

Nechita, L. C., Nechita, A., Voipan, A. E., Voipan, D., Debita, M., Fulga, A., & Musat, C. L. (2024). AI-Enhanced ECG Applications in Cardiology: Comprehensive Insights from the Current Literature with a Focus on COVID-19 and Multiple Cardiovascular Conditions. *Diagnostics (Basel)*, *14*(17), 1839. PMID: 39272624

Pham, S. D., Keijzer, H. M., Ruijter, B. J., Seeber, A. A., Scholten, E., Drost, G., & Tjepkema-Cloostermans, M. C. (2022). Outcome prediction of postanoxic coma: A comparison of automated electroencephalography analysis methods. *Neurocritical Care, 37*(Suppl 2), 248–258.

Plum, F., & Posner, J. B. (1982). *The diagnosis of stupor and coma* (Vol. 19). Oxford University Press.

Pradhan, D., Sahu, P. K., Tun, H. M., & Chatterjee, P. (Eds.). (2024). *Artificial and Cognitive Computing for Sustainable Healthcare Systems in Smart Cities*. John Wiley & Sons.

Reyna, M. A., Amorim, E., Sameni, R., Weigle, J., Elola, A., Rad, A. B., & Seyedi, S.. (2023). *"Predicting neurological recovery from coma after cardiac arrest: The George B. Moody PhysioNet Challenge 2023." In 2023 Computing in Cardiology (CinC)* (Vol. 50). IEEE.

. Sheikdavood, K., K. Soundar, M. G. Yaswanth, and P. TarunKumar. (2023). "Smart health monitoring system for coma patients using iot." In 2023 7th International Conference on Computing Methodologies and Communication (ICCMC), pp. 1342-1347. IEEE.

Silva, B., Contreras, M., Baslanti, T. O., Ren, Y., Guan, Z., Khezeli, K., Bihorac, A., & Rashidi, P. (2023). "Transformer models for acute brain dysfunction prediction." arXiv preprint arXiv:2303.07305.

Singh, A., Singh, U., Pandey, V., Deotale, N., & Talekar, P. (2024). Detecting Human Activities In COMA Patients Using ML Algorithm.

Sinha, N., Ghosh, M., Majumder, S., & Bhowmik, B. B. (2021). "Deep Learning based noise identification in the Optical fiber communication using Variational Mode Decomposition." In 2021 IEEE 2nd International Conference on Applied Electromagnetics, Signal Processing, & Communication (AESPC), pp. 1-5. IEEE.

Stevens, R. D., & Bhardwaj, A. (2006). Approach to the comatose patient. *Critical Care Medicine, 34*(1), 31–41. PMID: 16374153

Taherdoost, H. (2024). Wearable Healthcare and Continuous Vital Sign Monitoring with IoT Integration. *Computers, Materials & Continua, 81*(1).

Tsvetanov, F. (2024). Integrating AI technologies into remote monitoring patient systems. *Engineering Proceedings, 70*(1), 54.

Tu, K.-C., Nyam, T.-T. E., Wang, C.-C., Chen, N.-C., Chen, K.-T., Chen, C.-J., Liu, C.-F., & Kuo, J.-R. (2022). A computer-assisted system for early mortality risk prediction in patients with traumatic brain injury using artificial intelligence algorithms in emergency room triage. *Brain Sciences*, *12*(5), 612. PMID: 35624999

van der Harst, P., & Nathoe, H. (2025). Transforming cardiology with AI: The eko CORE 500 digital stethoscope. *Netherlands Heart Journal; Monthly Journal of the Netherlands Society of Cardiology and the Netherlands Heart Foundation*, •••, 1–2. PMID: 40138099

van Uum, R. T., Breteler, M., Hardeman, H., van de Pol, A. C., Smit, K., Boeijen, J. A., & Zwart, D. L. (2025). How Dutch initiatives to early discharge COVID-19 patients were organised during the pandemic: A scoping review. *BMJ Open*, *15*(8), e097839. PMID: 40858380

Venkatesan, M., Kandalkar, S. K., Menon, R., Kulkarni, A. V., & Prasad, S. Predictive Internet of Things Based Detection Model of Comatose Patient using Deep Learning.

Windle, N., Alam, A., Patel, H., Street, J. M., Lathwood, M., Farrington, T., & Maruthappu, M. (2024). Predicting Hospitalization Risk Among Home Care Residents in the United Kingdom: Development and Validation of a Machine Learning-Based Predictive Model. *Home Health Care Management & Practice*, *36*(4), 253–261.

Yimer, H. L., Degefa, H. D., Cristani, M., & Cunico, F. (2024). *"loT-Based Coma Patient Monitoring System." In 2024 IEEE International Multi-Conference on Smart Systems & Green Process (IMC-SSGP)*. IEEE.

Yimer, H., Dereje Degefa, H., Cristani, M., & Cunico, F. (2024). IoT-Based Coma Patient Monitoring System. arXiv e-prints, arXiv-2411.

Zheng, W.-L., Amorim, E., Jing, J., Ge, W., Hong, S., Wu, O., & Ghassemi, M.. (2021). Predicting neurological outcome in comatose patients after cardiac arrest with multiscale deep neural networks. *Resuscitation*, *169*, 86–94. PMID: 34699925

Chapter 7
Factors Influencing Consumers' Acceptance and Use of Wearable Devices in Ehealth:
A Study Using the UTAUT2 Model

Seema Rajesh Laddha
https://orcid.org/0000-0003-2673-2704
Universal AI University, India

ABSTRACT

This research aimed to investigate the factors influencing the usage intention of healthcare technology among patients in a developing country. A total of 500 patients participated in the study and completed a structured questionnaire that included measures of perceived usefulness, perceived ease of use, facilitating conditions, hedonic motivation, price, trust, social influence, habit, trial, SIFR, and perceived risk. The results indicated that perceived usefulness, perceived ease of use, facilitating conditions, hedonic motivation, price, and trust were positively related to usage intention, while perceived risk was negatively related. Social influence - specialist, habit, trial, and SIFR were found to have a significant positive correlation with usage intention but were not predictive factors.

INTRODUCTION

The acceptance and use of wearable devices in eHealth are increasingly significant topics within the realm of technology adoption, particularly as health-related

DOI: 10.4018/979-8-3373-2545-3.ch007

technologies continue to advance globally. This phenomenon is notably explored through the lens of the Unified Theory of Acceptance and Use of Technology 2 (UTAUT2) model, which identifies key factors influencing consumer behavior. The UTAUT2 model enhances its predecessor by incorporating constructs such as hedonic motivation, price value, and habit, providing a comprehensive framework for understanding adoption dynamics among different demographics, particularly older adults (Yin et al., 2022; Gao et al., 2015; Lee & Lee, 2020).

Research highlights several critical predictors of acceptance, including performance expectancy, effort expectancy, social influence, and facilitating conditions. For older adults, the perceived benefits of wearable technology—such as improved health monitoring and enhanced quality of life—play a crucial role in shaping their willingness to adopt these devices (Ma, 2022). Furthermore, emotional factors like hedonic motivation significantly impact acceptance, suggesting that the enjoyment and satisfaction derived from using technology can be just as influential as functional utility (Ma, 2022).

Despite the growing global interest in wearable health technology, several unresolved issues remain, especially within the context of developing countries. Challenges such as limited digital infrastructure, varying levels of health literacy, and socio-economic disparities often exacerbate the digital divide, particularly among older populations in low- and middle-income nations. Privacy concerns, data security, and affordability further complicate the adoption landscape in these regions (Chandrasekaran et al., 2020; Meier et al., 2020). In such settings, cultural attitudes, resource availability, and public health system limitations become crucial contextual factors influencing the uptake of wearable health devices.

This study specifically focuses on the various elements influencing consumers' acceptance of wearable health devices in eHealth contexts within a developing country setting. Employing the UTAUT2 model, the research explores the behavioral and cultural factors affecting technology adoption among healthcare professionals in Southwest Ethiopia. Findings reveal not only the significance of consumer innovativeness in enhancing perceived usefulness but also underscore the importance of tailoring interventions to fit local cultural contexts and resource constraints. These insights are essential for developing inclusive marketing strategies and product designs that respond to the needs of underserved populations, thereby supporting more equitable technology adoption in eHealth (Meier et al., 2020;).

The healthcare industry has undergone a significant transformation with the emergence of digital healthcare technologies, including telemedicine, mHealth, personal health records, mobile apps, artificial intelligence, and robotics. Among these, wearable devices have emerged as one of the most promising technologies for facilitating preventive healthcare, remote monitoring, and chronic disease management. However, successful adoption is not solely driven by technological functionality; user perceptions, cultural acceptability, and trust in digital health ecosystems are equally critical. Therefore, understanding the behavioral drivers of wearable device usage, particularly in resource-constrained contexts, is imperative.

To investigate these dynamics, this study applies the UTAUT2 model, originally developed by (Venkatesh et al.,2012), which is well-suited for exploring technology acceptance from a consumer perspective. The model includes core constructs—performance expectancy, effort expectancy, social influence, and facilitating conditions—moderated by demographic variables such as age, gender, and experience. Additionally, it incorporates hedonic motivation, price value, and habit to offer a more nuanced understanding of use behavior.

Through this model, the present research aims to explore how these constructs manifest in the socio-cultural and economic realities of a developing country. The findings contribute to the literature on technology adoption in emerging markets and provide valuable implications for designing more accessible and culturally aligned eHealth solutions that can better serve diverse populations.

LITERATURE REVIEW

The Unified Theory of Acceptance and Use of Technology 2 (UTAUT2) extends the original UTAUT model proposed by Venkatesh et al. in 2003, incorporating additional constructs such as hedonic motivation, price value, and habit, which are vital for understanding technology adoption behaviors . The UTAUT2 framework provides a robust basis for examining the factors influencing older adults' acceptance of smart wearable devices, particularly in developing countries, where access, affordability, and digital literacy significantly shape technology adoption patterns (Krogoll, 2015)

Perceived usefulness significantly influences the adoption of wearable devices for health monitoring among patients, as these technologies provide real-time data collection and personalized care, enhancing patient engagement and outcomes. This is particularly relevant in developing countries, where healthcare infrastructure is often strained, and wearable technologies offer a potential solution to bridge the healthcare delivery gap. Studies indicate that wearable devices, such as smartwatches and fitness trackers, facilitate continuous monitoring of vital signs and health indicators, empowering patients to take an active role in their health management (Ahlan, 2015).

Furthermore, the integration of wearable technology in chronic disease management has been shown to improve adherence and health outcomes across various medical fields, including cardiology and oncology . In developing country contexts, these benefits are critical in addressing the growing burden of non-communicable diseases. However, challenges such as data accuracy, privacy concerns, technological infrastructure gaps, and the need for reciprocal interaction between patients and healthcare providers remain critical barriers to widespread adoption (Collinson et al., 2024;). These challenges are often exacerbated in low-resource settings, making it imperative to design context-sensitive interventions.

Overall, the perceived benefits of these devices, particularly in enhancing health monitoring and enabling timely interventions, are pivotal in driving their acceptance among patients in resource-constrained environments. The use of wearable devices in the healthcare industry has been increasing rapidly in recent years, with the potential to transform healthcare delivery and improve patient outcomes in low- and middle-income countries (LMICs). However, despite these potential benefits, the adoption and acceptance of these devices by consumers have been relatively slow, especially in developing countries. Understanding the socioeconomic and cultural factors that influence consumers' acceptance and use of wearable devices in eHealth is crucial for healthcare providers and device manufacturers aiming to penetrate these markets.

The UTAUT2 model serves as a widely recognized theoretical framework to investigate such factors. This literature review explores the current state of research on the factors influencing consumers' acceptance and use of wearable devices in eHealth using the UTAUT2 model, particularly within the developing country context.

Within the context of this study, perceived usefulness is defined as the health benefits that consumers can achieve from using technology. Previous studies have consistently demonstrated a significant relationship between perceived usefulness and technology adoption in healthcare settings. For example, Carolyn Krogoll (2015) found that perceived usefulness is positively associated with the adoption and use of wearable devices in healthcare, a finding that resonates with populations in developing countries where health system accessibility is limited.

Perceived Usefulness (PU) is an important factor that influences the adoption and use of wearable devices in eHealth. It refers to the user's perception of the degree to which using a wearable device would be beneficial to their health. PU has been found to be a strong predictor of technology usage intention in many studies, including those related to consumer healthcare. For instance Venkatesh et al. (2012), Yu (2012), and Zhou et al. (2010) have all found that perceived usefulness is a significant predictor of technology adoption and use.

This suggests that if consumers perceive that using a wearable device would be beneficial to their health, they are more likely to adopt and use it—especially in developing countries, where healthcare challenges and unmet needs are more acute. (Davis, 1989) has argued that perceived usefulness is a critical determinant of technology acceptance and use. If users do not perceive that using technology would be beneficial to them, they are less likely to adopt and use it. Therefore, it is important to understand the contextual, economic, and infrastructural factors that influence users' perceptions of the usefulness of wearable devices in eHealth in developing countries, in order to promote their widespread adoption and sustained use.

H1: Perceived Usefulness significantly affects the adoption of wearable device for monitoring health for patients.

Perceived Ease of Use (PEOU) is an important factor that influences the adoption and use of wearable devices in eHealth. PEOU refers to the user's perception of the degree to which using a wearable device would be effortless. Previous studies have shown that ease of use is an important determinant of user adoption in healthcare settings (Or et al., 2010; Venkatesh et al., 2012).

Effort expectancy, which reflects the ease at which technology can be used, is a key component of PEOU (Venkatesh et al., 2012). In the context of this study, effort expectancy refers to the ease of use associated with using a wearable device. Several studies have shown that ease of use significantly affects user adoption and usage intention (Or et al., 2010; Venkatesh et al., 2012).

Recent studies also support the importance of PEOU in technology adoption in healthcare. A study by Lee and Kim (2021) found that PEOU significantly affects the adoption of wearable devices in older adults for healthcare purposes. Another study by Li et al. (2020) found that PEOU significantly affects the adoption of wearable devices for health monitoring in patients with chronic diseases. These findings highlight the importance of considering PEOU in promoting the adoption and use of wearable devices in eHealth..

If users perceive that using a wearable device would be effortless, they are more likely to adopt and use it. However, if the ease of use is not achieved, it can negatively impact the adoption and usage intention (PWC, 2013). Therefore, it is important to understand the factors that influence users' perceptions of the ease of use of wearable devices in eHealth to promote their adoption and use.

H2: Perceived Ease of Use significantly affects adoption of wearable device for monitoring health for patients.

The literature suggests that social influence plays an important role in the adoption of technology in healthcare. According to Venkatesh et al. (2003), the perception of important others believing that an individual should use wearable devices increases the likelihood of adoption. This notion is supported by several studies in healthcare, which have revealed the importance of the influence that comes from friends, relatives, superiors, and healthcare specialists (Or et al., 2010).

Theoretical notions of social influence are based on subjective norms from the Theory of Reasoned Action (TRA) and Planned Behavior (TPB), which refer to "the perceived social pressure to perform or not to perform the behavior" (Ajzen, 1991, p.188). However, it has been found that social influence does not always show consistent impacts and is largely dependent on the situation (Escobar-Rodriguez & Carvajal-Trujillo, 2014; Or et al., 2010). Additionally, there is a construct issue in many cases because of which this factor could not be adequately operationalized (Holden & Karsh, 2010), as social influence is considering only a selected few and the so-called "important others," regardless of the research context (Krogoll, 2015).

Overall, the literature suggests that social influence is an important factor to consider when examining the adoption of technology in healthcare, and it has both positive and negative impacts depending on the situation and context.

> H3: Social influence by friends and relatives significantly affects the adoption of wearable device for monitoring health for patients.
> H4:Social Influence by healthcare specialist significantly affects adoption of wearable device for monitoring health for patients.

The degree to which an individual believes that there is organizational and technical infrastructure to support the use of wearable devices is known as Facilitation Condition (FC) (Venkatesh et al., 2012). This factor can impact the adoption and usage of wearable devices as it makes it easier for users to access and use the technology. Several studies have found FC to be a significant predictor of usage intention in various domains, including healthcare (Or et al., 2010; Zhou et al., 2010). In our study, FC refers to the availability, accessibility, compatibility, and features of hardware and software resources, such as wearables, smartwatches, fitness bands, and other applications. Therefore, it can be argued that a sufficient amount of resources has a positive effect on technology adoption.

> H5: FC significantly affects the adoption of wearable device for monitoring health for patients..

Venkatesh et al. (2012) defines hedonic motivation as the pleasure or enjoyment that individuals derive from using a technology, which complements extrinsic motivation, such as perceived usefulness, in technology acceptance models. Numerous studies have demonstrated the significance of hedonic motivation in technology usage, especially in internet-related technologies like social media (Brown & Venkatesh, 2005; Venkatesh et al., 2012; Wang et al., 2003). Recent research has also supported the importance of hedonic motivation in technology adoption. For instance Venkatesh,(2012) found that hedonic motivation had a significant positive impact on users' intention to use a mobile health application, while Wang et al. (2020) found that hedonic motivation was a significant predictor of users' intention to adopt wearable fitness devices. Therefore, it can be argued that hedonic motivation plays a crucial role in predicting technology adoption among patients in the healthcare context.

H6: Hedonic motivation significantly influences patients' adoption of wearable device for monitoring health.

According to Venkatesh et al. (2012), habit refers to the involvement due to long-term usage of a particular service or product. Habitual behavior can be an important predictor of technology usage, as repeated usage can lead to the development of habits that become automatic and ingrained in an individual's daily routine (Kim & Malhotra, 2005; Kim, Limayem, Hirt & Cheung, 2007). In the context of this study, habit is seen as the behavioral pattern that is acquired and triggers the need to regularly use wearable technology, leading to its adoption by patients.

Recent studies have also shown the importance of habit in predicting technology adoption. For example, a study by Fu et al. (2021) found that habit was a significant predictor of users' intention to use telemedicine services. Similarly, a study by Kim et al. (2016) found that habit had a significant positive effect on users' intention to use healthcare wearable devices.

H7: Habit significantly influences the adoption of wearable devices by patients.

Price, which refers to the monetary value that consumers are willing to pay for a product or service, has been found to influence their intention to use technology (Dodds, Monroe & Grewal, 1991; Escobar-Rodriguez & Yu, 2012). According to Venkatesh et al. (2012), price value is the trade-off between the benefits and costs associated with a product or service. Price, along with facilitating conditions, is a key factor in technology adoption models. For consumers to perceive the value of a product or service positively, the benefits must outweigh the costs. In the case of technology, the potential benefits include improved health and disease prevention, which should be perceived as more important than the price to consumers.

H8: Price significantly affects the adoption of wearable devices.

Trust refers to a user's confidence in the quality and reliability of a particular service or technology (Gefen et al., 2003). Numerous studies have demonstrated that trust plays a critical role in consumer acceptance and use of technology (Gefen, Karahanna & Straub, 2003; Zhou et al., 2010). In the case of healthcare technology, it can be argued that trust in the technology provider system is crucial for user adoption (Akter et al., 2010; PWC, 2013). Specifically, consumers who trust the wearable devices provider to provide reliable health services and to satisfy their health needs are more likely to adopt technology than those who doubt the provider's commitment (Krogoll, 2015).

H9: Trust in the technology provider significantly influences patients' adoption of wearable device for monitoring health for patients.

Trialability refers to the extent to which an innovation can be experimented with on a limited basis. Essentially, it means that if consumers can try a solution before committing to it, they are more likely to adopt it since they have practical information about the solution, which reduces uncertainty (Krogoll, 2015). With the emergence of new technologies and ways of doing things, the trend of offering triability, demos, freebies, and proof of concept has become popular in attracting initial users. Users believe that these solutions can easily be put into trial, gain positive reviews, and are therefore willing to try them. In the context of this research, it is hypothesized that triability will significantly influence usage intention.

H10: Triability significantly influences the adoption of wearable device for monitoring health for patients.

Perceived Privacy Risk refers to the potential for regulatory or safety errors that a consumer may experience while using a health-related system (El Wajeeh et al., 2014). Privacy risk is a significant concern for consumers who use health-related applications, as there may be a lack of transparency between the consumer and the provider, leading to potential privacy breaches (West 2006). In addition to the importance of trusting the technology provider in healthcare, consumers also consider the perceived privacy risks of using wearable devices and would be the barrier for mobile health services (PWC, 2019). Based on these findings, it can be argued that consumers who perceive greater privacy risks with using a healthcare technology are less likely to adopt such a service (Krogoll, 2015).

H11: Perceived privacy risks significantly influence patients' adoption of wearable device for monitoring health for patients.

METHODOLOGY

The research methodology for this study will be descriptive and explanatory, and it will involve the use of a quantitative research design. The study will investigate the factors influencing the adoption of wearable devices for health monitoring purposes among patients in Mumbai, India. The research question is: What are the factors that influence the adoption of wearable devices for health monitoring purposes among patients in Mumbai, India?

Data Collection:

The data for this study will be collected through an online survey. The survey questionnaire will be developed based on the UTAUT2 model, which includes constructs such as performance expectancy, effort expectancy, social influence, facilitating conditions, hedonic motivation, and price value. The questionnaire will be administered to a sample of 670 individuals who have used wearable devices for health monitoring purposes. The sampling method will be convenience sampling, where respondents will be selected based on their availability and voluntariness.

Data Analysis:

The collected data will be analyzed using statistical techniques such as descriptive statistics, factor analysis, correlation analysis, and regression analysis. The analysis will be conducted using software such as SPSS and AMOS. The study will test a total of 11 hypotheses related to the independent constructs of perceived usefulness, perceived ease of use, social influence – friends, social influence – specialist, facilitating conditions, hedonic motivation, habit, price, trust, triability, perceived risk, and usage intention (UI) or behavioral intention.

In conclusion, this research methodology aims to investigate the factors influencing the adoption of wearable devices for health monitoring purposes among patients in Mumbai, India. The study will employ a quantitative research design, and data will be collected through an online survey method. The data collected will be analyzed using statistical techniques, and ethical considerations will be ensured. The results of this study will help healthcare providers understand the factors influencing the adoption of wearable devices and develop strategies to promote their use among patients.

THEORETICAL FRAMEWORK

UTAUT2 Model

The Unified Theory of Acceptance and Use of Technology 2 (UTAUT2) extends the original UTAUT model proposed by Venkatesh et al. in 2003, incorporating additional constructs such as hedonic motivation, price value, and habit, which are vital for understanding technology adoption behaviors(Sun, 2021). The UTAUT2 framework provides a robust basis for examining the factors influencing older adults' acceptance of smart wearable devices, highlighting the importance of user perceptions and contextual factors in shaping technology adoption .

Performance Expectancy

Performance expectancy refers to the extent to which individuals believe that using a system will enhance their work performance. In the context of older adults, this includes their expectations regarding the benefits of smart wearable devices in improving health management and overall well-being. Research indicates that when elderly users anticipate positive outcomes from technology, their willingness to adopt such devices increases significantly

Effort Expectancy

Effort expectancy is defined as an individual's perception of the effort required to use new technology. For older adults, this construct relates to their ease of learning and operating smart wearable devices. Studies have shown that higher levels of perceived ease of use correlate with greater intentions to adopt technology. This finding underscores the necessity for user-friendly designs that cater to the specific needs of older adults.

Price Value

Price value reflects the perceived balance between the benefits of using a system and its associated costs. Older adults are often more price-sensitive compared to younger demographics, which affects their evaluation of technology's cost-effectiveness. Their acceptance of smart wearable devices hinges on a clear perception of benefits that outweigh financial costs, suggesting that manufacturers should consider this demographic's budgetary constraints when marketing their products.

Facilitating Conditions

Facilitating conditions pertain to the availability of resources and support systems that assist users in employing new technology. In the case of older adults, having access to adequate technical support can enhance their confidence in using smart wearable devices, ultimately fostering a more favourable adoption attitude. Empirical evidence highlights that when older users perceive sufficient support, their likelihood of continuous usage increases.

Hedonic Motivation

Hedonic motivation refers to the enjoyment or pleasure derived from using technology. For older adults, devices that evoke positive emotions and satisfaction can significantly enhance their willingness to adopt and regularly use wearable technology. Research shows that hedonic motivations are crucial drivers of user behaviour, thus emphasizing the importance of developing engaging and enjoyable devices for this demographic.

Data Analysis:

Descriptive analysis

Table 1. Demographics Age - Patients

Age-Patients					
		Frequency	**Percent**	**Valid Percent**	**Cumulative Percent**
Valid	<25	91	13.6	13.6	13.6
	26-35	141	21.0	21.0	34.6
	36-45	96	14.3	14.3	49.0
	46-55	313	46.7	46.7	95.7
	>56	29	4.3	4.3	100.0
	Total	670	100.0	100.0	

Table 2. Gender-Patients

	Frequency		**Percent**	**Valid Percent**	**Cumulative Percent**
Valid	Male	399	59.6	59.6	59.6
	Female	271	40.4	40.4	100.0

Table 3. Income-Patients

Frequency			Percent	Valid Percent	Cumulative Percent
Valid	<5	125	18.7	18.7	18.7
	6-10	41	6.1	6.1	24.8
	11-30	184	27.5	27.5	52.2
	31-50	308	46.0	46.0	98.2
	>50	12	1.8	1.8	100.0
	Total	670	100.0	100.0	

Table 4. Daily Internet Usage

Frequency			Percent	Valid Percent	Cumulative Percent
Valid	<1	66	9.9	9.9	9.9
	1-2	45	6.7	6.7	16.6
	2-4	222	33.1	33.1	49.7
	4-6	207	30.9	30.9	80.6
	>6	130	19.4	19.4	100.0
	Total	670	100.0	100.0	

Figure 1. Correlation Matrix

Construct	PU	PEOU	SIFR	SISP	FC	HM	HAB	PRI	TR	TRL	PRI	UI
PERCEIVED USEFULNESS (PU)	1	.770**	.160**	.336**	.627**	.715**	.212**	.731**	.504**	.213**	-.518**	.768**
PERCEIVED EASE OF USE (PEOU)	.770**	1	.143**	.307**	.578**	.825**	.220**	.724**	.551**	.173**	-.653**	.776**
SOCIAL INFLUENCE -FRIENDS (SIFR)	.160**	.143**	1	.107**	.562**	0	.608**	0	.258**	.538**	0	.105**
SOCIAL INFLUENCE-SPECIALIST (SISP)	.336**	.307**	.107**	1	.305**	.276**	.086*	.285**	.084*	.159**	-.280**	.231**
FACILITATING CONDITION (FC)	.627**	.578**	.562**	.305**	1	.481**	.593**	.586**	.460**	.478**	-.255**	.517**
HEDONIC MOTIVATION (HM)	.715**	.825**	0	.276**	.481**	1	.165**	.701**	.497**	.094*	-.583**	.817**
HABIT (HAB)	.212**	.220**	.608**	.086*	.593**	.165**	1	.138**	.314**	.525**	0	.221**
PRICE (PRI)	.731**	.724**	0	.285**	.586**	.701**	.138**	1	.500**	.193**	-.500**	.768**
TRUST (TR)	.504**	.551**	.258**	.084*	.460**	.497**	.314**	.500**	1	.258**	-.387**	.568**
TRIABIITY (TRL)	.213**	.173**	.538**	.159**	.478**	.094*	.525**	.193**	.258**	1	0	.142**
PERCEIVED RISK (PR)	-.518**	-.653**	0	-.280**	-.255**	-.583**	0	-.500**	-.387**	0	1	-.461**
USAGE INTENTION (UI)	.768**	.776**	.105**	.231**	.517**	.817**	.221**	.768**	.568**	.142**	-.461**	1

*** Correlation significant at .01 level(2 tailed)*
**Correlation Significant at .05 level(2 tailed)*

In addition, Facilitating condition (r=.517) and Trust (.568) also have significant positive correlations with usage intention. On the other hand, Perceived Risk (r=-.461) has a significant negative correlation with usage intention, indicating that patients are less likely to use wearables if they perceive it as risky.

Social Influence – Specialist (r=.231), Habit (r=.221), Trial (r=.142), and SIFR (r=.105) have positive correlations with usage intention, but they are not as strong as the other predictors and are not significant predictors of usage intention. Overall, it appears that patients are more likely to use these devices if they perceive it as useful, easy to use, hedonically motivating, and if it is priced reasonably. It is also important for patients to feel that the service is trustworthy and that potential risks are minimized.

Hierarchical Regression on usage Intention for Proposed factors – Patients

The present study aimed to examine the factors influencing Patients' usage intention of wearable devices for health monitoring purposes using the UTAUT2 model. Hierarchical regression analysis was conducted to test the hypotheses proposed in the study.

The results indicated that the factors proposed in the UTAUT2 model significantly impact Patients' usage intention of wearable devices. Model 1, which included performance expectancy, effort expectancy, social influence, facilitating conditions, hedonic motivation, trust, and price value, explained 75.8% of the variability in Patients' usage intention. Model 2, which added perceived risk and triability, accounted for an additional 2% of the variance in Patients' usage intention.

Out of the 11 hypothesized factors, 8 were found to be significant predictors of Patients' usage intention, with performance expectancy being the strongest predictor, followed by effort expectancy, social influence, facilitating conditions, hedonic motivation, trust, perceived risk, and triability. Price value was not a significant predictor in Model 2.

The overall fit of the model improved slightly when perceived risk and triability were added, suggesting that these factors are relevant for Patients' adoption of wearable devices, but to a lesser extent than the factors included in Model 1.

In conclusion, healthcare providers and policymakers should focus on improving Patients' performance expectancy, effort expectancy, social influence, facilitating conditions, hedonic motivation, trust, perceived risk, and triability to increase the adoption of wearable devices for health monitoring purposes. The successful regression analysis of the proposed research model suggests that the model is a valid and reliable tool for predicting Patients' usage intention of wearable devices.

Table 5. Overview of tested hypotheses and results

Hypothesized Factor	Model 1 Beta	Model 2 Beta
Performance Expectancy	0.494***	0.447***
Effort Expectancy	0.364***	0.277***
Social Influence	0.200***	0.183***
Facilitating Conditions	0.173***	0.171***
Hedonic Motivation	0.167***	0.160***
Trust	0.136***	0.145***
Perceived Risk	-0.073***	-0.089***
Triability	0.060***	0.044*
Price Value	-0.006	-0.021

*** $p < 0.001$, ** $p < 0.01$, * $p < 0.05$

Note: β represents standardized coefficients; t represents t-values; ΔR2 represents change in R2 between models; F Change represents the F-value for the change in R2. All predictors are significant at $p < .05$, except for price value in Figure 2.

Figure 2.

Model		Unstandardized Coefficients		zed Coefficien					
		B	Std. Error	Beta	t	Sig.	R^2	Adjusted R^2	Difference R^2
UTAUT 2							0.758	0.755	
1	(Constant)	-0.116	0.611		-0.190	0.850			
	PERCEIVED USEFULNESS (PU)	0.040	0.031	0.178	1.312	0.019			
	PERCEIVED EASE OF USE (PEOU)	0.089	0.023	0.153	3.907	0.000			
	SOCIAL INFLUENCE -FRIENDS (SIFR)	0.002	0.045	0.001	0.053	0.958			
	SOCIAL INFLUENCE-SPECIALIST (SISP)	-0.135	0.065	-0.043	-2.085	0.037			
	FACILITATING CONDITION (FC)	-0.047	0.032	-0.052	-1.478	0.140			
	HEDONIC MOTIVATION (HM)	0.469	0.037	0.445	12.605	0.000			
	HABIT (HAB)	0.117	0.035	0.089	3.339	0.001			
	PRICE (PRI)	0.323	0.061	0.303	5.333	0.000			
PROPOSED MODEL							0.778	0.774	0.020
2	(Constant)	-4.078	0.833		-4.896	0.000			
	PERCEIVED USEFULNESS (PU)	0.046	0.030	0.189	1.542	0.024			
	PERCEIVED EASE OF USE (PEOU)	0.114	0.024	0.196	4.789	0.000			
	SOCIAL INFLUENCE -FRIENDS (SIFR)	-0.027	0.046	-0.016	-0.580	0.562			
	SOCIAL INFLUENCE-SPECIALIST (SISP)	-0.028	0.064	-0.009	-0.438	0.662			
	FACILITATING CONDITION (FC)	-0.061	0.031	-0.068	-1.999	0.046			
	HEDONIC MOTIVATION (HM)	0.464	0.036	0.441	12.845	0.000			
	HABIT (HAB)	0.105	0.035	0.080	3.006	0.003			
	PRICE (PRI)	0.299	0.060	0.280	5.030	0.000			
	TRUST (TR)	0.159	0.028	0.134	5.631	0.000			
	TRIABIITY (TRL)	-0.056	0.032	-0.042	-1.754	0.080			
	PERCEIVED RISK (PR)	0.092	0.016	0.144	5.621	0.000			
a. Dependent Variable: TUI									

Figure 3. Research results for the factors predicting Wearable device for monitoring health usage intention for Patients

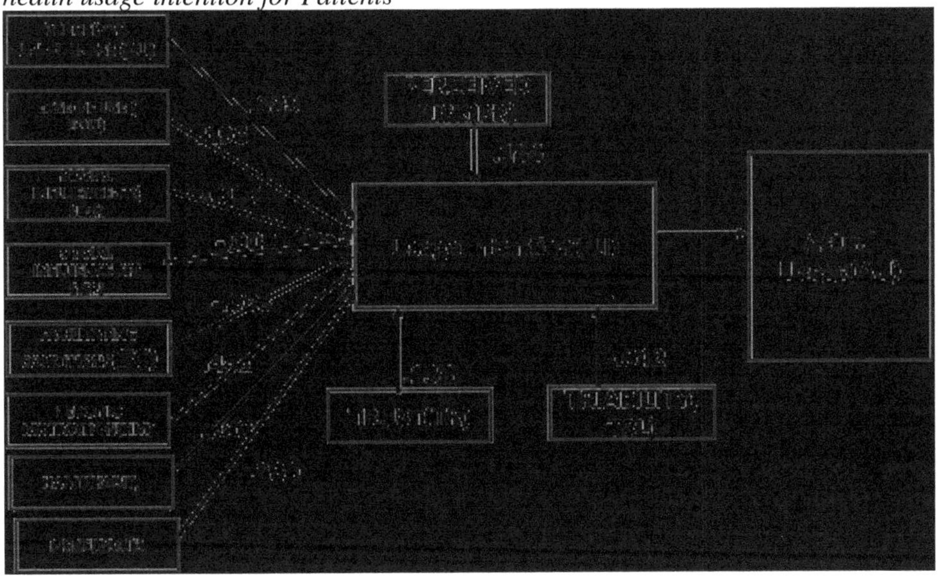

DISCUSSION

The analysis conducted in this study reveals several important factors that influence patient adoption of wearable devices for monitoring health within the context of a developing country. The findings suggest that healthcare providers and developers operating in such environments must emphasize improving the user-friendliness, utilitarian value, hedonic appeal, and trustworthiness of wearable health-monitoring devices to boost adoption and improve patient outcomes. These findings are particularly relevant given the increasing importance of remote healthcare and technology-enabled health solutions in developing countries, where access to healthcare facilities can be limited and managing chronic illnesses and promoting preventative care are pressing public health concerns.

One of the key findings of this study is the significance of Hedonic Motivation, which was found to be a strong positive predictor of consumers' usage intention. This aligns well with prior research (Venkatesh & Brown, 2005; Venkatesh et al., 2012) that demonstrated how enjoyment, fun, and engagement play crucial roles in the adoption of internet-based technologies. In the context of a developing country, this indicates that user experience design is critical—not just for functionality but also to drive engagement. Patients in these settings are not merely passive recipients of healthcare technology; they desire engaging, satisfying, and even entertaining health-monitoring experiences. The importance of hedonic value implies that devices with pleasant interfaces, gamification, and visual appeal could significantly influence long-term use, even among populations less familiar with advanced technologies. As noted, hedonic motivation serves as a key driver in sustaining health-related behaviors, especially among younger and tech-savvy patients, which also applies in developing nations with growing mobile penetration.

Secondly, Perceived Usefulness emerged as a critical determinant of consumers' intention to use wearable health-monitoring devices. This is consistent with Davis et al.'s (1989) Technology Acceptance Model (TAM), which identified perceived usefulness as a central factor influencing technology adoption. Patients must perceive wearable devices as capable of offering meaningful benefits such as early diagnosis, tracking of vital health indicators, and reminders for medication or appointments. Especially in the case of chronic disease management and elderly care, the assurance that these devices can actively contribute to health improvement strengthens the rationale for their adoption. Therefore, it becomes crucial for healthcare providers to emphasize and communicate these practical advantages clearly. Marketing communications and user onboarding should focus on the functional utility of the devices, such as improved health outcomes, prevention of disease escalation, and greater independence for patients.

Another compelling factor is Price Value, which confirms the high price sensitivity of consumers in developing countries when it comes to adopting wearable health technology. Affordability remains a major concern, and adoption is strongly influenced by the perceived return on investment. However, value should be viewed not only in terms of the device's direct cost but also the indirect savings it enables—such as reduced travel to healthcare centers, fewer work absences, and lower hospitalization rates. In remote or underserved regions, where routine healthcare access is costly or time-consuming, wearable devices can serve as an economical and efficient alternative. Thus, affordability models—possibly through public insurance, government subsidies, or rental schemes—should be considered to increase accessibility.

Ease of Use of wearable devices also emerged as a significant predictor of adoption, especially relevant in a developing country context where levels of digital literacy vary significantly across age groups and geographies. A complicated or intimidating user interface can hinder adoption among elderly users or those with limited exposure to digital tools. Designing user-friendly devices that incorporate voice guidance, simple visuals, or language options can greatly enhance usability. Furthermore, supporting this with accessible customer training or helplines is crucial to foster confidence and continued use.

Habit was found to be among the strongest predictors of wearable device usage. This aligns with previous findings (Venkatesh et al., 2003) and highlights the role of repeated use in building comfort and reliance on the device. In a developing country setting, where healthcare services may not always be available, establishing habitual use of health-monitoring technology could help patients independently manage chronic conditions. Behavioral nudges, reminders, and periodic health insights delivered via devices could support habit formation and ultimately improve health self-management.

Trust in the device and in the healthcare provider or brand behind it was another crucial factor influencing usage intentions. In developing countries, where skepticism towards digital platforms and concerns about data privacy may be more prevalent, building trust is essential. Users need assurance that the device functions reliably, their data is secure, and the information provided is medically sound. Transparency regarding data usage, endorsements from healthcare professionals, and clear privacy policies can play a significant role in overcoming these concerns and enhancing user confidence.

The study also underscores the impact of Social Influence from Friends (SIFR) and Social Influence from Specialists (SISP). SIFR refers to peer influence and the extent to which individuals observe and emulate the behaviors of friends or family members. If someone in a patient's social circle is already using a wearable device and shares a positive experience, the likelihood of that patient adopting the technology increases. This supports the diffusion of innovation theory, where early adopters influence the majority through social proof. Strategies such as referral incentives, group challenges, or community success stories can capitalize on peer influence.

SISP, on the other hand, involves influence from professionals such as doctors, fitness experts, or health coaches. Professional endorsement serves as validation of the technology's efficacy and safety. In many cases, patients may hesitate to adopt a device until it is recommended by a trusted healthcare provider. This underscores the importance of involving professionals in the promotion and onboarding process of wearable technology. Hospitals and clinics can integrate these devices into care plans, prescribe their use post-treatment, or offer demonstrations during check-ups.

In addition to these core predictors, Trialability and Perceived Risk also significantly influence the adoption process. Trialability allows hesitant users—especially those unfamiliar with digital health tools—to experiment without financial commitment, a critical feature in low-trust, resource-constrained settings. Providing demo units or short-term rentals could mitigate user anxiety. On the other hand, perceived risk—whether due to fears of technical failure or data misuse—can discourage adoption. In developing countries, where technical support may be less available, addressing these risks through quality assurance, certifications, and visible service support is essential.

Perceived Risk refers to the fear of potential negative consequences such as data breaches, malfunctioning devices, or incorrect readings. If the risks are perceived as high, users are likely to reject the technology irrespective of its benefits. To mitigate this, manufacturers and healthcare providers must prioritize quality assurance, offer robust customer support, and provide clear usage instructions. Additionally, third-party evaluations, consumer reports, and user reviews can help lower the perceived risk by providing objective performance metrics.

Moreover, demographic and contextual factors—such as age, gender, health status, and digital literacy—moderate the influence of these predictors. For example, younger individuals may prioritize hedonic features and design aesthetics, while older adults may focus more on perceived usefulness and ease of use. Understanding these user segments allows for the customization of marketing and training interventions.

The integration of wearable devices into broader health ecosystems is another area worth exploring. Linking devices with telehealth platforms, electronic medical records, and personalized care plans can significantly enhance their utility. The interoperability of devices with existing health infrastructure ensures that data collected from wearables translate into actionable insights, both for patients and providers.

Furthermore, demographic and contextual factors—such as age, gender, health status, and digital literacy—moderate the effects of the above constructs. For instance, older adults may prioritize perceived usefulness and trust, while younger users may respond more to hedonic motivation. Recognizing these segments within the population is necessary for crafting effective awareness, education, and marketing strategies tailored to each group's priorities.

The integration of wearable devices into developing country health ecosystems presents a vital opportunity. Linking these devices to telemedicine platforms, public health records, or chronic disease management programs can greatly enhance their utility. Ensuring that such technologies are interoperable with national digital health missions or e-health records will increase their relevance and acceptance among patients and providers.

Finally, policy-level support is critical. In developing countries, adoption can be scaled through initiatives such as preventive health incentives, government procurement of devices for public health distribution, campaigns to raise digital health awareness, and legal frameworks to regulate data use and privacy. Multi-sector partnerships between governments, NGOs, and the private sector can create an enabling ecosystem for digital health technologies like wearables.

CONCLUSION

In conclusion, the adoption of wearable devices for health monitoring is shaped by a multifaceted interplay of psychological, social, economic, and technological factors. Key determinants such as hedonic motivation, perceived usefulness, ease of use, price value, habit, and trust must be addressed in a holistic manner. Social influences, trialability, and perceived risk further refine the adoption curve, indicating that user engagement is as much about emotional comfort as it is about technical capability. By leveraging these insights, healthcare providers, policymakers, and device manufacturers can craft strategies that not only encourage adoption but also sustain long-term usage, ultimately leading to better health outcomes and more efficient care delivery systems.

Limitation and future scope of study

Despite the valuable insights gained from our study, it is important to acknowledge its limitations. The sample size of our study was 500, which although significant, may not be large enough to represent the entire population of interest. There may be some subgroups or demographics that are not fully represented in our sample, which could affect the generalizability of our findings.

Furthermore, given the rapid development of wearable technology, it is important to conduct ongoing research to assess the current state of usage and adoption, as well as to identify emerging trends and barriers. Such studies could inform the development of new strategies and interventions aimed at promoting the widespread adoption of wearable devices for health monitoring, ultimately leading to improved health outcomes for individuals and populations.

Secondly, given the rapidly evolving nature of wearable technology, it would be valuable to investigate the impact of newer features and functionalities on patients' usage intention and behavior. For example, features like AI-driven analytics and personalized health coaching could significantly impact patients' motivation to use these devices for monitoring their health.

Thirdly, future research could explore the role of cultural factors in patients' usage intention and behavior. The current study was conducted in a specific cultural context, and it would be interesting to see if the results hold true in other cultures and settings.

Fourth, as wearable devices become more prevalent and integrated into healthcare systems, it would be valuable to investigate the impact of these devices on healthcare outcomes, such as patient satisfaction, treatment adherence, and overall health outcomes. Such research could provide valuable insights into the effectiveness of wearable technology as a tool for improving patient outcomes in the healthcare setting.

Although the present research hass carried out using the cross-sectional design which provides a snapshot of technology adoption intention, future studies employing longitudinal methods are essential to confirm causal pathways and behavioral evolution. Additionally, cross-cultural comparative studies involving both developed and developing nations would provide deeper insights into the moderating role of socio-economic and technological infrastructure in shaping adoption behavior.

Managerial Implications

The findings of this study have several managerial implications for healthcare organizations and practitioners. Firstly, perceived usefulness, perceived ease of use, facilitating conditions, hedonic motivation, price, and trust were found to be significant predictors of usage intention for wearable health monitoring devices among patients. Therefore, healthcare providers should focus on enhancing the usefulness and ease of use of wearable devices, providing necessary facilitating conditions, and offering devices at a reasonable price to increase patients' adoption and usage intention.

Secondly, perceived risk was found to have a significant negative effect on usage intention. Therefore, healthcare organizations should take measures to reduce patients' perceived risk by providing clear and transparent information about the benefits and risks associated with the use of wearable health monitoring devices.

Finally, social influence, habit, trial, and SIFR were found to have a positive but insignificant effect on usage intention. Healthcare organizations should still consider these factors in their marketing and promotional efforts to increase patients' awareness and interest in wearable health monitoring devices.

In conclusion, healthcare providers should consider the significant predictors of usage intention identified in this study when developing strategies for promoting wearable health monitoring devices among patients.

REFERENCES

Ahlan, A. R., & Ahmad, B. I. (2015). An overview of patient acceptance of health information technology in developing countries: A review and conceptual model. *International Journal of Information Systems and Project Management*, *3*(1), 29–48.

Ajzen, I. (1991). The theory of planned behavior. *Organizational Behavior and Human Decision Processes*, *50*(2), 179–211. DOI: 10.1016/0749-5978(91)90020-T

Akter, S., D'Ambra, J., & Ray, P. (2010). Trustworthiness in health information services: An assessment of a hierarchical model with mediating and moderating effects using partial least squares (PLS). *Journal of the American Society for Information Science and Technology*, *62*(1), 100–116. DOI: 10.1002/asi.21442

Brown, S. A., & Venkatesh, V. (2005). Model of adoption of technology in households: A baseline model test and extension incorporating household life cycle. *Management Information Systems Quarterly*, *29*(3), 399–426. DOI: 10.2307/25148690

Chandrasekaran, R., Katthula, V., & Moustakas, E. (2020). Patterns of use and key predictors for the use of wearable health care devices by US adults: Insights from a national survey. *Journal of Medical Internet Research*, *22*(10), e22443. DOI: 10.2196/22443 PMID: 33064083

Davis, F. D. (1989). Perceived usefulness, perceived ease of use, and user acceptance of information technology. *Management Information Systems Quarterly*, *13*(3), 319–340. DOI: 10.2307/249008

Davis, F. D., Bagozzi, R. P., & Warshaw, P. R. (1989). User acceptance of computer technology: A comparison of two theoretical models. *Management Science*, *35*(8), 982–1003. DOI: 10.1287/mnsc.35.8.982

Dodds, W. B., Monroe, K. B., & Grewal, D. (1991). Effects of price, brand, and store information on buyers' product evaluations. *JMR, Journal of Marketing Research*, *28*(3), 307–319. DOI: 10.1177/002224379102800305

Escobar-Rodríguez, T., & Carvajal-Trujillo, E. (2014). Online purchasing tickets for low cost carriers: An application of the unified theory of acceptance and use of technology (UTAUT) model. *Tourism Management*, *43*, 70–88. DOI: 10.1016/j.tourman.2014.01.017

Gao, Y., Li, H., & Luo, Y. (2015). An empirical study of wearable technology acceptance in healthcare. *Industrial Management & Data Systems*, *115*(10), 1704–1723. DOI: 10.1108/IMDS-03-2015-0087

Gefen, D., Karahanna, E., & Straub, D. W. (2003). Trust and TAM in online shopping: An integrated model. *Management Information Systems Quarterly*, *27*(1), 51–90. DOI: 10.2307/30036519

Holden, R. J., & Karsh, B. T. (2010). The technology acceptance model: Its past and its future in health care. *Journal of Biomedical Informatics*, *43*(1), 159–172. DOI: 10.1016/j.jbi.2009.07.002 PMID: 19615467

Kim, S., Lee, K. H., Hwang, H., & Yoo, S. (2016). Analysis of the factors influencing healthcare professionals' adoption of mobile electronic medical record (EMR) using the unified theory of acceptance and use of technology (UTAUT). *BMC Medical Informatics and Decision Making*, *20*(1), 1–10. DOI: 10.1186/s12911-016-0249-8 PMID: 26831123

Kim, S. S., & Malhotra, N. K. (2005). A longitudinal model of continued IS use: An integrative view of four mechanisms underlying postadoption phenomena. *Management Science*, *51*(5), 741–755. DOI: 10.1287/mnsc.1040.0326

Krogoll, C. (2015). ICT in healthcare: A review of literature and implications for developing countries.

Krogoll, C., Schmidt, L., & Hoffmann, W. (2015). Use of wearables in healthcare–a systematic review. *Proceedings of the 48th Hawaii International Conference on System Sciences*.

Lee, S. M., & Lee, D. (2020). Healthcare wearable devices: An analysis of key factors for continuous use intention. *Service Business*, *14*(4), 503–531. DOI: 10.1007/s11628-020-00428-3

Limayem, M., Hirt, S. G., & Cheung, C. M. (2007). How habit limits the predictive power of intention: The case of information systems continuance. *Management Information Systems Quarterly*, *31*(4), 705–737. DOI: 10.2307/25148817

Ma, Z., Gao, Q., & Yang, M. (2022). Adoption of Wearable Devices by Older People: Changes in Use Behaviors and User Experiences. *International Journal of Human-Computer Interaction*, *39*, 1–24. DOI: 10.1080/10447318.2022.2083573

Meier, D. Y., Barthelmess, P., Sun, W., & Liberatore, F. (2020). Wearable technology acceptance in health care based on national culture differences: Cross-country analysis between Chinese and Swiss consumers. *Journal of Medical Internet Research*, *22*(10), e18801. DOI: 10.2196/18801 PMID: 33090108

Or, C. K., Karsh, B. T., Severtson, D. J., Burke, L. J., Brown, R. L., & Brennan, P. F. (2010). Factors affecting home care patients' acceptance of a web-based interactive self-management technology. *Journal of the American Medical Informatics Association : JAMIA, 18*(1), 51–59. DOI: 10.1136/jamia.2010.007336 PMID: 21131605

PWC. (2013). Healthcare's new entrants: Who will be the industry's Amazon.com? Retrieved from https://www.pwc.com/us/en/health-industries/top-health-industry-issues/assets/pwc-hri-top-issues-2013.pdf

PWC. (n.d.). Digital healthcare.

Sun, J., Williams, D., & Li, Y. (2021). Let's Bail!: The evolution of individual-group affiliation in an online gaming community. *Computers in Human Behavior, 121*, 106818. DOI: 10.1016/j.chb.2021.106818

Venkatesh, V., & Brown, S. A. (2005). A longitudinal investigation of personal computers in homes: Adoption determinants and emerging challenges. *Management Information Systems Quarterly, 29*(3), 425–478.

Venkatesh, V., Morris, M. G., Davis, G. B., & Davis, F. D. (2003). User acceptance of information technology: Toward a unified view. *Management Information Systems Quarterly, 27*(3), 425–478. DOI: 10.2307/30036540

Venkatesh, V., Thong, J. Y. L., & Xu, X. (2012). Consumer acceptance and use of information technology: Extending the unified theory of acceptance and use of technology. *Management Information Systems Quarterly, 36*(1), 157–178. DOI: 10.2307/41410412

Wang, Y., Kung, L., & Byrd, T. A. (2020). Big data analytics: Understanding its capabilities and potential benefits for healthcare organizations. *Technological Forecasting and Social Change, 126*, 3–13. DOI: 10.1016/j.techfore.2020.120004

Wang, Y. S., Wang, Y. M., Lin, H. H., & Tang, T. I. (2003). Determinants of user acceptance of Internet banking: An empirical study. *International Journal of Service Industry Management, 14*(5), 501–519. DOI: 10.1108/09564230310500192

West, D., & Miller, E. (2006). The Digital Divide in Public E-Health: Barriers to Accessibility and Privacy in State Health Department Websites. *Journal of Health Care for the Poor and Underserved, 17*, 652–667. DOI: 10.1353/hpu.2006.0115 PMID: 16960328

Wu, M., & Luo, J. (n.d.). *Wearable Technology Applications in Healthcare: A Literature Review*. Digital Health, Online Journal of Nursing Informatics Contributors. Retrieved from Kruse, C., Betancourt, J., Ortiz, S., Valdes Luna, S. M., Bamrah, I. K., & Segovia, N. (2019). Barriers to the use of mobile health in improving health outcomes in developing countries: Systematic review. *Journal of Medical Internet Research, 21*(10), e13263. DOI: 10.2196/13263

Yang, H. J., Lee, J.-H., & Lee, W. (2025, March 28). Factors Influencing Health Care Technology Acceptance in Older Adults Based on the Technology Acceptance Model and the Unified Theory of Acceptance and Use of Technology: Meta-Analysis. *Journal of Medical Internet Research, 27*(e65269). Advance online publication. DOI: 10.2196/65269 PMID: 40153796

Yin, Z., Yan, J., Fang, S., Wang, D., & Han, D. (2022). User acceptance of wearable intelligent medical devices through a modified unified theory of acceptance and use of technology. *Annals of Translational Medicine, 10*(11), 629. DOI: 10.21037/atm-21-5510 PMID: 35813345

Yu, C. S. (2012). Factors affecting individuals to adopt mobile banking: Empirical evidence from the UTAUT model. *Journal of Electronic Commerce Research, 13*(2), 104–121.

Zhou, T., Lu, Y., & Wang, B. (2010). Integrating TTF and UTAUT to explain mobile banking user adoption. *Computers in Human Behavior, 26*(4), 760–767. DOI: 10.1016/j.chb.2010.01.013

Chapter 8

First Insights in Video-Based Patient Monitoring in the Long-Time Care Setting

Marcel Sailer
https://orcid.org/0009-0000-3825-3984
Rosenheim Technical University of Applied Sciences, Germany

Alena Sofie Fischer
https://orcid.org/0009-0009-4179-0057
Ulm University Hospital, Germany

Sarah Kaiser
Ulm University Hospital, Germany

Amelie Münzing
https://orcid.org/0009-0009-4364-1848
Ulm University Hospital, Germany

Mina Julie Schmachtel
Weleda AG, Germany

ABSTRACT

Video-based monitoring systems in long-term inpatient care represent an opportunity to increase patient safety. This paper intends to provide a basis for discussion for the use of video-based monitoring systems, focusing on nursing an public acceptance. Method Interviews were conducted with nursing care professionals (n=4) and people from the public (n=244) were surveyed via an online survey. Results and

DOI: 10.4018/979-8-3373-2545-3.ch008

Discussion The results clearly show that video-based monitoring systems have both advantages and disadvantages as well as ethical aspects and factors that influence the acceptance of video-based monitoring which must be weighed up individually. From the total responses of n=244, 47,1% (n=115) of survey participants are in favour of the use of monitoring systems in nursing, while 40,1% are undecided. The most frequently mentioned advantages from the interviews included continual vital sign monitoring, faster reactions in emergencies, a reduction in the workload of nursing staff and an increase in patient safety, for example through improved fall prevention for patients.

1. INTRODUCTION / THEORETICAL BACKGROUND

Video-based health monitoring systems in long-term residential care wards offer a potential for enhanced patient safety. This approach involves huge technological applications such as infrared, RGB cameras and sensors, video and audio transmission, real-time imaging, remote photopletysmography (rPPG) as well as artificial intelligence (AI) and machine learning (ML) (Wright & Singh, 2022, He et al. 2023, Mujirishvili et al. 2023, Romeo et al. 2023; Ferreira et al. 2024, Ergai et al. 2024). The use of such systems can enable monitoring the detection of falls, action and activity monitoring, sleep monitoring, respiration, epilepsy, vital signs of facial expressions and others (Sathyanarayana et al. 2018; Hun et al., 2020; Guo et al. 2021; Wright & Singh, 2022; Lear et al. 2023; Ergai et al. 2024). Visual sensing technologies hold significant promise for improving care quality. The capability to remotely monitor health-related variables is particularly beneficial for disease management, early risk detection and continuous health status assessment (Ferreira et al. 2024, p. 10). There is substantial experience in clinical and outpatient settings with video-based monitoring of vital signs in critically ill patients, including assessments of activity, agitation, falls and delirium. The demand for unobtrusive, continuous health monitoring methods is increasingly evident, particularly in contexts where conventional monitoring methods are insufficient (Guo et al., 2021). However, acceptance of visual-sensor monitoring among potential users remains limited in some settings (Seigel et al., 2024). Ensuring the consistency and quality of video data collection and processing in an ethically responsible manner is a critical challenge (Ferreira et al., 2024).

Within the scope of this project, experiences with the video-based patient monitoring system Oxevision™ were studied. Oxevision™ as a product of Oxehealth enables video-based patient monitoring intended to enhance patient safety and quality of care (Oxehealth, 2023). It was developed for psychiatric inpatient care and is used in collaboration with the National Health Service (NHS) in psychiatric facilities, including clinics and nursing homes. Oxevision™ comprises the modules Observation, Vital Signs, Notifications, and Activity Reports. This study focuses on the "Vital Signs" module. Using an infrared camera, pulse rate and respiratory rate can be measured contactlessly, and a 15-second still image can be displayed. The camera is installed within an "Oxevision™ Unit" mounted in the patient's room (Oxehealth, 2023). According to the manufacturer, this component has been approved as a Class IIa medical device in Europe since 2018 and was first used in Sweden. FDA approval followed in 2021, with a market launch in the United States. There is, however, no publicly available information on its use in Germany (Oxehealth, 2023). This raises the question of whether Germany might consider adopting the system, drawing on experiences from Sweden and the United States.

Social acceptance and opinions of professionals and the public are vital for a successful implementation of this system. This paper aims to frame the discussion on the use of monitoring systems in long-term residential care facilities, using Oxevision™ as an example. The goal is to conduct qualitative and quantitative foundational research to generate data and critically analyze the topic. Alongside gathering a depiction of the public opinion, this study will highlight potential benefits and limitations of its technology and discuss ethical aspects.

2. STUDY DESIGN

This study employed a mixed-method design to support the analysis. Qualitative data were collected first via semi-structured interviews with nursing experts, followed by quantitative validation through an online survey conducted from February to April 2024.

An extensive literature review preceded data collection. Research was conducted in the Cochrane Library, PubMed, ScienceDirect and CINAHL using the keywords "vision-based monitoring" and "vision-based monitoring in nursing." Sources in German and English were included, spanning publications from 2008 to 2024.

2.1. Study population

To provide a reliable study, professional nurses (n = 4) with relevant experience in patient monitoring systems and expert knowledge on the topic were selected and interviewed. The interview sample included senior nurse managers, practicing nurses, and a certified nursing educator specializing in healthcare technology in nursing. To capture broader perspectives, an open online survey was also conducted (n = 244). No dropouts or incomplete data were identified among the study participants.

2.1.1. Characteristics of Interview Participants

To illustrate the selection of interview participants, Table 1 below summarizes the professional backgrounds of all interview participants (n=4) and their associated are of expertise.

Table 1. Characteristics of Interview Participants

Interview 1	No age provided Training as a retail salesperson, 1-year training as a geriatric care assistant, further training to become a registered geriatric nurse, training as a nursing service manager. Currently serving as the nursing service manager of a stationary long-term care facility.
Interview 2	53 years old Registered geriatric nurse at a stationary long-term care facility, practice educator, currently undergoing further education in organisation and leadership in social and health services, team leader, future nursing service manager at his facility.
Interview 3	No age provided Initially a geriatric care assistant, further training as a nursing professional, further training as a gerontopsychiatric specialist, business administrator for organization and leadership, facility management, practice instruction, ward management, deputy nursing service manager, nursing service manager since 2020 at a stationary long-term care facility, and deputy facility manager specializing in gerontopsychiatry.
Interview 4	59 years old Expert at the State Competence Center Baden-Württemberg, nurse, former role as a nursing school principal and nursing educator.

2.2. Interview

To gather the perspectives of professional nurses on video-based patient monitoring systems, semi-structured interviews (n=4) were conducted. The (expert) interviews were conducted methodologically in five stages: development of the interview guide, selection and contact of experts, execution, securing of results, and analysis of results (Kaiser, 2021). Prior written consent for participation, interview recording and data usage was obtained from all participants before conducting the interviews. Participants were questioned about themselves, opportunities and risks, ethical dilemmas and prior experiences (e.g., Oxevision™ system). Interview analysis, transcription and coding were performed using MAXQDA24 software (MAXQDA 2024). Subsequently, the interviews were evaluated using structured inductive content analysis following Mayring's approach (Mayring & Fenzl, 2019, pp. 638f.).

2.3. Survey

Figure 1. Schematic Representation of Online Survey (Original Illustration)

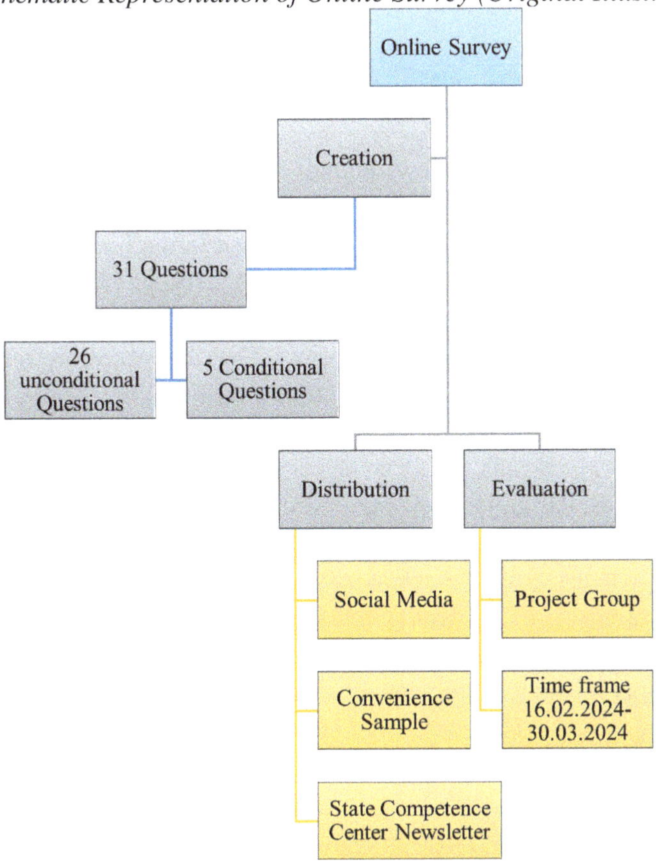

In order to inquire the public opinion on video-based surveillance systems in long-term care facilities, a quantitative survey was conducted using an online questionnaire (n=244). Prior to the survey, a pretest was conducted. The survey was primarily disseminated through social media channels. Participation was voluntary, adhering to data protection regulations, and responses were anonymized. Data collection was carried out using a nominal scale, and analysis involved frequency-based evaluation using R-Commander and R-Studio. No hypothesis-testing, statistical procedures, confidence intervals, or p-values were computed. Median was chosen as the measure of central tendency to minimize the impact of outliers compared to the mean. Survey questions were categorized and clustered beforehand, covering demographic information, opinions on care facilities using surveillance systems, concerns, benefits of usage and types of surveillance methods. The questionnaire comprised a total of 25 questions, plus a withdrawal question allowing participants to retract previously provided answers, with subsequent sub-questions dependent on initial responses.

3. RESULTS

The evaluation of the interviews employed predefined categories: Advantages, Disadvantages, Ethical Dilemmas, Oxevision™ and Other Systems, Desired Additions and Concluding Statements – developed through an inductive analysis following Mayring's approach (Mayring & Fenzl, 2019, p. 637). These categories emerged from the analysis of interview transcripts using Mayring's method and a structured literature review conducted a priori. The categorization framework was also applied to the quantitative data collection.

Definitions of categories:

- Advantages: All subjectively perceived and empirically identifiable benefits reported by interview participants.
- Disadvantages (Critical Aspects): Statements involving concerns, fears, legal considerations and significant challenges or limitations in the use of patient monitoring systems.
- Ethical Dilemmas: Statements or aspects that present moral considerations regarding criticisms and perceived benefits.
- Acceptance: The endorsement or rejection of patient monitoring systems in nursing.
- Oxevision™/Other Systems: Experiences, opinions and statements regarding patient monitoring systems applicable to daily routines in residential long-term care, including wearables and video surveillance systems such as Oxevision™.
- Additions/Desired Changes: Statements expressing desires for changes, expansions or enhancements to the Oxevision™ system.
- Concluding Statements: Expressions or reflections of personal views on video-based surveillance in nursing.

3.1. Interview

3.1.1. Advantages

From the conducted semi-structured interviews, various advantages for both patients and nursing professionals are highlighted by the nursing experts. Table 2 presents a comparison of the advantages mentioned by the nursing professionals and care recipients.

According to the experts, clear benefits for nursing professionals include gaining an overall overview, facilitating quicker responses in emergency situations and the prioritization of tasks. Additionally, these systems are said to alleviate staff workload, as the necessary care cannot always be guaranteed due to staffing ratios (see Interview 3). Care planning could be supplemented and adjusted through the monitoring of movements or micro-movements by surveillance systems. Furthermore, these systems would help minimize residents' fall risks through movement detection. Systems such as Oxevision™ would enable continuous vital sign monitoring, particularly at night and during end-of-life care, enhancing situational assessment.

Table 2. Overview of advantages for nurses and care recipients

Nurses	**Care recipients**
Creation of an overall overview	Fall prevention
Quicker response in emergency situations	Detection of bed exits
Prioritization of tasks	Quicker response in emergency situations
Staff relief	Undisturbed sleep
Monitoring of (micro-) movements	Increased patient safety
Assurance through documentation in care planning	
Continuous vital sign monitoring	
End-of-life care	

The use in psychiatric facilities, forensic institutions, and for self- or third-party endangerment was endorsed to ensure greater security (see Interview 1). For individuals with dementia, the use was considered positive as it can positively impact quality of life by enabling undisturbed sleep or ensuring freedom within the facility (see Interview 3).

3.1.2. Disadvantages and Critical Points

Several benefits for both nursing staff and patients were noted by the participants regarding the use of monitoring systems, yet they also mentioned negative or critically assessed aspects related to system implementation. A critical aspect mentioned in three out of four interviews is the intrusion into privacy or infringement of personal rights. To generate a comprehensive picture, monitoring would need to cover living areas, rooms, and corridors, which means capturing images of all residents, including those who do not require it. It is also necessary to consider whether video surveillance systems restrict the autonomy of residents. This raises the question of whether and to what extent restricted autonomy falls under deprivation of liberty measures. In Germany, this requires a judicial decision and are only used to prevent self-endangerment, and does not represent a permanent solution (StrUG, 2024). Furthermore, potential misuse of these systems, the data they generate and neglect of hands-on patient care are viewed critically.

Table 3. Disadvantage Overview for Nurses and Care Recipients

Nurses	Care Recipients
Privacy	Privacy
Infringement of personal rights	Infringement on personal rights
Feeling of being observed and controlled	Interference of autonomy
No faster response possible in case of multiple simultaneous events	Potential misuse of the systems
Patient observation is lost	Data misuse
Challenge in implementation	Neglect of hands-on patient care
High costs	

Additionally, according to experts, the use of patient monitoring systems could also trigger a feeling of continuous observation and control among nursing professionals. Furthermore, it is noted that these systems cannot replace insufficient staffing, and in the event of multiple simultaneous incidents, a quicker response may not be achievable. There is also concern that "[...] contacts may decrease, and people or nursing professionals may also forget to observe to some extent. [...] This sometimes worries me that we are only focusing on numbers and data" (see Interview 4).

Nurses also face a potential hurdle in maintaining their competence. "You go into a room and perceive something. Something that cannot immediately be proven with numbers, data, facts, that's what we also need to think about" (see Interview 4).

Another drawback or challenge in the implementation of monitoring systems is the partially inadequate technical equipment and the associated expertise, which is currently lacking in many long-term residential care facilities (Hülsken-Giesler, 2010, p. 238). Additionally, high implementation costs are expected, which need to be assessed in regards to their cost-effectiveness.

3.1.3. Ethical Dilemma

From an ethical perspective, the intrusion into privacy represents an aspect that must be specifically considered and discussed when using such monitoring systems. Particularly, the infringement of personal rights must be scrutinized and critically examined (see Interview 2). Moreover, both autonomy and self-determined living, which are also associated with privacy, are significant considerations. The topic of sexuality in old age can potentially be influenced by these surveillance systems, as individuals may experience constant monitoring. Ethical questioning in this context also includes whether those affected or their relatives have the possibility to independently deactivate the device in such cases (see Interview 2). Therefore, it remains to be discussed whether the disadvantages mentioned above can be justified by the benefits outlined in Chapter 1.3.1.

A possible question here is the over- or under-provisioning of certain groups of patients (see Interview 4). The use of monitoring systems could also lead to a reduction in personal interactions between nursing staff and the residents of the respective facility, which in turn could alter the professional relationship.

"[...] To what extent will nurses visits to patients in their rooms be decreased by? This needs to be examined very specifically at this stage. Clearly, we need relief and help in our job that is not the issue. However, when the relief leads to less personal contact with the care recipient, it needs to be carefully analyzed first. I'm not saying it shouldn't happen, [...] but it needs to be critically examined" (Interview expert 4).

One interviewee mentioned some of the employees' concerns about being monitored and filmed at all times in their own actions (see Interview 3).

Finally, it is important to discuss whether these systems provide space or restrict freedom.

3.1.4. Acceptance

The application of monitoring systems in psychiatric and disability facilities was widely accepted (cf. Interview 1). The aspect of security was particularly emphasized, which is often perceived as important by relatives based on their own experiences. Additionally, the use of monitoring systems during night shifts also garnered high acceptance, as staffing ratios are often smaller during these times, allowing for better oversight and prioritization of actions. Nonetheless, it is important not to overlook the importance of autonomous decision-making. Furthermore, there was a desire expressed for people to "think about such things as long as they are capable of doing so and then make decisions accordingly..." (Interview 4).

To increase the acceptance of monitoring systems, it was emphasized that nursing perspectives and the integration of these systems into care planning are essential. This includes prior risk assessment, individual consultation with residents and their families and transparent explanation or presentation of the facility and the current situation (see Interview 3). The focus here was on gaining the understanding of those affected, "because when the other person understands its benefits and sees the purpose behind it [...] then I always receive good feedback..." (Interview 3).

3.1.5. Oxevision™ and Other Systems

In the context of expert interviews, participants were asked about their experiences with patient monitoring systems. This included experiences with their own use of such systems, monitoring of family members or exposure to surveillance.

One interviewee mentioned knowing colleagues who work in forensic and psychiatric settings using infrared surveillance (see Interview 2).

Furthermore, in one of the facilities real-time monitoring is already being used to oversee common areas, corridors, and gardens. However, there is no monitoring in patient rooms (see Interview 3).

There was also mention of awareness regarding the use of patient-focused monitoring systems that do not include a camera function, such as MOJO™ or Wisbi™. Some advantages of these systems were also highlighted (see Interview 4). None of the interview participants had heard of the Oxevision™ monitoring system.

3.1.6. Additions or Desired Changes

There was mention of video-based monitoring being used during rest periods. Infrared surveillance was considered sufficient in this regard (see Interview 2).

Additionally, before implementing such surveillance systems in many facilities, structural changes and technical adjustments would be necessary, along with expansion of IT systems (see Interview 2).

One interview discussed the combination of camera-based surveillance with resident-specific monitoring systems like MOJO™ and sensor mattresses. It was also deemed important to be able to customize camera system functions for each resident and deactivate certain functions as and when needed (see Interview 4).

A benefit of clear image transmission was seen in assessing facial expressions, which is crucial for recognizing epileptic seizures, for example (cf. Interview 3). However, pixelated images would suffice for a brief glimpse into each patient's room (see Interview 3).

Furthermore, it was noted that surveillance systems could be used to justify specific care measures in care planning, such as monitoring positioning. However, this must be justified from a nursing perspective, applied individually and needs to be well-documented (see Interview 3).

3.1.7. Conclusion

Although patient monitoring systems offer significant benefits, critical aspects remain subject to discussion. The interview participants reject a generalized application and emphasize the need for justification at all times: “I can do everything, but I always have to justify why I don't do something or why I do something... and quality of life must always be paramount, it must always make sense. And then I think you can do anything" (Interview 3).

An expert in digitalization in nursing summarized the topic of surveillance in her statement: "[...] I see great potential in support technologies for professional nursing practice, both in outpatient and long-term residential care, as well as in acute care. The challenge will be for our discipline to establish criteria for decision-making and for targeted implementation, which is a major concern for me" (Interview 4).

3.2. Questionnaire

3.2.1. Characteristics and Distribution

From 16th February 2024 to 30th March 2024, a total of 244 individuals from various age groups participated in the online survey. Among them, 34,8% (n=85) are working actively in the healthcare sector. The majority of all participants reside in Germany. Regarding the age distribution, 4,5% were under 20 years old, 38,10% were 20-29 years, 9,4% 30-39 years, 9,4% 40-49 years, 26,2% 50-59 years and 12,3% 60-69 years.

3.2.2. Support for Surveillance Systems in Nursing Care

Overall, 40% of respondents support the use of surveillance systems in nursing care, while 48,2% are undecided. The median age of those undecided is "30-39 years". The median age of those who reject surveillance systems in nursing care is "50-59 years", whereas the median age of supporters is "40-49 years". Figure f shows a histogram depicting the absolute frequency of responses to the question "Do you support the use of surveillance systems in nursing care?"

3.2.3. Reported Experiences with Surveillance Systems

Figure 2. Bubble-Chart connection between profession in healthcare and advocacy

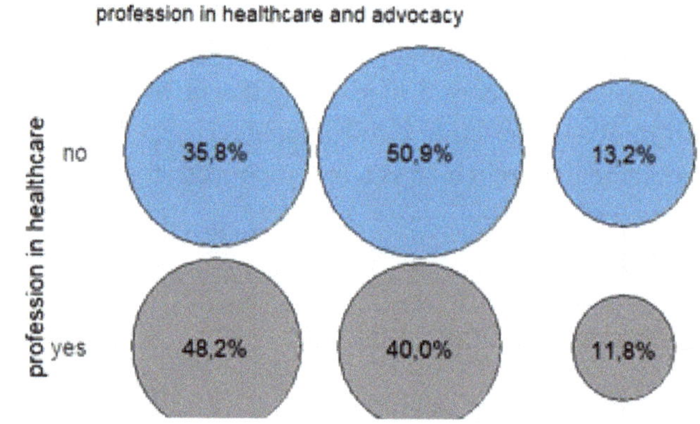

Figure 3. Histogramm of advocacy

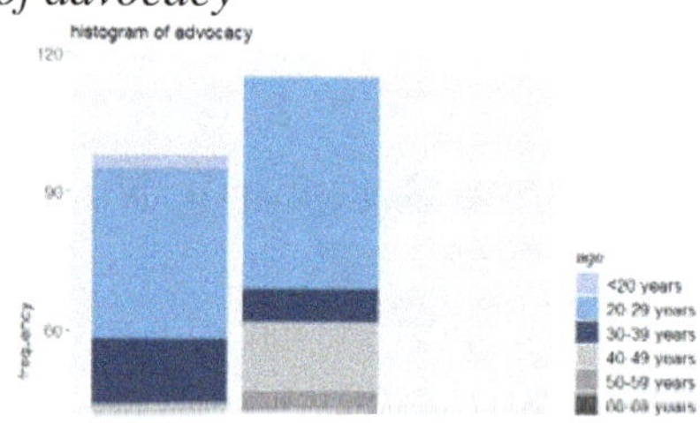

Among all participants, 30,7% (n=75) have heard of surveillance systems in nursing care, regardless of the care setting, with only two individuals specifically mentioning Oxevision™. Frequently mentioned systems included mobile monitors such as ECG applications and vital sign monitoring systems. Additionally, the sample indicated frequent use of emergency buttons and baby monitors in home settings.

3.2.4. Benefits and Concerns

Table 3 provides an overview of all questions regarding the benefits of surveillance systems. It includes both closed multiple-choice questions and suggestive questions with open-ended responses.

Table 4. Overview of the category "advantages" with answer frequency

Questions						
R: Do you think surveillance systems can enhance patient safety?	Yes 77% n=188	No 5,3% n=13	Undecided 17,6% n=43			
W: What advantage do surveillance systems offer patients?	Security 64,8% n=158	Undisturbed sleep 41,8% n=102	Quick response to events 82% n=200		It offers no advantage for patients 5,3% n=13	
X: What advantages do surveillance systems offer caregivers?	Security 36,9% n=90	Structured work 35,7% n=87	Relief through coordination 50,8% n=124	Relief through prioritization 45,5% n=111	It offers no advantage for caregivers 3,7% n=9	I cannot make a statement on this 13,5% n=33

Contrary to the results in Table 3, 70,9% (n=173) consider invasion of privacy as one of the critical issues. Upon further analysis, 76,2% (n=186) are against continuous monitoring of their own person. Compared to checks by nursing staff, 15-second recordings are seen as a greater invasion of privacy, mentioned by 54,5% (n=133) as a decisive concern that needs careful consideration.

The questionnaire (n=244) captured concerns through a free-text field with the question "What concerns do you have regarding the use of surveillance systems?" Subsequently, the free-text responses were systematically analyzed. Categories were formed based on frequently repeated keywords, and the responses were assigned to these categories. If multiple keywords were mentioned, the response was assigned to multiple categories.

The most frequently mentioned concern is privacy violation, which appears in 92 (n=244) responses, accounting for over 37% of the total. In this context, privacy primarily refers to the privacy of those in need of care, although some responses explicitly include the privacy of caregivers, which can also be violated by surveillance systems.

Table 5. Overview of the most frequently mentioned concerns in the survey

Categories	Definition	Number of Answers (n=244)
Privacy	All free-text responses containing the word "privacy."	**92**
Data Protection, Data Security, Data Abuse, and Hacking	All free-text responses containing the words "data protection," "data security," "data abuse," or "hacking." Additionally, responses questioning the security of data or implying that third parties could access the data or spread/misuse it without consent.	**60**
Lack of Human Contact	All free-text responses implying a lack of human contact or that caregiving becomes less personal. Also, responses implying that surveillance systems lead to dehumanization.	**24**
(Continuous) Monitoring and Discomfort	All free-text responses addressing surveillance or control, or describing how systems could be used for excessive or continuous monitoring. Additionally, responses describing feelings of being observed and associated negative emotions (e.g., discomfort or feelings of shame).	**24**
None	All free-text responses indicating that there are no concerns.	**23**
Deterioration of Care or Working Conditions	All free-text responses implying that the use of a system leads to a deterioration in care, for example, due to staff reductions or because certain aspects of care are no longer performed due to the system. Additionally, responses implying that the use of a system worsens working conditions for caregivers. Since poorer working conditions often coincide with staff shortages, which in turn affect the quality of care, these categories are combined.	**16**

Furthermore, many of the respondents have concerns about data privacy. This category includes responses that question the security of data or imply that third parties could access or misuse data without consent.

Also frequently mentioned is the lack of human contact, which could negatively impact the care recipients. Other concerns include the risk of excessive surveillance and the discomfort associated with the feeling of being observed. Additionally, there are concerns that the use of monitoring systems could lead to a deterioration of the care system, manifesting in reduced care services and worsened working conditions for nurses. Further concerns include technical errors and system failures, high costs, potential misuse and the worry that such systems could lead to unwanted life-prolonging measures. The violation of intimacy as well as personal rights were also mentioned as major concerns.

3.2.5. Acceptance

To determine acceptance, participants were asked if a nursing home with monitoring systems would be suitable for their relatives or themselves. Figure 4 shows that 112 individuals (45.9%) would choose a facility with video surveillance for their relatives. Overall, 15,6% (n=38) are not willing to, and 38,5% (n=94) are undecided about making the decision for others. Participants were also asked whether a nursing home with a monitoring system would be an option for themselves. It should be noted that the question regarding oneself was only asked if the question about relatives was answered with "yes". Among those who answered "yes" to this question, only 84,8% (n=95) would consider a nursing home with surveillance for themselves. More than 14% (n=16) of those who would consider such a nursing home for their relatives are unsure about it for themselves. It is evident that individuals have higher concerns regarding the use of video surveillance systems when it comes to themselves.

Figure 4. Choice of nursing home for yourself and others

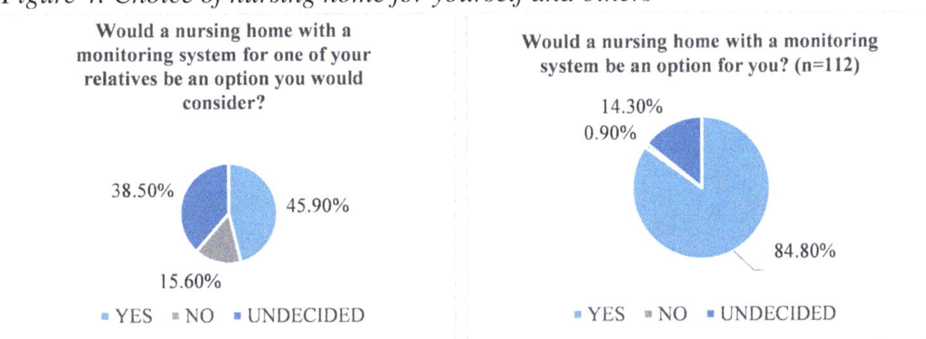

Figure 5.

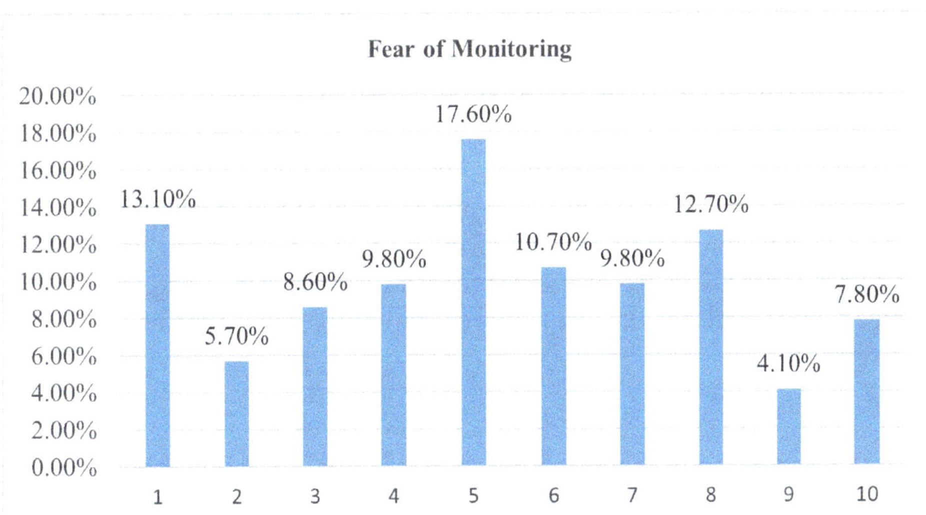

A potential reason could be a perceived fear among participants regarding video surveillance. Figure 8 depicts the distribution of fear among all 244 participants on a scale from 1 (no fear of video surveillance) to 10 (great fear of video surveillance). Supporting this depiction and figures, 76.2% (n=186) expressed that they do not want to be monitored permanently.

Figure 6 illustrates the distribution of acceptance based on the type of patient monitoring. It shows that infrared monitoring systems, in particular, receive strong support with 82% (n=200). In contrast, systems with audio recordings experience low acceptance among participants. Specifically, systems monitoring with continuous audio recordings are only supported by 3.3% (n=8).

Figure 6. Types of Monitoring

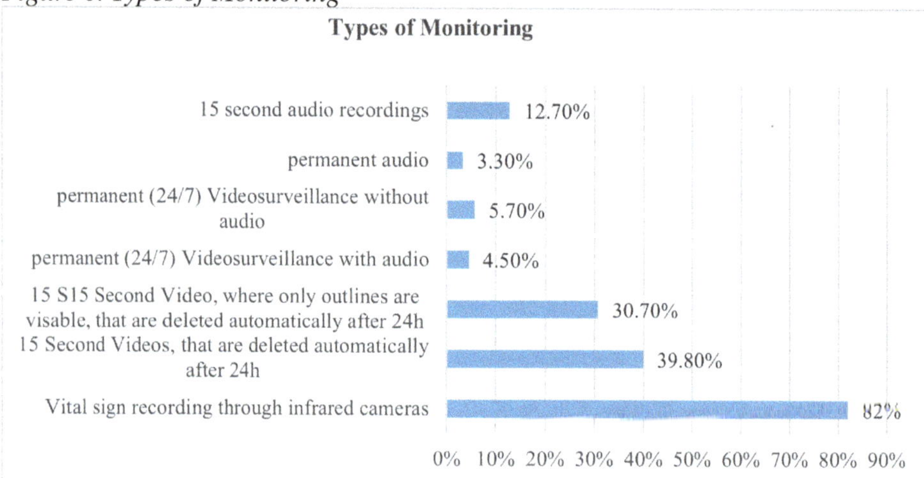

185 individuals (75.8%) of all respondents also believe that video surveillance systems should not have a blanket application and that different groups of people must therefore be considered separately. Among these 185 individuals, 153 agree on the necessity of monitoring for dementia patients, 115 support monitoring for mentally ill individuals, and 134 agree on the necessity of monitoring for people at increased risk of falls. Other indicated monitoring needs mentioned by respondents include diabetics, delirious individuals, people in nursing homes, infants, and people with epilepsy.

4. DISCUSSION

Observations from the interviews and the online questionnaire provide insights into the views of professional stakeholders and society regarding the use of video-based surveillance systems in long-term care facilities. Equally salient concerns raised in both the interviews and the survey include potential privacy intrusions, the risk of altered nurse–patient relationships, data protection/misuse concerns and cost considerations.

Patient Safety

The interviews particularly highlighted perceived relief among nursing staff, potential mitigation of the skilled-worker shortage through time savings and enhanced patient safety. These aspects were corroborated by the online questionnaire analysis. Supportive findings come from a study in a 115-bed rehabilitation facility, where most nurses favored video surveillance (only 4% described it as restrictive) and reported improvements in patient safety (reductions in falls from 6.34 to 5.09 per month) and in satisfaction among patients and staff (Cournan et al., 2016, pp. 3ff.). In psychiatry, video surveillance is also viewed as beneficial for reducing self-harming behaviors (Kekić et al., 2024). Consequently, it remains crucial to evaluate whether similar positive effects on patient safety can be achieved for gerontopsychiatric patients in long-term residential care. Improved patient safety through real-time video surveillance was already noted in Interview 3.

Privacy and security of data

Ferreira et al. (2025) identified three key challenges in video-based health monitoring: data collection, data processing and ethical considerations. Regarding data protection and privacy, the application of video-based surveillance should be evaluated on a case-by-case basis, necessitating in-depth research. In Germany, potential privacy interventions are governed by stringent regulations; patient data are accessible only when required for a predetermined purpose (§§ 47–48 BDSG). Ongoing data use is similarly regulated (see §§ 47(1) sentence 2, 48(1) BDSG). Furthermore, continuation of research to examine the relationship between surveillance type, acceptance and privacy intrusion remains desirable. Integrating surveillance systems as components of care planning and providing relevant nursing perspectives, explanations and education may increase acceptance and provide legal protection for facilities. Transparency within the facility is crucial in this regard (Interview 3).

Economic implications

The economic implications of such systems warrant careful consideration, as surveillance solutions of this type can entail high initial and ongoing costs due to complex production and deployment processes (Sathyanarayana et al., 2018). In addition, prioritization was discussed in the interview context, noting that some facilities still lack digital documentation methods or devices (Interview 2). While facilities face the financial hurdle of system acquisition, later-installed systems must also be financed by service users, potentially increasing the self-contribution of the amounts to be paid (Interview 4). It is then ethically questionable whether the use of such systems is linked to the financial means of those in need of care. Consequently, initial efforts should focus on digitalizing the entire facility. Additionally, a general cost reduction for facilities through the use of video surveillance systems, which enable a lower nurse-to-resident ratio, is supported by the aforementioned study (Cournan, M. et al., 2016, p. 3ff.).

Acceptance among younger individuals

Regarding the data depicted in Figure f, acceptance appears higher among younger individuals (20–29 years), likely due to earlier exposure to contemporary technologies. Individuals under 20 responded uniformly with "unsure" regarding their support for such surveillance (Figure f). This may reflect their extensive exposure to technology but relatively limited exposure to caregiving issues compared with older cohorts. Conversely, older generations may experience challenges stemming from the lack of transparency surrounding surveillance systems and technologies. Additionally, there is a paucity of publicly available data, hindering societal understanding of the benefits.

Application of Surveillance systems

As indicated in Figure g, respondents with health-care affiliations (n = 85) exhibited notable uncertainty (16.8%) regarding the application of surveillance systems. This suggests that health-care professionals, given their proximity to the care setting, may hold more nuanced views on the pros and cons, complicating a single, overarching stance. In comparison to these findings, Ergai et al. showed moderate nurses acceptance and perceived usefulness, even when video systems significantly reduced fall incidents (Ergai et al. 2024). Online survey respondents not engaged in health-care (n = 159) demonstrated substantial uncertainty (23.4%), although tendencies toward firm opinions were observed.

5. LIMITATIONS

Although user perspectives were obtained indirectly through population surveys, it remains important to note that the present study did not directly interview the primary affected group—the recipients of care. We acknowledge that their perspective is a central determinant in assessing the utility and acceptance of video-based monitoring and should be considered a core input for decision-making. Several studies across diverse settings indicate that acceptance of monitoring declines particularly in spaces associated with caregiving activities that involve privacy and personal intimacy (Lear et al. 2023), such as bathrooms and bedrooms, where visible skin heightens aversion, whereas daily-living-activities like cooking and eating are more tolerable (Maidhof et al., 2023; Himmel & Ziefle, 2016; Ziefle et al. 2011). Importantly, in the context of inpatient long-term care, caring in an environment characterized by high levels of intimacy; these considerations should lead decision-making processes.

The data presented reflect responses collected from February 16, 2024, to March 30, 2024, which is quite a short time-period. Across both interviews and questionnaire evaluation, data protection was repeatedly identified as a critical issue that requires case-by-case assessment. This topic was only superficially explored in the present analysis. A more in-depth examination would require an extended literature review and a discussion of the relevant legal considerations for individuals. The chosen data-collection approach is suitable for generating general data. In particular, the heterogeneity of all participants (see Table 1, Figures c–e) enhances insight generation but necessitates concise presentation of results. The online survey (n = 244) provides a relatively large sample, and we anticipate further increases in sample size; nonetheless, generalization to the broader population should be interpreted with caution. However, given the consistency of results between the interviews and the survey, which collectively included a substantially larger sample size (n = 244 for the survey), the validity of the qualitative findings is strengthened. For more in-depth analysis, an expanded qualitative interview component would be warranted. Additionally, the current data is cross-sectional and does not capture future developments. Potential technological advancements and broader application areas for video-based surveillance in general nursing care were not addressed. The literature to date has focused largely on functional areas and psychiatric care; consequently, some references dating back to 2008 were included to provide context.

6. CONCLUSION

In summary, the data collected here suggests a general interest in the population for implementation. However, for increased acceptance, aspects such as data protection, privacy and potential misuse (e.g., unauthorized access to the camera, sharing with third parties, hacking attacks and security of the storage medium) need further investigation. According to Lear et al., video recording patients for direct care purposes appears to be acceptable, despite concerns about privacy, technical considerations and how to incorporate recording into clinical workflows (see Lear et al. 2023). In a scoping review, Mujrishvilli et al. (2023) identified thematic categories that appear fundamental to acceptance and privacy perceptions:

1. Privacy: Informational privacy attitudes and handling and access to the video material
2. Necessity: Medical necessity; social environment and its influence
3. Benefits: Security and medical safety; being independent; remain at home
4. Barriers: Dignity and confidentiality; interference with normal routine, cyber dependency; decreased human contact

According to our findings, easily accessible information to the population, possibly through articles in popular magazines or consultations by nursing support centers on surveillance systems and their management, is also essential for this purpose. This should include mentioning the benefits, such as relieving caregivers, increasing patient safety, improving fall prevention, as well as the disadvantages, such as increased risk of reduced human contact leading to impaired personal relationships and potential of feeling surveyed. Particularly, the critically viewed aspect of data misuse can lead to hesitation in potential implementation and use, necessitating case-by-case evaluation. Further information for healthcare personnel is also important to reduce the number of undecided individuals and increase acceptance among them. Experts also describe the importance of a nursing-based and well-founded use of surveillance systems: "[...] great potential in support technologies for professional nursing practice, both in outpatient and long-term residential care, as well as in acute care. However, the challenge will be for our discipline to devise criteria on how we make decisions and specifically for targeted use that would be a major concern for me" (see Interview 4).

CONFLICT OF INTEREST

The authors have no conflicts of interest to declare. All co-authors have seen and agree with the contents of the manuscript and there is no financial interest to report. We certify that the submission is original work and is not under review at any other publication.

ACKNOWLEDGMENT

We would like to thank all participants of the survey and interviews for their willingness to participate in the surveys. Above all, we thank the State Competence Center for Nursing and Digitalization Baden-Württemberg (PflegeDigital@BW) for their support in distributing our online survey.

REFERENCES

Cournan, M., Fusco-Gessick, B., & Wright, L. (2016). Improving patient Safety through Video Monitoring. *Rehabilitation Nursing*, *0*, 1–6. DOI: 10.1002/rnj.308

Ergai, A., Spiva, L. A., Thurman, S., Hatfield, M., McCollum, M., & Holmes, M. (2024). The effectiveness of remote video monitoring on fall prevention and nurses acceptance. *Journal of Nursing Care Quality*, *39*, 24–30. DOI: 10.1097/NCQ.0000000000000716

Ferreira, S., Marinheiro, C., Mateus, C., Rodrigues, P. P., Rodrigues, M. A., & Rocha, N. (2024). Overcoming challenges in video-based health monitoring: Real-world implementation, ethics, and data considerations. *Sensors (Basel)*, *25*, 1–15. DOI: 10.3390/s25051357

Guo, Y., Liu, X., Peng, S., Jiang, X., Xu, K., Chen, C., Wang, Z., Dai, C., & Chen, W. (2021). A review of wearable and unobtrusive sensing technologies for chronic disease management. *Computers in Biology and Medicine*, *2021*(129), 104163.

He, M., Iwai, M., Nishino, T., Miura, K., Watanabe, R., & Kobayashi, K. (2023). Night-Time Monitoring System for Getting-up Action of Older Person Based on Single Camera and Infrared Reflective Sheets. *Advanced Biomedical Engineering*, *12*, 214–224. DOI: 10.14326/abe.12.214

Himmel, S., & Ziefle, M. (2016). Smart home medical technologies: Users'requirements for conditional acceptance. *I-Com*, *15*, 39–50. DOI: 10.1515/icom-2016-0007

Hülsken-Giesler, M. (2010). Zur systematischen Integration einer professionalisierten Pflege in das System der Gesundheitsversorgung – Computer in der Intensivpflege. *Intensiv*, *18*, 238–241. DOI: 10.1055/s-0030-1264126

Kaiser, R. (2021). *Qualitative Experteninterviews – konzeptionelle Grundlagen und praktische Durchführung* (2. aktualisierte Auflage). Springer VS.

Kekic, M., Rose, A., Baker, C., & Bayley, D. (2024). RETRACTED: Reduced self-harm on acute mental health wards following the implementation of a vision-based patient monitoring system: Evidence from five NHS trusts. *Journal of Psychiatric and Mental Health Nursing*, *00*, 1–9. DOI: 10.1111/jpm.13036

Lear, R., Ellis, S., Ollivierre-Harris, T., Long, S. & Mayer, E.K. (2023). Video recording patients for direct care purposes: Systematic review and narrative synthesis of international empirical studies and UK professional guidance. Journal of Medical Internet Research, 16, 25:e46478. DOI: DOI: 10.2196/46478

Maidhof, C., Offermann, J. & Ziefle, M. (2023). Eyes on privacy: acceptance of video-based AAL impacted by activities being filmed. Front Public Health, 4, 11:1186944. DOI: DOI: 10.3389/fpubh.2023.1186944

Mayring, P., & Fenzl, T. (2019). Qualitative Inhaltsanalyze. In Baur, N., & Blasius, J. (Eds.), *Handbuch Methoden der empirischen Sozialforschung*. Springer VS., DOI: 10.1007/978-3-658-21308-4_42

Mujirishvili, T., Maidhof, C., Florez-Revuelta, F., Ziefle, M., & Richart-Martinez, M. & Cabrero- Garcia, J. (2023). Acceptance and privacy perceptions toward video-based active and assisted living technologies: Scoping Review. *Journal of Medical Internet Research*, *25*, e45297. DOI: 10.2196/45297

Romeo, L.Marani, R., DÓrazio, T. & Cicirelli, G. (2023). Video based mobility monitoring of elderly people using deep learning models. *IEEE Access : Practical Innovations, Open Solutions*, *11*, 2804–2819. DOI: 10.1109/ACCESS.2023.3234421

Sathyanarayana, S., Satzoda, R. K., Sathyanarayana, S., & Thambipillai, S. (2018). Vision-based patient monitoring: A comprehensive review of algorithms and technologies. *Journal of Ambient Intelligence and Humanized Computing*, *9*, 225–251. DOI: 10.1007/s12652-015-0328-1

Seigel, C. R., Holly, M., Bastin, G., Myers, L. J., Taylor, S., Pike, F., Wilkinson, J., & Williams, L. S. (2024). Patient acceptance of teleneurology across neurologic conditions. *Journal of Neurology*, *271*, 2850–2858. DOI: 10.1007/s00415-024-12200-y

oVerf. (2023). Oxehealth. Abgerufen von https://www.oxehealth.com/oxevision (17.04.2024)

Wright, K., & Singh, S. (2022). Reducing Falls in Dementia Inpatients Using Vision-Based Technology. *Journal of Patient Safety*, *18*(3), 177–181. DOI: 10.1097/PTS.0000000000000882

Ziefle, M., Himmel, S., & Wilkowska, W. (2011). When your living space knows what you do: acceptance of medical home monitoring by different technologies. Information quality in e-health: 7th conference of the workgroup human-computer interaction and usability engineering of the Austrian computer society, USAB 2011. Springer, 607-624. DOI: DOI: 10.1007/978-3-642-25364-5_43

KEY TERMS AND DEFINITIONS

Long-term care: Long-term care provides nursing care (e.g. in a nursing home or ambulatory care setting), medical health, social and residential services to individuals with self-care demands.

Nursing perspective: A nursing perspective on the elderly focuses on the multifaceted needs (physical, psychological, social, cultural) of older adults and their families/caring persons through comprehensive assessment and individualized care.

Oxevision™: A product of Oxehealth enables video-based patient monitoring intended to enhance patient safety and quality of care

Video-based monitoring technologies: Infrared, RGB cameras and sensors, video and audio transmission, real-time imaging, remote photopletysmography (rPPG) artificial intelligence (AI) and machine learning (ML) applications

Video-based patient monitoring: Fall detection, action and activity monitoring, sleep monitoring, respiration, epilepsy, vital signs, facial expressions

Video-based privacy perceptions: Informational privacy and handling and access, medical necessity, social environment, security and medical safety, being independent, dignity and confidentiality

Vital Signs: Body´s most basic functions: Pulse rate, blood pressure, body temperature, respiration and -rate, oxygen saturation. Additional parameter: Vigilance, physical activities and action, facial expression, verbal expression and others

Chapter 9
Improved Public Health Ontologies in the Era of Generative AI Technologies

Dilek Küçük
https://orcid.org/0000-0003-2656-1300
TÜBİTAK Marmara Research Center, Turkey

Emine Ela Küçük
Giresun University, Turkey

ABSTRACT

Generative artificial intelligence (AI) technologies have common applications in different domains including medicine or health in general, law, education, and finance. Large language models (LLMs) constitute a subset of generative AI, that are trained on large text datasets to automatically generate natural language content. LLMs, similarly, are used to facilitate different tasks, and ontology engineering is among these tasks. Related research shows that LLMs can achieve promising performance in different ontology engineering tasks, particularly in ontology construction from text descriptions. In this book chapter, we first review the literature on ontology engineering and LLMs, and next, the literature on the use of this generative AI technology (namely, LLMs) for improved health, and public health, ontologies is reviewed. We also outline the main findings of the reviewed studies and present significant future research directions regarding the use of the recent generative AI technologies for improving public health ontologies.

DOI: 10.4018/979-8-3373-2545-3.ch009

INTRODUCTION

Ontologies are defined as semantic resources that organize the knowledge in a given domain by defining the terms, their attributes, and interrelationships. Domain ontologies serve various purposes; such as improved information system modeling, reasoning, and interoperability. Hence, ontologies have long been created for various domains and utilized in related domain-specific software.

Related literature shows that there are significant ontologies proposed and utilized for public health and healthcare domains as well. SNOMED-CT clinical ontology (Donnelly, 2006), international classification of diseases (ICD) ontology (Harrison et al., 2021), and human disease ontology (Schriml et al., 2022) are among the most common medical ontologies employed so far.

On the other hand, there are dramatic developments taking place in artificial intelligence (AI) research. It has been quite hard for related researchers to keep up with latest developments in AI, including deep learning models, generative AI models, and large language models (LLMs). Generative AI mainly refers to AI models that generative new content (in the form of text, image, video etc.) as defined in the related work (Goodfellow et al., 2014). Large Language Models (LLMs) are a subset of generative AI, specializing in natural language processing (NLP). LLMs are built on transformer architectures (Vaswani et al., 2017), and are trained on vast text datasets to understand and generate human-like text (Brown et al., 2020).

The outputs of chatbots based on these emerging AI technologies have shown that many natural language problems (NLP) problems such as language understanding and text generation can now be solved (using these technologies) with high accuracies, even close to human performance.

As these sophisticated AI technologies have affected many domains and related problems since their inception, it is currently emphasized in the literature that ontology engineering can also benefit considerably from these technologies.

In this book chapter, we will elaborate the effects of generative AI technologies, with a particular emphasis on LLMs, on the medical and public health domains, and on public health and healthcare ontologies. Particularly, we will investigate how these technologies can help improve ontology generation (or, engineering), ontology alignment, refinement, and extension, among others. We will compile the findings of the related studies and suggest pointers to fruitful future research directions on the use of generative AI models for health-related ontology engineering. We believe that the observations and points of the current chapter will constitute a solid contribution to related research topics of health-related ontologies and applications of generative AI in the medical domain.

The rest of the chapter is organized as follows: The first of the remaining sections is devoted to a brief survey of those studies on the use of LLMs for ontology engineering tasks, and the next section presents related work on the use of LLMs and AI technologies for ontologies in health-related domains including healthcare, medicine, and nursing. The last three sections of this chapter cover significant findings of the surveyed related studies, future research directions based on the presented studies, and main conclusions of the chapter, respectively.

ONTOLOGY ENGINEERING AND LARGE LANGUAGE MODELS

As outlined below, most of the studies on the use of LLMs in ontology engineering have been published after 2023, due to the relative recency of the emergence of generative AI and LLMs.

The paper by Neuhaus (2023) focuses on various aspects regarding the employment of LLMs for applied ontology tasks. It is emphasized that LLMs lack controlled vocabularies and logical consistency, hence, they cannot completely replace ontologies. Although they can help during ontology development processes, their outputs may still suffer from inconsistencies and ambiguities, and hence, they can best be used as part of semi-automatic tools during ontology generation from natural language (Neuhaus, 2023).

Funk et al. (2023) present the results of their experiments on using LLMs to automatically create concept hierarchies of ontologies for different domains. Based on the results of the related experiments using GPT-3.5 as the LLM, it is suggested that LLMs can considerably contribute to the building of concept hierarchies for ontologies, and testing for the outcome of fully expressive ontology creation by LLMs is left as future work, along with other future work directions (Funk et al., 2023).

Similarly, Mateiu and Groza (2023) leverage GPT-3 LLM model to transform natural language texts into OWL (Web Ontology Language) description logic, for ontology engineering. A set of 150 pairs of text prompts and their corresponding conversions is compiled and used for fine-tuning purposes. A Protégé plugin is also developed by the authors to extend existing ontologies by adding new axioms to ontologies using natural language texts. The experiments indicate that the fine-tuned LLM model attains the most convenient and accurate results when compared to zero-shot and few-shot settings (Mateiu and Groza, 2023).

The research by Babaei Giglou et al. (2023) introduces the LLMs4OL paradigm with the intention of using LLMs for automatic ontology learning which covers the process of extracting information from natural language texts and cerate the required domain ontology based on the extracted information. Various LLMs have been tested for this purpose and an a fine-tuned LLM, namely Flan-T5, has shown promising performance. The study suggests that domain-specific fine-tuning and advanced prompting techniques will further improve ontology learning using LLMs (Babaei Giglou et al., 2023).

The study by Garbacz (2024) similarly elaborates whether LLMs can be used to create formal ontologies, when descriptions of the domain in natural language text are provided. Particularly, GPT-4 is used as the selected LLM to translate given descriptions into an ontological framework. The study suggests that LLMs show promising performance on this task, yet, by fine-tuning these models for this task, better performance can be obtained. Additionally, it is reported that scarcity of relevant training data for the task is another challenge to be tackled with (Garbacz, 2024).

Another related paper by Kommineni et al. (2024) presents a semi-automatic approach for constructing ontologies and knowledge graphs, based on LLMs. After the first two stages (data collection, competency question (CQ) generation) of the proposed pipelined approach, an LLM (Mixtral) is used to carry out the remaining stages of ontology creation, CQ answering, knowledge graph construction, and evaluation. The experiments reveal that LLMs are promising for ontology and knowledge graph construction, nevertheless, shortcomings such as the hallucinations of LLMs and the need for human-in-the-loop for validations should be taken into account (Kommineni et al., 2024).

The paper by Saeedizade and Blomqvist (2024) also investigates the potential of LLMs in OWL ontology generation from descriptions given in the form of ontology questions or competency questions. They carry out their related generation experiments with GPT-3.5, GPT-4, and other open-source LLMs. It is emphasized that LLMs show promising performance in ontology development although limitations such as high costs persist (Saeedizade and Blomqvist, 2024).

Fathallah et al. (2024) propose an ontology development pipeline, also utilizing an LLM, namely GPT-3.5. This pipeline aims to automatically convert natural language descriptions of ontologies into formal ontologies, similar to the recent related work. Based on the experimentation results, it is concluded that LLMs are helpful in alleviating the time and effort required to create ontologies, but on the other hand, they suffer from shortcomings such as the lack of reasoning skills and domain expertise (Fathallah et al., 2024).

Various LLMs (including Llama-2-70b, Mistral 7B, and Flan-t5-xl) are tested for the purpose of generating competency questions for existing ontologies in (Alharbi et al., 2024). The results demonstrate that Flan-t5-xl outperforms the other LLMs for this task. Based on the results, it is also suggested that using context improves the quality of competency questions, and that data leakage and replicability are important issues to consider (Alharbi et al., 2024).

The research conducted by Tsaneva et al. (2024) is on the use of LLMs for ontology evaluation, where ChatGPT-4 is used for evaluating ontology restrictions and its performance is compared with that of humans. The experiments with 30 axioms from an ontology reveal that the performance of ChatGPT-4 at ontology evaluation is comparable to human performance. It is concluded that LLMs can be used to support ontology evaluation, and the main challenges include the need to replicate the experiments on diverse ontologies and more complex domains (Tsaneva et al., 2024).

A framework for utilizing LLMs in ontology requirements engineering tasks, called OntoChat, is described in (Zhao et al., 2024). OntoChat aims to streamline various related subtasks such as user story creation, competency question creation, and ontology testing. The main focus of the related study is to use and test GPT-4o as the selected LLM during the task of ontology user story creation by improving prompting at this stage with a method called participative prompting which includes researcher-mediated interactions. Hence, the participants of the study created user stories and refined queries with researcher assistance using GPT-4o, resulting in high satisfaction, during the user story creation phase of the overall ontology engineering pipeline (Zhao et al., 2024).

Zhao (2025) explores the potential contribution of LLMs on ontology requirements engineering, using insights from the domain of software requirements engineering. It is concluded that LLMs can act as knowledge engineers and thereby help domain experts during the requirements elicitation phase of ontology requirements engineering. Yet, there are limitations related to the robustness and adaptability of the models (Zhao, 2025).

The work by Lippolis et al. (2025) investigates the use of LLMs to automate the generation of ontology drafts from user stories and competency questions, by introducing two prompting techniques: memoryless CQbyCQ and Ontogenia. Presented experiments, conducted on a dataset of 10 ontologies with 100 competency questions and 29 user stories, demonstrate that LLMs can produce effective ontology drafts. The study highlights the potential of LLMs to streamline the complex, time-consuming, and error-prone ontology engineering process while emphasizing the need for multi-dimensional evaluation to ensure quality and usability (Lippolis et al., 2025).

PUBLIC HEALTH ONTOLOGIES AND LARGE LANGUAGE MODELS

In this section, we cover relevant studies that have been published between 2021 and 2025, due to the relative recency of the research topic considered in the chapter.

MedGPT is a deep learning-based tool described in (Kraljevic et al., 2021) which aims to predict future disorders from clinical narratives (in electronic health records) in the form of free text. MedGPT is based on GPT-2 (as the LLM), and a previously described tool called MedCAT (Kraljevic et al., 2019) which is proposed for named entity recognition and linking. It takes free natural language text as input and extracts SNOMED-CT clinical ontology (Donnelly, 2006) concepts from this text. MedGPT is also reported to outperform other models such as SVM and LSTM (Kraljevic et al., 2021).

The study by (Singhal et al., 2023) evaluates the clinical capabilities of LLMs using a new benchmark, called MultiMedQA, which includes six existing medical question-answering datasets and a novel dataset, called HealthSearchQA, covering professional, research, and consumer queries. The study evaluates the Pathways Language Model (PaLM) and its instruction-tuned variant, called Flan-PaLM, and state-of-the-art performance is achieved on multiple-choice datasets like MedQA. This study emphasizes the potential of the use of LLMs in the medical domain, however, the authors also indicate that further research is necessary to ensure safety and efficacy in clinical settings (Singhal et al., 2023).

Huatuo is an LLM for the medical domain, based on the LLaMa model, which is fine-tuned for Chinese biomedical domain (Wang et al., 2023). Medical information from semantic resources such as Chinese Medical Knowledge Graph (Byambasuren et al., 2019) is integrated into this domain-specific LLM, in order to alleviate the disadvantages of general-purpose LLMs for the medical domain. Based on the related experiments, it is reported to outperform baselines including LLaMA, Alpaca, and ChatGLM, in terms of usability and smoothness metrics.

Karabacak and Margetis (2023) emphasize the impact of LLMs in medicine, through disease progress prediction, improved diagnosis, and clinical decision support. Also pointed out in the paper are the related learning algorithms such as transfer learning, domain-specific fine-tuning, few-shot and zero-shot learning, and reinforcement learning, which will improve the implications of LLMs in the medical domain. Challenges such as privacy issues and bias within LLMs are also discussed in the paper (Karabacak and Margetis, 2023).

The study by Zaitoun et al. (2023) focuses on the potential use of LLMs in finding missing concepts and relations in existing biomedical ontologies and augmenting the ontologies with these missing items. Particularly, ChatGPT is used as the underlying LLM-based tool to augment SNOMED-CT clinical ontology (Donnelly, 2006) with missing concepts and relations. The experiments reveal that ChatGPT achieves promising performance by identifying 14 gold standard relations, missing 38, and proposing 39 additional valid relations. It is claimed that multiple LLMs, and biomedical-specific models can be used to achieve superior performance (Zaitoun et al., 2023).

In the review article by Thirunavukarasu et al. (2023), studies on the development, applications, and challenges of LLMs in the healthcare domain are considered. Fine-tuning is emphasized as it is an important stage when building domain-specific

LLMs. The application areas of medical LLMs include their use in clinical settings, in medical research, and education, among others. The article also covers common shortcomings of the use of LLMs in the medical domain such as fabricated facts, biases, and high computational costs. Ethical implications stand as a significant future research topic to be dealt with (Thirunavukarasu et al., 2023).

In (Küçük and Küçük, 2024), a public health ontology in Turkish is extended using ChatGPT prompts. The original public health ontology has been generated in a semi-automatic manner, and used in a social media application to extract health related phenomena from social media posts (Küçük et al., 2017) During the ontology extension procedure, new concepts (diseases and symptoms) for the domain are extracted from the outputs of the conversational LLM agent, after providing it with the relevant prompts. It is emphasized that the existing ontology is extended by 43% in terms of the included public health-related concepts, using ChatGPT (Küçük and Küçük, 2024).

Cao et al. (2024) present AutoRD which is an automated system to extract rare disease information from natural language texts and create knowledge graphs, using LLMs and medical ontologies. The proposed system outperforms baseline LLMs and fine-tuned AI models (based on the BERT model (Devlin et al., 2019)) during entity and relation extraction. It is pointed out that the system's integration with medical ontologies is one of the factors that improve performance, yet, the system suffers from some entity misclassifications which should be dealt with, as part of future work (Cao et al., 2024).

The review study by Liu et al. (2024a) focuses on the applications of LLMs in the general domain of healthcare. These application areas include decision support in the healthcare domain, disease diagnosis, medical knowledge dissemination, and analysis of medical images, among others. ChatGPT, BioBERT, and MedGPT are listed as plausible tools for consideration to be used in the related applications. The study also highlights important challenges such as interpretability, data protection and privacy, and other ethical concerns (Liu et al., 2024a).

A related study (Liu et al., 2024b) explores the use of LLMs in determining the is-a relations in medical ontologies such as SNOMED-CT (Donnelly, 2006), and human disease ontology (Schriml et al., 2022). Eight open-source LLMs or LLM-based chatbots are used for the task without fine-tuning, and among these tools, OpenChat has achieved the best performance rates. The study also points out current limitations of LLMs such as semantic ambiguity, and contextual sensitivity and specificity, when dealing with the task of predicting hierarchical relationships in medical ontologies (Liu et al., 2024b).

Zhang and Hao (2024) propose their approach to construct a knowledge graph for traditional Chinese medicine (TCM) knowledge graph using an LLM. The LLM is basically used to enhance the organization, storage, and application of the

TCM data. The TCM knowledge graph is evaluated, along with ChatGPT, and has achieves superior performance. It is highlighted that the medical knowledge graph can facilitate related diagnosis, treatment, and teaching tasks (Zhang and Hao, 2024).

The authors of the paper (Chen and Esmaeilzadeh, 2024) emphasize the two significant challenges of using generative AI technologies in the medical domain, namely privacy and security, after pointing out that these AI technologies have several application areas in the domain, including medical diagnosis, drug research, and virtual health assistants. The related threats are categorized and presented in different phases AI life cycle (data collection and processing, model training and building, and implementation phases) as data poisoning, sensor data tampering, fake data, data and privacy breaches, AI hallucinations, and data extraction from the AI model (Chen and Esmaeilzadeh, 2024).

In another related review paper (He et al., 2025), the potential of LLMs in enhancing healthcare applications is emphasized. It is suggested that LLMs' capabilities in various natural language processing (NLP) tasks such as text classification and information extraction can be used to handle complex and context-rich healthcare data. Similarly, multimodal applications such as medical image analysis are also considered. This review paper also addresses the related challenges of using LLMs in healthcare applications, such as accountability, and ethical considerations (He et al., 2025).

MedCT is a clinical terminology graph which is created by using SNOMED-CT (Donnelly, 2006) as the underlying foundational ontology, by translating the concepts in Chinese (Chen et al., 2025). The aim of building MEdCT is to improve the application of generative AI applications in the healthcare domain. When used together with other related AI models built for the medical domain (such as a pre-trained language model for the domain), MedCT is reported to achieve state-of-the-art performance in semantic matching and entity linking tasks for both Chinese and English. It is also reported that MedCT-augmented LLMs outperformed human and standalone LLM summaries with respect to depth and relevance (Chen et al., 2025).

Farmer et al. (2025) leverage an LLM to create a taxonomy for the 4M (for four evidence-based concepts including What Matters, Medication, Mentation, Mobility) framework of the Age-Friendly Health Systems. The dataset includes 21,209 text messages sent by healthcare workers from 12 nursing homes. Gemma 2 9b open-source LLM is employed, and fined-tuned with annotated subset 860 annotated messages. The study highlights the LLM's effectiveness in automating taxonomy creation for this domain, particularly for Medication and Mentation concepts, and also notes challenges with the What Matters and Mobility concepts, due to informal language (Farmer et al., 2025).

The recent survey by Zheng et al. (2025) presents a review of the studies on the development, applications, and challenges of LLMs in the medical field. It is emphasized that medical LLMs have a diverse set of application areas such as clinical medicine as in (Singhal et al., 2023), doctor-patient communication, supplementary diagnosis, drug design, medical image segmentation, and radiology. The review study is concluded with outstanding issues such as ethical aspects, and interpretability of medical LLMs (Zheng et al., 2025).

A recent related survey targets at trustworthiness of LLMs in healthcare (Aljohani et al., 2025). Main dimensions of trustworthiness like truthfulness, privacy, safety, robustness, fairness and bias, and explainability are examined, related issues of LLMs such as hallucinations, data privacy risks, and biased responses are mentioned. It is pointed out that although there exists progress on this topic, still, regulatory oversight and work from different disciplines are required for improved trustworthiness of the use LLMs in the healthcare domain (Aljohani et al., 2025).

The main topic in the recent related survey paper by Li et al. (2025) is the integration of clinical information with LLMs for better use of this technology in the medical domain, i.e., for improved medical artificial intelligence. The roles of existing clinical databases and datasets during the pre-training and fine-tuning phases of LLMs are explored. The lack of integration among related theoretical (or, academic) studies on the topic and practical applications is also highlighted in the paper (Li et al. (2025).

The final study to be covered is by Feng et al. (2025) where the study proposes a retrieval-augmented generation (RAG) pipeline that enhances biomedical code mapping by integrating ontology knowledge graphs with LLMs, called OntologyRAG. This pipeline leverages in-context learning, and eliminates the need for frequent LLM retraining. OntologyRAG has three modules: indexing module to create knowledge graphs from ontology data, retrieval module to extract the relevant subgraphs from the graphs, and reasoning module. It is indicated that OntologyRAG outperforms standalone LLMs in terms of accuracy and speed (Feng et al., 2025).

FINDINGS OF THE RELATED WORK

Significant findings of the papers reviewed in the previous sections on the use of generative AI and LLM technologies and tools, such as chatbots, in ontology engineering tasks and also the use of these technologies and tools for health-related ontologies are listed below:

- Generative AI and LLM technologies have been tested for various ontology engineering tasks, but most frequently, they are used to generate the ontologies (mainly concepts and relationships) from natural language texts, or competency questions. Other ontology engineering tasks that these technologies have been tested for include ontology evaluation and prediction of the hierarchical structure in ontologies.

- Based on the related experiments, these AI technologies demonstrate promising performance in ontology engineering tasks. Nevertheless, it is also emphasized in the literature that these technologies still have some disadvantages such as high costs, hallucinations, and bias which may hurt their employment in practical settings.
- AI technologies have been used in the health domain for various purposes including, but not limited to, medical diagnosis, medical research and education, medical image processing, drug research and design, radiological evaluations, virtual health assistants, doctor-patient communication, and decision support in clinical settings.
- There are several studies that present LLMs and other deep learning models trained or fine-tuned on medical datasets or existing medical databases.
- Related research has also shown that generative AI and LLM technologies and related tools like conversational chatbots contribute to automatic generation of health-related ontologies, improvement of existing health ontologies, automatic creation of medical taxonomies as well as medical knowledge graphs, to a large extent.

FUTURE RESEARCH DIRECTIONS

The following research directions can be specified as part of future work based on the reviewed papers in this book chapter:

- The use of generative AI and LLMs in the medical domain poses many issues including privacy and security challenges, and related ethical implications. Another covering concept for these issues is trustworthiness which also include other aspects such as truthfulness, robustness, fairness and bias, and explainability. Further studies on ontology engineering in the medical domain should also address these important issues.
- There are also technical issues such as hallucinations or fabricated facts that LLMs may produce, and high computational costs (Samsi et al., 2023) of using these technologies in practical settings. These issues should also be considered as part of future work.
- Related work on the use of these technologies for health-related ontologies have also specified limitations like semantic ambiguity, and contextual sensitivity and specificity than hinder their performance during the ontology engineering tasks in the domain. Hence, further studies can also be conducted on these

limitations and strategies to alleviate their negative effects during ontological research in the medical domain with LLMs.

• Overall, the reviewed papers present extensive experiments with a wide range of LLMs, including different versions of GPT, LLaMa, Flan-T5, Mistral, Mixtral, Alpaca, and ChatGLM. Although different papers report the superiority of different models, these results can be used as baselines, as part of future work.

CONCLUSION

In this book chapter, we focus on the applications of generative artificial intelligence (AI) and large language models (LLMs) in the medical domain, with a particular emphasis on ontology engineering and health-related ontologies. We briefly review those studies on the use of LLMs for ontology engineering tasks such as ontology requirements elicitation. Next, significant studies on the use of LLMs in the domain of medicine, and on the applications of LLMs related to medical, or public health-related, ontologies are reviewed. The findings of the reviewed papers are summarized, and related challenges and future research topics are also outlined. The current book chapter can serve as a significant resource for public health researchers and professionals, as well as for ontology researchers and engineers, particularly on the applications of the recent generative AI and LLM technologies in the medical domain and on ontology engineering, particularly for health-related ontologies.

REFERENCES

Alharbi, R., Tamma, V., Grasso, F., & Payne, T. R. (2024). Investigating open source LLMs to retrofit competency questions in ontology engineering. In *Proceedings of the AAAI Symposium Series* (Vol. 4, No. 1, pp. 188-198).

Aljohani, M., Hou, J., Kommu, S., & Wang, X. (2025). A comprehensive survey on the trustworthiness of large language models in healthcare. *arXiv preprint arXiv:2502.15871.*

Babaei Giglou, H., D'Souza, J., & Auer, S. (2023). LLMs4OL: Large language models for ontology learning. In *Proceedings of International Semantic Web Conference* (pp. 408-427).

Brown, T. B., Mann, B., Ryder, N., Subbiah, M., Kaplan, J., Dhariwal, P., & Amodei, D. (2020). Language models are few-shot learners. *Advances in Neural Information Processing Systems*, *33*, 1877–1901.

Byambasuren, O., Yang, Y., Sui, Z., Dai, D., Chang, B., Li, S., & Zan, H. (2019). Preliminary study on the construction of Chinese medical knowledge graph. *Journal of Chinese Information Processing*, *33*(10), 1–9.

Cao, L., Sun, J., & Cross, A. (2024). An automatic and end-to-end system for rare disease knowledge graph construction based on ontology-enhanced large language models: Development study. *JMIR Medical Informatics*, *12*(1), e60665.

Chen, Y., & Esmaeilzadeh, P. (2024). Generative AI in medical practice: In-depth exploration of privacy and security challenges. *Journal of Medical Internet Research*, *26*, e53008.

Chen, Y., Huang, D., Xu, H., Fu, C., Sheng, L., Zhou, Q., Shen, Y., & Wang, K. (2025). MedCT: A clinical terminology graph for generative AI applications in healthcare. *arXiv preprint arXiv:2501.06465.*

Devlin, J., Chang, M. W., Lee, K., & Toutanova, K. (2019). BERT: Pre-training of deep bidirectional transformers for language understanding. In *Proceedings of the Conference of the North American Chapter of the Association for Computational Linguistics: Human Language Technologies,* Volume 1 *(Long and Short papers)* (pp. 4171-4186).

Donnelly, K. (2006). SNOMED-CT: The advanced terminology and coding system for eHealth. *Studies in Health Technology and Informatics*, *121*, 279.

Farmer, M. S., Popescu, M., & Powell, K. (2025). Development and evaluation of a 4M taxonomy from nursing home staff text messages using a fine-tuned generative language model. *Journal of the American Medical Informatics Association : JAMIA*, *32*(3), 535–544.

Fathallah, N., Das, A., Giorgis, S. D., Poltronieri, A., Haase, P., & Kovriguina, L. (2024). Neon-GPT: A large language model-powered pipeline for ontology learning. In *Proceedings of the European Semantic Web Conference* (pp. 36-50).

Feng, H., Yin, Y., Reynares, E., & Nanavati, J. (2025). OntologyRAG: Better and faster biomedical code mapping with retrieval-augmented generation (RAG) leveraging ontology knowledge graphs and large language models. *arXiv preprint arXiv:2502.18992*.

Funk, M., Hosemann, S., Jung, J. C., & Lutz, C. (2023). Towards ontology construction with language models. *arXiv preprint arXiv:2309.09898*.

Garbacz, P. (2024). Large language models and foundational ontologies. In *Formal Ontology in Information Systems* (pp. 89–103). IOS Press.

Goodfellow, I. J., Pouget-Abadie, J., Mirza, M., Xu, B., Warde-Farley, D., Ozair, S., & Bengio, Y. (2014). Generative adversarial nets. *Advances in Neural Information Processing Systems*, •••, 27.

Harrison, J. E., Weber, S., Jakob, R., & Chute, C. G. (2021). ICD-11: An international classification of diseases for the twenty-first century. *BMC Medical Informatics and Decision Making*, *21*, 1–10.

He, K., Mao, R., Lin, Q., Ruan, Y., Lan, X., Feng, M., & Cambria, E. (2025). A survey of large language models for healthcare: From data, technology, and applications to accountability and ethics. *Information Fusion*, •••, 102963.

Karabacak, M., & Margetis, K. (2023). Embracing large language models for medical applications: Opportunities and challenges. *Cureus*, *15*(5).

Kommineni, V. K., König-Ries, B., & Samuel, S. (2024). From human experts to machines: An LLM supported approach to ontology and knowledge graph construction. *arXiv preprint arXiv:2403.08345*.

Kraljevic, Z., Bean, D., Mascio, A., Roguski, L., Folarin, A., Roberts, A., Bendayan, Y., & Dobson, R. (2019). MedCAT - Medical concept annotation tool. *arXiv preprint arXiv:1912.10166*.

Kraljevic, Z., Shek, A., Bean, D., Bendayan, R., Teo, J., & Dobson, R. (2021). MedGPT: Medical concept prediction from clinical narratives. *arXiv preprint arXiv:2107.03134.*

Küçük, E. E., & Küçük, D. (2024). Enhancing a public health ontology using ChatGPT. In *Proceedings of the 7th International Health Science and Life Congress* (pp. 143-145).

Küçük, E. E., Yapar, K., Küçük, D., & Küçük, D. (2017). Ontology-based automatic identification of public health-related Turkish tweets. *Computers in Biology and Medicine*, *83*, 1–9.

Li, Q., Liu, H., Guo, C., Chen, D., Wang, M., Gao, F., & Gu, J. (2025). Merging clinical knowledge into large language models for medical research and applications: A survey. *arXiv preprint arXiv:2502.20988.*

Lippolis, A. S., Saeedizade, M. J., Keskisärkkä, R., Zuppiroli, S., Ceriani, M., Gangemi, A., . . . Nuzzolese, A. G. (2025). Ontology generation using large language models. In *Proceedings of European Semantic Web Conference* (pp. 321-341). Cham: Springer Nature Switzerland.

Liu, H., Zhou, S., Chen, Z., Perl, Y., & Wang, J. (2024b). Using generative large language models for hierarchical relationship prediction in medical ontologies. In *Proceedings of IEEE 12th International Conference on Healthcare Informatics (ICHI)* (pp. 248-256).

Liu, Q., Yang, R., Gao, Q., Liang, T., Wang, X., Li, S., Lei, B., & Gao, K. (2024a). A review of applying large language models in healthcare. *IEEE Access : Practical Innovations, Open Solutions*, *13*, 6878–6892.

Mateiu, P., & Groza, A. (2023). Ontology engineering with large language models. In *Proceedings of IEEE 25th International Symposium on Symbolic and Numeric Algorithms for Scientific Computing (SYNASC)* (pp. 226-229).

Neuhaus, F. (2023). Ontologies in the era of large language models–a perspective. *Applied Ontology*, *18*(4), 399–407.

Saeedizade, M. J., & Blomqvist, E. (2024). Navigating ontology development with large language models. In *Proceedings of the European Semantic Web Conference* (pp. 143-161).

Samsi, S., Zhao, D., McDonald, J., Li, B., Michaleas, A., Jones, M., & Gadepally, V. (2023). From words to watts: Benchmarking the energy costs of large language model inference. In *Proceedings of IEEE High Performance Extreme Computing Conference (HPEC)* (pp. 1-9).

Schriml, L. M., Munro, J. B., Schor, M., Olley, D., McCracken, C., Felix, V., & Greene, C. (2022). The human disease ontology 2022 update. *Nucleic Acids Research*, *50*(D1), D1255–D1261.

Singhal, K., Azizi, S., Tu, T., Mahdavi, S. S., Wei, J., Chung, H. W., & Natarajan, V. (2023). Large language models encode clinical knowledge. *Nature*, *620*(7972), 172–180.

Thirunavukarasu, A. J., Ting, D. S. J., Elangovan, K., Gutierrez, L., Tan, T. F., & Ting, D. S. W. (2023). Large language models in medicine. *Nature Medicine*, *29*(8), 1930–1940.

Tsaneva, S., Vasic, S., & Sabou, M. (2024). LLM-driven ontology evaluation: Verifying ontology restrictions with ChatGPT. In *Proceedings of The Semantic Web: ESWC Satellite Events.*

Vaswani, A., Shazeer, N., Parmar, N., Uszkoreit, J., Jones, L., Gomez, A. N., & Polosukhin, I. (2017). Attention is all you need. *Advances in Neural Information Processing Systems*, •••, 30.

Wang, H., Liu, C., Xi, N., Qiang, Z., Zhao, S., Qin, B., & Liu, T. (2023). Huatuo: Tuning Llama model with Chinese medical knowledge. *arXiv preprint arXiv:2304.06975.*

Zaitoun, A., Sagi, T., Wilk, S., & Peleg, M. (2023). Can large language models augment a biomedical ontology with missing concepts and relations? *arXiv preprint arXiv:2311.06858.*

Zhang, Y., & Hao, Y. (2024). Traditional Chinese medicine knowledge graph construction based on large language models. *Electronics (Basel)*, *13*(7), 1395.

Zhao, Y. (2025). Leveraging large language models for ontology requirements engineering. In *Proceedings of the Extended Semantic Web Conference (ESWC).*

Zhao, Y., Zhang, B., Hu, X., Ouyang, S., Kim, J., Jain, N., & de Berardinis, J., Meroño-Peñuela & Simperl, E. (2024). Improving ontology requirements engineering with OntoChat and participatory prompting. In *Proceedings of the AAAI Symposium Series* (Vol. 4, No. 1, pp. 253-257).

Zheng, Y., Gan, W., Chen, Z., Qi, Z., Liang, Q., & Yu, P. S. (2025). Large language models for medicine: A survey. *International Journal of Machine Learning and Cybernetics*, *16*(2), 1015–1040.

Chapter 10

Integrating Generative AI, Blockchain, and Smart Health Technologies for Intelligent Clinical Decision Support

F. Sammy
SRM Institute of Science and Technology, India

P. Gajalakshmi
Adhiparasakthi Engineering College, India

R. Veerasundari
Vel Tech High Tech Dr. Rangarajan Dr. Sakunthala Engineering College, India

T. Thilagam
https://orcid.org/0000-0002-7657-0726
Vel Tech Rangarajan Dr. Sagunthala R&D Institute of Science and Technology, India

L. A. Anto Gracious
https://orcid.org/0000-0003-2386-9182
R.M.K. College of Engineering and Technology, India

ABSTRACT

Generative AI, blockchain, mobile health (mHealth), wearables, sensors, and smart CDSS are emerging trends in healthcare. Generative AI using deep learning and NLP improves diagnosis, treatment planning, and outcome prediction. Blockchain

DOI: 10.4018/979-8-3373-2545-3.ch010

ensures secure, transparent, and patient-owned medical records. mHealth apps support communication, monitoring, and AI-driven diagnosis, while wearables and sensors enable real-time health tracking and personalized care. The integration of these technologies has some considerations like data harmonization, compatibility, legal issues and security vulnerabilities. This chapter explores the use, benefits, and limits of these technologies, with real-world examples and a look at future directions. It highlights the need for multidisciplinary work on AI interpretability, federated learning, and ethical guidelines. In conclusion, integrating these technologies can transform clinical decision-making and enhance patient-centered care.

1. INTRODUCTION

1.1 Background and Motivation

AI is transforming the world and has been of great impact in various sectors including the healthcare industry. Artificial intelligence solutions are becoming integrated into various aspects of the healthcare industry for improving patient's care, operational efficiency, as well as in decision making. Because of its capacity to look, comprehend, and recommend on big amounts of data, AI is making considerable progress in diagnostics, treatment, as well as individualized medication. Generative AI technique has turned out to be one of the most revolutionary techniques in the field of AI as it can create high-quality data representations, medical images, and predictive models. Deep learning, neural networks, and transformer models can be used to generate synthetic patient data, improve medical imaging analysis and augment CDSS. They help the health care practitioners to decide on the best course of action, minimize mistakes and enhance the quality of the final results. CDSS has emerged as an important tool in the contemporary healthcare systems due to the advancement in artificial intelligence technologies. These systems use artificial intelligence, NLP and predictive analytics to provide real time information to clinicians. They are designed to aid in the diagnosis of diseases and the prescription of the right treatment to the patient. The conventional model of decision-making in the healthcare sector is highly dependent on the physician's judgment, knowledge, and interpretation of data on paper records. However, the rise of big data has made it challenging for the medical practitioners to analyze the large amounts of data that they receive. The integration of AI-powered CDSS will help achieving this goal by offering evidence-based suggestions, risk assessment, and treatment plan. Whichever the case, AI-based CDSS is not without its limitations and disadvantages: data protection concerns, ethical considerations, and the cost of fitting into the current framework of the healthcare system. It is so because the information generated by AI in clinical practice must be reliable and secure to be accepted in clinical practice. Moreover, the advancement of portable devices, wearable devices, and sensors has also contributed to the capabilities of AI-CDSS. These technologies enable the continuous monitoring of patients, early diagnoses of pathologies, and personalized therapy. However, the inability to integrate the healthcare information and the risks associated with cybercrimes render it relevant to come up with effective security mechanisms such as the blockchain system, which will improve the security & sharing of such data. Blockchain technology is a decentralized, immutable, and secure method of managing health records to enhance transparency and deter intrusions. Combined with CDSS, blockchain can ensure the security of patient data, adhere to data security regulations and promote the sharing of health information. The largest game-changers in clinical decision-making are the generative AI, blockchain, mobile technologies, and wearables and sensors. These technologies are interconnected and create a system that is capable of addressing existing problems in healthcare and, at the same time, preparing the future of personalized medicine and patient-centered care(Siva, S. R et al., 2024).

1.2 Objectives of the Survey

The aim of this chapter survey is to provide a general overview regarding the application of generative AI, blockchain, mHealth solutions, wearable and sensors in clinical decision making. The objectives are as follows: It has been demonstrated that generative AI can support clinical decision-making by generating quality medical knowledge, processing patient information and making diagnostics more precise. This survey aims at finding out how generative AI can complement CDSS in the following ways: Helping in disease diagnosis by using the AI analysis of medical images. Surveillance and monitoring of patient health status in the light of pre-existing and current data. Developing specific treatment plans with regard to each patient. Improving the development of new drugs and the concept of personalized medicine with the help of the AI-generated representations of molecules and their interaction. Security and confidentiality of data are paramount in the healthcare sector since patients' records are prone to cyber-attacks, unauthorized access, and alteration. Blockchain technology is again a good bet since it provides the following: Decentralization: Avoiding the problem of having a single database and the associated dangers of data centralization. Non- alterability: It means that once the data has been put, it cannot be changed to prevent data corruption. Smart Contracts: Facilitating timely and secure sharing of information between the members of the healthcare sector. Auditability and Transparency: The ability of including an accounting record of all data exchanges for increased confidence and to meet an organisation's legal requirements. The questionnaire focuses on the possibilities of applying blockchain in AI-based CDSS to protect the data and promote compliance with the legislation. Monitoring Mobile Solutions Wearables Sensors in Real-Time: A Review. There are numerous solutions in this area that include mHealth, wearable devices, and sensors that facilitate the monitoring of patients beyond clinical settings. These technologies provide information on the state of health of the patient and can be used in early diagnosis of health complications. This survey evaluates: Smartphone applications for Clinical Decision Support: Applications that can be downloaded to support patients in self-diagnosis, medication, and tele consultancy. Wearable technology (smart watches, ECG monitors, glucose sensors): Gathering physiological information for detecting abnormality and possibilities of disease. AI-driven Remote Monitoring: Enhancing disease management for chronic conditions such as diabetes, cardiovascular diseases, & respiratory disorders. The integration of these technologies with the AI powered CDSS in the care delivery process helps in proactive care management, patient centered care planning and increased patient involvement. However, there are some issues that have to be solved to increase their efficiency: data unification, compatibility, and privacy.

1.3 Organization of the chapter

For the purpose of making this survey chapter well-structured and exhaustive, the following sections are presented below. Section 2: Generative AI in Clinical Decision Support. Explores the fundamental principles of generative AI, its applications in healthcare, and its role in clinical decision-making. Speaks about the use of artificial intelligence in the prediction of diseases, diagnosis, and management. Section 3: Blockchain for Secure Healthcare Data Management. Evaluates blockchain's applicability in protecting patient's records, maintaining the accuracy of the information, and facilitating secure exchanges of health information. Explains how blockchain can improve clinical decision making, patient consents as well as compliance. Section 4: Mobile Solutions for Intelligent Clinical Decision-Making. Reviews AI-powered mobile health applications, virtual assistants, and remote patient monitoring systems. Assesses the role of m-CDSS in enhancing the availability of health services, minimizing hospitalization, and facilitating telemedicine. Section 5: Wearables and Sensors in Intelligent Clinical Decision Support. Examines the use of wearable technologies for continuous patient monitoring, real-time diagnosis, and predictive analytics. It draws focus on issues concerning privacy and security of customers' data as well as compatibility of the devices. Section 6: Integration of AI, Blockchain, Mobile, and Wearables in Clinical Decision-Making. Explores the synergy between AI, blockchain, and IoT-based healthcare technologies. Describes examples of the application of these integrated solutions in various case studies that are relevant in business environments. The chapter also outlines the areas of further research studies such as federated learning, decentralised care contexts for the future, and new advancements in AI. Section 7: Conclusion. Summarizes the study conclusions, emphasizes the importance of the described generative AI-enabled intelligent CDSS, and discusses the future research opportunities. Based on the applied decision support techniques, generative AI, blockchain technology, mobile health solutions for handheld devices, wearables, and sensors are some of the trends that are defining the future of clinical decision-making. It is clear that through the use of AI's prescriptive analytics, blockchain's security features, and the real-time tracking in the use of mobile and wearable devices, healthcare can provide better care to patients, make sound decisions, and protect the privacy of the patient's information. However, the ethical issues, data security issues and the regulatory issues remain a problem for the large scale implementation of this solution. This survey will help in identifying the current state of research, existing issues and potential future trends in creating an integrated and smart health care environment.

2. GENERATIVE AI IN CLINICAL DECISION SUPPORT

CDSS is one of the major areas where Generative AI has come up with newer possibilities in the healthcare sector. As a result, generative AI allows for a higher level of diagnostics, treatment, and individualized therapy based on ML and DL methods. This section explains what generative AI is and how it may be applied to clinical decision making and the challenges that clinicians encounter when using this technology.

2.1 Overview of Generative AI

Generative AI can be defined as a form of artificial intelligence that can generate new samples of data that are similar to the real ones. In comparison to classical AI, which is primarily applied in classification and prediction, generative AI creates new data, enhances medical images, and supports in decision-making.

Figure 1. Overview of Generative AI

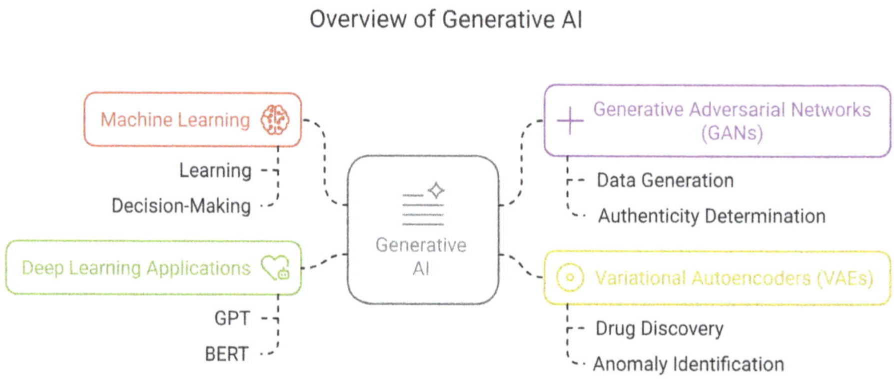

Among the key concepts that must be considered when generating AI is the following: Machine Learning: The idea of replicating the functioning of the human brain to learn and make decisions(Yamini et al., 2023). GAN: a framework consisting of two neural networks; one that creates new data and the other that is used to assess the authenticity of the data created by the former one [Sudha, K. et al 2023]. GANs have been used in the medical industry to enhance medical images and generate synthetic data. Variational Autoencoders (VAEs): A kind of deep learning model that helps in learning data distributions and generating realistic outputs in order to assist in drug discovery and identifying anomalies in medical images. Deep Learning Applications: Transformer models that can handle large medical texts, history of patients and diagnose a patient automatically.

Applications in Healthcare

1.Medical Imaging & Diagnostics: Generating synthetic medical images for training AI models. Detecting abnormalities in MRI, CT scans, and X-rays with high precision.
2.Drug Discovery and Development: AI models generating molecular structures for drug screening. Predicting interactions between drugs and biological systems.
3.Electronic Health Records (EHR) Augmentation: Integrating the patient data for better predictive modeling. To refine the strategy of treatment it is necessary to find out some patterns in the medical histories that are not obvious.
4.Interrogating the Human Disease Risk & the Concept of Personalized Medicine. Generating patient-specific treatment plans. Using predictive modeling for

early disease detection. Thus, if CDSS integrates these applications, generative AI will be beneficial in the enhancement of clinical decision-making, better diagnostic capacities, and decreased workload of clinicians(Priyadharshini et al., 2025).

2.2 Clinical Decision Support Systems

AI-based CDSS are used to help the clinicians to identify the diseases, suggest the best treatments and evaluate the risks related to the patient history and real time information. These systems rely on the generative AI to manage large volumes of data feeding it into the system in order to draw valuable lessons from it.

1. Diagnosis Assistance: Therefore, generative AI improves the diagnostic performance in the following ways: Matching the patient symptoms with millions of other patients' cases to possible diseases. Creating artificial medical images to enhance the training of deep learning systems that help in detection of the diseases. Applying NLP models for text-mining to obtain valuable information from the medical articles. For instance, the AI models developed can detect early signs of pneumonia from lung X-ray images and thus recommend an early treatment.
2. Treatment Recommendations. This is because it is possible for the AI-driven CDSS to: Review of patient's medical records and genetic information. Using placebo drugs to avoid side effects on patients. Developing programs for chronic disease rehabilitation. Such as in oncology, generative AI can advise the best option of chemotherapy depending on tumor type.
3. Risk Assessment and Predictive Analytics. In this aspect, generative AI benefits risk assessment in the following ways: Using the data of past outcomes to predict the further development of the disease. Targeting and enrolling high-risk patients into the care management program. To create some synthetic patient populations for clinical trial simulations. In cardiology, the AI models can identify the probability of heart attack by analyzing ECG signals and patient's parameters, thus allowing to prevent it.
4. Predictive Analytics and Personalized Medicine: Another significant aspect of AI in CDSS is on the capability of the use of predictive analytics in order to be able to determine disease occurrence and progression. Thus, using the information of patients, the generative AI can: Assess the potential issues that may arise in diabetic patients through the glucose level and the patient's lifestyle [Ghorbian, M. et al 2025]. Diagnose possible cancer relapse by reviewing subsequent medical imaging. Creating individualized wellness plans that will help the treatment outcome to be effective. With the integration of healthcare

wearable, sensors, clinical decision support system using AI and blockchain technology for data protection, healthcare providers can help patients to deliver tailored interventions at the point-of-care for optimum results(Shiny Irene et al., 2025).

2.3 Challenges and Limitations

However, there are some factors that need to be considered for proper implementation of generative AI in clinical decision support.

Data Quality and Bias

The generative AI models require high quality and diverse data to be fed to them so that they can make relevant suggestions. Nonetheless, the health care data have the following challenges: Lack of Data: There are cases when some patients' information is not recorded, and hence the AI system will not be accurate. Imbalanced Data: This is a major concern since AI models rely on data and if the data they are fed is imbalanced, the result will also be imbalanced in the same way. These problems can be addressed through federated learning methods, which can be used to train the AI models with data collected in other locations without compromising the patient information.

Ethical Concerns and Trust in AI

The ethical concerns associated with using the CDSS, which is driven by artificial intelligence, are as follows: Interpretability and explainability: AI judgments must be understandable to the healthcare professional. Patient Consent & Data Ownership: Ensuring patients retain control over their health data. Liability Issues: Who bears responsibility to the errors committed by AI in the medical field. Thus, to increase the degree of trust towards the use of AI in the CDSS, regulation and ethical standards should be created, which will regulate the system usage.

Integration with Existing Healthcare Systems

In the case of CDSS integrated with AI, it is crucial to be compatible with EHRs, telemedicine, and other hospital information systems. Some of the challenges in integration are: Interoperability Problem: Data is provided in different formats by different healthcare providers which does not favor well with AI. Computational Costs: Deep learning models take time to run in real-time and this greatly demands for the computational resources. Change Resistance: This is because clinicians may resist using AI as a basis for making decisions due to the unreliability and lack of interpretability of the results.

The need to overcome these barriers is important in the participation of AI researchers, clinical practitioners, and policy makers in the formulation of norms on the use of AI systems (Kamala, S. P. R. et al., 2023). The following are examples of applications of generative models in the medical field: diagnosis and treatment planning and evaluating the risk factors of the patient. CDSS with the help of artificial intelligence and predictive analysis aim at enhancing the patient's health. Nevertheless, there are some limitations such as data quality, ethical issues, and system implementation that have to be noted in order to advance the use of generative AI in healthcare. Several technologies such as federated learning, blockchain for data security, and explainable AI will go a long way in making AI-based CDSS more profound, trustworthy, as well as efficient. When applied to healthcare, generative AI should be used in conjunction with the latest technologies so that the sector can become smarter, data-focused, and more focused on patients(Ponnuviji, N. P et al., 2024).

3. BLOCKCHAIN FOR SECURE HEALTHCARE DATA MANAGEMENT

The advancement in technology has seen most of the health records of patients being collected, stored, processed and transmitted electronically. This is particularly the case given the need to maintain the security, integrity, & transparency of the data. Blockchain has become a revolutionary approach to safekeeping the data of healthcare by providing decentralized, non-tamper able, and transparent transactions. It also describes the basic concepts of blockchain technology and its use in CDS, as well as the barriers to its application.

3.1 Overview of Blockchain in Healthcare

Decentralization, Immutability, and Security Benefits

Blockchain is a DLT that provides secure and decentralised data sharing across a distributed network of computers in a way that prevents any alteration. In contrast to the traditional centralized healthcare databases, blockchain has the advantage of no single point where failure can occur, and data breaches or unauthorized data manipulation can take place.

Figure 2. Blockchain in Healthcare

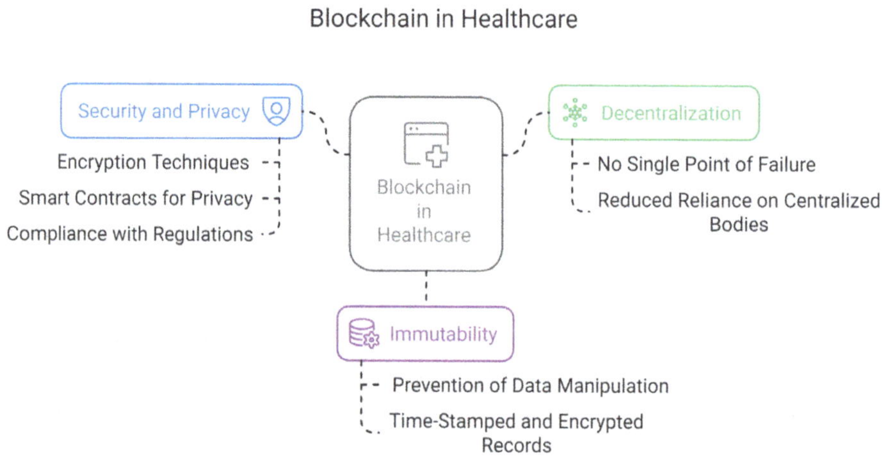

1. Decentralization: In a traditional health care system the patient's records are stored in centralized databases with the hospitals, clinics, or with the third-party cloud services. These databases are thus subject to hacking, data leakage and system breakdowns. With blockchain, information is dispersed over the nodes so that no individual or group has exclusive authority over the data. This increases security and also minimizes reliance with the centralised bodies. Patients, doctors and health care centres can have a common record of records in a block chain so that the record can be shared easily without any hassles.
2. Immutability: They are secure as once data is recorded in the ledger, it cannot be changed without the approval of the other nodes in the network. This helps to reduce cases of alteration, forgery or any other form of manipulation of the patient information. All prescription, diagnosis, and test results are stamped with time and encrypted to provide data integrity.
3. Security and Privacy Benefits: Encryption is achieved by using the more elaborate techniques such as hashing and public-key encryption on the record of the patient. Contracts that are self-executing and are based on the block-chain technology can be employed to enhance the privacy of data sharing through compliance with the privacy regulations (Mazhar, T. et al., 2025). It also made use of smart contract to allow only the authorized healthcare provider access and/or modify certain records. Through the use of blockchain in healthcare

systems, medical institutions can increase the safety of data, gain patient's trust, and meet the requirements of the law.

3.2 Role in Clinical Decision Support:

CDSS will benefit from blockchain as it provides for an efficient and secure way of managing patient data.

Secure Patient Data Sharing: Interoperability is another major issue in today's health care where various systems can only exchange and utilize patient information. Blockchain enhances secure and standard means of data exchange by:

Creating a Unified Patient Record: Blockchain allows for the generation of a single patient record for the lifetime of an individual that is integrated with various health institutions and wearables, and mHealth apps. This has the effect of keeping the records of the patients' health less fragmented and makes sure that the clinicians have an access to the patients' records.

Enhancing Data Accessibility for CDSS: As mentioned earlier, AI-based CDSS needs large data to create the prediction and recommendation systems. Blockchain also provides a way of accessing real-time patient data since the information is encrypted through cryptographic means. It is important to note that patients' consent for access to their records can be provided or withdrawn through blockchain-based consent management.

Supporting Cross-Border Healthcare Services: People go to different parts of the country for treatment and therefore, require their records to be secure and easily accessible. Blockchain enables the sharing of patient records by the healthcare providers across the globe without the need to compromise on the security of the records.

Enhancing Transparency and Auditability:

Transparency and auditability are important factors that should be considered while providing health care decision. In this respect, blockchain improves the following elements in CDSS: Providing a Tamper-Proof Audit Trail: Each operation performed on a blockchain is dated, and that means that the actions in the medical field, including prescriptions, diagnoses, and lab results, can be traced to the source. This is useful in problem solving, investigations, and in that regard enhancing on accountability in the practice of health care. To mitigate this risk and ensure that AI models are valid and reliable, the following techniques can be applied to ensure that medical AI models are trustworthy: Most of the AI models that are incorporated in CDSS require big data for both learning and performing predictions (Reddy, S. 2024). Blockchain can be used to prevent the use of fake training data and therefore eliminate cases of bias or manipulation of the model. Due to the provenance of data, the blockchain guarantees that the AI decisions made in the medical field are derived from legitimate and quality sources.

Facilitating Real-Time Monitoring and Alerts: It can also complement IoT devices that include wearable health tracking gadgets to capture real-time data of patients. If there are abnormalities in the physiological parameters such as pulse rate, blood sugar level, etc., an alarm can be triggered and the record can be safely stored in the blockchain. These functionalities put the role of blockchain in enhancing the transparency, security and trust in the clinical decision making based on AI in a proper perspective(Shiny Irene et al., 2024).

3.3 Challenges and Future Directions

However, there are some limitations of the blockchain technology in the healthcare settings and they are as follows;

Scalability:

Costs: The main costs include high computation costs especially for the PoW based systems since they consume high computational power. Data Storage: It is impossible to store large medical records such as MRI scans and genomic sequences directly on the blockchain due to the storage problem. There are already active work on growing Aion onto a full hybrid, which means that metadata will be on-chain while the actual files will remain off chain. Transaction Throughput: The speed at which the transactions occur in the public blockchains is low. For this reason, it is possible to optimize Ethereum by adopting other consensus algorithms like Proof-of-Stake (PoS) or sharding.

Regulatory Compliance

Privacy and Security: The privacy and security of blockchain remain questionable since there are no laws to regulate blockchain in many countries. One of the ongoing issues is the non- compliance with the data protection laws. Patient Consent Management: This means that patients should be able to provide and revoke access to their data on blockchain easily and at the same time meet legal requirements of privacy laws.

Interoperability

Lack of Standardization: Various healthcare organizations have adopted different EHR systems, thus making it hard to have a perfect compatibility with the blockchain network. There are initiatives made by organizations such as HL7 to develop frameworks of blockchain in the healthcare sector. Platform Integration: Blockchain must also be compatible with the AI-based CDSS, mobile health applications, and IoT. It is possible to note that the use of open-source blockchain platforms can enhance the integration to a greater extent.

Future Directions

Based on these challenges, the following should be the focus of future research and development; Federated Learning with Blockchain: The integration of decentralized AI training and the use of blockchain for CDSS improvement without compromising the patient's privacy. Quantum-Resistant Blockchain: Coming up with ways of creating blockchain that is immune to quantum computing risks. AI-Based Smart Contracts: Employing artificial intelligence technologies to enhance the efficiency of the patient data transactions by using smart contracts (Ramesh, J. V. N. et al., 2025). Decentralized Identity Management: Self-sovereign identity that will enable the patients to be in full control of their digital health identity. Blockchain technology provides an innovative solution to the challenge of patient data security, increased information openness, and CDS system credibility. This makes it difficult to alter or corrupt the data, protect the patient's data and keep it auditable while at the same time making it easily accessible to the medical practitioners. However, there are some drawbacks to the system such as scalability, regulatory compliance and interoperability issues which should be overcome in order to realize the full potential of the system. With the help of blockchain, AI-based CDSS, mHealth application, and IoT wearables, the prospective healthcare can be patient-oriented, evidence-based, and safe. The developments of new multi-layered blockchain system, federated learning systems and decentralized identity infrastructure will remain key areas of focus in future intelligent health care system.

4. MOBILE SOLUTIONS FOR INTELLIGENT CLINICAL DECISION-MAKING

Mobile health technologies have become popular and widely adopted in healthcare since they allow making clinical decisions on the go through smartphones, AI-based chatbots, and remote monitoring systems. These solutions enable patients and healthcare professionals to diagnose diseases at a tender stage, to monitor patients, and to access medical advice easily. The application of mobile applications based on artificial intelligence, cloud, and telemedicine technologies is altering the face of the future healthcare industry.

4.1 Mobile Health Technologies

mHealth is defined as the provision of healthcare through the use of mobile devices, applications and wireless technologies. It is very vital in providing support to the clinical decisions, decreasing the number of visits to the hospital, and encouraging preventive measures.

Smartphone-Based Clinical Decision Tools

Smartphones are versatile in nature and act as useful tools in clinical decision making processes and come with different AI applications. Some key functionalities include:

1.Decision Support Apps: This analyzes the patient data and provides the respective evidence based treatment options. Medscape: Offers drug interaction checks, medical calculators, and diagnostic support.

2. AI-Based Symptom Checkers: It uses artificial intelligence to calculate the symptoms and give possible diseases. The tools assist the patients in making a decision on whether to visit a hospital or not, thus reducing the number of individuals seeking medical care without need.

3.Point-of-Care Diagnostic Apps: ECG monitoring in a mobile application, blood pressure monitoring, and glucose monitoring allow real-time measurement of key health parameters. These mobile applications increase productivity, mobility, and reliability of clinical diagnoses.

Figure 3. Mobile Health Technologies and Applications

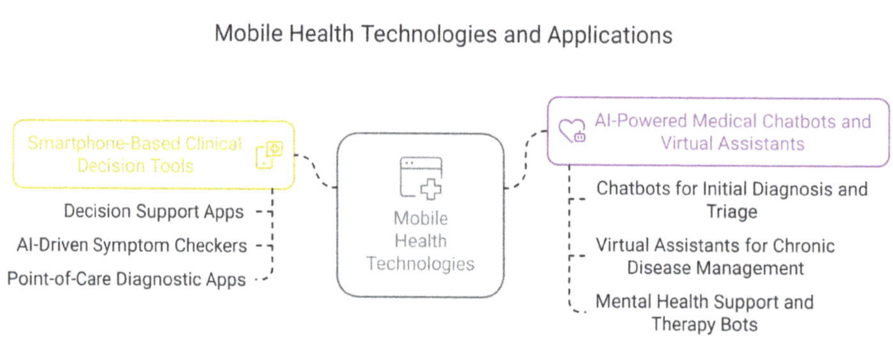

AI-Powered Medical Chatbots and Virtual Assistants

1. Chatbots for Initial Diagnosis and Triage: AI-based chatbots converse with the patients, inquire about their symptoms, and inform them of initial suggestions before consulting a doctor.
2. Virtual Assistants for Chronic Disease Management: Healthcare applications for the platforms like Amazon Alexa and Google Assistant help in reminding patients about medications and appointments.
3. Mental Health Support and Therapy Bots: Mental health chatbots use artificial intelligence to offer CBT and support for patients with mental disorders.

These chatbots help in increasing patient interaction, decreasing physicians' burden, and increasing the availability of health assistance.

4.2 Real-Time Monitoring and Diagnosis

The use of mobile technologies in healthcare helps in monitoring the patients' conditions and diagnosing the diseases at an early stage.

AI-Driven Mobile Diagnostics: These mobile diagnostic tools improve early diagnosis of the disease and clinical decision-making.

1. AI-Based Medical Imaging on Smartphones: Digital imaging solutions include the use of mobile applications that have the capability of analyzing X-rays, MRI, and ultrasound scan in a shorter time.
2. Smartphone Sensors for Disease Detection: There are modern cameras, accelerometers, gyroscopes and microphones integrated in the current smart phones that enable mobile diagnostic systems.
3. AI-Powered Digital Pathology: There are mobile application for digital pathology used in the identification of cancerous tissues through artificial intelligence(Rosaline, R et al., 2023).

Remote Patient Management and Telemedicine

Telemedicine with an integration of mobile health solutions enables facility of remote consultation, chronic disease management, and postoperative care.

1. Virtual Consultations and Telehealth Platforms: Software applications that are developed with the use of AI are used to analyze speech, facial expressions, and symptoms to diagnose the state of the patient.

2. Wearable-Connected Mobile Monitoring: Many people use mobile devices to connect with wearables such as smartwatches, ECG monitor, and glucose sensors to monitor their health. These findings provide DSS with superior diagnostic opportunities such as among them cardiovascular diseases diabetes and respiratory disorders.
3. Chronic Disease Management and Home-Based Care: Mobile applications serve remote patient monitoring of chronic illnesses such as hypertension, diabetes and COPD.

4.3 Implementation Challenges

1. Connectivity and Infrastructure Limitations: A significant concern is that low-bandwidth areas are a challenge to telemedicine services where patient care is concerned. In rural areas, internet connection is scarce and thus the real-time transfer of data is not possible. AI solutions based on cloud computing are high in terms of computational power, so their implementation is nearly impossible in low-resource environments.
2. Usability and Patient Adoption: Currently, most of the mHealth apps have many features and have a complicated design that would not be easily understandable by the elderly or less computer literate patients (Jayaprakasam, B. S. 2025). Lack of multilingual support may also be a problem for other groups of individuals who do not understand English well. AI diagnosis results in distrust among patients and therefore, there is need to increase the level of transparency in artificial intelligence.
3. Integration with Existing Healthcare Systems: Currently, most healthcare facilities are using systems that are incompatible with the mobile health platforms. Securing communication between mobile applications, wearables, and EHRs is still a problem to be solved.

Solutions to Overcome Challenges: 5G and Edge Computing: Enhances connectivity to real-time AI analysis on mobile devices. User-Centric Design: Increases patient and healthcare provider app usability. Interoperability Standards: The implementation of the FHIR allows the smooth integration of the EHR. Federated learning: This implies that an artificial intelligence model can be trained in several networks, enhancing the speed of data protection and privacy.

Smartphones applications, artificial intelligence in diagnosing and telemedicine solutions are contemporary methods of health management that improve the decision-making process of clinicians with the help of continuous monitoring, effective diagnosis, and other methods of care. However, issues to do with connectivity, ease of use and compatibility with the existing health care system need to be resolved to support wide use of the technology. The promising advancements in this area include 5G-based AI diagnostic systems, use of block chain technology for data sharing and protecting patient data as well as, decentralized AI models to offer better clinical decision making models.

5. WEARABLES AND SENSORS IN INTELLIGENT CLINICAL DECISION SUPPORT

Wearable technologies from sensors are becoming more prevalent in the contemporary world of health and are being used to monitor patients, detect diseases at an early stage, and support the CDSS. These devices help in constant monitoring of the health of the patients and give important information about the patients' physiological status. Wearable technology and sensors improve diagnosis, treatment, and prevention through the application of AI, IoT, and cloud computing.

5.1 Overview of Wearable Technologies and Sensors

Wearable devices and biosensors are portable, compact, and intelligent devices that capture and share the vital health information in real time. They contain artificial intelligence that helps in analyzing physiological patterns and making clinical decisions.

Types of Wearables

Wearable devices can be divided in to various types depending on their usage and data capturing mechanism.

Figure 4. Wearable Technologies and Sensors: Types and Applications

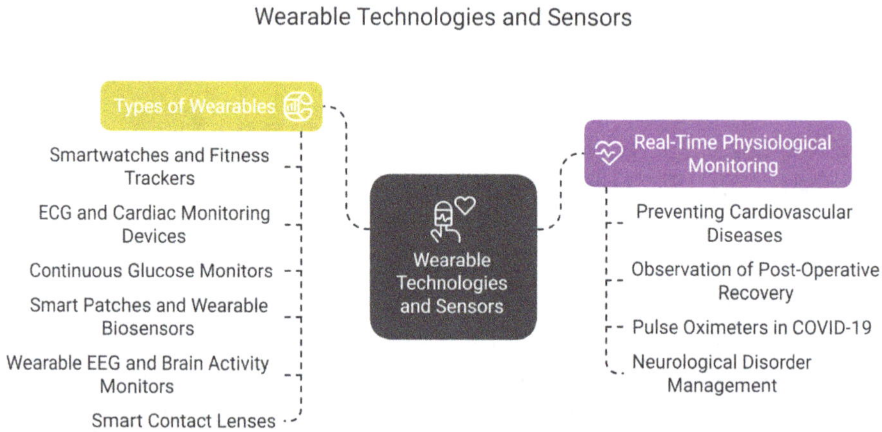

1. **Smartwatches and Fitness Trackers:** Measure heart rate, blood oxygen (SpO2), activity levels, and sleep patterns.
2. **ECG and Cardiac Monitoring Devices:** Track electrocardiogram (ECG), heart rhythm, and blood pressure.
3. **Continuous Glucose Monitors (CGMs):** Monitor the level of the blood sugar, in order to make sure that the type II patient with diabetes can be properly managed.
4. **Smart Patches and Wearable Biosensors:** Measure real-time biomarkers, including sweat composition, temperature and hydration levels.
5. **Wearable EEG and Brain Activity Monitors:** To regulate the brain waves, identify seizures and test cognitive abilities.
6. **Smart Contact Lenses:** Measures glucose and intraocular pressure (IOP) in diabetic retinopathy and glaucoma.

Real-Time Physiological Monitoring: Wearable devices keep track of the health parameters of the patients and the clinicians are able to take the necessary actions in a timely manner. This causes them to perform the following functions in real-time monitoring: Preventing cardiovascular diseases: ECG-enabled wearable smartwatches detect arrhythmias, reducing the risk of a stroke (Kovacova, M. et al., 2023). Observation of the post-operative recovery: Smart biosensors enable tracking of the recovery process of a patient. Pulse oximeters: The wearables come in handy in checking the respiratory complications in case of COVID-19. Wearable

EEG headsets are useful in managing neurological disorders such as the tracking of epileptic seizures and Parkinson diseases. Using wearables, clinicians can be notified about any alterations in the patient condition and increase timely intervention with the help of AI.

5.2 Data Collection and AI-Based Analysis

Intelligent algorithms analyze patterns, variations, and diseases based on a large volume of health related information gathered by sensors.

Continuous Patient Monitoring and Early Disease Detection

1. **AI-Enhanced Predictive Healthcare:** Wearables receive data on the patient regarding various bio signals and vital signs, such as pulse, physical activity, and temperature. AI is also used to identify symptoms of diseases based on regularities in the behavior of a patient. Example: CGMs are able to forecast instances of hypoglycemia prior to occurrence.
2. **Early Disease Detection with ML:** A plethora of wearable-based health informatics to AI models. Predicting chronic diseases based on wearables (Maithili et al., 2024; Sudha, K et al., 2024).
3. **AI-Powered Behavioral Analysis for Mental Health:** There are wearables that monitor sleep, movement, and speech to diagnose depression and anxiety disorders

AI Models for Real-Time Analysis and Alerts

1. **Anomaly Detection Algorithms:** The AI-based system can identify the critical anomalies in patient vitals by using such algorithms as Random Forest, XGBoost, LSTM, and others. As an example, AI will detect instances of irregular heartbeats and alert the emergency services.
2. **AI-Powered Remote Patient Monitoring (RPM):** Wearable technology transmits constant patient status to the AI-controlled CDSS, which notifies the physicians of the worsening conditions.
3. **Edge AI for Wearable Devices:** AI processing occurs on the actual wearables themselves (Wearable or Edge AI) to minimize latency when making decisions.

Such prognosis boost accuracy in diagnosis and prognosis, allow early actions to be taken prior to the occurrence of a specified event, and minimize the risk to the patient.

5.3 Privacy, Security, and Reliability Concerns

Nevertheless, wearables hold several issues of privacy, security, and reliability that must be solved.

1. **Data Ownership and Patient Consent:** Personal tracking devices produce huge amounts of health-related information; nevertheless, ownership of this information is undefined. According to laws, the patients have a right to control over their health data, while many wearables monetize the users' data. *Potential Solution:* Wearable-generated data is to be controlled by the patients, and blockchain-based decentralized health records makes it possible.
2. **Accuracy and Reliability of Wearable Data:** There are issues of low accuracy of wearables, which means that they can give wrong results or be interpreted wrongly. Example: Misdiagnosing the atrial fibrillation in early smartwatch ECGs led to anxiety among the patients (De Novi, G. et al., 2023). Most importantly the calibration of the sensors is not consistent and this is likely to impact the quality of the data being supplied to the AI to make clinical decisions. *Potential Solution:* Standardization and FDA/CE approvals of wearables mean that the devices will be more accurate and reliable.
3. **Cybersecurity Risks in Wearable Data Transmission:** As for the manner of functioning, the mentioned wearable devices work with Bluetooth, Wi-Fi, or cloud networks and are prone to MITM attacks – hackers intercept real-time health data. Ransomware targeting personal medical data. Sensor data manipulation through the wearable firmware vulnerabilities that an attacker can exploit. *Potential Solution:* Wearable has an advantage in terms of end-to-end encryption and MFA. Federated learning with AI models can assist healthcare algorithms to avoid exposing raw data to training. Therefore, by resolving these issues, wearables can reach their potential in delivering safe and smart clinical decision support.

The most popular innovations in the healthcare industry are smart clothes and digitized biosensors because they cut across the ability to track the condition of patients, diagnosing them with artificial intelligence and even making clinical decisions immediately. It informs patients, advances health and delivers helpful information to health practitioners. Nonetheless, the area of concern is data privacy, security & accuracy, which need to be considered to see their applicability grow. The future work is to be geared towards additional research in the machine learning of wearables, distributed health data management through blockchains, and how to devise legal and ethical regulations and controls to radical progress without compromising the privacy of the patient. This development will make wearables the future of intelligent, per patient, and data-driven healthcare.

6. INTEGRATION OF AI, BLOCKCHAIN, MOBILE, AND WEARABLES IN CLINICAL DECISION-MAKING

The advent of AI, blockchain, mobile health technologies and wearable sensors are transforming the process of clinical decision-making through patient-centered, interoperable, real-time, and evidence-based applications. It enhances the degree of integration and collaboration, enhances the prediction model, customized treatment of patients, and the decentralized storage and sharing of health data. Nevertheless, all these technologies should be coordinated, interoperable, and demand innovative solutions to data confidentiality and protection.

6.1 Interoperability and Data Fusion

AI-CDSS combined with blockchain enhances the security of the data, its transparency, and trustworthiness of the data.

1. **Role of Blockchain in AI-Driven Healthcare:** Blockchain also guarantees the integrity and un alterability of the data as well as the records' integrity to prevent any form of tampering. Decentralized data access: Electronic health records can be shared among the hospitals & research institutions and AI health platforms without having data island. Automated Transactions in Health care Industry using Smart Contracts: Smart contracts enhance the use of insurance claims, treatment approval, and prescription verifications.
2. **AI-Enhanced Blockchain Analytics for Healthcare Decision-Making:** AI models use the data that is blockchain-verified which means that the data is genuine, uncompromised, and of high quality. Example: Algorithms made using machine learning algorithms for learning purpose on cancer data which can be obtained using block chain with ensuring data verification on imaging tests, would increase the probability of cancer diagnoses(Rajendran et al., 2023). Of the four borderline nanoscale technologies, the synchronization of mobile health data and wearable sensor outputs shows the largest difference between professionals and non-professionals (Alabdulatif, A. et al., 2023). mHealth applications and wearable devices, for example, produce huge real-time health data that have to be interfaced with AI-based CDSS and blockchain-based Health Record Electronic (HRE).

3. **Challenges in Data Fusion from Mobile and Wearables:** Data Format Variability: Since every device employs its format, the similarity in this field is quite low. Sensitivity in Real-Time Processing: Wearable AI devices include ECG monitors, glucose sensors, etc., that produce real-time data for AI processing. Data Privacy Issues: There are privacy concerns when it comes to the integration of the health data generated by the mobile into the blockchain-based records through the use of AI.
4. **AI-Blockchain Integration for Wearable and Mobile Data:** Sensors on the wearables detect and transmit vital signs as heart rate, glucose levels, and SpO2, and the AI models analyze and alert on deviations. Blockchain makes it possible to record insights from AI in a secure manner to avoid tampering or interference. Edge AI on Wearables: It works by processing data within the wearable device, and therefore there is no need to transmit data to clouds frequently. The combination of integration of AI, blockchain, mobility and wearable technology in the context of healthcare can provide precise, secure and real-time data related to the clinical environment.

6.2 Future Research Directions

It describes key trends in artificial intelligence, such as its enhancement with blockchain, mobile health, and wearable devices, which will define the intelligent, decentralized, and secure decision-making systems in the near future.

1. **AI Advancements for Clinical Decision Support: Federated Learning (FL):** AI models trained across various multiple decentralized facilities without surrender patient data for data analysis and improving privacy-preserving AI in the healthcare facility. Explainable AI (XAI): Ensures that the clinicians have confidence in the CDSS recommendations made by the AI system. Multimodal Artificial Intelligence: They are formed by integrating EHRs, wearable devices, imaging, and genomic data for accurate diseases diagnosis.
2. **Blockchain for Decentralized Healthcare Systems:** Self-Sovereign Identity (SSI): Patient owns their data and control information on the blockchain by selecting a specific person/organization to share the data with. Interoperable Blockchain Networks: Refers to the implementation of blockchain solutions that will connect multiple hospitals and allow them to share EHRs. Quantum-Secure Blockchain: It provides better safeguard against any future quantum computing threats to the medical data.
3. **Mobile and Wearable Innovations for Smart Healthcare:** Mobile Edge Computing on Smartphones and Wearables: The AI models can be implemented on mobile phones and wearable devices, therefore there is no need to send the

data to the cloud for diagnosis. Telemedicine: With the help of the high speed of the 5G networks, remote patient monitoring and diagnosis using artificial intelligence become more effective. Wearable-Based Biometric Authentication: Ensures that there is no healthcare fraud by incorporating continuous authentication through wearable biometrics. Future work will then focus on resolving the current issues in data security, compatibility, and decentralized AI management to enable better and improved AI solutions in the field of healthcare. AI, blockchain, mobile health, and wearables are the four factors that have led to the emergence of the new intelligent clinical decision-making systems. In diagnostics, analytics is employed to make a better diagnosis, blockchain is used to protect the patient records, mobile applications make the health care services more accessible and wearable technology offer on-going monitoring. Despite these issues of interoperability, data privacy, and system integration, there are emerging technologies such as federated learning, decentralized identity management, and 5G-driven AI analytics that will revolutionalise the future of the personalized, predictive, and secure healthcare. It is evident that by integrating AI in CDSS with decentralized and privacy-protected blockchain structures, the envisioned clinical decision-making process will be smarter, easily scalable, and even more patient-centered.

7. CONCLUSION

The amalgamation of the four technologies such as AI, Blockchain, Mobile Technologies, and Wearables contribute positively in clinical decision making since they deliver real-time, intelligent and secured healthcare solutions. CDSS based on AI help improve diagnostics, planning of treatment processes, and monitoring of patients due to the application of predictive analysis and neural networks. Blockchain resolves the concern of data privacy and decentralized record keeping by providing data security, and data integration. Nevertheless, it has certain problems like data standardization, interoperability of the various systems, security, and adherence to the laws. In the massive deployments, the capability to deliver reliable AI models, the means of sharing patient data safely without compromising privacy, and appropriate alignments of these technologies are some of the challenges. Federated Learning (FL): The next generation of model based self-governing AI systems of privacy preserving clinical decision support with data centralization levels. Explainable Artificial Intelligence (XAI): Improving the acceptability of the clinical suggestions of AI. Quantum-Resistant Blockchain: The development of well-established systems that would safeguard health information databases in the future due to quantum computers. Integration of AI & IoT with 5G in healthcare: It is concerned with the way the use of 5G technology will advance near real-time and precise health diagnosis, monitoring, and telemedicine. When these challenges are managed and the opportunities of the new innovations are accepted, then the future of clinical choices will become more precise, safe, patient-focused, and effective in the future.

REFERENCES

Alabdulatif, A., Al Asqah, M., Moulahi, T., & Zidi, S. (2023). Leveraging artificial intelligence in blockchain-based e-health for safer decision making framework. *Applied Sciences (Basel, Switzerland)*, *13*(2), 1035.

De Novi, G., Sofia, N., Vasiliu-Feltes, I., Zang, C. Y., & Ricotta, F. (2023). Blockchain technology predictions 2024: Transformations in healthcare, patient identity, and public health. *Blockchain in Healthcare Today*, *6*, 10–30953.

Ghorbian, M., & Ghorbian, S. (2025). Empowering Clinical Decision-Making with Generative AI in Intelligent Decision Support Systems. In *Generative Artificial Intelligence (AI) Approaches for Industrial Applications* (pp. 241–259). Springer Nature Switzerland.

Jayaprakasam, B. S. (2025). AI and Big Data-Driven m-Health: Integrating Cloud Computing, Remote Patient Monitoring, Clinical Decision Support Systems, and Self-Supervised Learning with FHIR for Scalable Healthcare Systems. *Indo-American Journal of Life Sciences and Biotechnology*, *22*(1), 11–25.

Kamala, S. P. R., Gayathri, S., Pillai, N. M., Gracious, L. A., Varun, C. M., & Subramanian, R. S. (2023, July). Predictive analytics for heart disease detection: a machine learning approach. In 2023 4th International Conference on Electronics and Sustainable Communication Systems (ICESC) (pp. 1583-1589). IEEE.

Kovacova, M., Kevicky, F., & Popescu, G. H. (2023). Generative Artificial Intelligence-driven Healthcare Systems in Patient Record Analysis, in Disease Diagnosis and Monitoring, and in Customized Treatment Plans. *Contemporary Readings in Law and Social Justice*, *15*(1).

Maithili, K., Ponmalar, A., Yamini, B., Karthikeyan, M., Anish, T. P., Maheswari, B., & Subramanian, R. S. (2024). Advances in AI and Machine Learning for Healthcare Informatics. In Machine Learning and Generative AI in Smart Healthcare (pp. 1-22). IGI Global.

Mazhar, T., khan, S., Shahzad, T., khan, M. A., Saeed, M. M., Awotunde, J. B., & Hamam, H. (2025). Generative AI, IoT, and blockchain in healthcare: Application, issues, and solutions. *Discover Internet of Things*, *5*(1), 5.

Ponnuviji, N. P., Elangovan, G., Sujatha, K., Jambulingam, U., Ganesan, I., & Lalitha, S. D. (2024). IoT-Enabled Assistive Technologies Approach for Personalized Geriatric Health Monitoring and Safety. In Future of AI in Biomedicine and Biotechnology (pp. 125-146). IGI Global.

Priyadharshini, S. I., Irene, D. S., Beulah, J. R., & Ponnuviji, N. P. (2025). Enhancing real-time health monitoring with hybrid recurrent long short-term tyrannosaurus search for menstrual cups. *Biomedical Signal Processing and Control, 100*, 107065.

Rajendran, T., Rajathi, S. A., Balakrishnan, C., Aswini, J., Prakash, R. B., & Subramanian, R. S. (2023, December). Risk prediction modeling for breast cancer using supervised machine learning approaches. In 2023 2nd International Conference on Automation, Computing and Renewable Systems (ICACRS) (pp. 702-708). IEEE.

Ramesh, J. V. N., Talukdar, V., Kurniullah, A. Z., Jain, S. K., Anand, R., & Gupta, A. (2025). Integration of Generative AI System to IoT Based Healthcare Systems 5.0. In *Revolutionizing Healthcare 5.0: The Power of Generative AI: Advancements in Patient Care Through Generative AI Algorithms* (pp. 199–217). Springer Nature Switzerland.

Reddy, S. (2024). Generative AI in healthcare: An implementation science informed translational path on application, integration and governance. *Implementation Science : IS*, *19*(1), 27.

Rosaline, R. A. A., & Ponnuviji, N. P., TC, S. L., & Manisha, G. (2023). Enhancing lifestyle and health monitoring of elderly populations using CSA-TkELM classifier. *Knowledge-Based Systems*, *276*, 110758.

Shiny Irene, D., Indra Priyadharshini, S., Ponnuviji, N. P., & Kalaivani, A. (2024). Technological advancements in menstrual health: The role of generative pre trained transformer and bees algorithm. *Journal of the Institution of Electronics and Telecommunication Engineers*, *70*(12), 8476–8491.

Shiny Irene, D., Ponnuviji, N. P., & Kalaivani, A. (2025). EHECA-HSWS: A Holistic Method for Improving Menstrual Health App User Experience. *Journal of the Institution of Electronics and Telecommunication Engineers*, •••, 1–12.

Siva, S. R., Sudha, K., Pooja, E., Maheswari, B., & Girija, P. (2024). Revolutionizing Healthcare Delivery: Applications and Impact of Cutting-Edge Technologies. AI and IoT Technology and Applications for Smart Healthcare Systems, 75-91.

Sudha, K., Ambhika, C., Maheswari, B., Girija, P., & Nalini, M. (2023). AI and IoT applications in medical domain enhancing healthcare through technology integration. In *AI and IoT-Based Technologies for Precision Medicine* (pp. 280–294). IGI Global.

Sudha, K., Lakshmipriya, C., Pajila, P. B., Venitha, E., & Anita, M. (2024, January). Enhancing Diabetes Prediction and Management through Machine Learning: A Comparative Study. In *2024 Fourth International Conference on Advances in Electrical, Computing, Communication and Sustainable Technologies (ICAECT)* (pp. 1-6). IEEE.

Yamini, B., Sudha, K., Nalini, M., Kavitha, G., Subramanian, R. S., & Sugumar, R. (2023, June). Predictive modelling for lung cancer detection using machine learning techniques. In 2023 8th International Conference on Communication and Electronics Systems (ICCES) (pp. 1220-1226). IEEE.

Chapter 11

MENTORd: A Responsible mHealth Artifact for Empowering Type II Diabetes Self-Management

Shane Joachim
https://orcid.org/0000-0002-3687-4346
Swinburne University of Technology, Australia

Abdur Rahim Mohammad Forkan
https://orcid.org/0000-0003-0237-1705
Swinburne University of Technology, Australia

Prem Prakash Jayaraman
Swinburne University of Technology, Australia

Muhammad Ali Chaudhry
Emerging Health International, UAE

Zeina Khouri-Stevens
Emerging Health International, UAE

Nilmini Wickramasinghe
https://orcid.org/0000-0002-1314-8843
La Trobe University, Australia

ABSTRACT

This chapter presents MENTORd, a responsible mHealth artifact supporting Type II Diabetes self-management. While diabetes apps are widely available, most lack theoretical grounding, personalisation, and responsible data practices, limiting adoption and impact. MENTORd addresses these gaps through a co-designed platform integrating behaviour change techniques and AI-driven analytics. Developed using an Adapted 4-Cycle Design Science Research Methodology (A4C-DSRM), it combines a cross-platform patient app with a clinician dashboard. Key features include a Macronutrient Detection Algorithm (MDA), Glucometer Detection Model (GDM), Nudge rule engine, and tracking of blood glucose, medication, and physical activity. Behavioural interventions are guided by Nudge Theory, with

DOI: 10.4018/979-8-3373-2545-3.ch011

Task-Technology Fit ensuring user alignment. Responsible analytics principles such as secure data handling, contextual AI, and iterative stakeholder engagement are integrated throughout. This chapter provides a structured artifact description and insights into ethical mHealth design for chronic disease management.

INTRODUCTION

Type II Diabetes Mellitus (T2DM) is becoming increasingly common, affecting over 460 million people worldwide and is projected to impact 578 million individuals by 2030 (Cho et al., 2018; Saeedi et al., 2019). This chronic condition not only increases morbidity and mortality, but also imposes significant strain on healthcare systems, especially in low-socio economic settings (Adu et al., 2019; Cho et al., 2018). Self-management is essential to an effective diabetes care, involving ongoing tasks such as monitoring blood glucose levels, maintaining a balanced diet, exercise, and adhering to medication (Khan et al., 2019; Wickramasinghe et al., 2019). However, for many individuals, sustaining these practices is challenging due to various factors such as low sustained motivation, low health literacy, and limited access to continuous care (Oftedal et al., 2011).

With the arrival of mobile health (mHealth) technologies has introduced the ability for enabling self-management through real-time data collection, personalised feedback, and digital intervention. With the wide availability and uptake of smartphones, mHealth apps have emerged as scalable tools to deliver support outside clinical environments. These apps offer functionalities such as in app logging functionality, step counters, and meal trackers, often bundled into seemingly user-friendly interfaces. Yet, despite their attempt, most diabetes-focused mHealth solutions have demonstrated limited real-world impact in the short and long term (Cortez et al., 2014). A key challenge lies in the lack of theoretical grounding, responsible design practices, and meaningful personalisation, which is critical to have sustained engagement and effective behaviour change (Fu et al., 2017).

While commercial health apps are abundant within the various relevant app stores, they are often built without rigorous input from clinical, behavioural, or ethical frameworks (Brew-Sam, 2020; Jennings et al., 2019). Many are generic, designed for broad use cases, and lack specificity for individual needs. This results in features that are not necessarily fit-for-purpose for the users (Fu et al., 2017). Moreover, ethical considerations such as data privacy, transparency, and equitable access are frequently overlooked, raising concerns about trust, security, and long-term sustainability with the development and usage of these mHealth solutions (Morley et al., 2020; WHO, 2021). Additionally, these tools rarely accommodate the dynamic nature of patient behaviours, preferences, and contextual factors that influence self-management decisions in daily life.

This chapter introduces MENTORd, a responsible mHealth artifact specifically designed to support the self-management of individuals living with Type II Diabetes. MENTORd integrates behavioural intervention techniques, artificial intelligence (AI), and responsible analytics approaches to offer a novel approach to digital health design. Developed using an Adapted 4-Cycle Design Science Research Methodology (A4C-DSRM), MENTORd is a platform that is co-designed with patients and clinicians. It features a cross-platform mobile patient interface and a companion clinician dashboard that together enable real-time data collection, and clinical oversight.

At the core of MENTORd are features informed by Adapted Task-Technology Fit (ATTF), Nudge Theory, and Responsible Analytics centric practices. It employs machine learning for dietary logging via a Macronutrient Detection Algorithm (MDA), logging of blood glucose through a Glucometer Detection Model (GDM), and an Adaptive Nudge Rule Engine that delivers personalised motivational cues. These capabilities are designed to work in harmony, ensuring users are not just nudged into healthier behaviours but do so in a way that respects their agency, autonomy, and privacy. Responsible design principles underpin every layer of the system, from secure API communication and secured data storage to iterative stakeholder engagement.

This chapter provides a structured artifact description, theoretical foundations, development methodology, ethical design decisions, and planned evaluation of MENTORd. It aims to contribute to the emerging field of responsible digital health innovation by showcasing how design science and stakeholder co-design can lead to more ethical, effective, and sustainable mHealth interventions.

BACKGROUND AND GAPS

Type II Diabetes Mellitus (T2DM)

Diabetes is considered a metabolic disorder caused by issues in insulin secretion, insulin action, or both (Alberti & Zimmet, 1998). While Type I Diabetes is due to genetic and autoimmune factors, whereas Type II Diabetes is largely influenced by consistent lifestyle choices, and environmental conditions (Alberti & Zimmet, 1998).

T2DM, accounting for roughly 90% of global cases, is characterised by the body's inability to respond properly to insulin, resulting in insulin resistance and elevated blood glucose levels (Federation, 2019). Though symptoms such as excessive thirst, frequent urination, blurred vision, and weight loss may occur, they are often milder than in Type I, and many individuals remain symptom-free for years (Federation,

2019). This makes early detection difficult, with a significant portion of cases going undiagnosed for extended periods (Federation, 2019).

Currently affecting over 416 million people worldwide, T2DM is still under active research (Federation, 2019). However, a strong link has been established between the condition and factors such as obesity, aging, certain ethnic backgrounds, and family history. Lifestyle factors such as inactivity, smoking, and alcohol use also play a major role in increasing the risk of developing T2DM (Wu et al., 2014).

Ongoing effective management of T2DM requires daily decision-making, behavioural self-regulation, and lifestyle adjustments (Wu et al., 2014). Patients with T2DM are often required to engage in self-management routines which include various logging and tracking of their blood sugar levels, medication, physical activity, and nutrition (Federation, 2019). These tasks, while critical for effective management of T2DM, are difficult to maintain over a long period of time without ongoing support. Studies show that many individuals struggle with overall adherence, leading to poor glycaemic control and higher risk of more serious complications such as cardiovascular disease and stroke (scheme).

The traditional model of T2DM care is clinic-centric and offers limited time and communication periods between patients and their healthcare providers. The ever-growing strain in primary and specialist healthcare provider settings (Adu et al., 2019; Cho et al., 2018), coupled with increasing rates of T2DM diagnosis (Federation, 2019), the healthcare system's capacity to provide individualised, continuous care for T2DM is under spotlight.

In this context, mHealth emerges as a potential enabler of self-management, offering scalable and remote support that can extend the reach of traditional model of T2DM care.

MHealth for Diabetes Self-Management: Advances and Limitations

The mHealth landscape has been a part of an expansive growth, with thousands of health-related applications now available on commercial app stores (Huang et al., 2018; Jimenez et al., 2019). However, only a small number of these is dedicated to diabetes, and even fewer are backed by research, evidence or grounded in behavioural theory (Joachim et al., 2022). Many apps offer one-size-fits-all features with limited adaptability, user engagement strategies, or alignment with the lived experience of managing chronic illness. Most fall short in delivering sustained impact on self-management behaviours or clinical outcomes (Brew-Sam, 2020; Jennings et al., 2019) (Chavez et al., 2017).

Research highlights that some of T2DM self-management solutions are increasingly integrating essential features such as blood glucose tracking, nutrition logging, physical activity monitoring, medication adherence tools, and links to clinical services (Joachim et al., 2022). In addition, platforms are evolving to offer personalised components, including tailored nutrition and fitness recommendations, and predictive analytics for calorie, by integrating with external sensors and capturing more data. However, most existing T2DM solutions incorporate these core features only in isolated fragments, rather than offering a holistic and research-grounded solutions that addresses the requirements to self-manage T2DM effectively (Cortez et al., 2014; Villalba-Mora et al., 2017).

As mentioned earlier, while there is a disconnect between the innovation in T2DM solutions, there is an underlying disconnect between mHealth and adoption of behavioural science theories (Fu et al., 2017). Most diabetes-focused apps overlook evidence-based behaviour change frameworks such as Nudge Theory (Thaler & Sunstein, 2008) or Task-Technology Fit (D. Goodhue & R. Thompson, 1995; Goodhue, 1998), which are known to improve engagement and adherence. In addition, there is a general lack of attention to personalisation, cultural nuance, and context-aware design features essential for relevance and improve user uptake (Brew-Sam, 2020; Jennings et al., 2019). This is compounded by a lack of user co-design, resulting in apps that are functionally adequate but poorly aligned with the fit-for-purpose needs of users.

Moreover, user's nutrition, one of the most critical aspects of T2DM self-management, remains insufficiently supported in most existing mHealth solutions (Joachim et al., 2022). As demonstrated in Table 2 from our previously published study (Joachim et al., 2022), very few applications incorporate a personalised nutrition recommender system that considers the interaction between blood glucose levels, physical activity, medication use, and dietary intake. While some apps include fitness tracking or clinical logging features, a truly integrated solution that addresses all key self-management tasks is rarely observed. This fragmented functionality limits the overall impact of these tools and adds to the reason behind to uptake of mHealth solutions.

The same comparative analysis (Table 2, (Joachim et al., 2022)) highlighted widespread issues with user satisfaction, retention, and perceived utility. Many applications are used only briefly or intermittently before being abandoned, often due to poor user experience, lack of personalisation, or limited relevance (Brew-Sam, 2020; Fu et al., 2017; Jennings et al., 2019). Similar patterns are observed in web-based portals, particularly those that rely on proprietary hardware like connected glucometers, which introduce additional burdens and barriers to sustained use (Giardina et al., 2015; Kruse et al., 2015). These issues collectively point to a need for more inclusive, integrated, and user-centred mHealth solution that align with the lived experience of diabetes self-management.

Furthermore, while AI and data analytics have rapidly grown over the last year, they are now appearing integrated into commercial health tools, and they are often implemented with minimal transparency or validation. This raises concerns about explainability, bias, and ethical data governance.

Within mHealth, specifically in the responsible design and development of these tools. Few solutions leverage established models of behaviour change, such as Nudge Theory or Task-Technology Fit, to inform their design choices. Even fewer consider principles of responsible data governance such as transparency, privacy, ethical AI design, and co-design with vulnerable populations. This results in an ecosystem where apps are downloaded, utilised for a period, but not retained. The apps are used when the user motivation is high, however over a sustained period, they are abandoned altogether due to lack of relevance, trust, or utility.

This persistent pattern of early adoption followed by lack of ongoing engagement highlights a gap in the field. While many mHealth tools are functional in parts, few are grounded in behavioural theory, co-designed with end users, or built with ethical and transparent data governance in mind. Addressing this gap requires a shift toward the responsible design of mHealth solutions, for tools that are not only usable, but trustworthy, adaptive, and sustained over time.

Responsible MHEALTH Design

While there has been unprecedented growth in mHealth solutions, the need for the design and development of these solutions to adhere to a clear standard of responsible design is more important than ever. While these technologies offer immense potential for empowering patients, most current implementations lack robust theoretical foundations, transparent data practices, and meaningful user involvement (Danaher et al., 2015; Fu et al., 2017). As highlighted in the gaps identified earlier, this has led to short-lived engagement and meaningful clinical utility.

In the context of T2DM, responsible design needs to go beyond base functionality. It requires solutions that are not only usable but trustworthy. The platforms should be designed to respect user autonomy, safeguard personal data, support diverse populations, and promote sustained behaviour change. This involves embedding ethical principles directly into the design process, selecting behavioural frameworks that align with real-world self-management needs, and adopting development methodologies that prioritise stakeholder inclusion and accountability.

The MENTORd platform was conceptualised in response to these needs. It aims to fill the gap left by current T2DM self-management solutions available by combining behavioural theory, personalised analytics, and co-design within a fit-for-purpose framework that integrates user feedback into each design cycle. The MENTORd platforms theoretical underpinnings ensure that features are not just functional, but meaningful and aligns with user self-management need. In doing so, MENTORd addresses a systematic gap in the field, where there is absence of a holistic, theory-informed, co-designed, ethically grounded mHealth platform that support long-term, patient-centric T2DM self-management through mHealth.

THEORETICAL FOUNDATIONS

The MENTORd platform is built on two theoretical frameworks: Adapted Task-Technology Fit (ATTF) and Nudge Theory (Thaler & Sunstein, 2008). These design and behavioural frameworks are further informed by the principles of Responsible Analytics, which help guide the ethical aspects of the artifact. Together, these provide the foundation for the artifact's architecture, and user interface design, while being ethically aligned.

Adapted Task Technology FIT (ATTF)

The original Task Technology Fit (TTF) model (Goodhue, 1998; D. L. Goodhue & R. L. Thompson, 1995) is a theory that suggests that the technology in question is more likely to enhance performance and user adoption rates when its features are closely aligned with the specific tasks the users much performs. In the context of T2DM self-management, these tasks include logging meals, blood glucose, medication, and any fitness. Within the MENTORd platform, TTF served as a foundational theory, in guiding the identification and development of features that ensure the tasks are fit-for-purpose. To do this and ensure that TTF can be applied to this context, an Adapted Task Technology Fit (ATTF) model was developed by (Joachim, 2021). ATTF follows the core principles of TTF, in which it follows a fit-viability model, however, ATTF is specifically adapter for T2DM self-management mHealth solutions.

In the ATTF model, the external, organisational, and individual factors are considered in assessing how well a system aligns with the real-world needs. While preserving the original fit-viability process of the original TTF, the ATTF model incorporates the following three dimensions:

- **External Factors,** such as policies, digital infrastructure, and the overall Australian Healthcare Environment.
- **Organisational Factors,** including clinical setting processes and digital infrastructure of the hospital and/or primary care settings.

- **Individual Factors,** such as preferences, experiences, digital literacy, of both the healthcare professional and the patients who interact with the MENTORd platform.

By evaluating identified tasks in line with the above factors, the ATTF model enables a structured assessment of the system's "fit", which explains how well its functionalities align with the originally identified requirements. This approach not only evaluates whether user needs are translated effectively into system features but also captures key performance attributes such as timeliness, reliability, and accuracy.

For example, the Macronutrient Detection Algorithm (MDA) replaces traditional text-based food logging with automated visual detection, addressing the user-reported burden of manually entering meal details. Similarly, the Glucometer Detection Model (GDM) aims to streamline glucose tracking by extracting readings from images of device screens and syncing data directly into the MENTORd system, allowing migration of information regardless of the type of glucometer used. This helps minimising redundancy and manual effort. The Adaptive Nudge Rule Engine aims to align behavioural prompts with users' daily routines, offering feedback that fits into existing lifestyle patterns and context, rather than imposing generic or untimely advice. These features were iteratively refined during co-design cycles, where users actively provided feedback, which was used to assess relevance, usability and the level of motivation. Features that were perceived as unengaging or irrelevant with the user's needs were either redesigned (if deemed essential) or removed entirely, to support sustained uptake.

While the ATTF model ensured that the MENTORd platforms features were aligned with real-world self-management tasks and user contexts, the Responsible Analytics principles aspect provided the ethical and socio-technical lens necessary to guide how these features were implemented and improved upon. Beyond the fit-viability alignment, the platform was designed to prioritise user autonomy, transparency, and explainability which are some of the core principles of Responsible Analytics (Dignum, 2019; Mittelstadt et al., 2016). An example of this is, although some of the prior identified features automate logging and nudging are technologically feasible and is fit-for-purpose in relation to T2DM self-management, they are only activated with explicit user consent, and every prediction that is made is presented to the user, who accepts or edits the entry. This allows for a degree of trust where the user can make changes to any of the automated workflows, ultimately remain as the decision makers.

This approach ensures that features are not only useful and usable, but is also justified, trustworthy, and aligned with user immediate needs. By ensuring both ATTF and Responsible Analytics are present, MENTORd advances a model of digital health that is both effective in practice and but stays responsible in principle.

Nudge Theory

Nudge Theory (Thaler & Sunstein, 2008), introduced by Thaler and Sunstein, provides a behavioural economics framework which supports interventions that aren't forceful, however aims to be interventional by subtly structuring choices to influence the decision-making of an individual without removing their autonomy. These non-coercive interventions are called "nudges" and as mentioned, they act as a cue for users to make "better" decisions. In mHealth, nudges can take shape in many forms, including reminders, default settings, visual feedback, social comparison, and progress tracking (Kwan et al., 2020). Each of the mentioned nudges attempts to guide user behaviour, while preserving user autonomy.

The MENTORd platform's nudging features ensure to reinforces the foundational principle of nudge theory, which suggests that nudges guide rather than coerce. Thaler and Sunstein famously illustrate this distinction by stating, "Placing fruit at eye level counts as a nudge. Banning junk food does not" (Thaler & Sunstein, 2008). In the context of MENTORd, this means behavioural suggestions are presented as subtle prompts and interactions, not as a mandatory directive. The goal is to influence healthier choices, such as suggesting a making them feel better about their meal choices or highlighting their consistency with their fitness, without making users feel forced or overwhelmed. These cues are deliberately designed to be non-intrusive, subtle, in which users can either act upon or ignore without any retribution.

While there has been growing research into the use of nudging to influence dietary choices, obesity-related behaviours, and health decision-making more broadly, there remains a clear gap in applying nudging as part of a holistic T2DM self-management solution. Most interventions focus on influencing a specific behaviour or outcome, rather than supporting comprehensive, sustained self-management for individuals living with T2DM. A systematic review conducted by Kwan et al. examined how nudge theories and strategies have been used to influence adult health behaviours and outcomes in diabetes care (Kwan et al., 2020). The review identified five distinct nudging techniques across the included studies: Framing, Reminders, Gamification, Social modelling, and social influence (Kwan et al., 2020). Kwan et at., noted that the distinct techniques, worked best for certain domains. For instance, the study suggested that reminders were most effective in relation of medication adherence but lacked effectiveness with dietary behaviour. This finding suggests that mHealth solutions should support various distinct nudges to support intended behaviour change.

In the MENTORd platform, as mentioned earlier, nudging is not treated as a superficial or aesthetic feature, but is designed as core behavioural intervention that is grounded in theory, user context and co-design insights. Nudges are generated uniquely based on users' interaction history and patterns. An example, of a nudge that may occur within MENTORd is when a user learns that a meal they are about to consume or already have consumed, is high in certain macronutrients, such as fats. The visualisation of this information does not forbid the meal, but instead invites reflection, potentially encouraging a healthier choice. Over time, this repeated exposure hopes to foster increased nutritional awareness, which may help gradually shape users' dietary behaviours at a subconscious level. One implementation of this principle is the Macronutrient Detection Algorithm (MDA). When a user photographs their meal, the MDA identifies the food item and provides a breakdown of its macronutrient content. This creates a moment of insight that can act as a subtle behavioural cue, helping the users to align their choices with their health goals, without any external pressure or judgement.

By integrating nudge theory in this intentional and ethical manner, the MENTORd platform ensures it aligns with the principles of responsible analytics. The platform attempts to foster a sustained behavioural engagement through an autonomy and supportive design, making positive T2DM self-management behaviours not only more likely, but more personally meaningful and ethically aligned.

Responsible Analytics in MHEALTH

Responsible Analytics (RA), while not explicitly defined in the mHealth space, it generally refers to the ethical design and governance of data-driven systems, ensuring that technologies like AI are developed and deployed in ways that respect human dignity, autonomy, and justice (Dignum, 2019; Mittelstadt et al., 2016). In the context of mHealth, where digital tools influence personal health decisions, RA plays a vital role in safeguarding trust, mitigating harm, and enabling user empowerment.

Rather than focusing solely on predictive accuracy or automation, RA in digital health prioritises transparency, explainability, inclusivity, and meaningful consent (Floridi et al., 2018; WHO, 2021). It addresses risks such as involuntary data collection and biased interventions that may worsen disparities in health (Morley et al., 2020; Vayena et al., 2018).

MENTORd integrates relevant RA practices through a range of socio-technical safeguards and principles:

- **User Autonomy, Control, Transparency and explainability:** All AI-powered and algorithmic processes such as the Macronutrient Detection Algorithm (MDA) and Glucometer Detection Model (GDM) generate interpretable, human-readable outputs. Users can review, accept, or update the outputs, reinforcing trust and intelligibility of system behaviour.
- **Privacy by Design:** Potentially sensitive operations like MDA and GDM, which involves image processing, is handled entirely on-device. No user images are stored unless explicitly permitted, and all personal data is encrypted.

- **Fairness and Inclusivity:** MENTORd is designed to function in low-connectivity, mobile-first environments and supports variable digital literacy levels. Co-design sessions ensured we prevent bias, support equity, and identify overlooked user needs.
- **Accountability and Auditability:** All nudges, AI outputs, and data entry is logged with traceable metadata. This ensures auditability and supports ethical oversight.

These design choices align with ethical frameworks such as AI4People (Floridi et al., 2018) and WHO's AI guidance for health (WHO, 2021), which call for health technologies that are not only effective, but also transparent, equitable, and contextually appropriate. MENTORd displays how Responsible Analytics can move from principles into practical, feasible features in mHealth.

To incorporate the theoretical foundations into a functioning, real-world system, a structured design methodology is utilised. The next section outlines the methodological approach taken to develop MENTORd, an Adapted 4-Cycle Design Science Research Methodology (A4C-DSRM).

METHODOLOGY

The development of the MENTORd platform was guided by the Design Science Research Methodology (DSRM), which provided a structured approach for the co-design and co-development of a responsible mHealth solution aimed at supporting self-management in individuals living with T2DM. While the process is anchored in the Adapted 4-Cycle DSRM (A4C-DSRM) model established in our prior work (Joachim, 2021), this section focuses specifically on how the methodology was applied throughout the design, development, and refinement of the MENTORd platform.

Overview

The DSRM approach, which is widely used in information systems and socio-technical design to guide the development and evaluation of artifacts with a focus on ensuring the final output is fit-for-purpose (Hevner et al., 2004). DSRM is characterised by iterative cycles of problem identification, artifact design, demonstration, evaluation, and knowledge contribution. While it can be applied in a wide range of fields of research, it is particularly well-suited for health technology design (Hevner et al., 2004), where systems must balance technical feasibility, behavioural impact, and ethical responsibility.

Building on top of Design Science Research Methodology (DSRM), this research adopts an Adapted 4-Cycle Design Science Research Methodology (A4C-DSRM) (Joachim, 2021), specifically ported over to support the responsible development of mHealth artifacts. While the core principles of the design evaluation loops are retained, the adaptation expands on four interrelated cycles of Change & Impact, Relevance, Design, and Rigor. The adaptation attempts to address the demands of healthcare contexts, behavioural co-design, and responsible analytics. This MENTORd platform applies A4C-DSRM as the methodological framework to guide the iterative design, implementation, and refinement.

Adapted 4-Cycle DSRM (A4C-DSRM)

Aforementioned, we adopted the four-cycle DSRM (Drechsler & Hevner, 2016) to ensure that the platform was developed in a way that is contextually grounded, informed by stakeholder needs, rigorously evaluated, and capable of producing transferable knowledge. The adapted four cycles as follows:

1. **Change & Impact Cycle:** This cycle ensured the platform was relevant within the Australian healthcare environment. Regulatory compliance, patient environmental factors, and mobile access constraints were considered early in the design process through consultations with clinicians, digital health experts, and healthcare administrators.
2. **Relevance Cycle:** We conducted interviews, focus groups, and co-design workshops with T2DM patients and clinicians to better understand platform requirements. These sessions revealed nuanced needs, such as the importance and potential benefits of visual meal feedback, automated glucose tracking, and culturally relevant meal recommendations. A design utility model was used to map these insights to functional design components.
3. Co-Design Cycles (I-III):
    - I. **Cycle I:** Mock-ups and sketches of feature ideas were created based on initial requirements and tested with users.
    - II. **Cycle II:** Paper prototypes integrated feedback, emphasising user interface simplicity and fit-for-purpose nature of the features. Specific changes included enhancements to blood glucose visualisation and the integration of nudge feedback based on macronutrient analysis.
    - III. **Cycle III:** A functional MENTORd prototype, both mobile and clinician dashboard, were developed. Regular feedback loops with clinical and other

stakeholders ensured that features such as the previously identified were refined based on user experience.

4. **Rigor Cycle:** This cycle enabled systematic verification of our contributions to the field, ensuring the development of a novel, ethically grounded digital health artifact. Some of the contributions from this cycle include domain-specific extensions to TTF theory (e.g., ATTF), A4C-DSRM itself, the insights into co-design of mHealth solutions for chronic care – specifically T2DM, and a working system for the future pilot studies.

This methodology demonstrates how DSRM can be operationalised in health contexts to build responsible, fit-for-purpose digital solutions. While the theoretical model has been articulated elsewhere, this section adds a practical summarised depth on the implementation and refinement of the MENTORd artifact. Furthermore, the application of A4C-DSRM offers a transferable methodological approach, enabling improved stakeholder engagement, integration of behavioural theory, and alignment with responsible data practices in this context.

ARTIFACT DESCRIPTION

This section presents the MENTORd platform as a responsible mHealth artifact designed to support the self-management of T2DM. It outlines the system's architecture, core components, and key functionalities which were identified via co-design processes and grounded in theory.

Overview of the Mentord Platform

The MENTORd platform is a responsible mHealth solution, that is co-designed to support the long-term self-management of T2DM. Developed through the Adapted 4-Cycle Design Science Research Methodology (A4C-DSRM) (Joachim, 2021), MENTORd integrates behavioural science, patient and clinician insights, and responsible data practices to address identified gaps in mHealth solutions for T2DM self-management.

The platform is interactable by two user interfaces: a cross-platform mobile app for patients and a web-based clinician dashboard. These are underpinned by a set of embedded AI features that drive key system functionalities and automations. The Macronutrient Detection Algorithm (MDA) and Glucometer Detection Model (GDM) are designed as on-device models, deployed directly within the mobile application frontend, allowing for offline and on-device inference. In contrast, the Adaptive Nudge Rule Engine is designed as part of the backend API layer, responsible for generating context-aware behavioural prompts for each user based on their interactions and trends.

MENTORd follows a simple monolithic architecture at this stage of development, optimised for stability, maintainability, and ease of deployment during pilot trials. This structure enables streamlined and simplified data flow between the app, backend services, and database, while still accommodating modular growth in future iterations.

Currently, not all features are at the same stage of implementation. The MDA is fully implemented and is ready for internal testing. The GDM and Nudge Engine are currently under active development and will be progressively rolled out in alignment with upcoming pilot and evaluation phases. This staged implementation approach enables early user feedback while more complex AI features are still in development, reflecting a deliberate commitment to responsible and iterative development and deployment.

While MENTORd is a functional T2DM self-management solution, it is not solely a technical solution, but a socio-technical mHealth artifact shaped by behavioural theory, co-design with relevant stakeholders, and a commitment to responsible analytics practices. The following sections outline the platform's architecture, feature set, and ethical design principles in detail.

Platform Architecture

The MENTORd platform is structured using a simple, monolithic architecture, intentionally chosen to support a stable and manageable deployment during its upcoming pilot trial. While designed for future modularity, the current implementation prioritises reliability, robustness, and streamlined integration of backend services and user interfaces. When the architecture is simplified, it can be explained with the three key layers: *(1) the user interface layer, (2) the application logic layer, and (3) the data and services layer.* See figure 1.

Figure 1. Simple Layer based Platform Architecture

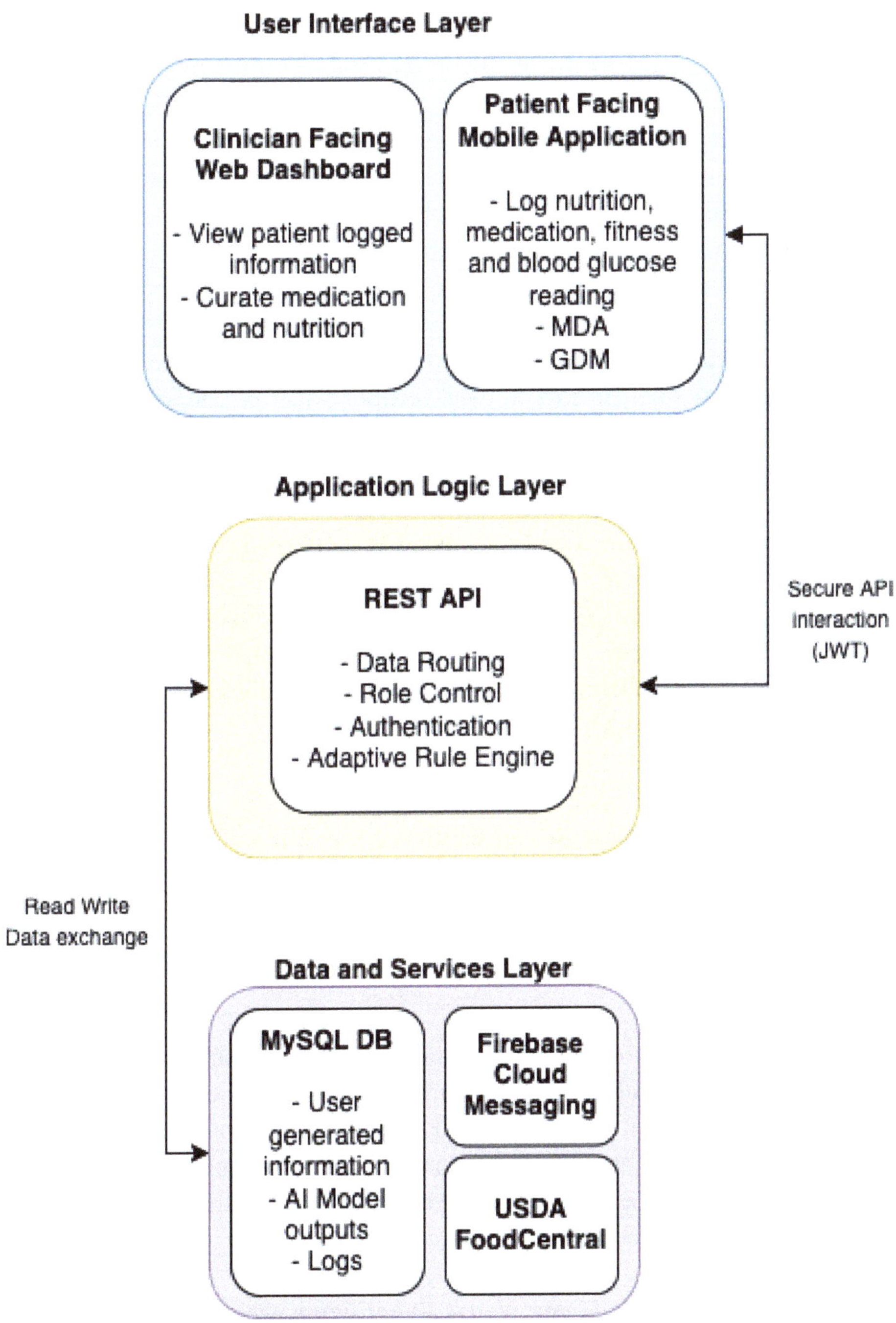

User Interface Layer

The user interface layer includes the two primary frontends that was co-designed and developed for the identified primary stakeholders of the MENTORd platform. The frontends are:

- The ***patient-facing mobile application*** which contains features required for daily self-management of T2DM, including logging of nutrition, blood sugar level, medication, and fitness. The mobile app also contains various visualisations, a simple learn page and user details update feature. The mobile app is developed using Flutter (Community., 2017), allowing the app to be cross-platform and supports offline functionality.
- The ***clinician-facing web-dashboard*** allows healthcare professionals to view aggregated patient logged data, monitor patterns, and support remote engagement. It includes tools for trend visualisation and holistic patient review.

While briefly mentioned earlier, the two AI models utilised in MENTORd are integrated directly within the mobile app using TensorFlow Lite (TFLite):

- ***The Macronutrient Detection Algorithm (MDA)*** enables real-time, on-device meal analysis via photo input.
- ***The Glucometer Detection Model (GDM)***, currently under development, is attempting to extract blood glucose values from glucometer screen images and aid blood glucose logging.

Embedding these models on-device ensures responsible analytics principles are followed as we preserve user privacy, minimise unnecessary data transmission, and ensures that the functionality, at its core, is present without the need for internet access.

Application Logic Layer

The aforementioned patient mobile app and clinician web dashboard both interact with a centralised backend through a secure, RESTful application programming interface (API). This layer facilitates and manages all data transmission, authentication, user role management, and interaction logging. All communication between clients and APIs is encrypted and governed by token-based authentication (Auth0, 2010) with role-based access controls, ensuring data security and privacy across the platform.

The API also hosts the ***Adaptive Nudge Rule Engine***, which is currently under development. This engine generates personalised behavioural nudges based on user data, system rules, and usage patterns. Designed with responsible analytics in mind, the adaptive nudge rule engine generates relevant nudges based on predefined, rule-based logic to ensure that prompts are consistent, context-aware, and free from unexplainable algorithmic decision-making.

Data and Services Layer

While the previous layer handles data transmission and communication between components, the Data and Services Layer is responsible for securely storing and managing all platform data.

To support its core features, the MENTORd platform uses a centralised MySQL (Oracle Corporation, 1995) database that holds user-generated entries, clinician notes, AI model outputs, and system-level logs. Responsible data design is embedded throughout this layer, some examples include:

- Users retain control over what they input and share.
- Users need to consent before the metadata is attached to all personal records.
- AI generated outputs are stored with associated confidence scores to support auditability and traceability.

Additionally, certain external services are integrated where required to ensure feature completion. For example, the USDA FoodCentral API (Agriculture) is used to retrieve detailed nutritional composition data for logged food items; and the Firebase Cloud Messaging (FCM) client is also being integrated and currently is being utilised to support the in-development Adaptive Nudge Rule Engine, enabling the delivery of timely, context-aware notification nudges to users.

In summary, the MENTORd platform architecture is intentionally designed for simplicity, stability, and responsible deployment in preparation for its pilot study. The monolithic structure enables for a relatively simplified integration of user interfaces, AI components, and backend services while maintaining clear data flows and secure interactions. On-device AI model interacts supports privacy and offline functionality, while the centralised API and database ensure consistency and traceability. Together, these layers allow for the delivery of key T2DM self-management features in a way that aligns with both clinical goals and responsible analytics principles.

The following sections outline the core functionalities in more detail provided to patients and clinicians through their respective interfaces.

Patient-Facing Mobile Application

In the MENTORd platform, the patient-facing mobile app is the main interface in which users/patients interact with the MENTORd platform in their daily self-management of T2DM. Designed through co-design sessions with patients and informed by behavioural theory, the app is purposefully built to prioritise user needs, usability, and task alignment. It offers a relevant suite of features that support logging of various parameter, receiving feedback, and monitoring personal trends, while maintaining user control over data entry and visibility. The application is built using Flutter (Community., 2017) for cross-platform compatibility to ensure wide support across a range of real-world environments. Each feature has been carefully implemented or planned to reduce burden and encourage engagement.

Core Logging Features

A core component of the patient-facing mobile app is the daily logging suite, which enables users to record and monitor key self-management activities related to T2DM. This includes logging of nutrition, blood glucose levels, medication intake, and physical activity. These features were identified as critical during co-design sessions, where users consistently highlighted the need for a simple, low-effort method to track their behaviours without feeling overwhelmed.

Each logging function is presented through an intuitive interface using large tiles, icons, and visual cues to support quick input and minimise cognitive load. Users can:

- Enter meals through selecting from a personalised clinician curated list, searching for a meal manually or via a photo-based input (MDA).
- Log blood glucose levels manually or through GDM (in development).
- Track medication adherence using simple dropdowns and reminders.
- Record physical activity

Figure 2. MENTORd Mobile App – Logging Blood Sugar Level Manually

As illustrated in Figure 2, the MENTORd mobile app supports intuitive, tile-based interfaces for core logging functions, including manual blood glucose entry. Further, these features also offer timestamped entries, history views, and visual feedback elements such as streaks and progress charts. While subtle, these design elements function as embedded nudges, encouraging users to maintain consistent engagement by promoting self-reflection, highlighting behavioural patterns, and reinforcing a sense of progress over time.

Importantly, the design emphasises user autonomy, as all inputs are editable, and under user control. This aligns with the platform's commitment to responsible analytics by reducing data fatigue, supporting informed participation, and avoiding coercive data collection practices.

Macronutrient Detection Algorithm (MDA)

To reduce the burden of manual food logging, the MENTORd mobile application integrates an AI-powered Macronutrient Detection Algorithm (MDA) that enables users to log meals using photos. This feature was prioritised during co-design workshops, where participants consistently reported an easier way to log their meals, particularly when logging multiple meals, snack and drinks a day.

The MDA was introduced and evaluated in (Joachim et al., 2022), and has since been present as a core feature in the MENTORd patient-facing app. The current implementation of the MDA integrates Google's pre-trained *food_v1 (Google AIY)* model for on-device image classification, as previously disclosed in (Joachim et al., 2022). Within the MENTORd app, users can capture a meal image, which is then processed locally to identify the type of meal, which is then processed by the API to then estimate its macronutrient composition, such as carbohydrates, proteins, and fats. The resulting values are presented in a viewable and editable summary, allowing users to accept or make changes to the entry as needed.

The MDA is fully implemented using a TFLite model within the mobile app, ensuring accessibility in low-connectivity environments while enhancing data privacy by avoiding cloud-based image processing. Logged meals are also visible to clinicians through the dashboard, supporting shared understanding and enabling personalised dietary guidance.

What makes the MDA particularly valuable from a Nudge Theory standpoint is that it functions not only as a logging tool but also as a subtle behavioural nudge. By prompting users to photograph their meals, the feature encourages greater mindfulness and self-awareness about food choices. The act of taking a photo becomes a moment of reflection, reinforcing conscious eating habits. Over time, this images also provides clinicians with concrete, user logged evidence to support personalised dietary discussions, grounded in what patients are consuming, rather than relying on verbal discussions or incomplete physical logs. This kind of context-rich feedback loop is difficult to achieve through traditional self-management routines. Additionally, the visual display of estimated macronutrient serves as a secondary nudge, helping users better understand their nutritional intake in real time based on simply the meal they are having.

Figure 3. MENTORd Mobile App – Adding through MDA

As shown in Figure 3, the MENTORd mobile app enables users to log meals through the Macronutrient Detection Algorithm (MDA) feature. This process begins with capturing a food image, which is then analysed on-device to the user can review the AI-generated details and confirm.

This feature reflects strong Task-Technology Fit (TTF) (Goodhue, 1998) by addressing a high-friction task such as meal logging, with a low-effort, context-aware alternative. It also operationalises responsible analytics principles by avoiding image storage by default, maintaining transparency of AI-driven estimates, and preserving user control throughout the interaction.

Glucometer Detection Model (GDM)

The Glucometer Detection Model (GDM) is a planned feature of the MENTORd mobile app, which is currently under active development. It aims to reduce the manual burden of entering blood glucose readings by enabling users to simply take a photo of their glucometer screen. The model then extracts the displayed value using optical character recognition (OCR) pipeline and logs it automatically within the app once the user accepts it.

This feature emerged through co-design sessions, where stakeholders described the inconvenience of manually inputting glucose data, particularly when readings are taken multiple times per day. Bluetooth glucometers were discussed as a possible solution; however, integration with such devices was found to be commercially restrictive due to licensing requirements and compatibility limitations.

Instead, the decision was made to pursue a more inclusive approach that would support any type of glucometer, regardless of brand or cost. Users will also have the option to upload multiple images in bulk for faster entry.

From a technical standpoint, the initial implementation will rely on a lightweight OCR pipeline to extract numerical values from glucometer screen images. However, if OCR performance proves insufficient, a fallback plan includes developing a custom convolutional neural network (CNN), potentially using MobileNet or a similar architecture. Further evaluation and prototyping are required to determine the optimal approach.

The GDM is being designed to run fully on-device using TensorFlow Lite (TFLite), ensuring that all image processing remains local to the user's phone. No images will be stored or transmitted externally. This aligns with the platform's commitment to responsible analytics, supporting user privacy, offline accessibility, and users retain full control over model detected values, with the ability to review, edit, or override outputs as needed.

Although still under development, the GDM reflects the principles of Task-Technology Fit (TTF) by addressing a repetitive, high-frequency task with a streamlined, low-effort alternative. It also supports Responsible Analytics by avoiding unnecessary data exposure, enhancing accessibility across device types, and preserving user control over logged data. Once implemented, the GDM is expected to streamline glucose tracking and provide clinicians with more complete and consistent insight into patient glucose patterns.

Adaptive Nudge Rule Engine

The MENTORd platform includes a rule-based nudging system designed to gently encourage consistent self-management behaviours for the mobile app users. These adaptive nudges are delivered through push notifications or in-app messages and are intended to support daily engagement without overwhelming the user.

Nudges are generated by a backend Adaptive Nudge Rule Engine, which evaluates user activity and interaction patterns to trigger context-aware prompts. For example, a user may receive a reminder to log a meal if no entry is detected during a typical mealtime, or a motivational message after maintaining a consistent logging streak. While the current system relies on predefined behavioural rules, future versions aim to incorporate personalisation and configurable settings based on user preferences or feedback on the nudges.

From a design standpoint, these nudges are intentionally lightweight, non-intrusive, and actionable. They are guided by principles of Nudge Theory, which emphasises subtle environmental cues that influence behaviour without limiting user choice. By embedding these cues into everyday interactions, MENTORd aims to help users stay engaged in their self-care routines with minimal friction.

In summary, the patient-facing MENTORd mobile app integrates a range of co-designed features to support the daily self-management of T2DM. From AI-powered components such as the Macronutrient Detection Algorithm (MDA) and Glucometer Detection Model (GDM), to core logging functions, visual feedback mechanisms, and the backend-driven Adaptive Nudge Rule Engine, the app has been developed with a strong focus on usability, privacy, and behavioural reinforcement. In addition to these core features, the platform includes several lightweight but meaningful tools that further support user engagement and reflection, such as blood glucose charting with customisable minimum and maximum ranges, a daily macronutrient and calorie intake counter, a statistics card displaying relevant metrics like average glucose readings, and a fully customisable, user-editable profile page.

The patient-facing mobile app operates in parallel with the clinician-facing dashboard, which is described in the following section.

Clinician-Facing Web Dashboard

The clinician-facing dashboard is a lightweight web-based interface designed to provide healthcare professionals with a consolidated view of patient-logged data. Developed alongside the patient-facing mobile app, this component supports remote monitoring, trend identification, and more personalised engagement during clinical consultations.

Clinicians here can view key data entries, including blood glucose logs, nutrition records (along with an image if applicable), and behavioural patterns over time. Further, the clinician can assign medication and meals to a curated list for their patients. This will appear when the patient is using their mobile app to log entries. The interface is intentionally simple, offering summary views rather than detailed analytics, in line with feedback from co-design sessions that emphasised the importance of clarity, ease of use, and clinical relevance.

From a system architecture perspective, the dashboard connects to the same backend API as the mobile app and adheres to strict role-based access controls to ensure data privacy and patient consent compliance. It is not designed for real-time monitoring, but rather for retrospective review, enabling more informed and collaborative conversations between clinicians and patients. The dashboard is built using Vue.js (You, 2014) and Bootstrap, providing a responsive interface optimised for desktop use and ensuring compatibility across a range of screen sizes and browsers.

The clinician dashboard also functions as a lightweight management portal. Each clinician can only access data for patients specifically assigned to them, ensuring strict adherence to privacy and access control. A designated head clinician role has extended privileges, including the ability to create new clinician accounts, assign patients, and register new patient profiles within the system.

From a behavioural standpoint, having a clinician dashboard also serves as a reverse nudge for patients, as it reinforces accountability and encourages them to be more consistent with the engagement with the MENTORd mobile app. Knowing that their logged data may be reviewed in future consultations subtly motivates users to maintain accurate records, without applying coercion. This also enhances patient clinician communication, grounding discussions in shared data rather than recollection. By enabling this collaborative review process while upholding strict access controls and consent-based visibility, the dashboard supports the platform's commitment to Responsible Analytics fostering trust, transparency, and meaningful use of patient-generated data.

Figure 4. MENTORd Web App – Viewing logged blood sugar and MDA

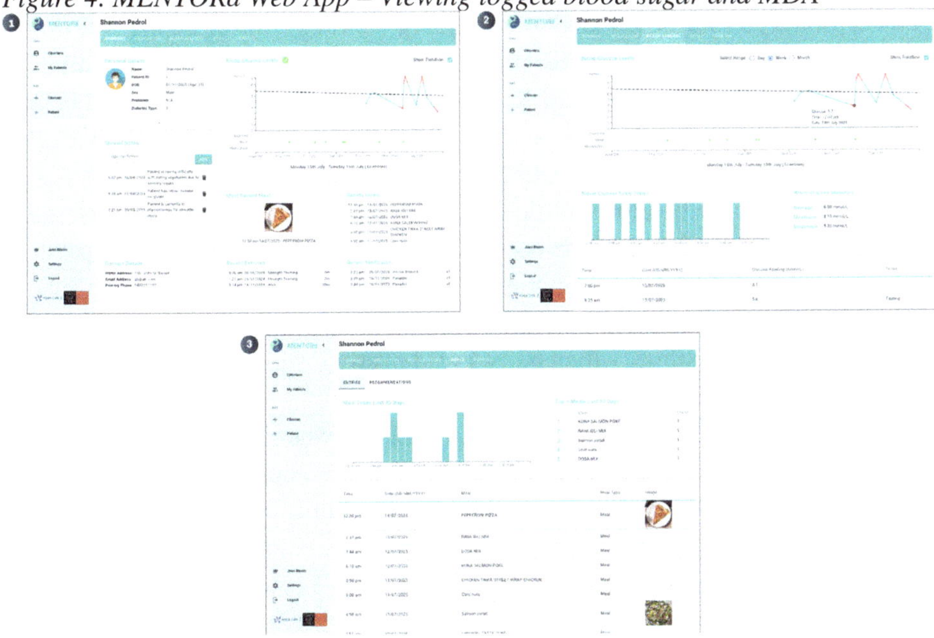

While streamlined in functionality, the clinician-facing dashboard plays a critical role in bridging patient self-management data with clinical oversight. By offering accessible, relevant summaries and secure management tools, it complements the patient app and reinforces the platform's commitment to collaborative, responsible, and context-aware care delivery.

Mentord and Responsible Analytics

Responsible Analytics (RA) was not only a guiding theoretical lens for the MENTORd platform but acted as an implicit set of principles that were translated into platform system decisions throughout the artifact's development. Rather than treating ethical concerns as secondary to functionality, the platform was built from the outset with privacy, transparency, user autonomy, and equity as central design goals.

An example is the use of on-device AI model processing for features like the Macronutrient Detection Algorithm (MDA) and Glucometer Detection Model (GDM). By leveraging TensorFlow Lite models that run entirely on the user's device, MENTORd avoids transmitting images to external servers and ensures that no visual data is stored unless explicitly permitted. This reduces both data exposure risk and reliance on continuous connectivity, making the system more secure and accessible.

The MENTORd platform also enforces user control for all AI-generated outputs. Outputs produced by MDA, and glucose readings extracted by the GDM, follow the same screen flows, which ensure that the outputted value is presented in an editable, human-readable format. Users can review, accept, or modify these values before submission. This ensures that the system remains assistive. This aligns with RA principles by avoiding decision-making that remove user autonomy.

Further, MENTORd follows a strict access control measure in which the users are on a role-based permissions in the backend API. Clinicians can only view patients explicitly assigned to them, and patient profiles include consent metadata linked to their generated records. Additionally, the clinician-facing dashboard is built for retrospective, not real-time, which helps avoid overly intrusive oversight, which is generally not required for T2DM self-management.

The Adaptive Nudge Rule Engine, while still in development, is also grounded in RA principles. The responsible design of this feature delivers relevant prompts through predefined rules rather than black-box algorithms. Nudges are transparent, simple, and designed to avoid manipulation or excessive intrusion to be in line with Nudge Theory, and it continues to reflect the platform's commitment non-coercive behavioural reinforcement and RA.

Across these features, the MENTORd platform, demonstrates how RA can be utilised not only through technical safeguards but through intentional design decisions and ethical awareness. From co-design with the stakeholders of this solution to role-specific data access and transparency in automation, the platform makes a case for the importance and need for RA in the mHealth space.

Summary

Table 1. Summary of MENTORd Features, Theoretical Basis, and Implementation Status

Feature	Interface	Theory	RA Element	Status
Nutrition Logging	Patient Mobile	TTF	User control, editable inputs	Implemented
Blood Glucose Logging	Patient Mobile	TTF, RA	User control, editable entries	Implemented
Medication Tracking	Patient Mobile	TTF	Simple dropdowns, autonomy	Implemented
Physical Activity Log	Patient Mobile	TTF	Low-effort, visual summaries	Implemented

continued on following page

Table 1. Continued

Feature	Interface	Theory	RA Element	Status
Macronutrient Detection Algorithm (MDA)	Patient Mobile App	TTF, Responsible Analytics (RA), Nudge Theory	On-device AI, privacy-by-design, editable predications	Implemented
Glucometer Detection Model (GDM)	Patient Mobile App	TTF, RA	On-device AI, privacy-by-design, editable predications	*In Development*
Adaptive Nudge Rule Engine	Backend & Mobile App	Nudge Theory, RA	Transparent, rule-based nudging	*In Development*
Visual Feedback (Streaks, Charts)	Patient Mobile App	Nudge Theory	Behavioural cues, passive reflection	Implemented
Clinician Dashboard	Web-based Dashboard	Responsible Analytics (RA)	Role-based access, consent-aware data handling	Implemented

Table 1 summarises the key features of the MENTORd platform, outlining their associated user interface, theoretical foundation, responsible design alignment, and current implementation status.

This section has detailed the architecture, core components, and responsible design strategies that exist within the MENTORd platform. From the Macronutrient Detection Algorithm (MDA) and Glucometer Detection Model (GDM) to the Adaptive Nudge Rule Engine and co-designed user interfaces, each element has been purposefully developed to support T2DM self-management through a blend of behavioural theory, stakeholder input, and responsible analytics. See Figure 5.

Figure 5. MENTORd Full Platform Architecture

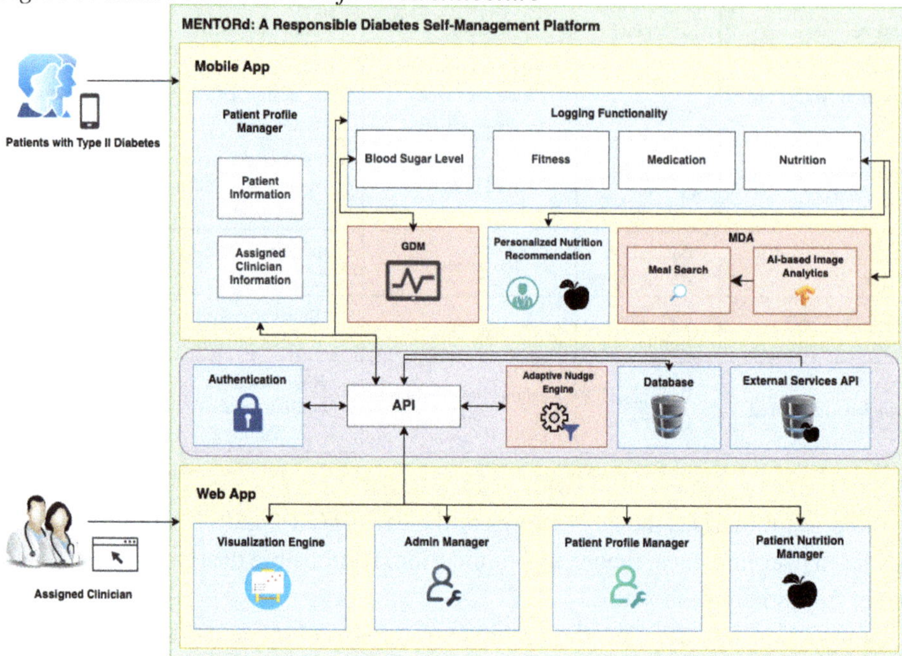

While several advanced features such as the AI-driven modules remain in active development or phased rollout, the MENTORd platform as a whole represents a functionally integrated, ethically grounded mHealth artifact. It is designed not only to deliver key self-management capabilities but to do so in a way that prioritises transparency, autonomy, and clinical relevance.

The following section outlines how MENTORd is planned to being evaluated through pilot trials.

PLANNED EVALUATION AND PILOT TRIAL

To assess the real-world usability of the MENTORd platform, a structured, two-phase evaluation has been conditionally approved by Swinburne University of Technology, Australia for implementation in collaboration with the Noor Care Health Network (NCHN), Pakistan. The study adopts a mixed-method approach designed to capture both quantitative metrics and in-depth user feedback, ensuring that the platform is not only functional but also ethically aligned, trusted, and practically usable.

Phase 1: Usability Study (1 Week)

The first phase will involve a usability study with six patients diagnosed with T2DM and two clinicians, recruited through NCHN. Participants will engage with the MENTORd mobile and web applications for a period of one week.

A purpose-built questionnaire, adapted version of Enlight (Baumel et al., 2017), will be provided at the end of the study, measuring five key dimensions: (i) Usability; (ii) Visual Design; (iii) User Engagement; (iv) Content; and (v) General Evaluation.

In addition, semi-structured interviews will be conducted to gather qualitative insights about user expectations, barriers, and perceived benefits. This early feedback will guide interface and feature refinement prior to the larger pilot rollout.

Phase 2: Pilot Trial (6 Months)

The second phase involves a 6-month pilot study with 30 patients and 5 clinicians, where participants use MENTORd in parallel with their ongoing clinical care. Each participant will actively engage with the platform for an 8-week window, logging meals, glucose levels, medications, and physical activity.

Clinicians will use the web-based dashboard to monitor assigned patients and use the tool during their standard care appointments. The same evaluation tools, purpose-built questionnaires and semi-structured interviews, will be repeated post the 8-week participation for the user, to track changes in perception, usability, and general thoughts.

Evaluation Metrics

The evaluation metrics used in this study were carefully selected to align with the theoretical underpinnings and design priorities of the MENTORd platform. Drawing from frameworks such as Task-Technology Fit (TTF) (Goodhue, 1998), Nudge Theory (Thaler & Sunstein, 2008), and Responsible Analytics (RA), the evaluation goes beyond functional performance to assess how well the system fit-for-purpose, enables and user empowerment. The core questionnaire, developed as part of the approved study protocol, captures standard dimensions such as usability, visual design, engagement, content quality and some general evaluation questions.

In addition, the evaluation includes targeted metrics that reflect the platform's responsible design. These include user trust in AI-generated outputs (e.g., from the MDA), the perceived clarity and usefulness of behavioural nudges, and the level of control users feel over their data and decisions.

Together, these metrics provide a holistic view of the MENTORd platforms functional value, measuring not only what the platform does, but how it is experienced, and interpreted by the end users.

DISCUSSION

This section reflects critically on the development of MENTORd as a responsible mHealth artifact, drawing insights from the integration of the utilised theoretical frameworks, stakeholder collaboration, and practical design trade-offs. The aim was not simply to build a functional diabetes self-management tool, but to create a digital health intervention that embodied ethical principles, behavioural insight, and user-centred relevance. By doing so, our fundamental goal was to create a platform that closely aligned with what users not only wanted but genuinely needed. The combined application of ATTF, Nudge Theory, and Responsible Analytics (RA) offered a structured lens through which key design decisions were reviewed, evaluated and implemented.

Adapted Task-Technology Fit (ATTF) played a critical role in ensuring that the MENTORd platforms features aligned with users' actual self-management behaviours and needs, particularly in relation to logging meals, medications, and blood glucose readings. More than just a usability check, ATTF served as a lens to interrogate which tasks imposed the most cognitive or behavioural burdens on users. Through the fit-viability approach, we assessed not only whether a feature was theoretically aligned with a task, but also whether it could be meaningfully integrated into daily routines without becoming coercive or overwhelming. This helped prioritise design solutions that were not only functional but also realistically adoptable and responsive to the user. Nudge Theory complemented this by providing a behavioural scaffold for designing feedback and decision support mechanisms. Rather than relying on static reminders or preconfigured generic prompts, nudging in MENTORd was structured to be adaptive, supportive, and context aware. Nudges were designed to be subtly reinforcing health behaviours decisions, through personalised prompts and visual cues, all while still allowing users full control over their experience. Responsible Analytics (RA) further shaped the ethical backbone of the system by ensuring that the design of the platform was conscious of the concerns around autonomy, privacy, transparency, and fairness. Translating RA into practice meant prioritising capabilities such as on-device AI to minimise data exposure, offering verbose, consent-based data sharing, and designing a clinician dashboard that supported retrospective review without enabling overreach or surveillance. Additionally, users retained the ability to edit AI-generated entries, reinforcing their role as the final decision-maker and avoiding deterministic interpretations of machine outputs.

These decisions collectively aimed to build trust, reduce dependency, and ensure that the automated functionalities of MENTORd served to present the output to human judgment rather than replace it. However, such commitments came with trade-offs. Deploying AI on-device limited the size, complexity and updatability of the models, in return, directly effecting the performance of the model. Yet these constraints were accepted in favour of preserving user control, ensuring ethical alignment, and supporting long-term sustained user engagement.

Co-design played a foundational role in shaping the MENTORd artifact, surfacing real-world needs, values, and constraints that would not have been visible through theoretical framing alone. By engaging patients and clinicians throughout the design process, the team was able to iteratively refine features to reflect both practical utility and ethical acceptability. For instance, consistent feedback from stakeholders highlighted the burden of manual food logging was not just as a usability issue but had stemmed as a significant barrier to sustained engagement with the platform. This insight directly informed the development of the Macronutrient Detection Algorithm (MDA), the AI-powered tool designed to reduce friction in logging by allowing users to take a photo of their meal. Co-design with RA, helped ensure that the MDA output was editable and transparent, addressing participant concerns about accuracy, autonomy, and cultural dietary variation. Similarly, stakeholder discussions revealed frustration with the cost, limitations, and connectivity challenges of bluetooth-enabled glucometers, particularly in under-resourced settings. We identified that given a hospital environment at a under-resourced setting, the glucometer used firstly may not have the Bluetooth functionality, but the brand and model different as there was no set standard. These insights led to the design of the Glucometer Detection Model (GDM), which enabled camera-based digit recognition as a more inclusive and device-agnostic alternative which aims to utilise an on-device model with offline capabilities. This shift not only reduced technical barriers but also aligned with RA principles by removing dependence on closed ecosystems and preserving user choice. These examples illustrate how co-design informed not just what was built, but why and reinforced the importance of ethics in responsible digital health advancements.

These insights were crucial in shaping a system that responded not only to clinical goals but also to the everyday realities and preferences of the users. By grounding feature decisions in real feedback, MENTORd was able to prioritise functionalities that were both useful and acceptable to those managing their T2DM in their daily lives. At the same time, the project faced technical challenges that placed natural limits on what could be implemented given the timeframe. Using AI on-device, for example, meant working within the processing and storage limits of mobile devices, which restricted the complexity and flexibility of certain features. Device compatibility posed a significant challenge, requiring careful design to ensure that MENTORd patient facing mobile app could run smoothly on older or less powerful smartphones. Beyond performance constraints, supporting both major mobile platforms such as Android and iOS, introduced its own set of complexities in code architecture, as each operating system demanded different permissions, and integration workflows. While the Flutter library used made this process immensely easier, there were issues for example regarding access to camera roll, as each operating system has different regulations on accessing hardware through apps. This significantly expanded the test cases, as now we had to account for various screen sizes, chipsets, and OS versions to ensure that the same functionality and user experience across devices is consistent. Throughout development, striking a balance between offering rich, meaningful features and maintaining a simple, intuitive interface was an ongoing challenge. These decisions could not be made once, as they had to be revisited in each design iteration to avoid overengineering and ensure that core functionality were being met, but also remained usable and accessible. Upholding the principles of RA added another layer of complexity. It was not enough to ensure that features were technically robust or secure; but every functionality had to uphold transparency, support user autonomy, and avoid creating full black-box experiences – even if that may seem like the easiest method. Ethical design required continuous reflection to ensure that convenience or efficiency did not come at the cost of user control or trust.

Ultimately, the MENTORd platform demonstrates how theory, ethics, and stakeholder engagement can converge in the design of responsible mHealth solutions. The resulting artifact is not simply a technological solution, but a socio-technical system that embeds values like trust, autonomy, and fairness into its architecture and user experience. While this chapter has focused on T2DM, the lessons extend more broadly to other aspects of digital health. The approach used to develop MENTORd, built on Responsible Analytics, co-design with relevant stakeholders, and behavioural intervention, can be applied to many other digital health systems, especially for self-managing other chronic conditions. These types of conditions often require daily self-management, personalisation, and support that is fit-for-purpose. The learnings from this research can help guide the development of future mHealth tools that aim to be not only effective, but also fair, respectful, and user centred. Scaling such systems will require infrastructure, regulatory support, and ongoing clinical validation. However, this work affirms that ethical, inclusive, and digital health platforms is not just aspirational it is achievable through intentional design and sustained engagement with users, theory, and practice.

CONCLUSION AND FUTURE WORKS

This chapter has presented the design, development, and planned evaluation of MENTORd, an ethically grounded, theory-informed mHealth platform for the self-management of Type II Diabetes. Developed using an Adapted 4-Cycle Design Science Research Methodology (A4C-DSRM), the MENTORd artifact integrates co-design principles, behavioural intervention theory, and responsible analytics to address long-standing challenges in chronic care mHealth. Unlike conventional digital health apps, MENTORd is built not only to support self-tracking and clinician communication, but to do so in a way that protects user autonomy, privacy, and engagement over time.

At the core of the platform are AI-powered features like the Macronutrient Detection Algorithm (MDA), the Glucometer Detection Model (GDM), and the Adaptive Nudge Rule Engine, each developed with transparency, on-device processing, and user control in mind. The patient-facing mobile app and clinician-facing web dashboard are designed to work together, offering a socio-technical solution that promotes trust, accountability, and contextual relevance in diabetes management. The discussion throughout this chapter has shown that embedding ethical principles into technical design is not only feasible, but essential for digital health innovation.

The upcoming usability and pilot studies will provide empirical insights into how the platform performs in real-world settings, including user trust, engagement, and usability. Feedback from these evaluations will guide the refinement of features, particularly the GDM and Adaptive Nudge Rule Engine, which are still under active development. Further work will also involve the extension of the MENTORd platform's functionalities. Potentially integrating more advanced nutrition related features such as a context-aware nutrition recommendation system.

In doing so, MENTORd contributes to a broader shift in digital health, toward mHealth solutions that are not only technically sophisticated, but also fit-for-purpose, inclusive, and ethically responsible. It stands as a practical example of how theory, stakeholder collaboration, and Responsible Analytics can converge to support more meaningful and sustainable health outcomes.

REFERENCES

Adu, M. D., Malabu, U. H., Malau-Aduli, A. E. O., & Malau-Aduli, B. S. (2019). Enablers and barriers to effective diabetes self-management: A multi-national investigation. *PLoS One*, *14*(6), e0217771. DOI: 10.1371/journal.pone.0217771 PMID: 31166971

Agriculture, U. S. D. o. FoodData Central. https://fdc.nal.usda.gov/

Alberti, K. G. M. M., & Zimmet, P. Z. (1998). Definition, diagnosis and classification of diabetes mellitus and its complications. Part 1: Diagnosis and classification of diabetes mellitus. Provisional report of a WHO Consultation. *Diabetic Medicine*, *15*(7), 539–553. https://doi.org/https://doi.org/10.1002/(SICI)1096-9136(199807)15:7<539:AID-DIA668>3.0.CO;2-S PMID: 9686693

Auth0. (2010). *JSON Web Tokens (JWT)*. https://jwt.io/

Baumel, A., Faber, K., Mathur, N., Kane, J. M., & Muench, F. (2017). Enlight: A Comprehensive Quality and Therapeutic Potential Evaluation Tool for Mobile and Web-Based eHealth Interventions [Original Paper]. *Journal of Medical Internet Research*, *19*(3), e82. DOI: 10.2196/jmir.7270 PMID: 28325712

Brew-Sam, N. (2020). Diabetes App Use – Previous mHealth Research. In *App Use and Patient Empowerment in Diabetes Self-Management: Advancing Theory-Guided mHealth Research* (pp. 29–38). Springer Fachmedien Wiesbaden., DOI: 10.1007/978-3-658-29357-4_4

Chavez, S., Fedele, D., Guo, Y., Bernier, A., Smith, M., Warnick, J., & Modave, F. (2017). Mobile Apps for the Management of Diabetes. *Diabetes Care*, *40*(10), e145–e146. DOI: 10.2337/dc17-0853 PMID: 28774944

Cho, N. H., Shaw, J. E., Karuranga, S., Huang, Y., da Rocha Fernandes, J. D., Ohlrogge, A. W., & Malanda, B. (2018). IDF Diabetes Atlas: Global estimates of diabetes prevalence for 2017 and projections for 2045. *Diabetes Research and Clinical Practice*, *138*, 271–281. DOI: 10.1016/j.diabres.2018.02.023 PMID: 29496507

Community, G. (2017). *Flutter*. Google and Community. https://flutter.dev/

Cortez, N. G., Cohen, I. G., & Kesselheim, A. S. (2014). FDA Regulation of Mobile Health Technologies. *The New England Journal of Medicine*, *371*(4), 372–379. DOI: 10.1056/NEJMhle1403384 PMID: 25054722

Danaher, B. G., Brendryen, H., Seeley, J. R., Tyler, M. S., & Woolley, T. (2015). From black box to toolbox: Outlining device functionality, engagement activities, and the pervasive information architecture of mHealth interventions. *Internet Interventions : the Application of Information Technology in Mental and Behavioural Health, 2*(1), 91–101. DOI: 10.1016/j.invent.2015.01.002 PMID: 25750862

Dignum, V. (2019). Ensuring Responsible AI in Practice. In Dignum, V. (Ed.), *Responsible Artificial Intelligence: How to Develop and Use AI in a Responsible Way* (pp. 93–105). Springer International Publishing., DOI: 10.1007/978-3-030-30371-6_6

Drechsler, A., & Hevner, A. (2016). A four-cycle model of IS design science research: capturing the dynamic nature of IS artifact design.

Federation, I. D. (2019). *IDF Diabetes Atlas* (9th ed.)., https://www.diabetesatlas.org

Floridi, L., Cowls, J., Beltrametti, M., Chatila, R., Chazerand, P., Dignum, V., Luetge, C., Madelin, R., Pagallo, U., Rossi, F., Schafer, B., Valcke, P., & Vayena, E. (2018). AI4People—An Ethical Framework for a Good AI Society: Opportunities, Risks, Principles, and Recommendations. *Minds and Machines, 28*(4), 689–707. DOI: 10.1007/s11023-018-9482-5 PMID: 30930541

Fu, H., McMahon, S. K., Gross, C. R., Adam, T. J., & Wyman, J. F. (2017). Usability and clinical efficacy of diabetes mobile applications for adults with type 2 diabetes: A systematic review. *Diabetes Research and Clinical Practice, 131*, 70–81. DOI: 10.1016/j.diabres.2017.06.016 PMID: 28692830

Giardina, T., Modi, V., Parrish, D., & Singh, H. (2015). The patient portal and abnormal test results: An exploratory study of patient experiences. *Patient Experience Journal, 2*(1), 148–154. PMID: 28345018

Goodhue, D., & Thompson, R. (1995). Task-Technology Fit and Individual Performance. *Management Information Systems Quarterly, 19*, 213–236.

Goodhue, D. L. (1998). Development and Measurement Validity of a Task-Technology Fit Instrument for User Evaluations of Information System. *Decision Sciences, 29*(1), 105–138. https://doi.org/https://doi.org/10.1111/j.1540-5915.1998.tb01346.x

Goodhue, D. L., & Thompson, R. L. (1995). Task-Technology Fit and Individual Performance. *Management Information Systems Quarterly, 19*(2), 213–236. DOI: 10.2307/249689

Google, A. I. Y. V. *Food_v1*. Google AIY, TenserflowHub. https://tfhub.dev/google/aiy/vision/classifier/food_V1/1

Hevner, A. R., March, S. T., Park, J., & Ram, S. (2004). Design Science in Information Systems Research. *Management Information Systems Quarterly*, *28*(1), 75–105. DOI: 10.2307/25148625

Huang, Z., Soljak, M., Boehm, B., & Car, J. (2018). Clinical relevance of smartphone apps for diabetes management: A global overview. *Diabetes/Metabolism Research and Reviews*, •••, 34. PMID: 29431916

Jennings, H. M., Morrison, J., Akter, K., Kuddus, A., Ahmed, N., Kumer Shaha, S., Nahar, T., Haghparast-Bidgoli, H., Khan, A. A., Azad, K., & Fottrell, E. (2019). Developing a theory-driven contextually relevant mHealth intervention. *Global Health Action*, *12*(1), 1550736. DOI: 10.1080/16549716.2018.1550736 PMID: 31154988

Jimenez, G., Lum, E., & Car, J. (2019). Examining Diabetes Management Apps Recommended From a Google Search: Content Analysis. *JMIR mHealth and uHealth*, *7*(1), e11848. DOI: 10.2196/11848 PMID: 30303485

Joachim, S., Forkan, A. R. M., Jayaraman, P. P., Morshed, A., & Wickramasinghe, N. (2022). A Nudge-Inspired AI-Driven Health Platform for Self-Management of Diabetes. *Sensors (Basel)*, *22*(12), 4620. https://www.mdpi.com/1424-8220/22/12/4620 PMID: 35746402

Joachim, S. J. Prem Prakash. Forkan, Abdur Rahim Mohammad. Morshed, Ahsan. Wickramasinghe, Nilmini. (2021, Jan, 2021.). *Design and Development of a Diabetes Self-Management Platform: A Case for Responsible Information System Development* Proceedings of the 54th Hawaii International Conference on System Sciences | 2021, Hawaii.

Khan, R. M. M., Chua, Z. J. Y., Tan, J. C., Yang, Y., Liao, Z., & Zhao, Y. (2019). From Pre-Diabetes to Diabetes: Diagnosis, Treatments and Translational Research. *Medicina (Kaunas, Lithuania)*, *55*(9). Advance online publication. DOI: 10.3390/medicina55090546 PMID: 31470636

Kruse, C. S., Argueta, D. A., Lopez, L., & Nair, A. (2015). Patient and provider attitudes toward the use of patient portals for the management of chronic disease: A systematic review. *Journal of Medical Internet Research*, *17*(2), e40. DOI: 10.2196/jmir.3703 PMID: 25707035

Kwan, Y. H., Cheng, T. Y., Yoon, S., Ho, L. Y. C., Huang, C. W., Chew, E. H., Thumboo, J., Østbye, T., & Low, L. L. (2020). A systematic review of nudge theories and strategies used to influence adult health behaviour and outcome in diabetes management. *Diabetes & Metabolism*, *46*(6), 450–460. https://doi.org/https://doi.org/10.1016/j.diabet.2020.04.002 PMID: 32387700

Mittelstadt, B. D., Allo, P., Taddeo, M., Wachter, S., & Floridi, L. (2016). The ethics of algorithms: Mapping the debate. *Big Data & Society*, *3*(2), 2053951716679679. DOI: 10.1177/2053951716679679

Morley, J., Machado, C. C. V., Burr, C., Cowls, J., Joshi, I., Taddeo, M., & Floridi, L. (2020). The ethics of AI in health care: A mapping review. *Social Science & Medicine*, *260*, 113172. DOI: 10.1016/j.socscimed.2020.113172 PMID: 32702587

Oftedal, B., Bru, E., & Karlsen, B. (2011). Motivation for diet and exercise management among adults with type 2 diabetes. *Scandinavian Journal of Caring Sciences*, *25*(4), 735–744. DOI: 10.1111/j.1471-6712.2011.00884.x PMID: 21443543

Oracle Corporation. M. A. (1995). *MySQL*. https://www.mysql.com/

Saeedi, P., Petersohn, I., Salpea, P., Malanda, B., Karuranga, S., Unwin, N., Colagiuri, S., Guariguata, L., Motala, A. A., Ogurtsova, K., Shaw, J. E., Bright, D., Williams, R., & Committee, I. D. F. D. A. (2019). Global and regional diabetes prevalence estimates for 2019 and projections for 2030 and 2045: Results from the International Diabetes Federation Diabetes Atlas, 9(th) edition. *Diabetes Research and Clinical Practice*, *157*, 107843. DOI: 10.1016/j.diabres.2019.107843 PMID: 31518657

scheme, N. D. s. *Diabetes-related complication*. Retrieved 7/2/2022 from https://www.ndss.com.au/

Thaler, R. H., & Sunstein, C. R. (2008). *Nudge: Improving decisions about health, wealth, and happiness*. Yale University Press.

Vayena, E., Blasimme, A., & Cohen, I. G. (2018). Machine learning in medicine: Addressing ethical challenges. *PLoS Medicine*, *15*(11), e1002689. DOI: 10.1371/journal.pmed.1002689 PMID: 30399149

Villalba-Mora, E., Peinado-Martínez, I., & Pozo, F. (2017). eHealth and diabetes: Designing a novel system for remotely monitoring older adults with type 2 diabetes.

WHO. (2021). *Ethics and governance of artificial intelligence for health: WHO guidance*. World Health Organization.

Wickramasinghe, N., John, B., George, J., & Vogel, D. (2019). Achieving Value-Based Care in Chronic Disease Management: Intervention Study. *JMIR Diabetes*, *4*(2), e10368. DOI: 10.2196/10368 PMID: 31066699

Wu, Y., Ding, Y., Tanaka, Y., & Zhang, W. (2014). Risk factors contributing to type 2 diabetes and recent advances in the treatment and prevention. *International Journal of Medical Sciences*, *11*(11), 1185–1200. DOI: 10.7150/ijms.10001 PMID: 25249787

You, E. (2014). *Vue.js*. https://vuejs.org/

Chapter 12

Precision and Accuracy Management for PROMs: A Model for Data Integrity in Value-Based Healthcare

Thais Spiegel
https://orcid.org/0000-0002-7801-8492
Universidade do Estado do Rio de Janeiro, Brazil

Daniel Bouzon Nagem Assad
https://orcid.org/0000-0003-3911-4323
Universidade do Estado do Rio de Janeiro, Brazil

ABSTRACT

Rising healthcare expenses, along with the need to improve patient outcomes, have led to the faster implementation of a value-based healthcare (VBHC) model. This approach aims to ensure the effectiveness of Patient-Reported Outcome Measures (PROMs) data gathering by suggesting a systematic framework for executing precision and accuracy management practices within a specialized governance structure, like a Value Management Office that allows healthcare institutions to effectively improve their data accuracy and reduce measurement bias. The proposed framework incorporates five essential practices—specifically, questionnaire design, standardized data collection, data quality assurance, statistical validation, and risk adjustment—to guarantee that PROM data is trustworthy, comparable, and functional. It also allows fair comparisons among healthcare providers, encouraging evidence-driven choices, and fostering trust between patients and clinicians that contributes to methodological foundations of VBHC.

DOI: 10.4018/979-8-3373-2545-3.ch012

INTRODUCTION

Globally, healthcare expenditures are rising at a pace that outstrips the growth of national Gross Domestic Products (GDPs), a trajectory of unsustainability that is expected to persist (OECD, 2023). Porter and Teisberg (2006), whose work remains the most widely cited reference point for addressing this challenge, attribute such unsustainability to a constellation of systemic "asymmetries" that inhibit value creation within health systems. A key example is the "zero-sum" competition among system actors, a dynamic that fosters rising costs and prices without commensurate improvements in quality.

To counter this, Porter and Teisberg (2006) proposed the Value-Based Healthcare (VBHC) model, which addresses what they identified as the fundamental dysfunction of health systems: the absence of the patient at the true center of care. In most other sectors of the economy, the user acts as the primary driver and legitimizer of innovations that enhance quality while reducing costs; in healthcare, this mechanism is often absent. The VBHC transformation agenda, further elaborated by Porter and Lee (2013), is grounded in the systematic measurement and disclosure of clinical outcomes associated with medical interventions. VBHC models prioritize patient outcomes over service volume, with Patient-Reported Outcome Measures (PROMs) serving as a critical instrument for assessing those outcomes (Porter & Teisberg, 2006). PROMs capture patients' perspectives on their health and quality of life, providing essential insights into the effectiveness of care interventions and informing strategies for improved health system performance. They form a crucial link between healthcare delivery and patient-centered objectives (Strougo et al., 2021).

As a key performance indicator (KPI) in VBHC, PROMs enable the evaluation of treatment effectiveness and service quality from the patient's perspective, allowing alignment with individual goals and needs (Bianchim et al., 2023). They assess changes in health-related quality of life before and after treatment, thus clarifying the real-world impact of care (Makhni & Hennekes, 2023). PROMs also promote patient awareness of symptoms, support self-management, and strengthen patient empowerment—important markers of effective care delivery (Bianchim et al., 2023). Standardized PROMs, such as those developed by the International Consortium for Health Outcomes Measurement (ICHOM), further allow for valid comparisons across contexts and over time, optimizing outcomes on a global scale (De Silva et al., 2022).

Despite their centrality to VBHC, significant challenges persist in the implementation and optimal use of PROMs. Evidence remains limited regarding the most effective methods for data collection, measurement, and integration into clinical and management workflows. Overemphasis on patient-reported experiences (PREMs) rather than outcomes can obscure the identification of effective therapeutic strategies (Bianchim et al., 2023; De Silva et al., 2022).

To operationalize VBHC, Kaplan et al. (2015) and Makdisse et al. (2018) proposed the establishment of a Value Management Office (VMO), a central unit responsible for coordinating the resources, activities, and information needed for outcome and cost measurement initiatives. Yet, the creation of such infrastructure alone does not equate to full organizational transformation; rather, it represents the starting point for a longer journey toward value-oriented operations.

This chapter presents a structured framework of precision and accuracy management practices designed to support the implementation of a VMO—or analogous structure—capable of driving transformation in line with VBHC principles. These practices focus on designing rigorous data collection instruments, implementing reliable data capture processes, and ensuring systematic review and analysis to guarantee trustworthy, valid results.

THEORETICAL BACKGROUND

Value-Based Healthcare (VBHC)

The consolidation of Value-Based Healthcare (VBHC) as a paradigm for reorganizing health systems represents a profound structural shift, aiming to align economic incentives and clinical outcomes in favor of the patient (Porter, 2010). In this model, the fundamental performance metric is not the volume of services delivered, but the value created, understood as the relationship between achieved outcomes and incurred costs. However, the effectiveness of this approach critically depends on the precision and accuracy with which outcomes are measured, since unreliable data undermine the validity of the very concept of value (Avula & Tummala, 2021; Khalil et al., 2025).

Systematic and scoping reviews published over the past decade have revealed the inherent complexity of VBHC implementation. Khalil et al. (2020) and Abdalla et al. (2023) show that reported outcomes cover a broad spectrum, ranging from patient-centered indicators to organizational and financial metrics. While this diversity illustrates the richness of the concept, it also generates significant methodological heterogeneity. Studies such as van Elten et al. (2023) emphasize that this variability hinders the development of robust comparative models and limits the generalizability of findings. In many healthcare contexts, outcome measurement remains fragmented, often restricted to isolated components of the strategic agenda, such as cost recording or immediate clinical results (Nilsson et al., 2017; van Staalduinen et al., 2022).

This fragmentation has direct implications for the measurement of value. The German Institute for Quality and Efficiency in Health Care (IQWiG, 2022) argues that the lack of standardized metrics prevents consistent cost-effectiveness analyses. Complementarily, Vijverberg et al. (2022), in their comprehensive review of VBHC research over the 15 years since the concept's introduction, highlight that while the body of literature is growing, it remains dispersed and lacks consensus on best practices. Thus, the central challenge is not merely expanding outcome measurement, but ensuring that such measures are valid, reproducible, and comparable across diverse clinical and geographic contexts.

Within this framework, the use of standardized instruments such as Patient-Reported Outcome Measures (PROMs) emerges as a cornerstone of VBHC (Black, 2013; Porter et al., 2016). PROMs allow for the integration of the patient perspective, aligning evaluation processes with real experiences and needs. However, evidence suggests that PROM implementation faces substantial barriers, including lack of system interoperability, inconsistencies in data collection, and organizational resistance (Van Egdom et al., 2019; van Elten et al., 2023). Moreover, even when applied, PROMs are often limited by inadequate methodological validation and insufficient standardization, which undermines their capacity to generate robust evidence (Khalil et al., 2025).

Another critical aspect concerns the role of digital technologies and artificial intelligence in outcome measurement. Machine learning models have been increasingly applied to uncover hidden patterns within large clinical datasets, enhancing predictive capabilities and decision support (Crowson & Chan, 2020). Yet, the quality of these models' outputs is entirely contingent upon the accuracy and reliability of the underlying data. Bouhouita-Guermech and Haidar (2024) further warn of the "algorithmic black box," where the opacity of models complicates accountability and erodes trust in their results. Consequently, data governance and algorithmic transparency become essential dimensions for the responsible integration of these technologies into the VBHC paradigm.

Therefore, advancing the VBHC agenda requires progress on two complementary fronts. First, it is imperative to overcome conceptual and methodological variability through the standardization of metrics, the strengthening of health information infrastructures, and the integration of clinical, organizational, and financial dimensions (van Elten et al., 2023). Second, strategies must be adopted to ensure data quality, precision, and reliability, embedding governance and transparency practices throughout the measurement process (Vijverberg et al., 2022; Khalil et al., 2025). Only through this dual approach will it be possible to sustain valid comparisons, guarantee the trust of patients and professionals, and consistently evaluate the effectiveness of value-driven healthcare practices.

Patient-Reported Outcome Measures (PROMs)

The historical evaluation of healthcare organizations has largely been based on service volume. This paradigm began to shift with the introduction of "person-centered" approaches, a concept first applied to psychotherapy by Carl Rogers in the 1950s under the term "client-centered," and later refined in the 1960s (Sanchez-Gavilan et al., 2022). In 2010, Michael Porter advanced a new healthcare paradigm that placed patients and their definition of value at the core of clinical practice, giving rise to VBHC as the dominant model for clinical management. Achieving VBHC requires a nuanced understanding of patients' values and the establishment of effective communication across clinical teams and the broader health network, with the twin goals of optimizing patient care and managing costs (Strougo et al., 2021).

PROMs are a key instrument for capturing information about patient outcomes, integrating both expectations and values. They may be classified as generic or disease-specific (Brooks, 1996). Generic PROMs assess health outcomes from a broad perspective, enabling cross-condition comparisons and providing an overall measure of health status or quality of life—examples include the EQ-5D and the WHO-5 (Devlin & Brooks, 2017). Disease-specific PROMs, by contrast, focus on symptoms, functional status, and quality-of-life aspects tied to a specific condition or group of conditions.

The accuracy of PROMs is critical to ensuring that they reflect patients' true experiences and can reliably inform clinical decision-making. Evidence shows variable reliability across contexts and populations. In primary care, PROMs measuring physical function and pain interference achieved accuracies between 71.7% and 79.1% in predicting Patient Acceptable Symptom States (PASS). Certain PROMIS measures maintained predictive accuracy over time, improving interpretability and clinical relevance (Jacobson et al., 2020). In contrast, studies in older adults have shown lower sensitivity; for example, intracranial hemorrhage PROMs achieved only 36.7% sensitivity despite 97.2% specificity, highlighting limits in detecting critical health events (Selvanayagam et al., 2021).

Effective PROMs are comprehensive, relevant, and informed by patient input to ensure that the questions are meaningful and actionable (Temple & Morris, 2020; Labban et al., 2021). Nonetheless, variability in accuracy underscores the need for ongoing refinement and validation, especially for specific populations or complex conditions.

Standardizing PROM implementation can enhance individualized treatment decisions and enable precise comparisons across interventions (Chaudhury et al., 2023). Tools such as the PROMIS platform facilitate efficient, cost-effective collection of patient-reported data while reducing respondent burden compared to traditional instruments. Comprehensive PROM questionnaires should have clearly defined objectives—whether to assess health status, quality of life, or treatment effectiveness—and be tailored to the target population (Ahern et al., 2017). They should undergo rigorous validation (Madan et al., 2020) and address multiple health domains, including physical, mental, and social dimensions (Porter, 2024).

Some specific and isolated initiatives can already be seen as Ayers (2017) that discusses the strategic use of PROMs in total knee arthroplasty, emphasizing the shift towards value-based care and the use of electronic platforms for PROM data collection and benchmarking; Pasqualini & Piuzzi (2023) that discusses the role of PROMs in assessing performance and making clinical decisions in the context of lower extremity orthopaedics highlighting the importance of a comprehensive PROM collection system to enhance preoperative optimization and surgical outcomes; and Meço et al. (2023) that introduces the Safe Brain Initiative, focusing on leveraging PROMs to enhance patient-centered precision care, particularly in perioperative settings.

Bates et al. (2023) explores the integration of PROMs into global hospital rankings to enhance the value of care by incorporating patient outcome–focused indicators using Publicly Reported Global Hospital Rankings to improve PROMs dissemination.

Despite their promise, PROM implementation faces persistent challenges. Data collection and management can be resource-intensive, requiring robust systems to process large volumes of information (Jeyaraman et al., 2024). Integration into clinical workflows may be hindered by technological barriers and professional resistance (Biondi-Zoccai et al., 2025). Skepticism among patients and clinicians about PROMs' utility further necessitates educational initiatives to foster engagement (Adeghe et al., 2024).

Potential solutions include leveraging mobile health applications and AI-enabled tools to streamline data capture and enhance patient participation (Biondi-Zoccai et al., 2025). Research priorities should include adapting PROMs for diverse demographic groups to ensure inclusivity and equitable relevance (Shapiro et al., 2024). However, careful implementation is critical to avoid exacerbating health disparities. Continuous evaluation and iterative refinement are essential to ensure that PROMs effectively serve all patient populations.

Patient-Reported Outcome Measures (PROMs) play a crucial role in assessing healthcare quality, converging with various tools and discussions in the literature. They are used to capture the patient experience, complementing traditional clinical outcomes and informing the effectiveness of interventions. The following presents the main aspects of the convergence of PROMs with the aforementioned tools.

Integration with Observational Health Data Sciences and Informatics (OHDSI) proposed in Hripcsak et al. (2015).

- PROMs are used to monitor the quality of care and the effectiveness of clinical teams, aligning with the OHDSI data approach to health outcomes analysis (Zuenkova, 2024).
- The implementation of PROMs can be integrated into healthcare systems to improve treatment personalization and resource allocation (Kyte et al., 2016).

Connection with Grading of Recommendations Assessment, Development and Evaluation (GRADE) and COnsensus-based Standards for the selection of health Measurement INstruments (COSMIN) proposed in Guyatt et al. (2008) and Mokkink et al. (2018), respectively.

- PROMs are evaluated for their validity and reliability, central aspects of the GRADE and COSMIN guidelines, which aim to ensure the quality of health evidence (Muller & Biberthaler, 2021; Biondi-Zoccai et al., 2025).
- The choice of PROMs should consider clinical relevance and sensitivity to change, as recommended by COSMIN (Kostuj & Niemeyer, 2022).

Relevance to Generating Evidence & Methods to improve patient outcomes (eGEMs) and Substitutable Medical Applications and Reusable Technologies (SMART) proposed in Kahn et al. (2016) and Mandel et al (2016), respectively.

- PROMs are fundamental to health research, as evidenced by eGEMs, where they are used to generate data on the patient experience (Biondi-Zoccai et al., 2025).
- The SMART approach emphasizes the importance of integrating PROMs into clinical practices to improve patient adherence and quality of care (Kostuj & Niemeyer, 2022).

While PROMs offer valuable insight into the patient experience, their implementation faces challenges, such as a lack of awareness among healthcare professionals and the need for cultural validation for different populations. This suggests that, despite their usefulness, widespread adoption of PROMs still requires significant efforts to overcome practical and educational barriers.

Data quality in healthcare

The measurement of value in healthcare is intrinsically dependent on the reliability of the data employed in the assessment of clinical and operational outcomes. Within this framework, the precision and accuracy of measurement processes constitute fundamental dimensions to ensure that comparative, predictive, and evaluative analyses faithfully reflect both patients' clinical realities and the performance of health systems.

The specialized literature emphasizes that the effectiveness of analytical and predictive models is directly contingent upon data quality, particularly with regard to the dimensions of accuracy, completeness, and timeliness (Avula & Tummala, 2021). Inaccurate or inconsistent records—often stemming from failures in data collection, processing, or integration—undermine the validity of results and may lead to misguided clinical decisions. Thus, data accuracy should be conceived not merely as a technical requirement but as a crucial element of patient safety.

Integrative reviews on data quality in health research reveal the heterogeneity of metrics employed to evaluate precision and reliability, as well as the existence of technical and methodological barriers that hinder standardization and interoperability (Bernardi et al., 2023). These limitations compromise both scientific reproducibility and the practical applicability of research findings, underscoring the need for consistent methodologies across all stages of data production and management. Digital technologies—including data mining, business intelligence, and advanced statistical models—have been identified as promising instruments to mitigate such weaknesses and to enhance the accuracy of health data.

In the context of value-based care, machine learning (ML) tools have emerged as catalysts of diagnostic precision and operational efficiency (Crowson & Chan, 2020). The ability of these algorithms to process large volumes of clinical information enables pattern recognition, risk stratification, and real-time decision support, often achieving performance that rivals or even surpasses human accuracy in specific tasks, such as medical imaging interpretation. Nonetheless, the effectiveness of ML models remains dependent on the availability of high-quality data—properly curated and free from bias—thus reaffirming the centrality of accurate outcome measurement as a determinant of healthcare value.

The integration of artificial intelligence-based technologies introduces ethical and accountability challenges. Recent studies highlight that algorithmic opacity—commonly referred to as the "black box problem"—complicates the attribution of responsibility and may erode trust in the generated results (Bouhouita-Guermech & Haidar, 2024). The lack of clarity regarding the origin of measurement errors and the accountability of stakeholders involved in decision-making processes carries significant implications for the validity of value assessments in healthcare and for the legitimacy of subsequent policies and practices.

Discussions of healthcare value must necessarily incorporate the dimension of data quality and the precision of outcome measurement. Measurement accuracy not only sustains the validity of value indicators but also ensures evidence-based decision-making processes while promoting ethically responsible and patient-centered practices. Advancing toward value-based health systems, therefore, requires continuous investments in data standardization, governance, and algorithmic transparency, ensuring that measured outcomes faithfully represent the realities of care delivery.

MODEL OVERVIEW: PURPOSE, DEVELOPMENT, AND CONTRIBUTIONS

As presented in Strougo et al (2021), the proposed capability-based reference model was designed to guide healthcare organizations in implementing Value-Based Healthcare (VBHC) through structured, evidence-informed management practices. Its central purpose is to enable organizations to plan, assess, and improve their maturity in delivering patient-centered value—defined as outcomes that matter to patients relative to the resources required to achieve them (Porter & Teisberg, 2006; Porter, 2010). In doing so, the model addresses a critical gap in the VBHC literature: the absence of operational frameworks that connect strategic intent with systematic, organization-wide transformation.

The model was constructed through an integration approach (Pagliuso et al., 2010), combining and adapting elements from established maturity and reference models—including the eSourcing Capability Models for Service Providers and Client Organizations (Hyder et al., 2010; Hefley & Loesche, 2010), ISO 9001 (ABNT, 2015), and the Capability Maturity Model Integration (CMMI Product Team, 2006)—as well as the *Guia de projeto de serviços de saúde baseados em valor* (Strougo et al., 2021). Its development involved iterative literature review, identification of critical issues through multidisciplinary workshops, and consensus-building with healthcare professionals and service operations experts. This process yielded 40 best practices organized into eight capability areas, mapped across five maturity levels, and structured to support progressive, context-sensitive adoption.

The capability areas are:

- Strategic management (str): definition of long-term objectives, alignment with organizational strategy and establishment of the organizational structure and programs needed to achieve the objectives.
- People management (peo): identifying and assigning roles and responsibilities to qualified people and managing and motivating employees to implement activities eëciently and eëciently.
- Knowledge management (kno): managing information systems and knowledge to ensure that the right person has access to the information needed to carry out the activity at the right time.
- Technology management (tec): managing the technological infrastructure used to support service provision. Relationship and communication manage-

ment (rel): managing relationships with patients, other internal departments and partners and suppliers.

- Relationship and communication management (rel): managing relationships with patients, other internal departments and partners and suppliers.
- Process and performance management (per): measuring and reviewing processes and performance against objectives, taking the necessary measures to ensure compliance of activities or improve results.
- Risk management (ris): managing the processes of identifying, analyzing and mitigating risk, protecting the VMO and the institution.
- Precision and accuracy management (acc): managing the rigor of the activities of capturing, processing and analyzing outcomes.

Precision and accuracy management (acc) capability practices are the focus of this chapter and are highlighted in Figure 1. These practices will be properly described below.

The organizational maturity level presented in Figure 1 has five different levels that are divided into:

- Level 1 (Initial): consists of activities that are unstructured or minimally structured for outcome collection. The work is ad hoc, sponsored by enthusiasts within the organization, but with little or no connection to the organization's strategy.
- Level 2 (Repeatable): represents the evolution to managed work at the level of each medical condition. Projects are planned, executed, monitored, and controlled. At this stage, a clear and well-defined strategy is essential, providing a basis for risk management, resource management, relationship management, and process management.
- Level 3 (Defined): organization standards and norms provide guidance on projects, programs, and portfolios related to the Practices. At this stage, managed outcome capture processes and obtaining a sufficient volume of consistent information pave the way for data processing and analysis to ensure result rigor.
- Level 4 (Quantitatively Managed): assumes an organization driven by data and reliable quantitative performance improvement objectives. Here, the focus is on redesigning care and proactive, preventive management to improve outcomes.
- Level 5 (Optimized): concerns the maintenance of all Practices and results, implying a stable and flexible organization, focused on continuous improvement and able to respond to opportunities and changes. At this level, the institution's stability provides a platform for agility and innovation.

Figure 1. Logical sequence for implementing the practices

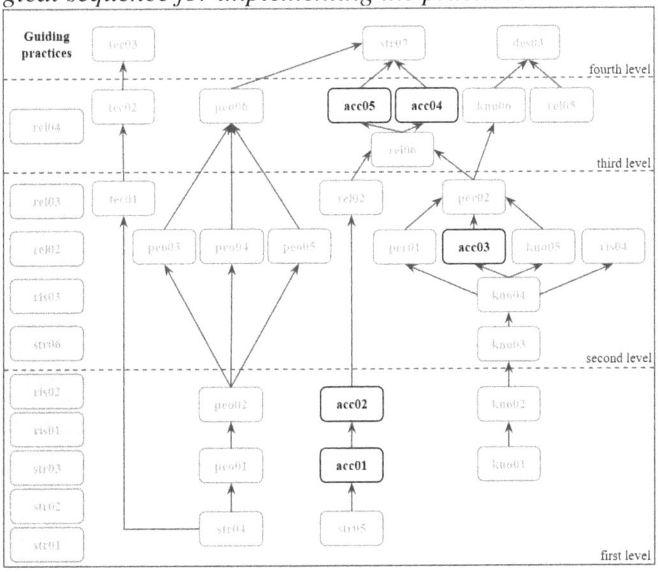

Source: The authors.

By consolidating strategic, organizational, technical, and analytical dimensions into a coherent maturity framework, the model contributes to both theory and practice. It offers a replicable, flexible blueprint for healthcare providers seeking to embed VBHC principles in governance, process design, workforce development, technology use, stakeholder engagement, and outcome measurement. For researchers, it serves as a conceptual bridge between maturity model methodology and healthcare transformation agendas, opening avenues for empirical validation and contextual adaptation. For policymakers, it provides a reference architecture to promote more transparent, efficient, and patient-oriented health systems.

While all eight capability areas are essential for a comprehensive transformation, the model places particular emphasis on *Precision and Accuracy Management* as a foundation for trustworthy analytics and evidence-based decision-making. The subsequent section will examine these practices in detail, highlighting their role in ensuring the rigor, validity, and comparability of outcome data across diverse healthcare contexts.

PRECISION AND ACCURACY MANAGEMENT PRACTICES

Precision and accuracy management practices focus on creating mechanisms that ensure reliable and trustworthy data. They focus on the design of the questionnaires used and on the collection, processing, and review of the data obtained from outcomes and risks. All precision and accuracy management practices are ongoing.

Table 1. Precision and accuracy management practices.

ID	Practice title	Practice statement	ML
acc01	Survey design	Design questionnaires for collecting and analyzing risk variables and outcomes	1
acc02	Data capture	Design and document data capture processes during and after intervention	1
acc03	Data capture quality	Establish and implement procedures to ensure data capture quality	2
acc04	Statistical validity	Establish and implement statistical validity analysis techniques for the outcomes collected	3
acc05	Risk adjustment	Establish and implement risk adjustment procedures for outcome indicators	3

Source: The authors.

acc01: Design questionnaires for collecting and analyzing risk variables and outcomes

Defining and documenting the questionnaires that will be applied for each line of care is essential for data reliability. Defining and documenting the questionnaires ensures a standard for the attributes measured for each patient and allows new evaluators to be trained in the same standards.

The use of previously tested and validated questionnaires ensures that the attributes measured are those that really matter for that specific line of care.

Activities

a. Provide support to create and maintain the products and work tasks to design questionnaires for collecting and analyzing risk variables and outcomes.
b. Document and implement the products and work tasks necessary to design questionnaires for the collection and analysis of risk variables and outcomes. Documentation and implementation include the following activities:
    1. Survey and document existing questionnaires for each care pathway.
        i. Review questionnaires used in the literature.
        ii. Analyze questionnaires used in the market and by competitors.
    2. Review the surveyed questionnaires for validity and reliability and define those that will be used. The use of previously tested and validated questionnaires is recommended. The use of proprietary questionnaires, created by the VMO or the organization, will be subject to review for reliability and relevance by the appropriate technical teams.

   i. Analyze experimental results from the literature resulting from the application of the questionnaires.
   ii. Obtain review and approval of the questionnaire selection from relevant stakeholders. Experts in the medical condition can assess the relevance of the questions contained in the questionnaires.
   iii. Obtain senior management review and approval of the choice of questionnaires. Senior management approval is required especially when it involves the acquisition of licenses.
3. Acquire the questionnaires that will be used. Some questionnaires are available free of charge, while others require a license to use.
4. Document the questionnaires used in each care pathway.
5. Identify and document the scoring techniques inherent in each questionnaire.
6. Identify and document the indicators obtained from the questionnaires and their scoring techniques.
7. Periodically review the validity and reliability of the questionnaire based on the results obtained from its application.

c. Support the implementation of the questionnaire design for the collection and analysis of risk variables and outcomes.

acc02: Design and document data capture processes during and after intervention

Designing and documenting data capture processes ensures standardization in collection and increases data reliability. It also provides support for training new professionals and analyzing VMO performance.

The capture process involves the available data sources, collection times, techniques and equipment used to extract the data, and the respective storage of the information.

Activities

a. Provide support to create and maintain work products and tasks to design and document data collection processes during and after intervention.
b. Document and implement the products and work tasks necessary to design and document data collection processes during and after intervention. Documentation and implementation include the following activities:
   1. Identify and document information sources and consultation methods to answer each question on the questionnaires. Sources of information may include patients themselves and their families, patient records, patient movement records, healthcare staff, among others.

2. Define and document data collection times for each question on the questionnaires.
3. Define and document the roles and responsibilities of the personnel assigned to data collection. Refer to Practices peo01, Definition of functions and peo02, Assignment of responsibilities.
4. Establish a method for storing the collected data. Data storage can occur through physical or digital means and use existing structures within the organization or new structures.
5. Define and document the processes, techniques, and equipment used to extract data from information sources and enter it into the storage system.
   i. Identify data that is automatically obtained by technology and the possibility of integration into the storage system.
   ii. Define and document data extraction processes from systems and the respective software used.
   iii. Define and document the information input processes into the storage system.
   iv. Identify points of contact with the healthcare team.
   v. Establish and document contact and relationship protocols with the healthcare team.
   vi. Identify points of contact with the patient and their family members within the healthcare unit.
   vii. Establish mechanisms for contact with the patient and their family members outside the healthcare unit. Contact mechanisms may include email, telephone, visit, among others.
   viii. Establish and document contact and relationship protocols with the patient and their family members.
6. Keep processes and documentation up to date. Modifications may be necessary due to the insertion of new technologies, care lines, among others.

c. Support project implementation and documentation of data collection processes during and after the intervention.

acc03: Establish and implement procedures to ensure data capture quality

Data capture quality assurance is essential for information reliability. Unprepared professionals, ineffective training, and poorly designed questionnaires can generate biases in information collection and result in indicators that are not representative of reality. Reviewing collection processes reduces the risk of these biases.

Activities

a. Provide support to create and maintain work products and tasks to establish and implement procedures for reviewing data capture processes.
b. Document and implement the work products and tasks necessary to establish and implement procedures for reviewing data collection processes. Documentation and implementation include the following activities:
   1. Define and document the types of review that will be adopted for each capture mechanism. Data capture mechanisms include telephone collection, email collection, system extraction, and others. Each mechanism should be covered by at least one type of review, which may involve observation of the collection, conducting a second collection, or interviewing a sample of patients. The ability to select a sample of patients and independently assess whether their outcomes are consistent with those reported in the questionnaires is essential to this practice.
   2. Define the frequency of the review.
   3. Document the information obtained in the reviews.
   4. Analyze the information obtained in the reviews and check for possible biases in the collection.
   5. Establish and execute action plans to mitigate the identified biases.
      i. Perform necessary actions and monitor them until completion.
      ii. Document planned and implemented corrective actions, including monitoring and completion.
c. Support the implementation of the establishment and implementation of review procedures for data capture processes.

acc04: Establish and implement analysis techniques that ensure the validity of the outcomes collected

Statistical validity analyses are necessary to ensure that the outcome indicators obtained from a sample of patients are reliable.

For this practice, the term statistical validity is used instead of statistical significance. This is due to the restrictive nature of the term significance in statistics, which is not capable of encompassing all the activities described here.

Statistical significance analysis is considered a statistical test to verify the discrepancy of a (null) hypothesis in relation to the observed data for a given confidence interval or significance level. The difference between a sample statistic and a hypothetical value is statistically significant if a hypothesis test indicates that it is very unlikely to have occurred by chance.

The concept of statistical validity, on the other hand, can include both the concepts of significance and others that may be necessary for the performance of activities.

Activities

a. Provide support to create and maintain work products and tasks to establish and implement analysis techniques that ensure the validity of the collected outcomes.
b. Document and implement the work products and tasks necessary to establish and implement analysis techniques that ensure the validity of the collected outcomes. Documentation and implementation include the following activities:
    1. Identify and document the types of variables obtained in the questionnaires that will be used by statistical techniques.
        i. Identify and document the discrete and continuous quantitative variables used in the questionnaires.
        ii. Identify and document the nominal and ordinary qualitative variables used in the questionnaires.
    2. Identify and document the objectives of statistical analyses. Statistical analyses typically have one or more of the following objectives: estimating a proportion (e.g., the mortality rate); estimating a mean (e.g., the mean obtained from a pain scale); comparing proportions between two populations (e.g., comparing two hospitals' mortality rates); and comparing two means. These objectives are influenced by the types of variables available and identified previously. It should be noted that the comparison objectives can only be achieved after estimating the proportions and means for the two populations being compared.
    3. Identify the most appropriate statistical techniques. The objectives, the types of variables used, the number of observations of the variables, among other relevant factors, must be taken into account.
    4. Define and document the statistical techniques that will be used.
        i. Define and document the statistical techniques used to achieve the defined objectives.
        ii. Define and document the statistical techniques used to evaluate and determine the required sample size.
        iii. Define and document the assumptions adopted, including the sources of information, when necessary. The assumptions may include estimates of the population mean and standard deviation that are unknown but necessary for the calculations. Also included are the mathematical and statistical techniques, pilot projects, assumptions, or data sources that supported the adopted assumptions.
        iv. Define and document the significance level used.

v. Define and document the software or processing methods used.
vi. Define and document the methods and procedures for applying the statistical techniques.
5. Perform statistical analyses and document the results obtained.
6. Analyze the results and take action as necessary.
7. Update the techniques and assumptions adopted as necessary.

c. Support the establishment and implementation of statistical validity analysis techniques for the outcomes collected.

acc05: Establish and implement risk adjustment procedures for outcome indicators

Assess patient risk and adjust outcome indicators to reduce the potential for false judgments about care practices due to unwanted outcomes whose prevention or control are beyond the provider's scope.

Risk adjustment (or standardization for severity) is a process that aims to adjust the outcomes found for the patient's prior risk (demographic, socioeconomic, diagnostic data, among others), establishing a baseline against which patients and providers can be compared more rigorously.

Activities

a. Provide support to create and maintain work products and tasks to establish and implement risk adjustment procedures for outcome indicators.
b. Document and implement the work products and tasks necessary to establish and implement risk adjustment procedures for outcome indicators. Documentation and implementation include the following activities:
   1. Identify and select risk variables with the potential to impact outcomes for each care pathway. Risk variables can be selected from the literature on a specific line of care, clinical trials, specialist consultations, and other sources. Risk variables include demographic and socioeconomic factors, comorbidities, prior treatments, and disease-related factors (e.g., severity).
   2. Identify and document the available data sources for the selected risk factors.
      i. Verify that all selected risk variables are covered by the care pathway questionnaires or care assessment.
      ii. Identify the location of risk variable information in systems and databases.
      iii. Ensure that relevant internal stakeholders have access to risk variable information.
   3. Establish and document procedures for collecting and storing risk variables.

4. Identify potential risk adjustment models for each care pathway.
5. Evaluate and select risk adjustment models for lines of care.
6. Identify and acquire the tools and software used by the model, as necessary.
7. Establish and document procedures for performing risk adjustments according to the selected models.
8. Apply risk assessment and adjustment models to the variables collected and document their results.
9. Assess whether the results of the risk assessment are consistent with the outcomes obtained, taking action when appropriate.
10. Periodically assess the need for a new risk adjustment model or its update.

c. Support the establishment and implementation of risk adjustment procedures for outcome indicators.

ROADMAP FOR IMPLEMENTING PRECISION AND ACCURACY MANAGEMENT PRACTICES

The effective implementation of precision and accuracy management practices necessitates a structured and phased approach to ensure methodological rigor, operational feasibility, and sustainable adoption. The proposed roadmap organizes the five core practices (acc01 through acc05) into a logical sequence, enabling organizations to build capabilities progressively while mitigating risks associated with abrupt, large-scale transformations. Despite being presented in a linear sequence, these phases may overlap, particularly during iterative refinements. To ensure strategic alignment and institutional oversight, these phases should be governed by a dedicated structure such as a Value Management Office (VMO).

The initial phase, designated as Practice acc01, entails the conceptualization and standardization of questionnaires for the collection and analysis of risk variables and outcomes. At this stage, organizations review existing validated instruments relevant to each care pathway, engage subject matter experts to assess content validity and clinical applicability, and, when necessary, secure licenses for proprietary tools. The scoring methodologies and associated outcome indicators are documented with the objective of establishing a consistent foundation for measurement. This phase is instrumental in ensuring that constructs are both meaningful and reliable, aligned with the intended analytical objectives, and capable of supporting comparative analysis over time.

The second phase, related to Practice acc02, involves the development and documentation of robust data capture processes to be applied during and after clinical interventions. This encompasses the mapping of data sources, the establishment of standardized collection timelines, the allocation of explicit responsibilities to personnel, and the implementation of procedures for both in-clinic and remote data acquisition. Secure storage methods are defined with an emphasis on interoperability to facilitate integration with existing health information systems. The outputs of this phase constitute a comprehensive operational blueprint, thereby enabling consistent and replicable data collection across diverse contexts.

In the third phase, associated with Practice acc03, the focus shifts to ensuring data capture quality through continuous monitoring and targeted interventions. Organizations delineate the types of reviews deemed suitable for each data collection method, including re-interviews, observational audits, and secondary verification, in addition to the frequency and documentation standards for these activities. The information obtained from quality reviews is analyzed to detect systematic errors or biases, leading to the implementation of corrective and preventive measures. When incorporated into organizational routines, these actions contribute to the reduction of variability, the enhancement of the trustworthiness of outcome indicators, and the safeguarding of compliance with methodological standards.

The fourth phase, which is aligned with Practice acc04, emphasizes the establishment and application of statistical techniques that ensure the validity of the outcomes collected. This process entails the classification of variables, the establishment of analytical objectives, and the selection of statistical methods that are commensurate with the characteristics of the data and the intended comparisons. Assumptions, significance levels, and analytical procedures are thoroughly documented to maintain transparency and reproducibility. Validity analyses are performed, results interpreted, and methodologies refined when necessary, ensuring that the conclusions drawn from patient-reported outcome data are both statistically defensible and clinically meaningful.

The fifth and final phase, corresponding to Practice acc05, addresses the implementation of risk adjustment procedures for outcome indicators, thereby enhancing fairness and comparability in performance assessment. In this stage, organizations identify and prioritize risk variables that may influence outcomes, select appropriate adjustment models, and validate these models in the context of each care pathway. Procedures have been developed for the collection and integration of risk data into analytical workflows. Regular reviews are conducted to update the models based on new evidence or changing population characteristics. This ensures that performance comparisons between providers are not confounded by differences in patient case mix, thereby supporting equitable benchmarking and informed decision-making.

Throughout all phases of the project, governance plays a central role in coordinating resources, monitoring progress, and maintaining stakeholder engagement. The VMO or analogous governance structure should oversee implementation, allocate the necessary resources, ensure compliance with data protection and ethical standards, and promote a culture of continuous improvement. Capacity-building initiatives, such as training for data collectors and analysts, in conjunction with sustained communication with clinicians and patients, are imperative to cultivate adoption and trust in the resulting outcome measurements. By following this roadmap, healthcare organizations can embed precision and accuracy management practices into their operational fabric. This will enhance the integrity of patient-reported data and reinforce the evidentiary foundation of value-based healthcare.

DISCUSSION

The precision and accuracy management practices delineated in this study address a critical, yet often underestimated, dimension of value-based healthcare (VBHC) implementation: the integrity of patient-reported outcome measures (PROMs) as a foundation for trustworthy decision-making. While PROMs have been widely recognized as indispensable for aligning care delivery with patient-centered outcomes (Porter & Teisberg, 2006; Strougo et al., 2021), their effectiveness is contingent upon the quality of the underlying data. The findings in this framework demonstrate that the validity and reliability of PROM-derived indicators are contingent on methodological rigor at each stage of the process, including questionnaire design, data capture, quality assurance, statistical validation, and risk adjustment.

Existing literature emphasizes the variability in PROM accuracy across settings and populations (Jacobson et al., 2020; Selvanayagam et al., 2021), a limitation that can compromise both clinical and managerial decision-making. Standardizing survey instruments, collection protocols, and analytical techniques is a proposed practice that directly addresses the heterogeneity and potential biases identified in earlier research (Ahern et al., 2017; Chaudhury et al., 2023; Madan et al., 2020). Furthermore, the integration of these practices within a Value Management Office (VMO) or analogous governance structure—as advocated by Kaplan et al. (2015) and Makdisse et al. (2018)—ensures institutional oversight and facilitates continuous improvement cycles.

To operationalize these practices effectively, this study proposes a structured roadmap that sequences their implementation into progressive, interlinked phases. The initial phase entails the design and standardization of questionnaires for the collection and analysis of risk variables and outcomes (acc01). This process entails the evaluation of validated instruments, the engagement of clinical experts to ensure content relevance, and the documentation of scoring methodologies to establish a consistent measurement framework. The subsequent phase pertains to the development and documentation of data capture processes during and following interventions (acc02), encompassing the mapping of information sources, the delineation of collection timelines, the allocation of responsibilities, and the establishment of secure, interoperable storage systems. The third phase places significant emphasis on ensuring data capture quality (acc03) through the definition of review types, monitoring frequencies, and corrective action protocols. These measures are implemented to minimize biases and maintain methodological integrity. In the fourth phase, statistical techniques are applied to ensure the validity of collected outcomes (acc04), with clear documentation of analytical objectives, assumptions, and procedures to ensure both transparency and reproducibility. The fifth phase entails the implementation of risk adjustment procedures for outcome indicators (acc05), the identification of pertinent risk variables, the selection of validated adjustment models, and the periodic updating of these models to ensure fair benchmarking and comparability across providers.

From a systems perspective, the integration of statistical validity testing and risk adjustment models—embedded within the latter phases of the roadmap—is particularly relevant for enabling fair benchmarking and inter-organizational comparisons (De Silva et al., 2022). Absent these safeguards, performance indicators risk being distorted by variations in patient case-mix or measurement error, potentially undermining the fairness and credibility of VBHC programs. The extant literature supports the notion that methodological robustness not only strengthens accountability but also enhances clinician engagement by providing data that is both interpretable and actionable (Bianchim et al., 2023; Makhni & Hennekes, 2023).

However, the operationalization of precision and accuracy management is not without challenges. The demands for resources in the context of training, technological integration, and ongoing quality assurance can be considerable (Biondi-Zoccai et al., 2025; Jeyaraman et al., 2025). The successful implementation of these practices is contingent upon cultural congruence within organizations, necessitating stakeholder engagement, patient involvement, and clinician confidence (Adeghe et al., 2024; Shapiro et al., 2024). The roadmap's phased approach has the potential to help mitigate these barriers by enabling gradual capacity building, aligning technical advancements with organizational readiness, and promoting iterative refinement of processes. It is imperative to couple this structured implementation pathway with robust governance mechanisms and change management strategies to realize the full potential of PROM-driven VBHC transformation.

CONCLUSION

This study aims to add to the discussion on Value-Based Health Care (VBHC) by turning the rather broad idea of precision and accuracy management into a practical, structured set of steps. The intention is not only to outline what these practices are, but to make them workable in real healthcare settings. The framework, along with its implementation roadmap, moves through a sequence of stages: questionnaire design, data collection, quality checks, statistical validation, and risk adjustment. By tackling each stage in turn, the approach reduces the risk of measurement bias, makes results easier to compare across different contexts, and provides stronger evidence for both clinical and organisational decisions.

Governance is central here. For example, a Value Management Office (VMO) is not simply a bureaucratic layer; it is meant to anchor these practices in the daily routine of an institution. When backed by ongoing cycles of improvement, this structure reflects the thinking behind established maturity models (CMMI Product Team, 2006; Hyder et al., 2010; Hefley & Loesche, 2010). In this way, the framework works on two fronts: as a tool that providers can actually use, and as a link between theory and the operational demands of value-based care.

The next step is to see how this holds up in the real world. Empirical studies should test whether the framework and roadmap improve the quality, usability, and fairness of Patient-Reported Outcome Measures (PROMs) in a variety of settings. There is also a need to look closely at digital health tools — AI-assisted data gathering, adaptive questionnaires, automated risk adjustment — not just for their efficiency, but for their ability to keep the rigour expected in clinical trials. In the end, managing precision and accuracy carefully is not only a technical necessity; it is a strategic choice that can help build trust, improve health results, and push the shift toward VBHC forward.

REFERENCES

Abdalla, R., Pavlova, M., & Groot, W. (2023). Prioritizing outcome measures for value-based healthcare: Physicians' perspectives in Saudi Arabia. *Value in Health Regional Issues*, *37*, 62–70. DOI: 10.1016/j.vhri.2023.05.002 PMID: 37327619

Adeghe, E. P., Okolo, C. A., & Ojeyinka, O. T. (2024). The influence of patient-reported outcome measures on healthcare delivery: A review of methodologies and applications. *Open Access Research Journal of Biology and Pharmacy*, *10*(2), 13–21. DOI: 10.53022/oarjbp.2024.10.2.0014

Ahern, S., Ruseckaite, R., & Ackerman, I. N. (2017). Collecting patient-reported outcome measures. *Internal Medicine Journal*, *47*(12), 1454–1457. DOI: 10.1111/imj.13633 PMID: 29224197

Associação Brasileira de Normas Técnicas. (2015). *NBR ISO 9001: Sistemas de gestão da qualidade: Requisitos*. ABNT.

Avula, R., & Tummala, S. (2021). Assessing the Impact of Data Quality on Predictive Analytics in Healthcare: Strategies, Tools, and Techniques for Ensuring Accuracy, Completeness, and Timeliness in Electronic Health Records. *Sage Science Review of Applied Machine Learning*, 4(2), 31–47. Retrieved from https://journals.sagescience.org/index.php/ssraml/article/view/203

Ayers, D. C. (2017). Implementation of patient-reported outcome measures in total knee arthroplasty. *JAAOS-Journal of the American Academy of Orthopaedic Surgeons*, *25*, S48–S50. DOI: 10.5435/JAAOS-D-16-00631 PMID: 27941415

Bates, D. W., Deerberg-Wittram, J., Katz, G., Braeger, K., Hirsch, L. S., Kaplan, G. S., Kwietniewski, L., Meier, C. A., Laifer, C. P., & Zimlichman, E. (2023). Using publicly reported global hospital rankings to improve dissemination of patient-reported outcome measures (PROMs). *NEJM Catalyst Innovations in Care Delivery*, *4*(11), CAT-23. DOI: 10.1056/CAT.23.0097

Bernardi, F. A., Alves, D., Crepaldi, N., Yamada, D. B., Lima, V. C., & Rijo, R. (2023). Data Quality in Health Research: Integrative Literature Review. *Journal of Medical Internet Research*, *25*, e41446. DOI: 10.2196/41446 PMID: 37906223

Bianchim, M. S., Crane, E., Jones, A., Neukirchinger, B., Roberts, G., & McLaughlin, L.. (2023). The implementation, use, and impact of patient-reported outcome measures in value-based healthcare programmes: A scoping review. *PLoS One*, *18*(12), e0290976. DOI: 10.1371/journal.pone.0290976 PMID: 38055759

Biondi-Zoccai, G., Frati, G., Peruzzi, M., Bernardi, M., Spadafora, L., & Tremoli, E. (2025). Patient-reported outcome measures in cardiovascular research and care: PRO(M)s and CONS. *Journal of Cardiovascular Pharmacology, 85*(4), 261–266. DOI: 10.1097/FJC.0000000000001669 PMID: 39847595

Black, N. (2013). Patient reported outcome measures could help transform healthcare. *BMJ (Clinical Research Ed.), 346*. Advance online publication. DOI: 10.1136/bmj.f167 PMID: 23358487

Bouhouita-Guermech, S., & Haidar, H. (2024). Scoping review shows the dynamics and complexities inherent to the notion of "responsibility" in artificial intelligence within the healthcare context. *ABR, 16*, 315–344. https://doi.org/DOI: 10.1007/s41649-024-00292-7

Brooks, R. (1996). EuroQol: The current state of play. *Health Policy (Amsterdam), 37*(1), 53–72. DOI: 10.1016/0168-8510(96)00822-6 PMID: 10158943

Chaudhury, A. S.. (2023). Bringing patient-reported outcome measures (PROMs) into practice: A review of the latest developments in PROM use in the evaluation and treatment of carpal tunnel syndrome. *Journal of Hand Surgery Global Online, 5*(4), 492–497. DOI: 10.1016/j.jhsg.2023.03.002 PMID: 37521564

CMMI Institute. (n.d.). *What is a maturity level? Capability level? How are they different?* https://cmmiinstitute.zendesk.com/hc/en-us/articles/216334148-What-is-a-maturity-level-Capability-level-How-are-they-different-

CMMI Product Team. (2006, August). *CMMI for development* (Version 1.2). Software Engineering Institute, Carnegie Mellon University.

Crowson, M. G., & Chan, T. C. Y. (2020). Machine learning as a catalyst for value-based health care. *Journal of Medical Systems, 44*(1), 139. DOI: 10.1007/s10916-020-01607-5 PMID: 32681388

de Silva, U., Connell, S., Tapela, N., & Bright, J. (2023). Driving value through standardized measurement of patient-reported outcomes. *Journal of Patient Experience, 10*, 1–8. DOI: 10.1177/23743735231202373 PMID: 37720908

Devlin, N. J., & Brooks, R. (2017). EQ-5D and the EuroQol Group: Past, present and future. *Applied Health Economics and Health Policy, 15*(2), 127–137. DOI: 10.1007/s40258-017-0310-5 PMID: 28194657

Guyatt, G. H., Oxman, A. D., Vist, G. E., Kunz, R., Falck-Ytter, Y., Alonso-Coello, P., & Schünemann, H. J. (2008). GRADE: An emerging consensus on rating quality of evidence and strength of recommendations. *BMJ (Clinical Research Ed.), 336*(7650), 924–926. DOI: 10.1136/bmj.39489.470347.AD PMID: 18436948

Hefley, B., & Loesche, E. A. (2010). *eSourcing capability model for client organizations* (1st ed.). Van Haren Publishing.

Hripcsak, G., Duke, J. D., Shah, N. H., Reich, C. G., Huser, V., Schuemie, M. J., & Ryan, P. B. (2015). Observational Health Data Sciences and Informatics (OHDSI): Opportunities for observational researchers. *Studies in Health Technology and Informatics*, *216*, 574. PMID: 26262116

Hyder, E. B., ... (2010). *eSourcing capability model for service providers* (1st ed.). Van Haren Publishing.

Institut für Qualität und Wirtschaftlichkeit im Gesundheitswesen (IQWiG). (2022). General Methods Version 6.1. https://www.iqwig.de/methoden/general-methods_version-6-1.pdf

Jacobson, R. P., Kang, D., & Houck, J. (2020). Can Patient-Reported Outcomes Measurement Information System® (PROMIS) measures accurately enhance understanding of acceptable symptoms and functioning in primary care? *Journal of Patient-Reported Outcomes*, *4*, 39. DOI: 10.1186/s41687-020-00206-9 PMID: 32436001

Jeyaraman, N., Jeyaraman, M., Ramasubramanian, S., Balaji, S., & Muthu, S. (2025). Voices that matter: The impact of patient-reported outcome measures on clinical decision-making. *World Journal of Methodology*, *15*(2), 98066. DOI: 10.5662/wjm.v15.i2.98066 PMID: 40548214

Kahn, M. G., Callahan, T. J., Barnard, J., Bauck, A. E., Brown, J., Davidson, B. N., Estiri, H., Goerg, C., Holve, E., Johnson, S. G., Liaw, S. T., Hamilton-Lopez, M., Meeker, D., Ong, T. C., Ryan, P., Shang, N., Weiskopf, N. G., Weng, C., Zozus, M. N., & Schilling, L. (2016). A harmonized data quality assessment terminology and framework for the secondary use of electronic health record data. *EGEMS (Washington, DC)*, *4*(1), 1244. DOI: 10.13063/2327-9214.1244 PMID: 27713905

Kaplan, R. S., ... (2015). Health care providers need a value management office. *Harvard Business Review*. https://hbr.org/2015/12/health-care-providers-need-a-value-management-office

Khalil, H., Ameen, M., Davies, C., & Liu, C. (2025). Implementing value-based healthcare: A scoping review of key elements, outcomes, and challenges for sustainable healthcare systems. *Frontiers in Public Health*, *13*, 1514098. DOI: 10.3389/fpubh.2025.1514098 PMID: 40270723

Kostuj, T., & Niemeyer, A. (2022). Diagnostik und Therapie aus der Patientenperspektive-PROMs in der Chirurgie. *Zentralblatt für Chirurgie-Zeitschrift für Allgemeine, Viszeral-. Thorax-und Gefäßchirurgie*, *147*(02), 125–128. DOI: 10.1055/a-1213-0817 PMID: 35378548

Kyte, D., Cockwell, P., Lencioni, M., Skrybant, M., Hildebrand, M. V., Price, G., Cockwell, P., Lencioni, M., Skrybant, M., von Hildebrand, M., Price, G., Squire, K., Webb, S., Brookes, O., Fanning, H., Jones, T., & Calvert, M. (2016). Reflections on the national patient-reported outcome measures (PROMs) programme: Where do we go from here? *Journal of the Royal Society of Medicine*, *109*(12), 441–445. DOI: 10.1177/0141076816677856 PMID: 27923896

Labban, M., Briggs, L., Cole, A. P., & Trinh, Q. D. (2021). Measuring What Matters: Patient-Reported Outcome and Experience Measures for Men Undergoing Radical Prostatectomy. *European Urology Focus*, *7*(5), 913–915. DOI: 10.1016/j.euf.2021.09.010 PMID: 34556455

Madan, V., Elbaz, A., & Mor, A.. (2020). Using gold standard patient-reported outcome measures in clinical practice: A new approach to facilitate their use. *Authorea*. https://doi.org/DOI: 10.22541/au.159542470.03987631

Makdisse, M.. (2018). What is a value management office? An implementation experience in Latin America. *Value in Health Regional Issues*, *17*, 71–73. DOI: 10.1016/j.vhri.2018.04.001 PMID: 29729500

Makhni, E. C., & Hennekes, M. E. (2023). The use of patient-reported outcome measures in clinical practice and clinical decision making. *The Journal of the American Academy of Orthopaedic Surgeons*, *31*(20), 1059–1066. DOI: 10.5435/JAAOS-D-23-00040 PMID: 37364243

Mandel, J. C., Kreda, D. A., Mandl, K. D., Kohane, I. S., & Ramoni, R. B. (2016). SMART on FHIR: A standards-based, interoperable apps platform for electronic health records. *Journal of the American Medical Informatics Association : JAMIA*, *23*(5), 899–908. DOI: 10.1093/jamia/ocv189 PMID: 26911829

Meço, B. C., de Agua Reis, A. B., Berger-Estilita, J., Jakobsen, K., Alkış, N., & Radtke, F. M. (2023). Precision anaesthesia: Advancing patient-centered precision care through repetitive assessment of PROMs with the safe brain initiative approach. *Turkish Journal of Anaesthesiology and Reanimation*, *51*(5), 374. DOI: 10.4274/TJAR.2023.231420 PMID: 37747258

Mokkink, L. B., De Vet, H. C., Prinsen, C. A., Patrick, D. L., Alonso, J., Bouter, L. M., & Terwee, C. B. (2018). COSMIN risk of bias checklist for systematic reviews of patient-reported outcome measures. *Quality of Life Research: An International Journal of Quality of Life Aspects of Treatment, Care and Rehabilitation*, *27*(5), 1171–1179. DOI: 10.1007/s11136-017-1765-4 PMID: 29260445

Müller, M., & Biberthaler, P. (2021). Patient-Reported Outcome Measures (PROMs)–eine Übersicht. *OP-Journal*, *37*(01), 55–62. DOI: 10.1055/a-1203-3352

Nilsson, K., Bååthe, F., Erichsen Andersson, A., & Sandoff, M. (2017). Value-based healthcare as a trigger for improvement initiatives. *Leadership in Health Services*, *30*(4), 364–377. DOI: 10.1108/LHS-09-2016-0045 PMID: 28862085

OECD. (2023). *Health at a Glance 2023: OECD Indicators*. OECD Publishing., DOI: 10.1787/7a7afb35-

Pagliuso, A. T., Cardoso, R., & Spiegel, T. (2010). *Gestão organizacional: O desafio da construção do modelo de gestão*. Instituto Chiavenato (Org.), Saraiva.

Pasqualini, I., & Piuzzi, N. S. (2023). Patient-reported outcome measures: State of the art in patient-reported outcome measure application in lower extremity orthopaedics. *JAAOS-Journal of the American Academy of Orthopaedic Surgeons*, *31*(20), e883–e889. DOI: 10.5435/JAAOS-D-23-00586 PMID: 37543754

Porter, I. (2024). Patient-reported indicator surveys (PaRIS): Measuring patient-reported experiences and outcomes across populations and health systems. *European Journal of Public Health, 34*(Supplement_3), ckae144.367. https://doi.org/DOI: 10.1093/eurpub/ckae144.367

Porter, M. E. (2010). What is value in health care? *The New England Journal of Medicine*, *363*(26), 2477–2481. DOI: 10.1056/NEJMp1011024 PMID: 21142528

Porter, M. E., & Lee, T. H. (2013). The strategy that will fix health care. *Harvard Business Review*, *91*(10), 1–19.

Porter, M. E., & Teisberg, E. O. (2006). *Redefining health care: Creating value-based competition on results*. Harvard Business School Press.

Sanchez-Gavilan, E., Montiel, E., & Baladas, M.. (2022). Added value of patient-reported outcome measures (PROMs) after an acute stroke and early predictors of 90 days PROMs. *Journal of Patient-Reported Outcomes*, *6*, 66. DOI: 10.1186/s41687-022-00472-9 PMID: 35695977

Selvanayagam, N.. (2021). Reliability of patient-reported outcome measures: Hemorrhage, anticoagulant, antiplatelet medication use. *Research and Practice in Thrombosis and Haemostasis*, *5*(4), e12501. DOI: 10.1002/rth2.12501 PMID: 34027288

Shapiro, L. M., Katz, P., Stern, B. Z., & Kamal, R. N. (2024). Equitable integration of patient-reported outcomes into clinical practice—Opportunities, challenges, and a roadmap for implementation. *The Journal of the American Academy of Orthopaedic Surgeons*, *32*(5), 187–195. DOI: 10.5435/JAAOS-D-23-00798 PMID: 38194644

Strougo, A. D., Assad, D. B. N., Spiegel, T., & Nobrega, C. (2021). *Guia de projeto de serviços de saúde baseados em valor*. Eduerj. https://eduerj.com/produto/guia-de-projeto-de-servicos-de-saude-baseados-em-valor-ebook/

Temple, L. K. F., & Morris, A. M. (2020). Patient-reported outcomes in surgical research. In Dimick, J., & Lubitz, C. (Eds.), *Health services research* (pp. 105–113). Springer., DOI: 10.1007/978-3-030-28357-5_10

van Egdom, L. S. E., Lagendijk, M., Van Der Kemp, M. H., Van Dam, J. H., Mureau, M. A. M., Hazelzet, J. A., & Koppert, L. B. (2019). Implementation of value based breast cancer care. *European Journal of Surgical Oncology*, *45*(7), 1163–1170. PMID: 30638807

van Elten, H. J., Howard, S. W., De Loo, I., & Schaepkens, F. (2023). Reflections on Managing the Performance of Value-Based Healthcare: A Scoping Review. *International Journal of Health Policy and Management*, *12*, 7366. DOI: 10.34172/ijhpm.2023.7366 PMID: 37579381

van Staalduinen, D. J., van den Bekerom, P., Groeneveld, S., Kidanemariam, M., Stiggelbout, A. M., & van den Akker-van Marle, M. E. (2022). The implementation of value-based healthcare: A scoping review. *BMC Health Services Research*, *22*(1), 270. DOI: 10.1186/s12913-022-07489-2 PMID: 35227279

Vijverberg, J. R. G., Daniels, K., Steinmann, G., Garvelink, M. M., Rouppe van der Voort, M. B. V., Biesma, D., Bos, W. J. W., van Merode, F., & van der Nat, P. (2022). Mapping the extent, range and nature of research activity on value-based healthcare in the 15 years following its introduction (2006-2021): A scoping review. *BMJ Open*, *12*(8), e064983. DOI: 10.1136/bmjopen-2022-064983 PMID: 35973705

KEY TERMS AND DEFINITIONS

Precision and Accuracy Management: The capability to ensure the integrity and reliability of data used for measurement and analysis, supporting rigorous and responsible analytics in healthcare decision-making.

Value-Based Healthcare (VBHC): A healthcare delivery model that prioritizes outcomes that matter to patients in relation to the cost of delivering those outcomes, aiming to align stakeholders around value creation.

Patient-Reported Outcome Measures (PROMs): Standardized instruments that capture patients' self-reported assessments of their health status, quality of life, and treatment outcomes, providing essential data to inform patient-centered care and evaluate healthcare performance.

Reference Model: A structured framework that consolidates best practices, processes, and concepts to guide the design, implementation, or evaluation of systems or services within a specific context.

Maturity Model: A model that assesses the current state of an organization or process and outlines progressive levels of development, supporting continuous improvement and strategic alignment.

Chapter 13

Revolutionizing Digital Healthcare: The Role of AI Innovations in E-Health Transformation

Tarun Madan Kanade
https://orcid.org/0009-0002-0084-3107
Symbiosis Institute of Operations Management, India

Hetal Gaglani
https://orcid.org/0000-0002-1485-7422
Ramdeobaba University, India

Radhakrishna Bhaskar Batule
Vishwakarma University, India

Ashima Manoj Varghese
https://orcid.org/0009-0003-9006-2036
National Academy of Defence Production, India

ABSTRACT

Artificial intelligence and the internet of things have revolutionized healthcare administration and delivery. "AI Innovations Transforming E-Health Systems" examines how AI affects digital health. Outline the current state of AIoT's impact on healthcare and how it is changing the course of future research. Using historical context, we may deduce how we progressed from healthcare AI to AIoT system development via IoT integration. The state-of-the-art in artificial intelligence (AI) research and development in the domains of e-health robots, computer vision (CV),

DOI: 10.4018/979-8-3373-2545-3.ch013

and natural language processing (NLP) will be our next destination. Among the many applications of this technology are the following: medical record management made easier, more precise operations, better imaging, and predictive analytics.

The proliferation of IoT-enabled wearable health gadgets, smart healthcare facilities, telemedicine, and remote patient monitoring is a direct result of this phenomenon. Through the use of networked environments and real-time data analytics, these apps enhance patient outcomes and personalized treatment. Case studies have shown the pros and cons of AIoT installations. There are several advantages to e-health AI breakthroughs, but the paper also discusses their disadvantages. To ensure equity, we look at financial, legal, privacy and security, data integration, and technical limitations. Advancements in AI are expected to revolutionize healthcare. It foretells developments in e-health and proposes solutions that may revolutionize digital health systems.

According to the study's findings, AI revolutionized e-health platforms. Optimizing AIoT in healthcare is the main focus, along with overcoming obstacles.

1. INTRODUCTION

AI and IoT have transformed medical care, management, and consumption. Several AI systems can mimic human behavior. Examples include ML, NLP, and computer vision. But IoT is the internet-connected network of gadgets that collect and exchange data.

Digital health's strong AIoT ecosystem combines IoT and AI. AI analysis and IoT connection enhance healthcare. This combination monitors, predicts, and controls health issues in real time to improve patient outcomes and healthcare resource optimization.

1.1 Importance of AIoT in Modern Healthcare Systems

AIoT is vital to contemporary healthcare. Slow diagnosis, reactive therapy, and inefficiency characterize traditional healthcare. AIoT offered real-time data processing and continuous monitoring for early health problem identification and speedier action.

AIoT enhances patient monitoring. Wearables and sensors track heart rate, blood pressure, glucose, and more. AI algorithms warn for early action and treatment of problems. Real-time analysis improves patient outcomes by helping clinicians respond quickly with accurate, current information. (Kunal, 2023)

The utilization of historical and real-time data in predictive analytics for health risks is another use of AIoT. Patients may be alerted about chronic disease using prediction algorithms. Patient health is improved and long-term costs are reduced via this predictive and preventative strategy.

Through the use of patient data, AIoT offers personalized treatment. Treatment outcomes are enhanced by this client-centered approach. By analyzing medical records and patient profiles, AIoT enhances medical diagnosis and therapy. (Sarah A. Alzakari, 2024)

Allocation of hospital resources, wait times, and patient management are all enhanced by AIoT. For the purpose of staffing need estimation, smart hospitals track patient intake, supplier chains, and bed occupancy. Better patient care and lower costs are the results of efficient utilization of resources. Ai technology enhances remote telemedicine. Patients living in rural areas or with low incomes might benefit from remote healthcare. Everyone can get the medical care they need thanks to this technology, which remotely pairs patients with top doctors.

1.2 Objective of the research

This study describes how AI advances are transforming e-health. It covers AI and IoT integration history, digital health applications, and successful case studies. The paper addresses present patterns and future prospects for these technologies, which raise ethical, regulatory, and technical challenges. It highlights AIoT's disruptive potential in healthcare and the necessity to overcome present challenges to realize its benefits.

Figure 1. Graphical abstract of the chapter

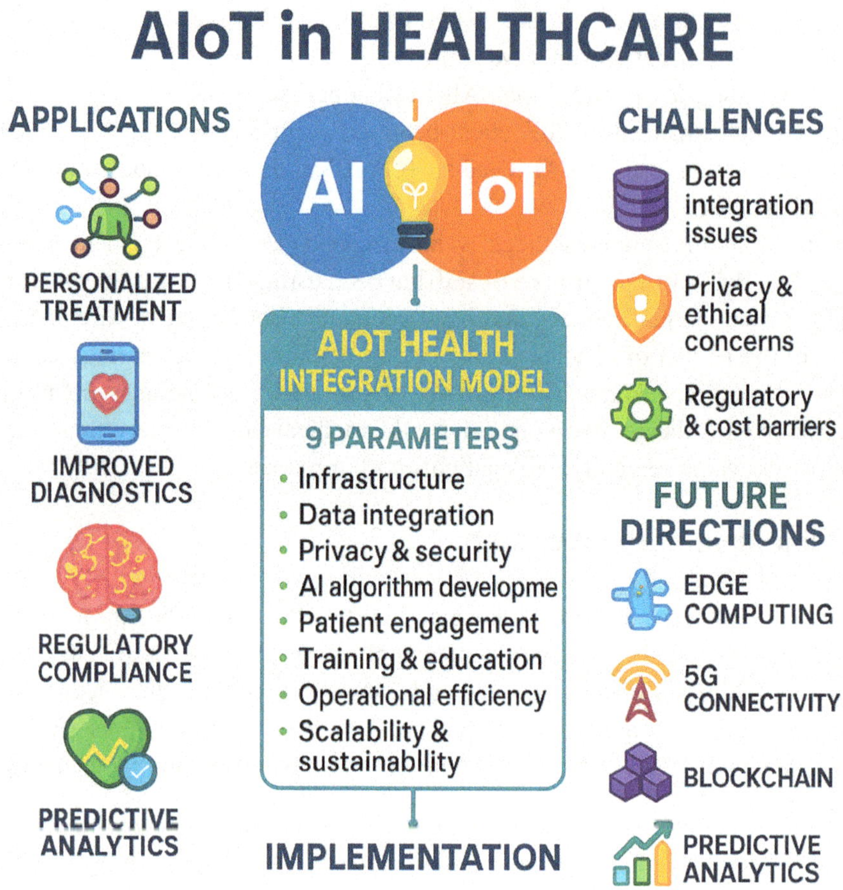

The above illustration showcases the graphical illustration of the flow of the chapter given in figure 1.

2. STUDY OF LITERATURE

AI in healthcare has evolved and complex. Early AI was limited to diagnostic expert systems. The 1970s MYCIN system diagnosed and treated germs using rule-based algorithms. Although inventive, these early systems were limited by frameworks and inability to respond to new data.

AI's machine learning subset enabled computers to learn from data and improve without programming in the 1990s and 2000s. Diagnostic accuracy and large dataset handling increased substantially. Neural networks and decision trees for medical imaging, predictive analytics, and patient care. Watson, launched in 2011, assessed medical data and helped cancer treatments using natural language processing. (Javanmard, 2024)

2.1 Integration of IoT with AI in Health Systems

IoT and AI synergistically changed healthcare. IoT's massive network of connected gadgets collected and exchanged data in real time. This relationship makes healthcare more dynamic, responsive, and personalized utilizing AI's analytical power.

Remote patient monitoring, where wearable sensors measured heart rate, glucose, and physical activity, was one of the first integrations. AI algorithms found irregularities and predicted health concerns in this data for fast action. It also includes smart home systems with IoT devices monitoring the elderly or chronically ill and AI alerting caregivers and doctors. (Hoang, 2024)

2.2 Milestones and Key Developments

Numerous developments and breakthroughs have altered the integration of AI and IoT in healthcare. Fitbit and Apple Watch, two popular fitness trackers released in the early 2010s, demonstrated the enormous potential of the IoT for health monitoring. These gadgets enabled AI to detect trends and possible risks by gathering massive volumes of health data.

Artificial intelligence-enabled diagnoses were also an improvement. With the first artificial intelligence (AI) diabetic retinopathy detection gadget getting FDA approval in 2017, AI diagnostics took a giant leap forward. This certification increased the reliability of AI medical diagnosis.

Artificial intelligence has completely transformed the field of telemedicine. Telemedicine and the Internet of Things (IoT) improved patient monitoring, virtual consultations, and data management during COVID-19. Internet of Things devices collected data, and artificial intelligence algorithms ranked the severity of symptoms to determine the priority of treatment. Applications of AIoT are enhanced by machine learning and natural language processing. Unparalleled precision in analyzing complicated medical data, making real-time diagnoses, and predicting patient outcomes is achieved by AI systems. This field is working on smart prosthetics and robotic surgeries driven by artificial intelligence. (Imroz khan, 2024)

AI and IoT have ushered in digital health. The use of AI diagnostic tools and wearable gadgets shows their transformative potential. AI and IoT will make healthcare smarter, more efficient, and customized.

2.3 Gap in Research in Industry

Table 1. Research Gap in the industry

Research Area	Research Title	Findings	Gap or Limitation	Reference
Data Integration & Interoperability	AIoT-Based Smart Healthcare in Everyday Lives: Data Collection and Standardization from Smartphones and Smartwatches	AIoT systems utilizing smart devices can offer personalized, proactive care, reducing reliance on limited medical services.	Lack of compatibility in health data formats and services across devices from different manufacturers hinders growth.	(Geonwoo Ji, 2024)
	Enabling Artificial Intelligence of Things (AIoT) Healthcare Architectures and Listing Security Issues	Discusses AIoT healthcare applications and associated security concerns.	Limited exploration of standardized frameworks for data integration across diverse AIoT systems.	(Anil Audumbar Pise, 2022)
	An Extensive Survey of AIoT in Healthcare	Provides a comprehensive review of AIoT architectures and applications in healthcare.	Identifies the need for more robust interoperability standards to facilitate seamless data exchange.	(Gunjan, 2024)
	HealthAIoT: AIoT-driven smart healthcare system for sustainable development	Proposes a new architecture utilizing AIoT with cloud computing for smart healthcare systems.	Requires further validation in real-world settings to assess integration challenges.	(Han Wang, 2025)

continued on following page

Table 1. Continued

Research Area	Research Title	Findings	Gap or Limitation	Reference
Privacy, Security & Ethics	Exploring the Role of AIoT in Data Privacy and Security	Identifies key privacy and security challenges in AIoT and explores enhancement strategies.	Emphasizes the need for comprehensive regulatory frameworks to balance innovation and data protection.	(Sushil Bhardwaj, 2025)
	Federated Learning for Privacy Preservation in Smart Healthcare Systems: A Comprehensive Survey	Highlights federated learning as a means to preserve privacy in IoMT devices without accessing confidential data.	Points out challenges in implementing federated learning at scale across diverse healthcare systems.	(Mansoor Ali, 2022)
	FedBlockHealth: A Synergistic Approach to Privacy and Security in IoT-Enabled Healthcare through Federated Learning and Blockchain	Proposes a hybrid approach combining federated learning and blockchain for secure healthcare applications.	Requires further research to assess scalability and performance in large-scale deployments.	(Nazar Waheed, 2023)
	Secure Artificial Intelligence of Things (AIoT)-enabled authenticated key agreement technique for a smart living environment	Focuses on designing secure AIoT-enabled key agreement techniques for smart environments.	Limited discussion on integration with existing healthcare infrastructure and standards.	(Siddhant Thapliyal, 2024)

continued on following page

Table 1. Continued

Research Area	Research Title	Findings	Gap or Limitation	Reference
Regulatory Compliance & Governance	Ethical and Regulatory Challenges of AI Technologies in Healthcare	Provides an overview of ethical and regulatory concerns in deploying AI systems in clinical practice.	Highlights the need for robust governance frameworks to foster acceptance and successful implementation.	(Ciro Mennella, 2024)
	Global Regulatory Frameworks for the Use of Artificial Intelligence in the Healthcare Sector	Reviews existing regulatory landscapes for AI in healthcare services in developed nations.	Suggests the necessity for harmonized regulations to facilitate global AIoT healthcare solutions.	(Kavitha Palaniappan, 2024)
	Aligning AI Principles and Healthcare Delivery Organization Best Practices	Maps AI regulatory frameworks to recommended best practices for healthcare delivery organizations.	Indicates a gap in practical guidance for implementing AI principles in diverse healthcare settings.	(Alifia Hasan, 2025)
	AI and Healthcare Regulatory Compliance	Discusses the reliance of AI deployment on data and associated privacy concerns governed by regulations like HIPAA.	Emphasizes the complexity of ensuring compliance amidst evolving AI technologies.	(Wachler & Associates, P.C., 2024)
Cost, Accessibility & Equity	Economics of Artificial Intelligence in Healthcare: Diagnosis vs. Treatment	Evaluates AI technology in the context of healthcare costs, comparing it to traditional approaches.	Identifies the need for more comprehensive cost-benefit analyses across various healthcare settings.	(Narendra N Khanna, 2022)
	The Potential Impact of Artificial Intelligence on Healthcare Spending	Estimates that wider AI adoption could lead to significant savings in US healthcare spending.	Suggests further research to understand the long-term economic impacts of AI integration.	(Nikhil Sahni, 2023)
	How AI in Healthcare Increases Accessibility and Equity	Explores how AI enables a more accessible and equitable healthcare system.	Calls for strategies to ensure AI benefits are equitably distributed across different populations.	(Slalom Build)
	Lowering Health Care Costs Through AI: The Possibilities and Barriers	Examines AI's potential to reduce healthcare costs and improve quality.	Highlights barriers such as initial investment costs and the need for workforce training.	(Coleman, 2024)

3. CURRENT AI INNOVATIONS IN E-HEALTH

Advanced e-health AI enhances care. AI and analytics improve patient outcomes and disease progression prediction. NLP analyzes unstructured medical data to improve physician judgments. Real-time, precise computer vision scan analysis improves medical imaging. Robotic surgery and treatment improve accuracy, invasiveness, and recuperation. These innovations improve diagnosis, treatment, administration, and patient care.

3.1 Machine Learning and Predictive Analytics

Machine learning (ML) allows computers learn from massive data sets and generate accurate predictions, changing e-health. Patient outcomes and disease progression change with ML-powered predictive analytics. Patient data may assist ML systems predict hospital readmissions and help healthcare providers avoid them. Early intervention helps diabetes and heart disease.

Individualized medicine uses predictive analytics. ML models predict medication responses using genetics, lifestyle, and medical history. This personalizes medications, enhancing effectiveness and decreasing side effects. ML algorithms may uncover illness causes and therapies, but analysts may overlook patterns and connections. (Mohd Javaid, 2022)

3.2 Natural Language Processing in Medical Records

Unstructured medical data is handled and analyzed better using NLP. The text-heavy and unstructured medical records, clinical notes, and patient histories make data extraction problematic. NLP can organize text for searching and analysis.

Automatic medical billing and insurance coding using NLP is popular. Classifying medical procedures and diagnoses from clinical data using NLP simplifies administrative work and reduces mistakes. Clinical decision support systems aid physicians real-time using NLP. Based on medical history and symptoms, NLP may enhance clinical decision-making by proposing diagnoses and treatments.

NLP is needed for patient involvement. NLP chatbots and virtual assistants may answer questions regarding medications, symptoms, and follow-up. Improves patient satisfaction and treatment adherence, improving health. (Sofia C. Pereira, 2024)

3.3 Computer Vision in Medical Imaging

Computer vision analyzes visual data to improve medical imaging. AI systems can discover X-ray, MRI, and CT scan issues faster and better than radiologists.

Early illness detection is a popular computer vision use. AI can identify lung nodules and breast lesions early for diagnosis and treatment. AI can detect retinal illnesses in eye scans, allowing early treatment and perhaps averting vision loss.

Image-guided operations are more accurate using computer vision. AI helps surgeons comprehend real-time images, boosting results. Computer vision simplifies image processing for radiologists and speeds diagnosis. (Tetiana Habuza, 2021)

3.4 Robotics in Surgery and Patient Care

Robotic surgery improves accuracy, invasiveness, and recuperation. Consoles let surgeons perform sophisticated robotic surgeries more accurately. High-definition, 3D operating site imagery decreases patient trauma and recuperation time in minimally invasive surgery.

The da Vinci Surgical System does prostateectomy, heart valve repair, and gynecologic operations. For better performance and fewer difficulties, da Vinci technology converts the surgeon's hand gestures into tiny tool movements within the patient. (Pradipta Biswas, 2023)

Robotic surgery improves accuracy, invasiveness, and recuperation. Consoles let surgeons perform sophisticated robotic surgeries more accurately. High-definition, 3D operating site imagery decreases patient trauma and recuperation time in minimally invasive surgery.

The da Vinci Surgical System does prostateectomy, heart valve repair, and gynecologic operations. For better performance and fewer difficulties, da Vinci technology converts the surgeon's hand gestures into tiny tool movements within the patient. (Prof, 2008)

4. AIOT APPLICATIONS IN E-HEALTH

In e-health, AI and IoT improve care. Predictive analytics, individualized treatment plans, and streamlined healthcare administration are all made possible by AI's real-time analysis of vast amounts of data collected by the Internet of Things (3T). Examples include telemedicine, wearable health gadgets, smart healthcare facilities, remote patient monitoring, and individualized therapy. AI's analytics and IoT's data collecting improve e-health patient outcomes, resource utilization, and proactive, personalized treatment.

4.1 Remote Patient Monitoring and Telemedicine

Health care delivery is being transformed by internet of things (IoT) applications in e-health, such as telemedicine and RPM. RPM monitors patients' vitals with the use of wearable sensors and at-home medical equipment. These gadgets track glucose, heart rate, blood pressure, and other health markers. Medical professionals employ AI to sift through online data for anomalies and potential dangers to patients' health.

AI's predictive algorithms help RPM see issues early. Analysis of pulse rate and blood pressure may help AI identify heart attacks and strokes early. The early discovery saves lives. AI may help physicians manage resources by prioritizing urgent patients. (Luiza Palmieri Serrano, 2023)

Telemedicine provided by AIoT helps people get medical care remotely. Video conferencing and AI-powered diagnostic technologies let doctors diagnose patients remotely. Patients in remote or impoverished areas with poor healthcare access benefit. Virtual consultations may use AI to diagnose and treat patients.

4.2 Wearable Health Devices and Real-Time Data Analytics

Wearable health devices gather and monitor health data. Biosensors, fitness trackers, and smartwatches monitor heart rate, sleep, and other health markers. IoT devices may provide data to centralized platforms for real-time AI analysis.

AI is necessary for data analysis. It may reveal health trends and patterns, providing users actionable advice to improve their health. AI can alert people to irregular heart rhythms that need medical care. Lifestyle changes may help patients manage diabetes and hypertension using AI-driven insights.

Wearables track public and personal health. Data from several devices may help public health specialists spot health hazards and respond fast. (Mohsen Masoumian Hosseini, 2023)

4.3 Smart Healthcare Facilities and Connected Environments

AIoT enhances hospital efficiency while improving patient care. Through the use of the Internet of Things, these companies manage healthcare facilities. Smart beds have sensors that notify caretakers of a patient's vital signs and movement.

IoT and AI improve healthcare facility operations. Artificial intelligence-powered bed management and admission prediction systems maximize the use of available resources. Through the management of stocks and supply networks, AI can eradicate waste and guarantee the availability of key goods. Hospitalized patients may be given priority by AIoT systems that evaluate symptoms and vital signs. Hospital efficiency, wait times, and patient outcomes are all enhanced by this. (Stephanie B. Baker, 2017)

4.4 Personalized Medicine and Treatment Plans

Personalization is enhanced by AIoT. For treatment plan adjustments, doctors employ data collected in real-time by AI and IoT devices. AI studies genetic, lifestyle, medical, and IoT data. Individualized, efficient therapy is made possible by this comprehensive evaluation. More successful medicines may be on the horizon as a result of AI assisting doctors in selecting tumor genetic profile therapy.

AIoT has the capability to monitor and modify treatment plans. A.I. analyses data collected from wearable devices that track patients' responses to medications in real time. In order to improve patient care, AI may suggest tweaks to unsuccessful medications. Chronic diseases may be effectively treated with personalized therapy. Internet of Things (IoT) technologies improve hypertension and diabetes control via data monitoring and delivery. AI has the potential to enhance patient outcomes and quality of life by prescribing nutritional, pharmacological, and other treatments using real-time data. (Wu, 2022)

Electronic health Personalized care, smart healthcare facilities, real-time data analytics from wearable health devices, telemedicine, and remote patient monitoring are all made possible by AIoT applications. Improved patient outcomes, streamlined operations, and proactive, individualized, networked healthcare are all made possible by these technological advancements. On a worldwide scale, AIoT will improve patients' lives and revolutionize e-health.

5. CASE STUDIES

5.1 Successful Implementations of AIoT in Healthcare

5.1.1 Philips' HealthSuite Platform

The HealthSuite Platform from Philips makes use of healthcare AIoT by combining data from a variety of health devices. AI analyzes data collected from the Internet of Things (IoT) such medical records, imaging equipment, and wearable monitors. Software has the potential to identify a patient's decline in condition in real-time, enabling prompt medical intervention. By keeping tabs on patients and notifying hospitals of any problems, this technology enhances both patient outcomes and hospital efficiency. (FasterCapital)

5.1.2 Medtronic's AIoT Solutions

Medtronic uses AIoT in their diabetes management products. With glucose sensors, the MiniMed 670G is a hybrid closed-loop insulin delivery system. With this information, AI systems can fine-tune insulin dosing. By lowering the risk of hyperglycemia and hypoglycemia and enhancing quality of life, this technology helps diabetics maintain optimum glucose levels without human intervention. (Neumiller, 2019)

5.1.3 GE Healthcare's Edison Platform

AI and the Internet of Things improve operational efficiency and aid in clinical decision-making on the Edison platform of GE Healthcare. Data from medical devices and systems are analyzed in real-time by the platform. Radiologists may now more quickly and reliably detect problems in imaging data by analyzing it using AI algorithms. Medical imaging diagnosis and treatment times might be improved by AIoT, according to this integration. (Digital Healthcare: This Software Marketplace Lets Hospitals Test-Drive AI-Powered Apps, 2020)

5.2 Real-World Examples of AI-Driven Health Solutions

5.2.1 IBM Watson for Oncology

AI-driven health solutions include IBM Watson for Oncology. This AI system generates therapy suggestions using medical literature, clinical trials, and patient data. It helps oncologists create tailored treatment regimens by selecting the most effective treatments based on patient data. Memorial Sloan Kettering Cancer Center uses Watson for Oncology to enhance treatment planning and results. (Na Zhou, 2019)

5.2.2 Babylon Health's AI Chatbot

Babylon Health's AI-powered chatbot gives symptom-based medical advice. The chatbot analyzes patient inputs and suggests diagnosis and treatments using natural language processing and machine learning. The NHS uses Babylon's chatbot in its digital health services to provide people preliminary medical advice and decrease hospital workload. This adoption has simplified initial consultations and enhanced patient access to healthcare. (Lu Xu, 2021)

5.2.3 Aidoc's Radiology AI

Radiology AI firm Aidoc uses AI algorithms to spot abnormalities in medical imaging data and prioritize cases for radiologists. In many hospitals and imaging centers worldwide, Aidoc's solutions speed up diagnosis of cerebral hemorrhages and pulmonary embolisms. Aidoc's AI-driven diagnostic solutions improve patient outcomes and radiology department efficiency by expediting diagnosis. (Reiner, 2019)

5.3 Outcomes and Benefits of AIoT Applications

5.3.1 Enhanced Patient Outcomes

Healthcare AIoT has dramatically improved patient outcomes. Philips' HealthSuite Platform can identify patient deterioration early for urgent treatment. Medtronic's MiniMed 670G gadget improves diabetics' quality of life by managing glucose levels without human intervention. These examples show how real-time data processing and monitoring may enhance patient care using AIoT.

5.3.2 Operational Efficiency

Healthcare operations are more efficient using AIoT. To optimise operations, GE Healthcare's Edison platform combines and analyses medical device data. Clinicians are able to treat more patients because to this integration, which speeds up diagnosis and allocates resources more efficiently. Thanks to Aidoc's radiology AI, radiologists have less work to complete, critical cases get priority, and operations run more smoothly.

5.3.3 Cost Reduction

Healthcare spending is drastically reduced via AIoT. By rapidly evaluating enormous amounts of data, AI-driven systems such as IBM Watson for Oncology may expedite and reduce the cost of customized treatment plans. By decreasing the need for first in-person consultations, Babylon Health's AI chatbot helps healthcare institutions save money and improve patient outcomes. Potential savings might assist healthcare providers in better managing resources and sustaining systems.

5.3.4 Increased Accessibility

AIoT makes healthcare more accessible in remote areas. Patients who do not have simple access to healthcare may get advice from Babylon Health's AI chatbot.

Patients are able to get treatment remotely using telemedicine systems powered by AIoT, which eliminates boundaries between healthcare professionals and patients. More people will be able to get adequate and timely medical treatment as a result of this improvement in accessibility.

5.3.5 Data-Driven Insights

AIoT applications generate enormous data sets that may enhance patient health and healthcare operations. Doctors use data to improve patient care, treatment, and decision-making. The Medtronic diabetes management system tailor's insulin treatment using continuous glucose monitoring data, improving patient outcomes. Patient data is analyzed by Philips HealthSuite Platform AI algorithms to identify health concerns and provide preventive care.

AIoT applications in healthcare have improved patient outcomes, operational efficiency, cost, and accessibility. Philips, Medtronic, and GE Healthcare demonstrate AIoT's disruptive potential in healthcare. IBM Watson for Oncology, Babylon Health's chatbot, and Aidoc's radiology AI demonstrate AI's practical applications. AIoT's healthcare applications will undoubtedly grow, improving patient care and delivery. (Shreyas Suresh Rao, 2023)

6. CHALLENGES AND LIMITATIONS

Technical obstacles with data integration, privacy and security concerns, and ethical considerations including bias and patient permission restrict AIoT in healthcare. Regulations and compliance complicate everything, demanding strict standards and constant monitoring. High implementation costs and the digital divide may increase health inequities. Technological advances, legislative adaption, and healthcare system equality and inclusion are needed to address these difficulties.

6.1 Technical Challenges and Data Integration Issues

Technical complexity and data integration are major obstacles to healthcare AIoT deployment. Healthcare systems create massive volumes of data from EHRs, wearable devices, imaging systems, and lab testing. Building an interoperable system with this data is difficult. Healthcare providers create data silos when their systems are siloed and do not share information.

Data for AI systems has to be of good quality and well labeled. It is difficult to handle and analyze healthcare data because it is often unstructured, missing, or inconsistent. Although they are necessary, data preparation and cleansing take a lot of time. Processing data in real-time requires a lot of resources and knowledge in computing, which may be hard to come by. (V. Dankan Gowda, 2024)

6.2 Privacy, Security, and Ethical Concerns

Patient data is sensitive, thus healthcare privacy and security are crucial. AI health data systems need strong data security to prevent breaches and unauthorized access. Patients' right to privacy in their health records is jeopardized by cyberattacks and ransomware. AI in healthcare raises ethical considerations. AI algorithms may create discriminatory outcomes. If training data does not represent all demographics, AI-driven conclusions may prejudice particular groups. In order for AI systems to address ethical concerns, they need to be accountable, open, and fair. Patients' autonomy and permission are also vital. Through AIoT solutions, patients need to be educated and given ownership over their data. The continuous challenge is to balance the advantages of the AIoT with patients' right to privacy and autonomy. (Olaoye, 2024)

6.3 Regulatory and Compliance Hurdles

New compliance and regulatory challenges have emerged as a result of AIoT in the heavily regulated healthcare sector. All software and hardware used in healthcare, including AI-powered solutions, must first get approval from the FDA and the EMA. AIoT systems are subject to data protection regulations such as GDPR and HIPAA in the eurozone. These limitations impede the processing, storage, and interchange of AIoT data, which in turn slows down adoption. It may become more difficult to regulate AI if it learns and adapts. For AI systems to be safe, effective, and compliant, they need to be assessed and monitored at every stage of their lifespan. The implementation of AIoT in healthcare is sluggish and challenging, necessitating changes to regulations. (Heinz-Uwe Dettling, 2022)

6.4 Cost and Accessibility Barriers

Expensive Medical Care Deploying AIoT. A lot of money goes into AI software and internet of things gadgets. Healthcare costs might go increase due to cybersecurity, maintenance, and upgrade costs. Affordable healthcare providers in rural areas and those with lower incomes may find it difficult to afford these modifications. Because of the digital divide, access is reduced. Patients living in rural areas or with little financial resources may not have access to the internet or other necessary equipment to take advantage of AIoT solutions. Health inequalities may widen as a result of this digital divide, as more individuals may not have access to AIoT innovations.

Equally important are training and the development of employees. There has to be an investment of time and money to educate healthcare staff on AIoT. Because of the possible changes that AIoT may bring about, healthcare procedures may have to be modified. (C. V. Suresh Babu, 2024)

AIoT has positives and downsides in healthcare. Data integration and technological issues make deployment privacy, security, and ethics problematic. Costly and inaccessible compliance and regulatory issues may slow AIoT development. We must improve technology, change legislation, and make healthcare accessible and egalitarian to address these obstacles. If the proper challenges are addressed, the IoT might improve healthcare operational efficiency and patient outcomes.

7. FUTURE TRENDS AND DIRECTIONS

Telemedicine and the real-time monitoring of healthcare via the Internet of Things are now within reach, all because of 5G and edge computing. While state-of-the-art robotics will improve surgical operations and patient care, blockchain technology will guarantee the safety of medical data. Patients' health results may be enhanced with the use of telemedicine, predictive analytics, and personalized treatment plans. The use of AI in preventative medicine, seamless data integration, and clinical decision assistance will greatly improve the accessibility, efficiency, and quality of healthcare.

7.1 Emerging Technologies and Innovations on the Horizon

Emerging technology is revolutionizing the healthcare AIoT. Operations, patient care, and results in healthcare might all be improved via innovation.

7.1.1 Edge Computing

Edge computing processes data from nearby IoT devices. Real-time healthcare decision-making is possible because to speedier sensor and wearable device data processing and analysis. Edge computing improves data privacy by minimizing sensitive health data transferred across networks.

7.1.2 5G Connectivity

Edge computing processes data from nearby IoT devices. Healthcare practitioners may improve real-time decision-making and minimize latency via faster data analysis and processing from wearable devices and sensors. Edge computing reduces network transfers of sensitive medical data, improving data privacy.

7.1.3 Blockchain for Data Security

Blockchain guarantees privacy and transparency in patient records. Blockchain medical records cannot be destroyed, protecting patients' privacy. This technology securely transfers patient data across healthcare professionals and systems, improving care coordination and outcomes.

7.1.4 Advanced Robotics

Surgical robots, which enhance accuracy and recovery time, and robotic support for the crippled and old will soon be common in hospitals. Blockchain technology secures and transparently handles health records. The integration of IoT, AI, and robots will enable autonomous medical solutions. Blockchain records are secure because they cannot be changed. This includes health statistics. Healthcare practitioners and systems may now securely share patient data, improving care coordination and results.

7.2 Potential Advancements in AIoT for Healthcare

Through the integration of genetic and real-time health data, the Internet of Things (IoT) has tremendous potential for enhancing personalized therapy. The use of predictive analytics may one day make it easier to spot and stop diseases in their tracks. Remote diagnostics and consultations will be made better using telemedicine. Clinical decision support for diagnosis and therapy has greatly improved using AI. Changes are coming to the healthcare system that will make it better at what it does, simpler for people, and more proactive in preserving their health.

7.2.1 Personalized Medicine

AIoT-guided therapy will use genetic, lifestyle, and real-time health data. AI systems searching this mountain of data for effective medicines, illness projections, and preventative actions may improve health and cut healthcare costs.

7.2.2 Predictive Analytics and Early Intervention

AI-powered predictive analytics will enable early health diagnosis. AI that collects and analyzes data might prevent medical emergencies and unneeded hospitalizations. Active care reduces healthcare expenses and improves patient outcomes.

7.2.3 Telemedicine and Remote Care

The IoT will improve telemedicine's capacity for remote monitoring and diagnosis. During virtual consultations, physicians will get precise insights and recommendations backed by AI-based patient data analysis. Because it increases healthcare access and the treatment of chronic diseases, remote care is particularly useful in economically constrained places.

7.3 Predictions for the Future of Digital Health Systems

Digital health systems of the future will be able to integrate data from many sources. Care coordination and patient outcomes might be improved with the use of standardized data formats and the facilitation of interactions between systems and providers. Treatment that is focused on the individual patient will be enhanced by the IoT. Lives will be improved with the help of wearable electronics and health apps that provide personalized health recommendations and real-time feedback. With the use of patient portals and telemedicine, physicians and patients will be able to interact more effectively. Internet of Things (IoT) will identify potential dangers and provide ways to prevent diseases before they start. These preventative measures are beneficial to healthcare expenditures and public health. Clinical decision support systems driven by AI will analyze massive amounts of medical data to make diagnoses, plans, and predictions. Artificial intelligence that is based on evidence will improve diagnosis and treatment. (Božić, 2024)

7.4 Suggested Model to Industry with 9 Parameters and Its Implementation Path

To help healthcare stakeholders grasp the potential of AIoT, a detailed implementation strategy with nine important criteria might be helpful. Various aspects of AIoT integration are discussed, including technology, data management, regulatory compliance, and patient interaction.

7.4.1 Infrastructure

You need a solid IT system to back up the AIoT. 5G connection and edge computing allow for dependable communication and fast data processing. In order to accommodate new technology and fluctuating needs, infrastructure must be scalable and adaptable.

7.4.2 Data Integration

Healthcare data integration formats and protocols must work with systems and devices. Improve these standards to simplify healthcare platform data interchange and processing. Standardizing EHR, wearable, and diagnostic data requires complex data integration standards. These systems must handle and interpret data well to provide physicians reliable patient data. This improves healthcare integration, coordination, clinical decision-making, and responsiveness.

7.4.3 Privacy and Security

Use blockchain to protect and disclose patient data. Protecting patient data is ethical business. Both HIPAA and GDPR protect patients' medical records. Encryption, access limits, and audits safeguard private data. Healthcare privacy and security policies reduce risks and protect patient data.

7.4.4 AI Algorithm Development

Make AI algorithm development and testing transparent and fair. Large, representative datasets with various patient demographics and medical conditions are essential for AI model training. When changing algorithms, medical developments must be considered. Improved AI-powered insights and judgments will lead to more equal healthcare solutions. Better AI models for healthcare's ever-changing environment are needed.

7.4.5 Patient Engagement

Health management requires patient input. These services should educate patients with current medical facts and user-friendly interfaces. Help people make educated health decisions with individualized advice. Interactive, accessible technology enhances health management by customizing therapy.

7.4.6 Regulatory Compliance

Maintain compliance with AI and medical device regulations and communicate with authorities. Ensure AIoT systems meet requirements. To achieve this, systems must be regularly examined for effectiveness and safety and adjusted to reflect legal changes. Organizations may assure compliant, safe, and successful AIoT systems by actively interacting with authorities and monitoring their activities.

7.4.7 Training and Education

Make sure medical staff are well-versed on AIoT. The greatest approach to keep up with the latest AIoT innovations and best practices is to promote lifelong learning.

7.4.8 Operational Efficiency

Full training increases healthcare workers' AIoT skills. These training should teach staff how to use current technology. AIoT technology and best practices must be studied regularly. Continuous learning and professional development may enhance healthcare AIoT system utilization and patient care.

7.4.9 Scalability and Sustainability

Scale and sustain AIoT. Ensure systems can manage growing data and healthcare. Provide long-term support for changing technology and needs. Flexible designs enable technology upgrades and integration, keeping solutions current. A resilient healthcare system can adapt to changing technology and healthcare environments with scalability and sustainability.

Figure 2. AIoT Health Integration Model (AIM)

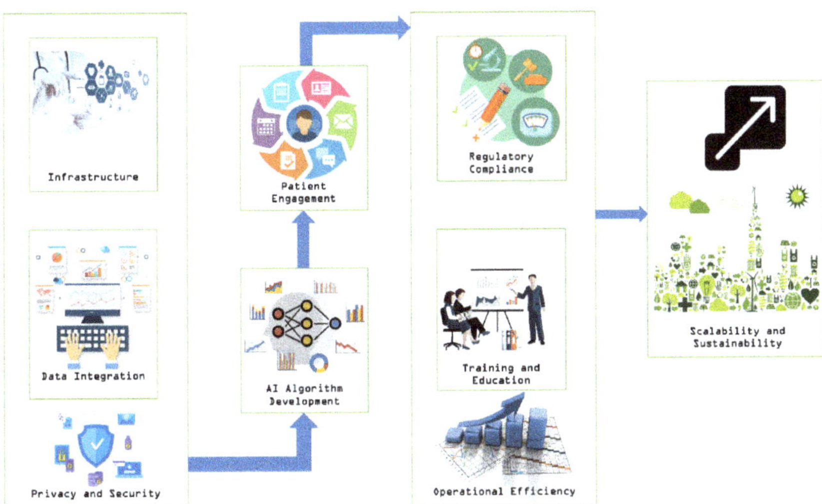

Suggested framework to the industry

To expedite healthcare AIoT implementation, the AIoT Health Integration Model (AIM) focuses infrastructure, data integration, privacy and security, AI algorithm development, patient engagement, regulatory compliance, training and education, operational efficiency, and scalability AIM advises methodically integrating new technologies, ensuring compatibility, and addressing data privacy and cost. AIM focuses on these traits to enhance healthcare delivery, patient outcomes, and digital health system development. Same is given as an illustration form in figure 1.

7.5 Implementation Path

Healthcare AIoT needs infrastructure evaluation, pilot projects, stakeholder involvement, and technology integration. Educate doctors, comply with regulations, and grow successful initiatives. Digital health systems require continual monitoring and updates to last.

7.5.1 Assessment and Planning

Evaluate infrastructure, data management, and technology. Your AIoT goals should fit your company strategy and patient care. This study will provide the framework for a tailored AIoT solution design that satisfies current and future needs and connects with existing systems.

7.5.2 Pilot Projects

Learn more about how telemedicine and RPM might benefit from AI research. It is possible to evaluate the practicality and efficacy of solutions via pilot projects. Statistical analysis of user experience, performance, and impact may reveal possible issues. Improving technology and methods according to outcomes should be done before extending applications. This approach enhances the integration and scalability of healthcare AIoT systems by addressing issues as they come up.

7.5.3 Stakeholder Collaboration

Healthcare providers, regulators, and patients may all benefit from an IT alliance's collaborative efforts to develop and implement AIoT solutions. Getting involved in these organizations could be a great way to meet new people, get insight into issues, and set some objectives for yourself. Getting everyone on the same page, considering other points of view, and winning over project backers all need open lines of communication and teamwork. As a result of its comprehensive design, this method streamlines installation, boosts AIoT utilization in healthcare, and finds problems early on.

7.5.4 Technology Integration

IoT security, data integration, and IT infrastructure are crucial. Strong, secure tech should support AIoT applications. Develop and thoroughly evaluate clinical and regulatory-compliant AI algorithms. For accuracy, effectiveness, and safety, extensive testing and verification are needed. All of this produces a robust and consistent healthcare AIoT ecosystem.

7.5.5 Training and Education

Healthcare practitioners and patients may be educated about AIoT to encourage its adoption. These efforts must include technological innovation, benefits, and best practices. Updating training materials and providing ongoing education may boost innovation and development. This method improves proactive healthcare technology and AIoT tool adoption via user education.

7.5.6 Monitoring and Evaluation

Comprehensive healthcare worker and patient education may increase AIoT deployment. These efforts need cutting-edge tech, perks, and best practices. Updated training materials and ongoing instruction may foster creativity and growth. This technique enhances AIoT tools and proactive healthcare technologies by training users.

7.5.7 Scaling and Sustainability

An flexible and lasting AIoT may be created by building on pilot initiatives in several fields. Increase efficiency while expanding systems to meet demand. Support and maintenance help fix problems and keep the system running. New system updates should offer limits and improvements. This strategy makes AIoT systems versatile, compliant, and profitable.

Healthcare was able to fully embrace AIoT because to the design and implementation methodology, which improved patient care, operational efficiency, and health outcomes.

8. CONCLUSION

AI and IoT are changing e-health. Technological advances are changing healthcare administration and delivery. AIoT was ahead of its time in several areas, including robots, computer vision, and NLP. These advances may enable more efficient and accurate personalized treatment, predictive analytics, and remote patient monitoring. Machine learning algorithms anticipate health risks from historical and real-time data, while natural language processing streamlines medical record maintenance. Medical imaging and surgery have advanced using computer vision and robots.

However, many issues remain. We must address the challenges of data integration, privacy and security, bias in artificial intelligence, and the morality of patient consent. Cost and restrictions are also major issues. These issues must be solved to employ AIoT technology successfully and fairly. (Timothy Malche, 2022)

However, many issues remain. Privacy, security, and patient consent ethics are among the numerous challenges that need to be addressed. Financial commitments and laws may be major hurdles. To use AIoT technology efficiently and fairly, these issues must be addressed. The Internet of Things has immense healthcare potential. IoT, edge computing, 5G, and blockchain will make healthcare safer, more efficient, more customized. Artificial intelligence will become more important in threat detection and mitigation.

Healthcare stakeholders must overcome challenges and invest in long-term, sustainable solutions to reap these benefits. E-health data may change substantially as the Internet of Things (IoT) grows and rules ease.

Finally, AIoT will improve healthcare personalization, efficiency, and patient outcomes. The future holds problem-solving, progress, and improved digital health systems for everyone.

REFERENCES

Alifia Hasan, N. P. (2025). Aligning AI principles and healthcare delivery organization best practices to navigate the shifting regulatory landscape. *npj digital medicine, 8*(278). https://doi.org/https://doi.org/10.1038/s41746-025-01605-2

Anil Audumbar Pise, K. K. (2022). Enabling Artificial Intelligence of Things (AIoT) Healthcare Architectures and Listing Security Issues. *Computational Intelligence and Neuroscience, 2022*, •••. https://doi.org/https://doi.org/10.1155/2022/8421434 PMID: 36911247

Božić, V. (2024). DIGITAL HEALTH AND COMMUNICATION -A REVOLUTION WITH CAUTIONS. https://doi.org/https://www.researchgate.net/publication/379823590_DIGITAL_HEALTH_AND_COMMUNICATION_-A_REVOLUTION_WITH_CAUTIONS

Build, S. (n.d.). *AI in healthcare: How Intelligent Products increase accessibility and equity.* Slalom Build. https://www.slalombuild.com/thinking/ai-in-healthcare-how-intelligent-products-increase-accessibility-and-equity

Ciro Mennella, U. M. (2024). Ethical and regulatory challenges of AI technologies in healthcare: A narrative review. *Heliyon, 10*(4). https://doi.org/https://doi.org/10.1016/j.heliyon.2024.e26297 PMID: 38384518

Coleman, K. (2024). *Lowering Health Care Costs Through AI The Possibilities and Barriers*. Paragon Health Institute.

Dankan Gowda, V. M. K. (2024). AIoT Integration Advancements and Challenges in Smart Sensing Technologies for Smart Devices. In *AIoT and Smart Sensing Technologies for Smart Devices.* IGI Global.

Digital Healthcare: This Software Marketplace Lets Hospitals Test-Drive AI-Powered Apps. (2020, December 14). General Electric Company. https://www.ge.com/news/reports/digital-healthcare-this-software-marketplace-lets-hospitals-test-drive-ai-powered-apps-0

FasterCapital. (n.d.). *Successful Business Applications Of Iot And Smart Devices.* Faster Capital. https://fastercapital.com/topics/successful-business-applications-of-iot-and-smart-devices.html

Geonwoo Ji, J. W. (2024). AIoT-Based Smart Healthcare in Everyday Lives: Data Collection and Standardization From Smartphones and Smartwatches. *IEEE Internet of Things Journal, 11*(16), 27597–27619. https://doi.org/https://doi.org/10.1109/JIOT.2024.3400509

Gunjan, I. S. (2024). An Extensive Survey of AIoT in Healthcare. In *N. D.-N. Surjeet Dalal, Reshaping Intelligent Business and Industry: Convergence of AI and IoT at the Cutting Edge*. Wiley Online Library.

Heinz-Uwe Dettling, K. J. (2022, July 27). *How the challenge of regulating AI in healthcare is escalating*. EY. https://www.ey.com/en_gl/insights/law/how-the-challenge-of-regulating-ai-in-healthcare-is-escalating

Hoang, T. V. (2024). Impact of Integrated Artificial Intelligence and Internet of Things Technologies on Smart City Transformation. *Journal of Technical Education Science, 19*(1), 64–73. DOI: 10.54644/jte.2024.1532

. Javanmard, S. (2024). Revolutionizing Medical Practice: The Impact of Artificial Intelligence (AI). *Journal of Applied Science and Technology, 2*(1), 01-16. https://doi.org/DOI: 10.33140/OAJAST.02.01.07

Kavitha Palaniappan, E. Y. (2024). Global Regulatory Frameworks for the Use of Artificial Intelligence (AI) in the Healthcare Services Sector. *Health Care, 15*(5). https://doi.org/https://doi.org/10.3390/healthcare12050562

Kunal, A. P. (2023). Modern Healthcare Systems: Unveiling the Possibility of AIoT for Remote Patient Monitoring. In *Developments Towards Next Generation Intelligent Systems for Sustainable Development* (pp. 180-203). IGI Global.

Lu Xu, M. L. (2021). Chatbot for Health Care and Oncology Applications Using Artificial Intelligence and Machine Learning: Systematic Review. *JMIR Cancer, 7*(4). Advance online publication. DOI: 10.2196/27850 PMID: 34847056

Luiza Palmieri Serrano, K. C.-G. (2023). Benefits and Challenges of Remote Patient Monitoring as Perceived by Health Care Practitioners: A Systematic Review. *The Permanente Journal, 27*(4), 100–111. DOI: 10.7812/TPP/23.022 PMID: 37735970

Mansoor Ali, F. N. (2022, Mar 18). Federated Learning for Privacy Preservation in Smart Healthcare Systems: A Comprehensive Survey. arxiv. https://arxiv.org/abs/2203.09702

Mohd Javaid, A. H. (2022). Significance of machine learning in healthcare: Features, pillars and applications. *International Journal of Intelligent Networks, 3*, 58–73. https://doi.org/https://doi.org/10.1016/j.ijin.2022.05.002

Mohsen Masoumian Hosseini, S. T. (2023). Smartwatches in healthcare medicine: Assistance and monitoring; a scoping review. *BMC Medical Informatics and Decision Making, 23*. Advance online publication. DOI: 10.1186/s12911-023-02350-w PMID: 37924029

Na Zhou, C.-T. Z.-Y. (2019). Concordance Study Between IBM Watson for Oncology and Clinical Practice for Patients with Cancer in China. *The Oncologist, 24*(6), 812–819. DOI: 10.1634/theoncologist.2018-0255 PMID: 30181315

Narendra, N., & Khanna, M. A. (2022). Economics of Artificial Intelligence in Healthcare: Diagnosis vs. Treatment. *Healthcare (Basel), 10*(12). https://doi.org/ https://doi.org/10.3390/healthcare10122493 PMID: 36554017

Nazar Waheed, A. U. (2023, Apr 16). *FedBlockHealth: A Synergistic Approach to Privacy and Security in IoT-Enabled Healthcare through Federated Learning and Blockchain.* arxiv logo. https://arxiv.org/abs/2304.07668

Neumiller, T. K. (2019). Medtronic MiniMed 670G Hybrid Closed-Loop System. *Clinical Diabetes : a Publication of the American Diabetes Association, 37*(1), 94–95. DOI: 10.2337/cd18-0067 PMID: 30705505

Nikhil Sahni, G. S. (2023, Jan). *The Potential Impact of Artificial Intelligence on Healthcare Spending.* National Bureau of Economic Research. https://www.nber .org/papers/w30857

Olaoye, E. F. (2024). Privacy and data protection in AI-enabled healthcare systems. https://doi.org/https://www.researchgate.net/publication/378287462_Privacy_and _data_protection_in_AI-enabled_healthcare_systems

Pradipta Biswas, S. S. (2023). Recent advances in robot-assisted surgical systems. *Biomedical Engineering Advances, 6*, •••. https://doi.org/https://doi.org/10.1016/ j.bea.2023.100109

Prof, H. M. (2008). Rehabilitation and Health Care Robotics. In *Springer Handbook of Robotics.* Springer.

Reiner, G. (2019). *Aidoc Brings Lifesaving AI Advancements to Medical Imaging on AWS.* Amazon Web Services. https://aws.amazon.com/solutions/case-studies/ aidoc-case-study/

Imroz khan, D. A. 2024. Internet of Things IoT Its Applications and Enabling Technologies in Healthcare: Review, A. *Educational Administration: Theory and Practice, 30*(4). https://doi.org/https://doi.org/10.53555/kuey.v30i4.5031

Sarah, A., & Alzakari, A. A. (2024). Enhanced heart disease prediction in remote healthcare monitoring using IoT-enabled cloud-based XGBoost and Bi-LSTM. *Alexandria Engineering Journal, 105*, 280–291. https://doi.org/https://doi.org/10 .1016/j.aej.2024.06.036

Shreyas Suresh Rao, S. L. (2023). *AIoT and Big Data Analytics for Smart Healthcare Applications*. Bentham Science Publishers., DOI: 10.2174/97898151960541230501

Siddhant Thapliyal, M. W. (2024). Secure Artificial Intelligence of Things (AIoT)-enabled authenticated key agreement technique for smart living environment. *Computers & Electrical Engineering, 118*, •••. https://doi.org/https://doi.org/10.1016/j.compeleceng.2024.109353

Sofia, C., & Pereira, A. M. (2024). Automated image label extraction from radiology reports — A review. *Artificial Intelligence in Medicine, 149*, •••. https://doi.org/https://doi.org/10.1016/j.artmed.2024.102814

. Stephanie B. Baker, W. X. (2017). Internet of Things for Smart Healthcare: Technologies, Challenges, and Opportunities. *IEEE Xplore*, 26521 - 26544. https://doi.org/DOI: 10.1109/ACCESS.2017.2775180

Suresh Babu, C. V. M. S. (2024). AIoT Revolution: Transforming Networking Productivity for the Digital Age. In *Artificial Intelligence of Things (AIoT) for Productivity and Organizational Transition*. IGI Global.

Sushil Bhardwaj, I. S. (2025). Exploring the Role of AIoT in Data Privacy and Security. In M. U. Tariq, *Merging Artificial Intelligence With the Internet of Things* (pp. 75-102). IGI Global.

Tetiana Habuza, A. N. (2021). AI applications in robotics, diagnostic image analysis and precision medicine: Current limitations, future trends, guidelines on CAD systems for medicine. *Informatics in Medicine Unlocked, 24*, •••. https://doi.org/https://doi.org/10.1016/j.imu.2021.100596

Timothy Malche, S. T. (2022). Artificial Intelligence of Things- (AIoT-) Based Patient Activity Tracking System for Remote Patient Monitoring. *Journal of Healthcare Engineering*. https://doi.org/ https://doi.org/10.1155/2022/8732213

Wachler., & Associates. P.C. (2024, Feb 16). *AI and Healthcare Regulatory Compliance*. Wachler & Associates, P.C. https://www.wachlerblog.com/ai-and-healthcare-regulatory-compliance/

Wang, H. K. A. (2025). HealthAIoT: AIoT-driven smart healthcare system for sustainable cloud computing environments. *Internet of Things, 31*. https://doi.org/https://doi.org/10.1016/j.iot.2025.101555

Wu, B. L. (2022). Digital Transformation in Personalized Medicine with Artificial Intelligence and the Internet of Medical Things. *OMICS: A Journal of Integrative Biology, 26*(2). https://doi.org/https://doi.org/10.1089/omi.2021.0037 PMID: 33887155

Compilation of References

Aakula, A., Zhang, C., & Ahmad, T. (2024). Leveraging AI And Blockchain For Strategic Advantage In Digital Transformation. *Journal of Artificial Intelligence Research*, *4*(1), 356–395.

Abbasi, S., Saeideh, S., Farbod, E., & Yousefi, M. (2024). Hybrid data mining and data-driven algorithms for a green logistics transportation network in the post-COVID era : A case study in the USA. *Systems and Soft Computing*, *6*(July), 200156. DOI: 10.1016/j.sasc.2024.200156

Abdalla, R., Pavlova, M., & Groot, W. (2023). Prioritizing outcome measures for value-based healthcare: Physicians' perspectives in Saudi Arabia. *Value in Health Regional Issues*, *37*, 62–70. DOI: 10.1016/j.vhri.2023.05.002 PMID: 37327619

Adeghe, E. P., Okolo, C. A., & Ojeyinka, O. T. (2024). The influence of patient-reported outcome measures on healthcare delivery: A review of methodologies and applications. *OARJ of Biology and Pharmacy, 10*(02), 013-021.

Adeghe, E. P., Okolo, C. A., & Ojeyinka, O. T. (2024). The influence of patient-reported outcome measures on healthcare delivery: A review of methodologies and applications. *Open Access Research Journal of Biology and Pharmacy*, *10*(2), 13–21. DOI: 10.53022/oarjbp.2024.10.2.0014

Adu, M. D., Malabu, U. H., Malau-Aduli, A. E. O., & Malau-Aduli, B. S. (2019). Enablers and barriers to effective diabetes self-management: A multi-national investigation. *PLoS One*, *14*(6), e0217771. DOI: 10.1371/journal.pone.0217771 PMID: 31166971

Adusumilli, S., Damancharla, H., & Metta, A. (2023). Enhancing Data Privacy in Healthcare Systems Using Blockchain Technology. *Transactions on Latest Trends in Artificial Intelligence*, *4*(4), 1–19.

Aellen, F. M., Alnes, S. L., Loosli, F., Rossetti, A. O., Zubler, F., De Lucia, M., & Tzovara, A. (2023). Auditory stimulation and deep learning predict awakening from coma after cardiac arrest. *Brain, 146*(2), 778–788. PMID: 36637902

Agriculture, U. S. D. o. FoodData Central. https://fdc.nal.usda.gov/

Ahern, S., Ruseckaite, R., & Ackerman, I. N. (2017). Collecting patient-reported outcome measures. *Internal Medicine Journal, 47*(12), 1454–1457. DOI: 10.1111/imj.13633 PMID: 29224197

Ahlan, A. R., & Ahmad, B. I. (2015). An overview of patient acceptance of health information technology in developing countries: A review and conceptual model. *International Journal of Information Systems and Project Management, 3*(1), 29–48.

Ahmed, M., Dar, A. R., Helfert, M., Khan, A., & Kim, J. (2023). Data provenance in healthcare: Approaches, challenges, and future directions. *Sensors (Basel), 23*(14), 6495. PMID: 37514788

Ahmed, T., Mosaddeque, A., Hossain, A., Twaha, U., Rowshon, M., & Babu, B. (2022). The Dynamics of AI and Automation in Financial Forecasting, Human Resources Planning, and Resources Optimization for Designing an Effective National Healthcare Policy. *Journal of Business Insight and Innovation, 1*(2), 78–88.

Ait Abdelouahid, R., Debauche, O., Mahmoudi, S., & Marzak, A. (2023). Literature review: Clinical data interoperability models. *Information (Basel), 14*(7), 364.

Ajzen, I. (1991). The theory of planned behavior. *Organizational Behavior and Human Decision Processes, 50*(2), 179–211. DOI: 10.1016/0749-5978(91)90020-T

Akter, S., D'Ambra, J., & Ray, P. (2010). Trustworthiness in health information services: An assessment of a hierarchical model with mediating and moderating effects using partial least squares (PLS). *Journal of the American Society for Information Science and Technology, 62*(1), 100–116. DOI: 10.1002/asi.21442

Al Sayah, F., Jin, X., & Johnson, J. A. (2021). Selection of patient-reported outcome measures (PROMs) for use in health systems. *Journal of Patient-Reported Outcomes, 5*, 1–5. PMID: 34637010

Alabdulatif, A., Al Asqah, M., Moulahi, T., & Zidi, S. (2023). Leveraging artificial intelligence in blockchain-based e-health for safer decision making framework. *Applied Sciences (Basel, Switzerland), 13*(2), 1035.

Alberti, K. G. M. M., & Zimmet, P. Z. (1998). Definition, diagnosis and classification of diabetes mellitus and its complications. Part 1: Diagnosis and classification of diabetes mellitus. Provisional report of a WHO Consultation. *Diabetic Medicine*, *15*(7), 539–553. https://doi.org/https://doi.org/10.1002/(SICI)1096-9136(199807)15:7<539:AID-DIA668>3.0.CO;2-S PMID: 9686693

Alharbi, R., Tamma, V., Grasso, F., & Payne, T. R. (2024). Investigating open source LLMs to retrofit competency questions in ontology engineering. In *Proceedings of the AAAI Symposium Series* (Vol. 4, No. 1, pp. 188-198).

Alhasani, A. T., Alkattan, H., Subhi, A. A., & Eid, M. M. (2023). *A Comparative Analysis of Methods for Detecting and Diagnosing Breast Cancer Based on Data Mining*. *04*(02), 8–17.

Ali, A., Almaiah, M. A., Hajjej, F., Pasha, M. F., Fang, O. H., Khan, R., Teo, J., & Zakarya, M. (2022). An Industrial IoT-Based Blockchain-Enabled Secure Searchable Encryption Approach for Healthcare Systems Using Neural Network. *Sensors (Basel)*, *22*(2), 572. DOI: 10.3390/s22020572 PMID: 35062530

Alifia Hasan, N. P. (2025). Aligning AI principles and healthcare delivery organization best practices to navigate the shifting regulatory landscape. *npj digital medicine*, *8*(278). https://doi.org/https://doi.org/10.1038/s41746-025-01605-2

Aljohani, M., Hou, J., Kommu, S., & Wang, X. (2025). A comprehensive survey on the trustworthiness of large language models in healthcare. *arXiv preprint arXiv:2502.15871*.

Alowais, S. A., Alghamdi, S. S., Alsuhebany, N., Alqahtani, T., Alshaya, A. I., Almohareb, S. N., & Albekairy, A. M. (2023). Revolutionizing healthcare: The role of artificial intelligence in clinical practice. *BMC Medical Education*, *23*(1), 689. PMID: 37740191

Alrabei, A. M. (2023). Green electronic auditing and accounting information reliability in the Jordanian social security corporation: The mediating role of cloud computing. *International Journal of Financial Studies*, *11*(3), 114.

Alsahli, S. S., Almalki, M. H. M., Alkhathami, A. M., Alharbi, A. A., Alhawit, M. E., Albalawi, K. I., & Binselm, K. R. A. (2020). Quality Improvement and Patient Safety: Strategies and Challenges in Healthcare System Transformation. *International Journal of Health Sciences*, *4*(S1), 478–497.

Al-shanableh, N., Al-zyoud, M., Al-husban, R. Y., Al-shdayfat, N., & Alkhawaldeh, J. M. (2024). *Data Mining to Reveal Factors Associated with Quality of life among Jordanian Women with Breast Cancer*. *408*(2), 403–408.

Alsubaie, S. S., Bukhamseen, Z. F. A., Alyami, F. S. A., Alotaibi, M. F., Alkahtani, F. A., Alkhamsan, M. S., & Al Khamees, Z. H. (2024). Multidisciplinary Approaches in General Medical Practice: Enhancing Collaboration for Better Patient Care. *Journal of Ecohumanism*, *3*(7), 2659–2669.

Alty, S. R., Millasseau, S. C., Chowienczyk, P. J., & Jakobsson, A. (2003). Cardiovascular Disease Prediction Using Support Vector Machines. *Midwest Symposium on Circuits and Systems, 1*(August 2015), 376–379. https://doi.org/DOI: 10.1109/MWSCAS.2003.1562297

Andrew, J., Isravel, D. P., Sagayam, K. M., Bhushan, B., Sei, Y., & Eunice, J. (2023). Blockchain for healthcare systems: Architecture, security challenges, trends and future directions. *Journal of Network and Computer Applications*, *215*, 103633.

Andrikopoulou, E. (2023). The rise of AI in telehealth. In *Emerging Practices in Telehealth* (pp. 183–207). Academic Press., DOI: 10.1016/B978-0-443-15980-0.00011-9

Androulaki, E., Barger, A., Bortnikov, V., Cachin, C., Christidis, K., De Caro, A., . . . Yellick, J. (2018). Hyperledger Fabric: a distributed operating system for permissioned blockchains. In *Proceedings of the thirteenth EuroSys conference*. Available at: https://dl.acm.org/doi/pdf/10.1145/3190508.3190538

Angeioplastis, A., Aliprantis, J., & Konstantakis, M. (2025). *Predicting Student Performance and Enhancing Learning Outcomes : A Data-Driven Approach Using Educational Data Mining Techniques*. 1–21.

Anil Audumbar Pise, K. K. (2022). Enabling Artificial Intelligence of Things (AIoT) Healthcare Architectures and Listing Security Issues. *Computational Intelligence and Neuroscience, 2022*, •••. https://doi.org/https://doi.org/10.1155/2022/8421434 PMID: 36911247

Ante, L. (2021). Smart contracts on the blockchain–A bibliometric analysis and review. *Telematics and Informatics*, *57*, 101519.

Antonio, J., Torres, O., Santiago, A. M., Manuel, J., Izaguirre, V., García, M. A., & Hernández, A. D. (2022). *Hypertension Diagnosis with Backpropagation Neural Networks for Sustainability in Public Health*. 1–20.

Antunes, R. S., André da Costa, C., Küderle, A., Yari, I. A., & Eskofier, B. (2022). Federated learning for healthcare: Systematic review and architecture proposal. [TIST]. *ACM Transactions on Intelligent Systems and Technology*, *13*(4), 1–23.

Armitage, H. (2019). Any way you slice it, there's a lot to say about nutrition studies. Scope blog Stanford, accessed 28-2-2025: https://scopeblog.stanford.edu/2019/01/28/any-way-you-slice-it-nutrition-studies-are-controversial/

Associação Brasileira de Normas Técnicas. (2015). *NBR ISO 9001: Sistemas de gestão da qualidade: Requisitos*. ABNT.

Auth0. (2010). *JSON Web Tokens (JWT)*. https://jwt.io/

Avula, R., & Tummala, S. (2021). Assessing the Impact of Data Quality on Predictive Analytics in Healthcare: Strategies, Tools, and Techniques for Ensuring Accuracy, Completeness, and Timeliness in Electronic Health Records. *Sage Science Review of Applied Machine Learning*, 4(2), 31–47. Retrieved from https://journals.sagescience.org/index.php/ssraml/article/view/203

Aydoğan, Ş. K., Pura, T., & BİngüI, F. (2024). *Predicting Students ' Academic Performances Using Machine Learning Algorithms in Educational Data Mining. 12*(4).

Ayers, D. C. (2017). Implementation of patient-reported outcome measures in total knee arthroplasty. *JAAOS-Journal of the American Academy of Orthopaedic Surgeons, 25*, S48–S50. DOI: 10.5435/JAAOS-D-16-00631 PMID: 27941415

Azad, C., Bhushan, B., Sharma, R., Shankar, A., & Kant, K. (2022). Prediction model using SMOTE, genetic algorithm and decision tree (PMSGD) for classification of diabetes mellitus. *Multimedia Systems*, •••, 1289–1307. DOI: 10.1007/s00530-021-00817-2

Babaei Giglou, H., D'Souza, J., & Auer, S. (2023). LLMs4OL: Large language models for ontology learning. In *Proceedings of International Semantic Web Conference* (pp. 408-427).

Badimon, L., Chagas, P., & Chiva-Blanch, G. (2019). Diet and Cardiovascular Disease: Effects of Foods and Nutrients in Classical and Emerging Cardiovascular Risk Factors. *Current Medicinal Chemistry, 26*(19), 3639–3651.

Bahani, K., Moujabbir, M., & Ramdani, M. (2021). An accurate fuzzy rule-based classification systems for heart disease diagnosis. *Scientific African, 14*, e01019. DOI: 10.1016/j.sciaf.2021.e01019

Bahrami Rad, A., Kirsch, M., Li, Q., Xue, J., Sameni, R., Albert, D., & Clifford, G. D. (2024). A crowdsourced AI framework for atrial fibrillation detection in Apple watch and Kardia mobile ECGs. *Sensors (Basel), 24*(17), 5708. PMID: 39275619

Balch, J. A., Chatham, A. H., Hong, P. K., Manganiello, L., Baskaran, N., Bihorac, A., & Loftus, T. J. (2024). Predicting patient-reported outcome measures: A scoping review for the artificial intelligence-guided patient preference predictor. *Frontiers in Artificial Intelligence*, *7*, 1477447. PMID: 39564457

Baliga, A., Subhod, I., Kamat, P., & Chatterjee, S. (2018). Performance evaluation of the quorum blockchain platform. *Available at:* https://arxiv.org/pdf/1809.03421

Barnard, R. J. (2018). How the Egg Industry Skews Science. YouTube, accessed 26-2-2024: https://www.youtube.com/watch?v=FyG8wr0gWIA

Barnard, N. D., Long, M. B., Ferguson, J. M., Flores, R., & Kahleova, H. (2021). Industry funding and cholesterol research: A systematic review. *American Journal of Lifestyle Medicine*, *15*(2), 165–172.

Bates, D. W., Deerberg-Wittram, J., Katz, G., Braeger, K., Hirsch, L. S., Kaplan, G. S., Kwietniewski, L., Meier, C. A., Laifer, C. P., & Zimlichman, E. (2023). Using publicly reported global hospital rankings to improve dissemination of patient-reported outcome measures (PROMs). *NEJM Catalyst Innovations in Care Delivery*, *4*(11), CAT-23. DOI: 10.1056/CAT.23.0097

Baumel, A., Faber, K., Mathur, N., Kane, J. M., & Muench, F. (2017). Enlight: A Comprehensive Quality and Therapeutic Potential Evaluation Tool for Mobile and Web-Based eHealth Interventions [Original Paper]. *Journal of Medical Internet Research*, *19*(3), e82. DOI: 10.2196/jmir.7270 PMID: 28325712

Beks, H., King, O., Clapham, R., Alston, L., Glenister, K., McKinstry, C., Quilliam, C., Wellwood, I., Williams, C., & Wong Shee, A. (2022). Community Health Programs Delivered Through Information and Communications Technology in High-Income Countries: Scoping Review. *Journal of Medical Internet Research*, *24*(3), e26515–e26515. DOI: 10.2196/26515 PMID: 35262498

Benjamens, S., Dhunnoo, P., & Meskó, B. (2020). The state of artificial intelligence-based FDA-approved medical devices and algorithms: An online database. *NPJ Digital Medicine*, *3*(1), 118. PMID: 32984550

Bensalloua, C. A., & Ahmed, O. (2018). Spatial OLAP and Multicriteria Integrated Approach for Decision Support System. *Application in Agroforestry Management.*, *10*(3), 1–26. DOI: 10.4018/IJDSST.2018070101

Bernardi, F. A., Alves, D., Crepaldi, N., Yamada, D. B., Lima, V. C., & Rijo, R. (2023). Data Quality in Health Research: Integrative Literature Review. *Journal of Medical Internet Research*, *25*, e41446. DOI: 10.2196/41446 PMID: 37906223

Bertoncelli, C. M., Altamura, P., Bagui, S., Bagui, S., Vieira, E. R., Costantini, S., Monticone, M., Solla, F., & Bertoncelli, D. (2022). *Predicting osteoarthritis in adults using statistical data mining and machine learning*. *X*, 1–12. https://doi.org/DOI: 10.1177/1759720X221104935

Bes-Rastrollo, M., Schulze, M. B., Ruiz-Canela, M., & Martinez-Gonzalez, M. A. (2013). Financial conflicts of interest and reporting bias regarding the association between sugar-sweetened beverages and weight gain: A systematic review of systematic reviews. *PLoS Medicine*, *10*(12), e1001578.

Bianchim, M. S., Crane, E., Jones, A., Neukirchinger, B., Roberts, G., & McLaughlin, L.. (2023). The implementation, use, and impact of patient-reported outcome measures in value-based healthcare programmes: A scoping review. *PLoS One*, *18*(12), e0290976. DOI: 10.1371/journal.pone.0290976 PMID: 38055759

Biao, Z. Z. (2023). Journal of King Saud University - Science Design and realization of data mining simulation and methodological models. *Journal of King Saud University. Science*, *35*(10), 102964. DOI: 10.1016/j.jksus.2023.102964

Biondi-Zoccai, G., Frati, G., Peruzzi, M., Bernardi, M., Spadafora, L., & Tremoli, E. (2025). Patient-reported outcome measures in cardiovascular research and care: PRO(M)s and CONS. *Journal of Cardiovascular Pharmacology*, *85*(4), 261–266. DOI: 10.1097/FJC.0000000000001669 PMID: 39847595

Black, N. (2013). Patient reported outcome measures could help transform healthcare. *BMJ (Clinical Research Ed.)*, *346*. Advance online publication. DOI: 10.1136/bmj.f167 PMID: 23358487

Bommu, R. (2022). Ethical Considerations in the Development and Deployment of AI-powered Medical Device Software: Balancing Innovation with Patient Welfare. *Journal of Innovative Technologies*, *5*(1), 1–7.

Bouhouita-Guermech, S., & Haidar, H. (2024). Scoping review shows the dynamics and complexities inherent to the notion of "responsibility" in artificial intelligence within the healthcare context. *ABR, 16*, 315–344. https://doi.org/DOI: 10.1007/s41649-024-00292-7

Božić, V. (2024). DIGITAL HEALTH AND COMMUNICATION -A REVOLUTION WITH CAUTIONS. https://doi.org/https://www.researchgate.net/publication/379823590_DIGITAL_HEALTH_AND_COMMUNICATION_-A_REVOLUTION_WITH_CAUTIONS

Braun, V., & Clarke, V. (2006). Using thematic analysis in psychology. *Qualitative Research in Psychology*, *3*(2), 77–101. https://url.au.m.mimecastprotect.com/s/VmMnCXLK3oUvE1JwtksxHWVmHz?domain=doi.org

Brew-Sam, N. (2020). Diabetes App Use – Previous mHealth Research. In *App Use and Patient Empowerment in Diabetes Self-Management: Advancing Theory-Guided mHealth Research* (pp. 29–38). Springer Fachmedien Wiesbaden., DOI: 10.1007/978-3-658-29357-4_4

Brooks, R. (1996). EuroQol: The current state of play. *Health Policy (Amsterdam)*, *37*(1), 53–72. DOI: 10.1016/0168-8510(96)00822-6 PMID: 10158943

Brown, S. A., & Venkatesh, V. (2005). Model of adoption of technology in households: A baseline model test and extension incorporating household life cycle. *Management Information Systems Quarterly*, *29*(3), 399–426. DOI: 10.2307/25148690

Brown, T. B., Mann, B., Ryder, N., Subbiah, M., Kaplan, J., Dhariwal, P., & Amodei, D. (2020). Language models are few-shot learners. *Advances in Neural Information Processing Systems*, *33*, 1877–1901.

Build, S. (n.d.). *AI in healthcare: How Intelligent Products increase accessibility and equity*. Slalom Build. https://www.slalombuild.com/thinking/ai-in-healthcare-how-intelligent-products-increase-accessibility-and-equity

Bul, K., Holliday, N., Magee, P., & Wark, P. (2020). From development to exploitation of digital health solutions: Lessons learnt through multidisciplinary research and consultancy. *Journal of Enabling Technologies*, *14*(4), 273–279.

Byambasuren, O., Yang, Y., Sui, Z., Dai, D., Chang, B., Li, S., & Zan, H. (2019). Preliminary study on the construction of Chinese medical knowledge graph. *Journal of Chinese Information Processing*, *33*(10), 1–9.

Callahan, A., & Shah, N. H. (2017). Machine learning in healthcare. In *Key Advances in Clinical Informatics* (pp. 279–291). Academic Press., DOI: 10.1016/B978-0-12-809523-2.00019-4

Campbell, T. C., & Campbell, T. M. (2016). *The China study: Revised and expanded edition: The most comprehensive study of nutrition ever conducted and the startling implications for diet, weight loss, and long-term health*. BenBella Books, Inc.

Cao, L., Sun, J., & Cross, A. (2024). An automatic and end-to-end system for rare disease knowledge graph construction based on ontology-enhanced large language models: Development study. *JMIR Medical Informatics*, *12*(1), e60665.

Carey, R. M., & Whelton, P. K. (2020). Evidence for the universal blood pressure goal of< 130/80 mm Hg is strong: Controversies in hypertension-pro side of the argument. *Hypertension*, *76*(5), 1384–1390.

Casas, L. A., Alarcón, J., Urbano, A., Peña-Zárate, E. E., Sangiovanni, S., Libreros-Peña, L., & Escobar, M. F. (2023). Telemedicine for the management of diabetic patients in a high-complexity Latin American hospital. *BMC Health Services Research*, *23*(1), 314–314. DOI: 10.1186/s12913-023-09267-0 PMID: 36997918

Casazza, K., Fontaine, K. R., Astrup, A., Birch, L. L., Brown, A. W., Bohan Brown, M. M., & Allison, D. B. (2013). Myths, presumptions, and facts about obesity. *The New England Journal of Medicine*, *368*(5), 446–454.

Chabot, P. J., Cirino, C. M., & Gulotta, L. V. (2023). Machine learning: The what, why, and how. *Seminars in Arthroplasty*, *33*(4), 857–861.

Chandrasekaran, R., Katthula, V., & Moustakas, E. (2020). Patterns of use and key predictors for the use of wearable health care devices by US adults: Insights from a national survey. *Journal of Medical Internet Research*, *22*(10), e22443. DOI: 10.2196/22443 PMID: 33064083

Chaudhury, A. S.. (2023). Bringing patient-reported outcome measures (PROMs) into practice: A review of the latest developments in PROM use in the evaluation and treatment of carpal tunnel syndrome. *Journal of Hand Surgery Global Online*, *5*(4), 492–497. DOI: 10.1016/j.jhsg.2023.03.002 PMID: 37521564

Chavez, S., Fedele, D., Guo, Y., Bernier, A., Smith, M., Warnick, J., & Modave, F. (2017). Mobile Apps for the Management of Diabetes. *Diabetes Care*, *40*(10), e145–e146. DOI: 10.2337/dc17-0853 PMID: 28774944

Chen, J., Li, P., Fang, W., Zhou, N., Yin, Y., Zheng, H., Xu, H., & Wang, R. (2021). *Fuzzy Frequent Pattern Mining Algorithm Based on Weighted Sliding Window and Type-2 Fuzzy Sets over Medical Data Stream. 2021*(1997). https://doi.org/DOI: 10.1155/2021/6662254

Chen, J., Yan, M., Howe, R. L. C., Tong, N. W., Chee, C. S., Niu, W., . . . Chen, G. (2019, July). Biovitals™: a personalized multivariate physiology analytics using continuous mobile biosensors. In 2019 41st Annual International Conference of the IEEE Engineering in Medicine and Biology Society (EMBC) (pp. 3243-3248). IEEE.

Chen, Y., Huang, D., Xu, H., Fu, C., Sheng, L., Zhou, Q., Shen, Y., & Wang, K. (2025). MedCT: A clinical terminology graph for generative AI applications in healthcare. *arXiv preprint arXiv:2501.06465.*

Cheng, L., Zhu, M., Poss, J. W., Hirdes, J. P., Glenny, C., & Stolee, P. (2015). Opinion versus practice regarding the use of rehabilitation services in-home care: An investigation using machine learning algorithms. *BMC Medical Informatics and Decision Making*, *15*, 1–11. PMID: 26453354

Chen, I. Y., Pierson, E., Rose, S., Joshi, S., Ferryman, K., & Ghassemi, M. (2021). Ethical machine learning in healthcare. *Annual Review of Biomedical Data Science*, *4*(1), 123–144. PMID: 34396058

Chen, Y., & Esmaeilzadeh, P. (2024). Generative AI in medical practice: In-depth exploration of privacy and security challenges. *Journal of Medical Internet Research*, *26*, e53008.

Chhajer, P., Shah, M., & Kshirsagar, A. (2022). The applications of artificial neural networks, support vector machines, and long – short term memory for stock market prediction. *Decision Analytics Journal, 2*(June 2021), 100015. https://doi.org/DOI: 10.1016/j.dajour.2021.100015

Cho, N. H., Shaw, J. E., Karuranga, S., Huang, Y., da Rocha Fernandes, J. D., Ohlrogge, A. W., & Malanda, B. (2018). IDF Diabetes Atlas: Global estimates of diabetes prevalence for 2017 and projections for 2045. *Diabetes Research and Clinical Practice*, *138*, 271–281. DOI: 10.1016/j.diabres.2018.02.023 PMID: 29496507

Chowdhury, R. H. (2024). Blockchain and AI: Driving the future of data security and business intelligence. *World Journal of Advanced Research and Reviews*, *23*(1), 2559–2570.

Chunara, R., Zhao, Y., Chen, J., Lawrence, K., Testa, P. A., Nov, O., & Mann, D. M. (2021). Telemedicine and healthcare disparities: A cohort study in a large healthcare system in New York City during COVID-19. *Journal of the American Medical Informatics Association : JAMIA*, *28*(1), 33–41. DOI: 10.1093/jamia/ocaa217 PMID: 32866264

Cimini, C. C. R., Maia, J. X., Pires, M. C., & Ribeiro, L. B., de Oliveira e Almeida Pinto, V. S., Batchelor, J., Ribeiro, A. L. P., & Marcolino, M. S. (2022). Pandemic-Related Impairment in the Monitoring of Patients With Hypertension and Diabetes and the Development of a Digital Solution for the Community Health Worker: Quasiexperimental and Implementation Study [Article]. *JMIR Medical Informatics*, *10*(3), e35216. Advance online publication. DOI: 10.2196/35216 PMID: 35191842

Cîmpan, I., & Cri an, E. L. (2025). Blockchain concepts in business research–a scoping review. *Management Matters*. Available at: https://www.emerald.com/insight/content/doi/10.1108/manm-06-2024-0034/full/pdf

Ciro Mennella, U. M. (2024). Ethical and regulatory challenges of AI technologies in healthcare: A narrative review. *Heliyon, 10*(4). https://doi.org/https://doi.org/10.1016/j.heliyon.2024.e26297 PMID: 38384518

CMMI Institute. (n.d.). *What is a maturity level? Capability level? How are they different?* https://cmmiinstitute.zendesk.com/hc/en-us/articles/216334148-What-is-a-maturity-level-Capability-level-How-are-they-different-

CMMI Product Team. (2006, August). *CMMI for development* (Version 1.2). Software Engineering Institute, Carnegie Mellon University.

Coleman, K. (2024). *Lowering Health Care Costs Through AI The Possibilities and Barriers*. Paragon Health Institute.

Community, G. (2017). *Flutter*. Google and Community. https://flutter.dev/

Contreras, M., Sena, J., Davidson, A., Zhang, J., Ozrazgat-Baslanti, T., Ren, Y., Guan, Z., ... (2025). "MANDARIN: Mixture-of-Experts Framework for Dynamic Delirium and Coma Prediction in ICU Patients: Development and Validation of an Acute Brain Dysfunction Prediction Model." arXiv preprint arXiv:2503.06059

Correia, P. H., Barcha, M. A., Marques, M. A., Simplicio, L., & Ermlivitch, C. C. Miers, and. Pillon, M. A. (2024). "Comparative Analysis of Permissioned Blockchains: Cosmos, Hyperledger Fabric, Quorum, and XRPL." In *2024 IEEE International Conference on Blockchain (Blockchain)*, pp. 464-469. Available at: https://ieeexplore.ieee.org/abstract/document/10664236

Cortez, N. G., Cohen, I. G., & Kesselheim, A. S. (2014). FDA Regulation of Mobile Health Technologies. *The New England Journal of Medicine, 371*(4), 372–379. DOI: 10.1056/NEJMhle1403384 PMID: 25054722

Cournan, M., Fusco-Gessick, B., & Wright, L. (2016). Improving patient Safety through Video Monitoring. *Rehabilitation Nursing, 0*, 1–6. DOI: 10.1002/rnj.308

Creswell, J. W., & Plano Clark, V. L. (2018). *Designing and conducting mixed methods research* (3rd ed.). Sage Publications.

Crowson, M. G., & Chan, T. C. Y. (2020). Machine learning as a catalyst for value-based health care. *Journal of Medical Systems, 44*(1), 139. DOI: 10.1007/s10916-020-01607-5 PMID: 32681388

Cuzzocrea, A. (2024). ScienceDirect ScienceDirect Evolving OLAP and BI towards Complex, High-Performance Big- OLAP-Data-Cube-Processing Analytics Frameworks : How to Speed-Up Large-Scale, High-Dimensional Queries over Clouds. *Procedia Computer Science, 246*, 4169–4175. DOI: 10.1016/j.procs.2024.09.256

Czmil, A. (2023). *Medical Applications*. 1–20.

Dafir, Z., Lamari, Y., & Chah, S. (2021). A survey on parallel clustering algorithms for Big Data. In *Artificial Intelligence Review* (Vol. 54, Issue 4). Springer Netherlands. https://doi.org/DOI: 10.1007/s10462-020-09918-2

Dahake, A., Adhau, R., Ghosh, M., & Thakre, L. (2025). "A Holistic Approach to Health Management and Integrated Fitness Mobile Application for Nutritionists, Dietitians, and Patients." In *2025 IEEE International Conference on Interdisciplinary Approaches in Technology and Management for Social Innovation (IATMSI)*, vol. 3, pp. 1-7. IEEE.

Dahr, J. M., Hamoud, A. K., Najm, I. A., & Ahmed, M. I. (2022). IMPLEMENTING SALES DECISION SUPPORT SYSTEM USING DATA MART BASED ON OLAP. *KPI, AND DATA MINING APPROACHES.*, *17*(1), 275–293.

Damoah, I. S., Ayakwah, A., & Tingbani, I. (2021). Artificial intelligence (AI)-enhanced medical drones in the healthcare supply chain (HSC) for sustainability development: A case study. *Journal of Cleaner Production*, *328*, 129598.

Danaher, B. G., Brendryen, H., Seeley, J. R., Tyler, M. S., & Woolley, T. (2015). From black box to toolbox: Outlining device functionality, engagement activities, and the pervasive information architecture of mHealth interventions. *Internet Interventions : the Application of Information Technology in Mental and Behavioural Health*, *2*(1), 91–101. DOI: 10.1016/j.invent.2015.01.002 PMID: 25750862

Daneshjou, R., Smith, M. P., Sun, M. D., Rotemberg, V., & Zou, J. (2021). Lack of transparency and potential bias in artificial intelligence data sets and algorithms: A scoping review. *JAMA Dermatology*, *157*(11), 1362–1369. PMID: 34550305

Dankan Gowda, V. M. K. (2024). AIoT Integration Advancements and Challenges in Smart Sensing Technologies for Smart Devices. In *AIoT and Smart Sensing Technologies for Smart Devices*. IGI Global.

Das, D., Ghosh, M., Raut, M., & Thakre, L. (2025, April). Enhancing Ophthalmologic Infrastructure: Seamless Integration. In Proceedings of the 15th International Conference on Soft Computing and Pattern Recognition (SoCPaR 2023): Volume 1: Smart Healthcare (Vol. 1243, p. 54). Springer Nature.

Das, D., Ghosh, M., Raut, M., Thakre, L., & Jichkar, R. (2023). "Enhancing Ophthalmologic Infrastructure: Seamless Integration of Deep Convolutional Neural Networks for Real-Time Ocular Disease Detection." In International Conference on Soft Computing and Pattern Recognition, pp. 54-65. Cham: Springer Nature Switzerland.

Davardoost, F., Sangar, A. B., & Majidzadeh, K. (2022). *An Innovative Model for Extracting OLAP Cubes from NOSQL Database Based on Scalable Na ̈ ıve Bayes Classifier. 2022.*

Davis, F. D. (1989). Perceived usefulness, perceived ease of use, and user acceptance of information technology. *Management Information Systems Quarterly*, *13*(3), 319–340. DOI: 10.2307/249008

Davis, F. D., Bagozzi, R. P., & Warshaw, P. R. (1989). User acceptance of computer technology: A comparison of two theoretical models. *Management Science*, *35*(8), 982–1003. DOI: 10.1287/mnsc.35.8.982

Davoudi, A., Malhotra, K. R., Shickel, B., Siegel, S., Williams, S., Ruppert, M., Bihorac, E., ... (2018). "The intelligent ICU pilot study: using artificial intelligence technology for autonomous patient monitoring." arXiv preprint arXiv:1804.10201

Dawidziuk, A., Butters, E., Lindegger, D. J., Foubister, C., Chrost, H., Wlodarski, M., Grogan, J., Rowicka, P. A., Bremner, F., & Manohar, S. G. (2025). Can the Pupillary Light Reflex and Pupillary Unrest Be Used as Biomarkers of Parkinson's Disease? A Systematic Review and Meta-Analysis. *Diagnostics (Basel)*, *15*(9), 1167. PMID: 40361985

De Novi, G., Sofia, N., Vasiliu-Feltes, I., Zang, C. Y., & Ricotta, F. (2023). Blockchain technology predictions 2024: Transformations in healthcare, patient identity, and public health. *Blockchain in Healthcare Today*, *6*, 10–30953.

de Silva, U., Connell, S., Tapela, N., & Bright, J. (2023). Driving value through standardized measurement of patient-reported outcomes. *Journal of Patient Experience*, *10*, 1–8. DOI: 10.1177/23743735231202373 PMID: 37720908

Denniss, E., Lindberg, R., & McNaughton, S. A. (2023). Quality and accuracy of online nutrition-related information: A systematic review of content analysis studies. *Public Health Nutrition*, *26*(7), 1345–1357.

Devlin, J., Chang, M. W., Lee, K., & Toutanova, K. (2019). BERT: Pre-training of deep bidirectional transformers for language understanding. In *Proceedings of the Conference of the North American Chapter of the Association for Computational Linguistics: Human Language Technologies,* Volume 1 *(Long and Short papers)* (pp. 4171-4186).

Devlin, N. J., & Brooks, R. (2017). EQ-5D and the EuroQol Group: Past, present and future. *Applied Health Economics and Health Policy*, *15*(2), 127–137. DOI: 10.1007/s40258-017-0310-5 PMID: 28194657

Dewasiri, N. J., Rathnasiri, M. S. H., & Karunarathna, K. S. S. N. (2025). Artificial Intelligence-Driven Technologies for Environmental Sustainability in the Healthcare Industry. In *Transforming Healthcare Sector Through Artificial Intelligence and Environmental Sustainability* (pp. 67–87). Springer Nature Singapore.

Dhayanidhi, G. (2022). Research on IoT threats & implementation of AI/ML to address emerging cybersecurity issues in IoT with cloud computing. Available at: https://era.library.ualberta.ca/items/72d03629-a6ac-4e5d-8528-3f10b552cda7

Dhingra, S., Raut, R., Naik, K., & Muduli, K. (2024). Blockchain technology applications in healthcare supply chains– A review. *IEEE Access*. Available at: https://ieeexplore.ieee.org/stamp/stamp.jsp?arnumber=10379101

Di Basilio, D., King, L., Lloyd, S., Michael, P., & Shardlow, M. (2024). Asking questions that are "close to the bone": Integrating thematic analysis and natural language processing to explore the experiences of people with traumatic brain injuries engaging with patient-reported outcome measures. *Frontiers in Digital Health*, *6*, 1387139. PMID: 38983792

Digital Healthcare: This Software Marketplace Lets Hospitals Test-Drive AI-Powered Apps. (2020, December 14). General Electric Company. https://www.ge.com/news/reports/digital-healthcare-this-software-marketplace-lets-hospitals-test-drive-ai-powered-apps-0

Dignum, V. (2019). Ensuring Responsible AI in Practice. In Dignum, V. (Ed.), *Responsible Artificial Intelligence: How to Develop and Use AI in a Responsible Way* (pp. 93–105). Springer International Publishing., DOI: 10.1007/978-3-030-30371-6_6

Dineen-Griffin, S., Garcia-Cardenas, V., Williams, K., & Benrimoj, S. I. (2019). Helping patients help themselves: A systematic review of self-management support strategies in primary health care practice. *PLoS One*, *14*(8), e0220116.

Dodds, W. B., Monroe, K. B., & Grewal, D. (1991). Effects of price, brand, and store information on buyers' product evaluations. *JMR, Journal of Marketing Research*, *28*(3), 307–319. DOI: 10.1177/002224379102800305

Donnelly, K. (2006). SNOMED-CT: The advanced terminology and coding system for eHealth. *Studies in Health Technology and Informatics*, *121*, 279.

Drechsler, A., & Hevner, A. (2016). A four-cycle model of IS design science research: capturing the dynamic nature of IS artifact design.

Dua, P., & Bais, S. (2014). Supervised learning methods for fraud detection in healthcare insurance. *Machine Learning in Healthcare Informatics*, 261-285. Available at: https://link.springer.com/chapter/10.1007/978-3-642-40017-9_12

Duman-Lubberding, S., van Uden-Kraan, C. F., Jansen, F., Witte, B. I., Eerenstein, S. E., Van Weert, S., & Verdonck-de Leeuw, I. M. (2017). Durable usage of patient-reported outcome measures in clinical practice to monitor health-related quality of life in head and neck cancer patients. *Supportive Care in Cancer, 25*, 3775–3783. PMID: 28702685

Duncan, E. A., & Murray, J. (2012). The barriers and facilitators to routine outcome measurement by allied health professionals in practice: A systematic review. *BMC Health Services Research, 12*, 1–9. PMID: 22506982

Duong-Trung, N., Son, H. X., Le, H. T., & Phan, T. T. (2020). On components of a patient-centered healthcare system using smart contract. In *Proceedings of the 2020 4th International Conference on Cryptography, Security and Privacy*. Available at: https://shorturl.at/o3dSF

East, S. A., Wang, Y., Yanamala, N., Maganti, K., & Sengupta, P. P. (2025). Artificial Intelligence-Enabled Point-of-Care Echocardiography: Bringing Precision Imaging to the Bedside. *Current Atherosclerosis Reports, 27*(1), 70.

Ekramifard, A., Amintoosi, H., Seno, A. H., Dehghantanha, A., & Parizi, R. M. (2020). A systematic literature review of integration of blockchain and artificial intelligence. *Blockchain Cybersecurity, Trust and Privacy*, 147-160. Available at: https://link.springer.com/chapter/10.1007/978-3-030-38181-3_8

Elsedimy, E. I., AboHashish, S. M. M., & Algarni, F. (2024). New cardiovascular disease prediction approach using support vector machine and quantum-behaved particle swarm optimization. *Multimedia Tools and Applications, 83*(8), 23901–23928. DOI: 10.1007/s11042-023-16194-z

Enad, A. J., & Aksu, M. (2024). *Early prediction of COVID-19 infection using data mining and multi machine learning algorithms. 13*(3). https://doi.org/DOI: 10.11591/eei.v13i3.6912

Ergai, A., Spiva, L. A., Thurman, S., Hatfield, M., McCollum, M., & Holmes, M. (2024). The effectiveness of remote video monitoring on fall prevention and nurses acceptance. *Journal of Nursing Care Quality, 39*, 24–30. DOI: 10.1097/NCQ.0000000000000716

Escobar-Rodríguez, T., & Carvajal-Trujillo, E. (2014). Online purchasing tickets for low cost carriers: An application of the unified theory of acceptance and use of technology (UTAUT) model. *Tourism Management, 43*, 70–88. DOI: 10.1016/j.tourman.2014.01.017

Fabbri, A., Lai, A., Grundy, Q., & Bero, L. A. (2018). The influence of industry sponsorship on the research agenda: A scoping review. *American Journal of Public Health*, *108*(11), e9–e16.

Fair, O., Ali, A. B., Haener, M., Plotnikoff, K., Schaaf, N., Schmitt-Boshnick, M., & Soprovich, A. (2025). Use of patient-reported outcome measures (PROMs) in primary care-based mental health programming: An environmental scan of Alberta, Canada. *BMC Primary Care*, *26*(1), 71. PMID: 40089665

Farmer, M. S., Popescu, M., & Powell, K. (2025). Development and evaluation of a 4M taxonomy from nursing home staff text messages using a fine-tuned generative language model. *Journal of the American Medical Informatics Association : JAMIA*, *32*(3), 535–544.

FasterCapital. (n.d.). *Successful Business Applications Of Iot And Smart Devices.* Faster Capital. https://fastercapital.com/topics/successful-business-applications-of-iot-and-smart-devices.html

Fathallah, N., Das, A., Giorgis, S. D., Poltronieri, A., Haase, P., & Kovriguina, L. (2024). Neon-GPT: A large language model-powered pipeline for ontology learning. In *Proceedings of the European Semantic Web Conference* (pp. 36-50).

Faulkner, L. (2003). Beyond the five-user assumption: Benefits of increased sample sizes in usability testing. *Behavior Research Methods, Instruments, & Computers*, *35*, 379–383.

Federal Communications Commission (FCC). (2024). 2024 Broadband Deployment Report. https://www.fcc.gov/reports-research/reports/broadband-progress-reports

Federation, I. D. (2019). *IDF Diabetes Atlas* (9th ed.)., https://www.diabetesatlas.org

Feng, H., Yin, Y., Reynares, E., & Nanavati, J. (2025). OntologyRAG: Better and faster biomedical code mapping with retrieval-augmented generation (RAG) leveraging ontology knowledge graphs and large language models. *arXiv preprint arXiv:2502.18992*.

Fennelly, O., Moroney, D., Doyle, M., Eustace-Cook, J., & Hughes, M. (2024). Key interoperability factors for patient portals and electronic health records: A scoping review. *International Journal of Medical Informatics*, *183*, 105335. PMID: 38266425

Ferreira, S., Marinheiro, C., Mateus, C., Rodrigues, P. P., Rodrigues, M. A., & Rocha, N. (2024). Overcoming challenges in video-based health monitoring: Real-world implementation, ethics, and data considerations. *Sensors (Basel)*, *25*, 1–15. DOI: 10.3390/s25051357

Field, J., Holmes, M. M., & Newell, D. (2019). PROMs data: Can it be used to make decisions for individual patients? A narrative review. *Patient Related Outcome Measures*, *10*, 233–241. PMID: 31534379

Filip, R., Gheorghita Puscaselu, R., Anchidin-Norocel, L., Dimian, M., & Savage, W. K. (2022). Global Challenges to Public Health Care Systems during the COVID-19 Pandemic: A Review of Pandemic Measures and Problems. *Journal of Personalized Medicine*, *12*(8), 1295. DOI: 10.3390/jpm12081295 PMID: 36013244

Floridi, L., Cowls, J., Beltrametti, M., Chatila, R., Chazerand, P., Dignum, V., Luetge, C., Madelin, R., Pagallo, U., Rossi, F., Schafer, B., Valcke, P., & Vayena, E. (2018). AI4People—An Ethical Framework for a Good AI Society: Opportunities, Risks, Principles, and Recommendations. *Minds and Machines*, *28*(4), 689–707. DOI: 10.1007/s11023-018-9482-5 PMID: 30930541

Forresi, C., Gallinucci, E., Golfarelli, M., & Ben Hamadou, H. (2021). A dataspace-based framework for OLAP analyses in a high-variety multistore. *The VLDB Journal*, *30*(6), 1017–1040. DOI: 10.1007/s00778-021-00682-5

Fugkeaw, S., & Hak, L. (2024). PPAC-CDW : A Privacy-Preserving Access Control Scheme With Fast OLAP Query and Efficient Revocation for Cloud Data Warehouse. *IEEE Access : Practical Innovations, Open Solutions*, *12*(June), 78743–78758. DOI: 10.1109/ACCESS.2024.3408221

Fu, H., McMahon, S. K., Gross, C. R., Adam, T. J., & Wyman, J. F. (2017). Usability and clinical efficacy of diabetes mobile applications for adults with type 2 diabetes: A systematic review. *Diabetes Research and Clinical Practice*, *131*, 70–81. DOI: 10.1016/j.diabres.2017.06.016 PMID: 28692830

Funk, M., Hosemann, S., Jung, J. C., & Lutz, C. (2023). Towards ontology construction with language models. *arXiv preprint arXiv:2309.09898.*

Gadde, S. S., & Kalli, V. D. R. (2020). Applications of Artificial Intelligence in Medical Devices and Healthcare. *International Journal of Computer Science Trends and Technology*, *8*, 182–188.

Gaidai, O., Cao, Y., & Loginov, S. (2023). Global Cardiovascular Diseases Death Rate Prediction. *Current Problems in Cardiology*, *48*(5), 101622.

Gao, Y., Xiong, Y., Gao, X., Jia, K., Pan, J., Bi, Y., . . . Wang, H. (2023). Retrieval-augmented generation for large language models: A survey. *arXiv preprint arXiv:2312.10997, 2.*

Gao, Y., Li, H., & Luo, Y. (2015). An empirical study of wearable technology acceptance in healthcare. *Industrial Management & Data Systems, 115*(10), 1704–1723. DOI: 10.1108/IMDS-03-2015-0087

Garbacz, P. (2024). Large language models and foundational ontologies. In *Formal Ontology in Information Systems* (pp. 89–103). IOS Press.

Gardner, R. S., Singh, J. P., Stancak, B., Nair, D. G., Cao, M., Schulze, C., & Boehmer, J. P. (2018). HeartLogic multisensor algorithm identifies patients during periods of significantly increased risk of heart failure events: Results from the MultiSENSE study. *Circulation: Heart Failure, 11*(7), e004669. PMID: 30002113

Gefen, D., Karahanna, E., & Straub, D. W. (2003). Trust and TAM in online shopping: An integrated model. *Management Information Systems Quarterly, 27*(1), 51–90. DOI: 10.2307/30036519

Geonwoo Ji, J. W. (2024). AIoT-Based Smart Healthcare in Everyday Lives: Data Collection and Standardization From Smartphones and Smartwatches. *IEEE Internet of Things Journal, 11*(16), 27597–27619. https://doi.org/https://doi.org/10.1109/JIOT.2024.3400509

Ge, Q., Huang, L., Fu, Q., Han, S., Wang, R., He, J., Li, C., Luo, J., & Xu, L. (2025). Bedside cerebral microvascular imaging of patients with disorders of consciousness: A feasibility study. *Frontiers in Neuroscience, 19*, 1518023. PMID: 40012684

Ghazal, T. M., Hussain, M. Z., Said, R. A., & Nadeem, A. (2021). *Performances of K-Means Clustering Algorithm with Different Distance Metrics*. https://doi.org/DOI: 10.32604/iasc.2021.019067

Ghorbian, M., & Ghorbian, S. (2025). Empowering Clinical Decision-Making with Generative AI in Intelligent Decision Support Systems. In *Generative Artificial Intelligence (AI) Approaches for Industrial Applications* (pp. 241–259). Springer Nature Switzerland.

Ghosh, M., Raut, M., Parteki, R., Das, D., Thakare, L. P., Jichkar, R., Rathore, S. S., & Bawankar, S. (2023). "An analysis of deep-neural-network model for the determination of the bit-rate of optical fiber signals." In 2023 11th International Conference on Emerging Trends in Engineering & Technology-Signal and Information Processing (ICETET-SIP), pp. 1-4. IEEE.

Ghosh, M. (2022). "Comparative DNN model analysis for detection of various types of optical noise." *Authorea Preprints*

Ghosh, M., & Bora, V. R. (2025). Evolution in blood glucose monitoring: A comprehensive review of invasive to non-invasive devices and sensors. *Discovery Medicine*, *2*(1), 74.

Ghosh, M., & Das, D. (2024). Voice-activated SOS: an AI-enabled wearable device. In *Impact of AI on Advancing Women's Safety* (pp. 251–277). IGI Global Scientific Publishing.

Ghosh, P. K., Chakraborty, A., Hasan, M., Rashid, K., & Siddique, A. H. (2023). Blockchain application in healthcare systems: A review. *Systems*, *11*(1), 38.

Giardina, T., Modi, V., Parrish, D., & Singh, H. (2015). The patient portal and abnormal test results: An exploratory study of patient experiences. *Patient Experience Journal*, *2*(1), 148–154. PMID: 28345018

Girgis, A., Durcinoska, I., Levesque, J. V., Gerges, M., Sandell, T., & Arnold, A.PROMPT-Care Program Group. (2017). eHealth system for collecting and utilizing patient-reported outcome measures for personalized treatment and care (PROMPT-Care) among cancer patients: Mixed methods approach to evaluate feasibility and acceptability. *Journal of Medical Internet Research*, *19*(10), e330. PMID: 28970188

Glenwright, B. G., Simmich, J., Cottrell, M., O'Leary, S. P., Sullivan, C., Pole, J. D., & Russell, T. (2023). Facilitators and barriers to implementing electronic patient-reported outcome and experience measures in a health care setting: A systematic review. *Journal of Patient-Reported Outcomes*, *7*(1), 13. PMID: 36786914

Gluyas, H. (2015). Patient-centred care: improving healthcare outcomes. *Nursing Standard (2014+)*, *30*(4), 50.

Goodfellow, I. J., Pouget-Abadie, J., Mirza, M., Xu, B., Warde-Farley, D., Ozair, S., & Bengio, Y. (2014). Generative adversarial nets. *Advances in Neural Information Processing Systems*, •••, 27.

Goodhue, D. L. (1998). Development and Measurement Validity of a Task-Technology Fit Instrument for User Evaluations of Information System. *Decision Sciences*, *29*(1), 105–138. https://doi.org/https://doi.org/10.1111/j.1540-5915.1998.tb01346.x

Goodhue, D., & Thompson, R. (1995). Task-Technology Fit and Individual Performance. *Management Information Systems Quarterly*, *19*, 213–236.

Google, A. I. Y. V. *Food_v1*. Google AIY, TenserflowHub. https://tfhub.dev/google/aiy/vision/classifier/food_V1/1

Greger, M. (2019). *How not to diet: the groundbreaking science of healthy, permanent weight loss*. Flatiron Books.

Greger, M. (2023). *How not to age: the scientific approach to getting healthier as you get older*. Flatiron Books.

Guido, R., Ferrisi, S., & Lofaro, D. (2024). An Overview on the Advancements of Support Vector Machine Models in Healthcare Applications. *RE:view*.

Guleria, P., & Sood, M. (2023). Explainable AI and machine learning : performance evaluation and explainability of classifiers on educational data mining inspired career counseling. In *Education and Information Technologies*. Springer US., DOI: 10.1007/s10639-022-11221-2

Guler, N., Ben, Z., & Gunes, A. (2025). Green Technologies and Sustainability Optimizing solar PV systems using fuzzy logic for Climate-Resilient Healthcare infrastructure in Kyrgyzstan. *Green Technologies and Sustainability*, *3*(3), 100190. DOI: 10.1016/j.grets.2025.100190

Gulzar, K., Memon, M. A., Mohsin, S. M., Aslam, S., Muhammad, S., Akber, A., & Nadeem, M. A. (2023). *An Efficient Healthcare Data Mining Approach Using Apriori Algorithm : A Case Study of Eye Disorders in Young Adults*. 1–14.

Gunjan, I. S. (2024). An Extensive Survey of AIoT in Healthcare. In *N. D.-N. Surjeet Dalal, Reshaping Intelligent Business and Industry: Convergence of AI and IoT at the Cutting Edge*. Wiley Online Library.

Guo, Y., Liu, X., Peng, S., Jiang, X., Xu, K., Chen, C., Wang, Z., Dai, C., & Chen, W. (2021). A review of wearable and unobtrusive sensing technologies for chronic disease management. *Computers in Biology and Medicine*, *2021*(129), 104163.

Guo, Z., Schlichtkrull, M., & Vlachos, A. (2022). A Survey on Automated Fact-Checking. arXiv:2108.11896 [cs].

Gu, W., Wang, J., Zhang, Y., Liang, S., Ai, Z., & Li, J. (2024). Evolution of digital health and exploration of patented Technologies (2017-2021): Bibliometric Analysis. *Interactive Journal of Medical Research*, *13*(1), e48259. PMID: 38991212

Guyatt, G. H., Oxman, A. D., Vist, G. E., Kunz, R., Falck-Ytter, Y., Alonso-Coello, P., & Schünemann, H. J. (2008). GRADE: An emerging consensus on rating quality of evidence and strength of recommendations. *BMJ (Clinical Research Ed.)*, *336*(7650), 924–926. DOI: 10.1136/bmj.39489.470347.AD PMID: 18436948

Hamid, Z., Khalique, F., Mahmood, S., Daud, A., Bukhari, A., & Alshemaimri, B. (2024). Healthcare insurance fraud detection using data mining. *BMC Medical Informatics and Decision Making*, *4*, 1–24. DOI: 10.1186/s12911-024-02512-4

Harris, J. L., Pomeranz, J. L., Lobstein, T., & Brownell, K. D. (2009). A crisis in the marketplace: How food marketing contributes to childhood obesity and what can be done. *Annual Review of Public Health*, *30*(1), 211–225.

Harrison, C. J., & Sidey-Gibbons, C. J. (2021). Machine learning in medicine: A practical introduction to natural language processing. *BMC Medical Research Methodology*, *21*(1), 158. PMID: 34332525

Harrison, J. E., Weber, S., Jakob, R., & Chute, C. G. (2021). ICD-11: An international classification of diseases for the twenty-first century. *BMC Medical Informatics and Decision Making*, *21*, 1–10.

Hasselgren, A., Hanssen Rensaa, J. A., Kralevska, K., Gligoroski, D., & Faxvaag, A. (2021). Blockchain for increased trust in virtual health care: Proof-of-concept study. *Journal of Medical Internet Research*, *23*(7), e28496. PMID: 34328437

Hassija, V., Chamola, V., Mahapatra, A., Singal, A., Goel, D., Huang, K., & Hussain, A. (2024). Interpreting black-box models: A review on explainable artificial intelligence. *Cognitive Computation*, *16*(1), 45–74.

Hays, R. D., & Quigley, D. D. (2025). A perspective on the use of patient-reported experience and patient-reported outcome measures in ambulatory healthcare. *Expert Review of Pharmacoeconomics & Outcomes Research*, *25*(4), 1–9. PMID: 39819211

Hazboun, F. H., & Owda, M. (2021). *A Natural Language Interface to Relational Databases Using an Online Analytic Processing Hypercube*. 720–737.

Hefley, B., & Loesche, E. A. (2010). *eSourcing capability model for client organizations* (1st ed.). Van Haren Publishing.

Heinz-Uwe Dettling, K. J. (2022, July 27). *How the challenge of regulating AI in healthcare is escalating*. EY. https://www.ey.com/en_gl/insights/law/how-the-challenge-of-regulating-ai-in-healthcare-is-escalating

He, K., Mao, R., Lin, Q., Ruan, Y., Lan, X., Feng, M., & Cambria, E. (2025). A survey of large language models for healthcare: From data, technology, and applications to accountability and ethics. *Information Fusion*, •••, 102963.

He, M., Iwai, M., Nishino, T., Miura, K., Watanabe, R., & Kobayashi, K. (2023). Night-Time Monitoring System for Getting-up Action of Older Person Based on Single Camera and Infrared Reflective Sheets. *Advanced Biomedical Engineering*, *12*, 214–224. DOI: 10.14326/abe.12.214

He, Q., Keith, D., Eckhoff, D. O., Park, C., & Ng, B. P. (2023). Accessibility and Utilization of Telehealth Services During the COVID-19 Pandemic Among Medicare Beneficiaries by Diabetes Status. *Research in Gerontological Nursing*, *16*(3), 134–146. DOI: 10.3928/19404921-20230301-01 PMID: 36881008

Hevner, A. R., March, S. T., Park, J., & Ram, S. (2004). Design Science in Information Systems Research. *Management Information Systems Quarterly*, *28*(1), 75–105. DOI: 10.2307/25148625

Himmel, S., & Ziefle, M. (2016). Smart home medical technologies: Users'requirements for conditional acceptance. *I-Com*, *15*, 39–50. DOI: 10.1515/icom-2016-0007

Hoang, T. V. (2024). Impact of Integrated Artificial Intelligence and Internet of Things Technologies on Smart City Transformation. *Journal of Technical Education Science*, *19*(1), 64–73. DOI: 10.54644/jte.2024.1532

Holden, R. J., & Karsh, B. T. (2010). The technology acceptance model: Its past and its future in health care. *Journal of Biomedical Informatics*, *43*(1), 159–172. DOI: 10.1016/j.jbi.2009.07.002 PMID: 19615467

Homayounfar, P. (2012). Process mining challenges in hospital information systems. In *2012, Federated Conference on Computer Science and Information Systems (FedCSIS)* (pp. 1135-1140). *IEEE*. Available at: https://annals-csis.org/proceedings/2012/pliks/376.pdf

Hripcsak, G., Duke, J. D., Shah, N. H., Reich, C. G., Huser, V., Schuemie, M. J., & Ryan, P. B. (2015). Observational Health Data Sciences and Informatics (OHDSI): Opportunities for observational researchers. *Studies in Health Technology and Informatics*, *216*, 574. PMID: 26262116

Huang, H., Lu, C., Jhou, M., Liu, T., Yang, C., Hsieh, S., Yang, W., Chang, H., Chen, M., Huang, H., Lu, C., & Jhou, M. (2023). *Using a Decision Tree Algorithm Predictive Model for Sperm Count Assessment and Risk Factors in Health Screening Population Using a Decision Tree Algorithm Predictive Model for Sperm Count Assessment and Risk Factors in Health Screening Population*. https://doi.org/DOI: 10.2147/RMHP.S433193

Huang, X., Lin, J., & Demner-Fushman, D. (2006). Evaluation of PICO as a knowledge representation for clinical questions. *AMIA Annual Symposium proceedings. AMIA Symposium*, 2006, 359–363.

Huang, Z., Soljak, M., Boehm, B., & Car, J. (2018). Clinical relevance of smartphone apps for diabetes management: A global overview. *Diabetes/Metabolism Research and Reviews*, •••, 34. PMID: 29431916

Hülsken-Giesler, M. (2010). Zur systematischen Integration einer professionalisierten Pflege in das System der Gesundheitsversorgung – Computer in der Intensivpflege. *Intensiv, 18*, 238–241. DOI: 10.1055/s-0030-1264126

Hyder, E. B., ... (2010). *eSourcing capability model for service providers* (1st ed.). Van Haren Publishing.

Ifty, S. M. H., Irin, F., Shovon, M. S. S., Amjad, M. H. H., Bhowmik, P. K., Ahmed, R., & Sunny, A. R. (2024). Advancements, Applications, and Future Directions of Artificial Intelligence in Healthcare. *Journal of Angiotherapy, 8*(8), 1–18.

Imroz khan, D. A. 2024. Internet of Things IoT Its Applications and Enabling Technologies in Healthcare: Review, A. *Educational Administration: Theory and Practice, 30*(4). https://doi.org/https://doi.org/10.53555/kuey.v30i4.5031

Institut für Qualität und Wirtschaftlichkeit im Gesundheitswesen (IQWiG). (2022). General Methods Version 6.1. https://www.iqwig.de/methoden/general-methods_version-6-1.pdf

Ioannidis, J. P. (2005). Contradicted and initially stronger effects in highly cited clinical research. *jama, 294*(2), 218-228.

IOM. (2001). Institute of Medicine: Crossing the Quality Chasm: Crossing the Quality Chasm: A new health system for the 21st century. In Book Crossing the Quality Chasm: A new health system for the 21st century. City: Institute of Medicine. Available at: https://shorturl.at/g5HIK

Jacobson, R. P., Kang, D., & Houck, J. (2020). Can Patient-Reported Outcomes Measurement Information System® (PROMIS) measures accurately enhance understanding of acceptable symptoms and functioning in primary care? *Journal of Patient-Reported Outcomes, 4*, 39. DOI: 10.1186/s41687-020-00206-9 PMID: 32436001

Jadhav, A. D., & Chobe, S. V. (2022). *Revue d ' Intelligence Artificielle Risk Assessment of Cardiovascular Diseases Using kNN and Decision Tree Classifier. 36*(1), 155–161.

Jain, S., Margetis, K., & Iverson, L. M. (2025). Glasgow coma scale. In *StatPearls* [internet]. StatPearls Publishing.

Jaleel, A., Mahmood, T., Hassan, M. A., Bano, G., & Khurshid, S. K. (2020). Towards medical data interoperability through collaboration of healthcare devices. *IEEE Access : Practical Innovations, Open Solutions, 8*, 132302–132319.

Jamil, A. S. A., Khalil, A., & Yunus, M. M. (2024). Empowering Predictive Maintenance of Medical Equipment Through AI-Driven Condition Monitoring. *Biomedical Engineering: AI and Technological Innovations*, 53.

Jamil, M., Warsito, B., & Wibowo, A. (2023). *Diabetes Mellitus Early Detection Simulation using The K-Nearest Neighbors Algorithm with Cloud-Based Runtime (COLAB). 15*(2), 215–221.

Jayaprakasam, B. S. (2025). AI and Big Data-Driven m-Health: Integrating Cloud Computing, Remote Patient Monitoring, Clinical Decision Support Systems, and Self-Supervised Learning with FHIR for Scalable Healthcare Systems. *Indo-American Journal of Life Sciences and Biotechnology*, *22*(1), 11–25.

Jennings, H. M., Morrison, J., Akter, K., Kuddus, A., Ahmed, N., Kumer Shaha, S., Nahar, T., Haghparast-Bidgoli, H., Khan, A. A., Azad, K., & Fottrell, E. (2019). Developing a theory-driven contextually relevant mHealth intervention. *Global Health Action*, *12*(1), 1550736. DOI: 10.1080/16549716.2018.1550736 PMID: 31154988

Jeyaraman, N., Jeyaraman, M., Ramasubramanian, S., Balaji, S., & Muthu, S. (2025). Voices that matter: The impact of patient-reported outcome measures on clinical decision-making. *World Journal of Methodology*, *15*(2), 98066. DOI: 10.5662/wjm.v15.i2.98066 PMID: 40548214

Jiang, F., Jiang, Y., Zhi, H., Dong, Y., Li, H., Ma, S., & Wang, Y. (2017). Artificial intelligence in healthcare: Past, present and future. *Stroke and Vascular Neurology*, *2*(4), e000101. PMID: 29507784

Jiang, P., Sinha, S., Aldape, K., Hannenhalli, S., Sahinalp, C., & Ruppin, E. (2022). Big data in basic and translational cancer research. *Nature Reviews. Cancer*, *22*(11), 625–639. PMID: 36064595

Jimenez, G., Lum, E., & Car, J. (2019). Examining Diabetes Management Apps Recommended From a Google Search: Content Analysis. *JMIR mHealth and uHealth*, *7*(1), e11848. DOI: 10.2196/11848 PMID: 30303485

Joachim, S. J. Prem Prakash. Forkan, Abdur Rahim Mohammad. Morshed, Ahsan. Wickramasinghe, Nilmini. (2021, Jan, 2021.). *Design and Development of a Diabetes Self-Management Platform: A Case for Responsible Information System Development* Proceedings of the 54th Hawaii International Conference on System Sciences | 2021, Hawaii.

Joachim, S., Forkan, A. R. M., Jayaraman, P. P., Morshed, A., & Wickramasinghe, N. (2022). A Nudge-Inspired AI-Driven Health Platform for Self-Management of Diabetes. *Sensors (Basel)*, *22*(12), 4620. https://www.mdpi.com/1424-8220/22/12/4620 PMID: 35746402

John, M. M., Olsson, H. H., & Bosch, J. (2023). Towards an AI-driven business development framework: A multi-case study. *Journal of Software (Malden, MA)*, *35*(6), e2432.

Kahn, M. G., Callahan, T. J., Barnard, J., Bauck, A. E., Brown, J., Davidson, B. N., Estiri, H., Goerg, C., Holve, E., Johnson, S. G., Liaw, S. T., Hamilton-Lopez, M., Meeker, D., Ong, T. C., Ryan, P., Shang, N., Weiskopf, N. G., Weng, C., Zozus, M. N., & Schilling, L. (2016). A harmonized data quality assessment terminology and framework for the secondary use of electronic health record data. *EGEMS (Washington, DC)*, *4*(1), 1244. DOI: 10.13063/2327-9214.1244 PMID: 27713905

Kaiser, R. (2021). *Qualitative Experteninterviews – konzeptionelle Grundlagen und praktische Durchführung* (2. aktualisierte Auflage). Springer VS.

Kalli, V. D. R., & Jonathan, E. (2023). AI-Driven Energy Management Solutions for Healthcare: Optimizing Medical Device Software. *International Journal of Advanced Engineering Technologies and Innovations*, *1*(01), 157–174.

Kamala, S. P. R., Gayathri, S., Pillai, N. M., Gracious, L. A., Varun, C. M., & Subramanian, R. S. (2023, July). Predictive analytics for heart disease detection: a machine learning approach. In 2023 4th International Conference on Electronics and Sustainable Communication Systems (ICESC) (pp. 1583-1589). IEEE.

Kaplan, R. S., ... (2015). Health care providers need a value management office. *Harvard Business Review*. https://hbr.org/2015/12/health-care-providers-need-a-value-management-office

Kaplan, R. S., Jehi, L., Ko, C. Y., Pusic, A., & Witkowski, M. (2021). Health care measurements that improve patient outcomes. *NEJM Catalyst Innovations in Care Delivery*, *2*(2), 1–21.

Karabacak, M., & Margetis, K. (2023). Embracing large language models for medical applications: Opportunities and challenges. *Cureus*, *15*(5).

Kaur, J., Khehra, B. S., & Singh, A. (2023). Back propagation artificial neural network for diagnose of the heart disease. *Journal of Reliable Intelligent Environments*, *9*(1), 57–85. DOI: 10.1007/s40860-022-00192-3

Kaushal, R. K., Kumar, N., Kukreja, V., & Boonchieng, E. (2025). Hyperledger fabric based remote patient monitoring solution and performance evaluation. *Peer-to-Peer Networking and Applications*, *18*(3), 105.

Kavitha Palaniappan, E. Y. (2024). Global Regulatory Frameworks for the Use of Artificial Intelligence (AI) in the Healthcare Services Sector. *Health Care*, *15*(5). https://doi.org/https://doi.org/10.3390/healthcare12050562

Kavitha, K. (2023). Optimal Stacked Sparse Auto-encoder based Online Analytic Processing (OLAP) Hypercube Text Analysis. *2023 Fifth International Conference on Electrical, Computer and Communication Technologies (ICECCT), February*, 1–5. https://doi.org/DOI: 10.1109/ICECCT56650.2023.10179777

Kekic, M., Rose, A., Baker, C., & Bayley, D. (2024). RETRACTED: Reduced self-harm on acute mental health wards following the implementation of a vision-based patient monitoring system: Evidence from five NHS trusts. *Journal of Psychiatric and Mental Health Nursing*, *00*, 1–9. DOI: 10.1111/jpm.13036

Kermany, D. S., Goldbaum, M., Cai, W., Valentim, C. C., Liang, H., Baxter, S. L., & Zhang, K. (2018). Identifying medical diagnoses and treatable diseases by image-based deep learning. *Cell*, *172*(5), 1122–1131. PMID: 29474911

Kerr, D., & Sabharwal, A. (2021). Principles for virtual health care to deliver real equity in diabetes. *The Lancet. Diabetes & Endocrinology*, *9*(8), 480–482. DOI: 10.1016/s2213-8587(21)00176-5 PMID: 34217405

Khalil, H., Ameen, M., Davies, C., & Liu, C. (2025). Implementing value-based healthcare: A scoping review of key elements, outcomes, and challenges for sustainable healthcare systems. *Frontiers in Public Health*, *13*, 1514098. DOI: 10.3389/fpubh.2025.1514098 PMID: 40270723

Khan, R. M. M., Chua, Z. J. Y., Tan, J. C., Yang, Y., Liao, Z., & Zhao, Y. (2019). From Pre-Diabetes to Diabetes: Diagnosis, Treatments and Translational Research. *Medicina (Kaunas, Lithuania)*, *55*(9). Advance online publication. DOI: 10.3390/medicina55090546 PMID: 31470636

Khatoon, A. (2020). A blockchain-based smart contract system for healthcare management. *Electronics (Basel)*, *9*(1), 94.

Khoruzhy, L. I., Katkov, Y. N., Katkova, E. A., Khoruzhy, V. I., & Dzhikiya, M. K. (2023). *Opportunities for the Application of a Model of Cost Management and Reduction of Risks in Financial and Economic Activity Based on the OLAP Technology : The Case of the Agro-Industrial Sector of Russia.*

Khoshgoftar, Z., Babaee, M., & Rouzbahani, A. K. (2025). *Educational data mining in medical education : A five - level approach.* https://doi.org/DOI: 10.4103/jehp.jehp

Khushal, R., & Fatima, U. (2025). MethodsX Machine learning and Fuzzy logic fusion approach for. *MethodsX, 14*(December 2024), 103152. https://doi.org/DOI: 10.1016/j.mex.2024.103152

Kim, K. A., Kim, H., Ha, E. J., Yoon, B. C., & Kim, D.-J. (2024). Artificial intelligence-enhanced neurocritical care for traumatic brain injury: Past, present and future. *Journal of Korean Neurosurgical Society*, *67*(5), 493–509. PMID: 38186369

Kim, S. S., & Malhotra, N. K. (2005). A longitudinal model of continued IS use: An integrative view of four mechanisms underlying postadoption phenomena. *Management Science*, *51*(5), 741–755. DOI: 10.1287/mnsc.1040.0326

Kim, S., Lee, K. H., Hwang, H., & Yoo, S. (2016). Analysis of the factors influencing healthcare professionals' adoption of mobile electronic medical record (EMR) using the unified theory of acceptance and use of technology (UTAUT). *BMC Medical Informatics and Decision Making*, *20*(1), 1–10. DOI: 10.1186/s12911-016-0249-8 PMID: 26831123

Kommineni, V. K., König-Ries, B., & Samuel, S. (2024). From human experts to machines: An LLM supported approach to ontology and knowledge graph construction. *arXiv preprint arXiv:2403.08345.*

Kostuj, T., & Niemeyer, A. (2022). Diagnostik und Therapie aus der Patientenperspektive-PROMs in der Chirurgie. *Zentralblatt für Chirurgie-Zeitschrift für Allgemeine, Viszeral-. Thorax-und Gefäßchirurgie*, *147*(02), 125–128. DOI: 10.1055/a-1213-0817 PMID: 35378548

Kovacova, M., Kevicky, F., & Popescu, G. H. (2023). Generative Artificial Intelligence-driven Healthcare Systems in Patient Record Analysis, in Disease Diagnosis and Monitoring, and in Customized Treatment Plans. *Contemporary Readings in Law and Social Justice*, *15*(1).

Kraljevic, Z., Bean, D., Mascio, A., Roguski, L., Folarin, A., Roberts, A., Bendayan, Y., & Dobson, R. (2019). MedCAT - Medical concept annotation tool. *arXiv preprint arXiv:1912.10166.*

Kraljevic, Z., Shek, A., Bean, D., Bendayan, R., Teo, J., & Dobson, R. (2021). MedGPT: Medical concept prediction from clinical narratives. *arXiv preprint arXiv:2107.03134.*

Krepper, D., Cesari, M., Hubel, N. J., Zelger, P., & Sztankay, M. J. (2024). Machine learning models including patient-reported outcome data in oncology: A systematic literature review and analysis of their reporting quality. *Journal of Patient-Reported Outcomes*, *8*(1), 126. PMID: 39499409

Krishnamoorthy, S., Dua, A., & Gupta, S. (2023). Role of emerging technologies in future IoT-driven Healthcare 4.0 technologies: A survey, current challenges and future directions. *Journal of Ambient Intelligence and Humanized Computing*, *14*(1), 361–407.

Krogoll, C. (2015). ICT in healthcare: A review of literature and implications for developing countries.

Krogoll, C., Schmidt, L., & Hoffmann, W. (2015). Use of wearables in healthcare–a systematic review. *Proceedings of the 48th Hawaii International Conference on System Sciences*.

Kruse, C. S., Argueta, D. A., Lopez, L., & Nair, A. (2015). Patient and provider attitudes toward the use of patient portals for the management of chronic disease: A systematic review. *Journal of Medical Internet Research*, *17*(2), e40. DOI: 10.2196/jmir.3703 PMID: 25707035

Küçük, E. E., & Küçük, D. (2024). Enhancing a public health ontology using ChatGPT. In *Proceedings of the 7th International Health Science and Life Congress* (pp. 143-145).

Küçük, E. E., Yapar, K., Küçük, D., & Küçük, D. (2017). Ontology-based automatic identification of public health-related Turkish tweets. *Computers in Biology and Medicine*, *83*, 1–9.

Kunal, A. P. (2023). Modern Healthcare Systems: Unveiling the Possibility of AIoT for Remote Patient Monitoring. In *Developments Towards Next Generation Intelligent Systems for Sustainable Development* (pp. 180-203). IGI Global.

Kurani, A., Doshi, P., Vakharia, A., & Shah, M. (2023). A Comprehensive Comparative Study of Artificial Neural Network (ANN) and Support Vector Machines (SVM) on Stock Forecasting. *Annals of Data Science*, *10*(1), 183–208. DOI: 10.1007/s40745-021-00344-x

Kushwaha, S. S., Joshi, S., Singh, D., Kaur, M., & Lee, H. N. (2022). Ethereum smart contract analysis tools: A systematic review. *IEEE Access : Practical Innovations, Open Solutions*, *10*, 57037–57062.

Kwan, Y. H., Cheng, T. Y., Yoon, S., Ho, L. Y. C., Huang, C. W., Chew, E. H., Thumboo, J., Østbye, T., & Low, L. L. (2020). A systematic review of nudge theories and strategies used to influence adult health behaviour and outcome in diabetes management. *Diabetes & Metabolism*, *46*(6), 450–460. https://doi.org/https://doi.org/10.1016/j.diabet.2020.04.002 PMID: 32387700

Kyrimi, E., Mclachlan, S., Neves, M. R., Fahmi, A., & Fenton, N. (n.d.). *A Comprehensive Scoping Review of Bayesian Networks in Healthcare : Past, Present and Future*. 1–32.

Kyte, D., Cockwell, P., Lencioni, M., Skrybant, M., Hildebrand, M. V., Price, G., Cockwell, P., Lencioni, M., Skrybant, M., von Hildebrand, M., Price, G., Squire, K., Webb, S., Brookes, O., Fanning, H., Jones, T., & Calvert, M. (2016). Reflections on the national patient-reported outcome measures (PROMs) programme: Where do we go from here? *Journal of the Royal Society of Medicine*, *109*(12), 441–445. DOI: 10.1177/0141076816677856 PMID: 27923896

Labban, M., Briggs, L., Cole, A. P., & Trinh, Q. D. (2021). Measuring What Matters: Patient-Reported Outcome and Experience Measures for Men Undergoing Radical Prostatectomy. *European Urology Focus*, *7*(5), 913–915. DOI: 10.1016/j.euf.2021.09.010 PMID: 34556455

Lai, W., Li, D., Yu, J., Huang, L., Zheng, M., Jiang, Y., Wang, S., Wen, J., Chen, S., Wen, C., & Jin, Y. (2022).. . *An Apriori Algorithm-Based Association Analysis of Analgesic Drugs in Chinese Medicine Prescriptions Recorded From Patients With Rheumatoid Arthritis*. , 3(July), 1–15. DOI: 10.3389/fpain.2022.937259

Lam, K., Lu, A. D., Shi, Y., & Covinsky, K. E. (2020). Assessing Telemedicine Unreadiness Among Older Adults in the United States During the COVID-19 Pandemic. *JAMA Internal Medicine*, *180*(10), 1389–1391. DOI: 10.1001/jamainternmed.2020.2671 PMID: 32744593

Latha, R., Raman, R., Kumar, T. S., Rawandale, C. J., Meenakshi, R., & Srinivasan, C. (2023, October). Automated health monitoring system for coma patients. In *2023 International Conference on Self Sustainable Artificial Intelligence Systems (ICSSAS)* (pp. 1475-1480). IEEE.

Latour, B. (1987). *Science in action: How to follow scientists and engineers through society*. Harvard UP.

Lax, G., Nardone, R., & Russo, A. (2024). Enabling secure health information sharing among healthcare organizations by public blockchain. *Multimedia Tools and Applications*, *83*(24), 64795–64811.

Lear, R., Ellis, S., Ollivierre-Harris, T., Long, S. & Mayer, E.K. (2023). Video recording patients for direct care purposes: Systematic review and narrative synthesis of international empirical studies and UK professional guidance. Journal of Medical Internet Research, 16, 25:e46478. DOI: DOI: 10.2196/46478

Lee, C.-j., Nagler, R. H., & Wang, N. (2018). Sourcespecific Exposure to Contradictory Nutrition Information: Documenting Prevalence and Effects on Adverse Cognitive and Behavioral Outcomes. *Health Communication*, *33*(4), 453–461.

Lee, S. M., & Lee, D. (2020). Healthcare wearable devices: An analysis of key factors for continuous use intention. *Service Business*, *14*(4), 503–531. DOI: 10.1007/s11628-020-00428-3

Lee, S., Kim, J., & Park, H. (2024). Digital literacy interventions for older adults: A systematic review. *Journal of Health Communication*, *29*(3), 145–156. DOI: 10.1080/10810730.2024.1234567

Lei, L., Wu, B., Fang, X., Chen, L., Wu, H., & Liu, W. (2023). A dynamic anomaly detection method of building energy consumption based on data mining technology. *Energy, 263*(PA), 125575. https://doi.org/DOI: 10.1016/j.energy.2022.125575

Lesser, L. I., Ebbeling, C. B., Goozner, M., Wypij, D., & Ludwig, D. S. (2007). Relationship between funding source and conclusion among nutrition-related scientific articles. *PLoS Medicine*, *4*(1), e5.

Levy, D. E., Bates, D., & Caronna, J. J. (1981). NIALL EF CARTLIDGE, ROBIN P. KNILL-JONES, ROBERT H. LAPINSKI, BURTON H. SINGER, DAVID A. SHAW, and FRED PLUM. "Prognosis in nontraumatic coma.". *Annals of Internal Medicine*, *94*(3), 293–301. PMID: 7224376

Li, J. (2022). *E-Commerce Fraud Detection Model by Computer Artificial Intelligence Data Mining. 2022*(Ml). https://doi.org/DOI: 10.1155/2022/8783783

Li, J., Li, J., Wang, C., & Verbeek, F. J. (2023). *Outlier detection using iterative adaptive mini-minimum spanning tree generation with applications on medical data. October*, 1–12. https://doi.org/DOI: 10.3389/fphys.2023.1233341

Li, J., Li, J., Wang, C., Verbeek, F. J., Schultz, T., & Liu, H. (2024). *MS2OD : outlier detection using minimum spanning tree and medoid selection OPEN ACCESS MS2OD : outlier detection using minimum spanning tree and medoid selection.* 0–15.

Li, Q., Liu, H., Guo, C., Chen, D., Wang, M., Gao, F., & Gu, J. (2025). Merging clinical knowledge into large language models for medical research and applications: A survey. *arXiv preprint arXiv:2502.20988.*

Li, F., Ruijs, N., & Lu, Y. (2022). Ethics & AI: A systematic review on ethical concerns and related strategies for designing with AI in healthcare. *AI*, *4*(1), 28–53.

Limayem, M., Hirt, S. G., & Cheung, C. M. (2007). How habit limits the predictive power of intention: The case of information systems continuance. *Management Information Systems Quarterly*, *31*(4), 705–737. DOI: 10.2307/25148817

Lippolis, A. S., Saeedizade, M. J., Keskisärkkä, R., Zuppiroli, S., Ceriani, M., Gangemi, A., . . . Nuzzolese, A. G. (2025). Ontology generation using large language models. In *Proceedings of European Semantic Web Conference* (pp. 321-341). Cham: Springer Nature Switzerland.

Lipton, Z. C. (2018). The mythos of model interpretability: In machine learning, the concept of interpretability is both important and slippery. *Queue*, *16*(3), 31–57.

Li, Q., Fan, Y., Luo, R., Hu, J., Wang, L., Ai, T., Li, Q., Fan, Y., Luo, R., Hu, J., Wang, L., & Ai, T. (2025). Related Risk Factors That Predict Moderate to Severe Asthma Attack in Children. *Analysis Based on Logistic Regression and Decision Tree Related Risk Factors That Predict Moderate to Severe Asthma Attack in Children : Analysis Based on Logistic Regression*, *7074*. Advance online publication. DOI: 10.2147/IJGM.S530736

Liu, F., Cao, Y., Luo, J., Zhi, J., & Yang, J. (2024). ScienceDirect A Boundary Partitioning Algorithm for Geometrical Product Deviation Evaluation. *Procedia CIRP*, *129*, 115–120. DOI: 10.1016/j.procir.2024.10.021

Liu, H., Soroush, A., Nestor, J. G., Park, E., Idnay, B., Fang, Y., Pan, J., Liao, S., Bernard, M., Peng, Y., & Weng, C. (2024). Retrieval augmented scientific claim verification. *JAMIA Open*, *7*(1), ooae021.

Liu, H., Zhou, S., Chen, Z., Perl, Y., & Wang, J. (2024b). Using generative large language models for hierarchical relationship prediction in medical ontologies. In *Proceedings of IEEE 12th International Conference on Healthcare Informatics (ICHI)* (pp. 248-256).

Liu, Q., Yang, R., Gao, Q., Liang, T., Wang, X., Li, S., Lei, B., & Gao, K. (2024a). A review of applying large language models in healthcare. *IEEE Access : Practical Innovations, Open Solutions*, *13*, 6878–6892.

Lu Xu, M. L. (2021). Chatbot for Health Care and Oncology Applications Using Artificial Intelligence and Machine Learning: Systematic Review. *JMIR Cancer*, *7*(4). Advance online publication. DOI: 10.2196/27850 PMID: 34847056

Luh, N., Purnama, P., Purnama, I. N., & Utami, N. W. (2022). *Penerapan Data Mining Untuk Clustering Penilaian Kinerja Dosen Menggunakan Algoritma K-Means (Studi Kasus : STMIK Primakara). 16*(2), 105–112.

Luiza Palmieri Serrano, K. C.-G. (2023). Benefits and Challenges of Remote Patient Monitoring as Perceived by Health Care Practitioners: A Systematic Review. *The Permanente Journal, 27*(4), 100–111. DOI: 10.7812/TPP/23.022 PMID: 37735970

Madan, V., Elbaz, A., & Mor, A.. (2020). Using gold standard patient-reported outcome measures in clinical practice: A new approach to facilitate their use. *Authorea*. https://doi.org/DOI: 10.22541/au.159542470.03987631

Mahmoud, Y., Horvath, K., & Zhou, Y. (2025). Deep Learning for Predicting Rehabilitation Success: Advancing Clinical and Patient-Reported Outcome Modeling. *Electronics (Basel), 14*(6), 1082.

Maidhof, C., Offermann, J. & Ziefle, M. (2023). Eyes on privacy: acceptance of video-based AAL impacted by activities being filmed. Front Public Health, 4, 11:1186944. DOI: DOI: 10.3389/fpubh.2023.1186944

Maithili, K., Ponmalar, A., Yamini, B., Karthikeyan, M., Anish, T. P., Maheswari, B., & Subramanian, R. S. (2024). Advances in AI and Machine Learning for Healthcare Informatics. In Machine Learning and Generative AI in Smart Healthcare (pp. 1-22). IGI Global.

Makdisse, M.. (2018). What is a value management office? An implementation experience in Latin America. *Value in Health Regional Issues, 17*, 71–73. DOI: 10.1016/j.vhri.2018.04.001 PMID: 29729500

Makhni, E. C., & Hennekes, M. E. (2023). The use of patient-reported outcome measures in clinical practice and clinical decision making. *The Journal of the American Academy of Orthopaedic Surgeons, 31*(20), 1059–1066. DOI: 10.5435/JAAOS-D-23-00040 PMID: 37364243

Maleki, N., Zeinali, Y., Taghi, S., & Niaki, A. (2021). A k-NN method for lung cancer prognosis with the use of a genetic algorithm for feature selection. *Expert Systems With Applications, 164*(July 2019), 113981. https://doi.org/DOI: 10.1016/j.eswa.2020.113981

Man, M., Ruslan, N. A., Jusoh, J. A., Aezwani, W., & Bakar, W. A. (2023). *IR-Eclat : A new algorithm of incremental R- Eclat for infrequent itemset mining IR-Eclat : A New Algorithm of Incremental R-Eclat for Infrequent Itemset Mining. 060012*(March).

Mandel, J. C., Kreda, D. A., Mandl, K. D., Kohane, I. S., & Ramoni, R. B. (2016). SMART on FHIR: A standards-based, interoperable apps platform for electronic health records. *Journal of the American Medical Informatics Association : JAMIA, 23*(5), 899–908. DOI: 10.1093/jamia/ocv189 PMID: 26911829

Maniaci, M. J., Torres-Guzman, R. A., Avila, F. R., Maita, K., Garcia, J. P., Forte, A. J., & Paulson, M. R. (2024). Development and evaluation of best practice advisory alert for patient eligibility in a hospital-at-home program: A multicenter retrospective study. *Journal of Hospital Medicine, 19*(3), 165–174. PMID: 38243666

Manickam, P., Mariappan, S. A., Murugesan, S. M., Hansda, S., Kaushik, A., Shinde, R., & Thipperudraswamy, S. P. (2022). Artificial intelligence (AI) and internet of medical things (IoMT) assisted biomedical systems for intelligent healthcare. *Biosensors (Basel), 12*(8), 562. PMID: 35892459

Manikandan, A., Prashanth, P. K., Ravindran, S., & Senthilnayaki, B. (2025). "Remote Health Monitoring for Empowering Patients with Intelligent." Advances in Communication and Applications: Proceedings of ERCICA 2024, Volume 2 1398: 101.

Mansoor Ali, F. N. (2022, Mar 18). Federated Learning for Privacy Preservation in Smart Healthcare Systems: A Comprehensive Survey. arxiv. https://arxiv.org/abs/2203.09702

Mastrototaro, J. J. (2000). The MiniMed continuous glucose monitoring system. *Diabetes Technology & Therapeutics, 2*(1, Supplement 1), 13–18. PMID: 11469627

Mateiu, P., & Groza, A. (2023). Ontology engineering with large language models. In *Proceedings of IEEE 25th International Symposium on Symbolic and Numeric Algorithms for Scientific Computing (SYNASC)* (pp. 226-229).

Mayring, P., & Fenzl, T. (2019). Qualitative Inhaltsanalyze. In Baur, N., & Blasius, J. (Eds.), *Handbuch Methoden der empirischen Sozialforschung*. Springer VS., DOI: 10.1007/978-3-658-21308-4_42

Ma, Z., Gao, Q., & Yang, M. (2022). Adoption of Wearable Devices by Older People: Changes in Use Behaviors and User Experiences. *International Journal of Human-Computer Interaction, 39*, 1–24. DOI: 10.1080/10447318.2022.2083573

Mazhar, T., khan, S., Shahzad, T., khan, M. A., Saeed, M. M., Awotunde, J. B., & Hamam, H. (2025). Generative AI, IoT, and blockchain in healthcare: Application, issues, and solutions. *Discover Internet of Things, 5*(1), 5.

McCurdy, D. (2022). Blockchain Governance Strategies. In *Blockchain in Life Sciences* (pp. 197–212). Springer Nature Singapore., Available at https://link.springer.com/chapter/10.1007/978-981-19-2976-2_9

McKay, C. A., & Crippen, L. (2008). Collaboration through clinical integration. *Nursing Administration Quarterly*, *32*(2), 109–116. PMID: 18360207

Meadows, K. A. (2011). Patient-reported outcome measures: An overview. *British Journal of Community Nursing*, *16*(3), 146–151. PMID: 21378658

Meço, B. C., de Agua Reis, A. B., Berger-Estilita, J., Jakobsen, K., Alkış, N., & Radtke, F. M. (2023). Precision anaesthesia: Advancing patient-centered precision care through repetitive assessment of PROMs with the safe brain initiative approach. *Turkish Journal of Anaesthesiology and Reanimation*, *51*(5), 374. DOI: 10.4274/TJAR.2023.231420 PMID: 37747258

Meenal, M. R., & Vennila, S. M. (2023). Bidirectional Recurrent Network and Neuro - fuzzy Frequent Pattern Mining for Heart Disease Prediction. *SN Computer Science*, *4*(4), 1–10. DOI: 10.1007/s42979-023-01711-6

Mehta, S., Grant, K., & Ackery, A. (2020). Future of blockchain in healthcare: Potential to improve the accessibility, security and interoperability of electronic health records. *BMJ Health & Care Informatics*, *27*(3), e100217. PMID: 33229440

Meier, D. Y., Barthelmess, P., Sun, W., & Liberatore, F. (2020). Wearable technology acceptance in health care based on national culture differences: Cross-country analysis between Chinese and Swiss consumers. *Journal of Medical Internet Research*, *22*(10), e18801. DOI: 10.2196/18801 PMID: 33090108

Mello, M. M., & Guha, N. (2024). Understanding liability risk from using health care artificial intelligence tools. *The New England Journal of Medicine*, *390*(3), 271–278. PMID: 38231630

Merrill, C. B., Roe, J. M., Seely, K. D., & Brooks, B. (2022). Advanced Telemedicine Training and Clinical Outcomes in Type II Diabetes: A Pilot Study. *Telemedicine Reports*, *3*(1), 15–23. DOI: 10.1089/tmr.2021.0039 PMID: 35720452

Mialon, M., Serodio, P., Crosbie, E., Teicholz, N., Naik, A., & Carriedo, A. (2022). Conflicts of interest for members of the US 2020 Dietary Guidelines Advisory Committee. *Public Health Nutrition*, •••, 1–28.

Migchels, C., Zerrouk, A., Crunelle, C. L., Matthys, F., Gremeaux, L., Fernandez, K., & Vanderplasschen, W. (2023). Patient Reported Outcome and Experience Measures (PROMs and PREMs) in substance use disorder treatment services: A scoping review. *Drug and Alcohol Dependence*, *253*, 111017. PMID: 37995391

Minvielle, E., Fierobe, A., Fourcade, A., Ferrua, M., Di Palma, M., Scotté, F., & Mir, O. (2023). The use of patient-reported outcome and experience measures for health policy purposes: A scoping review in oncology. *Health Policy (Amsterdam), 129*, 104702. PMID: 36588068

Mittal, N., Pal, S., Joshi, A., Sharma, A., Tayal, S., & Sharma, Y. (2021). Comparative analysis of various platforms of blockchain. *Smart and Sustainable Intelligent Systems*, 323-340.

Mittelstadt, B. D., Allo, P., Taddeo, M., Wachter, S., & Floridi, L. (2016). The ethics of algorithms: Mapping the debate. *Big Data & Society, 3*(2), 2053951716679679. DOI: 10.1177/2053951716679679

Mohd Javaid, A. H. (2022). Significance of machine learning in healthcare: Features, pillars and applications. *International Journal of Intelligent Networks, 3*, 58–73. https://doi.org/https://doi.org/10.1016/j.ijin.2022.05.002

Mohsen Masoumian Hosseini, S. T. (2023). Smartwatches in healthcare medicine: Assistance and monitoring; a scoping review. *BMC Medical Informatics and Decision Making, 23*. Advance online publication. DOI: 10.1186/s12911-023-02350-w PMID: 37924029

Mokkink, L. B., De Vet, H. C., Prinsen, C. A., Patrick, D. L., Alonso, J., Bouter, L. M., & Terwee, C. B. (2018). COSMIN risk of bias checklist for systematic reviews of patient-reported outcome measures. *Quality of Life Research: An International Journal of Quality of Life Aspects of Treatment, Care and Rehabilitation, 27*(5), 1171–1179. DOI: 10.1007/s11136-017-1765-4 PMID: 29260445

Monaghan, M., & Marks, B. (2020). Personal Experiences With COVID-19 and Diabetes Technology: All for Technology Yet Not Technology for All. *Journal of Diabetes Science and Technology, 14*(4), 762–763. DOI: 10.1177/1932296820930005 PMID: 32460543

Morley, J., Machado, C. C. V., Burr, C., Cowls, J., Joshi, I., Taddeo, M., & Floridi, L. (2020). The ethics of AI in health care: A mapping review. *Social Science & Medicine, 260*, 113172. DOI: 10.1016/j.socscimed.2020.113172 PMID: 32702587

Moxley-Wyles, B., Colling, R., & Verrill, C. (2020). Artificial intelligence in pathology: An overview. *Diagnostic Histopathology, 26*(11), 513–520.

Mudumba, B., & Kabir, F. (2024). Mine-first association rule mining : An integration of independent frequent patterns in distributed environments. *Decision Analytics Journal, 10*(February), 100434. DOI: 10.1016/j.dajour.2024.100434

Mujirishvili, T., Maidhof, C., Florez-Revuelta, F., Ziefle, M., & Richart-Martinez, M. & Cabrero- Garcia, J. (2023). Acceptance and privacy perceptions toward video-based active and assisted living technologies: Scoping Review. *Journal of Medical Internet Research*, *25*, e45297. DOI: 10.2196/45297

Müller, M., & Biberthaler, P. (2021). Patient-Reported Outcome Measures (PROMs)–eine Übersicht. *OP-Journal*, *37*(01), 55–62. DOI: 10.1055/a-1203-3352

Na Zhou, C.-T. Z.-Y. (2019). Concordance Study Between IBM Watson for Oncology and Clinical Practice for Patients with Cancer in China. *The Oncologist*, *24*(6), 812–819. DOI: 10.1634/theoncologist.2018-0255 PMID: 30181315

NABH. (2020). National Accreditation Standards for Hospitals April 2020 5th edition. Available at: https://healthcarearchitecture.in/wp-content/uploads/2022/01/NABH-5-STD-April-2020.pdf

Nagler, R. H. (2014). Adverse outcomes associated with media exposure to contradictory nutrition messages. *Journal of Health Communication*, *19*(1), 24–40.

Najm, I. A., Dahr, J. M., Hamoud, A. K., Alasady, A. S., Awadh, W. A., Alshawki, M. B., & Humadi, A. M. (2022). *OLAP Mining with Educational Data Mart to Predict Students ' Performance Literature r eview. 46*, 11–19.

Nakamoto, S. (2008). Bitcoin: A peer-to-peer electronic cash system. Available at: https://assets.pubpub.org/d8wct41f/31611263538139.pdf

Narendra, N., & Khanna, M. A. (2022). Economics of Artificial Intelligence in Healthcare: Diagnosis vs. Treatment. *Healthcare (Basel)*, *10*(12). https://doi.org/https://doi.org/10.3390/healthcare10122493 PMID: 36554017

Nazar Waheed, A. U. (2023, Apr 16). *FedBlockHealth: A Synergistic Approach to Privacy and Security in IoT-Enabled Healthcare through Federated Learning and Blockchain.* arxiv logo. https://arxiv.org/abs/2304.07668

Nechita, L. C., Nechita, A., Voipan, A. E., Voipan, D., Debita, M., Fulga, A., & Musat, C. L. (2024). AI-Enhanced ECG Applications in Cardiology: Comprehensive Insights from the Current Literature with a Focus on COVID-19 and Multiple Cardiovascular Conditions. *Diagnostics (Basel)*, *14*(17), 1839. PMID: 39272624

Nestle, M. (2018). *Unsavory truth: how food companies skew the science of what we eat*. Basic Books.

Neuhaus, F. (2023). Ontologies in the era of large language models–a perspective. *Applied Ontology*, *18*(4), 399–407.

Neumiller, T. K. (2019). Medtronic MiniMed 670G Hybrid Closed-Loop System. *Clinical Diabetes : a Publication of the American Diabetes Association, 37*(1), 94–95. DOI: 10.2337/cd18-0067 PMID: 30705505

Nikhil Sahni, G. S. (2023, Jan). *The Potential Impact of Artificial Intelligence on Healthcare Spending.* National Bureau of Economic Research. https://www.nber.org/papers/w30857

Nilsson, K., Bååthe, F., Erichsen Andersson, A., & Sandoff, M. (2017). Value-based healthcare as a trigger for improvement initiatives. *Leadership in Health Services, 30*(4), 364–377. DOI: 10.1108/LHS-09-2016-0045 PMID: 28862085

Noor, M., Khan, I., Alzahrani, A. R. R., Akkari, A. A., & Ahmad, B. (2024). Risk adjusted EWMA control chart based on support vector machine with application to cardiac surgery data. *Scientific Reports*, •••, 1–12. DOI: 10.1038/s41598-024-60285-2

Obermeyer, Z., Powers, B., Vogeli, C., & Mullainathan, S. (2019). Dissecting racial bias in an algorithm used to manage the health of populations. *Science, 366*(6464), 447–453. PMID: 31649194

OECD. (2023). *Health at a Glance 2023: OECD Indicators.* OECD Publishing., DOI: 10.1787/7a7afb35-

Oftedal, B., Bru, E., & Karlsen, B. (2011). Motivation for diet and exercise management among adults with type 2 diabetes. *Scandinavian Journal of Caring Sciences, 25*(4), 735–744. DOI: 10.1111/j.1471-6712.2011.00884.x PMID: 21443543

Okewu, E., Adewole, P., Misra, S., & Maskeliunas, R. (2021). Artificial Neural Networks for Educational Data Mining in Higher Education : A Sy ematic Literature Review Artificial Neural Networks for Educational Data Mining in Higher Education : A Systematic Literature Review. *Applied Artificial Intelligence, 35*(13), 983–1021. DOI: 10.1080/08839514.2021.1922847

Olaoye, E. F. (2024). Privacy and data protection in AI-enabled healthcare systems. https://doi.org/https://www.researchgate.net/publication/378287462_Privacy_and_data_protection_in_AI-enabled_healthcare_systems

Olatunji, I. E., Rauch, J., & Katzensteiner, M. (2021). *A Review of Anonymization for Healthcare Data.* 1–14.

Omidian, H. (2024). Synergizing blockchain and artificial intelligence to enhance healthcare. *Drug Discovery Today, 29*(9), 104111. PMID: 39034026

Oon, N. B., Khairudin, Z., Aryani, H., Rahman, A., Syamimi, N., Abu, H., Azimah, N., Aziz, A., Mara, U. T., Alam, S., Mara, U. T., & Buloh, S. (2024). *PREDICTION OF DIABETIC RETINOPATHY AMONG DIABETIC NEUROPATHY IN T2DM PATIENTS USING DATA. 9*(2), 1916–1929. https://doi.org/DOI: 10.24191/mjoc.v9i2.26720

Oracle Corporation. M. A. (1995). *MySQL.* https://www.mysql.com/

Or, C. K., Karsh, B. T., Severtson, D. J., Burke, L. J., Brown, R. L., & Brennan, P. F. (2010). Factors affecting home care patients' acceptance of a web-based interactive self-management technology. *Journal of the American Medical Informatics Association : JAMIA*, *18*(1), 51–59. DOI: 10.1136/jamia.2010.007336 PMID: 21131605

Ostchega, Y., Fryar, C. D., Nwankwo, T., & Nguyen, D. T. (2020). Hypertension prevalence among adults aged 18 and over: United States, 2017–2018, NCHS, National Health and Nutrition Examination Survey, 2017–2018: https://stacks.cdc.gov/view/cdc/87559, accessed 25-08-2023.

oVerf. (2023). Oxehealth. Abgerufen von https://www.oxehealth.com/oxevision (17.04.2024)

Owora, A. H., Tepper, R. S., Ramsey, C. D., & Becker, A. B. (2021). *Decision tree- based rules outperform risk scores for childhood asthma prognosis. January*, 1464–1473. https://doi.org/DOI: 10.1111/pai.13530

Pagliuso, A. T., Cardoso, R., & Spiegel, T. (2010). *Gestão organizacional: O desafio da construção do modelo de gestão.* Instituto Chiavenato (Org.), Saraiva.

Parcon, R. C. B., Setias, J. E. L., Holipas, M. T. M., & Ed, E. (2022). *Comparison of Transaction Reduction and Dynamic Itemset Counting Implementations of the Apriori algorithm in Python. 5*(1), 44–49.

Parekh, A. D. E., Shaikh, O. A., Manan, S., & Al Hasibuzzaman, M. (2023). Artificial intelligence (AI) in personalized medicine: AI-generated personalized therapy regimens based on genetic and medical history. *Annals of Medicine and Surgery (London)*, *85*(11), 5831–5833. PMID: 37915639

Pasdar, A., Lee, Y. C., & Dong, Z. (2023). Connect API with blockchain: A survey on blockchain oracle implementation. *ACM Computing Surveys*, *55*(10), 1–39.

Pasqualini, I., & Piuzzi, N. S. (2023). Patient-reported outcome measures: State of the art in patient-reported outcome measure application in lower extremity orthopaedics. *JAAOS-Journal of the American Academy of Orthopaedic Surgeons*, *31*(20), e883–e889. DOI: 10.5435/JAAOS-D-23-00586 PMID: 37543754

Patel, S. Y., Mehrotra, A., Huskamp, H. A., Uscher-Pines, L., Ganguli, I., & Barnett, M. L. (2021). Trends in Outpatient Care Delivery and Telemedicine During the COVID-19 Pandemic in the US. *JAMA Internal Medicine*, *181*(3), 388–391. DOI: 10.1001/jamainternmed.2020.5928 PMID: 33196765

Pathak, A., Abbott, J. H., Bajracharya, N., Gurung, G., Nepal, G. M., & Sharma, S. (2023). Barriers and facilitators to implementation of outcome measures among physiotherapists in Nepal: A mixed-methods study. *Musculoskeletal Science & Practice*, *68*, 102859. PMID: 37844424

Patil, S., Kanade, T. M., & Batule, R. (2024). Exploring digital healthcare trends: Integrating people, technology, and procedures for a comprehensive healthcare ecosystem. In *AIP Conference Proceedings. 3178*(1), 060002.

Peng, Y., Yang, Y., Xu, Y., Xue, Y., Song, R., Kang, J., Zhao, H., & Member, S. (2021). Electricity Theft Detection in AMI Based on Clustering and Local Outlier Factor. *IEEE Access : Practical Innovations, Open Solutions*, *9*, 107250–107259. DOI: 10.1109/ACCESS.2021.3100980

Petersen, F., Jacobs, M., & Pather, S. (2020, 2020//). Barriers for User Acceptance of Mobile Health Applications for Diabetic Patients: Applying the UTAUT Model. Responsible Design, Implementation and Use of Information and Communication Technology, Cham.

Peters, U. (2023). Explainable AI lacks regulative reasons: Why AI and human decision-making are not equally opaque. *AI and Ethics*, *3*(3), 963–974.

Pham, S. D., Keijzer, H. M., Ruijter, B. J., Seeber, A. A., Scholten, E., Drost, G., & Tjepkema-Cloostermans, M. C. (2022). Outcome prediction of postanoxic coma: A comparison of automated electroencephalography analysis methods. *Neurocritical Care*, *37*(Suppl 2), 248–258.

Philpot, L. M., Barnes, S. A., Brown, R. M., Austin, J. A., James, C. S., Stanford, R. H., & Ebbert, J. O. (2018). Barriers and benefits to the use of patient-reported outcome measures in routine clinical care: A qualitative study. *American Journal of Medical Quality*, *33*(4), 359–364. PMID: 29258323

Plum, F., & Posner, J. B. (1982). *The diagnosis of stupor and coma* (Vol. 19). Oxford University Press.

Polotskaya, K., Muñoz-valencia, C. S., Rabasa, A., Quesada-rico, J. A., Orozco-beltrán, D., & Barber, X. (2024). *Bayesian Networks for the Diagnosis and Prognosis of Diseases : A Scoping Review*. 1243–1262.

Ponnuviji, N. P., Elangovan, G., Sujatha, K., Jambulingam, U., Ganesan, I., & Lalitha, S. D. (2024). IoT-Enabled Assistive Technologies Approach for Personalized Geriatric Health Monitoring and Safety. In Future of AI in Biomedicine and Biotechnology (pp. 125-146). IGI Global.

Porter, I. (2024). Patient-reported indicator surveys (PaRIS): Measuring patient-reported experiences and outcomes across populations and health systems. *European Journal of Public Health, 34*(Supplement_3), ckae144.367. https://doi.org/DOI: 10.1093/eurpub/ckae144.367

Porter, M. E. (2010). What is value in health care? *The New England Journal of Medicine, 363*(26), 2477–2481. DOI: 10.1056/NEJMp1011024 PMID: 21142528

Porter, M. E., & Lee, T. H. (2013). The strategy that will fix health care. *Harvard Business Review, 91*(10), 1–19.

Porter, M. E., & Teisberg, E. O. (2006). *Redefining health care: Creating value-based competition on results*. Harvard Business School Press.

Pradeep, R., Ma, X., Nogueira, R., & Lin, J. (2021). Scientific Claim Verification with VerT5erini. In Holderness, E., Jimeno Yepes, A., Lavelli, A., Minard, A.-L., Pustejovsky, J., and Rinaldi, F., editors, *Proceedings of the 12th International Workshop on Health Text Mining and Information Analysis*, pages 94–103, online. Association for Computational Linguistics.

Pradhan, D., Sahu, P. K., Tun, H. M., & Chatterjee, P. (Eds.). (2024). *Artificial and Cognitive Computing for Sustainable Healthcare Systems in Smart Cities*. John Wiley & Sons.

Pradipta Biswas, S. S. (2023). Recent advances in robot-assisted surgical systems. *Biomedical Engineering Advances, 6*, •••. https://doi.org/https://doi.org/10.1016/j.bea.2023.100109

Priyadharshini, S. I., Irene, D. S., Beulah, J. R., & Ponnuviji, N. P. (2025). Enhancing real-time health monitoring with hybrid recurrent long short-term tyrannosaurus search for menstrual cups. *Biomedical Signal Processing and Control, 100*, 107065.

Prof, H. M. (2008). Rehabilitation and Health Care Robotics. In *Springer Handbook of Robotics*. Springer.

PWC. (2013). Healthcare's new entrants: Who will be the industry's Amazon.com? Retrieved from https://www.pwc.com/us/en/health-industries/top-health-industry-issues/assets/pwc-hri-top-issues-2013.pdf

PWC. (n.d.). Digital healthcare.

Qama, E., Rubinelli, S., & Diviani, N. (2022). Factors influencing the integration of self-management in daily life routines in chronic conditions: A scoping review of qualitative evidence. *BMJ Open*, *12*(12), e066647.

Queralt, M. S., Galofré, M., Tio, L., Monfort, J., Monllau, J. C., Piella, G., & Noailly, J. (2024). Characterization of clinical data for patient stratification in moderate osteoarthritis with support vector machines, regulatory network models, and verification against osteoarthritis Initiative data. *Scientific Reports*, *0123456789*, 1–11. DOI: 10.1038/s41598-024-62212-x

Raftari, A. (2022). *Framework for Evaluation of Blockchain-AI Technology and Governance to Secure Interoperable US Healthcare Data* (Doctoral dissertation, Northcentral University). Available at: https://shorturl.at/VuXNH

Rahman, M. H., Islam, T., Hossen, M. E., Chowdhury, M. E., Hayat, R., Shovon, M. S. S., & Sunny, A. R. (2024). Machine Learning in Healthcare: From Diagnostics to Personalized Medicine and Predictive Analytics. *Journal of Angiotherapy*, *8*(12), 1–8.

Raina, A., Mishra, P., & Kumar, D. (2024). AI as a Medical Ally: Evaluating ChatGPT's Usage and Impact in Indian Healthcare. *arXiv preprint arXiv:2401.15605*.

Rajendra, P., & Latifi, S. (2021). *Computer Methods and Programs in Biomedicine Update Prediction of diabetes using logistic regression and ensemble techniques. 1*, 1–8.

Rajendran, T., Rajathi, S. A., Balakrishnan, C., Aswini, J., Prakash, R. B., & Subramanian, R. S. (2023, December). Risk prediction modeling for breast cancer using supervised machine learning approaches. In 2023 2nd International Conference on Automation, Computing and Renewable Systems (ICACRS) (pp. 702-708). IEEE.

Ramesh, J. V. N., Talukdar, V., Kurniullah, A. Z., Jain, S. K., Anand, R., & Gupta, A. (2025). Integration of Generative AI System to IoT Based Healthcare Systems 5.0. In *Revolutionizing Healthcare 5.0: The Power of Generative AI: Advancements in Patient Care Through Generative AI Algorithms* (pp. 199–217). Springer Nature Switzerland.

Rao, T. V. N. (2011). 5g technologies–An anecdote of network service for the future. Journal of global research in computer science, 2(7), 164-170.

Rao, T. N., Tejaswini, V., & Preethi, K. (2012). Defending against web vulnerabilities and cross-site scripting. *Journal of Global Research in Computer Science*, *3*(5), 61–64.

Rastogi, R., & Bansal, M. (2023). Measurement : Sensors. *Measurement: Sensors, 25*(December 2022), 100605. https://doi.org/DOI: 10.1016/j.measen.2022.100605

Ratwani, R. M., Sutton, K., & Galarraga, J. E. (2024). Addressing AI algorithmic bias in health care. *Journal of the American Medical Association*, *332*(13), 1051–1052. PMID: 39230911

Razdan, S., & Sharma, S. (2022). Internet of medical things (IoMT): Overview, emerging technologies, and case studies. *IETE Technical Review*, *39*(4), 775–788.

Rb, A., & Kr, S. K. (2021). Credit card fraud detection using artificial neural network. *Global Transitions Proceedings*, *2*(1), 35–41. DOI: 10.1016/j.gltp.2021.01.006

Reddy, V. S., Rao, T. V., & Govardhan, A. (2017). Data mining techniques for data streams mining. Review of computer engineering studies, 4(1), 31-35.

Reddy, S. (2024). Generative AI in healthcare: An implementation science informed translational path on application, integration and governance. *Implementation Science : IS*, *19*(1), 27.

Rehan, H. (2023). Artificial intelligence and machine learning: The impact of machine learning on predictive analytics in healthcare. *Innovative Computer Sciences Journal*, *9*(1), 1–20.

Reine, S., Archer, H., Alshaikhsalama, A., Wells, J., Kohli, A., Xi, Y., & Chhabra, A. (2022). Deep Learning-Generated Radiographic Hip Dysplasia Parameters: Relationship to Postoperative Patient-Reported Outcome Measures. Available at: https://www.researchsquare.com/article/rs-1867063/v1

Reiner, G. (2019). *Aidoc Brings Lifesaving AI Advancements to Medical Imaging on AWS*. Amazon Web Services. https://aws.amazon.com/solutions/case-studies/aidoc-case-study/

Ressi, D., Romanello, R., Piazza, C., & Rossi, S. (2024). AI-enhanced blockchain technology: A review of advancements and opportunities. *Journal of Network and Computer Applications*, •••, 103858.

Rethlefsen, M. L., Kirtley, S., Waffenschmidt, S., Ayala, A. P., Moher, D., Page, M. J., & Koffel, J. B., & Group, P.-S. (2021). PRISMA-S: An extension to the PRISMA statement for reporting literature searches in systematic reviews. *Journal of the Medical Library Association: JMLA*, *109*(2), 174–200. DOI: 10.5195/jmla.2021.962 PMID: 34285662

Reyna, M. A., Amorim, E., Sameni, R., Weigle, J., Elola, A., Rad, A. B., & Seyedi, S.. (2023). *"Predicting neurological recovery from coma after cardiac arrest: The George B. Moody PhysioNet Challenge 2023." In 2023 Computing in Cardiology (CinC)* (Vol. 50). IEEE.

Richardson, W. S., Wilson, M. C., Nishikawa, J., & Hayward, R. S. (1995). The well-built clinical question: A key to evidence-based decisions. [Publisher: American College of Physicians.]. *ACP Journal Club*, *123*(3), A12.

Rivera, S. C., Liu, X., Hughes, S. E., Dunster, H., Manna, E., Denniston, A. K., & Calvert, M. J. (2023). Embedding patient-reported outcomes at the heart of artificial intelligence health-care technologies. *The Lancet. Digital Health*, *5*(3), e168–e173. PMID: 36828609

Romeo, L.Marani, R., DÓrazio, T. & Cicirelli, G. (2023). Video based mobility monitoring of elderly people using deep learning models. *IEEE Access : Practical Innovations, Open Solutions*, *11*, 2804–2819. DOI: 10.1109/ACCESS.2023.3234421

Rosa, M., & Gomez, C. De. (2024). *A Comprehensive Introduction to Healthcare Data Analytics*. *4*(1), 44–53.

Rosaline, R. A. A., & Ponnuviji, N. P., TC, S. L., & Manisha, G. (2023). Enhancing lifestyle and health monitoring of elderly populations using CSA-TkELM classifier. *Knowledge-Based Systems*, *276*, 110758.

Rosenstock, I. M., Strecher, V. J., & Becker, M. H. (1988). Social learning theory and the Health Belief Model. *Health Education Quarterly*, *15*(2), 175–183. DOI: 10.1177/109019818801500203 PMID: 3378902

Ruani, M. A., Reiss, M. J., & Kalea, A. Z. (2023). Diet-nutrition information seeking, source trustworthiness, and eating behavior changes: An international web-based survey. *Nutrients*, *15*(21), 4515.

Ruifeng, S. (2021). *Research on data mining system based on artificial intelligence and improved genetic algorithm*. *40*, 6731–6742. https://doi.org/DOI: 10.3233/JIFS-189507

Rummo, P. E., Cassidy, O., Wells, I., Coffino, J. A., & Bragg, M. A. (2020). Examining the relationship between youth-targeted food marketing expenditures and the demographics of social media followers. *International Journal of Environmental Research and Public Health*, *17*(5), 1631.

Saeedi, P., Petersohn, I., Salpea, P., Malanda, B., Karuranga, S., Unwin, N., Colagiuri, S., Guariguata, L., Motala, A. A., Ogurtsova, K., Shaw, J. E., Bright, D., Williams, R., & Committee, I. D. F. D. A. (2019). Global and regional diabetes prevalence estimates for 2019 and projections for 2030 and 2045: Results from the International Diabetes Federation Diabetes Atlas, 9(th) edition. *Diabetes Research and Clinical Practice*, *157*, 107843. DOI: 10.1016/j.diabres.2019.107843 PMID: 31518657

Saeedizade, M. J., & Blomqvist, E. (2024). Navigating ontology development with large language models. In *Proceedings of the European Semantic Web Conference* (pp. 143-161).

Saidi, M., Gheibi, M., Ghazikhani, A., Lotfata, A., Chahkandi, B., & Ghazikhani, A. (2025). Efficient COVID-19 detection using data mining algorithms : A comparison of basic and hybrid approaches. *Soft Computing*, *29*(3), 1437–1451. DOI: 10.1007/s00500-025-10538-7

Saint-Pierre, C., Herskovic, V., & Sepúlveda, M. (2018). Multidisciplinary collaboration in primary care: A systematic review. *Family Practice*, *35*(2), 132–141. PMID: 28973173

Sallam, M. (2023). ChatGPT utility in healthcare education, research, and practice: systematic review on the promising perspectives and valid concerns. In *Healthcare* MDPI, Vol. 11, No. 6, p. 887.

Samariya, D., & Thakkar, A. (2023). A Comprehensive Survey of Anomaly Detection Algorithms. *Annals of Data Science*, *10*(3), 829–850. DOI: 10.1007/s40745-021-00362-9

Samsi, S., Zhao, D., McDonald, J., Li, B., Michaleas, A., Jones, M., & Gadepally, V. (2023). From words to watts: Benchmarking the energy costs of large language model inference. In *Proceedings of IEEE High Performance Extreme Computing Conference (HPEC)* (pp. 1-9).

Sanchez-Gavilan, E., Montiel, E., & Baladas, M.. (2022). Added value of patient-reported outcome measures (PROMs) after an acute stroke and early predictors of 90 days PROMs. *Journal of Patient-Reported Outcomes*, *6*, 66. DOI: 10.1186/s41687-022-00472-9 PMID: 35695977

Sanjeev, C., Dash, K., Kumar, A., Dehuri, S., & Ghosh, A. (2023). An outliers detection and elimination framework in classification task of data mining. *Decision Analytics Journal*, *6*(January), 100164. DOI: 10.1016/j.dajour.2023.100164

Sarah, A., & Alzakari, A. A. (2024). Enhanced heart disease prediction in remote healthcare monitoring using IoT-enabled cloud-based XGBoost and Bi-LSTM. *Alexandria Engineering Journal*, *105*, 280–291. https://doi.org/https://doi.org/10.1016/j.aej.2024.06.036

Sathyanarayana, S., Satzoda, R. K., Sathyanarayana, S., & Thambipillai, S. (2018). Vision-based patient monitoring: A comprehensive review of algorithms and technologies. *Journal of Ambient Intelligence and Humanized Computing*, *9*, 225–251. DOI: 10.1007/s12652-015-0328-1 scheme, N. D. s. *Diabetes-related complication*. Retrieved 7/2/2022 from https://www.ndss.com.au/

Schrier, E., Schrier, I., Geertzen, J. H., & Dijkstra, P. U. (2016). Quality of life in rehabilitation outpatients: Normal values and a comparison with the general Dutch population and psychiatric patients. *Quality of Life Research: An International Journal of Quality of Life Aspects of Treatment, Care and Rehabilitation*, *25*, 135–142. PMID: 26159567

Schriml, L. M., Munro, J. B., Schor, M., Olley, D., McCracken, C., Felix, V., & Greene, C. (2022). The human disease ontology 2022 update. *Nucleic Acids Research*, *50*(D1), D1255–D1261.

Segado-Fernández, S. S., Gómez, B. J., Hidalgo, P. J., Lozano-Estevan, M. D. C., & Peco, I. H. (2025). Disinformation about diet and nutrition on social networks: A review of the literature. *Nutrición Hospitalaria*, *42*(2), 366–375. DOI: 10.20960/nh.05533

Seigel, C. R., Holly, M., Bastin, G., Myers, L. J., Taylor, S., Pike, F., Wilkinson, J., & Williams, L. S. (2024). Patient acceptance of teleneurology across neurologic conditions. *Journal of Neurology*, *271*, 2850–2858. DOI: 10.1007/s00415-024-12200-y

Selvanayagam, N.. (2021). Reliability of patient-reported outcome measures: Hemorrhage, anticoagulant, antiplatelet medication use. *Research and Practice in Thrombosis and Haemostasis*, *5*(4), e12501. DOI: 10.1002/rth2.12501 PMID: 34027288

Shapiro, L. M., Katz, P., Stern, B. Z., & Kamal, R. N. (2024). Equitable integration of patient-reported outcomes into clinical practice—Opportunities, challenges, and a roadmap for implementation. *The Journal of the American Academy of Orthopaedic Surgeons*, *32*(5), 187–195. DOI: 10.5435/JAAOS-D-23-00798 PMID: 38194644

Shawkat, M., Badawi, M., & El, S. (2022). An optimized FP - growth algorithm for discovery of association rules. *The Journal of Supercomputing*, *78*(4), 5479–5506. DOI: 10.1007/s11227-021-04066-y

Shiny Irene, D., Indra Priyadharshini, S., Ponnuviji, N. P., & Kalaivani, A. (2024). Technological advancements in menstrual health: The role of generative pre-trained transformer and bees algorithm. *Journal of the Institution of Electronics and Telecommunication Engineers*, *70*(12), 8476–8491.

Shiny Irene, D., Ponnuviji, N. P., & Kalaivani, A. (2025). EHECA-HSWS: A Holistic Method for Improving Menstrual Health App User Experience. *Journal of the Institution of Electronics and Telecommunication Engineers*, •••, 1–12.

Shreyas Suresh Rao, S. L. (2023). *AIoT and Big Data Analytics for Smart Healthcare Applications*. Bentham Science Publishers., DOI: 10.2174/97898151960541230501

Shukla, A., Chaurasia, S., Pandey, G., Shukla, S. K., & Parihar, S. S. (2025).. . *Privacy-Preserving Data Mining Methods Metrics and Applications in Healthcare Informatics., 04002*, 1–9.

Shukla, K., & Attar, A. (2024). The role of PROMs in mitigating infectious disease crises: A healthy ageing perspective. In *Sustainable Ageing: Reimagining Healthy Ageing Through the Lens of Flagship Campaigns* (pp. 189–209). Springer Nature Switzerland.

Siddhant Thapliyal, M. W. (2024). Secure Artificial Intelligence of Things (AIoT)-enabled authenticated key agreement technique for smart living environment. *Computers & Electrical Engineering, 118*, •••. https://doi.org/https://doi.org/10.1016/j.compeleceng.2024.109353

Silva, B., Contreras, M., Baslanti, T. O., Ren, Y., Guan, Z., Khezeli, K., Bihorac, A., & Rashidi, P. (2023). "Transformer models for acute brain dysfunction prediction." arXiv preprint arXiv:2303.07305.

Simons, L. P. A., Gerritsen, B., Wielaard, B., & Neerincx, M. A. (2022b). Health Self-Management Support with Microlearning to Improve Hypertension, pp. 511-524, 35th Bled eConference. June 26-29, Bled, Slovenia, from www.bledconference.org

Simons, L. P. A., Gerritsen, B., Wielaard, B., & Neerincx, M. A. (2023b). Hypertension Self-Management Success in 2 weeks; 3 Pilot Studies, pp.19-34, 36th Bled eConference. June 25-28, Bled, Slovenia.

Simons, L. P. A., Murukannaiah, P. K., & Neerincx, M. A. (2024b). Designing and Evaluating an LLM-based Health AI Research Assistant for Hypertension Self-Management; Using Health Claims Metadata Criteria, pp.283-298, 37th Bled eConference. June 9-12, Bled, Slovenia, Proceedings.

Simons, L. P. A., Neerincx, M. A., & Jonker, C. M. (2021). Health Literature Hybrid AI for Health Improvement; A Design Analysis for Diabetes & Hypertension, pp. 184-197, 34th Bled eConference. June 27-30, Bled, Slovenia, Retrieval www.bledconference.org

Simons, L., Gerritsen, B., Wielaard, B., & Neerincx, M. A. (2022). Health self-management support with microlearning to improve hypertension.

Simons, L., Wielaard, B., & Neerincx, M. A. (2025). Beyond Average Results in Hypertension E-Support and Self-Management: Three Pilot Studies With Social Learning. In *Impact of Digital Solutions for Improved Healthcare Delivery* (pp. 257-282). IGI Global.

Simon, S. J., Grant, A. R., Niu, R., Olatunbosun, S., Talmo, C. T., & Hollenbeck, B. L. (2025). Which patient factors influence pre-operative and post-operative completion of patient reported outcome surveys in total joint replacement surgery? *Journal of Orthopaedics*, *68*, 131–136. PMID: 40093815

Simons, L. P. A. (2023a). Health 2050: Faster Cure via Bioinformatics & Quantified Self; A Design Analysis. *International Journal of Networking and Virtual Organisations*, *28*(1), 36–52. DOI: 10.1504/IJNVO.2023.130957

Simons, L. P. A., Gerritsen, B., Wielaard, B., & Neerincx, M. A. (2024a). Employee Hypertension Self-Management Support with Microlearning and Social Learning. *International Journal of Networking and Virtual Organisations*, *30*(4), 350–365.

Simons, L. P. A., Neerincx, M. A., & Jonker, C. M. (2022a). Is Google Making us Smart? Health Self-Management for High Performance Employees & Organisations. *International Journal of Networking and Virtual Organisations*, *27*(3), 200–216.

Simons, L. P., Gerritsen, B., Wielaard, B., & Neerincx, M. A. (2024). Employee hypertension self-management support with microlearning and social learning. *International Journal of Networking and Virtual Organisations*, *30*(4), 350–365.

Singh, A., Singh, U., Pandey, V., Deotale, N., & Talekar, P. (2024). Detecting Human Activities In COMA Patients Using ML Algorithm.

Singhal, K., Azizi, S., Tu, T., Mahdavi, S. S., Wei, J., Chung, H. W., & Natarajan, V. (2023). Large language models encode clinical knowledge. *Nature*, *620*(7972), 172–180.

Singh, S., Bhatt, P., Sharma, S. K., & Rabiu, S. (2021). Digital transformation in healthcare: Innovation and technologies. In *Blockchain for Healthcare Systems* (pp. 61–79). CRC Press.

Sinha, N., Ghosh, M., Majumder, S., & Bhowmik, B. B. (2021). "Deep Learning based noise identification in the Optical fiber communication using Variational Mode Decomposition." In 2021 IEEE 2nd International Conference on Applied Electromagnetics, Signal Processing, & Communication (AESPC), pp. 1-5. IEEE.

Siva, S. R., Sudha, K., Pooja, E., Maheswari, B., & Girija, P. (2024). Revolutionizing Healthcare Delivery: Applications and Impact of Cutting-Edge Technologies. AI and IoT Technology and Applications for Smart Healthcare Systems, 75-91.

Soares, B., Ferreira, A., & Veiga, P. M. (2023). The Benefits and Challenges of Blockchain Technology and eHealth Implementation in Estonia-A Literature Review. *Applied Medical Informatics*, *45*(4).

Sofia, C., & Pereira, A. M. (2024). Automated image label extraction from radiology reports — A review. *Artificial Intelligence in Medicine*, *149*, •••. https://doi.org/https://doi.org/10.1016/j.artmed.2024.102814

Sohail, A. (2023). Genetic Algorithms in the Fields of Artificial Intelligence and Data Sciences. *Annals of Data Science*, *10*(4), 1007–1018. DOI: 10.1007/s40745-021-00354-9

Sokas, C., Hu, F., Edelen, M., Sisodia, R., Pusic, A., & Cooper, Z. (2022). A review of PROM implementation in surgical practice. *Annals of Surgery*, *275*(1), 85–90. PMID: 34183512

Soleimani, A., Monz, C., & Worring, M. (2020). BERT for Evidence Retrieval and Claim Verification. In Jose, J. M., Yilmaz, E., Magalhaes, J., Castells, P., Ferro, N., Silva, ˜. M. J., & Martins, F. (Eds.), *Advances in Information Retrieval* (pp. 359–366). Springer International Publishing.

Soydaner, D. (2022). Attention mechanism in neural networks: Where it comes and where it goes. *Neural Computing & Applications*, *34*(16), 13371–13385.

Stange, K. C. M. D. P. (2009). The Problem of Fragmentation and the Need for Integrative Solutions. *Annals of Family Medicine*, *7*(2), 100–103. DOI: 10.1370/afm.971 PMID: 19273863

Steinhardt, M. A., Brown, S. A., Lehrer, H. M., Dubois, S. K., Wright, J. I., Whyne, E. Z., Sumlin, L. L., Harrison, L.Jr, & Woo, J. (2021). Diabetes Self-Management Education and Support Culturally Tailored for African Americans: COVID-19-Related Factors Influencing Restart of the TX STRIDE Study. *The Science of Diabetes Self-Management and Care*, *47*(4), 290–301. DOI: 10.1177/26350106211027956 PMID: 34318725

Stevens, R. D., & Bhardwaj, A. (2006). Approach to the comatose patient. *Critical Care Medicine*, *34*(1), 31–41. PMID: 16374153

Stoumpos, A. I., Kitsios, F., & Talias, M. A. (2023). Digital transformation in healthcare: Technology acceptance and its applications. *International Journal of Environmental Research and Public Health*, *20*(4), 3407. PMID: 36834105

Strougo, A. D., Assad, D. B. N., Spiegel, T., & Nobrega, C. (2021). *Guia de projeto de serviços de saúde baseados em valor*. Eduerj. https://eduerj.com/produto/guia-de-projeto-de-servicos-de-saude-baseados-em-valor-ebook/

Suarez-Lledo, V., & Alvarez-Galvez, J. (2021). Prevalence of health misinformation on social media: Systematic review. *Journal of Medical Internet Research*, *23*(1), e17187.

Sudha, K., Ambhika, C., Maheswari, B., Girija, P., & Nalini, M. (2023). AI and IoT applications in medical domain enhancing healthcare through technology integration. In *AI and IoT-Based Technologies for Precision Medicine* (pp. 280–294). IGI Global.

Sudha, K., Lakshmipriya, C., Pajila, P. B., Venitha, E., & Anita, M. (2024, January). Enhancing Diabetes Prediction and Management through Machine Learning: A Comparative Study. In *2024 Fourth International Conference on Advances in Electrical, Computing, Communication and Sustainable Technologies (ICAECT)* (pp. 1-6). IEEE.

Sun, J., Williams, D., & Li, Y. (2021). Let's Bail!: The evolution of individual-group affiliation in an online gaming community. *Computers in Human Behavior*, *121*, 106818. DOI: 10.1016/j.chb.2021.106818

Sun, X., Yu, F. R., Zhang, P., Sun, Z., Xie, W., & Peng, X. (2021). A survey on zero-knowledge proof in blockchain. *IEEE Network*, *35*(4), 198–205.

Sun, Y. (2022)... *Multimedia Technology of Spatial Data Mining Based on Genetic Algorithm., 2022*. Advance online publication. DOI: 10.1155/2022/4835359

Suresh Babu, C. V. M. S. (2024). AIoT Revolution: Transforming Networking Productivity for the Digital Age. In *Artificial Intelligence of Things (AIoT) for Productivity and Organizational Transition*. IGI Global.

Sushil Bhardwaj, I. S. (2025). Exploring the Role of AIoT in Data Privacy and Security. In M. U. Tariq, *Merging Artificial Intelligence With the Internet of Things* (pp. 75-102). IGI Global.

Swarnakar, R., & Yadav, S. L. (2023). Artificial intelligence and machine learning in motor recovery: A rehabilitation medicine perspective. *World Journal of Clinical Cases*, *11*(29), 7258. PMID: 37946764

Tabianan, K., & Velu, S. (2022). *K-Means Clustering Approach for Intelligent Customer Segmentation Using Customer Purchase Behavior Data*. 1–15.

Taherdoost, H. (2024). Wearable Healthcare and Continuous Vital Sign Monitoring with IoT Integration. *Computers, Materials & Continua*, *81*(1).

Tarakanita, N. I., & Amaliah, Y. (2023)... *Analisa Metode Association Rule Untuk Penjualan Skincare Menggunakan Algoritma Pincer Serach Analysis of Association Rule Methods for Skincare Sales Using the Pincer Search Algorithm.*, *6*(2), 25–29.

Temple, L. K. F., & Morris, A. M. (2020). Patient-reported outcomes in surgical research. In Dimick, J., & Lubitz, C. (Eds.), *Health services research* (pp. 105–113). Springer., DOI: 10.1007/978-3-030-28357-5_10

Tetiana Habuza, A. N. (2021). AI applications in robotics, diagnostic image analysis and precision medicine: Current limitations, future trends, guidelines on CAD systems for medicine. *Informatics in Medicine Unlocked*, *24*, •••. https://doi.org/https://doi.org/10.1016/j.imu.2021.100596

Tewari, S., Coyne, K. D., Weinerman, R. S., Findley, J., Kim, S. T., & Flyckt, R. L. (2023). Racial Disparities in Telehealth Use During the COVID-19 Pandemic. *Fertility and Sterility*. Advance online publication. DOI: 10.1016/j.fertnstert.2023.05.159 PMID: 37244379

Thakkar, H., Shah, V., Yagnik, H., & Shah, M. (2022). Clinical eHealth Comparative anatomization of data mining and fuzzy logic techniques used in diabetes prognosis. *Clinical EHealth, 4*(2021), 12–23. https://doi.org/DOI: 10.1016/j.ceh.2020.11.001

Thakre, D., & Patel, J. (2024, November). The Advancements and Benefits of AI-Assisted Robotic Surgery. In *2024 2nd DMIHER International Conference on Artificial Intelligence in Healthcare, Education and Industry (IDICAIEI)* (pp. 1-5). IEEE.

Thaler, R. H., & Sunstein, C. R. (2008). *Nudge: Improving decisions about health, wealth, and happiness*. Yale University Press.

Thirunavukarasu, A. J., Ting, D. S. J., Elangovan, K., Gutierrez, L., Tan, T. F., & Ting, D. S. W. (2023). Large language models in medicine. *Nature Medicine*, *29*(8), 1930–1940.

Timothy Malche, S. T. (2022). Artificial Intelligence of Things- (AIoT-) Based Patient Activity Tracking System for Remote Patient Monitoring. *Journal of Healthcare Engineering*. https://doi.org/ https://doi.org/10.1155/2022/8732213

Topol, E. (2019). *Deep medicine: how artificial intelligence can make healthcare human again*. Hachette UK. Available at: https://shorturl.at/GYNij

Topol, E. J. (2019a). High-performance medicine: The convergence of human and artificial intelligence. *Nature Medicine*, *25*(1), 44–56. PMID: 30617339

Touati, S., Boumediri, H., Karmi, Y., & Chitour, M. (2025). Heliyon Performance analysis of steel W18CR4V grinding using RSM, DNN-GA, KNN, LM, DT, SVM models, and optimization via desirability function and MOGWO. *Heliyon*, *11*(4), e42640. DOI: 10.1016/j.heliyon.2025.e42640

Trautmann, F., Hentschel, L., Hornemann, B., Rentsch, A., Baumann, M., Ehninger, G., & Schuler, M. (2016). Electronic real-time assessment of patient-reported outcomes in routine care—First findings and experiences from the implementation in a comprehensive cancer center. *Supportive Care in Cancer*, *24*, 3047–3056. PMID: 26887586

Tsaneva, S., Vasic, S., & Sabou, M. (2024). LLM-driven ontology evaluation: Verifying ontology restrictions with ChatGPT. In *Proceedings of The Semantic Web: ESWC Satellite Events*.

Tsvetanov, F. (2024). Integrating AI technologies into remote monitoring patient systems. *Engineering Proceedings*, *70*(1), 54.

Tu, K.-C., Nyam, T.-T. E., Wang, C.-C., Chen, N.-C., Chen, K.-T., Chen, C.-J., Liu, C.-F., & Kuo, J.-R. (2022). A computer-assisted system for early mortality risk prediction in patients with traumatic brain injury using artificial intelligence algorithms in emergency room triage. *Brain Sciences*, *12*(5), 612. PMID: 35624999

Tyagi, A., & Singh, P. (2014). Asthma diagnosis and level of control using decision tree and fuzzy system. *Int. J. Biomedical Engineering and Technology J. Biomedical Engineering and Technology*, *16*(2), 169–181. DOI: 10.1504/IJBET.2014.065658

Upsher, R., Noori, Y., Kuriakose, L., Vassiliadou, I., Winkley, K., & Ismail, K. (2022). Needs, concerns and self-management experiences of people with type 2 diabetes during the COVID-19 pandemic: A qualitative study. *Diabetic medicine*, *39*(8), e14883-n/a. https://doi.org/DOI: 10.1111/dme.14883

van der Harst, P., & Nathoe, H. (2025). Transforming cardiology with AI: The eko CORE 500 digital stethoscope. *Netherlands Heart Journal; Monthly Journal of the Netherlands Society of Cardiology and the Netherlands Heart Foundation*, •••, 1–2. PMID: 40138099

van Egdom, L. S. E., Lagendijk, M., Van Der Kemp, M. H., Van Dam, J. H., Mureau, M. A. M., Hazelzet, J. A., & Koppert, L. B. (2019). Implementation of value based breast cancer care. *European Journal of Surgical Oncology*, *45*(7), 1163–1170. PMID: 30638807

van Elten, H. J., Howard, S. W., De Loo, I., & Schaepkens, F. (2023). Reflections on Managing the Performance of Value-Based Healthcare: A Scoping Review. *International Journal of Health Policy and Management*, *12*, 7366. DOI: 10.34172/ijhpm.2023.7366 PMID: 37579381 van Staalduinen, D. J., van den Bekerom, P., Groeneveld, S., Kidanemariam, M., Stiggelbout, A. M., & van den Akker-van Marle, M. E. (2022). The implementation of value-based healthcare: A scoping review. *BMC Health Services Research*, *22*(1), 270. DOI: 10.1186/s12913-022-07489-2 PMID: 35227279

van Uum, R. T., Breteler, M., Hardeman, H., van de Pol, A. C., Smit, K., Boeijen, J. A., & Zwart, D. L. (2025). How Dutch initiatives to early discharge COVID-19 patients were organised during the pandemic: A scoping review. *BMJ Open*, *15*(8), e097839. PMID: 40858380

Vasconcelos, C., Costa, R. L. D., Dias, Á. L., Pereira, L., & Santos, J. P. (2021). Online influencers: Healthy food or fake news. *International Journal of Internet Marketing and Advertising*, *15*(2), 149–175.

Vaswani, A., Shazeer, N., Parmar, N., Uszkoreit, J., Jones, L., Gomez, A. N., . . . Polosukhin, I. (2017). Attention is all you need. *Advances in Neural Information Processing Systems, 30*. Available at: https://proceedings.neurips.cc/paper/2017/file/3f5ee243547dee91fbd053c1c4a845aa-Paper.pdf

Vaswani, A., Shazeer, N., Parmar, N., Uszkoreit, J., Jones, L., Gomez, A. N., & Polosukhin, I. (2017). Attention is all you need. *Advances in Neural Information Processing Systems*, •••, 30.

Vaughan, E., Foreyt, J., Virani, S., Balasubramanyam, A., Ballantyne, C., Amspoker, A., & Landrum, J. (2022, 2022). Mentored implementation to initiate a diabetes program in an underserved community: A pilot study.

Vayena, E., Blasimme, A., & Cohen, I. G. (2018). Machine learning in medicine: Addressing ethical challenges. *PLoS Medicine*, *15*(11), e1002689. DOI: 10.1371/journal.pmed.1002689 PMID: 30399149

Velupillai, S., Suominen, H., Liakata, M., Roberts, A., Shah, A. D., Morley, K., & Dutta, R. (2018). Using clinical natural language processing for health outcomes research: Overview and actionable suggestions for future advances. *Journal of Biomedical Informatics*, *88*, 11–19. PMID: 30368002

Venkat Narayana Rao, T., & Govardhan, A. (2015). Efficient segmentation and classification of mammogram images with fuzzy filtering. *Indian Journal of Science and Technology*, *8*(15), 1–8.

Venkat Narayana Rao, T., Unnisa, A., & Sreni, K. (2022). Medicine recommendation system based on patient reviews. *Int J Sci Technol Res*, *9*, 3308–3312.

Venkatesan, M., Kandalkar, S. K., Menon, R., Kulkarni, A. V., & Prasad, S. Predictive Internet of Things Based Detection Model of Comatose Patient using Deep Learning.

Venkatesh, V., & Brown, S. A. (2005). A longitudinal investigation of personal computers in homes: Adoption determinants and emerging challenges. *Management Information Systems Quarterly*, *29*(3), 425–478.

Venkatesh, V., Morris, M. G., Davis, G. B., & Davis, F. D. (2003). User Acceptance of Information Technology: Toward a Unified View. *Management Information Systems Quarterly*, *27*(3), 425–478. DOI: 10.2307/30036540

Venkatesh, V., Thong, J. Y. L., & Xu, X. (2012). Consumer acceptance and use of information technology: Extending the unified theory of acceptance and use of technology. *Management Information Systems Quarterly*, *36*(1), 157–178. DOI: 10.2307/41410412

Verma, D., Bach, K., & Mork, P. J. (2021). Application of machine learning methods on patient reported outcome measurements for predicting outcomes: A literature review. *Informatics (MDPI)*, *8*(3), 56.

Vijverberg, J. R. G., Daniels, K., Steinmann, G., Garvelink, M. M., Rouppe van der Voort, M. B. V., Biesma, D., Bos, W. J. W., van Merode, F., & van der Nat, P. (2022). Mapping the extent, range and nature of research activity on value-based healthcare in the 15 years following its introduction (2006-2021): A scoping review. *BMJ Open*, *12*(8), e064983. DOI: 10.1136/bmjopen-2022-064983 PMID: 35973705

Villagra, V. G., Bhuva, B., Coman, E., Smith, D. O., & Fifield, J. (2019). Health insurance literacy: Disparities by race, ethnicity, and language preference. *The American Journal of Managed Care*, *25*(3), e71–e75. PMID: 30875174

Villalba-Mora, E., Peinado-Martínez, I., & Pozo, F. (2017). eHealth and diabetes: Designing a novel system for remotely monitoring older adults with type 2 diabetes.

Vishwakarma, L. P., Singh, R. K., Mishra, R., & Kumari, A. (2025). Application of artificial intelligence for resilient and sustainable healthcare system: Systematic literature review and future research directions. *International Journal of Production Research*, *63*(2), 822–844.

Wachler., & Associates. P.C. (2024, Feb 16). *AI and Healthcare Regulatory Compliance.* Wachler & Associates, P.C. https://www.wachlerblog.com/ai-and-healthcare-regulatory-compliance/

Wadden, D., Lin, S., Lo, K., Wang, L. L., van Zuylen, M., Cohan, A., & Hajishirzi, H. (2020). Fact or Fiction: Verifying Scientific Claims. In Webber, B., Cohn, T., He, Y., and Liu, Y., editors, *Proceedings of the 2020 Conference on Empirical Methods in Natural Language Processing (EMNLP)*, pages 7534–7550, Online. Association for Computational Linguistics.

Waizinger, O., Shpigelman, M., Shental, R., Yunis, B., Shimoni, P., Od Cohen, Y., & Kagan, I. (2022). Diabetes nurse practitioners in the shadow of the COVID-19 pandemic: Challenges, insights, and suggestions for improvement. *Journal of nursing scholarship: an official publication of Sigma Theta Tau International Honor Society of Nursing, 54*(4), 453-461. https://doi.org/https://dx.doi.org/10.1111/jnu.12754

Wang, H. K. A. (2025). HealthAIoT: AIoT-driven smart healthcare system for sustainable cloud computing environments. *Internet of Things, 31*. https://doi.org/https://doi.org/10.1016/j.iot.2025.101555

Wang, H., Liu, C., Xi, N., Qiang, Z., Zhao, S., Qin, B., & Liu, T. (2023). Huatuo: Tuning Llama model with Chinese medical knowledge. *arXiv preprint arXiv:2304.06975.*

Wang, S., Ouyang, L., Yuan, Y., Ni, X., Han, X., & Wang, F. Y. (2019). Blockchain-enabled smart contracts: Architecture, applications, and future trends. *IEEE Transactions on Systems, Man, and Cybernetics. Systems, 49*(11), 2266–2277.

Wang, Y. S., Wang, Y. M., Lin, H. H., & Tang, T. I. (2003). Determinants of user acceptance of Internet banking: An empirical study. *International Journal of Service Industry Management, 14*(5), 501–519. DOI: 10.1108/09564230310500192

Wang, Y., Kung, L., & Byrd, T. A. (2020). Big data analytics: Understanding its capabilities and potential benefits for healthcare organizations. *Technological Forecasting and Social Change, 126*, 3–13. DOI: 10.1016/j.techfore.2020.120004

Wansink, B., & Sobal, J. (2007). Mindless eating: The 200 daily food decisions we overlook. *Environment and Behavior, 39*(1), 106–123.

Wei, J., & Tan, C. (2025). *Volunteer Management : A Data Mining Approach. March.*

West, D., & Miller, E. (2006). The Digital Divide in Public E-Health: Barriers to Accessibility and Privacy in State Health Department Websites. *Journal of Health Care for the Poor and Underserved, 17*, 652–667. DOI: 10.1353/hpu.2006.0115 PMID: 16960328

WHO. (2021). *Ethics and governance of artificial intelligence for health: WHO guidance*. World Health Organization.

Wickramasinghe, N., John, B., George, J., & Vogel, D. (2019). Achieving Value-Based Care in Chronic Disease Management: Intervention Study. *JMIR Diabetes, 4*(2), e10368. DOI: 10.2196/10368 PMID: 31066699

Wijaya, R., Saeed, F., Samimi, P., & Albarrak, A. M. (2024). *An Ensemble Machine Learning and Data Mining Approach to Enhance Stroke Prediction.*

Williams, K., Sansoni, J., Darcy, M., Grootemaat, P., & Thompson, C. (2016). *Patient-reported outcome measures. Literature review*. Australian Commission on Safety and Quality in Health Care., Available at https://www.safetyandquality.gov.au/sites/default/files/migrated/PROMs-stakeholder-interviews-report-2018.pdf

Wilson, L., Horton, L., Polinder, S., Newcombe, V. F., Steinbuechel, N. V., & Maas, A. I. & CENTER-TBI participants and investigators. (2022). Tailoring multidimensional outcomes to level of functional recovery after traumatic brain injury. *Journal of Neurotrauma*, *39*(19-20), 1363–1381. PMID: 35607855

Windle, N., Alam, A., Patel, H., Street, J. M., Lathwood, M., Farrington, T., & Maruthappu, M. (2024). Predicting Hospitalization Risk Among Home Care Residents in the United Kingdom: Development and Validation of a Machine Learning-Based Predictive Model. *Home Health Care Management & Practice*, *36*(4), 253–261.

Wright, K., & Singh, S. (2022). Reducing Falls in Dementia Inpatients Using Vision-Based Technology. *Journal of Patient Safety*, *18*(3), 177–181. DOI: 10.1097/PTS.0000000000000882

Wu, M., Subramaniam, G., Li, Z., & Gao, X. (2025). Using AI Technology to Enhance Data-Driven Decision-Making in the Financial Sector. *Artificial Intelligence-Enabled Businesses: How to Develop Strategies for Innovation*, 187-207.

Wu, S., Xiong, Y., Cui, Y., Wu, H., Chen, C., Yuan, Y., . . . Xue, C. J. (2024). Retrieval-augmented generation for natural language processing: A survey. *arXiv preprint arXiv:2407.13193*.

Wu, W. T., Li, Y. J., Feng, A. Z., Li, L., Huang, T., Xu, A. D., & Lyu, J. (2021). *Data mining in clinical big data : the frequently used databases, steps, and methodological models*. 1–12. https://doi.org/DOI: 10.1186/s40779-021-00338-z

Wu, B. L. (2022). Digital Transformation in Personalized Medicine with Artificial Intelligence and the Internet of Medical Things. *OMICS: A Journal of Integrative Biology*, *26*(2). https://doi.org/https://doi.org/10.1089/omi.2021.0037 PMID: 33887155

Wu, M., & Luo, J. (n.d.). *Wearable Technology Applications in Healthcare: A Literature Review*. Digital Health, Online Journal of Nursing Informatics Contributors. Retrieved from Kruse, C., Betancourt, J., Ortiz, S., Valdes Luna, S. M., Bamrah, I. K., & Segovia, N. (2019). Barriers to the use of mobile health in improving health outcomes in developing countries: Systematic review. *Journal of Medical Internet Research*, *21*(10), e13263. DOI: 10.2196/13263

Wu, Y., Ding, Y., Tanaka, Y., & Zhang, W. (2014). Risk factors contributing to type 2 diabetes and recent advances in the treatment and prevention. *International Journal of Medical Sciences, 11*(11), 1185–1200. DOI: 10.7150/ijms.10001 PMID: 25249787

Xiong, L., Zhu, Y., & Zaza, S. (2024). Enhancing data diversity and traceability to mitigate bias in healthcare AI: a blockchain-driven approach. In *Proceedings of the 2024 Computers and People Research Conference* (pp. 1-2). Available at: https://dl.acm.org/doi/abs/10.1145/3632634.3655881

Xu, H. (2022). *Outlier detection algorithm based on k-nearest neighbors-local outlier factor*. https://doi.org/DOI: 10.1177/17483026221078111

Yadav, A., & Kumar, A. (2021). *Improving the Performance of Multidimensional Clinical Data for OLAP using an Optimized Data Clustering approach. 12*(3), 3269–3275.

Yamini, B., Sudha, K., Nalini, M., Kavitha, G., Subramanian, R. S., & Sugumar, R. (2023, June). Predictive modelling for lung cancer detection using machine learning techniques. In 2023 8th International Conference on Communication and Electronics Systems (ICCES) (pp. 1220-1226). IEEE.

Yang, H. J., Lee, J.-H., & Lee, W. (2025, March 28). Factors Influencing Health Care Technology Acceptance in Older Adults Based on the Technology Acceptance Model and the Unified Theory of Acceptance and Use of Technology: Meta-Analysis. *Journal of Medical Internet Research, 27*(e65269). Advance online publication. DOI: 10.2196/65269 PMID: 40153796

Yang, L., Peng, S., Othman, R., & Leren, Y. (2023). Cancer detection in breast cells using a hybrid method based on deep complex neural network and data mining. *Journal of Cancer Research and Clinical Oncology, 149*(14), 13331–13344. DOI: 10.1007/s00432-023-05191-2

Yao, K. (2024). Measurement : Sensors Application of sensor-based speech data mining in E-commerce operations data analysis. *Measurement: Sensors, 33*(June 2023), 101118. https://doi.org/DOI: 10.1016/j.measen.2024.101118

Ye, H. U. A., Wu, P., Zhu, T., Xiao, Z., Zhang, X. I. E., Zheng, L., Zheng, R., Sun, Y., Zhou, W., Fu, Q., Ye, X., Chen, A. L. I., Zheng, S., Heidari, A. L. I. A., Wang, M., Zhu, J., Chen, H., Member, A., & Li, J. (2021). Diagnosing Coronavirus Disease 2019 (COVID-19). *Efficient Harris Hawks-Inspired Fuzzy K-Nearest Neighbor Prediction Methods., 9*, 17787–17802. DOI: 10.1109/ACCESS.2021.3052835

Yimer, H., Dereje Degefa, H., Cristani, M., & Cunico, F. (2024). IoT-Based Coma Patient Monitoring System. arXiv e-prints, arXiv-2411.

Yimer, H. L., Degefa, H. D., Cristani, M., & Cunico, F. (2024). *"IoT-Based Coma Patient Monitoring System." In 2024 IEEE International Multi-Conference on Smart Systems & Green Process (IMC-SSGP)*. IEEE.

Yin, Z., Yan, J., Fang, S., Wang, D., & Han, D. (2022). User acceptance of wearable intelligent medical devices through a modified unified theory of acceptance and use of technology. *Annals of Translational Medicine*, *10*(11), 629. DOI: 10.21037/atm-21-5510 PMID: 35813345

Yogeshappa, V. G. (2024). AI-driven Precision medicine: Revolutionizing personalized treatment plans. [IJCET]. *International Journal of Computer Engineering and Technology*, *15*(5), 455–474.

You, E. (2014). *Vue.js*. https://vuejs.org/

Young, T., Hazarika, D., Poria, S., & Cambria, E. (2018). Recent trends in deep learning based natural language processing. *IEEE Computational Intelligence Magazine*, *13*(3), 55–75.

Yu, C. S. (2012). Factors affecting individuals to adopt mobile banking: Empirical evidence from the UTAUT model. *Journal of Electronic Commerce Research*, *13*(2), 104–121.

Zahmani, M. H., & Atmani, B. (2021). Multiple dispatching rules allocation in real time using data mining, genetic algorithms, and simulation. *Journal of Scheduling*, *24*(2), 175–196. DOI: 10.1007/s10951-020-00664-5

Zaitoun, A., Sagi, T., Wilk, S., & Peleg, M. (2023). Can large language models augment a biomedical ontology with missing concepts and relations? *arXiv preprint arXiv:2311.06858*.

Zhang, X., Yuan, Z., & Miao, D. (2023). Outlier Detection Using Three-Way Neighborhood Characteristic Regions and Corresponding Fusion Measurement. *IEEE Transactions on Knowledge and Data Engineering, PP*, 1–14. https://doi.org/DOI: 10.1109/TKDE.2023.3312108

Zhang, Z., Tan, L., & Tiong, R. (2024). *Research on fire accident prediction and risk assessment algorithm based on data mining and machine learning. 0*. https://doi.org/DOI: 10.1186/s13662-024-03845-0

Zhang, P., Schmidt, D. C., White, J., & Lenz, G. (2018). Blockchain technology use cases in healthcare. *Advances in Computers*, *111*, 1–41.

Zhang, Y., & Hao, Y. (2024). Traditional Chinese medicine knowledge graph construction based on large language models. *Electronics (Basel)*, *13*(7), 1395.

Zhao, Y., Zhang, B., Hu, X., Ouyang, S., Kim, J., Jain, N., & de Berardinis, J., Meroño-Peñuela & Simperl, E. (2024). Improving ontology requirements engineering with OntoChat and participatory prompting. In *Proceedings of the AAAI Symposium Series* (Vol. 4, No. 1, pp. 253-257).

Zhao, Y. (2025). Leveraging large language models for ontology requirements engineering. In *Proceedings of the Extended Semantic Web Conference (ESWC).*

Zheng, Z., Xie, S., Dai, H., Chen, X., & Wang, H. (2017). An overview of blockchain technology: Architecture, consensus, and future trends. In *2017 IEEE International Congress on Big Data (BigData Congress)* (pp. 557-564). IEEE. Available at: https://ieeexplore.ieee.org/abstract/document/8029379

Zheng, Q., Xu, Y., Liu, H., Shi, B., Wang, J., & Dong, B. (2024). Artificial Intelligence — Review A Survey of Tax Risk Detection Using Data Mining Techniques. *Engineering*, *34*, 43–59. DOI: 10.1016/j.eng.2023.07.014

Zheng, W.-L., Amorim, E., Jing, J., Ge, W., Hong, S., Wu, O., & Ghassemi, M.. (2021). Predicting neurological outcome in comatose patients after cardiac arrest with multiscale deep neural networks. *Resuscitation*, *169*, 86–94. PMID: 34699925

Zheng, Y., Gan, W., Chen, Z., Qi, Z., Liang, Q., & Yu, P. S. (2025). Large language models for medicine: A survey. *International Journal of Machine Learning and Cybernetics*, *16*(2), 1015–1040.

Zheng, Z., Xie, S., Dai, H. N., Chen, X., & Wang, H. (2018). Blockchain challenges and opportunities: A survey. *International Journal of Web and Grid Services*, *14*(4), 352–375.

Zhou, B., Perel, P., Mensah, G. A., & Ezzati, M. (2021). Global epidemiology, health burden and effective interventions for elevated blood pressure and hypertension. *Nature Reviews. Cardiology*, *18*(11), 785–802.

Zhou, T., Lu, Y., & Wang, B. (2010). Integrating TTF and UTAUT to explain mobile banking user adoption. *Computers in Human Behavior*, *26*(4), 760–767. DOI: 10.1016/j.chb.2010.01.013

Ziefle, M., Himmel, S., & Wilkowska, W. (2011). When your living space knows what you do: acceptance of medical home monitoring by different technologies. Information quality in e-health: 7th conference of the workgroup human-computer interaction and usability engineering of the Austrian computer society, USAB 2011. Springer, 607-624. DOI: DOI: 10.1007/978-3-642-25364-5_43

About the Contributors

Nilmini Wickramasinghe is the inaugural Optus Chair and Professor of Digital Health at La Trobe University. She is also an inaugural member of the Australian Centre for AI in Medical Innovation. She has held or holds honorary research professor positions at Epworth HealthCare, the Peter MacCallum Cancer Centre, MCRI and Northern Health in Australia and the Cleveland Clinic in the US. After completing 5 degrees at the University of Melbourne, she was awarded a full scholarship to complete PhD studies at Case Western Reserve University, Cleveland, OH, USA and later was sponsored to complete executive education at Harvard Business School, Harvard University, Cambridge, MA, USA in Value-based HealthCare. For over 20 years, Professor Wickramasinghe has been actively researching and teaching within the health informatics/digital health domain in the US, Germany and Australia with a particular focus on designing, developing and deploying suitable models, strategies and techniques grounded in various management principles to facilitate the implementation and adoption of technology solutions to effect superior, value-based patient centric care delivery. Professor Wickramasinghe collaborates with leading scholars at various premier healthcare organisations and universities throughout Australasia, US and Europe and is well published, with more than 400 referred scholarly articles, more than 25 books, numerous book chapters, an encyclopaedia and a well-established funded research track record securing over $25M in funding from grants in US, Australia, Germany and China as a chief investigator. She holds a patent around analytics solution for managing healthcare data and a trademark. She is the editor-in-chief of Intl. J Networking and virtual Organisations(www.inderscience.com/ijnvo) as well as the editor of the Springer book series Healthcare Delivery in the Information Age and the CRC Routledge book series on Analytics and AI in Healthcare. In 2020 she was awarded the prestigious Alexander von Humboldt life time award for outstanding contribution to Digital Health, the first time this honour has been bestowed to someone in the discipline of Digital Health worldwide.

***

Asiya Attar is a Dental Surgeon with over six years of clinical experience and is currently a Ph.D. Scholar and Senior Research Fellow (SRF) at Symbiosis International (Deemed) University, Pune, India. She holds a Master's degree in Healthcare and Pharmaceutical Management. Her research focuses on patient experience in dental care, patient-centred care, oral health-related quality of life, and dental patient-reported outcomes and experiences. Her work has been published in peer-reviewed, high-impact-factor journals within the area of patient-reported health outcomes. Her academic interests lie in improving healthcare quality through patient-reported data and outcomes-based research.

Radhakrishna Batule, PhD, is a distinguished academic leader in the field of management and senior faculty member in the Department of Management at Vishwakarma University, Pune, India. His research work has been published in reputed journals, and he has presented at numerous national and international conferences. His areas of interest are strategic marketing, branding, services, and the retail sector. He is also a research guide, and to date, two scholars have been awarded PhD degrees under his guidance. Dr. Batule holds an MBA in Marketing and a PhD in Management from Savitribai Phule Pune University, India. He has a wealth of experience and expertise spreading over two decades, encompassing teaching, research, and consultancy.

Sammy F is an Assistant Professor in the Department of Computing Technologies, School of Computing, at SRM Institute of Science and Technology, Kattankulathur. He is actively involved in teaching and mentoring students in the field of computing and technology. His academic interests include software development, data analytics, and emerging computing paradigms

Hetal Gaglani is an Assistant Professor at Ramdeobaba University, Nagpur. With a strong commitment to academic excellence and research, she has contributed significantly to her field through teaching, mentoring, and scholarly work. Her role at the university reflects her dedication to fostering student learning and academic development in a dynamic and evolving educational environment.

Tarun Madan Kanade, PhD, is a member of the faculty of operations management at the Symbiosis Institute of Operations Management, which is a constituent of Symbiosis International (Deemed University) in India. Through his deep thoughts and numerous works, he has made a significant contribution to the academic and literary realms, making him a young author who stands out as a respected figure. His enormous achievements include contributions to several books, incisive chapters, research articles that explore new ground, and keynote speeches at a variety of conferences both nationally and internationally. Dr. Kanade is a person who is passionate about traveling and has a strong desire to learn new things and experience new places. His excursions, which have brought him to more than eleven different nations, are more than just vacations; they are quests for knowledge, which he makes sure to properly chronicle for the benefit of both educators and practitioners. Because of his extensive expertise, which spans nine years and encompasses a wide range of subjects, he has a distinctive point of view that he applies to his work. Because of his strategic vision and his ability to prepare for the future, Dr. Kanade is renowned for his forward-thinking and inventive attitude. He is also acclaimed for his ability to plan for the future. To bridge the gap between theoretical concepts in academia and practical implementations in the real world, he can skilfully turn his observations and experiences gained from his trips into recorded knowledge. The captivating works that Dr. Kanade has produced continue to serve as a source of motivation and information for both academics and practitioners. His work combines elements of exploration and invention.

Dilek Küçük, Ph.D, is an associate professor and senior chief researcher at TÜBİTAK Marmara Research Center (MRC). She has obtained her B.S., M.S. and Ph.D. degrees all from Middle East Technical University in Ankara (Turkey), in 2003, 2005, and 2011, respectively. Between May 2013 and May 2014, she studied as a post-doctoral researcher at European Commission's Joint Research Centre in Italy. Her research interests include ontologies, stance detection, legal informatics, and energy informatics.

|Emine Küçük - Contributing Author|Emine Ela Küçük, Ph.D., is a full professor at the Faculty of Health Sciences, Giresun University. She received her B.Sc. degree from Giresun Health School of Karadeniz Technical University and her M.Sc. degree from the Public Health Department of the Faculty of Medicine in Karadeniz Technical University. She received her Ph.D. degree from the Public Health Department of the Faculty of Medicine in Erciyes University. Her research topics include public health, public health surveillance, women health, and adolescent health.

L. A. Anto Gracious is an accomplished academic professional in Information Technology and Computer Science, known for his dedication to education, technology, and research. He holds a B.Tech in IT from C.S.I Institute of Technology (2006), an MBA in Technology Management, and an M.Tech in IT from Francis Xavier Engineering College (2011). He began his career as a Programmer at Software Solutions Integrated Limited, later transitioning to academia in 2011 as an Assistant Professor at Marthandam College of Engineering and Technology. Over eight years, he excelled in teaching, led the Software Development Cell, and earned multiple awards for his contributions. He later served at St. Xavier's Catholic College of Engineering and currently holds a position at R.M.K. College of Engineering and Technology. A prolific researcher, Anto focuses on machine learning, wireless sensor networks, and healthcare technologies. His work is widely published, and he has received accolades such as the Best Paper Award and multiple Best Faculty Awards.

Seema Laddha is a distinguished academician and marketing expert, currently holding the position of Associate Professor and Head of Marketing at Universal AI University, Karjat. With a rich academic background that includes a PhD in Commerce (Management) from Amaravati University and an MBA specializing in Marketing and Finance, Dr. Laddha has consistently excelled in her educational pursuits. Her career has been marked by a passion for teaching, evident through her extensive experience as a professor at various esteemed institutions. Dr. Laddha's expertise extends to diverse areas of marketing, underpinned by a wide array of certifications, including those in digital marketing, strategic management, and marketing analytics. Beyond her academic achievements, Dr. Seema Laddha has made substantial contributions to the field of research Her role as a research supervisor for two universities underscores her commitment to nurturing the next generation of scholars. Furthermore, she has actively engaged in research projects and received grants, contributing to her publications and case studies. Her dynamic involvement in conferences, accreditation processes, and social groups showcases her leadership abilities and a commitment to the academic and social spheres. Dr. Laddha's impressive journey in academia and industry exemplifies her dedication to the advancement of marketing education and knowledge.

Mark A. Neerincx is a Professor in Human-Centered Computing and Senior Research Scientist at TNO Perceptual and Cognitive Systems. He focuses on the situated cognitive engineering of ePartners in health and safety, which enhance the social, cognitive and affective processes in human-automation teams.

Gajalakshmi P is an Assistant Professor in the Department of Computer Science and Engineering at Adhiparasakthi Engineering College. She specializes in teaching and research in emerging areas of computer science. With a passion for academic excellence, she actively contributes to student development and curriculum enhancement. Her areas of interest include machine learning, data analytics, and software engineering.

R. Veerasundari is a faculty member at Vel Tech High Tech Dr. Rangarajan Dr. Sakunthala Engineering College, Chennai. She is actively engaged in teaching, student mentoring, and academic development in the field of computer science.

Her areas of interest include programming, data structures, and modern software technologies.

Kasturi Shukla, is presently working as Associate Professor at Symbiosis International University, Pune, India. She is a trained Hospital Administrator with a Bachelor's and Master's degree in Hospital Administration from Devi Ahilya University, Indore, India and Ph.D. from King George's Medical University, Lucknow, India. She was awarded Senior Research Fellowship (SRF) by Indian Council of Medical Research (ICMR) for her research work during 2009-2011 and she was the recipient of the Vice Chancellor's Gold Medal for Best PhD thesis in 2012. With more than 18 years' experience in academia and industry she has published more than 30 original research articles in journals of national and international repute, and has 2 books and 3 registered patents to her credit. She has presented research papers in reputed conferences and is on the review board of some of the reputed health journals. She is a Life Member of many reputed professional bodies. Besides, hospital management her core research interest includes Quality of Life, Emotional Intelligence, Resilience, Project management and agile methodologies, Climate change and Green business.

Thaís Spiegel is a Full Professor at the Rio de Janeiro State University (UERJ), Brazil. She is the Coordinator of the Health Engineering and Management Laboratory (LEGOS) at UERJ, where she leads research focused on healthcare service design, operations design and management in health systems, and the integration of cognitive science perspectives into decision-making processes in operations. Her scholarship bridges engineering, design, and management to address complex challenges in healthcare delivery and service performance. Dr. Spiegel's research portfolio includes projects on the management and design of health operations, discrete-event simulation, and the development of tools and frameworks to support the redesign of health services and improve access, efficiency and quality of care. She teaches undergraduate and graduate courses in production engineering and design, and supervises master's and doctoral research in service design and health systems innovation.

Thilagam T is an faculty member at Vel Tech Rangarajan Dr. Sagunthala R&D Institute of Science and Technology, Chennai. She is actively engaged in research and teaching, contributing to advancements in her field of expertise. Her academic work reflects a commitment to innovation, knowledge dissemination, and student development.

Aman Tyagi obtained his BTech degree from Gurukula Kangri (Deemed to be University), Haridwar and MTech in Computer Science from Dayalbagh Educational

Institute, Dayalbagh, Agra. He obtained his PhD degree from Dayalbagh Educational Institute, Dayalbagh, Agra, India in 2019. He was awarded a Senior Research Fellowship by University Grant Commission, India. He worked as an Assistant Professor in Shri Rawatpura Sarkar Institute of Technology and Science, Datia, India and Himalayan Garhwal University, Pauri Garhwal, Uttarakhand, India. Currently, he is working as an Assistant Professor in the Department of computer science and engineering, Faculty of Engineering and Technology, Gurukula Kangri (Deemed to be University), Haridwar, India.

Ashima Manoj Varghese, currently pursuing her doctorate in Human Resource Management. She did UG and PG in Computer Science from RTM Nagpur University. She obtained her second Masters in Industrial Relations and Personnel Management & third Masters – MBA also qualified MH-SET exam & has acquired several certifications from AICTE, SWAYAM-NPTEL, IELTS-GRE, NLP, French Language, Search Engine Optimization, Prompt Engineering to ChatGPT, Generative AI Tools & more. Ashima started her career as a banker for 10 years, before switching to IT Industry as a domain expert (BFSI) for 7 years. She has 8 years of academic experience as an Assistant Professor at various reputed management institutions. She has been granted 3 patents by Indian and Australian Government. Ashima has contributed to various National & International Conferences, FDPs & Webinars and has published and presented 10 Research Papers Indexed in Google Scholar, Research Gate, UGC Care Listed Journal, ABDC and Korean Journals. She has published & co-authored 4 academic books also published 10 e-Books on Amazon Kindle Direct Publishing. Ms. Ashima has received an Indian Education Award 2024 among top 100 professors for teaching acumen, continued dedication & contribution in the field of education. She has also received four certificates of Excellence in Reviewing Articles for Advances in Research.

Nilmini Wickramasinghe, PhD, MBA, is the Professor and Optus chair of Digital Health at La Trobe University within the School of Computing, Engineering and Mathematical Sciences. She also holds honorary research professor positions at the Peter MacCallum Cancer Centre, MCRI, Epworth HealthCare and Northern Health. After completing 5 degrees at the University of Melbourne, she completed PhD studies at Case Western Reserve University, and later executive education at Harvard Business School, USA in Value-based HealthCare. For over 25 years, she has been actively, researching and teaching within the health informatics/ digital health domain with over 350 scholarly publications, a patent, 25 books, numerous posters and book chapters and a very successful grant funding portfolio. In 2020, she was awarded the prestigious Alexander von Humboldt award for her outstanding contribution to digital health. Professor Wickramasinghe is the editor in chief of International Journal Networking and Virtual Organisations, published by InderScience. In addition, she is the editor of two book series in digital health 1) Healthcare Delivery in the Information Age, published by Springer 2) Analytics and AI for healthcare Delivery, published by CRC Routledge.

Index

A

B

C

D

N

O

P

R

S

T

V

W